P9-DTE-170

McGraw-Hill's
Interest Amortization Tables

Second Edition

Jack C. Estes

Dennis R. Kelley

McGraw-Hill, Inc.

New York   St. Louis   San Francisco   Auckland   Bogotá
Caracas   Lisbon   London   Madrid   Mexico   Milan
Montreal   New Delhi   Paris   San Juan   São Paulo
Singapore   Sydney   Tokyo   Toronto

Library of Congress Cataloging-in-Publication Data

Estes, Jack C., 1922-1975
   McGraw-Hill's interest amortization tables. – 2nd ed. / Jack C.
Estes, Dennis R. Kelley.
     p.   cm.
   Rev. ed. of: Interest amortization tables. c1976.
   Includes index.
   ISBN 0-07-019696-6
   1. Interest –Tables. I. Kelley, Dennis R. II. Estes, Jack C.,
1922-1975. Interest amortization tables. III. Title. IV. Title:
Interest amortization tables.
HG1634.E79 1993
332.8′2′0212 – dc20   92-24724
                                            CIP

10 DOC/DOC 0 9 8 7 6 5 4 3 2

ISBN   0-07-019696-6

*The sponsoring editor for this book was David Conti, the
editing supervisor was Kimberly A. Goff, and the produc-
tion supervisor was Pamela A. Pelton.*

Composed by Realty Computing Company, Ltd.

Printed and bound by R. R. Donnelly & Sons Company.

Contents

Preface

This power-packed guide fills the need for quick, reliable data on today's complex mortgage loans. It was the intent of the late Jack C. Estes to provide a stockpile of mortgage information in a convenient form for mortgage and appraisal professionals, home buyers, educators, and students. This second edition has been completely updated to give a broader base of mortgage data, retaining the strengths of the perennially popular first edition.

Its tables provide mortgage payments on loans from $100 to $250,000, at interest rates from 5 percent to 20 percent. The tables also show the remaining balance on a loan at any year, and how to figure the interest on loans. Differing loan types include standard 30-year loans, adjustable rate mortgages (ARMs), and biweekly payment loans, and answer such questions as

Q What is the payment on a $150,000 loan for 30 years at 9 percent interest?

Q What are the payments on a biweekly loan? Would the loan term be shorter?

Q My loan has a balloon payment after seven years. How much will it be?

Q If my ARM can rise up to 3 percent, what payment keeps the same payoff schedule?

Q If I prepay a loan regularly, how much loan interest and time would I save?

Q What is my loan balance after four years?

Practical examples are fully worked out for each use of the tables, to let you apply the reasoning to your case.

In the office, at closings, or in the classroom, *Interest Amortization Tables* will furnish the real estate mortgage information you need.

What the Tables Show

Mortgage loans in the United States run for a period of five to thirty years, and typically call for monthly payments with a fixed rate of interest. The payments are calculated to pay the interest for the preceding month, plus a small amount that reduces the balance of the loan. These standard loans are covered in Table 1.

For less frequently used loan terms, Table 2 gives the monthly payment on $1000 for a wider variety of interest rates and amortization periods.

Table 3 gives the remaining balance of a loan at the end of each year. Balloon payment loans, where a lump sum payment of the entire balance comes due, are also covered under Table 3.

The interest on a loan for any number of days is shown in Table 4.

Loans with fixed rates are standard in the U.S., but adjustable rate mortgages (ARM) continue to grow in popularity. With an ARM, the interest rate moves up or down, usually once a year, according to an index. ARMs are covered in Table 5.

To build equity in real estate, nothing outscores making extra principal payments. Regular prepayments slash interest. Structuring a savings plan with regular prepayments is shown in Table 6.

Biweekly payments suit the convenience of many households, and offer a built-in prepayment feature to save interest and shorten the loan term. Table 7 gives the payments and shows the savings.

About the Authors

JACK C. ESTES (deceased) was owner and manager of Century 21-Estes, Inc., Realtors in Falls Church, Virginia. He was also president and director of his own real estate school, a real estate appraiser, and lecturer. Mr. Estes was the author of *Real Estate License Preparation Course for the Uniform Examinations* and the *Handbook of Loan Payment Tables*.

DENNIS R. KELLEY has 28 years of experience in investment, financing, appraising and management. He is head of the real estate advisory division of LaSalle National Trust. He is the author of *The McGraw-Hill Handbook of Financial Tables for Real Estate*.

Table 1
Monthly Payment Loans

By far the most common mortgage loan in the United States calls for equal monthly payments beginning one month after the loan closing.

Today's loans most often have an amortization period of 30 years, but loans amortized in 15 years are increasing in popularity. By amortization period is meant that, if the payments are continued for that time, the loan will be fully paid. Many loans are only offered for a shorter term than the amortization period. This results in a balloon payment, meaning that the entire balance remaining on the loan falls due in one payment.

When using the tables, be sure to look up the payment according to the amortization period, not the term. For example, if a lender quotes a loan that has a term of 7 years, but an amortization period of 30 years, use the column for 30 years.

When there is a balloon payment, the borrower takes the risk of higher interest rates at the end of the term. To compensate, many lenders offer a lower interest rate on balloons than on loans that will be fully amortized.

Example 1. Finding the Monthly Payment

The Selbins are seeking a $125,000 loan at the current 9.50 percent interest rate. The loan documents will call for monthly payments and will have a 30-year amortization period.

To find the monthly payment, turn to the page of Table 1 for 9.50 percent interest and 30 years. Read down the left-hand column to $125,000 and across on that line to the column headed 30 years. The answer there is $1051.07, the payment for a 9.50 percent loan with a 30-year amortization period.

Note that the monthly payment will be the same, even if the loan has a balloon payment earlier than 30 years.

Example 2.   Amount Not Shown in Table

Pauline and Jeremy are seeking an $87,000 loan, an amount not shown in Table 1. The payment can be quickly calculated in one of these two ways:

a) Find the payment for a $1000 loan with your interest rate and amortization. Multiply the payment for $1000 by the number of thousands, in this case, 87, as follows:

Payment on $1000   ×   Number of thousands

b) Take the payment shown for $85,000, and add to it the payment for $2,000.

Example 3.   Total Interest over the Life of a Loan

Jill Wrightwood has offers of two different loan plans for the $100,000 loan that she seeks. The first calls for amortization over 15 years and an interest rate of 8.25 percent. The second requires interest of 8.75 percent, but allows payment over a 30-year period. Obviously, 15-year amortization will mean higher payments than a 30-year plan, but she suspects the interest saved over time may be worth it.

To find the total interest cost, begin by finding the payments for each loan. On the page for 8.25 percent interest and 15-year amortization period, read on the $100,000 line under 15 years, $970.15. Multiply this payment by 180 months, the number of payments in the loan, to get

$$\$970.15 \times 180 = \$174,627$$

the total cost of the loan. Subtract the original loan amount from it to get $74,627, the total interest paid on the 15-year loan over its life.

Using the same procedure, on the 8.75 percent page, read across on the $100,000 line to 30 years, and find $786.71, the payment on the 30-year loan.

Multiply this payment by 360 for the thirty year term, to get

$$\$786.71 \times 360 = \$283,215$$

the total cost of a 30-year plan. Subtracting the original principal gives $183,215, the total interest paid in 30 years.

Jill Wrightwood concludes that not only does the lower interest rate save money, but more rapid amortization brings tremendous savings. In this example, $5300 of the $108,600 savings comes from the lower interest rate. The other $103,300 is saved by paying the loan off in 15 rather than 30 years.

Amortization Period in Years

	5	7	8	10	12
$ 100	1.89	1.42	1.27	1.07	0.93
200	3.78	2.83	2.54	2.13	1.85
300	5.67	4.25	3.80	3.19	2.78
400	7.55	5.66	5.07	4.25	3.70
500	9.44	7.07	6.33	5.31	4.63
600	11.33	8.49	7.60	6.37	5.55
700	13.21	9.90	8.87	7.43	6.48
800	15.10	11.31	10.13	8.49	7.40
900	16.99	12.73	11.40	9.55	8.33
1,000	18.88	14.14	12.66	10.61	9.25
2,000	37.75	28.27	25.32	21.22	18.50
3,000	56.62	42.41	37.98	31.82	27.75
4,000	75.49	56.54	50.64	42.43	37.00
5,000	94.36	70.67	63.30	53.04	46.25
6,000	113.23	84.81	75.96	63.64	55.50
7,000	132.10	98.94	88.62	74.25	64.75
8,000	150.97	113.08	101.28	84.86	74.00
9,000	169.85	127.21	113.94	95.46	83.25
10,000	188.72	141.34	126.60	106.07	92.49
15,000	283.07	212.01	189.90	159.10	138.74
20,000	377.43	282.68	253.20	212.14	184.98
25,000	471.79	353.35	316.50	265.17	231.23
30,000	566.14	424.02	379.80	318.20	277.47
35,000	660.50	494.69	443.10	371.23	323.72
40,000	754.85	565.36	506.40	424.27	369.96
45,000	849.21	636.03	569.70	477.30	416.21
50,000	943.57	706.70	633.00	530.33	462.45
55,000	1,037.92	777.37	696.30	583.37	508.69
60,000	1,132.28	848.04	759.60	636.40	554.94
65,000	1,226.64	918.71	822.90	689.43	601.18
70,000	1,320.99	989.38	886.20	742.46	647.43
75,000	1,415.35	1,060.05	949.50	795.50	693.67
80,000	1,509.70	1,130.72	1,012.80	848.53	739.92
85,000	1,604.06	1,201.39	1,076.10	901.56	786.16
90,000	1,698.42	1,272.06	1,139.40	954.59	832.41
95,000	1,792.77	1,342.73	1,202.70	1,007.63	878.65
100,000	1,887.13	1,413.40	1,266.00	1,060.66	924.90
110,000	2,075.84	1,554.73	1,392.60	1,166.73	1,017.38
120,000	2,264.55	1,696.07	1,519.20	1,272.79	1,109.87
125,000	2,358.91	1,766.74	1,582.50	1,325.82	1,156.12
130,000	2,453.27	1,837.41	1,645.79	1,378.86	1,202.36
140,000	2,641.98	1,978.75	1,772.39	1,484.92	1,294.85
150,000	2,830.69	2,120.09	1,898.99	1,590.99	1,387.34
160,000	3,019.40	2,261.43	2,025.59	1,697.05	1,479.83
170,000	3,208.11	2,402.77	2,152.19	1,803.12	1,572.32
175,000	3,302.47	2,473.44	2,215.49	1,856.15	1,618.56
180,000	3,396.83	2,544.11	2,278.79	1,909.18	1,664.81
190,000	3,585.54	2,685.45	2,405.39	2,015.25	1,757.30
200,000	3,774.25	2,826.79	2,531.99	2,121.32	1,849.79
220,000	4,151.68	3,109.46	2,785.19	2,333.45	2,034.76
225,000	4,246.03	3,180.13	2,848.49	2,386.48	2,081.01
230,000	4,340.39	3,250.80	2,911.79	2,439.51	2,127.25
240,000	4,529.10	3,392.14	3,038.39	2,545.58	2,219.74
$250,000	4,717.81	3,533.48	3,164.99	2,651.64	2,312.23

Monthly Payment Loans   **5.00%**

Amortization Period in Years

	15	16	17	18	20
$ 100	0.80	0.76	0.73	0.71	0.66
200	1.59	1.52	1.46	1.41	1.32
300	2.38	2.28	2.19	2.11	1.98
400	3.17	3.04	2.92	2.82	2.64
500	3.96	3.79	3.65	3.52	3.30
600	4.75	4.55	4.38	4.22	3.96
700	5.54	5.31	5.11	4.93	4.62
800	6.33	6.07	5.83	5.63	5.28
900	7.12	6.82	6.56	6.33	5.94
1,000	7.91	7.58	7.29	7.04	6.60
2,000	15.82	15.16	14.58	14.07	13.20
3,000	23.73	22.74	21.86	21.10	19.80
4,000	31.64	30.31	29.15	28.13	26.40
5,000	39.54	37.89	36.44	35.16	33.00
6,000	47.45	45.47	43.72	42.19	39.60
7,000	55.36	53.04	51.01	49.22	46.20
8,000	63.27	60.62	58.30	56.25	52.80
9,000	71.18	68.20	65.58	63.28	59.40
10,000	79.08	75.77	72.87	70.31	66.00
15,000	118.62	113.66	109.30	105.46	99.00
20,000	158.16	151.54	145.74	140.61	132.00
25,000	197.70	189.43	182.17	175.76	164.99
30,000	237.24	227.31	218.60	210.92	197.99
35,000	276.78	265.19	255.03	246.07	230.99
40,000	316.32	303.08	291.47	281.22	263.99
45,000	355.86	340.96	327.90	316.37	296.99
50,000	395.40	378.85	364.33	351.52	329.98
55,000	434.94	416.73	400.77	386.67	362.98
60,000	474.48	454.61	437.20	421.83	395.98
65,000	514.02	492.50	473.63	456.98	428.98
70,000	553.56	530.38	510.06	492.13	461.97
75,000	593.10	568.27	546.50	527.28	494.97
80,000	632.64	606.15	582.93	562.43	527.97
85,000	672.18	644.03	619.36	597.58	560.97
90,000	711.72	681.92	655.79	632.74	593.97
95,000	751.26	719.80	692.23	667.89	626.96
100,000	790.80	757.69	728.66	703.04	659.96
110,000	869.88	833.45	801.53	773.34	725.96
120,000	948.96	909.22	874.39	843.65	791.95
125,000	988.50	947.11	910.82	878.80	824.95
130,000	1,028.04	984.99	947.26	913.95	857.95
140,000	1,107.12	1,060.76	1,020.12	984.25	923.94
150,000	1,186.20	1,136.53	1,092.99	1,054.56	989.94
160,000	1,265.27	1,212.29	1,165.85	1,124.86	1,055.93
170,000	1,344.35	1,288.06	1,238.72	1,195.16	1,121.93
175,000	1,383.89	1,325.95	1,275.15	1,230.31	1,154.93
180,000	1,423.43	1,363.83	1,311.58	1,265.47	1,187.93
190,000	1,502.51	1,439.60	1,384.45	1,335.77	1,253.92
200,000	1,581.59	1,515.37	1,457.32	1,406.07	1,319.92
220,000	1,739.75	1,666.90	1,603.05	1,546.68	1,451.91
225,000	1,779.29	1,704.79	1,639.48	1,581.83	1,484.91
230,000	1,818.83	1,742.67	1,675.91	1,616.98	1,517.90
240,000	1,897.91	1,818.44	1,748.78	1,687.29	1,583.90
$250,000	1,976.99	1,894.21	1,821.64	1,757.59	1,649.89

Table 1   5

Amortization Period in Years

	21	22	23	24	25
$ 100	0.65	0.63	0.62	0.60	0.59
200	1.29	1.26	1.23	1.20	1.17
300	1.93	1.88	1.84	1.80	1.76
400	2.57	2.51	2.45	2.39	2.34
500	3.21	3.13	3.06	2.99	2.93
600	3.86	3.76	3.67	3.59	3.51
700	4.50	4.38	4.28	4.18	4.10
800	5.14	5.01	4.89	4.78	4.68
900	5.78	5.63	5.50	5.38	5.27
1,000	6.42	6.26	6.11	5.97	5.85
2,000	12.84	12.51	12.21	11.94	11.70
3,000	19.26	18.76	18.32	17.91	17.54
4,000	25.67	25.02	24.42	23.88	23.39
5,000	32.09	31.27	30.53	29.85	29.23
6,000	38.51	37.52	36.63	35.82	35.08
7,000	44.93	43.77	42.73	41.79	40.93
8,000	51.34	50.03	48.84	47.76	46.77
9,000	57.76	56.28	54.94	53.73	52.62
10,000	64.18	62.53	61.05	59.69	58.46
15,000	96.26	93.80	91.57	89.54	87.69
20,000	128.35	125.06	122.09	119.38	116.92
25,000	160.43	156.33	152.61	149.23	146.15
30,000	192.52	187.59	183.13	179.07	175.38
35,000	224.61	218.85	213.65	208.92	204.61
40,000	256.69	250.12	244.17	238.76	233.84
45,000	288.78	281.38	274.69	268.61	263.07
50,000	320.86	312.65	305.21	298.45	292.30
55,000	352.95	343.91	335.73	328.30	321.53
60,000	385.04	375.17	366.25	358.14	350.76
65,000	417.12	406.44	396.77	387.99	379.99
70,000	449.21	437.70	427.29	417.83	409.22
75,000	481.29	468.97	457.81	447.68	438.45
80,000	513.38	500.23	488.33	477.52	467.68
85,000	545.47	531.49	518.85	507.37	496.91
90,000	577.55	562.76	549.37	537.21	526.14
95,000	609.64	594.02	579.89	567.06	555.37
100,000	641.72	625.29	610.41	596.90	584.60
110,000	705.90	687.81	671.45	656.59	643.05
120,000	770.07	750.34	732.49	716.28	701.51
125,000	802.15	781.61	763.01	746.13	730.74
130,000	834.24	812.87	793.53	775.97	759.97
140,000	898.41	875.40	854.57	835.66	818.43
150,000	962.58	937.93	915.61	895.35	876.89
160,000	1,026.75	1,000.45	976.65	955.04	935.35
170,000	1,090.93	1,062.98	1,037.70	1,014.73	993.81
175,000	1,123.01	1,094.25	1,068.22	1,044.58	1,023.04
180,000	1,155.10	1,125.51	1,098.74	1,074.42	1,052.27
190,000	1,219.27	1,188.04	1,159.78	1,134.11	1,110.73
200,000	1,283.44	1,250.57	1,220.82	1,193.80	1,169.19
220,000	1,411.79	1,375.62	1,342.90	1,313.18	1,286.10
225,000	1,443.87	1,406.89	1,373.42	1,343.02	1,315.33
230,000	1,475.96	1,438.15	1,403.94	1,372.87	1,344.56
240,000	1,540.13	1,500.68	1,464.98	1,432.56	1,403.02
$250,000	1,604.30	1,563.21	1,526.02	1,492.25	1,461.48

Monthly Payment Loans   **5.00%**

Amortization Period in Years

	26	27	28	29	30
$ 100	0.58	0.57	0.56	0.55	0.54
200	1.15	1.13	1.11	1.09	1.08
300	1.73	1.69	1.67	1.64	1.62
400	2.30	2.26	2.22	2.18	2.15
500	2.87	2.82	2.77	2.73	2.69
600	3.45	3.38	3.33	3.27	3.23
700	4.02	3.95	3.88	3.82	3.76
800	4.59	4.51	4.43	4.36	4.30
900	5.17	5.07	4.99	4.91	4.84
1,000	5.74	5.64	5.54	5.45	5.37
2,000	11.47	11.27	11.08	10.90	10.74
3,000	17.21	16.90	16.61	16.35	16.11
4,000	22.94	22.53	22.15	21.80	21.48
5,000	28.67	28.16	27.68	27.25	26.85
6,000	34.41	33.79	33.22	32.70	32.21
7,000	40.14	39.42	38.76	38.15	37.58
8,000	45.87	45.05	44.29	43.59	42.95
9,000	51.61	50.68	49.83	49.04	48.32
10,000	57.34	56.31	55.36	54.49	53.69
15,000	86.01	84.46	83.04	81.73	80.53
20,000	114.67	112.61	110.72	108.98	107.37
25,000	143.34	140.76	138.40	136.22	134.21
30,000	172.01	168.92	166.08	163.46	161.05
35,000	200.68	197.07	193.76	190.71	187.89
40,000	229.34	225.22	221.43	217.95	214.74
45,000	258.01	253.37	249.11	245.19	241.57
50,000	286.68	281.52	276.79	272.44	268.42
55,000	315.34	309.68	304.47	299.68	295.26
60,000	344.01	337.83	332.15	326.92	322.10
65,000	372.68	365.98	359.83	354.16	348.94
70,000	401.35	394.13	387.51	381.41	375.78
75,000	430.01	422.28	415.19	408.65	402.62
80,000	458.68	450.44	442.86	435.89	429.46
85,000	487.35	478.59	470.54	463.14	456.30
90,000	516.01	506.74	498.22	490.38	483.14
95,000	544.68	534.89	525.90	517.62	509.99
100,000	573.35	563.04	553.58	544.87	536.83
110,000	630.68	619.35	608.94	599.35	590.51
120,000	688.02	675.65	664.29	653.84	644.19
125,000	716.68	703.80	691.97	681.08	671.03
130,000	745.35	731.96	719.65	708.32	697.87
140,000	802.69	788.26	775.01	762.81	751.56
150,000	860.02	844.56	830.37	817.30	805.24
160,000	917.35	900.87	885.72	871.78	858.92
170,000	974.69	957.17	941.08	926.27	912.60
175,000	1,003.36	985.32	968.76	953.51	939.44
180,000	1,032.02	1,013.48	996.44	980.75	966.28
190,000	1,089.36	1,069.78	1,051.80	1,035.24	1,019.97
200,000	1,146.69	1,126.08	1,107.15	1,089.73	1,073.65
220,000	1,261.36	1,238.69	1,217.87	1,198.70	1,181.01
225,000	1,290.03	1,266.84	1,245.55	1,225.94	1,207.85
230,000	1,318.70	1,294.99	1,273.23	1,253.18	1,234.69
240,000	1,376.03	1,351.30	1,328.58	1,307.67	1,288.38
$250,000	1,433.36	1,407.60	1,383.94	1,362.16	1,342.06

Table 1   7

5.25% — Monthly Payment Loans

Amortization Period in Years

	5	7	8	10	12
$ 100	1.90	1.43	1.28	1.08	0.94
200	3.80	2.86	2.56	2.15	1.88
300	5.70	4.28	3.84	3.22	2.82
400	7.60	5.71	5.12	4.30	3.75
500	9.50	7.13	6.39	5.37	4.69
600	11.40	8.56	7.67	6.44	5.63
700	13.30	9.98	8.95	7.52	6.57
800	15.19	11.41	10.23	8.59	7.50
900	17.09	12.83	11.51	9.66	8.44
1,000	18.99	14.26	12.78	10.73	9.38
2,000	37.98	28.51	25.56	21.46	18.75
3,000	56.96	42.76	38.34	32.19	28.13
4,000	75.95	57.01	51.12	42.92	37.50
5,000	94.93	71.26	63.90	53.65	46.88
6,000	113.92	85.52	76.68	64.38	56.25
7,000	132.91	99.77	89.46	75.11	65.63
8,000	151.89	114.02	102.24	85.84	75.00
9,000	170.88	128.27	115.02	96.57	84.38
10,000	189.86	142.52	127.80	107.30	93.75
15,000	284.79	213.78	191.69	160.94	140.63
20,000	379.72	285.04	255.59	214.59	187.50
25,000	474.65	356.30	319.49	268.23	234.38
30,000	569.58	427.56	383.38	321.88	281.25
35,000	664.51	498.81	447.28	375.53	328.12
40,000	759.44	570.07	511.18	429.17	375.00
45,000	854.37	641.33	575.07	482.82	421.87
50,000	949.30	712.59	638.97	536.46	468.75
55,000	1,044.23	783.85	702.87	590.11	515.62
60,000	1,139.16	855.11	766.76	643.76	562.49
65,000	1,234.09	926.36	830.66	697.40	609.37
70,000	1,329.02	997.62	894.55	751.05	656.24
75,000	1,423.95	1,068.88	958.45	804.69	703.12
80,000	1,518.88	1,140.14	1,022.35	858.34	749.99
85,000	1,613.81	1,211.40	1,086.24	911.98	796.86
90,000	1,708.74	1,282.66	1,150.14	965.63	843.74
95,000	1,803.67	1,353.91	1,214.04	1,019.28	890.61
100,000	1,898.60	1,425.17	1,277.93	1,072.92	937.49
110,000	2,088.46	1,567.69	1,405.73	1,180.21	1,031.23
120,000	2,278.32	1,710.21	1,533.52	1,287.51	1,124.98
125,000	2,373.25	1,781.46	1,597.42	1,341.15	1,171.86
130,000	2,468.18	1,852.72	1,661.31	1,394.80	1,218.73
140,000	2,658.04	1,995.24	1,789.10	1,502.09	1,312.48
150,000	2,847.90	2,137.76	1,916.90	1,609.38	1,406.23
160,000	3,037.76	2,280.27	2,044.69	1,716.67	1,499.98
170,000	3,227.62	2,422.79	2,172.48	1,823.96	1,593.72
175,000	3,322.55	2,494.05	2,236.38	1,877.61	1,640.60
180,000	3,417.48	2,565.31	2,300.28	1,931.26	1,687.47
190,000	3,607.34	2,707.82	2,428.07	2,038.55	1,781.22
200,000	3,797.20	2,850.34	2,555.86	2,145.84	1,874.97
220,000	4,176.92	3,135.37	2,811.45	2,360.42	2,062.46
225,000	4,271.85	3,206.63	2,875.34	2,414.07	2,109.34
230,000	4,366.78	3,277.89	2,939.24	2,467.71	2,156.21
240,000	4,556.64	3,420.41	3,067.03	2,575.01	2,249.96
$250,000	4,746.50	3,562.92	3,194.83	2,682.30	2,343.71

Monthly Payment Loans 5.25%

Amortization Period in Years

	15	16	17	18	20
$ 100	0.81	0.78	0.75	0.72	0.68
200	1.61	1.55	1.49	1.44	1.35
300	2.42	2.32	2.23	2.15	2.03
400	3.22	3.09	2.97	2.87	2.70
500	4.02	3.86	3.72	3.59	3.37
600	4.83	4.63	4.46	4.30	4.05
700	5.63	5.40	5.20	5.02	4.72
800	6.44	6.17	5.94	5.74	5.40
900	7.24	6.94	6.68	6.45	6.07
1,000	8.04	7.71	7.43	7.17	6.74
2,000	16.08	15.42	14.85	14.34	13.48
3,000	24.12	23.13	22.27	21.50	20.22
4,000	32.16	30.84	29.69	28.67	26.96
5,000	40.20	38.55	37.11	35.84	33.70
6,000	48.24	46.26	44.53	43.00	40.44
7,000	56.28	53.97	51.95	50.17	47.17
8,000	64.32	61.68	59.37	57.33	53.91
9,000	72.35	69.39	66.79	64.50	60.65
10,000	80.39	77.10	74.21	71.67	67.39
15,000	120.59	115.64	111.31	107.50	101.08
20,000	160.78	154.19	148.42	143.33	134.77
25,000	200.97	192.74	185.52	179.16	168.47
30,000	241.17	231.28	222.62	214.99	202.16
35,000	281.36	269.83	259.73	250.82	235.85
40,000	321.56	308.38	296.83	286.65	269.54
45,000	361.75	346.92	333.93	322.48	303.23
50,000	401.94	385.47	371.04	358.31	336.93
55,000	442.14	424.02	408.14	394.14	370.62
60,000	482.33	462.56	445.24	429.97	404.31
65,000	522.53	501.11	482.35	465.80	438.00
70,000	562.72	539.65	519.45	501.63	471.70
75,000	602.91	578.20	556.55	537.46	505.39
80,000	643.11	616.75	593.66	573.29	539.08
85,000	683.30	655.29	630.76	609.12	572.77
90,000	723.49	693.84	667.86	644.95	606.46
95,000	763.69	732.39	704.97	680.78	640.16
100,000	803.88	770.93	742.07	716.61	673.85
110,000	884.27	848.03	816.28	788.27	741.23
120,000	964.66	925.12	890.48	859.93	808.62
125,000	1,004.85	963.67	927.59	895.76	842.31
130,000	1,045.05	1,002.21	964.69	931.59	876.00
140,000	1,125.43	1,079.30	1,038.90	1,003.25	943.39
150,000	1,205.82	1,156.40	1,113.10	1,074.91	1,010.77
160,000	1,286.21	1,233.49	1,187.31	1,146.57	1,078.16
170,000	1,366.60	1,310.58	1,261.51	1,218.23	1,145.54
175,000	1,406.79	1,349.13	1,298.62	1,254.06	1,179.23
180,000	1,446.98	1,387.68	1,335.72	1,289.89	1,212.92
190,000	1,527.37	1,464.77	1,409.93	1,361.55	1,280.31
200,000	1,607.76	1,541.86	1,484.13	1,433.21	1,347.69
220,000	1,768.54	1,696.05	1,632.55	1,576.53	1,482.46
225,000	1,808.73	1,734.59	1,669.65	1,612.36	1,516.15
230,000	1,848.92	1,773.14	1,706.75	1,648.19	1,549.85
240,000	1,929.31	1,850.23	1,780.96	1,719.85	1,617.23
$250,000	2,009.70	1,927.33	1,855.17	1,791.52	1,684.62

Table 1   9

Monthly Payment Loans

Amortization Period in Years

	21	22	23	24	25
$ 100	0.66	0.64	0.63	0.62	0.60
200	1.32	1.28	1.25	1.23	1.20
300	1.97	1.92	1.88	1.84	1.80
400	2.63	2.56	2.50	2.45	2.40
500	3.28	3.20	3.13	3.06	3.00
600	3.94	3.84	3.75	3.67	3.60
700	4.60	4.48	4.38	4.28	4.20
800	5.25	5.12	5.00	4.90	4.80
900	5.91	5.76	5.63	5.51	5.40
1,000	6.56	6.40	6.25	6.12	6.00
2,000	13.12	12.79	12.50	12.23	11.99
3,000	19.68	19.19	18.75	18.35	17.98
4,000	26.24	25.58	25.00	24.46	23.97
5,000	32.79	31.98	31.24	30.58	29.97
6,000	39.35	38.37	37.49	36.69	35.96
7,000	45.91	44.77	43.74	42.80	41.95
8,000	52.47	51.16	49.99	48.92	47.94
9,000	59.02	57.56	56.23	55.03	53.94
10,000	65.58	63.95	62.48	61.15	59.93
15,000	98.37	95.93	93.72	91.72	89.89
20,000	131.16	127.90	124.96	122.29	119.85
25,000	163.95	159.88	156.20	152.86	149.82
30,000	196.73	191.85	187.43	183.43	179.78
35,000	229.52	223.82	218.67	214.00	209.74
40,000	262.31	255.80	249.91	244.57	239.70
45,000	295.10	287.77	281.15	275.14	269.67
50,000	327.89	319.75	312.39	305.71	299.63
55,000	360.68	351.72	343.62	336.28	329.59
60,000	393.46	383.69	374.86	366.85	359.55
65,000	426.25	415.67	406.10	397.42	389.52
70,000	459.04	447.64	437.34	427.99	419.48
75,000	491.83	479.62	468.58	458.56	449.44
80,000	524.62	511.59	499.81	489.13	479.40
85,000	557.40	543.56	531.05	519.70	509.37
90,000	590.19	575.54	562.29	550.27	539.33
95,000	622.98	607.51	593.53	580.84	569.29
100,000	655.77	639.49	624.77	611.41	599.25
110,000	721.35	703.43	687.24	672.55	659.18
120,000	786.92	767.38	749.72	733.69	719.10
125,000	819.71	799.36	780.96	764.26	749.06
130,000	852.50	831.33	812.19	794.83	779.03
140,000	918.07	895.28	874.67	855.97	838.95
150,000	983.65	959.23	937.15	917.11	898.88
160,000	1,049.23	1,023.18	999.62	978.25	958.80
170,000	1,114.80	1,087.12	1,062.10	1,039.39	1,018.73
175,000	1,147.59	1,119.10	1,093.34	1,069.96	1,048.69
180,000	1,180.38	1,151.07	1,124.57	1,100.53	1,078.65
190,000	1,245.96	1,215.02	1,187.05	1,161.67	1,138.58
200,000	1,311.53	1,278.97	1,249.53	1,222.81	1,198.50
220,000	1,442.69	1,406.86	1,374.48	1,345.10	1,318.35
225,000	1,475.47	1,438.84	1,405.72	1,375.67	1,348.31
230,000	1,508.26	1,470.81	1,436.96	1,406.24	1,378.27
240,000	1,573.84	1,534.76	1,499.43	1,467.38	1,438.20
$250,000	1,639.42	1,598.71	1,561.91	1,528.52	1,498.12

Monthly Payment Loans **5.25%**

Amortization Period in Years

	26	27	28	29	30
$ 100	0.59	0.58	0.57	0.57	0.56
200	1.18	1.16	1.14	1.13	1.11
300	1.77	1.74	1.71	1.69	1.66
400	2.36	2.32	2.28	2.25	2.21
500	2.95	2.89	2.85	2.81	2.77
600	3.53	3.47	3.42	3.37	3.32
700	4.12	4.05	3.99	3.93	3.87
800	4.71	4.63	4.55	4.49	4.42
900	5.30	5.21	5.12	5.05	4.97
1,000	5.89	5.78	5.69	5.61	5.53
2,000	11.77	11.56	11.38	11.21	11.05
3,000	17.65	17.34	17.07	16.81	16.57
4,000	23.53	23.12	22.75	22.41	22.09
5,000	29.41	28.90	28.44	28.01	27.62
6,000	35.29	34.68	34.13	33.61	33.14
7,000	41.18	40.46	39.81	39.21	38.66
8,000	47.06	46.24	45.50	44.81	44.18
9,000	52.94	52.02	51.19	50.41	49.70
10,000	58.82	57.80	56.87	56.02	55.23
15,000	88.23	86.70	85.31	84.02	82.84
20,000	117.64	115.60	113.74	112.03	110.45
25,000	147.04	144.50	142.17	140.03	138.06
30,000	176.45	173.40	170.61	168.04	165.67
35,000	205.86	202.30	199.04	196.04	193.28
40,000	235.27	231.20	227.47	224.05	220.89
45,000	264.67	260.10	255.91	252.05	248.50
50,000	294.08	289.00	284.34	280.06	276.11
55,000	323.49	317.90	312.77	308.06	303.72
60,000	352.90	346.80	341.21	336.07	331.33
65,000	382.30	375.70	369.64	364.07	358.94
70,000	411.71	404.60	398.08	392.08	386.55
75,000	441.12	433.50	426.51	420.08	414.16
80,000	470.53	462.40	454.94	448.09	441.77
85,000	499.93	491.30	483.38	476.09	469.38
90,000	529.34	520.20	511.81	504.10	496.99
95,000	558.75	549.10	540.24	532.10	524.60
100,000	588.16	578.00	568.68	560.11	552.21
110,000	646.97	635.80	625.54	616.12	607.43
120,000	705.79	693.60	682.41	672.13	662.65
125,000	735.19	722.50	710.85	700.13	690.26
130,000	764.60	751.39	739.28	728.14	717.87
140,000	823.42	809.19	796.15	784.15	773.09
150,000	882.23	866.99	853.01	840.16	828.31
160,000	941.05	924.79	909.88	896.17	883.53
170,000	999.86	982.59	966.75	952.18	938.75
175,000	1,029.27	1,011.49	995.18	980.18	966.36
180,000	1,058.68	1,040.39	1,023.61	1,008.19	993.97
190,000	1,117.49	1,098.19	1,080.48	1,064.20	1,049.19
200,000	1,176.31	1,155.99	1,137.35	1,120.21	1,104.41
220,000	1,293.94	1,271.59	1,251.08	1,232.23	1,214.85
225,000	1,323.34	1,300.49	1,279.52	1,260.23	1,242.46
230,000	1,352.75	1,329.39	1,307.95	1,288.24	1,270.07
240,000	1,411.57	1,387.19	1,364.82	1,344.25	1,325.29
$250,000	1,470.38	1,444.99	1,421.69	1,400.26	1,380.51

Table 1   11

5.50%   Monthly Payment Loans

Amortization Period in Years

	5	7	8	10	12
$ 100	1.92	1.44	1.29	1.09	0.96
200	3.83	2.88	2.58	2.18	1.91
300	5.74	4.32	3.87	3.26	2.86
400	7.65	5.75	5.16	4.35	3.81
500	9.56	7.19	6.45	5.43	4.76
600	11.47	8.63	7.74	6.52	5.71
700	13.38	10.06	9.03	7.60	6.66
800	15.29	11.50	10.32	8.69	7.61
900	17.20	12.94	11.61	9.77	8.56
1,000	19.11	14.38	12.90	10.86	9.51
2,000	38.21	28.75	25.80	21.71	19.01
3,000	57.31	43.12	38.70	32.56	28.51
4,000	76.41	57.49	51.60	43.42	38.01
5,000	95.51	71.86	64.50	54.27	47.51
6,000	114.61	86.23	77.40	65.12	57.02
7,000	133.71	100.60	90.30	75.97	66.52
8,000	152.81	114.97	103.20	86.83	76.02
9,000	171.92	129.34	116.10	97.68	85.52
10,000	191.02	143.71	129.00	108.53	95.02
15,000	286.52	215.56	193.49	162.79	142.53
20,000	382.03	287.41	257.99	217.06	190.04
25,000	477.53	359.26	322.49	271.32	237.55
30,000	573.04	431.11	386.98	325.58	285.06
35,000	668.55	502.96	451.48	379.85	332.57
40,000	764.05	574.81	515.98	434.11	380.07
45,000	859.56	646.66	580.47	488.37	427.58
50,000	955.06	718.51	644.97	542.64	475.09
55,000	1,050.57	790.36	709.47	596.90	522.60
60,000	1,146.07	862.21	773.96	651.16	570.11
65,000	1,241.58	934.06	838.46	705.43	617.62
70,000	1,337.09	1,005.91	902.96	759.69	665.13
75,000	1,432.59	1,077.76	967.45	813.95	712.63
80,000	1,528.10	1,149.61	1,031.95	868.22	760.14
85,000	1,623.60	1,221.46	1,096.45	922.48	807.65
90,000	1,719.11	1,293.31	1,160.94	976.74	855.16
95,000	1,814.62	1,365.16	1,225.44	1,031.00	902.67
100,000	1,910.12	1,437.01	1,289.94	1,085.27	950.18
110,000	2,101.13	1,580.71	1,418.93	1,193.79	1,045.19
120,000	2,292.14	1,724.41	1,547.92	1,302.32	1,140.21
125,000	2,387.65	1,796.26	1,612.42	1,356.58	1,187.72
130,000	2,483.16	1,868.11	1,676.92	1,410.85	1,235.23
140,000	2,674.17	2,011.81	1,805.91	1,519.37	1,330.25
150,000	2,865.18	2,155.51	1,934.90	1,627.90	1,425.26
160,000	3,056.19	2,299.21	2,063.90	1,736.43	1,520.28
170,000	3,247.20	2,442.91	2,192.89	1,844.95	1,615.30
175,000	3,342.71	2,514.76	2,257.39	1,899.21	1,662.81
180,000	3,438.21	2,586.61	2,321.88	1,953.48	1,710.31
190,000	3,629.23	2,730.31	2,450.88	2,062.00	1,805.33
200,000	3,820.24	2,874.01	2,579.87	2,170.53	1,900.35
220,000	4,202.26	3,161.41	2,837.86	2,387.58	2,090.38
225,000	4,297.77	3,233.26	2,902.35	2,441.85	2,137.89
230,000	4,393.27	3,305.11	2,966.85	2,496.11	2,185.40
240,000	4,584.28	3,448.82	3,095.84	2,604.64	2,280.42
$250,000	4,775.30	3,592.52	3,224.84	2,713.16	2,375.44

Monthly Payment Loans 5.50%

Amortization Period in Years

	15	16	17	18	20
$ 100	0.82	0.79	0.76	0.74	0.69
200	1.64	1.57	1.52	1.47	1.38
300	2.46	2.36	2.27	2.20	2.07
400	3.27	3.14	3.03	2.93	2.76
500	4.09	3.93	3.78	3.66	3.44
600	4.91	4.71	4.54	4.39	4.13
700	5.72	5.50	5.29	5.12	4.82
800	6.54	6.28	6.05	5.85	5.51
900	7.36	7.06	6.81	6.58	6.20
1,000	8.18	7.85	7.56	7.31	6.88
2,000	16.35	15.69	15.12	14.61	13.76
3,000	24.52	23.53	22.67	21.91	20.64
4,000	32.69	31.38	30.23	29.22	27.52
5,000	40.86	39.22	37.79	36.52	34.40
6,000	49.03	47.06	45.34	43.82	41.28
7,000	57.20	54.91	52.90	51.13	48.16
8,000	65.37	62.75	60.45	58.43	55.04
9,000	73.54	70.59	68.01	65.73	61.91
10,000	81.71	78.44	75.57	73.04	68.79
15,000	122.57	117.65	113.35	109.55	103.19
20,000	163.42	156.87	151.13	146.07	137.58
25,000	204.28	196.08	188.91	182.58	171.98
30,000	245.13	235.30	226.69	219.10	206.37
35,000	285.98	274.51	264.47	255.62	240.77
40,000	326.84	313.73	302.25	292.13	275.16
45,000	367.69	352.94	340.03	328.65	309.55
50,000	408.55	392.16	377.81	365.16	343.95
55,000	449.40	431.37	415.59	401.68	378.34
60,000	490.26	470.59	453.37	438.19	412.74
65,000	531.11	509.80	491.15	474.71	447.13
70,000	571.96	549.02	528.93	511.23	481.53
75,000	612.82	588.23	566.71	547.74	515.92
80,000	653.67	627.45	604.49	584.26	550.31
85,000	694.53	666.66	642.27	620.77	584.71
90,000	735.38	705.88	680.05	657.29	619.10
95,000	776.23	745.09	717.83	693.81	653.50
100,000	817.09	784.31	755.61	730.32	687.89
110,000	898.80	862.74	831.18	803.35	756.68
120,000	980.51	941.17	906.74	876.38	825.47
125,000	1,021.36	980.38	944.52	912.90	859.86
130,000	1,062.21	1,019.60	982.30	949.42	894.26
140,000	1,143.92	1,098.03	1,057.86	1,022.45	963.05
150,000	1,225.63	1,176.46	1,133.42	1,095.48	1,031.84
160,000	1,307.34	1,254.89	1,208.98	1,168.51	1,100.62
170,000	1,389.05	1,333.32	1,284.54	1,241.54	1,169.41
175,000	1,429.90	1,372.54	1,322.32	1,278.06	1,203.81
180,000	1,470.76	1,411.75	1,360.10	1,314.57	1,238.20
190,000	1,552.46	1,490.18	1,435.66	1,387.61	1,306.99
200,000	1,634.17	1,568.61	1,511.22	1,460.64	1,375.78
220,000	1,797.59	1,725.47	1,662.35	1,606.70	1,513.36
225,000	1,838.44	1,764.69	1,700.13	1,643.22	1,547.75
230,000	1,879.30	1,803.90	1,737.91	1,679.73	1,582.15
240,000	1,961.01	1,882.33	1,813.47	1,752.76	1,650.93
$250,000	2,042.71	1,960.76	1,889.03	1,825.80	1,719.72

Table 1   13

5.50% Monthly Payment Loans

Amortization Period in Years

	21	22	23	24	25
$ 100	0.67	0.66	0.64	0.63	0.62
200	1.34	1.31	1.28	1.26	1.23
300	2.01	1.97	1.92	1.88	1.85
400	2.68	2.62	2.56	2.51	2.46
500	3.35	3.27	3.20	3.14	3.08
600	4.02	3.93	3.84	3.76	3.69
700	4.69	4.58	4.48	4.39	4.30
800	5.36	5.24	5.12	5.01	4.92
900	6.03	5.89	5.76	5.64	5.53
1,000	6.70	6.54	6.40	6.27	6.15
2,000	13.40	13.08	12.79	12.53	12.29
3,000	20.10	19.62	19.18	18.79	18.43
4,000	26.80	26.16	25.58	25.05	24.57
5,000	33.50	32.70	31.97	31.31	30.71
6,000	40.20	39.24	38.36	37.57	36.85
7,000	46.90	45.77	44.76	43.83	42.99
8,000	53.60	52.31	51.15	50.09	49.13
9,000	60.30	58.85	57.54	56.35	55.27
10,000	67.00	65.39	63.93	62.61	61.41
15,000	100.50	98.08	95.90	93.92	92.12
20,000	134.00	130.77	127.86	125.22	122.82
25,000	167.50	163.47	159.83	156.53	153.53
30,000	201.00	196.16	191.79	187.83	184.23
35,000	234.49	228.85	223.76	219.14	214.94
40,000	267.99	261.54	255.72	250.44	245.64
45,000	301.49	294.24	287.68	281.75	276.34
50,000	334.99	326.93	319.65	313.05	307.05
55,000	368.49	359.62	351.61	344.35	337.75
60,000	401.99	392.31	383.58	375.66	368.46
65,000	435.49	425.01	415.54	406.96	399.16
70,000	468.98	457.70	447.51	438.27	429.87
75,000	502.48	490.39	479.47	469.57	460.57
80,000	535.98	523.08	511.44	500.88	491.27
85,000	569.48	555.78	543.40	532.18	521.98
90,000	602.98	588.47	575.36	563.49	552.68
95,000	636.48	621.16	607.33	594.79	583.39
100,000	669.98	653.85	639.29	626.09	614.09
110,000	736.97	719.24	703.22	688.70	675.50
120,000	803.97	784.62	767.15	751.31	736.91
125,000	837.47	817.32	799.11	782.62	767.61
130,000	870.97	850.01	831.08	813.92	798.32
140,000	937.96	915.39	895.01	876.53	859.73
150,000	1,004.96	980.78	958.94	939.14	921.14
160,000	1,071.96	1,046.16	1,022.87	1,001.75	982.54
170,000	1,138.95	1,111.55	1,086.79	1,064.36	1,043.95
175,000	1,172.45	1,144.24	1,118.76	1,095.66	1,074.66
180,000	1,205.95	1,176.93	1,150.72	1,126.97	1,105.36
190,000	1,272.95	1,242.32	1,214.65	1,189.57	1,166.77
200,000	1,339.95	1,307.70	1,278.58	1,252.18	1,228.18
220,000	1,473.94	1,438.47	1,406.44	1,377.40	1,351.00
225,000	1,507.44	1,471.17	1,438.40	1,408.71	1,381.70
230,000	1,540.94	1,503.86	1,470.37	1,440.01	1,412.41
240,000	1,607.93	1,569.24	1,534.30	1,502.62	1,473.81
$250,000	1,674.93	1,634.63	1,598.22	1,565.23	1,535.22

Monthly Payment Loans   **5.50%**

Amortization Period in Years

	26	27	28	29	30
$ 100	0.61	0.60	0.59	0.58	0.57
200	1.21	1.19	1.17	1.16	1.14
300	1.81	1.78	1.76	1.73	1.71
400	2.42	2.38	2.34	2.31	2.28
500	3.02	2.97	2.92	2.88	2.84
600	3.62	3.56	3.51	3.46	3.41
700	4.23	4.16	4.09	4.03	3.98
800	4.83	4.75	4.68	4.61	4.55
900	5.43	5.34	5.26	5.18	5.12
1,000	6.04	5.94	5.84	5.76	5.68
2,000	12.07	11.87	11.68	11.52	11.36
3,000	18.10	17.80	17.52	17.27	17.04
4,000	24.13	23.73	23.36	23.03	22.72
5,000	30.16	29.66	29.20	28.78	28.39
6,000	36.19	35.59	35.04	34.54	34.07
7,000	42.23	41.52	40.88	40.29	39.75
8,000	48.26	47.46	46.72	46.05	45.43
9,000	54.29	53.39	52.56	51.80	51.11
10,000	60.32	59.32	58.40	57.56	56.78
15,000	90.48	88.98	87.60	86.34	85.17
20,000	120.63	118.63	116.80	115.11	113.56
25,000	150.79	148.29	146.00	143.89	141.95
30,000	180.95	177.95	175.19	172.67	170.34
35,000	211.11	207.60	204.39	201.44	198.73
40,000	241.26	237.26	233.59	230.22	227.12
45,000	271.42	266.92	262.79	259.00	255.51
50,000	301.58	296.57	291.99	287.78	283.90
55,000	331.73	326.23	321.19	316.55	312.29
60,000	361.89	355.89	350.38	345.33	340.68
65,000	392.05	385.54	379.58	374.11	369.07
70,000	422.21	415.20	408.78	402.88	397.46
75,000	452.36	444.86	437.98	431.66	425.85
80,000	482.52	474.51	467.18	460.44	454.24
85,000	512.68	504.17	496.38	489.22	482.63
90,000	542.83	533.83	525.57	517.99	511.02
95,000	572.99	563.48	554.77	546.77	539.40
100,000	603.15	593.14	583.97	575.55	567.79
110,000	663.46	652.46	642.37	633.10	624.57
120,000	723.78	711.77	700.76	690.66	681.35
125,000	753.93	741.43	729.96	719.43	709.74
130,000	784.09	771.08	759.16	748.21	738.13
140,000	844.41	830.40	817.56	805.76	794.91
150,000	904.72	889.71	875.95	863.32	851.69
160,000	965.03	949.02	934.35	920.87	908.47
170,000	1,025.35	1,008.34	992.75	978.43	965.25
175,000	1,055.51	1,037.99	1,021.95	1,007.20	993.64
180,000	1,085.66	1,067.65	1,051.14	1,035.98	1,022.03
190,000	1,145.98	1,126.96	1,109.54	1,093.53	1,078.80
200,000	1,206.29	1,186.28	1,167.94	1,151.09	1,135.58
220,000	1,326.92	1,304.91	1,284.73	1,266.20	1,249.14
225,000	1,357.08	1,334.56	1,313.93	1,294.97	1,277.53
230,000	1,387.23	1,364.22	1,343.13	1,323.75	1,305.92
240,000	1,447.55	1,423.53	1,401.52	1,381.31	1,362.70
$250,000	1,507.86	1,482.85	1,459.92	1,438.86	1,419.48

Table 1   15

Amortization Period in Years

		5	7	8	10	12
$	100	1.93	1.45	1.31	1.10	0.97
	200	3.85	2.90	2.61	2.20	1.93
	300	5.77	4.35	3.91	3.30	2.89
	400	7.69	5.80	5.21	4.40	3.86
	500	9.61	7.25	6.52	5.49	4.82
	600	11.54	8.70	7.82	6.59	5.78
	700	13.46	10.15	9.12	7.69	6.75
	800	15.38	11.60	10.42	8.79	7.71
	900	17.30	13.05	11.72	9.88	8.67
	1,000	19.22	14.49	13.03	10.98	9.63
	2,000	38.44	28.98	26.05	21.96	19.26
	3,000	57.66	43.47	39.07	32.94	28.89
	4,000	76.87	57.96	52.09	43.91	38.52
	5,000	96.09	72.45	65.11	54.89	48.15
	6,000	115.31	86.94	78.13	65.87	57.78
	7,000	134.52	101.43	91.15	76.84	67.41
	8,000	153.74	115.92	104.17	87.82	77.04
	9,000	172.96	130.41	117.19	98.80	86.67
	10,000	192.17	144.90	130.21	109.77	96.30
	15,000	288.26	217.34	195.31	164.66	144.45
	20,000	384.34	289.79	260.41	219.54	192.60
	25,000	480.42	362.23	325.51	274.43	240.75
	30,000	576.51	434.68	390.61	329.31	288.89
	35,000	672.59	507.12	455.71	384.20	337.04
	40,000	768.68	579.57	520.81	439.08	385.19
	45,000	864.76	652.01	585.91	493.97	433.34
	50,000	960.84	724.46	651.01	548.85	481.49
	55,000	1,056.93	796.90	716.11	603.74	529.63
	60,000	1,153.01	869.35	781.21	658.62	577.78
	65,000	1,249.09	941.79	846.31	713.50	625.93
	70,000	1,345.18	1,014.24	911.41	768.39	674.08
	75,000	1,441.26	1,086.68	976.51	823.27	722.23
	80,000	1,537.35	1,159.13	1,041.61	878.16	770.37
	85,000	1,633.43	1,231.57	1,106.71	933.04	818.52
	90,000	1,729.51	1,304.02	1,171.81	987.93	866.67
	95,000	1,825.60	1,376.46	1,236.91	1,042.81	914.82
	100,000	1,921.68	1,448.91	1,302.01	1,097.70	962.97
	110,000	2,113.85	1,593.80	1,432.21	1,207.47	1,059.26
	120,000	2,306.02	1,738.69	1,562.41	1,317.24	1,155.56
	125,000	2,402.10	1,811.13	1,627.51	1,372.12	1,203.71
	130,000	2,498.18	1,883.58	1,692.61	1,427.00	1,251.86
	140,000	2,690.35	2,028.47	1,822.81	1,536.77	1,348.15
	150,000	2,882.52	2,173.36	1,953.01	1,646.54	1,444.45
	160,000	3,074.69	2,318.25	2,083.21	1,756.31	1,540.74
	170,000	3,266.86	2,463.14	2,213.41	1,866.08	1,637.04
	175,000	3,362.94	2,535.58	2,278.51	1,920.97	1,685.19
	180,000	3,459.02	2,608.03	2,343.61	1,975.85	1,733.34
	190,000	3,651.19	2,752.92	2,473.81	2,085.62	1,829.63
	200,000	3,843.36	2,897.81	2,604.01	2,195.39	1,925.93
	220,000	4,227.69	3,187.59	2,864.41	2,414.93	2,118.52
	225,000	4,323.78	3,260.03	2,929.51	2,469.81	2,166.67
	230,000	4,419.86	3,332.48	2,994.61	2,524.70	2,214.82
	240,000	4,612.03	3,477.37	3,124.81	2,634.47	2,311.11
$250,000		4,804.20	3,622.26	3,255.01	2,744.24	2,407.41

Monthly Payment Loans   **5.75%**

Amortization Period in Years

$	15	16	17	18	20
100	0.84	0.80	0.77	0.75	0.71
200	1.67	1.60	1.54	1.49	1.41
300	2.50	2.40	2.31	2.24	2.11
400	3.33	3.20	3.08	2.98	2.81
500	4.16	3.99	3.85	3.73	3.52
600	4.99	4.79	4.62	4.47	4.22
700	5.82	5.59	5.39	5.21	4.92
800	6.65	6.39	6.16	5.96	5.62
900	7.48	7.19	6.93	6.70	6.32
1,000	8.31	7.98	7.70	7.45	7.03
2,000	16.61	15.96	15.39	14.89	14.05
3,000	24.92	23.94	23.08	22.33	21.07
4,000	33.22	31.92	30.78	29.77	28.09
5,000	41.53	39.90	38.47	37.21	35.11
6,000	49.83	47.87	46.16	44.66	42.13
7,000	58.13	55.85	53.86	52.10	49.15
8,000	66.44	63.83	61.55	59.54	56.17
9,000	74.74	71.81	69.24	66.98	63.19
10,000	83.05	79.79	76.93	74.42	70.21
15,000	124.57	119.68	115.40	111.63	105.32
20,000	166.09	159.57	153.86	148.84	140.42
25,000	207.61	199.46	192.33	186.05	175.53
30,000	249.13	239.35	230.79	223.26	210.63
35,000	290.65	279.24	269.26	260.46	245.73
40,000	332.17	319.13	307.72	297.67	280.84
45,000	373.69	359.02	346.18	334.88	315.94
50,000	415.21	398.91	384.65	372.09	351.05
55,000	456.73	438.80	423.11	409.30	386.15
60,000	498.25	478.69	461.58	446.51	421.26
65,000	539.77	518.58	500.04	483.72	456.36
70,000	581.29	558.47	538.51	520.92	491.46
75,000	622.81	598.36	576.97	558.13	526.57
80,000	664.33	638.25	615.44	595.34	561.67
85,000	705.85	678.14	653.90	632.55	596.78
90,000	747.37	718.03	692.36	669.76	631.88
95,000	788.89	757.92	730.83	706.97	666.98
100,000	830.42	797.81	769.29	744.17	702.09
110,000	913.46	877.59	846.22	818.59	772.30
120,000	996.50	957.37	923.15	893.01	842.51
125,000	1,038.02	997.26	961.62	930.22	877.61
130,000	1,079.54	1,037.15	1,000.08	967.43	912.71
140,000	1,162.58	1,116.94	1,077.01	1,041.84	982.92
150,000	1,245.62	1,196.72	1,153.94	1,116.26	1,053.13
160,000	1,328.66	1,276.50	1,230.87	1,190.68	1,123.34
170,000	1,411.70	1,356.28	1,307.80	1,265.09	1,193.55
175,000	1,453.22	1,396.17	1,346.26	1,302.30	1,228.65
180,000	1,494.74	1,436.06	1,384.72	1,339.51	1,263.76
190,000	1,577.78	1,515.84	1,461.65	1,413.93	1,333.96
200,000	1,660.83	1,595.62	1,538.58	1,488.34	1,404.17
220,000	1,826.91	1,755.18	1,692.44	1,637.18	1,544.59
225,000	1,868.43	1,795.07	1,730.90	1,674.39	1,579.69
230,000	1,909.95	1,834.96	1,769.37	1,711.59	1,614.80
240,000	1,992.99	1,914.74	1,846.30	1,786.01	1,685.01
$250,000	2,076.03	1,994.52	1,923.23	1,860.43	1,755.21

Table 1   17

Amortization Period in Years

	21	22	23	24	25
$ 100	0.69	0.67	0.66	0.65	0.63
200	1.37	1.34	1.31	1.29	1.26
300	2.06	2.01	1.97	1.93	1.89
400	2.74	2.68	2.62	2.57	2.52
500	3.43	3.35	3.27	3.21	3.15
600	4.11	4.02	3.93	3.85	3.78
700	4.80	4.68	4.58	4.49	4.41
800	5.48	5.35	5.24	5.13	5.04
900	6.16	6.02	5.89	5.77	5.67
1,000	6.85	6.69	6.54	6.41	6.30
2,000	13.69	13.37	13.08	12.82	12.59
3,000	20.54	20.06	19.62	19.23	18.88
4,000	27.38	26.74	26.16	25.64	25.17
5,000	34.22	33.42	32.70	32.05	31.46
6,000	41.07	40.11	39.24	38.46	37.75
7,000	47.91	46.79	45.78	44.87	44.04
8,000	54.75	53.48	52.32	51.28	50.33
9,000	61.60	60.16	58.86	57.69	56.62
10,000	68.44	66.84	65.40	64.10	62.92
15,000	102.66	100.26	98.10	96.15	94.37
20,000	136.87	133.68	130.80	128.19	125.83
25,000	171.09	167.10	163.50	160.24	157.28
30,000	205.31	200.52	196.20	192.29	188.74
35,000	239.52	233.94	228.90	224.34	220.19
40,000	273.74	267.36	261.60	256.38	251.65
45,000	307.96	300.78	294.30	288.43	283.10
50,000	342.17	334.20	327.00	320.48	314.56
55,000	376.39	367.61	359.70	352.53	346.01
60,000	410.61	401.03	392.40	384.57	377.47
65,000	444.82	434.45	425.09	416.62	408.92
70,000	479.04	467.87	457.79	448.67	440.38
75,000	513.26	501.29	490.49	480.72	471.83
80,000	547.47	534.71	523.19	512.76	503.29
85,000	581.69	568.13	555.89	544.81	534.75
90,000	615.91	601.55	588.59	576.86	566.20
95,000	650.12	634.97	621.29	608.91	597.66
100,000	684.34	668.39	653.99	640.95	629.11
110,000	752.77	735.22	719.39	705.05	692.02
120,000	821.21	802.06	784.79	769.14	754.93
125,000	855.42	835.48	817.48	801.19	786.39
130,000	889.64	868.90	850.18	833.24	817.84
140,000	958.07	935.74	915.58	897.33	880.75
150,000	1,026.51	1,002.58	980.98	961.43	943.66
160,000	1,094.94	1,069.41	1,046.38	1,025.52	1,006.58
170,000	1,163.37	1,136.25	1,111.78	1,089.62	1,069.49
175,000	1,197.59	1,169.67	1,144.48	1,121.66	1,100.94
180,000	1,231.81	1,203.09	1,177.18	1,153.71	1,132.40
190,000	1,300.24	1,269.93	1,242.57	1,217.81	1,195.31
200,000	1,368.68	1,336.77	1,307.97	1,281.90	1,258.22
220,000	1,505.54	1,470.44	1,438.77	1,410.09	1,384.04
225,000	1,539.76	1,503.86	1,471.47	1,442.14	1,415.49
230,000	1,573.98	1,537.28	1,504.17	1,474.18	1,446.95
240,000	1,642.41	1,604.12	1,569.57	1,538.28	1,509.86
$250,000	1,710.84	1,670.96	1,634.96	1,602.37	1,572.77

Monthly Payment Loans　　5.75%

Amortization Period in Years

	26	27	28	29	30
$ 100	0.62	0.61	0.60	0.60	0.59
200	1.24	1.22	1.20	1.19	1.17
300	1.86	1.83	1.80	1.78	1.76
400	2.48	2.44	2.40	2.37	2.34
500	3.10	3.05	3.00	2.96	2.92
600	3.71	3.66	3.60	3.55	3.51
700	4.33	4.26	4.20	4.14	4.09
800	4.95	4.87	4.80	4.73	4.67
900	5.57	5.48	5.40	5.33	5.26
1,000	6.19	6.09	6.00	5.92	5.84
2,000	12.37	12.17	11.99	11.83	11.68
3,000	18.55	18.26	17.99	17.74	17.51
4,000	24.74	24.34	23.98	23.65	23.35
5,000	30.92	30.43	29.98	29.56	29.18
6,000	37.10	36.51	35.97	35.48	35.02
7,000	43.29	42.60	41.97	41.39	40.86
8,000	49.47	48.68	47.96	47.30	46.69
9,000	55.65	54.77	53.96	53.21	52.53
10,000	61.84	60.85	59.95	59.12	58.36
15,000	92.75	91.28	89.92	88.68	87.54
20,000	123.67	121.70	119.90	118.24	116.72
25,000	154.59	152.12	149.87	147.80	145.90
30,000	185.50	182.55	179.84	177.36	175.08
35,000	216.42	212.97	209.81	206.92	204.26
40,000	247.33	243.39	239.79	236.48	233.43
45,000	278.25	273.82	269.76	266.04	262.61
50,000	309.17	304.24	299.73	295.59	291.79
55,000	340.08	334.66	329.70	325.15	320.97
60,000	371.00	365.09	359.68	354.71	350.15
65,000	401.91	395.51	389.65	384.27	379.33
70,000	432.83	425.93	419.62	413.83	408.51
75,000	463.75	456.36	449.59	443.39	437.68
80,000	494.66	486.78	479.57	472.95	466.86
85,000	525.58	517.20	509.54	502.51	496.04
90,000	556.49	547.63	539.51	532.07	525.22
95,000	587.41	578.05	569.48	561.62	554.40
100,000	618.33	608.47	599.46	591.18	583.58
110,000	680.16	669.32	659.40	650.30	641.94
120,000	741.99	730.17	719.35	709.42	700.29
125,000	772.91	760.59	749.32	738.98	729.47
130,000	803.82	791.01	779.29	768.54	758.65
140,000	865.65	851.86	839.24	827.65	817.01
150,000	927.49	912.71	899.18	886.77	875.36
160,000	989.32	973.56	959.13	945.89	933.72
170,000	1,051.15	1,034.40	1,019.07	1,005.01	992.08
175,000	1,082.07	1,064.83	1,049.04	1,034.57	1,021.26
180,000	1,112.98	1,095.25	1,079.02	1,064.13	1,050.44
190,000	1,174.81	1,156.10	1,138.96	1,123.24	1,108.79
200,000	1,236.65	1,216.94	1,198.91	1,182.36	1,167.15
220,000	1,360.31	1,338.64	1,318.80	1,300.60	1,283.87
225,000	1,391.23	1,369.06	1,348.77	1,330.16	1,313.04
230,000	1,422.14	1,399.48	1,378.74	1,359.71	1,342.22
240,000	1,483.97	1,460.33	1,438.69	1,418.83	1,400.58
$250,000	1,545.81	1,521.18	1,498.63	1,477.95	1,458.94

Table 1　　19

6.00% Monthly Payment Loans

Amortization Period in Years

	5	7	8	10	12
$ 100	1.94	1.47	1.32	1.12	0.98
200	3.87	2.93	2.63	2.23	1.96
300	5.80	4.39	3.95	3.34	2.93
400	7.74	5.85	5.26	4.45	3.91
500	9.67	7.31	6.58	5.56	4.88
600	11.60	8.77	7.89	6.67	5.86
700	13.54	10.23	9.20	7.78	6.84
800	15.47	11.69	10.52	8.89	7.81
900	17.40	13.15	11.83	10.00	8.79
1,000	19.34	14.61	13.15	11.11	9.76
2,000	38.67	29.22	26.29	22.21	19.52
3,000	58.00	43.83	39.43	33.31	29.28
4,000	77.34	58.44	52.57	44.41	39.04
5,000	96.67	73.05	65.71	55.52	48.80
6,000	116.00	87.66	78.85	66.62	58.56
7,000	135.33	102.26	92.00	77.72	68.31
8,000	154.67	116.87	105.14	88.82	78.07
9,000	174.00	131.48	118.28	99.92	87.83
10,000	193.33	146.09	131.42	111.03	97.59
15,000	290.00	219.13	197.13	166.54	146.38
20,000	386.66	292.18	262.83	222.05	195.18
25,000	483.33	365.22	328.54	277.56	243.97
30,000	579.99	438.26	394.25	333.07	292.76
35,000	676.65	511.30	459.96	388.58	341.55
40,000	773.32	584.35	525.66	444.09	390.35
45,000	869.98	657.39	591.37	499.60	439.14
50,000	966.65	730.43	657.08	555.11	487.93
55,000	1,063.31	803.48	722.78	610.62	536.72
60,000	1,159.97	876.52	788.49	666.13	585.52
65,000	1,256.64	949.56	854.20	721.64	634.31
70,000	1,353.30	1,022.60	919.91	777.15	683.10
75,000	1,449.97	1,095.65	985.61	832.66	731.89
80,000	1,546.63	1,168.69	1,051.32	888.17	780.69
85,000	1,643.29	1,241.73	1,117.03	943.68	829.48
90,000	1,739.96	1,314.77	1,182.73	999.19	878.27
95,000	1,836.62	1,387.82	1,248.44	1,054.70	927.06
100,000	1,933.29	1,460.86	1,314.15	1,110.21	975.86
110,000	2,126.61	1,606.95	1,445.56	1,221.23	1,073.44
120,000	2,319.94	1,753.03	1,576.98	1,332.25	1,171.03
125,000	2,416.61	1,826.07	1,642.68	1,387.76	1,219.82
130,000	2,513.27	1,899.12	1,708.39	1,443.27	1,268.61
140,000	2,706.60	2,045.20	1,839.81	1,554.29	1,366.20
150,000	2,899.93	2,191.29	1,971.22	1,665.31	1,463.78
160,000	3,093.25	2,337.37	2,102.63	1,776.33	1,561.37
170,000	3,286.58	2,483.46	2,234.05	1,887.35	1,658.95
175,000	3,383.25	2,556.50	2,299.76	1,942.86	1,707.74
180,000	3,479.91	2,629.54	2,365.46	1,998.37	1,756.54
190,000	3,673.24	2,775.63	2,496.88	2,109.39	1,854.12
200,000	3,866.57	2,921.72	2,628.29	2,220.42	1,951.71
220,000	4,253.22	3,213.89	2,891.12	2,442.46	2,146.88
225,000	4,349.89	3,286.93	2,956.83	2,497.97	2,195.67
230,000	4,446.55	3,359.97	3,022.53	2,553.48	2,244.46
240,000	4,639.88	3,506.06	3,153.95	2,664.50	2,342.05
$250,000	4,833.21	3,652.14	3,285.36	2,775.52	2,439.63

Monthly Payment Loans   **6.00%**

Amortization Period in Years

	15	16	17	18	20
$ 100	0.85	0.82	0.79	0.76	0.72
200	1.69	1.63	1.57	1.52	1.44
300	2.54	2.44	2.35	2.28	2.15
400	3.38	3.25	3.14	3.04	2.87
500	4.22	4.06	3.92	3.80	3.59
600	5.07	4.87	4.70	4.55	4.30
700	5.91	5.69	5.49	5.31	5.02
800	6.76	6.50	6.27	6.07	5.74
900	7.60	7.31	7.05	6.83	6.45
1,000	8.44	8.12	7.84	7.59	7.17
2,000	16.88	16.23	15.67	15.17	14.33
3,000	25.32	24.35	23.50	22.75	21.50
4,000	33.76	32.46	31.33	30.33	28.66
5,000	42.20	40.58	39.16	37.91	35.83
6,000	50.64	48.69	46.99	45.49	42.99
7,000	59.07	56.81	54.82	53.08	50.16
8,000	67.51	64.92	62.65	60.66	57.32
9,000	75.95	73.03	70.48	68.24	64.48
10,000	84.39	81.15	78.32	75.82	71.65
15,000	126.58	121.72	117.47	113.73	107.47
20,000	168.78	162.29	156.63	151.64	143.29
25,000	210.97	202.86	195.78	189.55	179.11
30,000	253.16	243.44	234.94	227.45	214.93
35,000	295.35	284.01	274.09	265.36	250.76
40,000	337.55	324.58	313.25	303.27	286.58
45,000	379.74	365.15	352.40	341.18	322.40
50,000	421.93	405.72	391.56	379.09	358.22
55,000	464.13	446.30	430.71	416.99	394.04
60,000	506.32	486.87	469.87	454.90	429.86
65,000	548.51	527.44	509.02	492.81	465.69
70,000	590.70	568.01	548.18	530.72	501.51
75,000	632.90	608.58	587.33	568.63	537.33
80,000	675.09	649.16	626.49	606.53	573.15
85,000	717.28	689.73	665.64	644.44	608.97
90,000	759.48	730.30	704.80	682.35	644.79
95,000	801.67	770.87	743.95	720.26	680.61
100,000	843.86	811.44	783.11	758.17	716.44
110,000	928.25	892.59	861.42	833.98	788.08
120,000	1,012.63	973.73	939.73	909.80	859.72
125,000	1,054.83	1,014.30	978.88	947.71	895.54
130,000	1,097.02	1,054.87	1,018.04	985.62	931.37
140,000	1,181.40	1,136.02	1,096.35	1,061.43	1,003.01
150,000	1,265.79	1,217.16	1,174.66	1,137.25	1,074.65
160,000	1,350.18	1,298.31	1,252.97	1,213.06	1,146.29
170,000	1,434.56	1,379.45	1,331.28	1,288.88	1,217.94
175,000	1,476.75	1,420.02	1,370.43	1,326.79	1,253.76
180,000	1,518.95	1,460.59	1,409.59	1,364.70	1,289.58
190,000	1,603.33	1,541.74	1,487.90	1,440.51	1,361.22
200,000	1,687.72	1,622.88	1,566.21	1,516.33	1,432.87
220,000	1,856.49	1,785.17	1,722.83	1,667.96	1,576.15
225,000	1,898.68	1,825.74	1,761.98	1,705.87	1,611.97
230,000	1,940.88	1,866.31	1,801.14	1,743.78	1,647.80
240,000	2,025.26	1,947.46	1,879.45	1,819.59	1,719.44
$250,000	2,109.65	2,028.60	1,957.76	1,895.41	1,791.08

Table 1   21

Amortization Period in Years

	21	22	23	24	25
$ 100	0.70	0.69	0.67	0.66	0.65
200	1.40	1.37	1.34	1.32	1.29
300	2.10	2.05	2.01	1.97	1.94
400	2.80	2.74	2.68	2.63	2.58
500	3.50	3.42	3.35	3.28	3.23
600	4.20	4.10	4.02	3.94	3.87
700	4.90	4.79	4.69	4.60	4.52
800	5.60	5.47	5.36	5.25	5.16
900	6.29	6.15	6.02	5.91	5.80
1,000	6.99	6.84	6.69	6.56	6.45
2,000	13.98	13.67	13.38	13.12	12.89
3,000	20.97	20.50	20.07	19.68	19.33
4,000	27.96	27.33	26.76	26.24	25.78
5,000	34.95	34.16	33.45	32.80	32.22
6,000	41.94	40.99	40.14	39.36	38.66
7,000	48.92	47.82	46.82	45.92	45.11
8,000	55.91	54.65	53.51	52.48	51.55
9,000	62.90	61.48	60.20	59.04	57.99
10,000	69.89	68.31	66.89	65.60	64.44
15,000	104.83	102.47	100.33	98.40	96.65
20,000	139.78	136.62	133.77	131.20	128.87
25,000	174.72	170.77	167.22	164.00	161.08
30,000	209.66	204.93	200.66	196.80	193.30
35,000	244.60	239.08	234.10	229.60	225.51
40,000	279.55	273.23	267.54	262.40	257.73
45,000	314.49	307.39	300.99	295.20	289.94
50,000	349.43	341.54	334.43	327.99	322.16
55,000	384.38	375.70	367.87	360.79	354.37
60,000	419.32	409.85	401.31	393.59	386.59
65,000	454.26	444.00	434.76	426.39	418.80
70,000	489.20	478.16	468.20	459.19	451.02
75,000	524.15	512.31	501.64	491.99	483.23
80,000	559.09	546.46	535.08	524.79	515.45
85,000	594.03	580.62	568.53	557.59	547.66
90,000	628.98	614.77	601.97	590.39	579.88
95,000	663.92	648.93	635.41	623.18	612.09
100,000	698.86	683.08	668.85	655.98	644.31
110,000	768.75	751.39	735.74	721.58	708.74
120,000	838.63	819.69	802.62	787.18	773.17
125,000	873.58	853.85	836.06	819.98	805.38
130,000	908.52	888.00	869.51	852.78	837.60
140,000	978.40	956.31	936.39	918.37	902.03
150,000	1,048.29	1,024.62	1,003.28	983.97	966.46
160,000	1,118.18	1,092.92	1,070.16	1,049.57	1,030.89
170,000	1,188.06	1,161.23	1,137.05	1,115.17	1,095.32
175,000	1,223.00	1,195.39	1,170.49	1,147.97	1,127.53
180,000	1,257.95	1,229.54	1,203.93	1,180.77	1,159.75
190,000	1,327.83	1,297.85	1,270.81	1,246.36	1,224.18
200,000	1,397.72	1,366.15	1,337.70	1,311.96	1,288.61
220,000	1,537.49	1,502.77	1,471.47	1,443.16	1,417.47
225,000	1,572.43	1,536.92	1,504.91	1,475.96	1,449.68
230,000	1,607.38	1,571.08	1,538.35	1,508.75	1,481.90
240,000	1,677.26	1,639.38	1,605.24	1,574.35	1,546.33
$250,000	1,747.15	1,707.69	1,672.12	1,639.95	1,610.76

Monthly Payment Loans   6.00%

Amortization Period in Years

	26	27	28	29	30
$ 100	0.64	0.63	0.62	0.61	0.60
200	1.27	1.25	1.24	1.22	1.20
300	1.91	1.88	1.85	1.83	1.80
400	2.54	2.50	2.47	2.43	2.40
500	3.17	3.12	3.08	3.04	3.00
600	3.81	3.75	3.70	3.65	3.60
700	4.44	4.37	4.31	4.25	4.20
800	5.07	5.00	4.93	4.86	4.80
900	5.71	5.62	5.54	5.47	5.40
1,000	6.34	6.24	6.16	6.08	6.00
2,000	12.68	12.48	12.31	12.15	12.00
3,000	19.02	18.72	18.46	18.22	17.99
4,000	25.35	24.96	24.61	24.29	23.99
5,000	31.69	31.20	30.76	30.36	29.98
6,000	38.03	37.44	36.91	36.43	35.98
7,000	44.36	43.68	43.06	42.50	41.97
8,000	50.70	49.92	49.21	48.57	47.97
9,000	57.04	56.16	55.37	54.64	53.96
10,000	63.37	62.40	61.52	60.71	59.96
15,000	95.06	93.60	92.27	91.06	89.94
20,000	126.74	124.80	123.03	121.41	119.92
25,000	158.42	156.00	153.79	151.76	149.89
30,000	190.11	187.20	184.54	182.11	179.87
35,000	221.79	218.40	215.30	212.46	209.85
40,000	253.48	249.60	246.05	242.81	239.83
45,000	285.16	280.80	276.81	273.16	269.80
50,000	316.84	312.00	307.57	303.51	299.78
55,000	348.53	343.20	338.32	333.86	329.76
60,000	380.21	374.40	369.08	364.21	359.74
65,000	411.90	405.60	399.84	394.56	389.71
70,000	443.58	436.79	430.59	424.91	419.69
75,000	475.26	467.99	461.35	455.26	449.67
80,000	506.95	499.19	492.10	485.61	479.65
85,000	538.63	530.39	522.86	515.96	509.62
90,000	570.31	561.59	553.62	546.31	539.60
95,000	602.00	592.79	584.37	576.66	569.58
100,000	633.68	623.99	615.13	607.01	599.56
110,000	697.05	686.39	676.64	667.71	659.51
120,000	760.42	748.79	738.15	728.41	719.47
125,000	792.10	779.99	768.91	758.76	749.44
130,000	823.79	811.19	799.67	789.11	779.42
140,000	887.15	873.58	861.18	849.81	839.38
150,000	950.52	935.98	922.69	910.51	899.33
160,000	1,013.89	998.38	984.20	971.21	959.29
170,000	1,077.26	1,060.78	1,045.72	1,031.91	1,019.24
175,000	1,108.94	1,091.98	1,076.47	1,062.26	1,049.22
180,000	1,140.62	1,123.18	1,107.23	1,092.61	1,079.20
190,000	1,203.99	1,185.58	1,168.74	1,153.31	1,139.15
200,000	1,267.36	1,247.98	1,230.25	1,214.01	1,199.11
220,000	1,394.09	1,372.77	1,353.28	1,335.42	1,319.02
225,000	1,425.78	1,403.97	1,384.03	1,365.77	1,348.99
230,000	1,457.46	1,435.17	1,414.79	1,396.12	1,378.97
240,000	1,520.83	1,497.57	1,476.30	1,456.82	1,438.93
$250,000	1,584.20	1,559.97	1,537.82	1,517.52	1,498.88

Table 1   23

6.25%　Monthly Payment Loans

Amortization Period in Years

	5	7	8	10	12
$ 100	1.95	1.48	1.33	1.13	0.99
200	3.89	2.95	2.66	2.25	1.98
300	5.84	4.42	3.98	3.37	2.97
400	7.78	5.90	5.31	4.50	3.96
500	9.73	7.37	6.64	5.62	4.95
600	11.67	8.84	7.96	6.74	5.94
700	13.62	10.32	9.29	7.86	6.93
800	15.56	11.79	10.62	8.99	7.92
900	17.51	13.26	11.94	10.11	8.90
1,000	19.45	14.73	13.27	11.23	9.89
2,000	38.90	29.46	26.53	22.46	19.78
3,000	58.35	44.19	39.80	33.69	29.67
4,000	77.80	58.92	53.06	44.92	39.56
5,000	97.25	73.65	66.32	56.15	49.45
6,000	116.70	88.38	79.59	67.37	59.34
7,000	136.15	103.11	92.85	78.60	69.22
8,000	155.60	117.83	106.11	89.83	79.11
9,000	175.05	132.56	119.38	101.06	89.00
10,000	194.50	147.29	132.64	112.29	98.89
15,000	291.74	220.94	198.96	168.43	148.33
20,000	388.99	294.58	265.27	224.57	197.77
25,000	486.24	368.22	331.59	280.71	247.21
30,000	583.48	441.87	397.91	336.85	296.66
35,000	680.73	515.51	464.23	392.99	346.10
40,000	777.98	589.15	530.54	449.13	395.54
45,000	875.22	662.80	596.86	505.27	444.98
50,000	972.47	736.44	663.18	561.41	494.42
55,000	1,069.71	810.08	729.50	617.55	543.87
60,000	1,166.96	883.73	795.81	673.69	593.31
65,000	1,264.21	957.37	862.13	729.83	642.75
70,000	1,361.45	1,031.01	928.45	785.97	692.19
75,000	1,458.70	1,104.66	994.77	842.11	741.63
80,000	1,555.95	1,178.30	1,061.08	898.25	791.07
85,000	1,653.19	1,251.94	1,127.40	954.39	840.52
90,000	1,750.44	1,325.59	1,193.72	1,010.53	889.96
95,000	1,847.68	1,399.23	1,260.04	1,066.67	939.40
100,000	1,944.93	1,472.87	1,326.35	1,122.81	988.84
110,000	2,139.42	1,620.16	1,458.99	1,235.09	1,087.73
120,000	2,333.92	1,767.45	1,591.62	1,347.37	1,186.61
125,000	2,431.16	1,841.09	1,657.94	1,403.51	1,236.05
130,000	2,528.41	1,914.74	1,724.26	1,459.65	1,285.49
140,000	2,722.90	2,062.02	1,856.89	1,571.93	1,384.38
150,000	2,917.39	2,209.31	1,989.53	1,684.21	1,483.26
160,000	3,111.89	2,356.60	2,122.16	1,796.49	1,582.14
170,000	3,306.38	2,503.88	2,254.80	1,908.77	1,681.03
175,000	3,403.63	2,577.53	2,321.12	1,964.91	1,730.47
180,000	3,500.87	2,651.17	2,387.43	2,021.05	1,779.91
190,000	3,695.36	2,798.46	2,520.07	2,133.33	1,878.79
200,000	3,889.86	2,945.74	2,652.70	2,245.61	1,977.68
220,000	4,278.84	3,240.32	2,917.97	2,470.17	2,175.45
225,000	4,376.09	3,313.96	2,984.29	2,526.31	2,224.89
230,000	4,473.34	3,387.61	3,050.61	2,582.45	2,274.33
240,000	4,667.83	3,534.89	3,183.24	2,694.73	2,373.21
$250,000	4,862.32	3,682.18	3,315.88	2,807.01	2,472.10

Monthly Payment Loans   **6.25%**

Amortization Period in Years

	15	16	17	18	20
$ 100	0.86	0.83	0.80	0.78	0.74
200	1.72	1.66	1.60	1.55	1.47
300	2.58	2.48	2.40	2.32	2.20
400	3.43	3.31	3.19	3.09	2.93
500	4.29	4.13	3.99	3.87	3.66
600	5.15	4.96	4.79	4.64	4.39
700	6.01	5.78	5.58	5.41	5.12
800	6.86	6.61	6.38	6.18	5.85
900	7.72	7.43	7.18	6.96	6.58
1,000	8.58	8.26	7.98	7.73	7.31
2,000	17.15	16.51	15.95	15.45	14.62
3,000	25.73	24.76	23.92	23.17	21.93
4,000	34.30	33.01	31.89	30.90	29.24
5,000	42.88	41.26	39.86	38.62	36.55
6,000	51.45	49.52	47.83	46.34	43.86
7,000	60.02	57.77	55.80	54.07	51.17
8,000	68.60	66.02	63.77	61.79	58.48
9,000	77.17	74.27	71.74	69.51	65.79
10,000	85.75	82.52	79.71	77.23	73.10
15,000	128.62	123.78	119.56	115.85	109.64
20,000	171.49	165.04	159.41	154.46	146.19
25,000	214.36	206.30	199.27	193.08	182.74
30,000	257.23	247.56	239.12	231.69	219.28
35,000	300.10	288.82	278.97	270.31	255.83
40,000	342.97	330.08	318.82	308.92	292.38
45,000	385.85	371.34	358.68	347.54	328.92
50,000	428.72	412.60	398.53	386.15	365.47
55,000	471.59	453.86	438.38	424.77	402.02
60,000	514.46	495.12	478.23	463.38	438.56
65,000	557.33	536.38	518.08	502.00	475.11
70,000	600.20	577.64	557.94	540.61	511.65
75,000	643.07	618.90	597.79	579.23	548.20
80,000	685.94	660.16	637.64	617.84	584.75
85,000	728.81	701.42	677.49	656.45	621.29
90,000	771.69	742.68	717.35	695.07	657.84
95,000	814.56	783.94	757.20	733.68	694.39
100,000	857.43	825.20	797.05	772.30	730.93
110,000	943.17	907.72	876.75	849.53	804.03
120,000	1,028.91	990.24	956.46	926.76	877.12
125,000	1,071.78	1,031.50	996.31	965.37	913.67
130,000	1,114.65	1,072.76	1,036.16	1,003.99	950.21
140,000	1,200.40	1,155.28	1,115.87	1,081.22	1,023.30
150,000	1,286.14	1,237.80	1,195.57	1,158.45	1,096.40
160,000	1,371.88	1,320.32	1,275.28	1,235.67	1,169.49
170,000	1,457.62	1,402.84	1,354.98	1,312.90	1,242.58
175,000	1,500.50	1,444.09	1,394.83	1,351.52	1,279.13
180,000	1,543.37	1,485.35	1,434.69	1,390.13	1,315.68
190,000	1,629.11	1,567.87	1,514.39	1,467.36	1,388.77
200,000	1,714.85	1,650.39	1,594.10	1,544.59	1,461.86
220,000	1,886.34	1,815.43	1,753.50	1,699.05	1,608.05
225,000	1,929.21	1,856.69	1,793.36	1,737.67	1,644.59
230,000	1,972.08	1,897.95	1,833.21	1,776.28	1,681.14
240,000	2,057.82	1,980.47	1,912.91	1,853.51	1,754.23
$250,000	2,143.56	2,062.99	1,992.62	1,930.74	1,827.33

Table 1   25

Monthly Payment Loans

Amortization Period in Years

32$		21	22	23	24	25
	100	0.72	0.70	0.69	0.68	0.66
	200	1.43	1.40	1.37	1.35	1.32
	300	2.15	2.10	2.06	2.02	1.98
	400	2.86	2.80	2.74	2.69	2.64
	500	3.57	3.49	3.42	3.36	3.30
	600	4.29	4.19	4.11	4.03	3.96
	700	5.00	4.89	4.79	4.70	4.62
	800	5.71	5.59	5.48	5.37	5.28
	900	6.43	6.29	6.16	6.05	5.94
	1,000	7.14	6.98	6.84	6.72	6.60
	2,000	14.28	13.96	13.68	13.43	13.20
	3,000	21.41	20.94	20.52	20.14	19.80
	4,000	28.55	27.92	27.36	26.85	26.39
	5,000	35.68	34.90	34.20	33.56	32.99
	6,000	42.82	41.88	41.04	40.28	39.59
	7,000	49.95	48.86	47.88	46.99	46.18
	8,000	57.09	55.84	54.71	53.70	52.78
	9,000	64.22	62.82	61.55	60.41	59.38
	10,000	71.36	69.80	68.39	67.12	65.97
	15,000	107.04	104.69	102.59	100.68	98.96
	20,000	142.71	139.59	136.78	134.24	131.94
	25,000	178.39	174.49	170.97	167.80	164.92
	30,000	214.07	209.38	205.17	201.36	197.91
	35,000	249.74	244.28	239.36	234.92	230.89
	40,000	285.42	279.18	273.55	268.48	263.87
	45,000	321.10	314.07	307.75	302.03	296.86
	50,000	356.77	348.97	341.94	335.59	329.84
	55,000	392.45	383.87	376.14	369.15	362.82
	60,000	428.13	418.76	410.33	402.71	395.81
	65,000	463.80	453.66	444.52	436.27	428.79
	70,000	499.48	488.55	478.72	469.83	461.77
	75,000	535.16	523.45	512.91	503.39	494.76
	80,000	570.83	558.35	547.10	536.95	527.74
	85,000	606.51	593.24	581.30	570.51	560.72
	90,000	642.19	628.14	615.49	604.06	593.71
	95,000	677.86	663.04	649.69	637.62	626.69
	100,000	713.54	697.93	683.88	671.18	659.67
	110,000	784.89	767.73	752.27	738.30	725.64
	120,000	856.25	837.52	820.65	805.42	791.61
	125,000	891.92	872.41	854.85	838.98	824.59
	130,000	927.60	907.31	889.04	872.54	857.58
	140,000	998.95	977.10	957.43	939.65	923.54
	150,000	1,070.31	1,046.90	1,025.82	1,006.77	989.51
	160,000	1,141.66	1,116.69	1,094.20	1,073.89	1,055.48
	170,000	1,213.01	1,186.48	1,162.59	1,141.01	1,121.44
	175,000	1,248.69	1,221.38	1,196.79	1,174.57	1,154.43
	180,000	1,284.37	1,256.28	1,230.98	1,208.12	1,187.41
	190,000	1,355.72	1,326.07	1,299.37	1,275.24	1,253.38
	200,000	1,427.07	1,395.86	1,367.75	1,342.36	1,319.34
	220,000	1,569.78	1,535.45	1,504.53	1,476.60	1,451.28
	225,000	1,605.46	1,570.34	1,538.72	1,510.15	1,484.26
	230,000	1,641.13	1,605.24	1,572.92	1,543.71	1,517.24
	240,000	1,712.49	1,675.03	1,641.30	1,610.83	1,583.21
	$250,000	1,783.84	1,744.82	1,709.69	1,677.95	1,649.18

Monthly Payment Loans   <u>**6.25%**</u>

Amortization Period in Years

	26	27	28	29	30
$ 100	0.65	0.64	0.64	0.63	0.62
200	1.30	1.28	1.27	1.25	1.24
300	1.95	1.92	1.90	1.87	1.85
400	2.60	2.56	2.53	2.50	2.47
500	3.25	3.20	3.16	3.12	3.08
600	3.90	3.84	3.79	3.74	3.70
700	4.55	4.48	4.42	4.37	4.32
800	5.20	5.12	5.05	4.99	4.93
900	5.85	5.76	5.68	5.61	5.55
1,000	6.50	6.40	6.31	6.24	6.16
2,000	12.99	12.80	12.62	12.47	12.32
3,000	19.48	19.20	18.93	18.70	18.48
4,000	25.97	25.59	25.24	24.93	24.63
5,000	32.47	31.99	31.55	31.16	30.79
6,000	38.96	38.39	37.86	37.39	36.95
7,000	45.45	44.78	44.17	43.62	43.11
8,000	51.94	51.18	50.48	49.85	49.26
9,000	58.43	57.58	56.79	56.08	55.42
10,000	64.93	63.97	63.10	62.31	61.58
15,000	97.39	95.96	94.65	93.46	92.36
20,000	129.85	127.94	126.20	124.61	123.15
25,000	162.31	159.93	157.75	155.76	153.93
30,000	194.77	191.91	189.30	186.91	184.72
35,000	227.23	223.89	220.85	218.06	215.51
40,000	259.69	255.88	252.40	249.21	246.29
45,000	292.15	287.86	283.95	280.36	277.08
50,000	324.61	319.85	315.50	311.51	307.86
55,000	357.07	351.83	347.04	342.66	338.65
60,000	389.53	383.81	378.59	373.82	369.44
65,000	421.99	415.80	410.14	404.97	400.22
70,000	454.45	447.78	441.69	436.12	431.01
75,000	486.91	479.77	473.24	467.27	461.79
80,000	519.37	511.75	504.79	498.42	492.58
85,000	551.83	543.73	536.34	529.57	523.36
90,000	584.29	575.72	567.89	560.72	554.15
95,000	616.76	607.70	599.44	591.87	584.94
100,000	649.22	639.69	630.99	623.02	615.72
110,000	714.14	703.66	694.08	685.32	677.29
120,000	779.06	767.62	757.18	747.63	738.87
125,000	811.52	799.61	788.73	778.78	769.65
130,000	843.98	831.59	820.28	809.93	800.44
140,000	908.90	895.56	883.38	872.23	862.01
150,000	973.82	959.53	946.48	934.53	923.58
160,000	1,038.74	1,023.50	1,009.57	996.83	985.15
170,000	1,103.66	1,087.46	1,072.67	1,059.14	1,046.72
175,000	1,136.12	1,119.45	1,104.22	1,090.29	1,077.51
180,000	1,168.58	1,151.43	1,135.77	1,121.44	1,108.30
190,000	1,233.51	1,215.40	1,198.87	1,183.74	1,169.87
200,000	1,298.43	1,279.37	1,261.97	1,246.04	1,231.44
220,000	1,428.27	1,407.31	1,388.16	1,370.64	1,354.58
225,000	1,460.73	1,439.29	1,419.71	1,401.79	1,385.37
230,000	1,493.19	1,471.27	1,451.26	1,432.95	1,416.15
240,000	1,558.11	1,535.24	1,514.36	1,495.25	1,477.73
$250,000	1,623.03	1,599.21	1,577.46	1,557.55	1,539.30

Table 1   27

6.50% Monthly Payment Loans

Amortization Period in Years

	5	7	8	10	12
$ 100	1.96	1.49	1.34	1.14	1.01
200	3.92	2.97	2.68	2.28	2.01
300	5.87	4.46	4.02	3.41	3.01
400	7.83	5.94	5.36	4.55	4.01
500	9.79	7.43	6.70	5.68	5.01
600	11.74	8.91	8.04	6.82	6.02
700	13.70	10.40	9.38	7.95	7.02
800	15.66	11.88	10.71	9.09	8.02
900	17.61	13.37	12.05	10.22	9.02
1,000	19.57	14.85	13.39	11.36	10.02
2,000	39.14	29.70	26.78	22.71	20.04
3,000	58.70	44.55	40.16	34.07	30.06
4,000	78.27	59.40	53.55	45.42	40.08
5,000	97.84	74.25	66.94	56.78	50.10
6,000	117.40	89.10	80.32	68.13	60.12
7,000	136.97	103.95	93.71	79.49	70.14
8,000	156.53	118.80	107.09	90.84	80.16
9,000	176.10	133.65	120.48	102.20	90.18
10,000	195.67	148.50	133.87	113.55	100.20
15,000	293.50	222.75	200.80	170.33	150.29
20,000	391.33	296.99	267.73	227.10	200.39
25,000	489.16	371.24	334.66	283.87	250.49
30,000	586.99	445.49	401.59	340.65	300.58
35,000	684.82	519.74	468.52	397.42	350.68
40,000	782.65	593.98	535.45	454.20	400.77
45,000	880.48	668.23	602.39	510.97	450.87
50,000	978.31	742.48	669.32	567.74	500.97
55,000	1,076.14	816.72	736.25	624.52	551.06
60,000	1,173.97	890.97	803.18	681.29	601.16
65,000	1,271.80	965.22	870.11	738.07	651.25
70,000	1,369.64	1,039.47	937.04	794.84	701.35
75,000	1,467.47	1,113.71	1,003.97	851.61	751.45
80,000	1,565.30	1,187.96	1,070.90	908.39	801.54
85,000	1,663.13	1,262.21	1,137.83	965.16	851.64
90,000	1,760.96	1,336.45	1,204.77	1,021.94	901.73
95,000	1,858.79	1,410.70	1,271.70	1,078.71	951.83
100,000	1,956.62	1,484.95	1,338.63	1,135.48	1,001.93
110,000	2,152.28	1,633.44	1,472.49	1,249.03	1,102.12
120,000	2,347.94	1,781.94	1,606.35	1,362.58	1,202.31
125,000	2,445.77	1,856.18	1,673.28	1,419.35	1,252.41
130,000	2,543.60	1,930.43	1,740.22	1,476.13	1,302.50
140,000	2,739.27	2,078.93	1,874.08	1,589.68	1,402.69
150,000	2,934.93	2,227.42	2,007.94	1,703.22	1,502.89
160,000	3,130.59	2,375.91	2,141.80	1,816.77	1,603.08
170,000	3,326.25	2,524.41	2,275.66	1,930.32	1,703.27
175,000	3,424.08	2,598.66	2,342.60	1,987.09	1,753.37
180,000	3,521.91	2,672.90	2,409.53	2,043.87	1,803.46
190,000	3,717.57	2,821.40	2,543.39	2,157.42	1,903.66
200,000	3,913.23	2,969.89	2,677.25	2,270.96	2,003.85
220,000	4,304.56	3,266.88	2,944.98	2,498.06	2,204.23
225,000	4,402.39	3,341.13	3,011.91	2,554.83	2,254.33
230,000	4,500.22	3,415.38	3,078.84	2,611.61	2,304.42
240,000	4,695.88	3,563.87	3,212.70	2,725.16	2,404.62
$250,000	4,891.54	3,712.36	3,346.56	2,838.70	2,504.81

Monthly Payment Loans   **6.50%**

Amortization Period in Years

	15	16	17	18	20
$ 100	0.88	0.84	0.82	0.79	0.75
200	1.75	1.68	1.63	1.58	1.50
300	2.62	2.52	2.44	2.36	2.24
400	3.49	3.36	3.25	3.15	2.99
500	4.36	4.20	4.06	3.94	3.73
600	5.23	5.04	4.87	4.72	4.48
700	6.10	5.88	5.68	5.51	5.22
800	6.97	6.72	6.49	6.30	5.97
900	7.84	7.56	7.31	7.08	6.72
1,000	8.72	8.40	8.12	7.87	7.46
2,000	17.43	16.79	16.23	15.74	14.92
3,000	26.14	25.18	24.34	23.60	22.37
4,000	34.85	33.57	32.45	31.47	29.83
5,000	43.56	41.96	40.56	39.33	37.28
6,000	52.27	50.35	48.67	47.20	44.74
7,000	60.98	58.74	56.78	55.06	52.20
8,000	69.69	67.13	64.89	62.93	59.65
9,000	78.40	75.52	73.01	70.80	67.11
10,000	87.12	83.91	81.12	78.66	74.56
15,000	130.67	125.87	121.67	117.99	111.84
20,000	174.23	167.82	162.23	157.32	149.12
25,000	217.78	209.77	202.79	196.65	186.40
30,000	261.34	251.73	243.34	235.97	223.68
35,000	304.89	293.68	283.90	275.30	260.96
40,000	348.45	335.64	324.45	314.63	298.23
45,000	392.00	377.59	365.01	353.96	335.51
50,000	435.56	419.54	405.57	393.29	372.79
55,000	479.11	461.50	446.12	432.61	410.07
60,000	522.67	503.45	486.68	471.94	447.35
65,000	566.22	545.40	527.23	511.27	484.63
70,000	609.78	587.36	567.79	550.60	521.91
75,000	653.34	629.31	608.35	589.93	559.18
80,000	696.89	671.27	648.90	629.25	596.46
85,000	740.45	713.22	689.46	668.58	633.74
90,000	784.00	755.17	730.01	707.91	671.02
95,000	827.56	797.13	770.57	747.24	708.30
100,000	871.11	839.08	811.13	786.57	745.58
110,000	958.22	922.99	892.24	865.22	820.14
120,000	1,045.33	1,006.90	973.35	943.88	894.69
125,000	1,088.89	1,048.85	1,013.91	983.21	931.97
130,000	1,132.44	1,090.80	1,054.46	1,022.53	969.25
140,000	1,219.56	1,174.71	1,135.57	1,101.19	1,043.81
150,000	1,306.67	1,258.62	1,216.69	1,179.85	1,118.36
160,000	1,393.78	1,342.53	1,297.80	1,258.50	1,192.92
170,000	1,480.89	1,426.43	1,378.91	1,337.16	1,267.48
175,000	1,524.44	1,468.39	1,419.47	1,376.49	1,304.76
180,000	1,568.00	1,510.34	1,460.02	1,415.82	1,342.04
190,000	1,655.11	1,594.25	1,541.14	1,494.47	1,416.59
200,000	1,742.22	1,678.16	1,622.25	1,573.13	1,491.15
220,000	1,916.44	1,845.97	1,784.47	1,730.44	1,640.27
225,000	1,960.00	1,887.92	1,825.03	1,769.77	1,677.54
230,000	2,003.55	1,929.88	1,865.58	1,809.10	1,714.82
240,000	2,090.66	2,013.79	1,946.70	1,887.75	1,789.38
$250,000	2,177.77	2,097.69	2,027.81	1,966.41	1,863.94

Table 1   29

6.50%   Monthly Payment Loans

Amortization Period in Years

	21	22	23	24	25
$ 100	0.73	0.72	0.70	0.69	0.68
200	1.46	1.43	1.40	1.38	1.36
300	2.19	2.14	2.10	2.06	2.03
400	2.92	2.86	2.80	2.75	2.71
500	3.65	3.57	3.50	3.44	3.38
600	4.38	4.28	4.20	4.12	4.06
700	5.10	5.00	4.90	4.81	4.73
800	5.83	5.71	5.60	5.50	5.41
900	6.56	6.42	6.30	6.18	6.08
1,000	7.29	7.13	7.00	6.87	6.76
2,000	14.57	14.26	13.99	13.74	13.51
3,000	21.86	21.39	20.98	20.60	20.26
4,000	29.14	28.52	27.97	27.47	27.01
5,000	36.42	35.65	34.96	34.33	33.77
6,000	43.71	42.78	41.95	41.20	40.52
7,000	50.99	49.91	48.94	48.06	47.27
8,000	58.27	57.04	55.93	54.93	54.02
9,000	65.56	64.17	62.92	61.79	60.77
10,000	72.84	71.30	69.91	68.66	67.53
15,000	109.26	106.95	104.86	102.99	101.29
20,000	145.68	142.59	139.82	137.31	135.05
25,000	182.10	178.24	174.77	171.64	168.81
30,000	218.51	213.89	209.72	205.97	202.57
35,000	254.93	249.53	244.68	240.29	236.33
40,000	291.35	285.18	279.63	274.62	270.09
45,000	327.77	320.83	314.58	308.95	303.85
50,000	364.19	356.47	349.54	343.28	337.61
55,000	400.60	392.12	384.49	377.60	371.37
60,000	437.02	427.77	419.44	411.93	405.13
65,000	473.44	463.42	454.40	446.26	438.89
70,000	509.86	499.06	489.35	480.58	472.65
75,000	546.28	534.71	524.30	514.91	506.41
80,000	582.70	570.36	559.26	549.24	540.17
85,000	619.11	606.00	594.21	583.57	573.93
90,000	655.53	641.65	629.16	617.89	607.69
95,000	691.95	677.30	664.12	652.22	641.45
100,000	728.37	712.94	699.07	686.55	675.21
110,000	801.20	784.24	768.98	755.20	742.73
120,000	874.04	855.53	838.88	823.86	810.25
125,000	910.46	891.18	873.84	858.18	844.01
130,000	946.88	926.83	908.79	892.51	877.77
140,000	1,019.71	998.12	978.70	961.16	945.30
150,000	1,092.55	1,069.41	1,048.60	1,029.82	1,012.82
160,000	1,165.39	1,140.71	1,118.51	1,098.47	1,080.34
170,000	1,238.22	1,212.00	1,188.41	1,167.13	1,147.86
175,000	1,274.64	1,247.65	1,223.37	1,201.45	1,181.62
180,000	1,311.06	1,283.30	1,258.32	1,235.78	1,215.38
190,000	1,383.89	1,354.59	1,328.23	1,304.44	1,282.90
200,000	1,456.73	1,425.88	1,398.13	1,373.09	1,350.42
220,000	1,602.40	1,568.47	1,537.95	1,510.40	1,485.46
225,000	1,638.82	1,604.12	1,572.90	1,544.73	1,519.22
230,000	1,675.24	1,639.76	1,607.85	1,579.05	1,552.98
240,000	1,748.08	1,711.06	1,677.76	1,647.71	1,620.50
$250,000	1,820.91	1,782.35	1,747.67	1,716.36	1,688.02

Monthly Payment Loans   **6.50%**

Amortization Period in Years

	26	27	28	29	30
$ 100	0.67	0.66	0.65	0.64	0.64
200	1.33	1.32	1.30	1.28	1.27
300	2.00	1.97	1.95	1.92	1.90
400	2.66	2.63	2.59	2.56	2.53
500	3.33	3.28	3.24	3.20	3.17
600	3.99	3.94	3.89	3.84	3.80
700	4.66	4.59	4.53	4.48	4.43
800	5.32	5.25	5.18	5.12	5.06
900	5.99	5.90	5.83	5.76	5.69
1,000	6.65	6.56	6.48	6.40	6.33
2,000	13.30	13.12	12.95	12.79	12.65
3,000	19.95	19.67	19.42	19.18	18.97
4,000	26.60	26.23	25.89	25.57	25.29
5,000	33.25	32.78	32.36	31.97	31.61
6,000	39.90	39.34	38.83	38.36	37.93
7,000	46.55	45.89	45.30	44.75	44.25
8,000	53.20	52.45	51.77	51.14	50.57
9,000	59.85	59.00	58.24	57.53	56.89
10,000	66.50	65.56	64.71	63.93	63.21
15,000	99.74	98.34	97.06	95.89	94.82
20,000	132.99	131.12	129.41	127.85	126.42
25,000	166.23	163.89	161.76	159.81	158.02
30,000	199.48	196.67	194.11	191.77	189.63
35,000	232.73	229.45	226.46	223.73	221.23
40,000	265.97	262.23	258.81	255.69	252.83
45,000	299.22	295.00	291.16	287.65	284.44
50,000	332.46	327.78	323.51	319.61	316.04
55,000	365.71	360.56	355.86	351.57	347.64
60,000	398.96	393.34	388.21	383.53	379.25
65,000	432.20	426.12	420.57	415.49	410.85
70,000	465.45	458.89	452.92	447.45	442.45
75,000	498.69	491.67	485.27	479.41	474.06
80,000	531.94	524.45	517.62	511.38	505.66
85,000	565.19	557.23	549.97	543.34	537.26
90,000	598.43	590.00	582.32	575.30	568.87
95,000	631.68	622.78	614.67	607.26	600.47
100,000	664.92	655.56	647.02	639.22	632.07
110,000	731.41	721.12	711.72	703.14	695.28
120,000	797.91	786.67	776.42	767.06	758.49
125,000	831.15	819.45	808.78	799.02	790.09
130,000	864.40	852.23	841.13	830.98	821.69
140,000	930.89	917.78	905.83	894.90	884.90
150,000	997.38	983.34	970.53	958.82	948.11
160,000	1,063.87	1,048.89	1,035.23	1,022.75	1,011.31
170,000	1,130.37	1,114.45	1,099.93	1,086.67	1,074.52
175,000	1,163.61	1,147.23	1,132.28	1,118.63	1,106.12
180,000	1,196.86	1,180.00	1,164.63	1,150.59	1,137.73
190,000	1,263.35	1,245.56	1,229.34	1,214.51	1,200.93
200,000	1,329.84	1,311.11	1,294.04	1,278.43	1,264.14
220,000	1,462.82	1,442.23	1,423.44	1,406.27	1,390.55
225,000	1,496.07	1,475.00	1,455.79	1,438.23	1,422.16
230,000	1,529.32	1,507.78	1,488.14	1,470.19	1,453.76
240,000	1,595.81	1,573.34	1,552.84	1,534.12	1,516.97
$250,000	1,662.30	1,638.89	1,617.55	1,598.04	1,580.18

Table 1   31

6.75%   **Monthly Payment Loans**

Amortization Period in Years

	5	7	8	10	12
$ 100	1.97	1.50	1.36	1.15	1.02
200	3.94	3.00	2.71	2.30	2.04
300	5.91	4.50	4.06	3.45	3.05
400	7.88	5.99	5.41	4.60	4.07
500	9.85	7.49	6.76	5.75	5.08
600	11.82	8.99	8.11	6.89	6.10
700	13.78	10.48	9.46	8.04	7.11
800	15.75	11.98	10.81	9.19	8.13
900	17.72	13.48	12.16	10.34	9.14
1,000	19.69	14.98	13.51	11.49	10.16
2,000	39.37	29.95	27.02	22.97	20.31
3,000	59.06	44.92	40.53	34.45	30.46
4,000	78.74	59.89	54.04	45.93	40.61
5,000	98.42	74.86	67.55	57.42	50.76
6,000	118.11	89.83	81.06	68.90	60.91
7,000	137.79	104.80	94.57	80.38	71.06
8,000	157.47	119.77	108.08	91.86	81.21
9,000	177.16	134.74	121.59	103.35	91.36
10,000	196.84	149.71	135.10	114.83	101.52
15,000	295.26	224.57	202.65	172.24	152.27
20,000	393.67	299.42	270.20	229.65	203.03
25,000	492.09	374.27	337.75	287.07	253.78
30,000	590.51	449.13	405.29	344.48	304.54
35,000	688.93	523.98	472.84	401.89	355.29
40,000	787.34	598.84	540.39	459.30	406.05
45,000	885.76	673.69	607.94	516.71	456.80
50,000	984.18	748.54	675.49	574.13	507.56
55,000	1,082.60	823.40	743.04	631.54	558.31
60,000	1,181.01	898.25	810.58	688.95	609.07
65,000	1,279.43	973.10	878.13	746.36	659.82
70,000	1,377.85	1,047.96	945.68	803.77	710.58
75,000	1,476.26	1,122.81	1,013.23	861.19	761.33
80,000	1,574.68	1,197.67	1,080.78	918.60	812.09
85,000	1,673.10	1,272.52	1,148.32	976.01	862.84
90,000	1,771.52	1,347.37	1,215.87	1,033.42	913.60
95,000	1,869.93	1,422.23	1,283.42	1,090.83	964.35
100,000	1,968.35	1,497.08	1,350.97	1,148.25	1,015.11
110,000	2,165.19	1,646.79	1,486.07	1,263.07	1,116.62
120,000	2,362.02	1,796.50	1,621.16	1,377.89	1,218.13
125,000	2,460.44	1,871.35	1,688.71	1,435.31	1,268.88
130,000	2,558.85	1,946.20	1,756.26	1,492.72	1,319.64
140,000	2,755.69	2,095.91	1,891.35	1,607.54	1,421.15
150,000	2,952.52	2,245.62	2,026.45	1,722.37	1,522.66
160,000	3,149.36	2,395.33	2,161.55	1,837.19	1,624.17
170,000	3,346.19	2,545.03	2,296.64	1,952.01	1,725.68
175,000	3,444.61	2,619.89	2,364.19	2,009.43	1,776.43
180,000	3,543.03	2,694.74	2,431.74	2,066.84	1,827.19
190,000	3,739.86	2,844.45	2,566.84	2,181.66	1,928.70
200,000	3,936.70	2,994.16	2,701.93	2,296.49	2,030.21
220,000	4,330.37	3,293.57	2,972.13	2,526.14	2,233.23
225,000	4,428.78	3,368.43	3,039.67	2,583.55	2,283.99
230,000	4,527.20	3,443.28	3,107.22	2,640.96	2,334.74
240,000	4,724.04	3,592.99	3,242.32	2,755.78	2,436.25
$250,000	4,920.87	3,742.70	3,377.42	2,870.61	2,537.76

Monthly Payment Loans   **6.75%**

Amortization Period in Years

		15	16	17	18	20
$	100	0.89	0.86	0.83	0.81	0.77
	200	1.77	1.71	1.66	1.61	1.53
	300	2.66	2.56	2.48	2.41	2.29
	400	3.54	3.42	3.31	3.21	3.05
	500	4.43	4.27	4.13	4.01	3.81
	600	5.31	5.12	4.96	4.81	4.57
	700	6.20	5.98	5.78	5.61	5.33
	800	7.08	6.83	6.61	6.41	6.09
	900	7.97	7.68	7.43	7.21	6.85
	1,000	8.85	8.54	8.26	8.01	7.61
	2,000	17.70	17.07	16.51	16.02	15.21
	3,000	26.55	25.60	24.76	24.03	22.82
	4,000	35.40	34.13	33.02	32.04	30.42
	5,000	44.25	42.66	41.27	40.05	38.02
	6,000	53.10	51.19	49.52	48.06	45.63
	7,000	61.95	59.72	57.78	56.07	53.23
	8,000	70.80	68.25	66.03	64.08	60.83
	9,000	79.65	76.78	74.28	72.09	68.44
	10,000	88.50	85.31	82.54	80.10	76.04
	15,000	132.74	127.97	123.80	120.15	114.06
	20,000	176.99	170.62	165.07	160.20	152.08
	25,000	221.23	213.28	206.34	200.25	190.10
	30,000	265.48	255.93	247.60	240.29	228.11
	35,000	309.72	298.58	288.87	280.34	266.13
	40,000	353.97	341.24	330.14	320.39	304.15
	45,000	398.21	383.89	371.40	360.44	342.17
	50,000	442.46	426.55	412.67	400.49	380.19
	55,000	486.71	469.20	453.93	440.54	418.21
	60,000	530.95	511.85	495.20	480.58	456.22
	65,000	575.20	554.51	536.47	520.63	494.24
	70,000	619.44	597.16	577.73	560.68	532.26
	75,000	663.69	639.82	619.00	600.73	570.28
	80,000	707.93	682.47	660.27	640.78	608.30
	85,000	752.18	725.12	701.53	680.82	646.31
	90,000	796.42	767.78	742.80	720.87	684.33
	95,000	840.67	810.43	784.07	760.92	722.35
	100,000	884.91	853.09	825.33	800.97	760.37
	110,000	973.41	938.39	907.86	881.07	836.41
	120,000	1,061.90	1,023.70	990.40	961.16	912.44
	125,000	1,106.14	1,066.36	1,031.66	1,001.21	950.46
	130,000	1,150.39	1,109.01	1,072.93	1,041.26	988.48
	140,000	1,238.88	1,194.32	1,155.46	1,121.36	1,064.51
	150,000	1,327.37	1,279.63	1,237.99	1,201.45	1,140.55
	160,000	1,415.86	1,364.93	1,320.53	1,281.55	1,216.59
	170,000	1,504.35	1,450.24	1,403.06	1,361.64	1,292.62
	175,000	1,548.60	1,492.90	1,444.33	1,401.69	1,330.64
	180,000	1,592.84	1,535.55	1,485.59	1,441.74	1,368.66
	190,000	1,681.33	1,620.86	1,568.13	1,521.84	1,444.70
	200,000	1,769.82	1,706.17	1,650.66	1,601.93	1,520.73
	220,000	1,946.81	1,876.78	1,815.72	1,762.13	1,672.81
	225,000	1,991.05	1,919.44	1,856.99	1,802.18	1,710.82
	230,000	2,035.30	1,962.09	1,898.26	1,842.22	1,748.84
	240,000	2,123.79	2,047.40	1,980.79	1,922.32	1,824.88
$	250,000	2,212.28	2,132.71	2,063.32	2,002.42	1,900.92

6.75%   Monthly Payment Loans

Amortization Period in Years

	21	22	23	24	25
$ 100	0.75	0.73	0.72	0.71	0.70
200	1.49	1.46	1.43	1.41	1.39
300	2.24	2.19	2.15	2.11	2.08
400	2.98	2.92	2.86	2.81	2.77
500	3.72	3.65	3.58	3.52	3.46
600	4.47	4.37	4.29	4.22	4.15
700	5.21	5.10	5.01	4.92	4.84
800	5.95	5.83	5.72	5.62	5.53
900	6.70	6.56	6.43	6.32	6.22
1,000	7.44	7.29	7.15	7.03	6.91
2,000	14.87	14.57	14.29	14.05	13.82
3,000	22.31	21.85	21.44	21.07	20.73
4,000	29.74	29.13	28.58	28.09	27.64
5,000	37.17	36.41	35.73	35.11	34.55
6,000	44.61	43.69	42.87	42.13	41.46
7,000	52.04	50.97	50.01	49.15	48.37
8,000	59.47	58.25	57.16	56.17	55.28
9,000	66.91	65.53	64.30	63.19	62.19
10,000	74.34	72.82	71.45	70.21	69.10
15,000	111.51	109.22	107.17	105.32	103.64
20,000	148.67	145.63	142.89	140.42	138.19
25,000	185.84	182.03	178.61	175.52	172.73
30,000	223.01	218.44	214.33	210.63	207.28
35,000	260.18	254.84	250.05	245.73	241.82
40,000	297.34	291.25	285.77	280.83	276.37
45,000	334.51	327.65	321.49	315.94	310.92
50,000	371.68	364.06	357.21	351.04	345.46
55,000	408.84	400.46	392.93	386.14	380.01
60,000	446.01	436.87	428.65	421.25	414.55
65,000	483.18	473.27	464.37	456.35	449.10
70,000	520.35	509.68	500.09	491.45	483.64
75,000	557.51	546.08	535.82	526.56	518.19
80,000	594.68	582.49	571.54	561.66	552.73
85,000	631.85	618.89	607.26	596.77	587.28
90,000	669.01	655.30	642.98	631.87	621.83
95,000	706.18	691.70	678.70	666.97	656.37
100,000	743.35	728.11	714.42	702.08	690.92
110,000	817.68	800.92	785.86	772.28	760.01
120,000	892.02	873.73	857.30	842.49	829.10
125,000	929.18	910.14	893.02	877.59	863.64
130,000	966.35	946.54	928.74	912.70	898.19
140,000	1,040.69	1,019.35	1,000.18	982.90	967.28
150,000	1,115.02	1,092.16	1,071.63	1,053.11	1,036.37
160,000	1,189.35	1,164.97	1,143.07	1,123.32	1,105.46
170,000	1,263.69	1,237.78	1,214.51	1,193.53	1,174.55
175,000	1,300.86	1,274.19	1,250.23	1,228.63	1,209.10
180,000	1,338.02	1,310.59	1,285.95	1,263.73	1,243.65
190,000	1,412.36	1,383.40	1,357.39	1,333.94	1,312.74
200,000	1,486.69	1,456.22	1,428.83	1,404.15	1,381.83
220,000	1,635.36	1,601.84	1,571.72	1,544.56	1,520.01
225,000	1,672.53	1,638.24	1,607.44	1,579.66	1,554.56
230,000	1,709.69	1,674.65	1,643.16	1,614.77	1,589.10
240,000	1,784.03	1,747.46	1,714.60	1,684.98	1,658.19
$250,000	1,858.36	1,820.27	1,786.04	1,755.18	1,727.28

Monthly Payment Loans   **6.75%**

Amortization Period in Years

	26	27	28	29	30
$ 100	0.69	0.68	0.67	0.66	0.65
200	1.37	1.35	1.33	1.32	1.30
300	2.05	2.02	1.99	1.97	1.95
400	2.73	2.69	2.66	2.63	2.60
500	3.41	3.36	3.32	3.28	3.25
600	4.09	4.03	3.98	3.94	3.90
700	4.77	4.71	4.65	4.59	4.55
800	5.45	5.38	5.31	5.25	5.19
900	6.13	6.05	5.97	5.91	5.84
1,000	6.81	6.72	6.64	6.56	6.49
2,000	13.62	13.44	13.27	13.12	12.98
3,000	20.43	20.15	19.90	19.67	19.46
4,000	27.24	26.87	26.53	26.23	25.95
5,000	34.04	33.59	33.17	32.78	32.43
6,000	40.85	40.30	39.80	39.34	38.92
7,000	47.66	47.02	46.43	45.90	45.41
8,000	54.47	53.73	53.06	52.45	51.89
9,000	61.28	60.45	59.70	59.01	58.38
10,000	68.08	67.17	66.33	65.56	64.86
15,000	102.12	100.75	99.49	98.34	97.29
20,000	136.16	134.33	132.65	131.12	129.72
25,000	170.20	167.91	165.81	163.90	162.15
30,000	204.24	201.49	198.97	196.68	194.58
35,000	238.28	235.07	232.13	229.46	227.01
40,000	272.32	268.65	265.30	262.24	259.44
45,000	306.36	302.23	298.46	295.02	291.87
50,000	340.40	335.81	331.62	327.80	324.30
55,000	374.44	369.39	364.78	360.58	356.73
60,000	408.48	402.97	397.94	393.36	389.16
65,000	442.52	436.55	431.10	426.14	421.59
70,000	476.56	470.13	464.26	458.91	454.02
75,000	510.60	503.71	497.43	491.69	486.45
80,000	544.64	537.29	530.59	524.47	518.88
85,000	578.68	570.87	563.75	557.25	551.31
90,000	612.72	604.45	596.91	590.03	583.74
95,000	646.76	638.03	630.07	622.81	616.17
100,000	680.80	671.61	663.23	655.59	648.60
110,000	748.88	738.77	729.55	721.15	713.46
120,000	816.96	805.93	795.88	786.71	778.32
125,000	851.00	839.51	829.04	819.49	810.75
130,000	885.04	873.09	862.20	852.27	843.18
140,000	953.12	940.25	928.52	917.82	908.04
150,000	1,021.20	1,007.41	994.85	983.38	972.90
160,000	1,089.28	1,074.57	1,061.17	1,048.94	1,037.76
170,000	1,157.36	1,141.73	1,127.49	1,114.50	1,102.62
175,000	1,191.40	1,175.31	1,160.65	1,147.28	1,135.05
180,000	1,225.44	1,208.89	1,193.81	1,180.06	1,167.48
190,000	1,293.51	1,276.05	1,260.14	1,245.62	1,232.34
200,000	1,361.59	1,343.21	1,326.46	1,311.17	1,297.20
220,000	1,497.75	1,477.53	1,459.10	1,442.29	1,426.92
225,000	1,531.79	1,511.11	1,492.27	1,475.07	1,459.35
230,000	1,565.83	1,544.69	1,525.43	1,507.85	1,491.78
240,000	1,633.91	1,611.85	1,591.75	1,573.41	1,556.64
$250,000	1,701.99	1,679.01	1,658.07	1,638.97	1,621.50

Table 1   35

7.00% Monthly Payment Loans

Amortization Period in Years

	5	7	8	10	12
$ 100	1.99	1.51	1.37	1.17	1.03
200	3.97	3.02	2.73	2.33	2.06
300	5.95	4.53	4.10	3.49	3.09
400	7.93	6.04	5.46	4.65	4.12
500	9.91	7.55	6.82	5.81	5.15
600	11.89	9.06	8.19	6.97	6.18
700	13.87	10.57	9.55	8.13	7.20
800	15.85	12.08	10.91	9.29	8.23
900	17.83	13.59	12.28	10.45	9.26
1,000	19.81	15.10	13.64	11.62	10.29
2,000	39.61	30.19	27.27	23.23	20.57
3,000	59.41	45.28	40.91	34.84	30.86
4,000	79.21	60.38	54.54	46.45	41.14
5,000	99.01	75.47	68.17	58.06	51.42
6,000	118.81	90.56	81.81	69.67	61.71
7,000	138.61	105.65	95.44	81.28	71.99
8,000	158.41	120.75	109.07	92.89	82.28
9,000	178.22	135.84	122.71	104.50	92.56
10,000	198.02	150.93	136.34	116.11	102.84
15,000	297.02	226.40	204.51	174.17	154.26
20,000	396.03	301.86	272.68	232.22	205.68
25,000	495.03	377.32	340.85	290.28	257.10
30,000	594.04	452.79	409.02	348.33	308.52
35,000	693.05	528.25	477.19	406.38	359.94
40,000	792.05	603.71	545.35	464.44	411.36
45,000	891.06	679.18	613.52	522.49	462.78
50,000	990.06	754.64	681.69	580.55	514.20
55,000	1,089.07	830.10	749.86	638.60	565.61
60,000	1,188.08	905.57	818.03	696.66	617.03
65,000	1,287.08	981.03	886.20	754.71	668.45
70,000	1,386.09	1,056.49	954.37	812.76	719.87
75,000	1,485.09	1,131.96	1,022.53	870.82	771.29
80,000	1,584.10	1,207.42	1,090.70	928.87	822.71
85,000	1,683.11	1,282.88	1,158.87	986.93	874.13
90,000	1,782.11	1,358.35	1,227.04	1,044.98	925.55
95,000	1,881.12	1,433.81	1,295.21	1,103.04	976.97
100,000	1,980.12	1,509.27	1,363.38	1,161.09	1,028.39
110,000	2,178.14	1,660.20	1,499.71	1,277.20	1,131.22
120,000	2,376.15	1,811.13	1,636.05	1,393.31	1,234.06
125,000	2,475.15	1,886.59	1,704.22	1,451.36	1,285.48
130,000	2,574.16	1,962.05	1,772.39	1,509.42	1,336.90
140,000	2,772.17	2,112.98	1,908.73	1,625.52	1,439.74
150,000	2,970.18	2,263.91	2,045.06	1,741.63	1,542.58
160,000	3,168.20	2,414.83	2,181.40	1,857.74	1,645.41
170,000	3,366.21	2,565.76	2,317.74	1,973.85	1,748.25
175,000	3,465.21	2,641.22	2,385.91	2,031.90	1,799.67
180,000	3,564.22	2,716.69	2,454.07	2,089.96	1,851.09
190,000	3,762.23	2,867.61	2,590.41	2,206.07	1,953.93
200,000	3,960.24	3,018.54	2,726.75	2,322.17	2,056.77
220,000	4,356.27	3,320.39	2,999.42	2,554.39	2,262.44
225,000	4,455.27	3,395.86	3,067.59	2,612.45	2,313.86
230,000	4,554.28	3,471.32	3,135.76	2,670.50	2,365.28
240,000	4,752.29	3,622.25	3,272.10	2,786.61	2,468.12
$250,000	4,950.30	3,773.17	3,408.43	2,902.72	2,570.96

Monthly Payment Loans   **7.00%**

Amortization Period in Years

	15	16	17	18	20
$ 100	0.90	0.87	0.84	0.82	0.78
200	1.80	1.74	1.68	1.64	1.56
300	2.70	2.61	2.52	2.45	2.33
400	3.60	3.47	3.36	3.27	3.11
500	4.50	4.34	4.20	4.08	3.88
600	5.40	5.21	5.04	4.90	4.66
700	6.30	6.08	5.88	5.71	5.43
800	7.20	6.94	6.72	6.53	6.21
900	8.09	7.81	7.56	7.34	6.98
1,000	8.99	8.68	8.40	8.16	7.76
2,000	17.98	17.35	16.80	16.32	15.51
3,000	26.97	26.02	25.19	24.47	23.26
4,000	35.96	34.69	33.59	32.63	31.02
5,000	44.95	43.37	41.99	40.78	38.77
6,000	53.93	52.04	50.38	48.94	46.52
7,000	62.92	60.71	58.78	57.09	54.28
8,000	71.91	69.38	67.18	65.25	62.03
9,000	80.90	78.05	75.57	73.40	69.78
10,000	89.89	86.73	83.97	81.56	77.53
15,000	134.83	130.09	125.95	122.33	116.30
20,000	179.77	173.45	167.94	163.11	155.06
25,000	224.71	216.81	209.92	203.88	193.83
30,000	269.65	260.17	251.90	244.66	232.59
35,000	314.59	303.53	293.89	285.43	271.36
40,000	359.54	346.89	335.87	326.21	310.12
45,000	404.48	390.25	377.85	366.98	348.89
50,000	449.42	433.61	419.84	407.76	387.65
55,000	494.36	476.97	461.82	448.53	426.42
60,000	539.30	520.33	503.80	489.31	465.18
65,000	584.24	563.69	545.78	530.08	503.95
70,000	629.18	607.05	587.77	570.86	542.71
75,000	674.13	650.41	629.75	611.63	581.48
80,000	719.07	693.77	671.73	652.41	620.24
85,000	764.01	737.13	713.72	693.18	659.01
90,000	808.95	780.49	755.70	733.96	697.77
95,000	853.89	823.85	797.68	774.73	736.54
100,000	898.83	867.21	839.67	815.51	775.30
110,000	988.72	953.93	923.63	897.06	852.83
120,000	1,078.60	1,040.65	1,007.60	978.61	930.36
125,000	1,123.54	1,084.02	1,049.58	1,019.38	969.13
130,000	1,168.48	1,127.38	1,091.56	1,060.16	1,007.89
140,000	1,258.36	1,214.10	1,175.53	1,141.71	1,085.42
150,000	1,348.25	1,300.82	1,259.50	1,223.26	1,162.95
160,000	1,438.13	1,387.54	1,343.46	1,304.81	1,240.48
170,000	1,528.01	1,474.26	1,427.43	1,386.36	1,318.01
175,000	1,572.95	1,517.62	1,469.41	1,427.13	1,356.78
180,000	1,617.90	1,560.98	1,511.39	1,467.91	1,395.54
190,000	1,707.78	1,647.70	1,595.36	1,549.46	1,473.07
200,000	1,797.66	1,734.42	1,679.33	1,631.01	1,550.60
220,000	1,977.43	1,907.86	1,847.26	1,794.11	1,705.66
225,000	2,022.37	1,951.22	1,889.24	1,834.88	1,744.43
230,000	2,067.31	1,994.58	1,931.22	1,875.66	1,783.19
240,000	2,157.19	2,081.30	2,015.19	1,957.21	1,860.72
$250,000	2,247.08	2,168.03	2,099.16	2,038.76	1,938.25

Table 1   37

7.00%   Monthly Payment Loans

Amortization Period in Years

	21	22	23	24	25
$ 100	0.76	0.75	0.73	0.72	0.71
200	1.52	1.49	1.46	1.44	1.42
300	2.28	2.24	2.19	2.16	2.13
400	3.04	2.98	2.92	2.88	2.83
500	3.80	3.72	3.65	3.59	3.54
600	4.56	4.47	4.38	4.31	4.25
700	5.31	5.21	5.11	5.03	4.95
800	6.07	5.95	5.84	5.75	5.66
900	6.83	6.70	6.57	6.46	6.37
1,000	7.59	7.44	7.30	7.18	7.07
2,000	15.17	14.87	14.60	14.36	14.14
3,000	22.76	22.31	21.90	21.54	21.21
4,000	30.34	29.74	29.20	28.72	28.28
5,000	37.93	37.18	36.50	35.89	35.34
6,000	45.51	44.61	43.80	43.07	42.41
7,000	53.10	52.04	51.10	50.25	49.48
8,000	60.68	59.48	58.40	57.43	56.55
9,000	68.27	66.91	65.70	64.60	63.62
10,000	75.85	74.35	73.00	71.78	70.68
15,000	113.78	111.52	109.49	107.67	106.02
20,000	151.70	148.69	145.99	143.56	141.36
25,000	189.62	185.86	182.48	179.44	176.70
30,000	227.55	223.03	218.98	215.33	212.04
35,000	265.47	260.20	255.48	251.22	247.38
40,000	303.39	297.37	291.97	287.11	282.72
45,000	341.32	334.55	328.47	323.00	318.06
50,000	379.24	371.72	364.96	358.88	353.39
55,000	417.16	408.89	401.46	394.77	388.73
60,000	455.09	446.06	437.96	430.66	424.07
65,000	493.01	483.23	474.45	466.55	459.41
70,000	530.94	520.40	510.95	502.44	494.75
75,000	568.86	557.57	547.44	538.32	530.09
80,000	606.78	594.74	583.94	574.21	565.43
85,000	644.71	631.92	620.44	610.10	600.77
90,000	682.63	669.09	656.93	645.99	636.11
95,000	720.55	706.26	693.43	681.88	671.45
100,000	758.48	743.43	729.92	717.76	706.78
110,000	834.32	817.77	802.92	789.54	777.46
120,000	910.17	892.11	875.91	861.32	848.14
125,000	948.09	929.29	912.40	897.20	883.48
130,000	986.02	966.46	948.90	933.09	918.82
140,000	1,061.87	1,040.80	1,021.89	1,004.87	989.50
150,000	1,137.71	1,115.14	1,094.88	1,076.64	1,060.17
160,000	1,213.56	1,189.48	1,167.88	1,148.42	1,130.85
170,000	1,289.41	1,263.83	1,240.87	1,220.20	1,201.53
175,000	1,327.33	1,301.00	1,277.36	1,256.08	1,236.87
180,000	1,365.25	1,338.17	1,313.86	1,291.97	1,272.21
190,000	1,441.10	1,412.51	1,386.85	1,363.75	1,342.89
200,000	1,516.95	1,486.85	1,459.84	1,435.52	1,413.56
220,000	1,668.64	1,635.54	1,605.83	1,579.08	1,554.92
225,000	1,706.57	1,672.71	1,642.32	1,614.96	1,590.26
230,000	1,744.49	1,709.88	1,678.82	1,650.85	1,625.60
240,000	1,820.34	1,784.22	1,751.81	1,722.63	1,696.28
$250,000	1,896.18	1,858.57	1,824.80	1,794.40	1,766.95

Monthly Payment Loans   **7.00%**

Amortization Period in Years

	26	27	28	29	30
$ 100	0.70	0.69	0.68	0.68	0.67
200	1.40	1.38	1.36	1.35	1.34
300	2.10	2.07	2.04	2.02	2.00
400	2.79	2.76	2.72	2.69	2.67
500	3.49	3.44	3.40	3.37	3.33
600	4.19	4.13	4.08	4.04	4.00
700	4.88	4.82	4.76	4.71	4.66
800	5.58	5.51	5.44	5.38	5.33
900	6.28	6.20	6.12	6.05	5.99
1,000	6.97	6.88	6.80	6.73	6.66
2,000	13.94	13.76	13.60	13.45	13.31
3,000	20.91	20.64	20.39	20.17	19.96
4,000	27.88	27.52	27.19	26.89	26.62
5,000	34.85	34.40	33.99	33.61	33.27
6,000	41.82	41.27	40.78	40.33	39.92
7,000	48.78	48.15	47.58	47.05	46.58
8,000	55.75	55.03	54.37	53.78	53.23
9,000	62.72	61.91	61.17	60.50	59.88
10,000	69.69	68.79	67.97	67.22	66.54
15,000	104.53	103.18	101.95	100.82	99.80
20,000	139.37	137.57	135.93	134.43	133.07
25,000	174.21	171.96	169.91	168.04	166.33
30,000	209.06	206.35	203.89	201.64	199.60
35,000	243.90	240.74	237.87	235.25	232.86
40,000	278.74	275.13	271.85	268.86	266.13
45,000	313.58	309.52	305.83	302.46	299.39
50,000	348.42	343.91	339.81	336.07	332.66
55,000	383.27	378.30	373.79	369.68	365.92
60,000	418.11	412.69	407.77	403.28	399.19
65,000	452.95	447.08	441.75	436.89	432.45
70,000	487.79	481.48	475.73	470.50	465.72
75,000	522.63	515.87	509.71	504.10	498.98
80,000	557.48	550.26	543.69	537.71	532.25
85,000	592.32	584.65	577.67	571.32	565.51
90,000	627.16	619.04	611.65	604.92	598.78
95,000	662.00	653.43	645.63	638.53	632.04
100,000	696.84	687.82	679.61	672.14	665.31
110,000	766.53	756.60	747.57	739.35	731.84
120,000	836.21	825.38	815.54	806.56	798.37
125,000	871.05	859.77	849.52	840.17	831.63
130,000	905.89	894.16	883.50	873.77	864.90
140,000	975.58	962.95	951.46	940.99	931.43
150,000	1,045.26	1,031.73	1,019.42	1,008.20	997.96
160,000	1,114.95	1,100.51	1,087.38	1,075.41	1,064.49
170,000	1,184.63	1,169.29	1,155.34	1,142.63	1,131.02
175,000	1,219.47	1,203.68	1,189.32	1,176.23	1,164.28
180,000	1,254.31	1,238.07	1,223.30	1,209.84	1,197.55
190,000	1,324.00	1,306.85	1,291.26	1,277.05	1,264.08
200,000	1,393.68	1,375.63	1,359.22	1,344.27	1,330.61
220,000	1,533.05	1,513.20	1,495.14	1,478.69	1,463.67
225,000	1,567.89	1,547.59	1,529.12	1,512.30	1,496.94
230,000	1,602.73	1,581.98	1,563.10	1,545.90	1,530.20
240,000	1,672.42	1,650.76	1,631.07	1,613.12	1,596.73
$250,000	1,742.10	1,719.54	1,699.03	1,680.33	1,663.26

Table 1   39

7.25%   Monthly Payment Loans

Amortization Period in Years

	5	7	8	10	12
$ 100	2.00	1.53	1.38	1.18	1.05
200	3.99	3.05	2.76	2.35	2.09
300	5.98	4.57	4.13	3.53	3.13
400	7.97	6.09	5.51	4.70	4.17
500	9.96	7.61	6.88	5.88	5.21
600	11.96	9.13	8.26	7.05	6.26
700	13.95	10.66	9.64	8.22	7.30
800	15.94	12.18	11.01	9.40	8.34
900	17.93	13.70	12.39	10.57	9.38
1,000	19.92	15.22	13.76	11.75	10.42
2,000	39.84	30.44	27.52	23.49	20.84
3,000	59.76	45.65	41.28	35.23	31.26
4,000	79.68	60.87	55.04	46.97	41.68
5,000	99.60	76.08	68.80	58.71	52.09
6,000	119.52	91.30	82.56	70.45	62.51
7,000	139.44	106.51	96.31	82.19	72.93
8,000	159.36	121.73	110.07	93.93	83.35
9,000	179.28	136.94	123.83	105.67	93.76
10,000	199.20	152.16	137.59	117.41	104.18
15,000	298.80	228.23	206.38	176.11	156.27
20,000	398.39	304.31	275.17	234.81	208.36
25,000	497.99	380.38	343.97	293.51	260.44
30,000	597.59	456.46	412.76	352.21	312.53
35,000	697.18	532.54	481.55	410.91	364.62
40,000	796.78	608.61	550.34	469.61	416.71
45,000	896.38	684.69	619.14	528.31	468.80
50,000	995.97	760.76	687.93	587.01	520.88
55,000	1,095.57	836.84	756.72	645.71	572.97
60,000	1,195.17	912.92	825.51	704.41	625.06
65,000	1,294.76	988.99	894.30	763.11	677.15
70,000	1,394.36	1,065.07	963.10	821.81	729.23
75,000	1,493.96	1,141.14	1,031.89	880.51	781.32
80,000	1,593.55	1,217.22	1,100.68	939.21	833.41
85,000	1,693.15	1,293.30	1,169.47	997.91	885.50
90,000	1,792.75	1,369.37	1,238.27	1,056.61	937.59
95,000	1,892.34	1,445.45	1,307.06	1,115.31	989.67
100,000	1,991.94	1,521.52	1,375.85	1,174.02	1,041.76
110,000	2,191.13	1,673.68	1,513.44	1,291.42	1,145.94
120,000	2,390.33	1,825.83	1,651.02	1,408.82	1,250.11
125,000	2,489.93	1,901.90	1,719.81	1,467.52	1,302.20
130,000	2,589.52	1,977.98	1,788.60	1,526.22	1,354.29
140,000	2,788.72	2,130.13	1,926.19	1,643.62	1,458.46
150,000	2,987.91	2,282.28	2,063.77	1,761.02	1,562.64
160,000	3,187.10	2,434.43	2,201.36	1,878.42	1,666.81
170,000	3,386.30	2,586.59	2,338.94	1,995.82	1,770.99
175,000	3,485.89	2,662.66	2,407.74	2,054.52	1,823.08
180,000	3,585.49	2,738.74	2,476.53	2,113.22	1,875.17
190,000	3,784.68	2,890.89	2,614.11	2,230.62	1,979.34
200,000	3,983.88	3,043.04	2,751.70	2,348.03	2,083.52
220,000	4,382.26	3,347.35	3,026.87	2,582.83	2,291.87
225,000	4,481.86	3,423.42	3,095.66	2,641.53	2,343.96
230,000	4,581.46	3,499.50	3,164.45	2,700.23	2,396.04
240,000	4,780.65	3,651.65	3,302.04	2,817.63	2,500.22
$250,000	4,979.85	3,803.80	3,439.62	2,935.03	2,604.39

Monthly Payment Loans   7.25%

Amortization Period in Years

	15	16	17	18	20
$ 100	0.92	0.89	0.86	0.84	0.80
200	1.83	1.77	1.71	1.67	1.59
300	2.74	2.65	2.57	2.50	2.38
400	3.66	3.53	3.42	3.33	3.17
500	4.57	4.41	4.28	4.16	3.96
600	5.48	5.29	5.13	4.99	4.75
700	6.40	6.18	5.98	5.82	5.54
800	7.31	7.06	6.84	6.65	6.33
900	8.22	7.94	7.69	7.48	7.12
1,000	9.13	8.82	8.55	8.31	7.91
2,000	18.26	17.63	17.09	16.61	15.81
3,000	27.39	26.45	25.63	24.91	23.72
4,000	36.52	35.26	34.17	33.21	31.62
5,000	45.65	44.08	42.71	41.51	39.52
6,000	54.78	52.89	51.25	49.82	47.43
7,000	63.91	61.71	59.79	58.12	55.33
8,000	73.03	70.52	68.33	66.42	63.24
9,000	82.16	79.34	76.88	74.72	71.14
10,000	91.29	88.15	85.42	83.02	79.04
15,000	136.93	132.22	128.12	124.53	118.56
20,000	182.58	176.30	170.83	166.04	158.08
25,000	228.22	220.37	213.54	207.55	197.60
30,000	273.86	264.44	256.24	249.06	237.12
35,000	319.51	308.52	298.95	290.57	276.64
40,000	365.15	352.59	341.65	332.07	316.16
45,000	410.79	396.66	384.36	373.58	355.67
50,000	456.44	440.73	427.07	415.09	395.19
55,000	502.08	484.81	469.77	456.60	434.71
60,000	547.72	528.88	512.48	498.11	474.23
65,000	593.37	572.95	555.18	539.62	513.75
70,000	639.01	617.03	597.89	581.13	553.27
75,000	684.65	661.10	640.60	622.63	592.79
80,000	730.30	705.17	683.30	664.14	632.31
85,000	775.94	749.24	726.01	705.65	671.82
90,000	821.58	793.32	768.71	747.16	711.34
95,000	867.22	837.39	811.42	788.67	750.86
100,000	912.87	881.46	854.13	830.18	790.38
110,000	1,004.15	969.61	939.54	913.19	869.42
120,000	1,095.44	1,057.75	1,024.95	996.21	948.46
125,000	1,141.08	1,101.83	1,067.66	1,037.72	987.97
130,000	1,186.73	1,145.90	1,110.36	1,079.23	1,027.49
140,000	1,278.01	1,234.05	1,195.78	1,162.25	1,106.53
150,000	1,369.30	1,322.19	1,281.19	1,245.26	1,185.57
160,000	1,460.59	1,410.34	1,366.60	1,328.28	1,264.61
170,000	1,551.87	1,498.48	1,452.01	1,411.30	1,343.64
175,000	1,597.52	1,542.56	1,494.72	1,452.81	1,383.16
180,000	1,643.16	1,586.63	1,537.42	1,494.31	1,422.68
190,000	1,734.44	1,674.77	1,622.84	1,577.33	1,501.72
200,000	1,825.73	1,762.84	1,708.25	1,660.35	1,580.76
220,000	2,008.30	1,939.21	1,879.07	1,826.38	1,738.83
225,000	2,053.95	1,983.28	1,921.78	1,867.89	1,778.35
230,000	2,099.59	2,027.36	1,964.49	1,909.40	1,817.87
240,000	2,190.88	2,115.50	2,049.90	1,992.42	1,896.91
$250,000	2,282.16	2,203.65	2,135.31	2,075.44	1,975.94

Table 1   41

7.25%   Monthly Payment Loans

Amortization Period in Years

	21	22	23	24	25
$ 100	0.78	0.76	0.75	0.74	0.73
200	1.55	1.52	1.50	1.47	1.45
300	2.33	2.28	2.24	2.21	2.17
400	3.10	3.04	2.99	2.94	2.90
500	3.87	3.80	3.73	3.67	3.62
600	4.65	4.56	4.48	4.41	4.34
700	5.42	5.32	5.22	5.14	5.06
800	6.19	6.08	5.97	5.87	5.79
900	6.97	6.84	6.72	6.61	6.51
1,000	7.74	7.59	7.46	7.34	7.23
2,000	15.48	15.18	14.92	14.68	14.46
3,000	23.22	22.77	22.37	22.01	21.69
4,000	30.95	30.36	29.83	29.35	28.92
5,000	38.69	37.95	37.28	36.69	36.15
6,000	46.43	45.54	44.74	44.02	43.37
7,000	54.17	53.13	52.20	51.36	50.60
8,000	61.90	60.72	59.65	58.69	57.83
9,000	69.64	68.31	67.11	66.03	65.06
10,000	77.38	75.89	74.56	73.37	72.29
15,000	116.07	113.84	111.84	110.05	108.43
20,000	154.75	151.78	149.12	146.73	144.57
25,000	193.44	189.73	186.40	183.41	180.71
30,000	232.13	227.67	223.68	220.09	216.85
35,000	270.82	265.62	260.96	256.77	252.99
40,000	309.50	303.56	298.24	293.45	289.13
45,000	348.19	341.51	335.52	330.13	325.27
50,000	386.88	379.45	372.79	366.81	361.41
55,000	425.57	417.40	410.07	403.49	397.55
60,000	464.25	455.34	447.35	440.17	433.69
65,000	502.94	493.29	484.63	476.85	469.83
70,000	541.63	531.23	521.91	513.53	505.97
75,000	580.32	569.18	559.19	550.21	542.11
80,000	619.00	607.12	596.47	586.89	578.25
85,000	657.69	645.06	633.75	623.57	614.39
90,000	696.38	683.01	671.03	660.25	650.53
95,000	735.06	720.95	708.30	696.93	686.67
100,000	773.75	758.90	745.58	733.61	722.81
110,000	851.13	834.79	820.14	806.97	795.09
120,000	928.50	910.68	894.70	880.33	867.37
125,000	967.19	948.62	931.98	917.01	903.51
130,000	1,005.88	986.57	969.26	953.69	939.65
140,000	1,083.25	1,062.46	1,043.82	1,027.05	1,011.93
150,000	1,160.63	1,138.35	1,118.37	1,100.41	1,084.22
160,000	1,238.00	1,214.23	1,192.93	1,173.77	1,156.50
170,000	1,315.37	1,290.12	1,267.49	1,247.13	1,228.78
175,000	1,354.06	1,328.07	1,304.77	1,283.81	1,264.92
180,000	1,392.75	1,366.01	1,342.05	1,320.49	1,301.06
190,000	1,470.12	1,441.90	1,416.60	1,393.85	1,373.34
200,000	1,547.50	1,517.79	1,491.16	1,467.22	1,445.62
220,000	1,702.25	1,669.57	1,640.28	1,613.94	1,590.18
225,000	1,740.94	1,707.52	1,677.56	1,650.62	1,626.32
230,000	1,779.62	1,745.46	1,714.84	1,687.30	1,662.46
240,000	1,857.00	1,821.35	1,789.39	1,760.66	1,734.74
$250,000	1,934.37	1,897.24	1,863.95	1,834.02	1,807.02

Monthly Payment Loans   **7.25%**

Amortization Period in Years

	26	27	28	29	30
$ 100	0.72	0.71	0.70	0.69	0.69
200	1.43	1.41	1.40	1.38	1.37
300	2.14	2.12	2.09	2.07	2.05
400	2.86	2.82	2.79	2.76	2.73
500	3.57	3.53	3.49	3.45	3.42
600	4.28	4.23	4.18	4.14	4.10
700	5.00	4.93	4.88	4.83	4.78
800	5.71	5.64	5.57	5.52	5.46
900	6.42	6.34	6.27	6.20	6.14
1,000	7.14	7.05	6.97	6.89	6.83
2,000	14.27	14.09	13.93	13.78	13.65
3,000	21.40	21.13	20.89	20.67	20.47
4,000	28.53	28.17	27.85	27.56	27.29
5,000	35.66	35.21	34.81	34.45	34.11
6,000	42.79	42.26	41.77	41.34	40.94
7,000	49.92	49.30	48.74	48.22	47.76
8,000	57.05	56.34	55.70	55.11	54.58
9,000	64.18	63.38	62.66	62.00	61.40
10,000	71.31	70.42	69.62	68.89	68.22
15,000	106.96	105.63	104.43	103.33	102.33
20,000	142.61	140.84	139.24	137.77	136.44
25,000	178.27	176.05	174.04	172.22	170.55
30,000	213.92	211.26	208.85	206.66	204.66
35,000	249.57	246.47	243.66	241.10	238.77
40,000	285.22	281.68	278.47	275.54	272.88
45,000	320.87	316.89	313.28	309.98	306.98
50,000	356.53	352.10	348.08	344.43	341.09
55,000	392.18	387.31	382.89	378.87	375.20
60,000	427.83	422.52	417.70	413.31	409.31
65,000	463.48	457.73	452.51	447.75	443.42
70,000	499.14	492.94	487.31	482.20	477.53
75,000	534.79	528.15	522.12	516.64	511.64
80,000	570.44	563.36	556.93	551.08	545.75
85,000	606.09	598.57	591.74	585.52	579.85
90,000	641.74	633.78	626.55	619.96	613.96
95,000	677.40	668.99	661.35	654.41	648.07
100,000	713.05	704.20	696.16	688.85	682.18
110,000	784.35	774.62	765.78	757.73	750.40
120,000	855.66	845.04	835.39	826.62	818.62
125,000	891.31	880.25	870.20	861.06	852.73
130,000	926.96	915.46	905.01	895.50	886.83
140,000	998.27	985.88	974.62	964.39	955.05
150,000	1,069.57	1,056.30	1,044.24	1,033.27	1,023.27
160,000	1,140.87	1,126.72	1,113.86	1,102.15	1,091.49
170,000	1,212.18	1,197.13	1,183.47	1,171.04	1,159.70
175,000	1,247.83	1,232.34	1,218.28	1,205.48	1,193.81
180,000	1,283.48	1,267.55	1,253.09	1,239.92	1,227.92
190,000	1,354.79	1,337.97	1,322.70	1,308.81	1,296.14
200,000	1,426.09	1,408.39	1,392.32	1,377.69	1,364.36
220,000	1,568.70	1,549.23	1,531.55	1,515.46	1,500.79
225,000	1,604.35	1,584.44	1,566.36	1,549.90	1,534.90
230,000	1,640.00	1,619.65	1,601.17	1,584.34	1,569.01
240,000	1,711.31	1,690.07	1,670.78	1,653.23	1,637.23
$250,000	1,782.61	1,760.49	1,740.40	1,722.11	1,705.45

Table 1   43

7.50%   Monthly Payment Loans

Amortization Period in Years

	5	7	8	10	12
$ 100	2.01	1.54	1.39	1.19	1.06
200	4.01	3.07	2.78	2.38	2.12
300	6.02	4.61	4.17	3.57	3.17
400	8.02	6.14	5.56	4.75	4.23
500	10.02	7.67	6.95	5.94	5.28
600	12.03	9.21	8.34	7.13	6.34
700	14.03	10.74	9.72	8.31	7.39
800	16.04	12.28	11.11	9.50	8.45
900	18.04	13.81	12.50	10.69	9.50
1,000	20.04	15.34	13.89	11.88	10.56
2,000	40.08	30.68	27.77	23.75	21.11
3,000	60.12	46.02	41.66	35.62	31.66
4,000	80.16	61.36	55.54	47.49	42.21
5,000	100.19	76.70	69.42	59.36	52.77
6,000	120.23	92.03	83.31	71.23	63.32
7,000	140.27	107.37	97.19	83.10	73.87
8,000	160.31	122.71	111.08	94.97	84.42
9,000	180.35	138.05	124.96	106.84	94.98
10,000	200.38	153.39	138.84	118.71	105.53
15,000	300.57	230.08	208.26	178.06	158.29
20,000	400.76	306.77	277.68	237.41	211.05
25,000	500.95	383.46	347.10	296.76	263.81
30,000	601.14	460.15	416.52	356.11	316.57
35,000	701.33	536.84	485.94	415.46	369.33
40,000	801.52	613.54	555.36	474.81	422.10
45,000	901.71	690.23	624.78	534.16	474.86
50,000	1,001.90	766.92	694.20	593.51	527.62
55,000	1,102.09	843.61	763.62	652.86	580.38
60,000	1,202.28	920.30	833.04	712.22	633.14
65,000	1,302.47	996.99	902.46	771.57	685.90
70,000	1,402.66	1,073.68	971.88	830.92	738.66
75,000	1,502.85	1,150.38	1,041.30	890.27	791.42
80,000	1,603.04	1,227.07	1,110.71	949.62	844.19
85,000	1,703.23	1,303.76	1,180.13	1,008.97	896.95
90,000	1,803.42	1,380.45	1,249.55	1,068.32	949.71
95,000	1,903.61	1,457.14	1,318.97	1,127.67	1,002.47
100,000	2,003.80	1,533.83	1,388.39	1,187.02	1,055.23
110,000	2,204.18	1,687.22	1,527.23	1,305.72	1,160.75
120,000	2,404.56	1,840.60	1,666.07	1,424.43	1,266.28
125,000	2,504.75	1,917.29	1,735.49	1,483.78	1,319.04
130,000	2,604.94	1,993.98	1,804.91	1,543.13	1,371.80
140,000	2,805.32	2,147.36	1,943.75	1,661.83	1,477.32
150,000	3,005.70	2,300.75	2,082.59	1,780.53	1,582.84
160,000	3,206.08	2,454.13	2,221.42	1,899.23	1,688.37
170,000	3,406.46	2,607.51	2,360.26	2,017.94	1,793.89
175,000	3,506.65	2,684.20	2,429.68	2,077.29	1,846.65
180,000	3,606.84	2,760.89	2,499.10	2,136.64	1,899.41
190,000	3,807.22	2,914.28	2,637.94	2,255.34	2,004.93
200,000	4,007.59	3,067.66	2,776.78	2,374.04	2,110.46
220,000	4,408.35	3,374.43	3,054.46	2,611.44	2,321.50
225,000	4,508.54	3,451.12	3,123.88	2,670.79	2,374.26
230,000	4,608.73	3,527.81	3,193.30	2,730.15	2,427.03
240,000	4,809.11	3,681.19	3,332.13	2,848.85	2,532.55
$250,000	5,009.49	3,834.57	3,470.97	2,967.55	2,638.07

Monthly Payment Loans   **7.50%**

Amortization Period in Years

	15	16	17	18	20
$ 100	0.93	0.90	0.87	0.85	0.81
200	1.86	1.80	1.74	1.69	1.62
300	2.79	2.69	2.61	2.54	2.42
400	3.71	3.59	3.48	3.38	3.23
500	4.64	4.48	4.35	4.23	4.03
600	5.57	5.38	5.22	5.07	4.84
700	6.49	6.28	6.09	5.92	5.64
800	7.42	7.17	6.95	6.76	6.45
900	8.35	8.07	7.82	7.61	7.26
1,000	9.28	8.96	8.69	8.45	8.06
2,000	18.55	17.92	17.38	16.90	16.12
3,000	27.82	26.88	26.07	25.35	24.17
4,000	37.09	35.84	34.75	33.80	32.23
5,000	46.36	44.80	43.44	42.25	40.28
6,000	55.63	53.75	52.13	50.70	48.34
7,000	64.90	62.71	60.81	59.15	56.40
8,000	74.17	71.67	69.50	67.60	64.45
9,000	83.44	80.63	78.19	76.05	72.51
10,000	92.71	89.59	86.88	84.50	80.56
15,000	139.06	134.38	130.31	126.75	120.84
20,000	185.41	179.17	173.75	169.00	161.12
25,000	231.76	223.96	217.18	211.25	201.40
30,000	278.11	268.75	260.62	253.50	241.68
35,000	324.46	313.54	304.05	295.75	281.96
40,000	370.81	358.34	347.49	337.99	322.24
45,000	417.16	403.13	390.92	380.24	362.52
50,000	463.51	447.92	434.36	422.49	402.80
55,000	509.86	492.71	477.80	464.74	443.08
60,000	556.21	537.50	521.23	506.99	483.36
65,000	602.56	582.29	564.67	549.24	523.64
70,000	648.91	627.08	608.10	591.49	563.92
75,000	695.26	671.88	651.54	633.73	604.20
80,000	741.61	716.67	694.97	675.98	644.48
85,000	787.97	761.46	738.41	718.23	684.76
90,000	834.32	806.25	781.84	760.48	725.04
95,000	880.67	851.04	825.28	802.73	765.32
100,000	927.02	895.83	868.71	844.98	805.60
110,000	1,019.72	985.42	955.59	929.48	886.16
120,000	1,112.42	1,075.00	1,042.46	1,013.97	966.72
125,000	1,158.77	1,119.79	1,085.89	1,056.22	1,007.00
130,000	1,205.12	1,164.58	1,129.33	1,098.47	1,047.28
140,000	1,297.82	1,254.16	1,216.20	1,182.97	1,127.84
150,000	1,390.52	1,343.75	1,303.07	1,267.46	1,208.39
160,000	1,483.22	1,433.33	1,389.94	1,351.96	1,288.95
170,000	1,575.93	1,522.91	1,476.81	1,436.46	1,369.51
175,000	1,622.28	1,567.70	1,520.25	1,478.71	1,409.79
180,000	1,668.63	1,612.49	1,563.68	1,520.96	1,450.07
190,000	1,761.33	1,702.08	1,650.55	1,605.45	1,530.63
200,000	1,854.03	1,791.66	1,737.42	1,689.95	1,611.19
220,000	2,039.43	1,970.83	1,911.17	1,858.95	1,772.31
225,000	2,085.78	2,015.62	1,954.60	1,901.19	1,812.59
230,000	2,132.13	2,060.41	1,998.04	1,943.44	1,852.87
240,000	2,224.83	2,149.99	2,084.91	2,027.94	1,933.43
$250,000	2,317.54	2,239.57	2,171.78	2,112.44	2,013.99

Table 1   45

7.50%   Monthly Payment Loans

Amortization Period in Years

	21	22	23	24	25
$ 100	0.79	0.78	0.77	0.75	0.74
200	1.58	1.55	1.53	1.50	1.48
300	2.37	2.33	2.29	2.25	2.22
400	3.16	3.10	3.05	3.00	2.96
500	3.95	3.88	3.81	3.75	3.70
600	4.74	4.65	4.57	4.50	4.44
700	5.53	5.43	5.33	5.25	5.18
800	6.32	6.20	6.10	6.00	5.92
900	7.11	6.98	6.86	6.75	6.66
1,000	7.90	7.75	7.62	7.50	7.39
2,000	15.79	15.50	15.23	15.00	14.78
3,000	23.68	23.24	22.85	22.49	22.17
4,000	31.57	30.99	30.46	29.99	29.56
5,000	39.46	38.73	38.07	37.49	36.95
6,000	47.35	46.48	45.69	44.98	44.34
7,000	55.25	54.22	53.30	52.48	51.73
8,000	63.14	61.97	60.92	59.97	59.12
9,000	71.03	69.71	68.53	67.47	66.51
10,000	78.92	77.46	76.14	74.97	73.90
15,000	118.38	116.18	114.21	112.45	110.85
20,000	157.84	154.91	152.28	149.93	147.80
25,000	197.30	193.63	190.35	187.41	184.75
30,000	236.75	232.36	228.42	224.89	221.70
35,000	276.21	271.08	266.49	262.37	258.65
40,000	315.67	309.81	304.56	299.85	295.60
45,000	355.13	348.53	342.63	337.33	332.55
50,000	394.59	387.26	380.70	374.81	369.50
55,000	434.05	425.99	418.77	412.29	406.45
60,000	473.50	464.71	456.84	449.77	443.40
65,000	512.96	503.44	494.91	487.25	480.35
70,000	552.42	542.16	532.98	524.73	517.30
75,000	591.88	580.89	571.05	562.21	554.25
80,000	631.34	619.61	609.12	599.69	591.20
85,000	670.80	658.34	647.19	637.17	628.15
90,000	710.25	697.06	685.26	674.65	665.10
95,000	749.71	735.79	723.32	712.13	702.05
100,000	789.17	774.52	761.39	749.61	739.00
110,000	868.09	851.97	837.53	824.57	812.90
120,000	947.00	929.42	913.67	899.53	886.79
125,000	986.46	968.14	951.74	937.01	923.74
130,000	1,025.92	1,006.87	989.81	974.49	960.69
140,000	1,104.84	1,084.32	1,065.95	1,049.45	1,034.59
150,000	1,183.75	1,161.77	1,142.09	1,124.41	1,108.49
160,000	1,262.67	1,239.22	1,218.23	1,199.37	1,182.39
170,000	1,341.59	1,316.67	1,294.37	1,274.33	1,256.29
175,000	1,381.05	1,355.40	1,332.44	1,311.81	1,293.24
180,000	1,420.50	1,394.12	1,370.51	1,349.29	1,330.19
190,000	1,499.42	1,471.57	1,446.64	1,424.25	1,404.09
200,000	1,578.34	1,549.03	1,522.78	1,499.21	1,477.99
220,000	1,736.17	1,703.93	1,675.06	1,649.14	1,625.79
225,000	1,775.63	1,742.65	1,713.13	1,686.62	1,662.74
230,000	1,815.09	1,781.38	1,751.20	1,724.10	1,699.68
240,000	1,894.00	1,858.83	1,827.34	1,799.06	1,773.58
$250,000	1,972.92	1,936.28	1,903.48	1,874.02	1,847.48

Monthly Payment Loans **7.50%**

Amortization Period in Years

	26	27	28	29	30
$ 100	0.73	0.73	0.72	0.71	0.70
200	1.46	1.45	1.43	1.42	1.40
300	2.19	2.17	2.14	2.12	2.10
400	2.92	2.89	2.86	2.83	2.80
500	3.65	3.61	3.57	3.53	3.50
600	4.38	4.33	4.28	4.24	4.20
700	5.11	5.05	5.00	4.95	4.90
800	5.84	5.77	5.71	5.65	5.60
900	6.57	6.49	6.42	6.36	6.30
1,000	7.30	7.21	7.13	7.06	7.00
2,000	14.59	14.42	14.26	14.12	13.99
3,000	21.89	21.63	21.39	21.18	20.98
4,000	29.18	28.83	28.52	28.23	27.97
5,000	36.48	36.04	35.65	35.29	34.97
6,000	43.77	43.25	42.78	42.35	41.96
7,000	51.06	50.46	49.91	49.41	48.95
8,000	58.36	57.66	57.03	56.46	55.94
9,000	65.65	64.87	64.16	63.52	62.93
10,000	72.95	72.08	71.29	70.58	69.93
15,000	109.42	108.12	106.94	105.86	104.89
20,000	145.89	144.15	142.58	141.15	139.85
25,000	182.36	180.19	178.22	176.44	174.81
30,000	218.83	216.23	213.87	211.72	209.77
35,000	255.30	252.26	249.51	247.01	244.73
40,000	291.77	288.30	285.15	282.29	279.69
45,000	328.24	324.34	320.80	317.58	314.65
50,000	364.71	360.37	356.44	352.87	349.61
55,000	401.18	396.41	392.08	388.15	384.57
60,000	437.65	432.45	427.73	423.44	419.53
65,000	474.12	468.48	463.37	458.72	454.49
70,000	510.59	504.52	499.01	494.01	489.46
75,000	547.06	540.56	534.66	529.30	524.42
80,000	583.53	576.59	570.30	564.58	559.38
85,000	620.00	612.63	605.94	599.87	594.34
90,000	656.47	648.67	641.59	635.15	629.30
95,000	692.94	684.70	677.23	670.44	664.26
100,000	729.41	720.74	712.87	705.73	699.22
110,000	802.35	792.81	784.16	776.30	769.14
120,000	875.29	864.89	855.45	846.87	839.06
125,000	911.76	900.92	891.09	882.16	874.02
130,000	948.23	936.96	926.73	917.44	908.98
140,000	1,021.18	1,009.03	998.02	988.01	978.91
150,000	1,094.12	1,081.11	1,069.31	1,058.59	1,048.83
160,000	1,167.06	1,153.18	1,140.59	1,129.16	1,118.75
170,000	1,240.00	1,225.25	1,211.88	1,199.73	1,188.67
175,000	1,276.47	1,261.29	1,247.52	1,235.02	1,223.63
180,000	1,312.94	1,297.33	1,283.17	1,270.30	1,258.59
190,000	1,385.88	1,369.40	1,354.45	1,340.87	1,328.51
200,000	1,458.82	1,441.47	1,425.74	1,411.45	1,398.43
220,000	1,604.70	1,585.62	1,568.31	1,552.59	1,538.28
225,000	1,641.17	1,621.66	1,603.96	1,587.88	1,573.24
230,000	1,677.64	1,657.69	1,639.60	1,623.16	1,608.20
240,000	1,750.58	1,729.77	1,710.89	1,693.73	1,678.12
$250,000	1,823.52	1,801.84	1,782.17	1,764.31	1,748.04

Table 1   47

7.75%　Monthly Payment Loans

Amortization Period in Years

	5	7	8	10	12
$ 100	2.02	1.55	1.41	1.21	1.07
200	4.04	3.10	2.81	2.41	2.14
300	6.05	4.64	4.21	3.61	3.21
400	8.07	6.19	5.61	4.81	4.28
500	10.08	7.74	7.01	6.01	5.35
600	12.10	9.28	8.41	7.21	6.42
700	14.11	10.83	9.81	8.41	7.49
800	16.13	12.37	11.21	9.61	8.56
900	18.15	13.92	12.61	10.81	9.62
1,000	20.16	15.47	14.01	12.01	10.69
2,000	40.32	30.93	28.02	24.01	21.38
3,000	60.48	46.39	42.03	36.01	32.07
4,000	80.63	61.85	56.04	48.01	42.76
5,000	100.79	77.31	70.05	60.01	53.44
6,000	120.95	92.78	84.06	72.01	64.13
7,000	141.10	108.24	98.07	84.01	74.82
8,000	161.26	123.70	112.08	96.01	85.51
9,000	181.42	139.16	126.09	108.01	96.20
10,000	201.57	154.62	140.10	120.02	106.88
15,000	302.36	231.93	210.15	180.02	160.32
20,000	403.14	309.24	280.20	240.03	213.76
25,000	503.93	386.55	350.25	300.03	267.20
30,000	604.71	463.86	420.30	360.04	320.64
35,000	705.50	541.17	490.35	420.04	374.08
40,000	806.28	618.48	560.40	480.05	427.52
45,000	907.07	695.79	630.45	540.05	480.96
50,000	1,007.85	773.10	700.50	600.06	534.40
55,000	1,108.64	850.41	770.55	660.06	587.84
60,000	1,209.42	927.72	840.60	720.07	641.28
65,000	1,310.21	1,005.03	910.65	780.07	694.72
70,000	1,410.99	1,082.34	980.70	840.08	748.16
75,000	1,511.78	1,159.65	1,050.75	900.08	801.60
80,000	1,612.56	1,236.96	1,120.80	960.09	855.04
85,000	1,713.35	1,314.27	1,190.85	1,020.10	908.48
90,000	1,814.13	1,391.58	1,260.90	1,080.10	961.92
95,000	1,914.92	1,468.89	1,330.95	1,140.11	1,015.36
100,000	2,015.70	1,546.20	1,401.00	1,200.11	1,068.80
110,000	2,217.27	1,700.82	1,541.10	1,320.12	1,175.68
120,000	2,418.84	1,855.44	1,681.20	1,440.13	1,282.56
125,000	2,519.62	1,932.75	1,751.25	1,500.14	1,336.00
130,000	2,620.41	2,010.06	1,821.30	1,560.14	1,389.43
140,000	2,821.98	2,164.68	1,961.40	1,680.15	1,496.31
150,000	3,023.55	2,319.30	2,101.50	1,800.16	1,603.19
160,000	3,225.12	2,473.92	2,241.60	1,920.18	1,710.07
170,000	3,426.69	2,628.54	2,381.70	2,040.19	1,816.95
175,000	3,527.47	2,705.85	2,451.75	2,100.19	1,870.39
180,000	3,628.26	2,783.16	2,521.79	2,160.20	1,923.83
190,000	3,829.83	2,937.78	2,661.89	2,280.21	2,030.71
200,000	4,031.40	3,092.40	2,801.99	2,400.22	2,137.59
220,000	4,434.54	3,401.63	3,082.19	2,640.24	2,351.35
225,000	4,535.32	3,478.94	3,152.24	2,700.24	2,404.79
230,000	4,636.11	3,556.25	3,222.29	2,760.25	2,458.23
240,000	4,837.68	3,710.87	3,362.39	2,880.26	2,565.11
$250,000	5,039.24	3,865.49	3,502.49	3,000.27	2,671.99

Monthly Payment Loans   7.75%

Amortization Period in Years

$	15	16	17	18	20
100	0.95	0.92	0.89	0.86	0.83
200	1.89	1.83	1.77	1.72	1.65
300	2.83	2.74	2.66	2.58	2.47
400	3.77	3.65	3.54	3.44	3.29
500	4.71	4.56	4.42	4.30	4.11
600	5.65	5.47	5.31	5.16	4.93
700	6.59	6.38	6.19	6.02	5.75
800	7.54	7.29	7.07	6.88	6.57
900	8.48	8.20	7.96	7.74	7.39
1,000	9.42	9.11	8.84	8.60	8.21
2,000	18.83	18.21	17.67	17.20	16.42
3,000	28.24	27.31	26.51	25.80	24.63
4,000	37.66	36.42	35.34	34.40	32.84
5,000	47.07	45.52	44.18	43.00	41.05
6,000	56.48	54.62	53.01	51.60	49.26
7,000	65.89	63.73	61.84	60.20	57.47
8,000	75.31	72.83	70.68	68.80	65.68
9,000	84.72	81.93	79.51	77.40	73.89
10,000	94.13	91.04	88.35	86.00	82.10
15,000	141.20	136.55	132.52	128.99	123.15
20,000	188.26	182.07	176.69	171.99	164.19
25,000	235.32	227.58	220.86	214.98	205.24
30,000	282.39	273.10	265.03	257.98	246.29
35,000	329.45	318.62	309.20	300.97	287.34
40,000	376.52	364.13	353.37	343.97	328.38
45,000	423.58	409.65	397.54	386.96	369.43
50,000	470.64	455.16	441.72	429.96	410.48
55,000	517.71	500.68	485.89	472.95	451.53
60,000	564.77	546.20	530.06	515.95	492.57
65,000	611.83	591.71	574.23	558.94	533.62
70,000	658.90	637.23	618.40	601.94	574.67
75,000	705.96	682.74	662.57	644.93	615.72
80,000	753.03	728.26	706.74	687.93	656.76
85,000	800.09	773.77	750.91	730.92	697.81
90,000	847.15	819.29	795.08	773.92	738.86
95,000	894.22	864.81	839.26	816.91	779.91
100,000	941.28	910.32	883.43	859.91	820.95
110,000	1,035.41	1,001.35	971.77	945.90	903.05
120,000	1,129.54	1,092.39	1,060.11	1,031.89	985.14
125,000	1,176.60	1,137.90	1,104.28	1,074.88	1,026.19
130,000	1,223.66	1,183.42	1,148.45	1,117.88	1,067.24
140,000	1,317.79	1,274.45	1,236.80	1,203.87	1,149.33
150,000	1,411.92	1,365.48	1,325.14	1,289.86	1,231.43
160,000	1,506.05	1,456.51	1,413.48	1,375.85	1,313.52
170,000	1,600.17	1,547.54	1,501.82	1,461.84	1,395.62
175,000	1,647.24	1,593.06	1,545.99	1,504.84	1,436.66
180,000	1,694.30	1,638.58	1,590.16	1,547.83	1,477.71
190,000	1,788.43	1,729.61	1,678.51	1,633.82	1,559.81
200,000	1,882.56	1,820.64	1,766.85	1,719.81	1,641.90
220,000	2,070.81	2,002.70	1,943.53	1,891.79	1,806.09
225,000	2,117.88	2,048.22	1,987.70	1,934.79	1,847.14
230,000	2,164.94	2,093.73	2,031.87	1,977.78	1,888.19
240,000	2,259.07	2,184.77	2,120.22	2,063.77	1,970.28
$250,000	2,353.19	2,275.80	2,208.56	2,149.76	2,052.38

Table 1   49

7.75% Monthly Payment Loans

Amortization Period in Years

	21	22	23	24	25
$ 100	0.81	0.80	0.78	0.77	0.76
200	1.61	1.59	1.56	1.54	1.52
300	2.42	2.38	2.34	2.30	2.27
400	3.22	3.17	3.11	3.07	3.03
500	4.03	3.96	3.89	3.83	3.78
600	4.83	4.75	4.67	4.60	4.54
700	5.64	5.54	5.45	5.37	5.29
800	6.44	6.33	6.22	6.13	6.05
900	7.25	7.12	7.00	6.90	6.80
1,000	8.05	7.91	7.78	7.66	7.56
2,000	16.10	15.81	15.55	15.32	15.11
3,000	24.15	23.71	23.33	22.98	22.66
4,000	32.19	31.62	31.10	30.64	30.22
5,000	40.24	39.52	38.87	38.29	37.77
6,000	48.29	47.42	46.65	45.95	45.32
7,000	56.34	55.32	54.42	53.61	52.88
8,000	64.38	63.23	62.19	61.27	60.43
9,000	72.43	71.13	69.97	68.92	67.98
10,000	80.48	79.03	77.74	76.58	75.54
15,000	120.71	118.55	116.61	114.87	113.30
20,000	160.95	158.06	155.47	153.16	151.07
25,000	201.19	197.57	194.34	191.44	188.84
30,000	241.42	237.09	233.21	229.73	226.60
35,000	281.66	276.60	272.08	268.02	264.37
40,000	321.90	316.11	310.94	306.31	302.14
45,000	362.13	355.63	349.81	344.60	339.90
50,000	402.37	395.14	388.68	382.88	377.67
55,000	442.60	434.66	427.55	421.17	415.44
60,000	482.84	474.17	466.41	459.46	453.20
65,000	523.08	513.68	505.28	497.75	490.97
70,000	563.31	553.20	544.15	536.03	528.74
75,000	603.55	592.71	583.02	574.32	566.50
80,000	643.79	632.22	621.88	612.61	604.27
85,000	684.02	671.74	660.75	650.90	642.03
90,000	724.26	711.25	699.62	689.19	679.80
95,000	764.50	750.76	738.49	727.47	717.57
100,000	804.73	790.28	777.35	765.76	755.33
110,000	885.20	869.31	855.09	842.34	830.87
120,000	965.68	948.33	932.82	918.91	906.40
125,000	1,005.91	987.85	971.69	957.20	944.17
130,000	1,046.15	1,027.36	1,010.56	995.49	981.93
140,000	1,126.62	1,106.39	1,088.29	1,072.06	1,057.47
150,000	1,207.10	1,185.41	1,166.03	1,148.64	1,133.00
160,000	1,287.57	1,264.44	1,243.76	1,225.21	1,208.53
170,000	1,368.04	1,343.47	1,321.50	1,301.79	1,284.06
175,000	1,408.28	1,382.98	1,360.36	1,340.08	1,321.83
180,000	1,448.51	1,422.50	1,399.23	1,378.37	1,359.60
190,000	1,528.99	1,501.52	1,476.97	1,454.94	1,435.13
200,000	1,609.46	1,580.55	1,554.70	1,531.52	1,510.66
220,000	1,770.40	1,738.61	1,710.17	1,684.67	1,661.73
225,000	1,810.64	1,778.12	1,749.04	1,722.96	1,699.49
230,000	1,850.88	1,817.63	1,787.91	1,761.24	1,737.26
240,000	1,931.35	1,896.66	1,865.64	1,837.82	1,812.79
$250,000	2,011.82	1,975.69	1,943.38	1,914.39	1,888.33

Monthly Payment Loans   **7.75%**

Amortization Period in Years

	26	27	28	29	30
$ 100	0.75	0.74	0.73	0.73	0.72
200	1.50	1.48	1.46	1.45	1.44
300	2.24	2.22	2.19	2.17	2.15
400	2.99	2.95	2.92	2.90	2.87
500	3.73	3.69	3.65	3.62	3.59
600	4.48	4.43	4.38	4.34	4.30
700	5.23	5.17	5.11	5.06	5.02
800	5.97	5.90	5.84	5.79	5.74
900	6.72	6.64	6.57	6.51	6.45
1,000	7.46	7.38	7.30	7.23	7.17
2,000	14.92	14.75	14.60	14.46	14.33
3,000	22.38	22.13	21.90	21.69	21.50
4,000	29.84	29.50	29.19	28.92	28.66
5,000	37.30	36.88	36.49	36.14	35.83
6,000	44.76	44.25	43.79	43.37	42.99
7,000	52.22	51.63	51.09	50.60	50.15
8,000	59.68	59.00	58.38	57.83	57.32
9,000	67.14	66.37	65.68	65.05	64.48
10,000	74.60	73.75	72.98	72.28	71.65
15,000	111.89	110.62	109.47	108.42	107.47
20,000	149.19	147.49	145.95	144.56	143.29
25,000	186.49	184.36	182.44	180.69	179.11
30,000	223.78	221.23	218.93	216.83	214.93
35,000	261.08	258.11	255.41	252.97	250.75
40,000	298.38	294.98	291.90	289.11	286.57
45,000	335.67	331.85	328.39	325.25	322.39
50,000	372.97	368.72	364.87	361.38	358.21
55,000	410.26	405.59	401.36	397.52	394.03
60,000	447.56	442.46	437.85	433.66	429.85
65,000	484.86	479.33	474.33	469.80	465.67
70,000	522.15	516.21	510.82	505.93	501.49
75,000	559.45	553.08	547.31	542.07	537.31
80,000	596.75	589.95	583.79	578.21	573.13
85,000	634.04	626.82	620.28	614.35	608.96
90,000	671.34	663.69	656.77	650.49	644.78
95,000	708.64	700.56	693.25	686.62	680.60
100,000	745.93	737.44	729.74	722.76	716.42
110,000	820.52	811.18	802.71	795.04	788.06
120,000	895.12	884.92	875.69	867.31	859.70
125,000	932.41	921.79	912.18	903.45	895.52
130,000	969.71	958.66	948.66	939.59	931.34
140,000	1,044.30	1,032.41	1,021.64	1,011.86	1,002.98
150,000	1,118.90	1,106.15	1,094.61	1,084.14	1,074.62
160,000	1,193.49	1,179.89	1,167.58	1,156.41	1,146.26
170,000	1,268.08	1,253.64	1,240.56	1,228.69	1,217.91
175,000	1,305.38	1,290.51	1,277.04	1,264.83	1,253.73
180,000	1,342.67	1,327.38	1,313.53	1,300.97	1,289.55
190,000	1,417.27	1,401.12	1,386.50	1,373.24	1,361.19
200,000	1,491.86	1,474.87	1,459.48	1,445.52	1,432.83
220,000	1,641.04	1,622.35	1,605.42	1,590.07	1,576.11
225,000	1,678.34	1,659.22	1,641.91	1,626.21	1,611.93
230,000	1,715.64	1,696.10	1,678.40	1,662.34	1,647.75
240,000	1,790.23	1,769.84	1,751.37	1,734.62	1,719.39
$250,000	1,864.82	1,843.58	1,824.35	1,806.89	1,791.04

Table 1   51

8.00% Monthly Payment Loans

Amortization Period in Years

	5	7	8	10	12
$ 100	2.03	1.56	1.42	1.22	1.09
200	4.06	3.12	2.83	2.43	2.17
300	6.09	4.68	4.25	3.64	3.25
400	8.12	6.24	5.66	4.86	4.33
500	10.14	7.80	7.07	6.07	5.42
600	12.17	9.36	8.49	7.28	6.50
700	14.20	10.92	9.90	8.50	7.58
800	16.23	12.47	11.31	9.71	8.66
900	18.25	14.03	12.73	10.92	9.75
1,000	20.28	15.59	14.14	12.14	10.83
2,000	40.56	31.18	28.28	24.27	21.65
3,000	60.83	46.76	42.42	36.40	32.48
4,000	81.11	62.35	56.55	48.54	43.30
5,000	101.39	77.94	70.69	60.67	54.13
6,000	121.66	93.52	84.83	72.80	64.95
7,000	141.94	109.11	98.96	84.93	75.78
8,000	162.22	124.69	113.10	97.07	86.60
9,000	182.49	140.28	127.24	109.20	97.43
10,000	202.77	155.87	141.37	121.33	108.25
15,000	304.15	233.80	212.06	182.00	162.37
20,000	405.53	311.73	282.74	242.66	216.50
25,000	506.91	389.66	353.42	303.32	270.62
30,000	608.30	467.59	424.11	363.99	324.74
35,000	709.68	545.52	494.79	424.65	378.86
40,000	811.06	623.45	565.47	485.32	432.99
45,000	912.44	701.38	636.16	545.98	487.11
50,000	1,013.82	779.32	706.84	606.64	541.23
55,000	1,115.21	857.25	777.52	667.31	595.35
60,000	1,216.59	935.18	848.21	727.97	649.48
65,000	1,317.97	1,013.11	918.89	788.63	703.60
70,000	1,419.35	1,091.04	989.57	849.30	757.72
75,000	1,520.73	1,168.97	1,060.26	909.96	811.84
80,000	1,622.12	1,246.90	1,130.94	970.63	865.97
85,000	1,723.50	1,324.83	1,201.62	1,031.29	920.09
90,000	1,824.88	1,402.76	1,272.31	1,091.95	974.21
95,000	1,926.26	1,480.70	1,342.99	1,152.62	1,028.33
100,000	2,027.64	1,558.63	1,413.67	1,213.28	1,082.46
110,000	2,230.41	1,714.49	1,555.04	1,334.61	1,190.70
120,000	2,433.17	1,870.35	1,696.41	1,455.94	1,298.95
125,000	2,534.55	1,948.28	1,767.09	1,516.60	1,353.07
130,000	2,635.94	2,026.21	1,837.77	1,577.26	1,407.19
140,000	2,838.70	2,182.08	1,979.14	1,698.59	1,515.44
150,000	3,041.46	2,337.94	2,120.51	1,819.92	1,623.68
160,000	3,244.23	2,493.80	2,261.87	1,941.25	1,731.93
170,000	3,446.99	2,649.66	2,403.24	2,062.57	1,840.17
175,000	3,548.37	2,727.59	2,473.92	2,123.24	1,894.30
180,000	3,649.76	2,805.52	2,544.61	2,183.90	1,948.42
190,000	3,852.52	2,961.39	2,685.97	2,305.23	2,056.66
200,000	4,055.28	3,117.25	2,827.34	2,426.56	2,164.91
220,000	4,460.81	3,428.97	3,110.07	2,669.21	2,381.40
225,000	4,562.19	3,506.90	3,180.76	2,729.88	2,435.52
230,000	4,663.58	3,584.83	3,251.44	2,790.54	2,489.65
240,000	4,866.34	3,740.70	3,392.81	2,911.87	2,597.89
$250,000	5,069.10	3,896.56	3,534.17	3,033.19	2,706.14

Monthly Payment Loans **8.00%**

Amortization Period in Years

	15	16	17	18	20
$ 100	0.96	0.93	0.90	0.88	0.84
200	1.92	1.85	1.80	1.75	1.68
300	2.87	2.78	2.70	2.63	2.51
400	3.83	3.70	3.60	3.50	3.35
500	4.78	4.63	4.50	4.38	4.19
600	5.74	5.55	5.39	5.25	5.02
700	6.69	6.48	6.29	6.13	5.86
800	7.65	7.40	7.19	7.00	6.70
900	8.61	8.33	8.09	7.88	7.53
1,000	9.56	9.25	8.99	8.75	8.37
2,000	19.12	18.50	17.97	17.50	16.73
3,000	28.67	27.75	26.95	26.25	25.10
4,000	38.23	37.00	35.94	35.00	33.46
5,000	47.79	46.25	44.92	43.75	41.83
6,000	57.34	55.50	53.90	52.50	50.19
7,000	66.90	64.75	62.88	61.25	58.56
8,000	76.46	74.00	71.87	70.00	66.92
9,000	86.01	83.25	80.85	78.75	75.28
10,000	95.57	92.50	89.83	87.50	83.65
15,000	143.35	138.74	134.74	131.25	125.47
20,000	191.14	184.99	179.66	175.00	167.29
25,000	238.92	231.24	224.57	218.75	209.12
30,000	286.70	277.48	269.48	262.49	250.94
35,000	334.48	323.73	314.39	306.24	292.76
40,000	382.27	369.98	359.31	349.99	334.58
45,000	430.05	416.22	404.22	393.74	376.40
50,000	477.83	462.47	449.13	437.49	418.23
55,000	525.61	508.71	494.05	481.23	460.05
60,000	573.40	554.96	538.96	524.98	501.87
65,000	621.18	601.21	583.87	568.73	543.69
70,000	668.96	647.45	628.78	612.48	585.51
75,000	716.74	693.70	673.70	656.23	627.34
80,000	764.53	739.95	718.61	699.98	669.16
85,000	812.31	786.19	763.52	743.72	710.98
90,000	860.09	832.44	808.44	787.47	752.80
95,000	907.87	878.68	853.35	831.22	794.62
100,000	955.66	924.93	898.26	874.97	836.45
110,000	1,051.22	1,017.42	988.09	962.46	920.09
120,000	1,146.79	1,109.92	1,077.91	1,049.96	1,003.73
125,000	1,194.57	1,156.16	1,122.83	1,093.71	1,045.56
130,000	1,242.35	1,202.41	1,167.74	1,137.46	1,087.38
140,000	1,337.92	1,294.90	1,257.56	1,224.95	1,171.02
150,000	1,433.48	1,387.39	1,347.39	1,312.45	1,254.67
160,000	1,529.05	1,479.89	1,437.22	1,399.95	1,338.31
170,000	1,624.61	1,572.38	1,527.04	1,487.44	1,421.95
175,000	1,672.40	1,618.62	1,571.95	1,531.19	1,463.78
180,000	1,720.18	1,664.87	1,616.87	1,574.94	1,505.60
190,000	1,815.74	1,757.36	1,706.69	1,662.43	1,589.24
200,000	1,911.31	1,849.86	1,796.52	1,749.93	1,672.89
220,000	2,102.44	2,034.84	1,976.17	1,924.92	1,840.17
225,000	2,150.22	2,081.09	2,021.08	1,968.67	1,882.00
230,000	2,198.00	2,127.33	2,066.00	2,012.42	1,923.82
240,000	2,293.57	2,219.83	2,155.82	2,099.92	2,007.46
$250,000	2,389.14	2,312.32	2,245.65	2,187.41	2,091.11

Table 1   53

Monthly Payment Loans

Amortization Period in Years

	21	22	23	24	25
$ 100	0.83	0.81	0.80	0.79	0.78
200	1.65	1.62	1.59	1.57	1.55
300	2.47	2.42	2.39	2.35	2.32
400	3.29	3.23	3.18	3.13	3.09
500	4.11	4.04	3.97	3.92	3.86
600	4.93	4.84	4.77	4.70	4.64
700	5.75	5.65	5.56	5.48	5.41
800	6.57	6.45	6.35	6.26	6.18
900	7.39	7.26	7.15	7.04	6.95
1,000	8.21	8.07	7.94	7.83	7.72
2,000	16.41	16.13	15.87	15.65	15.44
3,000	24.62	24.19	23.81	23.47	23.16
4,000	32.82	32.25	31.74	31.29	30.88
5,000	41.03	40.31	39.68	39.11	38.60
6,000	49.23	48.38	47.61	46.93	46.31
7,000	57.43	56.44	55.55	54.75	54.03
8,000	65.64	64.50	63.48	62.57	61.75
9,000	73.84	72.56	71.42	70.39	69.47
10,000	82.05	80.62	79.35	78.21	77.19
15,000	123.07	120.93	119.02	117.31	115.78
20,000	164.09	161.24	158.70	156.42	154.37
25,000	205.11	201.55	198.37	195.52	192.96
30,000	246.13	241.86	238.04	234.62	231.55
35,000	287.15	282.17	277.71	273.72	270.14
40,000	328.18	322.48	317.39	312.83	308.73
45,000	369.20	362.79	357.06	351.93	347.32
50,000	410.22	403.09	396.73	391.03	385.91
55,000	451.24	443.40	436.40	430.13	424.50
60,000	492.26	483.71	476.08	469.24	463.09
65,000	533.28	524.02	515.75	508.34	501.69
70,000	574.30	564.33	555.42	547.44	540.28
75,000	615.33	604.64	595.09	586.55	578.87
80,000	656.35	644.95	634.77	625.65	617.46
85,000	697.37	685.26	674.44	664.75	656.05
90,000	738.39	725.57	714.11	703.85	694.64
95,000	779.41	765.87	753.78	742.96	733.23
100,000	820.43	806.18	793.46	782.06	771.82
110,000	902.48	886.80	872.80	860.26	849.00
120,000	984.52	967.42	952.15	938.47	926.18
125,000	1,025.54	1,007.73	991.82	977.57	964.78
130,000	1,066.56	1,048.04	1,031.49	1,016.68	1,003.37
140,000	1,148.60	1,128.65	1,110.84	1,094.88	1,080.55
150,000	1,230.65	1,209.27	1,190.18	1,173.09	1,157.73
160,000	1,312.69	1,289.89	1,269.53	1,251.29	1,234.91
170,000	1,394.73	1,370.51	1,348.87	1,329.50	1,312.09
175,000	1,435.75	1,410.82	1,388.55	1,368.60	1,350.68
180,000	1,476.78	1,451.13	1,428.22	1,407.70	1,389.27
190,000	1,558.82	1,531.74	1,507.56	1,485.91	1,466.46
200,000	1,640.86	1,612.36	1,586.91	1,564.11	1,543.64
220,000	1,804.95	1,773.60	1,745.60	1,720.52	1,698.00
225,000	1,845.97	1,813.91	1,785.27	1,759.63	1,736.59
230,000	1,886.99	1,854.21	1,824.95	1,798.73	1,775.18
240,000	1,969.03	1,934.83	1,904.29	1,876.93	1,852.36
$250,000	2,051.07	2,015.45	1,983.64	1,955.14	1,929.55

Monthly Payment Loans   **8.00%**

Amortization Period in Years

$	26	27	28	29	30
100	0.77	0.76	0.75	0.74	0.74
200	1.53	1.51	1.50	1.48	1.47
300	2.29	2.27	2.25	2.22	2.21
400	3.06	3.02	2.99	2.96	2.94
500	3.82	3.78	3.74	3.70	3.67
600	4.58	4.53	4.49	4.44	4.41
700	5.34	5.28	5.23	5.18	5.14
800	6.11	6.04	5.98	5.92	5.88
900	6.87	6.79	6.73	6.66	6.61
1,000	7.63	7.55	7.47	7.40	7.34
2,000	15.26	15.09	14.94	14.80	14.68
3,000	22.88	22.63	22.41	22.20	22.02
4,000	30.51	30.18	29.88	29.60	29.36
5,000	38.13	37.72	37.34	37.00	36.69
6,000	45.76	45.26	44.81	44.40	44.03
7,000	53.39	52.80	52.28	51.80	51.37
8,000	61.01	60.35	59.75	59.20	58.71
9,000	68.64	67.89	67.21	66.60	66.04
10,000	76.26	75.43	74.68	74.00	73.38
15,000	114.39	113.15	112.02	111.00	110.07
20,000	152.52	150.86	149.36	147.99	146.76
25,000	190.65	188.57	186.69	184.99	183.45
30,000	228.78	226.29	224.03	221.99	220.13
35,000	266.91	264.00	261.37	258.99	256.82
40,000	305.04	301.72	298.71	295.98	293.51
45,000	343.17	339.43	336.05	332.98	330.20
50,000	381.30	377.14	373.38	369.98	366.89
55,000	419.43	414.86	410.72	406.98	403.58
60,000	457.56	452.57	448.06	443.97	440.26
65,000	495.69	490.29	485.40	480.97	476.95
70,000	533.82	528.00	522.74	517.97	513.64
75,000	571.95	565.71	560.07	554.96	550.33
80,000	610.08	603.43	597.41	591.96	587.02
85,000	648.21	641.14	634.75	628.96	623.70
90,000	686.34	678.86	672.09	665.96	660.39
95,000	724.47	716.57	709.43	702.95	697.08
100,000	762.60	754.28	746.76	739.95	733.77
110,000	838.86	829.71	821.44	813.95	807.15
120,000	915.12	905.14	896.12	887.94	880.52
125,000	953.25	942.85	933.45	924.94	917.21
130,000	991.38	980.57	970.79	961.93	953.90
140,000	1,067.64	1,056.00	1,045.47	1,035.93	1,027.28
150,000	1,143.90	1,131.42	1,120.14	1,109.92	1,100.65
160,000	1,220.16	1,206.85	1,194.82	1,183.92	1,174.03
170,000	1,296.42	1,282.28	1,269.49	1,257.91	1,247.40
175,000	1,334.55	1,319.99	1,306.83	1,294.91	1,284.09
180,000	1,372.68	1,357.71	1,344.17	1,331.91	1,320.78
190,000	1,448.94	1,433.14	1,418.85	1,405.90	1,394.16
200,000	1,525.20	1,508.56	1,493.52	1,479.90	1,467.53
220,000	1,677.72	1,659.42	1,642.87	1,627.89	1,614.29
225,000	1,715.85	1,697.13	1,680.21	1,664.88	1,650.98
230,000	1,753.98	1,734.85	1,717.55	1,701.88	1,687.66
240,000	1,830.24	1,810.28	1,792.23	1,775.87	1,761.04
$250,000	1,906.50	1,885.70	1,866.90	1,849.87	1,834.42

Table 1   55

8.25%   Monthly Payment Loans

Amortization Period in Years

	5	7	8	10	12
$ 100	2.04	1.58	1.43	1.23	1.10
200	4.08	3.15	2.86	2.46	2.20
300	6.12	4.72	4.28	3.68	3.29
400	8.16	6.29	5.71	4.91	4.39
500	10.20	7.86	7.14	6.14	5.49
600	12.24	9.43	8.56	7.36	6.58
700	14.28	11.00	9.99	8.59	7.68
800	16.32	12.57	11.42	9.82	8.77
900	18.36	14.14	12.84	11.04	9.87
1,000	20.40	15.72	14.27	12.27	10.97
2,000	40.80	31.43	28.53	24.54	21.93
3,000	61.19	47.14	42.80	36.80	32.89
4,000	81.59	62.85	57.06	49.07	43.85
5,000	101.99	78.56	71.33	61.33	54.82
6,000	122.38	94.27	85.59	73.60	65.78
7,000	142.78	109.98	99.85	85.86	76.74
8,000	163.18	125.69	114.12	98.13	87.70
9,000	183.57	141.40	128.38	110.39	98.66
10,000	203.97	157.12	142.65	122.66	109.63
15,000	305.95	235.67	213.97	183.98	164.44
20,000	407.93	314.23	285.29	245.31	219.25
25,000	509.91	392.78	356.61	306.64	274.06
30,000	611.89	471.34	427.93	367.96	328.87
35,000	713.87	549.89	499.25	429.29	383.68
40,000	815.86	628.45	570.57	490.62	438.49
45,000	917.84	707.00	641.89	551.94	493.30
50,000	1,019.82	785.56	713.21	613.27	548.11
55,000	1,121.80	864.11	784.53	674.59	602.92
60,000	1,223.78	942.67	855.85	735.92	657.73
65,000	1,325.76	1,021.22	927.17	797.25	712.54
70,000	1,427.74	1,099.78	998.49	858.57	767.35
75,000	1,529.72	1,178.33	1,069.81	919.90	822.16
80,000	1,631.71	1,256.89	1,141.13	981.23	876.97
85,000	1,733.69	1,335.45	1,212.45	1,042.55	931.78
90,000	1,835.67	1,414.00	1,283.77	1,103.88	986.59
95,000	1,937.65	1,492.56	1,355.09	1,165.20	1,041.40
100,000	2,039.63	1,571.11	1,426.41	1,226.53	1,096.21
110,000	2,243.59	1,728.22	1,569.05	1,349.18	1,205.83
120,000	2,447.56	1,885.33	1,711.69	1,471.84	1,315.45
125,000	2,549.54	1,963.89	1,783.01	1,533.16	1,370.26
130,000	2,651.52	2,042.44	1,854.33	1,594.49	1,425.07
140,000	2,855.48	2,199.55	1,996.98	1,717.14	1,534.70
150,000	3,059.44	2,356.66	2,139.62	1,839.79	1,644.32
160,000	3,263.41	2,513.77	2,282.26	1,962.45	1,753.94
170,000	3,467.37	2,670.89	2,424.90	2,085.10	1,863.56
175,000	3,569.35	2,749.44	2,496.22	2,146.43	1,918.37
180,000	3,671.33	2,828.00	2,567.54	2,207.75	1,973.18
190,000	3,875.29	2,985.11	2,710.18	2,330.40	2,082.80
200,000	4,079.26	3,142.22	2,852.82	2,453.06	2,192.42
220,000	4,487.18	3,456.44	3,138.10	2,698.36	2,411.66
225,000	4,589.16	3,534.99	3,209.42	2,759.69	2,466.47
230,000	4,691.14	3,613.55	3,280.74	2,821.02	2,521.28
240,000	4,895.11	3,770.66	3,423.38	2,943.67	2,630.90
$250,000	5,099.07	3,927.77	3,566.02	3,066.32	2,740.52

Monthly Payment Loans   <u>8.25%</u>

Amortization Period in Years

	15	16	17	18	20
$ 100	0.98	0.94	0.92	0.90	0.86
200	1.95	1.88	1.83	1.79	1.71
300	2.92	2.82	2.74	2.68	2.56
400	3.89	3.76	3.66	3.57	3.41
500	4.86	4.70	4.57	4.46	4.27
600	5.83	5.64	5.48	5.35	5.12
700	6.80	6.58	6.40	6.24	5.97
800	7.77	7.52	7.31	7.13	6.82
900	8.74	8.46	8.22	8.02	7.67
1,000	9.71	9.40	9.14	8.91	8.53
2,000	19.41	18.80	18.27	17.81	17.05
3,000	29.11	28.19	27.40	26.71	25.57
4,000	38.81	37.59	36.53	35.61	34.09
5,000	48.51	46.99	45.67	44.51	42.61
6,000	58.21	56.38	54.80	53.41	51.13
7,000	67.91	65.78	63.93	62.32	59.65
8,000	77.62	75.18	73.06	71.22	68.17
9,000	87.32	84.57	82.19	80.12	76.69
10,000	97.02	93.97	91.33	89.02	85.21
15,000	145.53	140.95	136.99	133.53	127.81
20,000	194.03	187.94	182.65	178.03	170.42
25,000	242.54	234.92	228.31	222.54	213.02
30,000	291.05	281.90	273.97	267.05	255.62
35,000	339.55	328.88	319.63	311.56	298.23
40,000	388.06	375.87	365.29	356.06	340.83
45,000	436.57	422.85	410.95	400.57	383.43
50,000	485.08	469.83	456.61	445.08	426.04
55,000	533.58	516.81	502.27	489.59	468.64
60,000	582.09	563.80	547.93	534.09	511.24
65,000	630.60	610.78	593.59	578.60	553.85
70,000	679.10	657.76	639.25	623.11	596.45
75,000	727.61	704.74	684.92	667.62	639.05
80,000	776.12	751.73	730.58	712.12	681.66
85,000	824.62	798.71	776.24	756.63	724.26
90,000	873.13	845.69	821.90	801.14	766.86
95,000	921.64	892.67	867.56	845.65	809.47
100,000	970.15	939.66	913.22	890.15	852.07
110,000	1,067.16	1,033.62	1,004.54	979.17	937.28
120,000	1,164.17	1,127.59	1,095.86	1,068.18	1,022.48
125,000	1,212.68	1,174.57	1,141.52	1,112.69	1,065.09
130,000	1,261.19	1,221.55	1,187.18	1,157.20	1,107.69
140,000	1,358.20	1,315.52	1,278.50	1,246.21	1,192.90
150,000	1,455.22	1,409.48	1,369.83	1,335.23	1,278.10
160,000	1,552.23	1,503.45	1,461.15	1,424.24	1,363.31
170,000	1,649.24	1,597.41	1,552.47	1,513.26	1,448.52
175,000	1,697.75	1,644.39	1,598.13	1,557.76	1,491.12
180,000	1,746.26	1,691.38	1,643.79	1,602.27	1,533.72
190,000	1,843.27	1,785.34	1,735.11	1,691.29	1,618.93
200,000	1,940.29	1,879.31	1,826.43	1,780.30	1,704.14
220,000	2,134.31	2,067.24	2,009.08	1,958.33	1,874.55
225,000	2,182.82	2,114.22	2,054.74	2,002.84	1,917.15
230,000	2,231.33	2,161.20	2,100.40	2,047.34	1,959.76
240,000	2,328.34	2,255.17	2,191.72	2,136.36	2,044.96
$250,000	2,425.36	2,349.13	2,283.04	2,225.37	2,130.17

Table 1   57

8.25%   Monthly Payment Loans

Amortization Period in Years

	21	22	23	24	25
$ 100	0.84	0.83	0.81	0.80	0.79
200	1.68	1.65	1.62	1.60	1.58
300	2.51	2.47	2.43	2.40	2.37
400	3.35	3.29	3.24	3.20	3.16
500	4.19	4.12	4.05	4.00	3.95
600	5.02	4.94	4.86	4.80	4.74
700	5.86	5.76	5.67	5.59	5.52
800	6.70	6.58	6.48	6.39	6.31
900	7.53	7.41	7.29	7.19	7.10
1,000	8.37	8.23	8.10	7.99	7.89
2,000	16.73	16.45	16.20	15.97	15.77
3,000	25.09	24.67	24.30	23.96	23.66
4,000	33.46	32.89	32.39	31.94	31.54
5,000	41.82	41.12	40.49	39.93	39.43
6,000	50.18	49.34	48.59	47.91	47.31
7,000	58.54	57.56	56.68	55.90	55.20
8,000	66.91	65.78	64.78	63.88	63.08
9,000	75.27	74.01	72.88	71.87	70.97
10,000	83.63	82.23	80.97	79.85	78.85
15,000	125.44	123.34	121.46	119.78	118.27
20,000	167.26	164.45	161.94	159.70	157.70
25,000	209.07	205.56	202.43	199.63	197.12
30,000	250.88	246.67	242.91	239.55	236.54
35,000	292.70	287.78	283.40	279.48	275.96
40,000	334.51	328.89	323.88	319.40	315.39
45,000	376.32	370.01	364.37	359.33	354.81
50,000	418.14	411.12	404.85	399.25	394.23
55,000	459.95	452.23	445.34	439.18	433.65
60,000	501.76	493.34	485.82	479.10	473.08
65,000	543.58	534.45	526.31	519.03	512.50
70,000	585.39	575.56	566.79	558.95	551.92
75,000	627.20	616.67	607.28	598.88	591.34
80,000	669.02	657.78	647.76	638.80	630.77
85,000	710.83	698.89	688.25	678.73	670.19
90,000	752.64	740.01	728.73	718.65	709.61
95,000	794.46	781.12	769.22	758.58	749.03
100,000	836.27	822.23	809.70	798.50	788.46
110,000	919.90	904.45	890.67	878.35	867.30
120,000	1,003.52	986.67	971.64	958.20	946.15
125,000	1,045.34	1,027.78	1,012.13	998.13	985.57
130,000	1,087.15	1,068.90	1,052.61	1,038.05	1,024.99
140,000	1,170.78	1,151.12	1,133.58	1,117.90	1,103.84
150,000	1,254.40	1,233.34	1,214.55	1,197.75	1,182.68
160,000	1,338.03	1,315.56	1,295.52	1,277.60	1,261.53
170,000	1,421.66	1,397.78	1,376.49	1,357.45	1,340.37
175,000	1,463.47	1,438.90	1,416.98	1,397.38	1,379.79
180,000	1,505.28	1,480.01	1,457.46	1,437.30	1,419.22
190,000	1,588.91	1,562.23	1,538.43	1,517.15	1,498.06
200,000	1,672.54	1,644.45	1,619.40	1,597.00	1,576.91
220,000	1,839.79	1,808.90	1,781.34	1,756.70	1,734.60
225,000	1,881.60	1,850.01	1,821.83	1,796.62	1,774.02
230,000	1,923.42	1,891.12	1,862.31	1,836.55	1,813.44
240,000	2,007.04	1,973.34	1,943.28	1,916.40	1,892.29
$250,000	2,090.67	2,055.56	2,024.25	1,996.25	1,971.13

Monthly Payment Loans   **8.25%**

Amortization Period in Years

$	26	27	28	29	30
100	0.78	0.78	0.77	0.76	0.76
200	1.56	1.55	1.53	1.52	1.51
300	2.34	2.32	2.30	2.28	2.26
400	3.12	3.09	3.06	3.03	3.01
500	3.90	3.86	3.82	3.79	3.76
600	4.68	4.63	4.59	4.55	4.51
700	5.46	5.40	5.35	5.31	5.26
800	6.24	6.18	6.12	6.06	6.02
900	7.02	6.95	6.88	6.82	6.77
1,000	7.80	7.72	7.64	7.58	7.52
2,000	15.59	15.43	15.28	15.15	15.03
3,000	23.39	23.14	22.92	22.72	22.54
4,000	31.18	30.86	30.56	30.30	30.06
5,000	38.98	38.57	38.20	37.87	37.57
6,000	46.77	46.28	45.84	45.44	45.08
7,000	54.56	53.99	53.48	53.01	52.59
8,000	62.36	61.71	61.12	60.59	60.11
9,000	70.15	69.42	68.76	68.16	67.62
10,000	77.95	77.13	76.40	75.73	75.13
15,000	116.92	115.70	114.59	113.60	112.69
20,000	155.89	154.26	152.79	151.46	150.26
25,000	194.86	192.82	190.99	189.33	187.82
30,000	233.83	231.39	229.18	227.19	225.38
35,000	272.80	269.95	267.38	265.05	262.95
40,000	311.77	308.52	305.58	302.92	300.51
45,000	350.74	347.08	343.77	340.78	338.07
50,000	389.71	385.64	381.97	378.65	375.64
55,000	428.68	424.21	420.17	416.51	413.20
60,000	467.66	462.77	458.36	454.38	450.76
65,000	506.63	501.34	496.56	492.24	488.33
70,000	545.60	539.90	534.76	530.10	525.89
75,000	584.57	578.46	572.95	567.97	563.45
80,000	623.54	617.03	611.15	605.83	601.02
85,000	662.51	655.59	649.35	643.70	638.58
90,000	701.48	694.16	687.54	681.56	676.14
95,000	740.45	732.72	725.74	719.43	713.71
100,000	779.42	771.28	763.94	757.29	751.27
110,000	857.36	848.41	840.33	833.02	826.40
120,000	935.31	925.54	916.72	908.75	901.52
125,000	974.28	964.10	954.92	946.61	939.09
130,000	1,013.25	1,002.67	993.11	984.48	976.65
140,000	1,091.19	1,079.79	1,069.51	1,060.20	1,051.78
150,000	1,169.13	1,156.92	1,145.90	1,135.93	1,126.90
160,000	1,247.07	1,234.05	1,222.29	1,211.66	1,202.03
170,000	1,325.01	1,311.18	1,298.69	1,287.39	1,277.16
175,000	1,363.98	1,349.74	1,336.88	1,325.25	1,314.72
180,000	1,402.96	1,388.31	1,375.08	1,363.12	1,352.28
190,000	1,480.90	1,465.43	1,451.47	1,438.85	1,427.41
200,000	1,558.84	1,542.56	1,527.87	1,514.58	1,502.54
220,000	1,714.72	1,696.82	1,680.65	1,666.03	1,652.79
225,000	1,753.69	1,735.38	1,718.85	1,703.90	1,690.35
230,000	1,792.66	1,773.94	1,757.05	1,741.76	1,727.92
240,000	1,870.61	1,851.07	1,833.44	1,817.49	1,803.04
$250,000	1,948.55	1,928.20	1,909.83	1,893.22	1,878.17

Table 1   59

8.50%   Monthly Payment Loans

Amortization Period in Years

	5	7	8	10	12
$ 100	2.06	1.59	1.44	1.24	1.12
200	4.11	3.17	2.88	2.48	2.23
300	6.16	4.76	4.32	3.72	3.34
400	8.21	6.34	5.76	4.96	4.45
500	10.26	7.92	7.20	6.20	5.56
600	12.31	9.51	8.64	7.44	6.67
700	14.37	11.09	10.08	8.68	7.78
800	16.42	12.67	11.52	9.92	8.89
900	18.47	14.26	12.96	11.16	10.00
1,000	20.52	15.84	14.40	12.40	11.11
2,000	41.04	31.68	28.79	24.80	22.21
3,000	61.55	47.51	43.18	37.20	33.31
4,000	82.07	63.35	57.57	49.60	44.41
5,000	102.59	79.19	71.97	62.00	55.51
6,000	123.10	95.02	86.36	74.40	66.61
7,000	143.62	110.86	100.75	86.79	77.71
8,000	164.14	126.70	115.14	99.19	88.81
9,000	184.65	142.53	129.53	111.59	99.91
10,000	205.17	158.37	143.93	123.99	111.01
15,000	307.75	237.55	215.89	185.98	166.51
20,000	410.34	316.73	287.85	247.98	222.02
25,000	512.92	395.92	359.81	309.97	277.52
30,000	615.50	475.10	431.77	371.96	333.02
35,000	718.08	554.28	503.73	433.95	388.52
40,000	820.67	633.46	575.69	495.95	444.03
45,000	923.25	712.65	647.65	557.94	499.53
50,000	1,025.83	791.83	719.61	619.93	555.03
55,000	1,128.41	871.01	791.57	681.93	610.54
60,000	1,231.00	950.19	863.53	743.92	666.04
65,000	1,333.58	1,029.38	935.49	805.91	721.54
70,000	1,436.16	1,108.56	1,007.45	867.90	777.04
75,000	1,538.74	1,187.74	1,079.41	929.90	832.55
80,000	1,641.33	1,266.92	1,151.38	991.89	888.05
85,000	1,743.91	1,346.11	1,223.34	1,053.88	943.55
90,000	1,846.49	1,425.29	1,295.30	1,115.88	999.06
95,000	1,949.08	1,504.47	1,367.26	1,177.87	1,054.56
100,000	2,051.66	1,583.65	1,439.22	1,239.86	1,110.06
110,000	2,256.82	1,742.02	1,583.14	1,363.85	1,221.07
120,000	2,461.99	1,900.38	1,727.06	1,487.83	1,332.07
125,000	2,564.57	1,979.57	1,799.02	1,549.83	1,387.57
130,000	2,667.15	2,058.75	1,870.98	1,611.82	1,443.08
140,000	2,872.32	2,217.11	2,014.90	1,735.80	1,554.08
150,000	3,077.48	2,375.48	2,158.82	1,859.79	1,665.09
160,000	3,282.65	2,533.84	2,302.75	1,983.78	1,776.09
170,000	3,487.82	2,692.21	2,446.67	2,107.76	1,887.10
175,000	3,590.40	2,771.39	2,518.63	2,169.75	1,942.60
180,000	3,692.98	2,850.57	2,590.59	2,231.75	1,998.11
190,000	3,898.15	3,008.94	2,734.51	2,355.73	2,109.11
200,000	4,103.31	3,167.30	2,878.43	2,479.72	2,220.12
220,000	4,513.64	3,484.03	3,166.27	2,727.69	2,442.13
225,000	4,616.22	3,563.21	3,238.23	2,789.68	2,497.63
230,000	4,718.81	3,642.40	3,310.19	2,851.68	2,553.13
240,000	4,923.97	3,800.76	3,454.12	2,975.66	2,664.14
$250,000	5,129.14	3,959.13	3,598.04	3,099.65	2,775.14

Monthly Payment Loans   **8.50%**

Amortization Period in Years

	15	16	17	18	20
$ 100	0.99	0.96	0.93	0.91	0.87
200	1.97	1.91	1.86	1.82	1.74
300	2.96	2.87	2.79	2.72	2.61
400	3.94	3.82	3.72	3.63	3.48
500	4.93	4.78	4.65	4.53	4.34
600	5.91	5.73	5.57	5.44	5.21
700	6.90	6.69	6.50	6.34	6.08
800	7.88	7.64	7.43	7.25	6.95
900	8.87	8.60	8.36	8.15	7.82
1,000	9.85	9.55	9.29	9.06	8.68
2,000	19.70	19.09	18.57	18.11	17.36
3,000	29.55	28.64	27.85	27.17	26.04
4,000	39.39	38.18	37.14	36.22	34.72
5,000	49.24	47.73	46.42	45.28	43.40
6,000	59.09	57.27	55.70	54.33	52.07
7,000	68.94	66.82	64.99	63.39	60.75
8,000	78.78	76.36	74.27	72.44	69.43
9,000	88.63	85.91	83.55	81.50	78.11
10,000	98.48	95.45	92.83	90.55	86.79
15,000	147.72	143.18	139.25	135.82	130.18
20,000	196.95	190.90	185.66	181.10	173.57
25,000	246.19	238.63	232.08	226.37	216.96
30,000	295.43	286.35	278.49	271.64	260.35
35,000	344.66	334.08	324.91	316.92	303.74
40,000	393.90	381.80	371.32	362.19	347.13
45,000	443.14	429.53	417.74	407.46	390.53
50,000	492.37	477.25	464.15	452.73	433.92
55,000	541.61	524.98	510.57	498.01	477.31
60,000	590.85	572.70	556.98	543.28	520.70
65,000	640.09	620.42	603.39	588.55	564.09
70,000	689.32	668.15	649.81	633.83	607.48
75,000	738.56	715.87	696.22	679.10	650.87
80,000	787.80	763.60	742.64	724.37	694.26
85,000	837.03	811.32	789.05	769.64	737.65
90,000	886.27	859.05	835.47	814.92	781.05
95,000	935.51	906.77	881.88	860.19	824.44
100,000	984.74	954.50	928.30	905.46	867.83
110,000	1,083.22	1,049.95	1,021.13	996.01	954.61
120,000	1,181.69	1,145.39	1,113.96	1,086.55	1,041.39
125,000	1,230.93	1,193.12	1,160.37	1,131.83	1,084.78
130,000	1,280.17	1,240.84	1,206.78	1,177.10	1,128.18
140,000	1,378.64	1,336.29	1,299.61	1,267.65	1,214.96
150,000	1,477.11	1,431.74	1,392.44	1,358.19	1,301.74
160,000	1,575.59	1,527.19	1,485.27	1,448.74	1,388.52
170,000	1,674.06	1,622.64	1,578.10	1,539.28	1,475.30
175,000	1,723.30	1,670.36	1,624.52	1,584.56	1,518.70
180,000	1,772.54	1,718.09	1,670.93	1,629.83	1,562.09
190,000	1,871.01	1,813.54	1,763.76	1,720.37	1,648.87
200,000	1,969.48	1,908.99	1,856.59	1,810.92	1,735.65
220,000	2,166.43	2,099.89	2,042.25	1,992.01	1,909.22
225,000	2,215.67	2,147.61	2,088.66	2,037.28	1,952.61
230,000	2,264.91	2,195.33	2,135.08	2,082.56	1,996.00
240,000	2,363.38	2,290.78	2,227.91	2,173.10	2,082.78
$250,000	2,461.85	2,386.23	2,320.74	2,263.65	2,169.56

Table 1   61

8.50%   Monthly Payment Loans

Amortization Period in Years

	21	22	23	24	25
$ 100	0.86	0.84	0.83	0.82	0.81
200	1.71	1.68	1.66	1.64	1.62
300	2.56	2.52	2.48	2.45	2.42
400	3.41	3.36	3.31	3.27	3.23
500	4.27	4.20	4.14	4.08	4.03
600	5.12	5.04	4.96	4.90	4.84
700	5.97	5.87	5.79	5.71	5.64
800	6.82	6.71	6.61	6.53	6.45
900	7.68	7.55	7.44	7.34	7.25
1,000	8.53	8.39	8.27	8.16	8.06
2,000	17.05	16.77	16.53	16.31	16.11
3,000	25.57	25.16	24.79	24.46	24.16
4,000	34.09	33.54	33.05	32.61	32.21
5,000	42.62	41.93	41.31	40.76	40.27
6,000	51.14	50.31	49.57	48.91	48.32
7,000	59.66	58.69	57.83	57.06	56.37
8,000	68.18	67.08	66.09	65.21	64.42
9,000	76.71	75.46	74.35	73.36	72.48
10,000	85.23	83.85	82.61	81.51	80.53
15,000	127.84	125.77	123.92	122.27	120.79
20,000	170.45	167.69	165.22	163.02	161.05
25,000	213.06	209.61	206.53	203.78	201.31
30,000	255.68	251.53	247.83	244.53	241.57
35,000	298.29	293.45	289.14	285.28	281.83
40,000	340.90	335.37	330.44	326.04	322.10
45,000	383.51	377.29	371.74	366.79	362.36
50,000	426.12	419.21	413.05	407.55	402.62
55,000	468.74	461.13	454.35	448.30	442.88
60,000	511.35	503.05	495.66	489.05	483.14
65,000	553.96	544.97	536.96	529.81	523.40
70,000	596.57	586.89	578.27	570.56	563.66
75,000	639.18	628.81	619.57	611.32	603.93
80,000	681.80	670.73	660.87	652.07	644.19
85,000	724.41	712.65	702.18	692.82	684.45
90,000	767.02	754.57	743.48	733.58	724.71
95,000	809.63	796.49	784.79	774.33	764.97
100,000	852.24	838.41	826.09	815.09	805.23
110,000	937.47	922.25	908.70	896.60	885.75
120,000	1,022.69	1,006.09	991.31	978.10	966.28
125,000	1,065.30	1,048.01	1,032.61	1,018.86	1,006.54
130,000	1,107.92	1,089.93	1,073.92	1,059.61	1,046.80
140,000	1,193.14	1,173.77	1,156.53	1,141.12	1,127.32
150,000	1,278.36	1,257.61	1,239.13	1,222.63	1,207.85
160,000	1,363.59	1,341.45	1,321.74	1,304.14	1,288.37
170,000	1,448.81	1,425.30	1,404.35	1,385.64	1,368.89
175,000	1,491.42	1,467.22	1,445.66	1,426.40	1,409.15
180,000	1,534.04	1,509.14	1,486.96	1,467.15	1,449.41
190,000	1,619.26	1,592.98	1,569.57	1,548.66	1,529.94
200,000	1,704.48	1,676.82	1,652.18	1,630.17	1,610.46
220,000	1,874.93	1,844.50	1,817.40	1,793.19	1,771.50
225,000	1,917.54	1,886.42	1,858.70	1,833.94	1,811.77
230,000	1,960.16	1,928.34	1,900.00	1,874.69	1,852.03
240,000	2,045.38	2,012.18	1,982.61	1,956.20	1,932.55
$250,000	2,130.60	2,096.02	2,065.22	2,037.71	2,013.07

Monthly Payment Loans   **8.50%**

Amortization Period in Years

	26	27	28	29	30
$ 100	0.80	0.79	0.79	0.78	0.77
200	1.60	1.58	1.57	1.55	1.54
300	2.39	2.37	2.35	2.33	2.31
400	3.19	3.16	3.13	3.10	3.08
500	3.99	3.95	3.91	3.88	3.85
600	4.78	4.74	4.69	4.65	4.62
700	5.58	5.52	5.47	5.43	5.39
800	6.38	6.31	6.25	6.20	6.16
900	7.17	7.10	7.04	6.98	6.93
1,000	7.97	7.89	7.82	7.75	7.69
2,000	15.93	15.77	15.63	15.50	15.38
3,000	23.90	23.66	23.44	23.25	23.07
4,000	31.86	31.54	31.25	31.00	30.76
5,000	39.82	39.43	39.07	38.74	38.45
6,000	47.79	47.31	46.88	46.49	46.14
7,000	55.75	55.19	54.69	54.24	53.83
8,000	63.72	63.08	62.50	61.99	61.52
9,000	71.68	70.96	70.32	69.73	69.21
10,000	79.64	78.85	78.13	77.48	76.90
15,000	119.46	118.27	117.19	116.22	115.34
20,000	159.28	157.69	156.25	154.96	153.79
25,000	199.10	197.11	195.32	193.70	192.23
30,000	238.92	236.53	234.38	232.44	230.68
35,000	278.74	275.95	273.44	271.17	269.12
40,000	318.56	315.37	312.50	309.91	307.57
45,000	358.38	354.79	351.57	348.65	346.02
50,000	398.19	394.22	390.63	387.39	384.46
55,000	438.01	433.64	429.69	426.13	422.91
60,000	477.83	473.06	468.75	464.87	461.35
65,000	517.65	512.48	507.82	503.61	499.80
70,000	557.47	551.90	546.88	542.34	538.24
75,000	597.29	591.32	585.94	581.08	576.69
80,000	637.11	630.74	625.00	619.82	615.14
85,000	676.93	670.16	664.07	658.56	653.58
90,000	716.75	709.58	703.13	697.30	692.03
95,000	756.57	749.00	742.19	736.04	730.47
100,000	796.38	788.43	781.25	774.78	768.92
110,000	876.02	867.27	859.38	852.25	845.81
120,000	955.66	946.11	937.50	929.73	922.70
125,000	995.48	985.53	976.56	968.47	961.15
130,000	1,035.30	1,024.95	1,015.63	1,007.21	999.59
140,000	1,114.94	1,103.79	1,093.75	1,084.68	1,076.48
150,000	1,194.57	1,182.64	1,171.88	1,162.16	1,153.38
160,000	1,274.21	1,261.48	1,250.00	1,239.64	1,230.27
170,000	1,353.85	1,340.32	1,328.13	1,317.11	1,307.16
175,000	1,393.67	1,379.74	1,367.19	1,355.85	1,345.60
180,000	1,433.49	1,419.16	1,406.25	1,394.59	1,384.05
190,000	1,513.13	1,498.00	1,484.38	1,472.07	1,460.94
200,000	1,592.76	1,576.85	1,562.50	1,549.55	1,537.83
220,000	1,752.04	1,734.53	1,718.75	1,704.50	1,691.61
225,000	1,791.86	1,773.95	1,757.81	1,743.24	1,730.06
230,000	1,831.68	1,813.37	1,796.87	1,781.98	1,768.51
240,000	1,911.32	1,892.22	1,875.00	1,859.45	1,845.40
$250,000	1,990.95	1,971.06	1,953.12	1,936.93	1,922.29

Table 1   63

8.75%   Monthly Payment Loans

Amortization Period in Years

		5	7	8	10	12
$	100	2.07	1.60	1.46	1.26	1.13
	200	4.13	3.20	2.91	2.51	2.25
	300	6.20	4.79	4.36	3.76	3.38
	400	8.26	6.39	5.81	5.02	4.50
	500	10.32	7.99	7.27	6.27	5.62
	600	12.39	9.58	8.72	7.52	6.75
	700	14.45	11.18	10.17	8.78	7.87
	800	16.51	12.77	11.62	10.03	9.00
	900	18.58	14.37	13.07	11.28	10.12
	1,000	20.64	15.97	14.53	12.54	11.24
	2,000	41.28	31.93	29.05	25.07	22.48
	3,000	61.92	47.89	43.57	37.60	33.72
	4,000	82.55	63.85	58.09	50.14	44.96
	5,000	103.19	79.82	72.61	62.67	56.20
	6,000	123.83	95.78	87.13	75.20	67.44
	7,000	144.47	111.74	101.65	87.73	78.68
	8,000	165.10	127.70	116.17	100.27	89.92
	9,000	185.74	143.67	130.69	112.80	101.16
	10,000	206.38	159.63	145.21	125.33	112.40
	15,000	309.56	239.44	217.82	188.00	168.60
	20,000	412.75	319.25	290.42	250.66	224.80
	25,000	515.94	399.07	363.03	313.32	281.00
	30,000	619.12	478.88	435.63	375.99	337.20
	35,000	722.31	558.69	508.23	438.65	393.40
	40,000	825.49	638.50	580.84	501.31	449.60
	45,000	928.68	718.32	653.44	563.98	505.80
	50,000	1,031.87	798.13	726.05	626.64	562.00
	55,000	1,135.05	877.94	798.65	689.30	618.20
	60,000	1,238.24	957.75	871.26	751.97	674.40
	65,000	1,341.43	1,037.57	943.86	814.63	730.60
	70,000	1,444.61	1,117.38	1,016.46	877.29	786.80
	75,000	1,547.80	1,197.19	1,089.07	939.96	843.00
	80,000	1,650.98	1,277.00	1,161.67	1,002.62	899.20
	85,000	1,754.17	1,356.82	1,234.28	1,065.28	955.40
	90,000	1,857.36	1,436.63	1,306.88	1,127.95	1,011.60
	95,000	1,960.54	1,516.44	1,379.48	1,190.61	1,067.80
	100,000	2,063.73	1,596.25	1,452.09	1,253.27	1,124.00
	110,000	2,270.10	1,755.88	1,597.30	1,378.60	1,236.40
	120,000	2,476.47	1,915.50	1,742.51	1,503.93	1,348.80
	125,000	2,579.66	1,995.32	1,815.11	1,566.59	1,405.00
	130,000	2,682.85	2,075.13	1,887.71	1,629.25	1,461.20
	140,000	2,889.22	2,234.75	2,032.92	1,754.58	1,573.60
	150,000	3,095.59	2,394.38	2,178.13	1,879.91	1,686.00
	160,000	3,301.96	2,554.00	2,323.34	2,005.23	1,798.40
	170,000	3,508.33	2,713.63	2,468.55	2,130.56	1,910.80
	175,000	3,611.52	2,793.44	2,541.15	2,193.22	1,967.00
	180,000	3,714.71	2,873.25	2,613.76	2,255.89	2,023.20
	190,000	3,921.08	3,032.88	2,758.96	2,381.21	2,135.60
	200,000	4,127.45	3,192.50	2,904.17	2,506.54	2,248.00
	220,000	4,540.20	3,511.75	3,194.59	2,757.19	2,472.80
	225,000	4,643.38	3,591.57	3,267.19	2,819.86	2,529.00
	230,000	4,746.57	3,671.38	3,339.80	2,882.52	2,585.20
	240,000	4,952.94	3,831.00	3,485.01	3,007.85	2,697.60
$	250,000	5,159.31	3,990.63	3,630.21	3,133.17	2,810.00

Monthly Payment Loans   __8.75%__

Amortization Period in Years

	15	16	17	18	20
$ 100	1.00	0.97	0.95	0.93	0.89
200	2.00	1.94	1.89	1.85	1.77
300	3.00	2.91	2.84	2.77	2.66
400	4.00	3.88	3.78	3.69	3.54
500	5.00	4.85	4.72	4.61	4.42
600	6.00	5.82	5.67	5.53	5.31
700	7.00	6.79	6.61	6.45	6.19
800	8.00	7.76	7.55	7.37	7.07
900	9.00	8.73	8.50	8.29	7.96
1,000	10.00	9.70	9.44	9.21	8.84
2,000	19.99	19.39	18.87	18.42	17.68
3,000	29.99	29.09	28.31	27.63	26.52
4,000	39.98	38.78	37.74	36.84	35.35
5,000	49.98	48.48	47.18	46.05	44.19
6,000	59.97	58.17	56.61	55.26	53.03
7,000	69.97	67.87	66.05	64.47	61.86
8,000	79.96	77.56	75.48	73.68	70.70
9,000	89.96	87.26	84.92	82.89	79.54
10,000	99.95	96.95	94.35	92.09	88.38
15,000	149.92	145.42	141.53	138.14	132.56
20,000	199.89	193.89	188.70	184.18	176.75
25,000	249.87	242.37	235.88	230.23	220.93
30,000	299.84	290.84	283.05	276.27	265.12
35,000	349.81	339.31	330.23	322.32	309.30
40,000	399.78	387.78	377.40	368.36	353.49
45,000	449.76	436.26	424.58	414.41	397.67
50,000	499.73	484.73	471.75	460.45	441.86
55,000	549.70	533.20	518.92	506.49	486.05
60,000	599.67	581.67	566.10	552.54	530.23
65,000	649.65	630.15	613.27	598.58	574.42
70,000	699.62	678.62	660.45	644.63	618.60
75,000	749.59	727.09	707.62	690.67	662.79
80,000	799.56	775.56	754.80	736.72	706.97
85,000	849.54	824.03	801.97	782.76	751.16
90,000	899.51	872.51	849.15	828.81	795.34
95,000	949.48	920.98	896.32	874.85	839.53
100,000	999.45	969.45	943.49	920.90	883.72
110,000	1,099.40	1,066.40	1,037.84	1,012.98	972.09
120,000	1,199.34	1,163.34	1,132.19	1,105.07	1,060.46
125,000	1,249.32	1,211.81	1,179.37	1,151.12	1,104.64
130,000	1,299.29	1,260.29	1,226.54	1,197.16	1,148.83
140,000	1,399.23	1,357.23	1,320.89	1,289.25	1,237.20
150,000	1,499.18	1,454.18	1,415.24	1,381.34	1,325.57
160,000	1,599.12	1,551.12	1,509.59	1,473.43	1,413.94
170,000	1,699.07	1,648.06	1,603.94	1,565.52	1,502.31
175,000	1,749.04	1,696.54	1,651.11	1,611.56	1,546.50
180,000	1,799.01	1,745.01	1,698.29	1,657.61	1,590.68
190,000	1,898.96	1,841.95	1,792.63	1,749.70	1,679.06
200,000	1,998.90	1,938.90	1,886.98	1,841.79	1,767.43
220,000	2,198.79	2,132.79	2,075.68	2,025.96	1,944.17
225,000	2,248.76	2,181.26	2,122.86	2,072.01	1,988.35
230,000	2,298.74	2,229.73	2,170.03	2,118.05	2,032.54
240,000	2,398.68	2,326.68	2,264.38	2,210.14	2,120.91
$250,000	2,498.63	2,423.62	2,358.73	2,302.23	2,209.28

Table 1   65

8.75% **Monthly Payment Loans**

Amortization Period in Years

	21	22	23	24	25
$ 100	0.87	0.86	0.85	0.84	0.83
200	1.74	1.71	1.69	1.67	1.65
300	2.61	2.57	2.53	2.50	2.47
400	3.48	3.42	3.38	3.33	3.29
500	4.35	4.28	4.22	4.16	4.12
600	5.22	5.13	5.06	5.00	4.94
700	6.08	5.99	5.90	5.83	5.76
800	6.95	6.84	6.75	6.66	6.58
900	7.82	7.70	7.59	7.49	7.40
1,000	8.69	8.55	8.43	8.32	8.23
2,000	17.37	17.10	16.86	16.64	16.45
3,000	26.06	25.65	25.28	24.96	24.67
4,000	34.74	34.19	33.71	33.28	32.89
5,000	43.42	42.74	42.14	41.60	41.11
6,000	52.11	51.29	50.56	49.91	49.33
7,000	60.79	59.84	58.99	58.23	57.56
8,000	69.47	68.38	67.41	66.55	65.78
9,000	78.16	76.93	75.84	74.87	74.00
10,000	86.84	85.48	84.27	83.19	82.22
15,000	130.26	128.21	126.40	124.78	123.33
20,000	173.67	170.95	168.53	166.37	164.43
25,000	217.09	213.69	210.66	207.96	205.54
30,000	260.51	256.42	252.79	249.55	246.65
35,000	303.93	299.16	294.92	291.14	287.76
40,000	347.34	341.89	337.05	332.73	328.86
45,000	390.76	384.63	379.18	374.32	369.97
50,000	434.18	427.37	421.31	415.91	411.08
55,000	477.59	470.10	463.44	457.50	452.18
60,000	521.01	512.84	505.57	499.09	493.29
65,000	564.43	555.58	547.70	540.68	534.40
70,000	607.85	598.31	589.83	582.27	575.51
75,000	651.26	641.05	631.96	623.86	616.61
80,000	694.68	683.78	674.09	665.45	657.72
85,000	738.10	726.52	716.22	707.04	698.83
90,000	781.52	769.26	758.35	748.63	739.93
95,000	824.93	811.99	800.48	790.22	781.04
100,000	868.35	854.73	842.62	831.81	822.15
110,000	955.18	940.20	926.88	914.99	904.36
120,000	1,042.02	1,025.67	1,011.14	998.17	986.58
125,000	1,085.44	1,068.41	1,053.27	1,039.76	1,027.68
130,000	1,128.85	1,111.15	1,095.40	1,081.35	1,068.79
140,000	1,215.69	1,196.62	1,179.66	1,164.53	1,151.01
150,000	1,302.52	1,282.09	1,263.92	1,247.71	1,233.22
160,000	1,389.36	1,367.56	1,348.18	1,330.89	1,315.43
170,000	1,476.19	1,453.04	1,432.44	1,414.07	1,397.65
175,000	1,519.61	1,495.77	1,474.57	1,455.66	1,438.76
180,000	1,563.03	1,538.51	1,516.70	1,497.26	1,479.86
190,000	1,649.86	1,623.98	1,600.96	1,580.44	1,562.08
200,000	1,736.69	1,709.45	1,685.23	1,663.62	1,644.29
220,000	1,910.36	1,880.40	1,853.75	1,829.98	1,808.72
225,000	1,953.78	1,923.13	1,895.88	1,871.57	1,849.83
230,000	1,997.20	1,965.87	1,938.01	1,913.16	1,890.94
240,000	2,084.03	2,051.34	2,022.27	1,996.34	1,973.15
$250,000	2,170.87	2,136.82	2,106.53	2,079.52	2,055.36

Monthly Payment Loans   **8.75%**

Amortization Period in Years

	26	27	28	29	30
$ 100	0.82	0.81	0.80	0.80	0.79
200	1.63	1.62	1.60	1.59	1.58
300	2.45	2.42	2.40	2.38	2.37
400	3.26	3.23	3.20	3.17	3.15
500	4.07	4.03	4.00	3.97	3.94
600	4.89	4.84	4.80	4.76	4.73
700	5.70	5.64	5.60	5.55	5.51
800	6.51	6.45	6.39	6.34	6.30
900	7.33	7.26	7.19	7.14	7.09
1,000	8.14	8.06	7.99	7.93	7.87
2,000	16.27	16.12	15.98	15.85	15.74
3,000	24.41	24.18	23.97	23.78	23.61
4,000	32.54	32.23	31.95	31.70	31.47
5,000	40.68	40.29	39.94	39.62	39.34
6,000	48.81	48.35	47.93	47.55	47.21
7,000	56.95	56.40	55.91	55.47	55.07
8,000	65.08	64.46	63.90	63.40	62.94
9,000	73.22	72.52	71.89	71.32	70.81
10,000	81.35	80.58	79.88	79.24	78.68
15,000	122.03	120.86	119.81	118.86	118.01
20,000	162.70	161.15	159.75	158.48	157.35
25,000	203.38	201.43	199.68	198.10	196.68
30,000	244.05	241.72	239.62	237.72	236.02
35,000	284.72	282.00	279.55	277.34	275.35
40,000	325.40	322.29	319.49	316.96	314.69
45,000	366.07	362.57	359.42	356.58	354.02
50,000	406.75	402.86	399.36	396.20	393.36
55,000	447.42	443.14	439.29	435.82	432.69
60,000	488.10	483.43	479.23	475.44	472.03
65,000	528.77	523.71	519.16	515.06	511.36
70,000	569.44	564.00	559.10	554.68	550.70
75,000	610.12	604.28	599.03	594.30	590.03
80,000	650.79	644.57	638.97	633.92	629.37
85,000	691.47	684.85	678.90	673.54	668.70
90,000	732.14	725.14	718.84	713.16	708.04
95,000	772.81	765.42	758.77	752.78	747.37
100,000	813.49	805.71	798.71	792.40	786.71
110,000	894.84	886.28	878.58	871.64	865.38
120,000	976.19	966.85	958.45	950.88	944.05
125,000	1,016.86	1,007.14	998.39	990.50	983.38
130,000	1,057.53	1,047.42	1,038.32	1,030.12	1,022.72
140,000	1,138.88	1,127.99	1,118.19	1,109.36	1,101.39
150,000	1,220.23	1,208.56	1,198.06	1,188.60	1,180.06
160,000	1,301.58	1,289.13	1,277.93	1,267.84	1,258.73
170,000	1,382.93	1,369.70	1,357.80	1,347.08	1,337.40
175,000	1,423.60	1,409.99	1,397.74	1,386.70	1,376.73
180,000	1,464.28	1,450.27	1,437.67	1,426.32	1,416.07
190,000	1,545.62	1,530.84	1,517.54	1,505.56	1,494.74
200,000	1,626.97	1,611.41	1,597.42	1,584.80	1,573.41
220,000	1,789.67	1,772.56	1,757.16	1,743.28	1,730.75
225,000	1,830.34	1,812.84	1,797.09	1,782.90	1,770.08
230,000	1,871.02	1,853.13	1,837.03	1,822.52	1,809.42
240,000	1,952.37	1,933.70	1,916.90	1,901.76	1,888.09
$250,000	2,033.71	2,014.27	1,996.77	1,980.99	1,966.76

Table 1   67

9.00%   Monthly Payment Loans

Amortization Period in Years

	5	7	8	10	12
$ 100	2.08	1.61	1.47	1.27	1.14
200	4.16	3.22	2.94	2.54	2.28
300	6.23	4.83	4.40	3.81	3.42
400	8.31	6.44	5.87	5.07	4.56
500	10.38	8.05	7.33	6.34	5.70
600	12.46	9.66	8.80	7.61	6.83
700	14.54	11.27	10.26	8.87	7.97
800	16.61	12.88	11.73	10.14	9.11
900	18.69	14.49	13.19	11.41	10.25
1,000	20.76	16.09	14.66	12.67	11.39
2,000	41.52	32.18	29.31	25.34	22.77
3,000	62.28	48.27	43.96	38.01	34.15
4,000	83.04	64.36	58.61	50.68	45.53
5,000	103.80	80.45	73.26	63.34	56.91
6,000	124.56	96.54	87.91	76.01	68.29
7,000	145.31	112.63	102.56	88.68	79.67
8,000	166.07	128.72	117.21	101.35	91.05
9,000	186.83	144.81	131.86	114.01	102.43
10,000	207.59	160.90	146.51	126.68	113.81
15,000	311.38	241.34	219.76	190.02	170.71
20,000	415.17	321.79	293.01	253.36	227.61
25,000	518.96	402.23	366.26	316.69	284.51
30,000	622.76	482.68	439.51	380.03	341.41
35,000	726.55	563.12	512.76	443.37	398.32
40,000	830.34	643.57	586.01	506.71	455.22
45,000	934.13	724.01	659.26	570.05	512.12
50,000	1,037.92	804.46	732.52	633.38	569.02
55,000	1,141.71	884.90	805.77	696.72	625.92
60,000	1,245.51	965.35	879.02	760.06	682.82
65,000	1,349.30	1,045.80	952.27	823.40	739.72
70,000	1,453.09	1,126.24	1,025.52	886.74	796.63
75,000	1,556.88	1,206.69	1,098.77	950.07	853.53
80,000	1,660.67	1,287.13	1,172.02	1,013.41	910.43
85,000	1,764.47	1,367.58	1,245.27	1,076.75	967.33
90,000	1,868.26	1,448.02	1,318.52	1,140.09	1,024.23
95,000	1,972.05	1,528.47	1,391.77	1,203.42	1,081.13
100,000	2,075.84	1,608.91	1,465.03	1,266.76	1,138.04
110,000	2,283.42	1,769.80	1,611.53	1,393.44	1,251.84
120,000	2,491.01	1,930.69	1,758.03	1,520.11	1,365.64
125,000	2,594.80	2,011.14	1,831.28	1,583.45	1,422.54
130,000	2,698.59	2,091.59	1,904.53	1,646.79	1,479.44
140,000	2,906.17	2,252.48	2,051.03	1,773.47	1,593.25
150,000	3,113.76	2,413.37	2,197.54	1,900.14	1,707.05
160,000	3,321.34	2,574.26	2,344.04	2,026.82	1,820.85
170,000	3,528.93	2,735.15	2,490.54	2,153.49	1,934.66
175,000	3,632.72	2,815.59	2,563.79	2,216.83	1,991.56
180,000	3,736.51	2,896.04	2,637.04	2,280.17	2,048.46
190,000	3,944.09	3,056.93	2,783.54	2,406.84	2,162.26
200,000	4,151.68	3,217.82	2,930.05	2,533.52	2,276.07
220,000	4,566.84	3,539.60	3,223.05	2,786.87	2,503.67
225,000	4,670.63	3,620.05	3,296.30	2,850.21	2,560.57
230,000	4,774.43	3,700.49	3,369.55	2,913.55	2,617.48
240,000	4,982.01	3,861.38	3,516.05	3,040.22	2,731.28
$250,000	5,189.59	4,022.27	3,662.56	3,166.90	2,845.08

Monthly Payment Loans   **9.00%**

Amortization Period in Years

	15	16	17	18	20
$ 100	1.02	0.99	0.96	0.94	0.90
200	2.03	1.97	1.92	1.88	1.80
300	3.05	2.96	2.88	2.81	2.70
400	4.06	3.94	3.84	3.75	3.60
500	5.08	4.93	4.80	4.69	4.50
600	6.09	5.91	5.76	5.62	5.40
700	7.10	6.90	6.72	6.56	6.30
800	8.12	7.88	7.68	7.50	7.20
900	9.13	8.87	8.63	8.43	8.10
1,000	10.15	9.85	9.59	9.37	9.00
2,000	20.29	19.70	19.18	18.73	18.00
3,000	30.43	29.54	28.77	28.10	27.00
4,000	40.58	39.39	38.36	37.46	35.99
5,000	50.72	49.23	47.95	46.83	44.99
6,000	60.86	59.08	57.53	56.19	53.99
7,000	71.00	68.92	67.12	65.56	62.99
8,000	81.15	78.77	76.71	74.92	71.98
9,000	91.29	88.61	86.30	84.29	80.98
10,000	101.43	98.46	95.89	93.65	89.98
15,000	152.14	147.68	143.83	140.47	134.96
20,000	202.86	196.91	191.77	187.29	179.95
25,000	253.57	246.13	239.71	234.12	224.94
30,000	304.28	295.36	287.65	280.94	269.92
35,000	355.00	344.59	335.59	327.76	314.91
40,000	405.71	393.81	383.53	374.58	359.90
45,000	456.42	443.04	431.47	421.41	404.88
50,000	507.14	492.26	479.41	468.23	449.87
55,000	557.85	541.49	527.35	515.05	494.85
60,000	608.56	590.71	575.29	561.87	539.84
65,000	659.28	639.94	623.23	608.69	584.83
70,000	709.99	689.17	671.17	655.52	629.81
75,000	760.70	738.39	719.11	702.34	674.80
80,000	811.42	787.62	767.05	749.16	719.79
85,000	862.13	836.84	814.99	795.98	764.77
90,000	912.84	886.07	862.93	842.81	809.76
95,000	963.56	935.30	910.87	889.63	854.74
100,000	1,014.27	984.52	958.81	936.45	899.73
110,000	1,115.70	1,082.97	1,054.69	1,030.09	989.70
120,000	1,217.12	1,181.42	1,150.57	1,123.74	1,079.68
125,000	1,267.84	1,230.65	1,198.51	1,170.56	1,124.66
130,000	1,318.55	1,279.88	1,246.45	1,217.38	1,169.65
140,000	1,419.98	1,378.33	1,342.33	1,311.03	1,259.62
150,000	1,521.40	1,476.78	1,438.21	1,404.67	1,349.59
160,000	1,622.83	1,575.23	1,534.09	1,498.32	1,439.57
170,000	1,724.26	1,673.68	1,629.97	1,591.96	1,529.54
175,000	1,774.97	1,722.91	1,677.91	1,638.78	1,574.53
180,000	1,825.68	1,772.13	1,725.85	1,685.61	1,619.51
190,000	1,927.11	1,870.59	1,821.73	1,779.25	1,709.48
200,000	2,028.54	1,969.04	1,917.61	1,872.89	1,799.46
220,000	2,231.39	2,165.94	2,109.37	2,060.18	1,979.40
225,000	2,282.10	2,215.17	2,157.31	2,107.01	2,024.39
230,000	2,332.82	2,264.39	2,205.25	2,153.83	2,069.37
240,000	2,434.24	2,362.84	2,301.13	2,247.47	2,159.35
$250,000	2,535.67	2,461.29	2,397.01	2,341.12	2,249.32

9.00% Monthly Payment Loans

Amortization Period in Years

	21	22	23	24	25
$ 100	0.89	0.88	0.86	0.85	0.84
200	1.77	1.75	1.72	1.70	1.68
300	2.66	2.62	2.58	2.55	2.52
400	3.54	3.49	3.44	3.40	3.36
500	4.43	4.36	4.30	4.25	4.20
600	5.31	5.23	5.16	5.10	5.04
700	6.20	6.10	6.02	5.95	5.88
800	7.08	6.97	6.88	6.79	6.72
900	7.97	7.85	7.74	7.64	7.56
1,000	8.85	8.72	8.60	8.49	8.40
2,000	17.70	17.43	17.19	16.98	16.79
3,000	26.54	26.14	25.78	25.46	25.18
4,000	35.39	34.85	34.38	33.95	33.57
5,000	44.23	43.56	42.97	42.44	41.96
6,000	53.08	52.28	51.56	50.92	50.36
7,000	61.93	60.99	60.15	59.41	58.75
8,000	70.77	69.70	68.75	67.90	67.14
9,000	79.62	78.41	77.34	76.38	75.53
10,000	88.46	87.12	85.93	84.87	83.92
15,000	132.69	130.68	128.90	127.30	125.88
20,000	176.92	174.24	171.86	169.74	167.84
25,000	221.15	217.80	214.82	212.17	209.80
30,000	265.38	261.36	257.79	254.60	251.76
35,000	309.61	304.92	300.75	297.04	293.72
40,000	353.84	348.47	343.71	339.47	335.68
45,000	398.07	392.03	386.68	381.90	377.64
50,000	442.30	435.59	429.64	424.34	419.60
55,000	486.52	479.15	472.60	466.77	461.56
60,000	530.75	522.71	515.57	509.20	503.52
65,000	574.98	566.27	558.53	551.64	545.48
70,000	619.21	609.83	601.49	594.07	587.44
75,000	663.44	653.39	644.46	636.50	629.40
80,000	707.67	696.94	687.42	678.94	671.36
85,000	751.90	740.50	730.38	721.37	713.32
90,000	796.13	784.06	773.35	763.80	755.28
95,000	840.36	827.62	816.31	806.24	797.24
100,000	884.59	871.18	859.27	848.67	839.20
110,000	973.04	958.30	945.20	933.54	923.12
120,000	1,061.50	1,045.41	1,031.13	1,018.40	1,007.04
125,000	1,105.73	1,088.97	1,074.09	1,060.84	1,049.00
130,000	1,149.96	1,132.53	1,117.05	1,103.27	1,090.96
140,000	1,238.42	1,219.65	1,202.98	1,188.14	1,174.88
150,000	1,326.88	1,306.77	1,288.91	1,273.00	1,258.80
160,000	1,415.33	1,393.88	1,374.83	1,357.87	1,342.72
170,000	1,503.79	1,481.00	1,460.76	1,442.73	1,426.64
175,000	1,548.02	1,524.56	1,503.72	1,485.17	1,468.60
180,000	1,592.25	1,568.12	1,546.69	1,527.60	1,510.56
190,000	1,680.71	1,655.24	1,632.61	1,612.47	1,594.48
200,000	1,769.17	1,742.35	1,718.54	1,697.33	1,678.40
220,000	1,946.08	1,916.59	1,890.39	1,867.07	1,846.24
225,000	1,990.31	1,960.15	1,933.36	1,909.50	1,888.20
230,000	2,034.54	2,003.71	1,976.32	1,951.93	1,930.16
240,000	2,123.00	2,090.82	2,062.25	2,036.80	2,014.08
$250,000	2,211.46	2,177.94	2,148.18	2,121.67	2,098.00

Monthly Payment Loans   **9.00%**

Amortization Period in Years

	26	27	28	29	30
$ 100	0.84	0.83	0.82	0.82	0.81
200	1.67	1.65	1.64	1.63	1.61
300	2.50	2.47	2.45	2.44	2.42
400	3.33	3.30	3.27	3.25	3.22
500	4.16	4.12	4.09	4.06	4.03
600	4.99	4.94	4.90	4.87	4.83
700	5.82	5.77	5.72	5.68	5.64
800	6.65	6.59	6.54	6.49	6.44
900	7.48	7.41	7.35	7.30	7.25
1,000	8.31	8.24	8.17	8.11	8.05
2,000	16.62	16.47	16.33	16.21	16.10
3,000	24.93	24.70	24.49	24.31	24.14
4,000	33.23	32.93	32.66	32.41	32.19
5,000	41.54	41.16	40.82	40.51	40.24
6,000	49.85	49.39	48.98	48.61	48.28
7,000	58.16	57.62	57.15	56.72	56.33
8,000	66.46	65.86	65.31	64.82	64.37
9,000	74.77	74.09	73.47	72.92	72.42
10,000	83.08	82.32	81.63	81.02	80.47
15,000	124.61	123.47	122.45	121.53	120.70
20,000	166.15	164.63	163.26	162.04	160.93
25,000	207.69	205.79	204.08	202.54	201.16
30,000	249.22	246.94	244.89	243.05	241.39
35,000	290.76	288.10	285.71	283.56	281.62
40,000	332.29	329.26	326.52	324.07	321.85
45,000	373.83	370.41	367.34	364.58	362.09
50,000	415.37	411.57	408.15	405.08	402.32
55,000	456.90	452.72	448.97	445.59	442.55
60,000	498.44	493.88	489.78	486.10	482.78
65,000	539.98	535.04	530.60	526.61	523.01
70,000	581.51	576.19	571.41	567.12	563.24
75,000	623.05	617.35	612.23	607.62	603.47
80,000	664.58	658.51	653.04	648.13	643.70
85,000	706.12	699.66	693.86	688.64	683.93
90,000	747.66	740.82	734.67	729.15	724.17
95,000	789.19	781.97	775.49	769.65	764.40
100,000	830.73	823.13	816.30	810.16	804.63
110,000	913.80	905.44	897.93	891.18	885.09
120,000	996.87	987.76	979.56	972.19	965.55
125,000	1,038.41	1,028.91	1,020.38	1,012.70	1,005.78
130,000	1,079.95	1,070.07	1,061.19	1,053.21	1,046.01
140,000	1,163.02	1,152.38	1,142.82	1,134.23	1,126.48
150,000	1,246.09	1,234.69	1,224.45	1,215.24	1,206.94
160,000	1,329.16	1,317.01	1,306.08	1,296.26	1,287.40
170,000	1,412.23	1,399.32	1,387.71	1,377.27	1,367.86
175,000	1,453.77	1,440.47	1,428.53	1,417.78	1,408.09
180,000	1,495.31	1,481.63	1,469.34	1,458.29	1,448.33
190,000	1,578.38	1,563.94	1,550.97	1,539.30	1,528.79
200,000	1,661.45	1,646.26	1,632.60	1,620.32	1,609.25
220,000	1,827.60	1,810.88	1,795.86	1,782.35	1,770.17
225,000	1,869.13	1,852.04	1,836.68	1,822.86	1,810.41
230,000	1,910.67	1,893.19	1,877.49	1,863.37	1,850.64
240,000	1,993.74	1,975.51	1,959.12	1,944.38	1,931.10
$250,000	2,076.81	2,057.82	2,040.75	2,025.40	2,011.56

Table 1   71

9.25%   Monthly Payment Loans

Amortization Period in Years

	5	7	8	10	12
$ 100	2.09	1.63	1.48	1.29	1.16
200	4.18	3.25	2.96	2.57	2.31
300	6.27	4.87	4.44	3.85	3.46
400	8.36	6.49	5.92	5.13	4.61
500	10.44	8.11	7.40	6.41	5.77
600	12.53	9.73	8.87	7.69	6.92
700	14.62	11.36	10.35	8.97	8.07
800	16.71	12.98	11.83	10.25	9.22
900	18.80	14.60	13.31	11.53	10.37
1,000	20.88	16.22	14.79	12.81	11.53
2,000	41.76	32.44	29.57	25.61	23.05
3,000	62.64	48.65	44.35	38.41	34.57
4,000	83.52	64.87	59.13	51.22	46.09
5,000	104.40	81.09	73.91	64.02	57.61
6,000	125.28	97.30	88.69	76.82	69.13
7,000	146.16	113.52	103.47	89.63	80.66
8,000	167.04	129.73	118.25	102.43	92.18
9,000	187.92	145.95	133.03	115.23	103.70
10,000	208.80	162.17	147.81	128.04	115.22
15,000	313.20	243.25	221.71	192.05	172.83
20,000	417.60	324.33	295.61	256.07	230.44
25,000	522.00	405.41	369.51	320.09	288.04
30,000	626.40	486.49	443.41	384.10	345.65
35,000	730.80	567.57	517.31	448.12	403.26
40,000	835.20	648.65	591.21	512.14	460.87
45,000	939.60	729.74	665.11	576.15	518.48
50,000	1,044.00	810.82	739.02	640.17	576.08
55,000	1,148.40	891.90	812.92	704.18	633.69
60,000	1,252.80	972.98	886.82	768.20	691.30
65,000	1,357.20	1,054.06	960.72	832.22	748.91
70,000	1,461.60	1,135.14	1,034.62	896.23	806.51
75,000	1,566.00	1,216.22	1,108.52	960.25	864.12
80,000	1,670.40	1,297.30	1,182.42	1,024.27	921.73
85,000	1,774.80	1,378.39	1,256.32	1,088.28	979.34
90,000	1,879.20	1,459.47	1,330.22	1,152.30	1,036.95
95,000	1,983.60	1,540.55	1,404.13	1,216.32	1,094.55
100,000	2,087.99	1,621.63	1,478.03	1,280.33	1,152.16
110,000	2,296.79	1,783.79	1,625.83	1,408.36	1,267.38
120,000	2,505.59	1,945.95	1,773.63	1,536.40	1,382.59
125,000	2,609.99	2,027.04	1,847.53	1,600.41	1,440.20
130,000	2,714.39	2,108.12	1,921.43	1,664.43	1,497.81
140,000	2,923.19	2,270.28	2,069.24	1,792.46	1,613.02
150,000	3,131.99	2,432.44	2,217.04	1,920.50	1,728.24
160,000	3,340.79	2,594.60	2,364.84	2,048.53	1,843.46
170,000	3,549.59	2,756.77	2,512.64	2,176.56	1,958.67
175,000	3,653.99	2,837.85	2,586.54	2,240.58	2,016.28
180,000	3,758.39	2,918.93	2,660.44	2,304.59	2,073.89
190,000	3,967.19	3,081.09	2,808.25	2,432.63	2,189.10
200,000	4,175.98	3,243.25	2,956.05	2,560.66	2,304.32
220,000	4,593.58	3,567.58	3,251.65	2,816.72	2,534.75
225,000	4,697.98	3,648.66	3,325.55	2,880.74	2,592.36
230,000	4,802.38	3,729.74	3,399.46	2,944.76	2,649.96
240,000	5,011.18	3,891.90	3,547.26	3,072.79	2,765.18
$250,000	5,219.98	4,054.07	3,695.06	3,200.82	2,880.40

Monthly Payment Loans 9.25%

Amortization Period in Years

	15	16	17	18	20
$ 100	1.03	1.00	0.98	0.96	0.92
200	2.06	2.00	1.95	1.91	1.84
300	3.09	3.00	2.93	2.86	2.75
400	4.12	4.00	3.90	3.81	3.67
500	5.15	5.00	4.88	4.77	4.58
600	6.18	6.00	5.85	5.72	5.50
700	7.21	7.00	6.82	6.67	6.42
800	8.24	8.00	7.80	7.62	7.33
900	9.27	9.00	8.77	8.57	8.25
1,000	10.30	10.00	9.75	9.53	9.16
2,000	20.59	20.00	19.49	19.05	18.32
3,000	30.88	30.00	29.23	28.57	27.48
4,000	41.17	39.99	38.97	38.09	36.64
5,000	51.46	49.99	48.72	47.61	45.80
6,000	61.76	59.99	58.46	57.13	54.96
7,000	72.05	69.98	68.20	66.65	64.12
8,000	82.34	79.98	77.94	76.17	73.27
9,000	92.63	89.98	87.69	85.70	82.43
10,000	102.92	99.97	97.43	95.22	91.59
15,000	154.38	149.96	146.14	142.82	137.39
20,000	205.84	199.94	194.85	190.43	183.18
25,000	257.30	249.93	243.56	238.03	228.97
30,000	308.76	299.91	292.28	285.64	274.77
35,000	360.22	349.90	340.99	333.25	320.56
40,000	411.68	399.88	389.70	380.85	366.35
45,000	463.14	449.87	438.41	428.46	412.15
50,000	514.60	499.85	487.12	476.06	457.94
55,000	566.06	549.84	535.83	523.67	503.73
60,000	617.52	599.82	584.55	571.28	549.53
65,000	668.98	649.81	633.26	618.88	595.32
70,000	720.44	699.79	681.97	666.49	641.11
75,000	771.90	749.78	730.68	714.09	686.91
80,000	823.36	799.76	779.39	761.70	732.70
85,000	874.82	849.75	828.10	809.31	778.49
90,000	926.28	899.73	876.82	856.91	824.29
95,000	977.74	949.72	925.53	904.52	870.08
100,000	1,029.20	999.70	974.24	952.12	915.87
110,000	1,132.12	1,099.67	1,071.66	1,047.34	1,007.46
120,000	1,235.04	1,199.64	1,169.09	1,142.55	1,099.05
125,000	1,286.50	1,249.63	1,217.80	1,190.15	1,144.84
130,000	1,337.95	1,299.61	1,266.51	1,237.76	1,190.63
140,000	1,440.87	1,399.58	1,363.93	1,332.97	1,282.22
150,000	1,543.79	1,499.55	1,461.36	1,428.18	1,373.81
160,000	1,646.71	1,599.52	1,558.78	1,523.40	1,465.39
170,000	1,749.63	1,699.49	1,656.20	1,618.61	1,556.98
175,000	1,801.09	1,749.48	1,704.92	1,666.21	1,602.77
180,000	1,852.55	1,799.46	1,753.63	1,713.82	1,648.57
190,000	1,955.47	1,899.43	1,851.05	1,809.03	1,740.15
200,000	2,058.39	1,999.40	1,948.47	1,904.24	1,831.74
220,000	2,264.23	2,199.34	2,143.32	2,094.67	2,014.91
225,000	2,315.69	2,249.32	2,192.03	2,142.27	2,060.71
230,000	2,367.15	2,299.31	2,240.75	2,189.88	2,106.50
240,000	2,470.07	2,399.28	2,338.17	2,285.09	2,198.09
$250,000	2,572.99	2,499.25	2,435.59	2,380.30	2,289.67

Table 1   73

9.25%   Monthly Payment Loans

Amortization Period in Years

	21	22	23	24	25
$ 100	0.91	0.89	0.88	0.87	0.86
200	1.81	1.78	1.76	1.74	1.72
300	2.71	2.67	2.63	2.60	2.57
400	3.61	3.56	3.51	3.47	3.43
500	4.51	4.44	4.39	4.33	4.29
600	5.41	5.33	5.26	5.20	5.14
700	6.31	6.22	6.14	6.06	6.00
800	7.21	7.11	7.01	6.93	6.86
900	8.11	7.99	7.89	7.80	7.71
1,000	9.01	8.88	8.77	8.66	8.57
2,000	18.02	17.76	17.53	17.32	17.13
3,000	27.03	26.64	26.29	25.97	25.70
4,000	36.04	35.52	35.05	34.63	34.26
5,000	45.05	44.39	43.81	43.29	42.82
6,000	54.06	53.27	52.57	51.94	51.39
7,000	63.07	62.15	61.33	60.60	59.95
8,000	72.08	71.03	70.09	69.26	68.52
9,000	81.09	79.90	78.85	77.91	77.08
10,000	90.10	88.78	87.61	86.57	85.64
15,000	135.15	133.17	131.41	129.85	128.46
20,000	180.19	177.56	175.22	173.14	171.28
25,000	225.24	221.94	219.02	216.42	214.10
30,000	270.29	266.33	262.82	259.70	256.92
35,000	315.34	310.72	306.62	302.98	299.74
40,000	360.38	355.11	350.43	346.27	342.56
45,000	405.43	399.49	394.23	389.55	385.38
50,000	450.48	443.88	438.03	432.83	428.20
55,000	495.52	488.27	481.84	476.12	471.02
60,000	540.57	532.66	525.64	519.40	513.83
65,000	585.62	577.05	569.44	562.68	556.65
70,000	630.67	621.43	613.24	605.96	599.47
75,000	675.71	665.82	657.05	649.25	642.29
80,000	720.76	710.21	700.85	692.53	685.11
85,000	765.81	754.60	744.65	735.81	727.93
90,000	810.86	798.98	788.46	779.09	770.75
95,000	855.90	843.37	832.26	822.38	813.57
100,000	900.95	887.76	876.06	865.66	856.39
110,000	991.04	976.53	963.67	952.23	942.03
120,000	1,081.14	1,065.31	1,051.27	1,038.79	1,027.66
125,000	1,126.19	1,109.70	1,095.08	1,082.07	1,070.48
130,000	1,171.23	1,154.09	1,138.88	1,125.36	1,113.30
140,000	1,261.33	1,242.86	1,226.48	1,211.92	1,198.94
150,000	1,351.42	1,331.64	1,314.09	1,298.49	1,284.58
160,000	1,441.52	1,420.41	1,401.70	1,385.05	1,370.22
170,000	1,531.61	1,509.19	1,489.30	1,471.62	1,455.85
175,000	1,576.66	1,553.58	1,533.10	1,514.90	1,498.67
180,000	1,621.71	1,597.96	1,576.91	1,558.18	1,541.49
190,000	1,711.80	1,686.74	1,664.51	1,644.75	1,627.13
200,000	1,801.89	1,775.51	1,752.12	1,731.32	1,712.77
220,000	1,982.08	1,953.06	1,927.33	1,904.45	1,884.05
225,000	2,027.13	1,997.45	1,971.13	1,947.73	1,926.86
230,000	2,072.18	2,041.84	2,014.94	1,991.01	1,969.68
240,000	2,162.27	2,130.62	2,102.54	2,077.58	2,055.32
$250,000	2,252.37	2,219.39	2,190.15	2,164.14	2,140.96

Monthly Payment Loans   9.25%

Amortization Period in Years

	26	27	28	29	30
$ 100	0.85	0.85	0.84	0.83	0.83
200	1.70	1.69	1.67	1.66	1.65
300	2.55	2.53	2.51	2.49	2.47
400	3.40	3.37	3.34	3.32	3.30
500	4.25	4.21	4.18	4.15	4.12
600	5.09	5.05	5.01	4.97	4.94
700	5.94	5.89	5.84	5.80	5.76
800	6.79	6.73	6.68	6.63	6.59
900	7.64	7.57	7.51	7.46	7.41
1,000	8.49	8.41	8.35	8.29	8.23
2,000	16.97	16.82	16.69	16.57	16.46
3,000	25.45	25.23	25.03	24.85	24.69
4,000	33.93	33.63	33.37	33.13	32.91
5,000	42.41	42.04	41.71	41.41	41.14
6,000	50.89	50.45	50.05	49.69	49.37
7,000	59.37	58.85	58.39	57.97	57.59
8,000	67.85	67.26	66.73	66.25	65.82
9,000	76.33	75.67	75.07	74.53	74.05
10,000	84.81	84.07	83.41	82.81	82.27
15,000	127.22	126.11	125.11	124.21	123.41
20,000	169.62	168.14	166.81	165.62	164.54
25,000	212.03	210.17	208.51	207.02	205.67
30,000	254.43	252.21	250.21	248.42	246.81
35,000	296.84	294.24	291.91	289.82	287.94
40,000	339.24	336.28	333.62	331.23	329.08
45,000	381.65	378.31	375.32	372.63	370.21
50,000	424.05	420.34	417.02	414.03	411.34
55,000	466.46	462.38	458.72	455.43	452.48
60,000	508.86	504.41	500.42	496.84	493.61
65,000	551.27	546.45	542.12	538.24	534.74
70,000	593.67	588.48	583.82	579.64	575.88
75,000	636.08	630.51	625.52	621.04	617.01
80,000	678.48	672.55	667.23	662.45	658.15
85,000	720.89	714.58	708.93	703.85	699.28
90,000	763.29	756.62	750.63	745.25	740.41
95,000	805.70	798.65	792.33	786.65	781.55
100,000	848.10	840.68	834.03	828.06	822.68
110,000	932.91	924.75	917.43	910.86	904.95
120,000	1,017.72	1,008.82	1,000.84	993.67	987.22
125,000	1,060.13	1,050.85	1,042.54	1,035.07	1,028.35
130,000	1,102.53	1,092.89	1,084.24	1,076.47	1,069.48
140,000	1,187.34	1,176.96	1,167.64	1,159.28	1,151.75
150,000	1,272.15	1,261.02	1,251.04	1,242.08	1,234.02
160,000	1,356.96	1,345.09	1,334.45	1,324.89	1,316.29
170,000	1,441.77	1,429.16	1,417.85	1,407.69	1,398.55
175,000	1,484.17	1,471.19	1,459.55	1,449.09	1,439.69
180,000	1,526.58	1,513.23	1,501.25	1,490.50	1,480.82
190,000	1,611.39	1,597.29	1,584.66	1,573.30	1,563.09
200,000	1,696.20	1,681.36	1,668.06	1,656.11	1,645.36
220,000	1,865.82	1,849.50	1,834.86	1,821.72	1,809.89
225,000	1,908.22	1,891.53	1,876.56	1,863.12	1,851.02
230,000	1,950.63	1,933.57	1,918.27	1,904.52	1,892.16
240,000	2,035.44	2,017.63	2,001.67	1,987.33	1,974.43
$250,000	2,120.25	2,101.70	2,085.07	2,070.13	2,056.69

Table 1   75

9.50% Monthly Payment Loan

Amortization Period in Years

	5	7	8	10	12
$ 100	2.11	1.64	1.50	1.30	1.17
200	4.21	3.27	2.99	2.59	2.34
300	6.31	4.91	4.48	3.89	3.50
400	8.41	6.54	5.97	5.18	4.67
500	10.51	8.18	7.46	6.47	5.84
600	12.61	9.81	8.95	7.77	7.00
700	14.71	11.45	10.44	9.06	8.17
800	16.81	13.08	11.93	10.36	9.34
900	18.91	14.71	13.42	11.65	10.50
1,000	21.01	16.35	14.92	12.94	11.67
2,000	42.01	32.69	29.83	25.88	23.33
3,000	63.01	49.04	44.74	38.82	35.00
4,000	84.01	65.38	59.65	51.76	46.66
5,000	105.01	81.72	74.56	64.70	58.32
6,000	126.02	98.07	89.47	77.64	69.99
7,000	147.02	114.41	104.38	90.58	81.65
8,000	168.02	130.76	119.29	103.52	93.31
9,000	189.02	147.10	134.20	116.46	104.98
10,000	210.02	163.44	149.11	129.40	116.64
15,000	315.03	245.16	223.67	194.10	174.96
20,000	420.04	326.88	298.22	258.80	233.28
25,000	525.05	408.60	372.78	323.50	291.60
30,000	630.06	490.32	447.33	388.20	349.92
35,000	735.07	572.04	521.89	452.90	408.24
40,000	840.08	653.76	596.44	517.60	466.55
45,000	945.09	735.48	670.99	582.29	524.87
50,000	1,050.10	817.20	745.55	646.99	583.19
55,000	1,155.11	898.92	820.10	711.69	641.51
60,000	1,260.12	980.64	894.66	776.39	699.83
65,000	1,365.13	1,062.36	969.21	841.09	758.15
70,000	1,470.14	1,144.08	1,043.77	905.79	816.47
75,000	1,575.14	1,225.80	1,118.32	970.49	874.78
80,000	1,680.15	1,307.52	1,192.88	1,035.19	933.10
85,000	1,785.16	1,389.24	1,267.43	1,099.88	991.42
90,000	1,890.17	1,470.96	1,341.98	1,164.58	1,049.74
95,000	1,995.18	1,552.68	1,416.54	1,229.28	1,108.06
100,000	2,100.19	1,634.40	1,491.09	1,293.98	1,166.38
110,000	2,310.21	1,797.84	1,640.20	1,423.38	1,283.02
120,000	2,520.23	1,961.28	1,789.31	1,552.78	1,399.65
125,000	2,625.24	2,043.00	1,863.87	1,617.47	1,457.97
130,000	2,730.25	2,124.72	1,938.42	1,682.17	1,516.29
140,000	2,940.27	2,288.16	2,087.53	1,811.57	1,632.93
150,000	3,150.28	2,451.60	2,236.64	1,940.97	1,749.56
160,000	3,360.30	2,615.04	2,385.75	2,070.37	1,866.20
170,000	3,570.32	2,778.48	2,534.86	2,199.76	1,982.84
175,000	3,675.33	2,860.20	2,609.41	2,264.46	2,041.16
180,000	3,780.34	2,941.92	2,683.96	2,329.16	2,099.48
190,000	3,990.36	3,105.36	2,833.07	2,458.56	2,216.11
200,000	4,200.38	3,268.80	2,982.18	2,587.96	2,332.75
220,000	4,620.41	3,595.68	3,280.40	2,846.75	2,566.03
225,000	4,725.42	3,677.40	3,354.95	2,911.45	2,624.34
230,000	4,830.43	3,759.12	3,429.51	2,976.15	2,682.66
240,000	5,040.45	3,922.56	3,578.62	3,105.55	2,799.30
$250,000	5,250.47	4,086.00	3,727.73	3,234.94	2,915.94

Monthly Payment Loans   **9.50%**

Amortization Period in Years

	15	16	17	18	20
$ 100	1.05	1.02	0.99	0.97	0.94
200	2.09	2.03	1.98	1.94	1.87
300	3.14	3.05	2.97	2.91	2.80
400	4.18	4.06	3.96	3.88	3.73
500	5.23	5.08	4.95	4.84	4.67
600	6.27	6.09	5.94	5.81	5.60
700	7.31	7.11	6.93	6.78	6.53
800	8.36	8.12	7.92	7.75	7.46
900	9.40	9.14	8.91	8.72	8.39
1,000	10.45	10.15	9.90	9.68	9.33
2,000	20.89	20.30	19.80	19.36	18.65
3,000	31.33	30.45	29.70	29.04	27.97
4,000	41.77	40.60	39.60	38.72	37.29
5,000	52.22	50.75	49.49	48.40	46.61
6,000	62.66	60.90	59.39	58.08	55.93
7,000	73.10	71.05	69.29	67.76	65.25
8,000	83.54	81.20	79.19	77.44	74.58
9,000	93.99	91.35	89.09	87.12	83.90
10,000	104.43	101.50	98.98	96.80	93.22
15,000	156.64	152.25	148.47	145.19	139.82
20,000	208.85	203.00	197.96	193.59	186.43
25,000	261.06	253.75	247.45	241.98	233.04
30,000	313.27	304.50	296.94	290.38	279.64
35,000	365.48	355.25	346.43	338.77	326.25
40,000	417.69	406.00	395.92	387.17	372.86
45,000	469.91	456.75	445.41	435.57	419.46
50,000	522.12	507.50	494.90	483.96	466.07
55,000	574.33	558.25	544.38	532.36	512.68
60,000	626.54	609.00	593.87	580.75	559.28
65,000	678.75	659.75	643.36	629.15	605.89
70,000	730.96	710.50	692.85	677.54	652.50
75,000	783.17	761.25	742.34	725.94	699.10
80,000	835.38	812.00	791.83	774.33	745.71
85,000	887.60	862.75	841.32	822.73	792.32
90,000	939.81	913.50	890.81	871.13	838.92
95,000	992.02	964.25	940.30	919.52	885.53
100,000	1,044.23	1,014.99	989.79	967.92	932.14
110,000	1,148.65	1,116.49	1,088.76	1,064.71	1,025.35
120,000	1,253.07	1,217.99	1,187.74	1,161.50	1,118.56
125,000	1,305.29	1,268.74	1,237.23	1,209.89	1,165.17
130,000	1,357.50	1,319.49	1,286.72	1,258.29	1,211.78
140,000	1,461.92	1,420.99	1,385.70	1,355.08	1,304.99
150,000	1,566.34	1,522.49	1,484.68	1,451.87	1,398.20
160,000	1,670.76	1,623.99	1,583.65	1,548.66	1,491.41
170,000	1,775.19	1,725.49	1,682.63	1,645.45	1,584.63
175,000	1,827.40	1,776.24	1,732.12	1,693.85	1,631.23
180,000	1,879.61	1,826.99	1,781.61	1,742.25	1,677.84
190,000	1,984.03	1,928.49	1,880.59	1,839.04	1,771.05
200,000	2,088.45	2,029.98	1,979.57	1,935.83	1,864.27
220,000	2,297.30	2,232.98	2,177.52	2,129.41	2,050.69
225,000	2,349.51	2,283.73	2,227.01	2,177.81	2,097.30
230,000	2,401.72	2,334.48	2,276.50	2,226.20	2,143.91
240,000	2,506.14	2,435.98	2,375.48	2,322.99	2,237.12
$250,000	2,610.57	2,537.48	2,474.46	2,419.78	2,330.33

Table 1   77

9.50%   Monthly Payment Loans

Amortization Period in Years

		21	22	23	24	25
$	100	0.92	0.91	0.90	0.89	0.88
	200	1.84	1.81	1.79	1.77	1.75
	300	2.76	2.72	2.68	2.65	2.63
	400	3.67	3.62	3.58	3.54	3.50
	500	4.59	4.53	4.47	4.42	4.37
	600	5.51	5.43	5.36	5.30	5.25
	700	6.43	6.34	6.26	6.18	6.12
	800	7.34	7.24	7.15	7.07	6.99
	900	8.26	8.15	8.04	7.95	7.87
	1,000	9.18	9.05	8.93	8.83	8.74
	2,000	18.35	18.09	17.86	17.66	17.48
	3,000	27.53	27.14	26.79	26.49	26.22
	4,000	36.70	36.18	35.72	35.32	34.95
	5,000	45.88	45.23	44.65	44.14	43.69
	6,000	55.05	54.27	53.58	52.97	52.43
	7,000	64.23	63.32	62.51	61.80	61.16
	8,000	73.40	72.36	71.44	70.63	69.90
	9,000	82.57	81.41	80.37	79.45	78.64
	10,000	91.75	90.45	89.30	88.28	87.37
	15,000	137.62	135.67	133.95	132.42	131.06
	20,000	183.49	180.90	178.60	176.56	174.74
	25,000	229.36	226.12	223.25	220.70	218.43
	30,000	275.24	271.34	267.90	264.84	262.11
	35,000	321.11	316.57	312.55	308.98	305.80
	40,000	366.98	361.79	357.19	353.11	349.48
	45,000	412.85	407.01	401.84	397.25	393.17
	50,000	458.72	452.24	446.49	441.39	436.85
	55,000	504.59	497.46	491.14	485.53	480.54
	60,000	550.47	542.68	535.79	529.67	524.22
	65,000	596.34	587.90	580.44	573.81	567.91
	70,000	642.21	633.13	625.09	617.95	611.59
	75,000	688.08	678.35	669.74	662.09	655.28
	80,000	733.95	723.57	714.38	706.22	698.96
	85,000	779.82	768.80	759.03	750.36	742.65
	90,000	825.70	814.02	803.68	794.50	786.33
	95,000	871.57	859.24	848.33	838.64	830.02
	100,000	917.44	904.47	892.98	882.78	873.70
	110,000	1,009.18	994.91	982.28	971.06	961.07
	120,000	1,100.93	1,085.36	1,071.57	1,059.33	1,048.44
	125,000	1,146.80	1,130.58	1,116.22	1,103.47	1,092.13
	130,000	1,192.67	1,175.80	1,160.87	1,147.61	1,135.81
	140,000	1,284.41	1,266.25	1,250.17	1,235.89	1,223.18
	150,000	1,376.16	1,356.70	1,339.47	1,324.17	1,310.55
	160,000	1,467.90	1,447.14	1,428.76	1,412.44	1,397.92
	170,000	1,559.64	1,537.59	1,518.06	1,500.72	1,485.29
	175,000	1,605.52	1,582.81	1,562.71	1,544.86	1,528.97
	180,000	1,651.39	1,628.04	1,607.36	1,589.00	1,572.66
	190,000	1,743.13	1,718.48	1,696.66	1,677.28	1,660.03
	200,000	1,834.87	1,808.93	1,785.95	1,765.55	1,747.40
	220,000	2,018.36	1,989.82	1,964.55	1,942.11	1,922.14
	225,000	2,064.23	2,035.04	2,009.20	1,986.25	1,965.82
	230,000	2,110.10	2,080.27	2,053.85	2,030.39	2,009.51
	240,000	2,201.85	2,170.71	2,143.14	2,118.66	2,096.88
$	250,000	2,293.59	2,261.16	2,232.44	2,206.94	2,184.25

Monthly Payment Loans   **9.50%**

Amortization Period in Years

	26	27	28	29	30
$ 100	0.87	0.86	0.86	0.85	0.85
200	1.74	1.72	1.71	1.70	1.69
300	2.60	2.58	2.56	2.54	2.53
400	3.47	3.44	3.41	3.39	3.37
500	4.33	4.30	4.26	4.24	4.21
600	5.20	5.16	5.12	5.08	5.05
700	6.06	6.01	5.97	5.93	5.89
800	6.93	6.87	6.82	6.77	6.73
900	7.80	7.73	7.67	7.62	7.57
1,000	8.66	8.59	8.52	8.47	8.41
2,000	17.32	17.17	17.04	16.93	16.82
3,000	25.97	25.76	25.56	25.39	25.23
4,000	34.63	34.34	34.08	33.85	33.64
5,000	43.28	42.92	42.60	42.31	42.05
6,000	51.94	51.51	51.12	50.77	50.46
7,000	60.60	60.09	59.64	59.23	58.86
8,000	69.25	68.67	68.16	67.69	67.27
9,000	77.91	77.26	76.67	76.15	75.68
10,000	86.56	85.84	85.19	84.61	84.09
15,000	129.84	128.76	127.79	126.92	126.13
20,000	173.12	171.68	170.38	169.22	168.18
25,000	216.40	214.60	212.98	211.52	210.22
30,000	259.68	257.51	255.57	253.83	252.26
35,000	302.96	300.43	298.16	296.13	294.30
40,000	346.24	343.35	340.76	338.43	336.35
45,000	389.52	386.27	383.35	380.74	378.39
50,000	432.80	429.19	425.95	423.04	420.43
55,000	476.08	472.10	468.54	465.34	462.47
60,000	519.36	515.02	511.13	507.65	504.52
65,000	562.64	557.94	553.73	549.95	546.56
70,000	605.92	600.86	596.32	592.26	588.60
75,000	649.20	643.78	638.92	634.56	630.65
80,000	692.48	686.69	681.51	676.86	672.69
85,000	735.76	729.61	724.10	719.17	714.73
90,000	779.04	772.53	766.70	761.47	756.77
95,000	822.32	815.45	809.29	803.77	798.82
100,000	865.60	858.37	851.89	846.08	840.86
110,000	952.16	944.20	937.07	930.68	924.94
120,000	1,038.72	1,030.04	1,022.26	1,015.29	1,009.03
125,000	1,082.00	1,072.96	1,064.86	1,057.59	1,051.07
130,000	1,125.28	1,115.87	1,107.45	1,099.90	1,093.12
140,000	1,211.84	1,201.71	1,192.64	1,184.51	1,177.20
150,000	1,298.40	1,287.55	1,277.83	1,269.11	1,261.29
160,000	1,384.96	1,373.38	1,363.02	1,353.72	1,345.37
170,000	1,471.52	1,459.22	1,448.20	1,438.33	1,429.46
175,000	1,514.80	1,502.14	1,490.80	1,480.63	1,471.50
180,000	1,558.08	1,545.06	1,533.39	1,522.93	1,513.54
190,000	1,644.64	1,630.89	1,618.58	1,607.54	1,597.63
200,000	1,731.20	1,716.73	1,703.77	1,692.15	1,681.71
220,000	1,904.32	1,888.40	1,874.14	1,861.36	1,849.88
225,000	1,947.60	1,931.32	1,916.74	1,903.67	1,891.93
230,000	1,990.88	1,974.24	1,959.33	1,945.97	1,933.97
240,000	2,077.44	2,060.07	2,044.52	2,030.58	2,018.06
$250,000	2,164.00	2,145.91	2,129.71	2,115.18	2,102.14

Table 1   79

9.75%   Monthly Payment Loans

Amortization Period in Years

	5	7	8	10	12
$ 100	2.12	1.65	1.51	1.31	1.19
200	4.23	3.30	3.01	2.62	2.37
300	6.34	4.95	4.52	3.93	3.55
400	8.45	6.59	6.02	5.24	4.73
500	10.57	8.24	7.53	6.54	5.91
600	12.68	9.89	9.03	7.85	7.09
700	14.79	11.54	10.53	9.16	8.27
800	16.90	13.18	12.04	10.47	9.45
900	19.02	14.83	13.54	11.77	10.63
1,000	21.13	16.48	15.05	13.08	11.81
2,000	42.25	32.95	30.09	26.16	23.62
3,000	63.38	49.42	45.13	39.24	35.43
4,000	84.50	65.89	60.17	52.31	47.23
5,000	105.63	82.37	75.22	65.39	59.04
6,000	126.75	98.84	90.26	78.47	70.85
7,000	147.87	115.31	105.30	91.54	82.65
8,000	169.00	131.78	120.34	104.62	94.46
9,000	190.12	148.26	135.38	117.70	106.27
10,000	211.25	164.73	150.43	130.78	118.07
15,000	316.87	247.09	225.64	196.16	177.11
20,000	422.49	329.45	300.85	261.55	236.14
25,000	528.11	411.81	376.06	326.93	295.18
30,000	633.73	494.17	451.27	392.32	354.21
35,000	739.35	576.54	526.48	457.70	413.24
40,000	844.97	658.90	601.69	523.09	472.28
45,000	950.60	741.26	676.90	588.47	531.31
50,000	1,056.22	823.62	752.12	653.86	590.35
55,000	1,161.84	905.98	827.33	719.24	649.38
60,000	1,267.46	988.34	902.54	784.63	708.41
65,000	1,373.08	1,070.70	977.75	850.01	767.45
70,000	1,478.70	1,153.07	1,052.96	915.40	826.48
75,000	1,584.32	1,235.43	1,128.17	980.78	885.52
80,000	1,689.94	1,317.79	1,203.38	1,046.17	944.55
85,000	1,795.57	1,400.15	1,278.59	1,111.55	1,003.58
90,000	1,901.19	1,482.51	1,353.80	1,176.94	1,062.62
95,000	2,006.81	1,564.87	1,429.01	1,242.32	1,121.65
100,000	2,112.43	1,647.23	1,504.23	1,307.71	1,180.69
110,000	2,323.67	1,811.96	1,654.65	1,438.48	1,298.75
120,000	2,534.91	1,976.68	1,805.07	1,569.25	1,416.82
125,000	2,640.54	2,059.04	1,880.28	1,634.63	1,475.86
130,000	2,746.16	2,141.40	1,955.49	1,700.02	1,534.89
140,000	2,957.40	2,306.13	2,105.91	1,830.79	1,652.96
150,000	3,168.64	2,470.85	2,256.34	1,961.56	1,771.03
160,000	3,379.88	2,635.57	2,406.76	2,092.33	1,889.09
170,000	3,591.13	2,800.30	2,557.18	2,223.10	2,007.16
175,000	3,696.75	2,882.66	2,632.39	2,288.48	2,066.20
180,000	3,802.37	2,965.02	2,707.60	2,353.87	2,125.23
190,000	4,013.61	3,129.74	2,858.02	2,484.64	2,243.30
200,000	4,224.85	3,294.46	3,008.45	2,615.41	2,361.37
220,000	4,647.34	3,623.91	3,309.29	2,876.95	2,597.50
225,000	4,752.96	3,706.27	3,384.50	2,942.34	2,656.54
230,000	4,858.58	3,788.63	3,459.71	3,007.72	2,715.57
240,000	5,069.82	3,953.36	3,610.13	3,138.49	2,833.64
$250,000	5,281.07	4,118.08	3,760.56	3,269.26	2,951.71

Monthly Payment Loans   **9.75%**

Amortization Period in Years

	15	16	17	18	20
$ 100	1.06	1.04	1.01	0.99	0.95
200	2.12	2.07	2.02	1.97	1.90
300	3.18	3.10	3.02	2.96	2.85
400	4.24	4.13	4.03	3.94	3.80
500	5.30	5.16	5.03	4.92	4.75
600	6.36	6.19	6.04	5.91	5.70
700	7.42	7.22	7.04	6.89	6.64
800	8.48	8.25	8.05	7.88	7.59
900	9.54	9.28	9.05	8.86	8.54
1,000	10.60	10.31	10.06	9.84	9.49
2,000	21.19	20.61	20.11	19.68	18.98
3,000	31.79	30.92	30.17	29.52	28.46
4,000	42.38	41.22	40.22	39.36	37.95
5,000	52.97	51.52	50.28	49.20	47.43
6,000	63.57	61.83	60.33	59.03	56.92
7,000	74.16	72.13	70.39	68.87	66.40
8,000	84.75	82.44	80.44	78.71	75.89
9,000	95.35	92.74	90.49	88.55	85.37
10,000	105.94	103.04	100.55	98.39	94.86
15,000	158.91	154.56	150.82	147.58	142.28
20,000	211.88	206.08	201.09	196.77	189.71
25,000	264.85	257.60	251.36	245.96	237.13
30,000	317.81	309.12	301.64	295.15	284.56
35,000	370.78	360.64	351.91	344.34	331.99
40,000	423.75	412.16	402.18	393.53	379.41
45,000	476.72	463.68	452.45	442.72	426.84
50,000	529.69	515.20	502.72	491.92	474.26
55,000	582.65	566.72	553.00	541.11	521.69
60,000	635.62	618.24	603.27	590.30	569.12
65,000	688.59	669.76	653.54	639.49	616.54
70,000	741.56	721.28	703.81	688.68	663.97
75,000	794.53	772.80	754.08	737.87	711.39
80,000	847.50	824.32	804.36	787.06	758.82
85,000	900.46	875.84	854.63	836.25	806.24
90,000	953.43	927.36	904.90	885.44	853.67
95,000	1,006.40	978.88	955.17	934.63	901.10
100,000	1,059.37	1,030.40	1,005.44	983.83	948.52
110,000	1,165.30	1,133.44	1,105.99	1,082.21	1,043.37
120,000	1,271.24	1,236.47	1,206.53	1,180.59	1,138.23
125,000	1,324.21	1,287.99	1,256.80	1,229.78	1,185.65
130,000	1,377.18	1,339.51	1,307.08	1,278.97	1,233.08
140,000	1,483.11	1,442.55	1,407.62	1,377.35	1,327.93
150,000	1,589.05	1,545.59	1,508.16	1,475.74	1,422.78
160,000	1,694.99	1,648.63	1,608.71	1,574.12	1,517.63
170,000	1,800.92	1,751.67	1,709.25	1,672.50	1,612.48
175,000	1,853.89	1,803.19	1,759.52	1,721.69	1,659.91
180,000	1,906.86	1,854.71	1,809.80	1,770.88	1,707.34
190,000	2,012.79	1,957.75	1,910.34	1,869.26	1,802.19
200,000	2,118.73	2,060.79	2,010.88	1,967.65	1,897.04
220,000	2,330.60	2,266.87	2,211.97	2,164.41	2,086.74
225,000	2,383.57	2,318.39	2,262.24	2,213.60	2,134.17
230,000	2,436.54	2,369.91	2,312.52	2,262.79	2,181.59
240,000	2,542.48	2,472.94	2,413.06	2,361.17	2,276.45
$250,000	2,648.41	2,575.98	2,513.60	2,459.56	2,371.30

Table 1   81

9.75% Monthly Payment Loans
Amortization Period in Years

	21	22	23	24	25
$ 100	0.94	0.93	0.92	0.91	0.90
200	1.87	1.85	1.83	1.81	1.79
300	2.81	2.77	2.74	2.71	2.68
400	3.74	3.69	3.65	3.61	3.57
500	4.68	4.61	4.56	4.51	4.46
600	5.61	5.53	5.47	5.41	5.35
700	6.54	6.45	6.38	6.31	6.24
800	7.48	7.38	7.29	7.21	7.13
900	8.41	8.30	8.20	8.11	8.03
1,000	9.35	9.22	9.11	9.01	8.92
2,000	18.69	18.43	18.21	18.01	17.83
3,000	28.03	27.64	27.31	27.01	26.74
4,000	37.37	36.86	36.41	36.01	35.65
5,000	46.71	46.07	45.51	45.01	44.56
6,000	56.05	55.28	54.61	54.01	53.47
7,000	65.39	64.50	63.71	63.01	62.38
8,000	74.73	73.71	72.81	72.01	71.30
9,000	84.07	82.92	81.91	81.01	80.21
10,000	93.41	92.13	91.01	90.01	89.12
15,000	140.11	138.20	136.51	135.01	133.68
20,000	186.81	184.26	182.01	180.01	178.23
25,000	233.52	230.33	227.51	225.01	222.79
30,000	280.22	276.39	273.01	270.01	267.35
35,000	326.92	322.46	318.51	315.01	311.90
40,000	373.62	368.52	364.01	360.01	356.46
45,000	420.33	414.59	409.51	405.01	401.02
50,000	467.03	460.65	455.01	450.02	445.57
55,000	513.73	506.72	500.51	495.02	490.13
60,000	560.43	552.78	546.02	540.02	534.69
65,000	607.14	598.85	591.52	585.02	579.24
70,000	653.84	644.91	637.02	630.02	623.80
75,000	700.54	690.97	682.52	675.02	668.36
80,000	747.24	737.04	728.02	720.02	712.91
85,000	793.94	783.10	773.52	765.02	757.47
90,000	840.65	829.17	819.02	810.02	802.03
95,000	887.35	875.23	864.52	855.02	846.59
100,000	934.05	921.30	910.02	900.03	891.14
110,000	1,027.46	1,013.43	1,001.02	990.03	980.26
120,000	1,120.86	1,105.56	1,092.03	1,080.03	1,069.37
125,000	1,167.56	1,151.62	1,137.53	1,125.03	1,113.93
130,000	1,214.27	1,197.69	1,183.03	1,170.03	1,158.48
140,000	1,307.67	1,289.81	1,274.03	1,260.03	1,247.60
150,000	1,401.08	1,381.94	1,365.03	1,350.04	1,336.71
160,000	1,494.48	1,474.07	1,456.03	1,440.04	1,425.82
170,000	1,587.88	1,566.20	1,547.03	1,530.04	1,514.94
175,000	1,634.59	1,612.27	1,592.53	1,575.04	1,559.50
180,000	1,681.29	1,658.33	1,638.04	1,620.04	1,604.05
190,000	1,774.69	1,750.46	1,729.04	1,710.04	1,693.17
200,000	1,868.10	1,842.59	1,820.04	1,800.05	1,782.28
220,000	2,054.91	2,026.85	2,002.04	1,980.05	1,960.51
225,000	2,101.61	2,072.91	2,047.54	2,025.05	2,005.06
230,000	2,148.31	2,118.98	2,093.04	2,070.05	2,049.62
240,000	2,241.72	2,211.11	2,184.05	2,160.05	2,138.73
$250,000	2,335.12	2,303.24	2,275.05	2,250.06	2,227.85

Monthly Payment Loans   **9.75%**

Amortization Period in Years

	26	27	28	29	30
$ 100	0.89	0.88	0.87	0.87	0.86
200	1.77	1.76	1.74	1.73	1.72
300	2.65	2.63	2.61	2.60	2.58
400	3.54	3.51	3.48	3.46	3.44
500	4.42	4.39	4.35	4.33	4.30
600	5.30	5.26	5.22	5.19	5.16
700	6.19	6.14	6.09	6.05	6.02
800	7.07	7.01	6.96	6.92	6.88
900	7.95	7.89	7.83	7.78	7.74
1,000	8.84	8.77	8.70	8.65	8.60
2,000	17.67	17.53	17.40	17.29	17.19
3,000	26.50	26.29	26.10	25.93	25.78
4,000	35.33	35.05	34.80	34.57	34.37
5,000	44.17	43.81	43.50	43.22	42.96
6,000	53.00	52.58	52.20	51.86	51.55
7,000	61.83	61.34	60.90	60.50	60.15
8,000	70.66	70.10	69.59	69.14	68.74
9,000	79.50	78.86	78.29	77.78	77.33
10,000	88.33	87.62	86.99	86.43	85.92
15,000	132.49	131.43	130.48	129.64	128.88
20,000	176.65	175.24	173.98	172.85	171.84
25,000	220.81	219.05	217.47	216.06	214.79
30,000	264.97	262.86	260.96	259.27	257.75
35,000	309.13	306.66	304.46	302.48	300.71
40,000	353.30	350.47	347.95	345.69	343.67
45,000	397.46	394.28	391.44	388.90	386.62
50,000	441.62	438.09	434.94	432.11	429.58
55,000	485.78	481.90	478.43	475.32	472.54
60,000	529.94	525.71	521.92	518.53	515.50
65,000	574.10	569.51	565.41	561.74	558.46
70,000	618.26	613.32	608.91	604.96	601.41
75,000	662.43	657.13	652.40	648.17	644.37
80,000	706.59	700.94	695.89	691.38	687.33
85,000	750.75	744.75	739.39	734.59	730.29
90,000	794.91	788.56	782.88	777.80	773.24
95,000	839.07	832.37	826.37	821.01	816.20
100,000	883.23	876.17	869.87	864.22	859.16
110,000	971.55	963.79	956.85	950.64	945.07
120,000	1,059.88	1,051.41	1,043.84	1,037.06	1,030.99
125,000	1,104.04	1,095.22	1,087.33	1,080.27	1,073.95
130,000	1,148.20	1,139.02	1,130.82	1,123.48	1,116.91
140,000	1,236.52	1,226.64	1,217.81	1,209.91	1,202.82
150,000	1,324.85	1,314.26	1,304.80	1,296.33	1,288.74
160,000	1,413.17	1,401.88	1,391.78	1,382.75	1,374.65
170,000	1,501.49	1,489.49	1,478.77	1,469.17	1,460.57
175,000	1,545.65	1,533.30	1,522.26	1,512.38	1,503.53
180,000	1,589.81	1,577.11	1,565.75	1,555.59	1,546.48
190,000	1,678.14	1,664.73	1,652.74	1,642.01	1,632.40
200,000	1,766.46	1,752.34	1,739.73	1,728.43	1,718.31
220,000	1,943.10	1,927.58	1,913.70	1,901.28	1,890.14
225,000	1,987.27	1,971.38	1,957.19	1,944.49	1,933.10
230,000	2,031.43	2,015.19	2,000.69	1,987.70	1,976.06
240,000	2,119.75	2,102.81	2,087.67	2,074.12	2,061.98
$250,000	2,208.07	2,190.43	2,174.66	2,160.54	2,147.89

Table 1   83

10.00% Monthly Payment Loans

Amortization Period in Years

	5	7	8	10	12
$ 100	2.13	1.67	1.52	1.33	1.20
200	4.25	3.33	3.04	2.65	2.40
300	6.38	4.99	4.56	3.97	3.59
400	8.50	6.65	6.07	5.29	4.79
500	10.63	8.31	7.59	6.61	5.98
600	12.75	9.97	9.11	7.93	7.18
700	14.88	11.63	10.63	9.26	8.37
800	17.00	13.29	12.14	10.58	9.57
900	19.13	14.95	13.66	11.90	10.76
1,000	21.25	16.61	15.18	13.22	11.96
2,000	42.50	33.21	30.35	26.44	23.91
3,000	63.75	49.81	45.53	39.65	35.86
4,000	84.99	66.41	60.70	52.87	47.81
5,000	106.24	83.01	75.88	66.08	59.76
6,000	127.49	99.61	91.05	79.30	71.71
7,000	148.73	116.21	106.22	92.51	83.66
8,000	169.98	132.81	121.40	105.73	95.61
9,000	191.23	149.42	136.57	118.94	107.56
10,000	212.48	166.02	151.75	132.16	119.51
15,000	318.71	249.02	227.62	198.23	179.27
20,000	424.95	332.03	303.49	264.31	239.02
25,000	531.18	415.03	379.36	330.38	298.77
30,000	637.42	498.04	455.23	396.46	358.53
35,000	743.65	581.05	531.10	462.53	418.28
40,000	849.89	664.05	606.97	528.61	478.04
45,000	956.12	747.06	682.84	594.68	537.79
50,000	1,062.36	830.06	758.71	660.76	597.54
55,000	1,168.59	913.07	834.58	726.83	657.30
60,000	1,274.83	996.08	910.45	792.91	717.05
65,000	1,381.06	1,079.08	986.33	858.98	776.81
70,000	1,487.30	1,162.09	1,062.20	925.06	836.56
75,000	1,593.53	1,245.09	1,138.07	991.14	896.31
80,000	1,699.77	1,328.10	1,213.94	1,057.21	956.07
85,000	1,806.00	1,411.11	1,289.81	1,123.29	1,015.82
90,000	1,912.24	1,494.11	1,365.68	1,189.36	1,075.58
95,000	2,018.47	1,577.12	1,441.55	1,255.44	1,135.33
100,000	2,124.71	1,660.12	1,517.42	1,321.51	1,195.08
110,000	2,337.18	1,826.14	1,669.16	1,453.66	1,314.59
120,000	2,549.65	1,992.15	1,820.90	1,585.81	1,434.10
125,000	2,655.89	2,075.15	1,896.78	1,651.89	1,493.85
130,000	2,762.12	2,158.16	1,972.65	1,717.96	1,553.61
140,000	2,974.59	2,324.17	2,124.39	1,850.12	1,673.11
150,000	3,187.06	2,490.18	2,276.13	1,982.27	1,792.62
160,000	3,399.53	2,656.19	2,427.87	2,114.42	1,912.13
170,000	3,612.00	2,822.21	2,579.61	2,246.57	2,031.64
175,000	3,718.24	2,905.21	2,655.48	2,312.64	2,091.39
180,000	3,824.47	2,988.22	2,731.35	2,378.72	2,151.15
190,000	4,036.94	3,154.23	2,883.10	2,510.87	2,270.65
200,000	4,249.41	3,320.24	3,034.84	2,643.02	2,390.16
220,000	4,674.35	3,652.27	3,338.32	2,907.32	2,629.18
225,000	4,780.59	3,735.27	3,414.19	2,973.40	2,688.93
230,000	4,886.83	3,818.28	3,490.06	3,039.47	2,748.69
240,000	5,099.30	3,984.29	3,641.80	3,171.62	2,868.19
$250,000	5,311.77	4,150.30	3,793.55	3,303.77	2,987.70

Monthly Payment Loans   **10.00%**

Amortization Period in Years

	15	16	17	18	20
$ 100	1.08	1.05	1.03	1.00	0.97
200	2.15	2.10	2.05	2.00	1.94
300	3.23	3.14	3.07	3.00	2.90
400	4.30	4.19	4.09	4.00	3.87
500	5.38	5.23	5.11	5.00	4.83
600	6.45	6.28	6.13	6.00	5.80
700	7.53	7.33	7.15	7.00	6.76
800	8.60	8.37	8.17	8.00	7.73
900	9.68	9.42	9.20	9.00	8.69
1,000	10.75	10.46	10.22	10.00	9.66
2,000	21.50	20.92	20.43	20.00	19.31
3,000	32.24	31.38	30.64	30.00	28.96
4,000	42.99	41.84	40.85	40.00	38.61
5,000	53.74	52.30	51.07	50.00	48.26
6,000	64.48	62.76	61.28	60.00	57.91
7,000	75.23	73.22	71.49	69.99	67.56
8,000	85.97	83.68	81.70	79.99	77.21
9,000	96.72	94.14	91.91	89.99	86.86
10,000	107.47	104.60	102.13	99.99	96.51
15,000	161.20	156.89	153.19	149.98	144.76
20,000	214.93	209.19	204.25	199.97	193.01
25,000	268.66	261.48	255.31	249.97	241.26
30,000	322.39	313.78	306.37	299.96	289.51
35,000	376.12	366.07	357.43	349.95	337.76
40,000	429.85	418.37	408.49	399.94	386.01
45,000	483.58	470.66	459.55	449.93	434.26
50,000	537.31	522.96	510.61	499.93	482.52
55,000	591.04	575.25	561.67	549.92	530.77
60,000	644.77	627.55	612.73	599.91	579.02
65,000	698.50	679.84	663.79	649.90	627.27
70,000	752.23	732.14	714.85	699.90	675.52
75,000	805.96	784.43	765.91	749.89	723.77
80,000	859.69	836.73	816.97	799.88	772.02
85,000	913.42	889.02	868.03	849.87	820.27
90,000	967.15	941.32	919.09	899.86	868.52
95,000	1,020.88	993.61	970.15	949.86	916.78
100,000	1,074.61	1,045.91	1,021.22	999.85	965.03
110,000	1,182.07	1,150.50	1,123.34	1,099.83	1,061.53
120,000	1,289.53	1,255.09	1,225.46	1,199.82	1,158.03
125,000	1,343.26	1,307.38	1,276.52	1,249.81	1,206.28
130,000	1,396.99	1,359.68	1,327.58	1,299.80	1,254.53
140,000	1,504.45	1,464.27	1,429.70	1,399.79	1,351.04
150,000	1,611.91	1,568.86	1,531.82	1,499.77	1,447.54
160,000	1,719.37	1,673.45	1,633.94	1,599.75	1,544.04
170,000	1,826.83	1,778.04	1,736.06	1,699.74	1,640.54
175,000	1,880.56	1,830.33	1,787.12	1,749.73	1,688.79
180,000	1,934.29	1,882.63	1,838.18	1,799.72	1,737.04
190,000	2,041.75	1,987.22	1,940.30	1,899.71	1,833.55
200,000	2,149.22	2,091.81	2,042.43	1,999.69	1,930.05
220,000	2,364.14	2,300.99	2,246.67	2,199.66	2,123.05
225,000	2,417.87	2,353.28	2,297.73	2,249.65	2,171.30
230,000	2,471.60	2,405.58	2,348.79	2,299.65	2,219.55
240,000	2,579.06	2,510.17	2,450.91	2,399.63	2,316.06
$250,000	2,686.52	2,614.76	2,553.03	2,499.61	2,412.56

Table 1   85

10.00%　　Monthly Payment Loans

Amortization Period in Years

	21	22	23	24	25
$ 100	0.96	0.94	0.93	0.92	0.91
200	1.91	1.88	1.86	1.84	1.82
300	2.86	2.82	2.79	2.76	2.73
400	3.81	3.76	3.71	3.67	3.64
500	4.76	4.70	4.64	4.59	4.55
600	5.71	5.63	5.57	5.51	5.46
700	6.66	6.57	6.50	6.43	6.37
800	7.61	7.51	7.42	7.34	7.27
900	8.56	8.45	8.35	8.26	8.18
1,000	9.51	9.39	9.28	9.18	9.09
2,000	19.02	18.77	18.55	18.35	18.18
3,000	28.53	28.15	27.82	27.53	27.27
4,000	38.04	37.53	37.09	36.70	36.35
5,000	47.54	46.92	46.36	45.87	45.44
6,000	57.05	56.30	55.64	55.05	54.53
7,000	66.56	65.68	64.91	64.22	63.61
8,000	76.07	75.06	74.18	73.40	72.70
9,000	85.58	84.45	83.45	82.57	81.79
10,000	95.08	93.83	92.72	91.74	90.88
15,000	142.62	140.74	139.08	137.61	136.31
20,000	190.16	187.65	185.44	183.48	181.75
25,000	237.70	234.57	231.80	229.35	227.18
30,000	285.24	281.48	278.16	275.22	272.62
35,000	332.78	328.39	324.52	321.09	318.05
40,000	380.32	375.30	370.88	366.96	363.49
45,000	427.86	422.22	417.24	412.83	408.92
50,000	475.40	469.13	463.60	458.70	454.36
55,000	522.93	516.04	509.95	504.57	499.79
60,000	570.47	562.95	556.31	550.44	545.23
65,000	618.01	609.86	602.67	596.31	590.66
70,000	665.55	656.78	649.03	642.18	636.10
75,000	713.09	703.69	695.39	688.05	681.53
80,000	760.63	750.60	741.75	733.92	726.97
85,000	808.17	797.51	788.11	779.79	772.40
90,000	855.71	844.43	834.47	825.65	817.84
95,000	903.25	891.34	880.83	871.52	863.27
100,000	950.79	938.25	927.19	917.39	908.71
110,000	1,045.86	1,032.08	1,019.90	1,009.13	999.58
120,000	1,140.94	1,125.90	1,112.62	1,100.87	1,090.45
125,000	1,188.48	1,172.81	1,158.98	1,146.74	1,135.88
130,000	1,236.02	1,219.72	1,205.34	1,192.61	1,181.32
140,000	1,331.10	1,313.55	1,298.06	1,284.35	1,272.19
150,000	1,426.18	1,407.37	1,390.78	1,376.09	1,363.06
160,000	1,521.25	1,501.20	1,483.50	1,467.83	1,453.93
170,000	1,616.33	1,595.02	1,576.21	1,559.57	1,544.80
175,000	1,663.87	1,641.94	1,622.57	1,605.44	1,590.23
180,000	1,711.41	1,688.85	1,668.93	1,651.30	1,635.67
190,000	1,806.49	1,782.67	1,761.65	1,743.04	1,726.54
200,000	1,901.57	1,876.50	1,854.37	1,834.78	1,817.41
220,000	2,091.72	2,064.15	2,039.80	2,018.26	1,999.15
225,000	2,139.26	2,111.06	2,086.16	2,064.13	2,044.58
230,000	2,186.80	2,157.97	2,132.52	2,110.00	2,090.02
240,000	2,281.88	2,251.80	2,225.24	2,201.74	2,180.89
$250,000	2,376.96	2,345.62	2,317.96	2,293.48	2,271.76

Monthly Payment Loans   **10.00%**

Amortization Period in Years

	26	27	28	29	30
$ 100	0.91	0.90	0.89	0.89	0.88
200	1.81	1.79	1.78	1.77	1.76
300	2.71	2.69	2.67	2.65	2.64
400	3.61	3.58	3.56	3.53	3.52
500	4.51	4.48	4.44	4.42	4.39
600	5.41	5.37	5.33	5.30	5.27
700	6.31	6.26	6.22	6.18	6.15
800	7.21	7.16	7.11	7.06	7.03
900	8.11	8.05	8.00	7.95	7.90
1,000	9.01	8.95	8.88	8.83	8.78
2,000	18.02	17.89	17.76	17.65	17.56
3,000	27.03	26.83	26.64	26.48	26.33
4,000	36.04	35.77	35.52	35.30	35.11
5,000	45.05	44.71	44.40	44.13	43.88
6,000	54.06	53.65	53.28	52.95	52.66
7,000	63.07	62.59	62.16	61.78	61.44
8,000	72.08	71.53	71.04	70.60	70.21
9,000	81.09	80.47	79.92	79.43	78.99
10,000	90.10	89.41	88.80	88.25	87.76
15,000	135.15	134.12	133.20	132.38	131.64
20,000	180.20	178.82	177.60	176.50	175.52
25,000	225.25	223.53	222.00	220.62	219.40
30,000	270.30	268.23	266.39	264.75	263.28
35,000	315.35	312.94	310.79	308.87	307.16
40,000	360.40	357.64	355.19	353.00	351.03
45,000	405.44	402.35	399.59	397.12	394.91
50,000	450.49	447.05	443.99	441.24	438.79
55,000	495.54	491.76	488.38	485.37	482.67
60,000	540.59	536.46	532.78	529.49	526.55
65,000	585.64	581.17	577.18	573.62	570.43
70,000	630.69	625.87	621.58	617.74	614.31
75,000	675.74	670.58	665.98	661.86	658.18
80,000	720.79	715.28	710.37	705.99	702.06
85,000	765.84	759.99	754.77	750.11	745.94
90,000	810.88	804.69	799.17	794.23	789.82
95,000	855.93	849.40	843.57	838.36	833.70
100,000	900.98	894.10	887.97	882.48	877.58
110,000	991.08	983.51	976.76	970.73	965.33
120,000	1,081.18	1,072.92	1,065.56	1,058.98	1,053.09
125,000	1,126.23	1,117.63	1,109.96	1,103.10	1,096.97
130,000	1,171.28	1,162.33	1,154.35	1,147.23	1,140.85
140,000	1,261.37	1,251.74	1,243.15	1,235.47	1,228.61
150,000	1,351.47	1,341.15	1,331.95	1,323.72	1,316.36
160,000	1,441.57	1,430.56	1,420.74	1,411.97	1,404.12
170,000	1,531.67	1,519.97	1,509.54	1,500.22	1,491.88
175,000	1,576.71	1,564.68	1,553.94	1,544.34	1,535.76
180,000	1,621.76	1,609.38	1,598.33	1,588.46	1,579.63
190,000	1,711.86	1,698.79	1,687.13	1,676.71	1,667.39
200,000	1,801.96	1,788.20	1,775.93	1,764.96	1,755.15
220,000	1,982.15	1,967.02	1,953.52	1,941.45	1,930.66
225,000	2,027.20	2,011.72	1,997.92	1,985.58	1,974.54
230,000	2,072.25	2,056.43	2,042.31	2,029.70	2,018.42
240,000	2,162.35	2,145.84	2,131.11	2,117.95	2,106.18
$250,000	2,252.45	2,235.25	2,219.91	2,206.20	2,193.93

Table 1   87

10.25% Monthly Payment Loans

Amortization Period in Years

	5	7	8	10	12
$ 100	2.14	1.68	1.54	1.34	1.21
200	4.28	3.35	3.07	2.68	2.42
300	6.42	5.02	4.60	4.01	3.63
400	8.55	6.70	6.13	5.35	4.84
500	10.69	8.37	7.66	6.68	6.05
600	12.83	10.04	9.19	8.02	7.26
700	14.96	11.72	10.72	9.35	8.47
800	17.10	13.39	12.25	10.69	9.68
900	19.24	15.06	13.78	12.02	10.89
1,000	21.38	16.74	15.31	13.36	12.10
2,000	42.75	33.47	30.62	26.71	24.20
3,000	64.12	50.20	45.93	40.07	36.29
4,000	85.49	66.93	61.23	53.42	48.39
5,000	106.86	83.66	76.54	66.77	60.48
6,000	128.23	100.39	91.85	80.13	72.58
7,000	149.60	117.12	107.15	93.48	84.67
8,000	170.97	133.85	122.46	106.84	96.77
9,000	192.34	150.58	137.77	120.19	108.87
10,000	213.71	167.31	153.07	133.54	120.96
15,000	320.56	250.96	229.61	200.31	181.44
20,000	427.41	334.62	306.14	267.08	241.92
25,000	534.26	418.27	382.67	333.85	302.40
30,000	641.11	501.92	459.21	400.62	362.87
35,000	747.96	585.58	535.74	467.39	423.35
40,000	854.82	669.23	612.28	534.16	483.83
45,000	961.67	752.88	688.81	600.93	544.31
50,000	1,068.52	836.54	765.34	667.70	604.79
55,000	1,175.37	920.19	841.88	734.47	665.27
60,000	1,282.22	1,003.84	918.41	801.24	725.74
65,000	1,389.07	1,087.50	994.95	868.01	786.22
70,000	1,495.92	1,171.15	1,071.48	934.78	846.70
75,000	1,602.77	1,254.80	1,148.01	1,001.55	907.18
80,000	1,709.63	1,338.46	1,224.55	1,068.32	967.66
85,000	1,816.48	1,422.11	1,301.08	1,135.09	1,028.14
90,000	1,923.33	1,505.76	1,377.61	1,201.86	1,088.61
95,000	2,030.18	1,589.42	1,454.15	1,268.63	1,149.09
100,000	2,137.03	1,673.07	1,530.68	1,335.40	1,209.57
110,000	2,350.73	1,840.38	1,683.75	1,468.93	1,330.53
120,000	2,564.44	2,007.68	1,836.82	1,602.47	1,451.48
125,000	2,671.29	2,091.34	1,913.35	1,669.24	1,511.96
130,000	2,778.14	2,174.99	1,989.89	1,736.01	1,572.44
140,000	2,991.84	2,342.30	2,142.95	1,869.55	1,693.40
150,000	3,205.54	2,509.60	2,296.02	2,003.09	1,814.35
160,000	3,419.25	2,676.91	2,449.09	2,136.63	1,935.31
170,000	3,632.95	2,844.21	2,602.16	2,270.17	2,056.27
175,000	3,739.80	2,927.87	2,678.69	2,336.94	2,116.74
180,000	3,846.65	3,011.52	2,755.22	2,403.71	2,177.22
190,000	4,060.36	3,178.83	2,908.29	2,537.25	2,298.18
200,000	4,274.06	3,346.13	3,061.36	2,670.79	2,419.14
220,000	4,701.46	3,680.75	3,367.49	2,937.86	2,661.05
225,000	4,808.31	3,764.40	3,444.03	3,004.63	2,721.53
230,000	4,915.17	3,848.05	3,520.56	3,071.40	2,782.00
240,000	5,128.87	4,015.36	3,673.63	3,204.94	2,902.96
$250,000	5,342.57	4,182.67	3,826.70	3,338.48	3,023.92

Monthly Payment Loans   **10.25%**

Amortization Period in Years

	15	16	17	18	20
$ 100	1.09	1.07	1.04	1.02	0.99
200	2.18	2.13	2.08	2.04	1.97
300	3.27	3.19	3.12	3.05	2.95
400	4.36	4.25	4.15	4.07	3.93
500	5.45	5.31	5.19	5.08	4.91
600	6.54	6.37	6.23	6.10	5.89
700	7.63	7.44	7.26	7.12	6.88
800	8.72	8.50	8.30	8.13	7.86
900	9.81	9.56	9.34	9.15	8.84
1,000	10.90	10.62	10.38	10.16	9.82
2,000	21.80	21.24	20.75	20.32	19.64
3,000	32.70	31.85	31.12	30.48	29.45
4,000	43.60	42.47	41.49	40.64	39.27
5,000	54.50	53.08	51.86	50.80	49.09
6,000	65.40	63.70	62.23	60.96	58.90
7,000	76.30	74.31	72.60	71.12	68.72
8,000	87.20	84.93	82.97	81.28	78.54
9,000	98.10	95.54	93.34	91.44	88.35
10,000	109.00	106.16	103.71	101.60	98.17
15,000	163.50	159.23	155.57	152.40	147.25
20,000	218.00	212.31	207.42	203.20	196.33
25,000	272.49	265.38	259.28	254.00	245.42
30,000	326.99	318.46	311.13	304.80	294.50
35,000	381.49	371.54	362.99	355.60	343.58
40,000	435.99	424.61	414.84	406.40	392.66
45,000	490.48	477.69	466.70	457.20	441.74
50,000	544.98	530.76	518.55	508.00	490.83
55,000	599.48	583.84	570.41	558.79	539.91
60,000	653.98	636.92	622.26	609.59	588.99
65,000	708.47	689.99	674.11	660.39	638.07
70,000	762.97	743.07	725.97	711.19	687.16
75,000	817.47	796.14	777.82	761.99	736.24
80,000	871.97	849.22	829.68	812.79	785.32
85,000	926.46	902.30	881.53	863.59	834.40
90,000	980.96	955.37	933.39	914.39	883.48
95,000	1,035.46	1,008.45	985.24	965.19	932.57
100,000	1,089.96	1,061.52	1,037.10	1,015.99	981.65
110,000	1,198.95	1,167.68	1,140.81	1,117.58	1,079.81
120,000	1,307.95	1,273.83	1,244.51	1,219.18	1,177.98
125,000	1,362.44	1,326.90	1,296.37	1,269.98	1,227.06
130,000	1,416.94	1,379.98	1,348.22	1,320.78	1,276.14
140,000	1,525.94	1,486.13	1,451.93	1,422.38	1,374.31
150,000	1,634.93	1,592.28	1,555.64	1,523.98	1,472.47
160,000	1,743.93	1,698.44	1,659.35	1,625.57	1,570.63
170,000	1,852.92	1,804.59	1,763.06	1,727.17	1,668.80
175,000	1,907.42	1,857.66	1,814.92	1,777.97	1,717.88
180,000	1,961.92	1,910.74	1,866.77	1,828.77	1,766.96
190,000	2,070.91	2,016.89	1,970.48	1,930.37	1,865.13
200,000	2,179.91	2,123.04	2,074.19	2,031.97	1,963.29
220,000	2,397.90	2,335.35	2,281.61	2,235.16	2,159.62
225,000	2,452.39	2,388.42	2,333.46	2,285.96	2,208.70
230,000	2,506.89	2,441.50	2,385.32	2,336.76	2,257.78
240,000	2,615.89	2,547.65	2,489.02	2,438.36	2,355.95
$250,000	2,724.88	2,653.80	2,592.73	2,539.96	2,454.11

Table 1   89

10.25%   Monthly Payment Loans

Amortization Period in Years

	21	22	23	24	25
$ 100	0.97	0.96	0.95	0.94	0.93
200	1.94	1.92	1.89	1.87	1.86
300	2.91	2.87	2.84	2.81	2.78
400	3.88	3.83	3.78	3.74	3.71
500	4.84	4.78	4.73	4.68	4.64
600	5.81	5.74	5.67	5.61	5.56
700	6.78	6.69	6.62	6.55	6.49
800	7.75	7.65	7.56	7.48	7.42
900	8.71	8.60	8.51	8.42	8.34
1,000	9.68	9.56	9.45	9.35	9.27
2,000	19.36	19.11	18.89	18.70	18.53
3,000	29.03	28.66	28.34	28.05	27.80
4,000	38.71	38.22	37.78	37.40	37.06
5,000	48.39	47.77	47.23	46.75	46.32
6,000	58.06	57.32	56.67	56.10	55.59
7,000	67.74	66.88	66.12	65.45	64.85
8,000	77.42	76.43	75.56	74.80	74.12
9,000	87.09	85.98	85.01	84.14	83.38
10,000	96.77	95.54	94.45	93.49	92.64
15,000	145.15	143.30	141.67	140.24	138.96
20,000	193.53	191.07	188.90	186.98	185.28
25,000	241.91	238.83	236.12	233.72	231.60
30,000	290.29	286.60	283.34	280.47	277.92
35,000	338.68	334.37	330.57	327.21	324.24
40,000	387.06	382.13	377.79	373.96	370.56
45,000	435.44	429.90	425.01	420.70	416.88
50,000	483.82	477.66	472.24	467.44	463.20
55,000	532.20	525.43	519.46	514.19	509.52
60,000	580.58	573.20	566.68	560.93	555.83
65,000	628.97	620.96	613.91	607.67	602.15
70,000	677.35	668.73	661.13	654.42	648.47
75,000	725.73	716.49	708.35	701.16	694.79
80,000	774.11	764.26	755.58	747.91	741.11
85,000	822.49	812.03	802.80	794.65	787.43
90,000	870.87	859.79	850.02	841.39	833.75
95,000	919.25	907.56	897.25	888.14	880.07
100,000	967.64	955.32	944.47	934.88	926.39
110,000	1,064.40	1,050.86	1,038.92	1,028.37	1,019.03
120,000	1,161.16	1,146.39	1,133.36	1,121.86	1,111.66
125,000	1,209.54	1,194.15	1,180.59	1,168.60	1,157.98
130,000	1,257.93	1,241.92	1,227.81	1,215.34	1,204.30
140,000	1,354.69	1,337.45	1,322.26	1,308.83	1,296.94
150,000	1,451.45	1,432.98	1,416.70	1,402.32	1,389.58
160,000	1,548.22	1,528.51	1,511.15	1,495.81	1,482.22
170,000	1,644.98	1,624.05	1,605.60	1,589.30	1,574.86
175,000	1,693.36	1,671.81	1,652.82	1,636.04	1,621.18
180,000	1,741.74	1,719.58	1,700.04	1,682.78	1,667.49
190,000	1,838.50	1,815.11	1,794.49	1,776.27	1,760.13
200,000	1,935.27	1,910.64	1,888.94	1,869.76	1,852.77
220,000	2,128.79	2,101.71	2,077.83	2,056.73	2,038.05
225,000	2,177.18	2,149.47	2,125.05	2,103.48	2,084.37
230,000	2,225.56	2,197.24	2,172.28	2,150.22	2,130.69
240,000	2,322.32	2,292.77	2,266.72	2,243.71	2,223.32
$250,000	2,419.08	2,388.30	2,361.17	2,337.20	2,315.96

Monthly Payment Loans   **10.25%**

Amortization Period in Years

	26	27	28	29	30
$ 100	0.92	0.92	0.91	0.91	0.90
200	1.84	1.83	1.82	1.81	1.80
300	2.76	2.74	2.72	2.71	2.69
400	3.68	3.65	3.63	3.61	3.59
500	4.60	4.57	4.54	4.51	4.49
600	5.52	5.48	5.44	5.41	5.38
700	6.44	6.39	6.35	6.31	6.28
800	7.36	7.30	7.25	7.21	7.17
900	8.27	8.21	8.16	8.11	8.07
1,000	9.19	9.13	9.07	9.01	8.97
2,000	18.38	18.25	18.13	18.02	17.93
3,000	27.57	27.37	27.19	27.03	26.89
4,000	36.76	36.49	36.25	36.04	35.85
5,000	45.95	45.61	45.31	45.05	44.81
6,000	55.14	54.73	54.38	54.06	53.77
7,000	64.32	63.86	63.44	63.06	62.73
8,000	73.51	72.98	72.50	72.07	71.69
9,000	82.70	82.10	81.56	81.08	80.65
10,000	91.89	91.22	90.62	90.09	89.62
15,000	137.83	136.83	135.93	135.13	134.42
20,000	183.77	182.43	181.24	180.18	179.23
25,000	229.72	228.04	226.55	225.22	224.03
30,000	275.66	273.65	271.86	270.26	268.84
35,000	321.60	319.26	317.17	315.30	313.64
40,000	367.54	364.86	362.48	360.35	358.45
45,000	413.49	410.47	407.78	405.39	403.25
50,000	459.43	456.08	453.09	450.43	448.06
55,000	505.37	501.68	498.40	495.47	492.86
60,000	551.31	547.29	543.71	540.52	537.67
65,000	597.25	592.90	589.02	585.56	582.47
70,000	643.20	638.51	634.33	630.60	627.28
75,000	689.14	684.11	679.64	675.65	672.08
80,000	735.08	729.72	724.95	720.69	716.89
85,000	781.02	775.33	770.25	765.73	761.69
90,000	826.97	820.93	815.56	810.77	806.50
95,000	872.91	866.54	860.87	855.82	851.30
100,000	918.85	912.15	906.18	900.86	896.11
110,000	1,010.74	1,003.36	996.80	990.94	985.72
120,000	1,102.62	1,094.58	1,087.42	1,081.03	1,075.33
125,000	1,148.56	1,140.18	1,132.72	1,126.07	1,120.13
130,000	1,194.50	1,185.79	1,178.03	1,171.11	1,164.94
140,000	1,286.39	1,277.01	1,268.65	1,261.20	1,254.55
150,000	1,378.27	1,368.22	1,359.27	1,351.29	1,344.16
160,000	1,470.16	1,459.44	1,449.89	1,441.37	1,433.77
170,000	1,562.04	1,550.65	1,540.50	1,531.46	1,523.38
175,000	1,607.98	1,596.26	1,585.81	1,576.50	1,568.18
180,000	1,653.93	1,641.86	1,631.12	1,621.54	1,612.99
190,000	1,745.81	1,733.08	1,721.74	1,711.63	1,702.60
200,000	1,837.70	1,824.29	1,812.36	1,801.71	1,792.21
220,000	2,021.47	2,006.72	1,993.59	1,981.88	1,971.43
225,000	2,067.41	2,052.33	2,038.90	2,026.93	2,016.23
230,000	2,113.35	2,097.94	2,084.21	2,071.97	2,061.04
240,000	2,205.23	2,189.15	2,174.83	2,162.05	2,150.65
$250,000	2,297.12	2,280.36	2,265.44	2,252.14	2,240.26

Table 1   91

10.50%   Monthly Payment Loans

Amortization Period in Years

	5	7	8	10	12
$ 100	2.15	1.69	1.55	1.35	1.23
200	4.30	3.38	3.09	2.70	2.45
300	6.45	5.06	4.64	4.05	3.68
400	8.60	6.75	6.18	5.40	4.90
500	10.75	8.44	7.73	6.75	6.13
600	12.90	10.12	9.27	8.10	7.35
700	15.05	11.81	10.81	9.45	8.57
800	17.20	13.49	12.36	10.80	9.80
900	19.35	15.18	13.90	12.15	11.02
1,000	21.50	16.87	15.45	13.50	12.25
2,000	42.99	33.73	30.89	26.99	24.49
3,000	64.49	50.59	46.33	40.49	36.73
4,000	85.98	67.45	61.77	53.98	48.97
5,000	107.47	84.31	77.21	67.47	61.21
6,000	128.97	101.17	92.65	80.97	73.45
7,000	150.46	118.03	108.09	94.46	85.69
8,000	171.96	134.89	123.53	107.95	97.94
9,000	193.45	151.75	138.97	121.45	110.18
10,000	214.94	168.61	154.41	134.94	122.42
15,000	322.41	252.92	231.61	202.41	183.63
20,000	429.88	337.22	308.81	269.87	244.83
25,000	537.35	421.52	386.01	337.34	306.04
30,000	644.82	505.83	463.21	404.81	367.25
35,000	752.29	590.13	540.41	472.28	428.45
40,000	859.76	674.43	617.61	539.74	489.66
45,000	967.23	758.74	694.81	607.21	550.87
50,000	1,074.70	843.04	772.01	674.68	612.08
55,000	1,182.17	927.34	849.21	742.15	673.28
60,000	1,289.64	1,011.65	926.41	809.61	734.49
65,000	1,397.11	1,095.95	1,003.61	877.08	795.70
70,000	1,504.58	1,180.25	1,080.81	944.55	856.90
75,000	1,612.05	1,264.56	1,158.01	1,012.02	918.11
80,000	1,719.52	1,348.86	1,235.21	1,079.48	979.32
85,000	1,826.99	1,433.16	1,312.41	1,146.95	1,040.52
90,000	1,934.46	1,517.47	1,389.61	1,214.42	1,101.73
95,000	2,041.93	1,601.77	1,466.81	1,281.89	1,162.94
100,000	2,149.40	1,686.07	1,544.01	1,349.35	1,224.15
110,000	2,364.33	1,854.68	1,698.41	1,484.29	1,346.56
120,000	2,579.27	2,023.29	1,852.81	1,619.22	1,468.97
125,000	2,686.74	2,107.59	1,930.01	1,686.69	1,530.18
130,000	2,794.21	2,191.89	2,007.21	1,754.16	1,591.39
140,000	3,009.15	2,360.50	2,161.61	1,889.09	1,713.80
150,000	3,224.09	2,529.11	2,316.01	2,024.03	1,836.22
160,000	3,439.03	2,697.71	2,470.41	2,158.96	1,958.63
170,000	3,653.97	2,866.32	2,624.81	2,293.90	2,081.04
175,000	3,761.44	2,950.62	2,702.01	2,361.37	2,142.25
180,000	3,868.91	3,034.93	2,779.21	2,428.83	2,203.46
190,000	4,083.85	3,203.53	2,933.61	2,563.77	2,325.87
200,000	4,298.79	3,372.14	3,088.01	2,698.70	2,448.29
220,000	4,728.66	3,709.35	3,396.81	2,968.57	2,693.11
225,000	4,836.13	3,793.66	3,474.01	3,036.04	2,754.32
230,000	4,943.60	3,877.96	3,551.21	3,103.51	2,815.53
240,000	5,158.54	4,046.57	3,705.61	3,238.44	2,937.94
$250,000	5,373.48	4,215.17	3,860.01	3,373.38	3,060.36

Monthly Payment Loans   **10.50%**

Amortization Period in Years

	15	16	17	18	20
$ 100	1.11	1.08	1.06	1.04	1.00
200	2.22	2.16	2.11	2.07	2.00
300	3.32	3.24	3.16	3.10	3.00
400	4.43	4.31	4.22	4.13	4.00
500	5.53	5.39	5.27	5.17	5.00
600	6.64	6.47	6.32	6.20	6.00
700	7.74	7.55	7.38	7.23	6.99
800	8.85	8.62	8.43	8.26	7.99
900	9.95	9.70	9.48	9.30	8.99
1,000	11.06	10.78	10.54	10.33	9.99
2,000	22.11	21.55	21.07	20.65	19.97
3,000	33.17	32.32	31.60	30.97	29.96
4,000	44.22	43.09	42.13	41.29	39.94
5,000	55.27	53.87	52.66	51.62	49.92
6,000	66.33	64.64	63.19	61.94	59.91
7,000	77.38	75.41	73.72	72.26	69.89
8,000	88.44	86.18	84.25	82.58	79.88
9,000	99.49	96.96	94.78	92.91	89.86
10,000	110.54	107.73	105.31	103.23	99.84
15,000	165.81	161.59	157.97	154.84	149.76
20,000	221.08	215.45	210.62	206.45	199.68
25,000	276.35	269.32	263.28	258.06	249.60
30,000	331.62	323.18	315.93	309.67	299.52
35,000	386.89	377.04	368.58	361.28	349.44
40,000	442.16	430.90	421.24	412.90	399.36
45,000	497.43	484.76	473.89	464.51	449.28
50,000	552.70	538.63	526.55	516.12	499.19
55,000	607.97	592.49	579.20	567.73	549.11
60,000	663.24	646.35	631.85	619.34	599.03
65,000	718.51	700.21	684.51	670.95	648.95
70,000	773.78	754.07	737.16	722.56	698.87
75,000	829.05	807.94	789.82	774.18	748.79
80,000	884.32	861.80	842.47	825.79	798.71
85,000	939.59	915.66	895.12	877.40	848.63
90,000	994.86	969.52	947.78	929.01	898.55
95,000	1,050.13	1,023.39	1,000.43	980.62	948.47
100,000	1,105.40	1,077.25	1,053.09	1,032.23	998.38
110,000	1,215.94	1,184.97	1,158.39	1,135.46	1,098.22
120,000	1,326.48	1,292.70	1,263.70	1,238.68	1,198.06
125,000	1,381.75	1,346.56	1,316.36	1,290.29	1,247.98
130,000	1,437.02	1,400.42	1,369.01	1,341.90	1,297.90
140,000	1,547.56	1,508.14	1,474.32	1,445.12	1,397.74
150,000	1,658.10	1,615.87	1,579.63	1,548.35	1,497.57
160,000	1,768.64	1,723.59	1,684.93	1,651.57	1,597.41
170,000	1,879.18	1,831.32	1,790.24	1,754.79	1,697.25
175,000	1,934.45	1,885.18	1,842.90	1,806.40	1,747.17
180,000	1,989.72	1,939.04	1,895.55	1,858.01	1,797.09
190,000	2,100.26	2,046.77	2,000.86	1,961.24	1,896.93
200,000	2,210.80	2,154.49	2,106.17	2,064.46	1,996.76
220,000	2,431.88	2,369.94	2,316.78	2,270.91	2,196.44
225,000	2,487.15	2,423.80	2,369.44	2,322.52	2,246.36
230,000	2,542.42	2,477.66	2,422.09	2,374.13	2,296.28
240,000	2,652.96	2,585.39	2,527.40	2,477.35	2,396.12
$250,000	2,763.50	2,693.11	2,632.71	2,580.57	2,495.95

Table 1   93

10.50% Monthly Payment Loans

Amortization Period in Years

	21	22	23	24	25
$ 100	0.99	0.98	0.97	0.96	0.95
200	1.97	1.95	1.93	1.91	1.89
300	2.96	2.92	2.89	2.86	2.84
400	3.94	3.90	3.85	3.81	3.78
500	4.93	4.87	4.81	4.77	4.73
600	5.91	5.84	5.78	5.72	5.67
700	6.90	6.81	6.74	6.67	6.61
800	7.88	7.79	7.70	7.62	7.56
900	8.87	8.76	8.66	8.58	8.50
1,000	9.85	9.73	9.62	9.53	9.45
2,000	19.70	19.46	19.24	19.05	18.89
3,000	29.54	29.18	28.86	28.58	28.33
4,000	39.39	38.91	38.48	38.10	37.77
5,000	49.23	48.63	48.10	47.63	47.21
6,000	59.08	58.36	57.72	57.15	56.66
7,000	68.93	68.08	67.34	66.68	66.10
8,000	78.77	77.81	76.95	76.20	75.54
9,000	88.62	87.53	86.57	85.73	84.98
10,000	98.46	97.26	96.19	95.25	94.42
15,000	147.69	145.88	144.29	142.88	141.63
20,000	196.92	194.51	192.38	190.50	188.84
25,000	246.15	243.13	240.47	238.13	236.05
30,000	295.38	291.76	288.57	285.75	283.26
35,000	344.61	340.38	336.66	333.37	330.47
40,000	393.84	389.01	384.75	381.00	377.68
45,000	443.07	437.63	432.85	428.62	424.89
50,000	492.30	486.26	480.94	476.25	472.10
55,000	541.53	534.88	529.03	523.87	519.30
60,000	590.76	583.51	577.13	571.49	566.51
65,000	639.99	632.13	625.22	619.12	613.72
70,000	689.22	680.76	673.31	666.74	660.93
75,000	738.45	729.39	721.41	714.37	708.14
80,000	787.68	778.01	769.50	761.99	755.35
85,000	836.91	826.64	817.59	809.61	802.56
90,000	886.14	875.26	865.69	857.24	849.77
95,000	935.37	923.89	913.78	904.86	896.98
100,000	984.60	972.51	961.87	952.49	944.19
110,000	1,083.06	1,069.76	1,058.06	1,047.73	1,038.60
120,000	1,181.52	1,167.01	1,154.25	1,142.98	1,133.02
125,000	1,230.75	1,215.64	1,202.34	1,190.61	1,180.23
130,000	1,279.98	1,264.26	1,250.43	1,238.23	1,227.44
140,000	1,378.44	1,361.51	1,346.62	1,333.48	1,321.86
150,000	1,476.90	1,458.77	1,442.81	1,428.73	1,416.28
160,000	1,575.36	1,556.02	1,538.99	1,523.97	1,510.70
170,000	1,673.82	1,653.27	1,635.18	1,619.22	1,605.11
175,000	1,723.05	1,701.89	1,683.27	1,666.85	1,652.32
180,000	1,772.28	1,750.52	1,731.37	1,714.47	1,699.53
190,000	1,870.74	1,847.77	1,827.55	1,809.72	1,793.95
200,000	1,969.20	1,945.02	1,923.74	1,904.97	1,888.37
220,000	2,166.12	2,139.52	2,116.11	2,095.46	2,077.20
225,000	2,215.35	2,188.15	2,164.21	2,143.09	2,124.41
230,000	2,264.58	2,236.77	2,212.30	2,190.71	2,171.62
240,000	2,363.04	2,334.02	2,308.49	2,285.96	2,266.04
$250,000	2,461.50	2,431.27	2,404.67	2,381.21	2,360.46

Monthly Payment Loans   **10.50%**

Amortization Period in Years

	26	27	28	29	30
$ 100	0.94	0.94	0.93	0.92	0.92
200	1.88	1.87	1.85	1.84	1.83
300	2.82	2.80	2.78	2.76	2.75
400	3.75	3.73	3.70	3.68	3.66
500	4.69	4.66	4.63	4.60	4.58
600	5.63	5.59	5.55	5.52	5.49
700	6.56	6.52	6.48	6.44	6.41
800	7.50	7.45	7.40	7.36	7.32
900	8.44	8.38	8.33	8.28	8.24
1,000	9.37	9.31	9.25	9.20	9.15
2,000	18.74	18.61	18.50	18.39	18.30
3,000	28.11	27.91	27.74	27.59	27.45
4,000	37.48	37.22	36.99	36.78	36.59
5,000	46.85	46.52	46.23	45.97	45.74
6,000	56.21	55.82	55.48	55.17	54.89
7,000	65.58	65.13	64.72	64.36	64.04
8,000	74.95	74.43	73.97	73.55	73.18
9,000	84.32	83.73	83.21	82.75	82.33
10,000	93.69	93.04	92.46	91.94	91.48
15,000	140.53	139.55	138.68	137.91	137.22
20,000	187.37	186.07	184.91	183.87	182.95
25,000	234.21	232.58	231.13	229.84	228.69
30,000	281.05	279.10	277.36	275.81	274.43
35,000	327.90	325.61	323.58	321.77	320.16
40,000	374.74	372.13	369.81	367.74	365.90
45,000	421.58	418.64	416.03	413.71	411.64
50,000	468.42	465.16	462.26	459.68	457.37
55,000	515.26	511.67	508.48	505.64	503.11
60,000	562.10	558.19	554.71	551.61	548.85
65,000	608.94	604.70	600.93	597.58	594.59
70,000	655.79	651.22	647.16	643.54	640.32
75,000	702.63	697.73	693.38	689.51	686.06
80,000	749.47	744.25	739.61	735.48	731.80
85,000	796.31	790.76	785.83	781.44	777.53
90,000	843.15	837.28	832.06	827.41	823.27
95,000	889.99	883.79	878.28	873.38	869.01
100,000	936.83	930.31	924.51	919.35	914.74
110,000	1,030.52	1,023.34	1,016.96	1,011.28	1,006.22
120,000	1,124.20	1,116.37	1,109.41	1,103.21	1,097.69
125,000	1,171.04	1,162.88	1,155.63	1,149.18	1,143.43
130,000	1,217.88	1,209.40	1,201.86	1,195.15	1,189.17
140,000	1,311.57	1,302.43	1,294.31	1,287.08	1,280.64
150,000	1,405.25	1,395.46	1,386.76	1,379.02	1,372.11
160,000	1,498.93	1,488.49	1,479.21	1,470.95	1,463.59
170,000	1,592.61	1,581.52	1,571.66	1,562.88	1,555.06
175,000	1,639.46	1,628.04	1,617.89	1,608.85	1,600.80
180,000	1,686.30	1,674.55	1,664.11	1,654.82	1,646.54
190,000	1,779.98	1,767.58	1,756.56	1,746.75	1,738.01
200,000	1,873.66	1,860.61	1,849.01	1,838.69	1,829.48
220,000	2,061.03	2,046.67	2,033.91	2,022.55	2,012.43
225,000	2,107.87	2,093.19	2,080.14	2,068.52	2,058.17
230,000	2,154.71	2,139.70	2,126.36	2,114.49	2,103.91
240,000	2,248.40	2,232.73	2,218.81	2,206.42	2,195.38
$250,000	2,342.08	2,325.76	2,311.26	2,298.36	2,286.85

10.75% **Monthly Payment Loans**

Amortization Period in Years

		5	7	8	10	12
$	100	2.17	1.70	1.56	1.37	1.24
	200	4.33	3.40	3.12	2.73	2.48
	300	6.49	5.10	4.68	4.10	3.72
	400	8.65	6.80	6.23	5.46	4.96
	500	10.81	8.50	7.79	6.82	6.20
	600	12.98	10.20	9.35	8.19	7.44
	700	15.14	11.90	10.91	9.55	8.68
	800	17.30	13.60	12.46	10.91	9.92
	900	19.46	15.30	14.02	12.28	11.15
	1,000	21.62	17.00	15.58	13.64	12.39
	2,000	43.24	33.99	31.15	27.27	24.78
	3,000	64.86	50.98	46.73	40.91	37.17
	4,000	86.48	67.97	62.30	54.54	49.56
	5,000	108.09	84.96	77.87	68.17	61.95
	6,000	129.71	101.95	93.45	81.81	74.33
	7,000	151.33	118.94	109.02	95.44	86.72
	8,000	172.95	135.94	124.60	109.08	99.11
	9,000	194.57	152.93	140.17	122.71	111.50
	10,000	216.18	169.92	155.74	136.34	123.89
	15,000	324.27	254.87	233.61	204.51	185.83
	20,000	432.36	339.83	311.48	272.68	247.77
	25,000	540.45	424.79	389.35	340.85	309.71
	30,000	648.54	509.74	467.22	409.02	371.65
	35,000	756.63	594.70	545.09	477.19	433.59
	40,000	864.72	679.66	622.96	545.36	495.53
	45,000	972.81	764.61	700.83	613.53	557.47
	50,000	1,080.90	849.57	778.70	681.70	619.41
	55,000	1,188.99	934.52	856.57	749.87	681.35
	60,000	1,297.08	1,019.48	934.44	818.04	743.29
	65,000	1,405.17	1,104.44	1,012.31	886.21	805.23
	70,000	1,513.26	1,189.39	1,090.18	954.38	867.17
	75,000	1,621.35	1,274.35	1,168.05	1,022.55	929.11
	80,000	1,729.44	1,359.31	1,245.92	1,090.71	991.05
	85,000	1,837.53	1,444.26	1,323.79	1,158.88	1,052.99
	90,000	1,945.62	1,529.22	1,401.66	1,227.05	1,114.93
	95,000	2,053.71	1,614.18	1,479.53	1,295.22	1,176.87
	100,000	2,161.80	1,699.13	1,557.40	1,363.39	1,238.81
	110,000	2,377.98	1,869.04	1,713.13	1,499.73	1,362.69
	120,000	2,594.16	2,038.96	1,868.87	1,636.07	1,486.57
	125,000	2,702.25	2,123.91	1,946.74	1,704.24	1,548.51
	130,000	2,810.34	2,208.87	2,024.61	1,772.41	1,610.45
	140,000	3,026.52	2,378.78	2,180.35	1,908.75	1,734.33
	150,000	3,242.70	2,548.70	2,336.09	2,045.09	1,858.21
	160,000	3,458.88	2,718.61	2,491.83	2,181.42	1,982.09
	170,000	3,675.06	2,888.52	2,647.57	2,317.76	2,105.97
	175,000	3,783.15	2,973.48	2,725.44	2,385.93	2,167.91
	180,000	3,891.24	3,058.43	2,803.31	2,454.10	2,229.85
	190,000	4,107.42	3,228.35	2,959.05	2,590.44	2,353.73
	200,000	4,323.60	3,398.26	3,114.79	2,726.78	2,477.61
	220,000	4,755.95	3,738.08	3,426.26	2,999.46	2,725.37
	225,000	4,864.04	3,823.04	3,504.13	3,067.63	2,787.31
	230,000	4,972.13	3,908.00	3,582.00	3,135.79	2,849.25
	240,000	5,188.31	4,077.91	3,737.74	3,272.13	2,973.14
$250,000		5,404.49	4,247.82	3,893.48	3,408.47	3,097.02

Monthly Payment Loans   **10.75%**

Amortization Period in Years

	15	16	17	18	20
$ 100	1.13	1.10	1.07	1.05	1.02
200	2.25	2.19	2.14	2.10	2.04
300	3.37	3.28	3.21	3.15	3.05
400	4.49	4.38	4.28	4.20	4.07
500	5.61	5.47	5.35	5.25	5.08
600	6.73	6.56	6.42	6.30	6.10
700	7.85	7.66	7.49	7.35	7.11
800	8.97	8.75	8.56	8.39	8.13
900	10.09	9.84	9.63	9.44	9.14
1,000	11.21	10.94	10.70	10.49	10.16
2,000	22.42	21.87	21.39	20.98	20.31
3,000	33.63	32.80	32.08	31.46	30.46
4,000	44.84	43.73	42.77	41.95	40.61
5,000	56.05	54.66	53.46	52.43	50.77
6,000	67.26	65.59	64.16	62.92	60.92
7,000	78.47	76.52	74.85	73.41	71.07
8,000	89.68	87.45	85.54	83.89	81.22
9,000	100.89	98.38	96.23	94.38	91.38
10,000	112.10	109.31	106.92	104.86	101.53
15,000	168.15	163.97	160.38	157.29	152.29
20,000	224.19	218.62	213.84	209.72	203.05
25,000	280.24	273.27	267.30	262.15	253.81
30,000	336.29	327.93	320.76	314.58	304.57
35,000	392.34	382.58	374.22	367.01	355.34
40,000	448.38	437.23	427.68	419.44	406.10
45,000	504.43	491.89	481.14	471.87	456.86
50,000	560.48	546.54	534.59	524.30	507.62
55,000	616.53	601.19	588.05	576.73	558.38
60,000	672.57	655.85	641.51	629.16	609.14
65,000	728.62	710.50	694.97	681.59	659.90
70,000	784.67	765.15	748.43	734.01	710.67
75,000	840.72	819.81	801.89	786.44	761.43
80,000	896.76	874.46	855.35	838.87	812.19
85,000	952.81	929.11	908.81	891.30	862.95
90,000	1,008.86	983.77	962.27	943.73	913.71
95,000	1,064.91	1,038.42	1,015.72	996.16	964.47
100,000	1,120.95	1,093.07	1,069.18	1,048.59	1,015.23
110,000	1,233.05	1,202.38	1,176.10	1,153.45	1,116.76
120,000	1,345.14	1,311.69	1,283.02	1,258.31	1,218.28
125,000	1,401.19	1,366.34	1,336.48	1,310.74	1,269.04
130,000	1,457.24	1,421.00	1,389.94	1,363.17	1,319.80
140,000	1,569.33	1,530.30	1,496.85	1,468.02	1,421.33
150,000	1,681.43	1,639.61	1,603.77	1,572.88	1,522.85
160,000	1,793.52	1,748.92	1,710.69	1,677.74	1,624.37
170,000	1,905.62	1,858.22	1,817.61	1,782.60	1,725.89
175,000	1,961.66	1,912.88	1,871.07	1,835.03	1,776.66
180,000	2,017.71	1,967.53	1,924.53	1,887.46	1,827.42
190,000	2,129.81	2,076.84	2,031.44	1,992.32	1,928.94
200,000	2,241.90	2,186.14	2,138.36	2,097.17	2,030.46
220,000	2,466.09	2,404.76	2,352.20	2,306.89	2,233.51
225,000	2,522.14	2,459.41	2,405.66	2,359.32	2,284.27
230,000	2,578.19	2,514.07	2,459.11	2,411.75	2,335.03
240,000	2,690.28	2,623.37	2,566.03	2,516.61	2,436.55
$250,000	2,802.37	2,732.68	2,672.95	2,621.47	2,538.08

Table 1   97

10.75%　　Monthly Payment Loans

Amortization Period in Years

	21	22	23	24	25
$ 100	1.01	0.99	0.98	0.98	0.97
200	2.01	1.98	1.96	1.95	1.93
300	3.01	2.97	2.94	2.92	2.89
400	4.01	3.96	3.92	3.89	3.85
500	5.01	4.95	4.90	4.86	4.82
600	6.02	5.94	5.88	5.83	5.78
700	7.02	6.93	6.86	6.80	6.74
800	8.02	7.92	7.84	7.77	7.70
900	9.02	8.91	8.82	8.74	8.66
1,000	10.02	9.90	9.80	9.71	9.63
2,000	20.04	19.80	19.59	19.41	19.25
3,000	30.06	29.70	29.39	29.11	28.87
4,000	40.07	39.60	39.18	38.81	38.49
5,000	50.09	49.50	48.97	48.51	48.11
6,000	60.11	59.39	58.77	58.22	57.73
7,000	70.12	69.29	68.56	67.92	67.35
8,000	80.14	79.19	78.36	77.62	76.97
9,000	90.16	89.09	88.15	87.32	86.59
10,000	100.17	98.99	97.94	97.02	96.21
15,000	150.26	148.48	146.91	145.53	144.32
20,000	200.34	197.97	195.88	194.04	192.42
25,000	250.42	247.46	244.85	242.55	240.53
30,000	300.51	296.95	293.82	291.06	288.63
35,000	350.59	346.44	342.79	339.57	336.74
40,000	400.68	395.93	391.76	388.08	384.84
45,000	450.76	445.42	440.73	436.59	432.95
50,000	500.84	494.91	489.70	485.10	481.05
55,000	550.93	544.40	538.67	533.61	529.16
60,000	601.01	593.89	587.63	582.12	577.26
65,000	651.10	643.38	636.60	630.63	625.37
70,000	701.18	692.87	685.57	679.14	673.47
75,000	751.26	742.36	734.54	727.65	721.57
80,000	801.35	791.85	783.51	776.16	769.68
85,000	851.43	841.34	832.48	824.67	817.78
90,000	901.52	890.83	881.45	873.18	865.89
95,000	951.60	940.32	930.42	921.69	913.99
100,000	1,001.68	989.81	979.39	970.20	962.10
110,000	1,101.85	1,088.80	1,077.33	1,067.22	1,058.31
120,000	1,202.02	1,187.78	1,175.26	1,164.24	1,154.52
125,000	1,252.10	1,237.27	1,224.23	1,212.75	1,202.62
130,000	1,302.19	1,286.76	1,273.20	1,261.26	1,250.73
140,000	1,402.36	1,385.74	1,371.14	1,358.28	1,346.93
150,000	1,502.52	1,484.72	1,469.08	1,455.30	1,443.14
160,000	1,602.69	1,583.70	1,567.02	1,552.32	1,539.35
170,000	1,702.86	1,682.68	1,664.95	1,649.34	1,635.56
175,000	1,752.94	1,732.17	1,713.92	1,697.85	1,683.67
180,000	1,803.03	1,781.66	1,762.89	1,746.36	1,731.77
190,000	1,903.20	1,880.64	1,860.83	1,843.38	1,827.98
200,000	2,003.36	1,979.62	1,958.77	1,940.40	1,924.19
220,000	2,203.70	2,177.59	2,154.65	2,134.44	2,116.61
225,000	2,253.78	2,227.08	2,203.61	2,182.95	2,164.71
230,000	2,303.87	2,276.57	2,252.58	2,231.46	2,212.82
240,000	2,404.04	2,375.55	2,350.52	2,328.48	2,309.03
$250,000	2,504.20	2,474.53	2,448.46	2,425.50	2,405.24

Monthly Payment Loans **10.75%**

Amortization Period in Years

	26	27	28	29	30
$ 100	0.96	0.95	0.95	0.94	0.94
200	1.91	1.90	1.89	1.88	1.87
300	2.87	2.85	2.83	2.82	2.81
400	3.82	3.80	3.78	3.76	3.74
500	4.78	4.75	4.72	4.69	4.67
600	5.73	5.70	5.66	5.63	5.61
700	6.69	6.65	6.61	6.57	6.54
800	7.64	7.59	7.55	7.51	7.47
900	8.60	8.54	8.49	8.45	8.41
1,000	9.55	9.49	9.43	9.38	9.34
2,000	19.10	18.98	18.86	18.76	18.67
3,000	28.65	28.46	28.29	28.14	28.01
4,000	38.20	37.95	37.72	37.52	37.34
5,000	47.75	47.43	47.15	46.90	46.68
6,000	57.30	56.92	56.58	56.28	56.01
7,000	66.85	66.41	66.01	65.66	65.35
8,000	76.40	75.89	75.44	75.04	74.68
9,000	85.95	85.38	84.87	84.42	84.02
10,000	95.50	94.86	94.30	93.80	93.35
15,000	143.24	142.29	141.45	140.70	140.03
20,000	190.99	189.72	188.59	187.59	186.70
25,000	238.74	237.15	235.74	234.49	233.38
30,000	286.48	284.58	282.89	281.39	280.05
35,000	334.23	332.01	330.03	328.28	326.72
40,000	381.97	379.43	377.18	375.18	373.40
45,000	429.72	426.86	424.33	422.08	420.07
50,000	477.47	474.29	471.47	468.97	466.75
55,000	525.21	521.72	518.62	515.87	513.42
60,000	572.96	569.15	565.77	562.77	560.09
65,000	620.71	616.58	612.92	609.66	606.77
70,000	668.45	664.01	660.06	656.56	653.44
75,000	716.20	711.44	707.21	703.46	700.12
80,000	763.94	758.86	754.36	750.35	746.79
85,000	811.69	806.29	801.50	797.25	793.46
90,000	859.44	853.72	848.65	844.15	840.14
95,000	907.18	901.15	895.80	891.04	886.81
100,000	954.93	948.58	942.94	937.94	933.49
110,000	1,050.42	1,043.44	1,037.24	1,031.73	1,026.83
120,000	1,145.91	1,138.29	1,131.53	1,125.53	1,120.18
125,000	1,193.66	1,185.72	1,178.68	1,172.42	1,166.86
130,000	1,241.41	1,233.15	1,225.83	1,219.32	1,213.53
140,000	1,336.90	1,328.01	1,320.12	1,313.11	1,306.88
150,000	1,432.39	1,422.87	1,414.41	1,406.91	1,400.23
160,000	1,527.88	1,517.72	1,508.71	1,500.70	1,493.58
170,000	1,623.38	1,612.58	1,603.00	1,594.49	1,586.92
175,000	1,671.12	1,660.01	1,650.15	1,641.39	1,633.60
180,000	1,718.87	1,707.44	1,697.30	1,688.29	1,680.27
190,000	1,814.36	1,802.30	1,791.59	1,782.08	1,773.62
200,000	1,909.85	1,897.15	1,885.88	1,875.87	1,866.97
220,000	2,100.84	2,086.87	2,074.47	2,063.46	2,053.66
225,000	2,148.58	2,134.30	2,121.62	2,110.36	2,100.34
230,000	2,196.33	2,181.72	2,168.77	2,157.25	2,147.01
240,000	2,291.82	2,276.58	2,263.06	2,251.05	2,240.36
$250,000	2,387.32	2,371.44	2,357.35	2,344.84	2,333.71

Table 1   99

11.00%   **Monthly Payment Loans**

Amortization Period in Years

	5	7	8	10	12
$ 100	2.18	1.72	1.58	1.38	1.26
200	4.35	3.43	3.15	2.76	2.51
300	6.53	5.14	4.72	4.14	3.77
400	8.70	6.85	6.29	5.52	5.02
500	10.88	8.57	7.86	6.89	6.27
600	13.05	10.28	9.43	8.27	7.53
700	15.22	11.99	11.00	9.65	8.78
800	17.40	13.70	12.57	11.03	10.03
900	19.57	15.42	14.14	12.40	11.29
1,000	21.75	17.13	15.71	13.78	12.54
2,000	43.49	34.25	31.42	27.56	25.08
3,000	65.23	51.37	47.13	41.33	37.61
4,000	86.97	68.49	62.84	55.11	50.15
5,000	108.72	85.62	78.55	68.88	62.68
6,000	130.46	102.74	94.26	82.66	75.22
7,000	152.20	119.86	109.96	96.43	87.75
8,000	173.94	136.98	125.67	110.21	100.29
9,000	195.69	154.11	141.38	123.98	112.82
10,000	217.43	171.23	157.09	137.76	125.36
15,000	326.14	256.84	235.63	206.63	188.04
20,000	434.85	342.45	314.17	275.51	250.72
25,000	543.57	428.07	392.72	344.38	313.39
30,000	652.28	513.68	471.26	413.26	376.07
35,000	760.99	599.29	549.80	482.13	438.75
40,000	869.70	684.90	628.34	551.01	501.43
45,000	978.41	770.51	706.88	619.88	564.10
50,000	1,087.13	856.13	785.43	688.76	626.78
55,000	1,195.84	941.74	863.97	757.63	689.46
60,000	1,304.55	1,027.35	942.51	826.51	752.14
65,000	1,413.26	1,112.96	1,021.05	895.38	814.82
70,000	1,521.97	1,198.58	1,099.59	964.26	877.49
75,000	1,630.69	1,284.19	1,178.14	1,033.13	940.17
80,000	1,739.40	1,369.80	1,256.68	1,102.01	1,002.85
85,000	1,848.11	1,455.41	1,335.22	1,170.88	1,065.53
90,000	1,956.82	1,541.02	1,413.76	1,239.76	1,128.20
95,000	2,065.54	1,626.64	1,492.31	1,308.63	1,190.88
100,000	2,174.25	1,712.25	1,570.85	1,377.51	1,253.56
110,000	2,391.67	1,883.47	1,727.93	1,515.26	1,378.92
120,000	2,609.10	2,054.70	1,885.02	1,653.01	1,504.27
125,000	2,717.81	2,140.31	1,963.56	1,721.88	1,566.95
130,000	2,826.52	2,225.92	2,042.10	1,790.76	1,629.63
140,000	3,043.94	2,397.15	2,199.18	1,928.51	1,754.98
150,000	3,261.37	2,568.37	2,356.27	2,066.26	1,880.34
160,000	3,478.79	2,739.59	2,513.35	2,204.01	2,005.69
170,000	3,696.22	2,910.82	2,670.44	2,341.76	2,131.05
175,000	3,804.93	2,996.43	2,748.98	2,410.63	2,193.73
180,000	3,913.64	3,082.04	2,827.52	2,479.51	2,256.40
190,000	4,131.07	3,253.27	2,984.61	2,617.26	2,381.76
200,000	4,348.49	3,424.49	3,141.69	2,755.01	2,507.12
220,000	4,783.34	3,766.94	3,455.86	3,030.51	2,757.83
225,000	4,892.05	3,852.55	3,534.40	3,099.38	2,820.50
230,000	5,000.76	3,938.17	3,612.94	3,168.26	2,883.18
240,000	5,218.19	4,109.39	3,770.03	3,306.01	3,008.54
$250,000	5,435.61	4,280.61	3,927.11	3,443.76	3,133.89

Monthly Payment Loans **11.00%**

Amortization Period in Years

	15	16	17	18	20
$ 100	1.14	1.11	1.09	1.07	1.04
200	2.28	2.22	2.18	2.14	2.07
300	3.41	3.33	3.26	3.20	3.10
400	4.55	4.44	4.35	4.27	4.13
500	5.69	5.55	5.43	5.33	5.17
600	6.82	6.66	6.52	6.40	6.20
700	7.96	7.77	7.60	7.46	7.23
800	9.10	8.88	8.69	8.53	8.26
900	10.23	9.99	9.77	9.59	9.29
1,000	11.37	11.10	10.86	10.66	10.33
2,000	22.74	22.19	21.71	21.31	20.65
3,000	34.10	33.28	32.57	31.96	30.97
4,000	45.47	44.37	43.42	42.61	41.29
5,000	56.83	55.46	54.27	53.26	51.61
6,000	68.20	66.55	65.13	63.91	61.94
7,000	79.57	77.64	75.98	74.56	72.26
8,000	90.93	88.73	86.84	85.21	82.58
9,000	102.30	99.82	97.69	95.86	92.90
10,000	113.66	110.91	108.54	106.51	103.22
15,000	170.49	166.36	162.81	159.76	154.83
20,000	227.32	221.81	217.08	213.01	206.44
25,000	284.15	277.26	271.35	266.27	258.05
30,000	340.98	332.71	325.62	319.52	309.66
35,000	397.81	388.16	379.89	372.77	361.27
40,000	454.64	443.61	434.16	426.02	412.88
45,000	511.47	499.06	488.43	479.28	464.49
50,000	568.30	554.51	542.70	532.53	516.10
55,000	625.13	609.96	596.96	585.78	567.71
60,000	681.96	665.41	651.23	639.03	619.32
65,000	738.79	720.86	705.50	692.29	670.93
70,000	795.62	776.31	759.77	745.54	722.54
75,000	852.45	831.76	814.04	798.79	774.15
80,000	909.28	887.21	868.31	852.04	825.76
85,000	966.11	942.66	922.58	905.30	877.37
90,000	1,022.94	998.11	976.85	958.55	928.97
95,000	1,079.77	1,053.56	1,031.12	1,011.80	980.58
100,000	1,136.60	1,109.01	1,085.39	1,065.05	1,032.19
110,000	1,250.26	1,219.91	1,193.92	1,171.56	1,135.41
120,000	1,363.92	1,330.81	1,302.46	1,278.06	1,238.63
125,000	1,420.75	1,386.26	1,356.73	1,331.32	1,290.24
130,000	1,477.58	1,441.71	1,411.00	1,384.57	1,341.85
140,000	1,591.24	1,552.61	1,519.54	1,491.07	1,445.07
150,000	1,704.90	1,663.51	1,628.08	1,597.58	1,548.29
160,000	1,818.56	1,774.41	1,736.61	1,704.08	1,651.51
170,000	1,932.22	1,885.31	1,845.15	1,810.59	1,754.73
175,000	1,989.05	1,940.76	1,899.42	1,863.84	1,806.33
180,000	2,045.88	1,996.21	1,953.69	1,917.09	1,857.94
190,000	2,159.54	2,107.11	2,062.23	2,023.60	1,961.16
200,000	2,273.20	2,218.01	2,170.77	2,130.10	2,064.38
220,000	2,500.52	2,439.81	2,387.84	2,343.11	2,270.82
225,000	2,557.35	2,495.26	2,442.11	2,396.37	2,322.43
230,000	2,614.18	2,550.71	2,496.38	2,449.62	2,374.04
240,000	2,727.84	2,661.61	2,604.92	2,556.12	2,477.26
$250,000	2,841.50	2,772.51	2,713.46	2,662.63	2,580.48

Table 1   101

11.00%   Monthly Payment Loans

Amortization Period in Years

	21	22	23	24	25
$ 100	1.02	1.01	1.00	0.99	0.99
200	2.04	2.02	2.00	1.98	1.97
300	3.06	3.03	3.00	2.97	2.95
400	4.08	4.03	3.99	3.96	3.93
500	5.10	5.04	4.99	4.95	4.91
600	6.12	6.05	5.99	5.93	5.89
700	7.14	7.06	6.98	6.92	6.87
800	8.16	8.06	7.98	7.91	7.85
900	9.17	9.07	8.98	8.90	8.83
1,000	10.19	10.08	9.98	9.89	9.81
2,000	20.38	20.15	19.95	19.77	19.61
3,000	30.57	30.22	29.92	29.65	29.41
4,000	40.76	40.29	39.89	39.53	39.21
5,000	50.95	50.37	49.86	49.41	49.01
6,000	61.14	60.44	59.83	59.29	58.81
7,000	71.33	70.51	69.80	69.17	68.61
8,000	81.51	80.58	79.77	79.05	78.41
9,000	91.70	90.66	89.74	88.93	88.22
10,000	101.89	100.73	99.71	98.81	98.02
15,000	152.84	151.09	149.56	148.21	147.02
20,000	203.78	201.45	199.41	197.61	196.03
25,000	254.72	251.81	249.26	247.01	245.03
30,000	305.67	302.17	299.11	296.41	294.04
35,000	356.61	352.53	348.96	345.81	343.04
40,000	407.55	402.89	398.81	395.22	392.05
45,000	458.50	453.26	448.66	444.62	441.06
50,000	509.44	503.62	498.51	494.02	490.06
55,000	560.38	553.98	548.36	543.42	539.07
60,000	611.33	604.34	598.21	592.82	588.07
65,000	662.27	654.70	648.06	642.22	637.08
70,000	713.21	705.06	697.91	691.62	686.08
75,000	764.16	755.42	747.76	741.02	735.09
80,000	815.10	805.78	797.61	790.43	784.10
85,000	866.05	856.14	847.46	839.83	833.10
90,000	916.99	906.51	897.31	889.23	882.11
95,000	967.93	956.87	947.16	938.63	931.11
100,000	1,018.88	1,007.23	997.01	988.03	980.12
110,000	1,120.76	1,107.95	1,096.71	1,086.83	1,078.13
120,000	1,222.65	1,208.67	1,196.41	1,185.64	1,176.14
125,000	1,273.59	1,259.03	1,246.27	1,235.04	1,225.15
130,000	1,324.54	1,309.40	1,296.12	1,284.44	1,274.15
140,000	1,426.42	1,410.12	1,395.82	1,383.24	1,372.16
150,000	1,528.31	1,510.84	1,495.52	1,482.04	1,470.17
160,000	1,630.20	1,611.56	1,595.22	1,580.85	1,568.19
170,000	1,732.09	1,712.28	1,694.92	1,679.65	1,666.20
175,000	1,783.03	1,762.65	1,744.77	1,729.05	1,715.20
180,000	1,833.97	1,813.01	1,794.62	1,778.45	1,764.21
190,000	1,935.86	1,913.73	1,894.32	1,877.26	1,862.22
200,000	2,037.75	2,014.45	1,994.02	1,976.06	1,960.23
220,000	2,241.52	2,215.90	2,193.42	2,173.66	2,156.25
225,000	2,292.46	2,266.26	2,243.27	2,223.06	2,205.26
230,000	2,343.41	2,316.62	2,293.12	2,272.47	2,254.27
240,000	2,445.30	2,417.34	2,392.82	2,371.27	2,352.28
$250,000	2,547.18	2,518.06	2,492.53	2,470.07	2,450.29

Monthly Payment Loans   **11.00%**

Amortization Period in Years

	26	27	28	29	30
$ 100	0.98	0.97	0.97	0.96	0.96
200	1.95	1.94	1.93	1.92	1.91
300	2.92	2.91	2.89	2.87	2.86
400	3.90	3.87	3.85	3.83	3.81
500	4.87	4.84	4.81	4.79	4.77
600	5.84	5.81	5.77	5.74	5.72
700	6.82	6.77	6.74	6.70	6.67
800	7.79	7.74	7.70	7.66	7.62
900	8.76	8.71	8.66	8.61	8.58
1,000	9.74	9.67	9.62	9.57	9.53
2,000	19.47	19.34	19.23	19.14	19.05
3,000	29.20	29.01	28.85	28.70	28.57
4,000	38.93	38.68	38.46	38.27	38.10
5,000	48.66	48.35	48.08	47.84	47.62
6,000	58.39	58.02	57.69	57.40	57.14
7,000	68.12	67.69	67.31	66.97	66.67
8,000	77.86	77.36	76.92	76.54	76.19
9,000	87.59	87.03	86.54	86.10	85.71
10,000	97.32	96.70	96.15	95.67	95.24
15,000	145.97	145.05	144.23	143.50	142.85
20,000	194.63	193.40	192.30	191.33	190.47
25,000	243.29	241.74	240.37	239.16	238.09
30,000	291.94	290.09	288.45	286.99	285.70
35,000	340.60	338.44	336.52	334.83	333.32
40,000	389.26	386.79	384.60	382.66	380.93
45,000	437.91	435.13	432.67	430.49	428.55
50,000	486.57	483.48	480.74	478.32	476.17
55,000	535.23	531.83	528.82	526.15	523.78
60,000	583.88	580.18	576.89	573.98	571.40
65,000	632.54	628.52	624.97	621.81	619.02
70,000	681.19	676.87	673.04	669.65	666.63
75,000	729.85	725.22	721.11	717.48	714.25
80,000	778.51	773.57	769.19	765.31	761.86
85,000	827.16	821.91	817.26	813.14	809.48
90,000	875.82	870.26	865.34	860.97	857.10
95,000	924.48	918.61	913.41	908.80	904.71
100,000	973.13	966.96	961.48	956.63	952.33
110,000	1,070.45	1,063.65	1,057.63	1,052.30	1,047.56
120,000	1,167.76	1,160.35	1,153.78	1,147.96	1,142.79
125,000	1,216.41	1,208.69	1,201.85	1,195.79	1,190.41
130,000	1,265.07	1,257.04	1,249.93	1,243.62	1,238.03
140,000	1,362.38	1,353.74	1,346.08	1,339.29	1,333.26
150,000	1,459.70	1,450.43	1,442.22	1,434.95	1,428.49
160,000	1,557.01	1,547.13	1,538.37	1,530.61	1,523.72
170,000	1,654.32	1,643.82	1,634.52	1,626.28	1,618.95
175,000	1,702.98	1,692.17	1,682.59	1,674.11	1,666.57
180,000	1,751.63	1,740.52	1,730.67	1,721.94	1,714.19
190,000	1,848.95	1,837.21	1,826.82	1,817.60	1,809.42
200,000	1,946.26	1,933.91	1,922.96	1,913.26	1,904.65
220,000	2,140.89	2,127.30	2,115.26	2,104.59	2,095.12
225,000	2,189.54	2,175.64	2,163.33	2,152.42	2,142.73
230,000	2,238.20	2,223.99	2,211.41	2,200.25	2,190.35
240,000	2,335.51	2,320.69	2,307.56	2,295.92	2,285.58
$250,000	2,432.82	2,417.38	2,403.70	2,391.58	2,380.81

Table 1   103

11.25% Monthly Payment Loans

Amortization Period in Years

	5	7	8	10	12
$ 100	2.19	1.73	1.59	1.40	1.27
200	4.38	3.46	3.17	2.79	2.54
300	6.57	5.18	4.76	4.18	3.81
400	8.75	6.91	6.34	5.57	5.08
500	10.94	8.63	7.93	6.96	6.35
600	13.13	10.36	9.51	8.36	7.62
700	15.31	12.08	11.10	9.75	8.88
800	17.50	13.81	12.68	11.14	10.15
900	19.69	15.53	14.26	12.53	11.42
1,000	21.87	17.26	15.85	13.92	12.69
2,000	43.74	34.51	31.69	27.84	25.37
3,000	65.61	51.77	47.54	41.76	38.06
4,000	87.47	69.02	63.38	55.67	50.74
5,000	109.34	86.28	79.22	69.59	63.42
6,000	131.21	103.53	95.07	83.51	76.11
7,000	153.08	120.78	110.91	97.42	88.79
8,000	174.94	138.04	126.75	111.34	101.48
9,000	196.81	155.29	142.60	125.26	114.16
10,000	218.68	172.55	158.44	139.17	126.84
15,000	328.01	258.82	237.66	208.76	190.26
20,000	437.35	345.09	316.88	278.34	253.68
25,000	546.69	431.36	396.09	347.93	317.10
30,000	656.02	517.63	475.31	417.51	380.52
35,000	765.36	603.90	554.53	487.10	443.94
40,000	874.70	690.17	633.75	556.68	507.36
45,000	984.03	776.44	712.97	626.27	570.78
50,000	1,093.37	862.71	792.18	695.85	634.20
55,000	1,202.71	948.98	871.40	765.43	697.62
60,000	1,312.04	1,035.26	950.62	835.02	761.04
65,000	1,421.38	1,121.53	1,029.84	904.60	824.46
70,000	1,530.72	1,207.80	1,109.06	974.19	887.88
75,000	1,640.05	1,294.07	1,188.27	1,043.77	951.30
80,000	1,749.39	1,380.34	1,267.49	1,113.36	1,014.72
85,000	1,858.73	1,466.61	1,346.71	1,182.94	1,078.14
90,000	1,968.06	1,552.88	1,425.93	1,252.53	1,141.56
95,000	2,077.40	1,639.15	1,505.15	1,322.11	1,204.98
100,000	2,186.74	1,725.42	1,584.36	1,391.69	1,268.40
110,000	2,405.41	1,897.96	1,742.80	1,530.86	1,395.24
120,000	2,624.08	2,070.51	1,901.24	1,670.03	1,522.08
125,000	2,733.42	2,156.78	1,980.45	1,739.62	1,585.50
130,000	2,842.76	2,243.05	2,059.67	1,809.20	1,648.92
140,000	3,061.43	2,415.59	2,218.11	1,948.37	1,775.76
150,000	3,280.10	2,588.13	2,376.54	2,087.54	1,902.59
160,000	3,498.77	2,760.67	2,534.98	2,226.71	2,029.43
170,000	3,717.45	2,933.21	2,693.41	2,365.88	2,156.27
175,000	3,826.78	3,019.48	2,772.63	2,435.46	2,219.69
180,000	3,936.12	3,105.76	2,851.85	2,505.05	2,283.11
190,000	4,154.79	3,278.30	3,010.29	2,644.21	2,409.95
200,000	4,373.47	3,450.84	3,168.72	2,783.38	2,536.79
220,000	4,810.81	3,795.92	3,485.59	3,061.72	2,790.47
225,000	4,920.15	3,882.19	3,564.81	3,131.31	2,853.89
230,000	5,029.49	3,968.46	3,644.03	3,200.89	2,917.31
240,000	5,248.16	4,141.01	3,802.47	3,340.06	3,044.15
$250,000	5,466.83	4,313.55	3,960.90	3,479.23	3,170.99

Monthly Payment Loans **11.25%**

Amortization Period in Years

	15	16	17	18	20
$ 100	1.16	1.13	1.11	1.09	1.05
200	2.31	2.26	2.21	2.17	2.10
300	3.46	3.38	3.31	3.25	3.15
400	4.61	4.51	4.41	4.33	4.20
500	5.77	5.63	5.51	5.41	5.25
600	6.92	6.76	6.62	6.49	6.30
700	8.07	7.88	7.72	7.58	7.35
800	9.22	9.01	8.82	8.66	8.40
900	10.38	10.13	9.92	9.74	9.45
1,000	11.53	11.26	11.02	10.82	10.50
2,000	23.05	22.51	22.04	21.64	20.99
3,000	34.58	33.76	33.06	32.45	31.48
4,000	46.10	45.01	44.07	43.27	41.98
5,000	57.62	56.26	55.09	54.09	52.47
6,000	69.15	67.51	66.11	64.90	62.96
7,000	80.67	78.76	77.12	75.72	73.45
8,000	92.19	90.01	88.14	86.53	83.95
9,000	103.72	101.26	99.16	97.35	94.44
10,000	115.24	112.51	110.17	108.17	104.93
15,000	172.86	168.76	165.26	162.25	157.39
20,000	230.47	225.01	220.34	216.33	209.86
25,000	288.09	281.26	275.43	270.41	262.32
30,000	345.71	337.51	330.51	324.49	314.78
35,000	403.33	393.77	385.60	378.57	367.24
40,000	460.94	450.02	440.68	432.65	419.71
45,000	518.56	506.27	495.76	486.73	472.17
50,000	576.18	562.52	550.85	540.82	524.63
55,000	633.79	618.77	605.93	594.90	577.10
60,000	691.41	675.02	661.02	648.98	629.56
65,000	749.03	731.28	716.10	703.06	682.02
70,000	806.65	787.53	771.19	757.14	734.48
75,000	864.26	843.78	826.27	811.22	786.95
80,000	921.88	900.03	881.35	865.30	839.41
85,000	979.50	956.28	936.44	919.38	891.87
90,000	1,037.12	1,012.53	991.52	973.46	944.34
95,000	1,094.73	1,068.79	1,046.61	1,027.54	996.80
100,000	1,152.35	1,125.04	1,101.69	1,081.63	1,049.26
110,000	1,267.58	1,237.54	1,211.86	1,189.79	1,154.19
120,000	1,382.82	1,350.04	1,322.03	1,297.95	1,259.11
125,000	1,440.44	1,406.30	1,377.11	1,352.03	1,311.58
130,000	1,498.05	1,462.55	1,432.20	1,406.11	1,364.04
140,000	1,613.29	1,575.05	1,542.37	1,514.27	1,468.96
150,000	1,728.52	1,687.55	1,652.54	1,622.44	1,573.89
160,000	1,843.76	1,800.06	1,762.70	1,730.60	1,678.81
170,000	1,958.99	1,912.56	1,872.87	1,838.76	1,783.74
175,000	2,016.61	1,968.81	1,927.96	1,892.84	1,836.20
180,000	2,074.23	2,025.06	1,983.04	1,946.92	1,888.67
190,000	2,189.46	2,137.57	2,093.21	2,055.08	1,993.59
200,000	2,304.69	2,250.07	2,203.38	2,163.25	2,098.52
220,000	2,535.16	2,475.08	2,423.72	2,379.57	2,308.37
225,000	2,592.78	2,531.33	2,478.80	2,433.65	2,360.83
230,000	2,650.40	2,587.58	2,533.89	2,487.73	2,413.29
240,000	2,765.63	2,700.08	2,644.05	2,595.89	2,518.22
$250,000	2,880.87	2,812.59	2,754.22	2,704.06	2,623.15

Table 1   105

11.25%　　Monthly Payment Loans

Amortization Period in Years

	21	22	23	24	25
$ 100	1.04	1.03	1.02	1.01	1.00
200	2.08	2.05	2.03	2.02	2.00
300	3.11	3.08	3.05	3.02	3.00
400	4.15	4.10	4.06	4.03	4.00
500	5.19	5.13	5.08	5.03	5.00
600	6.22	6.15	6.09	6.04	5.99
700	7.26	7.18	7.11	7.05	6.99
800	8.29	8.20	8.12	8.05	7.99
900	9.33	9.23	9.14	9.06	8.99
1,000	10.37	10.25	10.15	10.06	9.99
2,000	20.73	20.50	20.30	20.12	19.97
3,000	31.09	30.75	30.45	30.18	29.95
4,000	41.45	40.99	40.59	40.24	39.93
5,000	51.81	51.24	50.74	50.30	49.92
6,000	62.18	61.49	60.89	60.36	59.90
7,000	72.54	71.74	71.04	70.42	69.88
8,000	82.90	81.98	81.18	80.48	79.86
9,000	93.26	92.23	91.33	90.54	89.85
10,000	103.62	102.48	101.48	100.60	99.83
15,000	155.43	153.72	152.22	150.90	149.74
20,000	207.24	204.95	202.95	201.20	199.65
25,000	259.05	256.19	253.69	251.50	249.56
30,000	310.86	307.43	304.43	301.79	299.48
35,000	362.66	358.67	355.16	352.09	349.39
40,000	414.47	409.90	405.90	402.39	399.30
45,000	466.28	461.14	456.64	452.69	449.21
50,000	518.09	512.38	507.38	502.99	499.12
55,000	569.90	563.62	558.11	553.28	549.04
60,000	621.71	614.85	608.85	603.58	598.95
65,000	673.52	666.09	659.59	653.88	648.86
70,000	725.32	717.33	710.32	704.18	698.77
75,000	777.13	768.56	761.06	754.48	748.68
80,000	828.94	819.80	811.80	804.77	798.60
85,000	880.75	871.04	862.54	855.07	848.51
90,000	932.56	922.28	913.27	905.37	898.42
95,000	984.37	973.51	964.01	955.67	948.33
100,000	1,036.18	1,024.75	1,014.75	1,005.97	998.24
110,000	1,139.79	1,127.23	1,116.22	1,106.56	1,098.07
120,000	1,243.41	1,229.70	1,217.70	1,207.16	1,197.89
125,000	1,295.22	1,280.94	1,268.43	1,257.46	1,247.80
130,000	1,347.03	1,332.17	1,319.17	1,307.76	1,297.72
140,000	1,450.64	1,434.65	1,420.64	1,408.35	1,397.54
150,000	1,554.26	1,537.12	1,522.12	1,508.95	1,497.36
160,000	1,657.88	1,639.60	1,623.59	1,609.54	1,597.19
170,000	1,761.50	1,742.07	1,725.07	1,710.14	1,697.01
175,000	1,813.30	1,793.31	1,775.80	1,760.44	1,746.92
180,000	1,865.11	1,844.55	1,826.54	1,810.74	1,796.84
190,000	1,968.73	1,947.02	1,928.01	1,911.33	1,896.66
200,000	2,072.35	2,049.50	2,029.49	2,011.93	1,996.48
220,000	2,279.58	2,254.45	2,232.44	2,213.12	2,196.13
225,000	2,331.39	2,305.68	2,283.17	2,263.42	2,246.04
230,000	2,383.20	2,356.92	2,333.91	2,313.72	2,295.96
240,000	2,486.82	2,459.39	2,435.39	2,414.31	2,395.78
$250,000	2,590.43	2,561.87	2,536.86	2,514.91	2,495.60

Monthly Payment Loans   11.25%

Amortization Period in Years

	26	27	28	29	30
$ 100	1.00	0.99	0.99	0.98	0.98
200	1.99	1.98	1.97	1.96	1.95
300	2.98	2.96	2.95	2.93	2.92
400	3.97	3.95	3.93	3.91	3.89
500	4.96	4.93	4.91	4.88	4.86
600	5.95	5.92	5.89	5.86	5.83
700	6.95	6.90	6.87	6.83	6.80
800	7.94	7.89	7.85	7.81	7.78
900	8.93	8.87	8.83	8.78	8.75
1,000	9.92	9.86	9.81	9.76	9.72
2,000	19.83	19.71	19.61	19.51	19.43
3,000	29.75	29.57	29.41	29.27	29.14
4,000	39.66	39.42	39.21	39.02	38.86
5,000	49.58	49.28	49.01	48.78	48.57
6,000	59.49	59.13	58.81	58.53	58.28
7,000	69.41	68.99	68.61	68.28	67.99
8,000	79.32	78.84	78.41	78.04	77.71
9,000	89.23	88.69	88.22	87.79	87.42
10,000	99.15	98.55	98.02	97.55	97.13
15,000	148.72	147.82	147.02	146.32	145.69
20,000	198.29	197.09	196.03	195.09	194.26
25,000	247.86	246.36	245.04	243.86	242.82
30,000	297.44	295.63	294.04	292.63	291.38
35,000	347.01	344.91	343.05	341.40	339.95
40,000	396.58	394.18	392.05	390.17	388.51
45,000	446.15	443.45	441.06	438.95	437.07
50,000	495.72	492.72	490.07	487.72	485.64
55,000	545.29	541.99	539.07	536.49	534.20
60,000	594.87	591.26	588.08	585.26	582.76
65,000	644.44	640.53	637.08	634.03	631.32
70,000	694.01	689.81	686.09	682.80	679.89
75,000	743.58	739.08	735.10	731.57	728.45
80,000	793.15	788.35	784.10	780.34	777.01
85,000	842.72	837.62	833.11	829.11	825.58
90,000	892.30	886.89	882.11	877.89	874.14
95,000	941.87	936.16	931.12	926.66	922.70
100,000	991.44	985.43	980.13	975.43	971.27
110,000	1,090.58	1,083.98	1,078.14	1,072.97	1,068.39
120,000	1,189.73	1,182.52	1,176.15	1,170.51	1,165.52
125,000	1,239.30	1,231.79	1,225.16	1,219.28	1,214.08
130,000	1,288.87	1,281.06	1,274.16	1,268.06	1,262.64
140,000	1,388.01	1,379.61	1,372.17	1,365.60	1,359.77
150,000	1,487.16	1,478.15	1,470.19	1,463.14	1,456.90
160,000	1,586.30	1,576.69	1,568.20	1,560.68	1,554.02
170,000	1,685.44	1,675.23	1,666.21	1,658.22	1,651.15
175,000	1,735.02	1,724.51	1,715.22	1,707.00	1,699.71
180,000	1,784.59	1,773.78	1,764.22	1,755.77	1,748.28
190,000	1,883.73	1,872.32	1,862.24	1,853.31	1,845.40
200,000	1,982.87	1,970.86	1,960.25	1,950.85	1,942.53
220,000	2,181.16	2,167.95	2,156.27	2,145.94	2,136.78
225,000	2,230.73	2,217.22	2,205.28	2,194.71	2,185.34
230,000	2,280.31	2,266.49	2,254.28	2,243.48	2,233.91
240,000	2,379.45	2,365.04	2,352.30	2,341.02	2,331.03
$250,000	2,478.59	2,463.58	2,450.31	2,438.56	2,428.16

Table 1   107

11.50% Monthly Payment Loans

Amortization Period in Years

	5	7	8	10	12
$ 100	2.20	1.74	1.60	1.41	1.29
200	4.40	3.48	3.20	2.82	2.57
300	6.60	5.22	4.80	4.22	3.85
400	8.80	6.96	6.40	5.63	5.14
500	11.00	8.70	7.99	7.03	6.42
600	13.20	10.44	9.59	8.44	7.70
700	15.40	12.18	11.19	9.85	8.99
800	17.60	13.91	12.79	11.25	10.27
900	19.80	15.65	14.39	12.66	11.55
1,000	22.00	17.39	15.98	14.06	12.84
2,000	43.99	34.78	31.96	28.12	25.67
3,000	65.98	52.16	47.94	42.18	38.50
4,000	87.98	69.55	63.92	56.24	51.34
5,000	109.97	86.94	79.90	70.30	64.17
6,000	131.96	104.32	95.88	84.36	77.00
7,000	153.95	121.71	111.86	98.42	89.84
8,000	175.95	139.10	127.84	112.48	102.67
9,000	197.94	156.48	143.82	126.54	115.50
10,000	219.93	173.87	159.80	140.60	128.34
15,000	329.89	260.80	239.70	210.90	192.50
20,000	439.86	347.73	319.59	281.20	256.67
25,000	549.82	434.67	399.49	351.49	320.83
30,000	659.78	521.60	479.39	421.79	385.00
35,000	769.75	608.53	559.28	492.09	449.17
40,000	879.71	695.46	639.18	562.39	513.33
45,000	989.67	782.40	719.08	632.68	577.50
50,000	1,099.64	869.33	798.97	702.98	641.66
55,000	1,209.60	956.26	878.87	773.28	705.83
60,000	1,319.56	1,043.19	958.77	843.58	769.99
65,000	1,429.52	1,130.12	1,038.66	913.88	834.16
70,000	1,539.49	1,217.06	1,118.56	984.17	898.33
75,000	1,649.45	1,303.99	1,198.46	1,054.47	962.49
80,000	1,759.41	1,390.92	1,278.35	1,124.77	1,026.66
85,000	1,869.38	1,477.85	1,358.25	1,195.07	1,090.82
90,000	1,979.34	1,564.79	1,438.15	1,265.36	1,154.99
95,000	2,089.30	1,651.72	1,518.05	1,335.66	1,219.16
100,000	2,199.27	1,738.65	1,597.94	1,405.96	1,283.32
110,000	2,419.19	1,912.52	1,757.74	1,546.55	1,411.65
120,000	2,639.12	2,086.38	1,917.53	1,687.15	1,539.98
125,000	2,749.08	2,173.31	1,997.43	1,757.45	1,604.15
130,000	2,859.04	2,260.24	2,077.32	1,827.75	1,668.32
140,000	3,078.97	2,434.11	2,237.12	1,968.34	1,796.65
150,000	3,298.90	2,607.97	2,396.91	2,108.94	1,924.98
160,000	3,518.82	2,781.84	2,556.70	2,249.53	2,053.31
170,000	3,738.75	2,955.70	2,716.50	2,390.13	2,181.64
175,000	3,848.71	3,042.64	2,796.40	2,460.43	2,245.81
180,000	3,958.67	3,129.57	2,876.29	2,530.72	2,309.97
190,000	4,178.60	3,303.43	3,036.09	2,671.32	2,438.31
200,000	4,398.53	3,477.30	3,195.88	2,811.91	2,566.64
220,000	4,838.38	3,825.03	3,515.47	3,093.10	2,823.30
225,000	4,948.34	3,911.96	3,595.36	3,163.40	2,887.47
230,000	5,058.30	3,998.89	3,675.26	3,233.70	2,951.63
240,000	5,278.23	4,172.76	3,835.05	3,374.30	3,079.96
$250,000	5,498.16	4,346.62	3,994.85	3,514.89	3,208.30

Monthly Payment Loans **11.50%**

Amortization Period in Years

	15	16	17	18	20
$ 100	1.17	1.15	1.12	1.10	1.07
200	2.34	2.29	2.24	2.20	2.14
300	3.51	3.43	3.36	3.30	3.20
400	4.68	4.57	4.48	4.40	4.27
500	5.85	5.71	5.60	5.50	5.34
600	7.01	6.85	6.71	6.59	6.40
700	8.18	7.99	7.83	7.69	7.47
800	9.35	9.13	8.95	8.79	8.54
900	10.52	10.28	10.07	9.89	9.60
1,000	11.69	11.42	11.19	10.99	10.67
2,000	23.37	22.83	22.37	21.97	21.33
3,000	35.05	34.24	33.55	32.95	32.00
4,000	46.73	45.65	44.73	43.94	42.66
5,000	58.41	57.06	55.91	54.92	53.33
6,000	70.10	68.47	67.09	65.90	63.99
7,000	81.78	79.89	78.27	76.89	74.66
8,000	93.46	91.30	89.45	87.87	85.32
9,000	105.14	102.71	100.63	98.85	95.98
10,000	116.82	114.12	111.81	109.83	106.65
15,000	175.23	171.18	167.72	164.75	159.97
20,000	233.64	228.24	223.62	219.66	213.29
25,000	292.05	285.30	279.53	274.58	266.61
30,000	350.46	342.35	335.43	329.49	319.93
35,000	408.87	399.41	391.34	384.41	373.26
40,000	467.28	456.47	447.24	439.32	426.58
45,000	525.69	513.53	503.15	494.24	479.90
50,000	584.10	570.59	559.05	549.15	533.22
55,000	642.51	627.65	614.96	604.07	586.54
60,000	700.92	684.70	670.86	658.98	639.86
65,000	759.33	741.76	726.77	713.90	693.18
70,000	817.74	798.82	782.67	768.81	746.51
75,000	876.15	855.88	838.58	823.73	799.83
80,000	934.56	912.94	894.48	878.64	853.15
85,000	992.97	970.00	950.39	933.56	906.47
90,000	1,051.38	1,027.05	1,006.29	988.47	959.79
95,000	1,109.79	1,084.11	1,062.20	1,043.39	1,013.11
100,000	1,168.19	1,141.17	1,118.10	1,098.30	1,066.43
110,000	1,285.01	1,255.29	1,229.91	1,208.13	1,173.08
120,000	1,401.83	1,369.40	1,341.72	1,317.96	1,279.72
125,000	1,460.24	1,426.46	1,397.63	1,372.87	1,333.04
130,000	1,518.65	1,483.52	1,453.53	1,427.79	1,386.36
140,000	1,635.47	1,597.64	1,565.34	1,537.62	1,493.01
150,000	1,752.29	1,711.75	1,677.15	1,647.45	1,599.65
160,000	1,869.11	1,825.87	1,788.96	1,757.28	1,706.29
170,000	1,985.93	1,939.99	1,900.77	1,867.11	1,812.94
175,000	2,044.34	1,997.04	1,956.67	1,922.02	1,866.26
180,000	2,102.75	2,054.10	2,012.58	1,976.94	1,919.58
190,000	2,219.57	2,168.22	2,124.39	2,086.77	2,026.22
200,000	2,336.38	2,282.33	2,236.20	2,196.60	2,132.86
220,000	2,570.02	2,510.57	2,459.82	2,416.25	2,346.15
225,000	2,628.43	2,567.63	2,515.72	2,471.17	2,399.47
230,000	2,686.84	2,624.68	2,571.63	2,526.08	2,452.79
240,000	2,803.66	2,738.80	2,683.44	2,635.91	2,559.44
$250,000	2,920.48	2,852.92	2,795.25	2,745.74	2,666.08

Table 1   109

11.50%　Monthly Payment Loans

Amortization Period in Years

	21	22	23	24	25
$ 100	1.06	1.05	1.04	1.03	1.02
200	2.11	2.09	2.07	2.05	2.04
300	3.17	3.13	3.10	3.08	3.05
400	4.22	4.17	4.14	4.10	4.07
500	5.27	5.22	5.17	5.13	5.09
600	6.33	6.26	6.20	6.15	6.10
700	7.38	7.30	7.23	7.17	7.12
800	8.43	8.34	8.27	8.20	8.14
900	9.49	9.39	9.30	9.22	9.15
1,000	10.54	10.43	10.33	10.25	10.17
2,000	21.08	20.85	20.66	20.49	20.33
3,000	31.61	31.28	30.98	30.73	30.50
4,000	42.15	41.70	41.31	40.97	40.66
5,000	52.68	52.12	51.63	51.21	50.83
6,000	63.22	62.55	61.96	61.45	60.99
7,000	73.76	72.97	72.29	71.69	71.16
8,000	84.29	83.39	82.61	81.93	81.32
9,000	94.83	93.82	92.94	92.17	91.49
10,000	105.36	104.24	103.26	102.41	101.65
15,000	158.04	156.36	154.89	153.61	152.48
20,000	210.72	208.48	206.52	204.81	203.30
25,000	263.40	260.60	258.15	256.01	254.12
30,000	316.08	312.72	309.78	307.21	304.95
35,000	368.76	364.84	361.41	358.41	355.77
40,000	421.44	416.95	413.04	409.61	406.59
45,000	474.11	469.07	464.67	460.81	457.42
50,000	526.79	521.19	516.30	512.01	508.24
55,000	579.47	573.31	567.92	563.21	559.06
60,000	632.15	625.43	619.55	614.41	609.89
65,000	684.83	677.55	671.18	665.61	660.71
70,000	737.51	729.67	722.81	716.81	711.53
75,000	790.19	781.79	774.44	768.01	762.36
80,000	842.87	833.90	826.07	819.21	813.18
85,000	895.55	886.02	877.70	870.41	864.00
90,000	948.22	938.14	929.33	921.61	914.83
95,000	1,000.90	990.26	980.96	972.81	965.65
100,000	1,053.58	1,042.38	1,032.59	1,024.01	1,016.47
110,000	1,158.94	1,146.62	1,135.84	1,126.41	1,118.12
120,000	1,264.30	1,250.85	1,239.10	1,228.81	1,219.77
125,000	1,316.98	1,302.97	1,290.73	1,280.01	1,270.59
130,000	1,369.66	1,355.09	1,342.36	1,331.21	1,321.41
140,000	1,475.01	1,459.33	1,445.62	1,433.61	1,423.06
150,000	1,580.37	1,563.53	1,548.88	1,536.01	1,524.71
160,000	1,685.73	1,667.80	1,652.14	1,638.41	1,626.36
170,000	1,791.09	1,772.04	1,755.39	1,740.81	1,728.00
175,000	1,843.77	1,824.16	1,807.02	1,792.01	1,778.83
180,000	1,896.44	1,876.28	1,858.65	1,843.21	1,829.65
190,000	2,001.80	1,980.52	1,961.91	1,945.61	1,931.30
200,000	2,107.16	2,084.75	2,065.17	2,048.01	2,032.94
220,000	2,317.88	2,293.23	2,271.68	2,252.81	2,236.24
225,000	2,370.55	2,345.35	2,323.31	2,304.01	2,287.06
230,000	2,423.23	2,397.47	2,374.94	2,355.21	2,337.88
240,000	2,528.59	2,501.70	2,478.20	2,457.61	2,439.53
$250,000	2,633.95	2,605.94	2,581.46	2,560.01	2,541.18

Monthly Payment Loans   **11.50%**

Amortization Period in Years

	26	27	28	29	30
$ 100	1.01	1.01	1.00	1.00	1.00
200	2.02	2.01	2.00	1.99	1.99
300	3.03	3.02	3.00	2.99	2.98
400	4.04	4.02	4.00	3.98	3.97
500	5.05	5.03	5.00	4.98	4.96
600	6.06	6.03	6.00	5.97	5.95
700	7.07	7.03	7.00	6.97	6.94
800	8.08	8.04	8.00	7.96	7.93
900	9.09	9.04	8.99	8.95	8.92
1,000	10.10	10.05	9.99	9.95	9.91
2,000	20.20	20.09	19.98	19.89	19.81
3,000	30.30	30.13	29.97	29.83	29.71
4,000	40.40	40.17	39.96	39.78	39.62
5,000	50.50	50.21	49.95	49.72	49.52
6,000	60.60	60.25	59.94	59.66	59.42
7,000	70.69	70.29	69.93	69.61	69.33
8,000	80.79	80.33	79.91	79.55	79.23
9,000	90.89	90.37	89.90	89.49	89.13
10,000	100.99	100.41	99.89	99.44	99.03
15,000	151.48	150.61	149.83	149.15	148.55
20,000	201.97	200.81	199.78	198.87	198.06
25,000	252.47	251.01	249.72	248.58	247.58
30,000	302.96	301.21	299.66	298.30	297.09
35,000	353.45	351.41	349.61	348.01	346.61
40,000	403.94	401.61	399.55	397.73	396.12
45,000	454.43	451.81	449.49	447.45	445.64
50,000	504.93	502.01	499.43	497.16	495.15
55,000	555.42	552.21	549.38	546.88	544.67
60,000	605.91	602.41	599.32	596.59	594.18
65,000	656.40	652.61	649.26	646.31	643.69
70,000	706.90	702.81	699.21	696.02	693.21
75,000	757.39	753.01	749.15	745.74	742.72
80,000	807.88	803.21	799.09	795.45	792.24
85,000	858.37	853.41	849.04	845.17	841.75
90,000	908.86	903.61	898.98	894.89	891.27
95,000	959.36	953.81	948.92	944.60	940.78
100,000	1,009.85	1,004.01	998.86	994.32	990.30
110,000	1,110.83	1,104.41	1,098.75	1,093.75	1,089.33
120,000	1,211.82	1,204.81	1,198.64	1,193.18	1,188.35
125,000	1,262.31	1,255.01	1,248.58	1,242.90	1,237.87
130,000	1,312.80	1,305.22	1,298.52	1,292.61	1,287.38
140,000	1,413.79	1,405.62	1,398.41	1,392.04	1,386.41
150,000	1,514.77	1,506.02	1,498.29	1,491.47	1,485.44
160,000	1,615.76	1,606.42	1,598.18	1,590.90	1,584.47
170,000	1,716.74	1,706.82	1,698.07	1,690.34	1,683.50
175,000	1,767.23	1,757.02	1,748.01	1,740.05	1,733.02
180,000	1,817.72	1,807.22	1,797.95	1,789.77	1,782.53
190,000	1,918.71	1,907.62	1,897.84	1,889.20	1,881.56
200,000	2,019.69	2,008.02	1,997.72	1,988.63	1,980.59
220,000	2,221.66	2,208.82	2,197.50	2,187.49	2,178.65
225,000	2,272.15	2,259.02	2,247.44	2,237.21	2,228.16
230,000	2,322.65	2,309.22	2,297.38	2,286.92	2,277.68
240,000	2,423.63	2,409.62	2,397.27	2,386.35	2,376.70
$250,000	2,524.61	2,510.02	2,497.15	2,485.79	2,475.73

Table 1   111

11.75%   Monthly Payment Loans

Amortization Period in Years

	5	7	8	10	12
$ 100	2.22	1.76	1.62	1.43	1.30
200	4.43	3.51	3.23	2.85	2.60
300	6.64	5.26	4.84	4.27	3.90
400	8.85	7.01	6.45	5.69	5.20
500	11.06	8.76	8.06	7.11	6.50
600	13.28	10.52	9.67	8.53	7.79
700	15.49	12.27	11.29	9.95	9.09
800	17.70	14.02	12.90	11.37	10.39
900	19.91	15.77	14.51	12.79	11.69
1,000	22.12	17.52	16.12	14.21	12.99
2,000	44.24	35.04	32.24	28.41	25.97
3,000	66.36	52.56	48.35	42.61	38.95
4,000	88.48	70.08	64.47	56.82	51.94
5,000	110.60	87.60	80.58	71.02	64.92
6,000	132.71	105.12	96.70	85.22	77.90
7,000	154.83	122.64	112.82	99.43	90.89
8,000	176.95	140.16	128.93	113.63	103.87
9,000	199.07	157.68	145.05	127.83	116.85
10,000	221.19	175.20	161.16	142.03	129.84
15,000	331.78	262.79	241.74	213.05	194.75
20,000	442.37	350.39	322.32	284.06	259.67
25,000	552.96	437.99	402.90	355.08	324.59
30,000	663.55	525.58	483.48	426.09	389.50
35,000	774.15	613.18	564.06	497.11	454.42
40,000	884.74	700.78	644.64	568.12	519.34
45,000	995.33	788.37	725.22	639.14	584.25
50,000	1,105.92	875.97	805.79	710.15	649.17
55,000	1,216.51	963.57	886.37	781.17	714.08
60,000	1,327.10	1,051.16	966.95	852.18	779.00
65,000	1,437.70	1,138.76	1,047.53	923.20	843.92
70,000	1,548.29	1,226.36	1,128.11	994.21	908.83
75,000	1,658.88	1,313.95	1,208.69	1,065.23	973.75
80,000	1,769.47	1,401.55	1,289.27	1,136.24	1,038.67
85,000	1,880.06	1,489.15	1,369.85	1,207.26	1,103.58
90,000	1,990.65	1,576.74	1,450.43	1,278.27	1,168.50
95,000	2,101.25	1,664.34	1,531.01	1,349.28	1,233.41
100,000	2,211.84	1,751.94	1,611.58	1,420.30	1,298.33
110,000	2,433.02	1,927.13	1,772.74	1,562.33	1,428.16
120,000	2,654.20	2,102.32	1,933.90	1,704.36	1,558.00
125,000	2,764.80	2,189.92	2,014.48	1,775.37	1,622.91
130,000	2,875.39	2,277.52	2,095.06	1,846.39	1,687.83
140,000	3,096.57	2,452.71	2,256.22	1,988.42	1,817.66
150,000	3,317.75	2,627.90	2,417.37	2,130.45	1,947.49
160,000	3,538.94	2,803.10	2,578.53	2,272.48	2,077.33
170,000	3,760.12	2,978.29	2,739.69	2,414.51	2,207.16
175,000	3,870.71	3,065.89	2,820.27	2,485.52	2,272.07
180,000	3,981.30	3,153.48	2,900.85	2,556.54	2,336.99
190,000	4,202.49	3,328.68	3,062.01	2,698.56	2,466.82
200,000	4,423.67	3,503.87	3,223.16	2,840.59	2,596.66
220,000	4,866.04	3,854.25	3,545.48	3,124.65	2,856.32
225,000	4,976.63	3,941.85	3,626.06	3,195.67	2,921.24
230,000	5,087.22	4,029.45	3,706.64	3,266.68	2,986.15
240,000	5,308.40	4,204.64	3,867.80	3,408.71	3,115.99
$250,000	5,529.59	4,379.83	4,028.95	3,550.74	3,245.82

Monthly Payment Loans   **11.75%**

Amortization Period in Years

	15	16	17	18	20
$ 100	1.19	1.16	1.14	1.12	1.09
200	2.37	2.32	2.27	2.24	2.17
300	3.56	3.48	3.41	3.35	3.26
400	4.74	4.63	4.54	4.47	4.34
500	5.93	5.79	5.68	5.58	5.42
600	7.11	6.95	6.81	6.70	6.51
700	8.29	8.11	7.95	7.81	7.59
800	9.48	9.26	9.08	8.93	8.67
900	10.66	10.42	10.22	10.04	9.76
1,000	11.85	11.58	11.35	11.16	10.84
2,000	23.69	23.15	22.70	22.31	21.68
3,000	35.53	34.73	34.04	33.46	32.52
4,000	47.37	46.30	45.39	44.61	43.35
5,000	59.21	57.87	56.74	55.76	54.19
6,000	71.05	69.45	68.08	66.91	65.03
7,000	82.89	81.02	79.43	78.06	75.86
8,000	94.74	92.60	90.77	89.21	86.70
9,000	106.58	104.17	102.12	100.36	97.54
10,000	118.42	115.74	113.47	111.51	108.38
15,000	177.62	173.61	170.20	167.27	162.56
20,000	236.83	231.48	226.93	223.02	216.75
25,000	296.04	289.35	283.66	278.77	270.93
30,000	355.24	347.22	340.39	334.53	325.12
35,000	414.45	405.09	397.12	390.28	379.30
40,000	473.66	462.96	453.85	446.03	433.49
45,000	532.86	520.83	510.58	501.79	487.67
50,000	592.07	578.70	567.31	557.54	541.86
55,000	651.28	636.57	624.04	613.29	596.04
60,000	710.48	694.44	680.77	669.05	650.23
65,000	769.69	752.31	737.50	724.80	704.41
70,000	828.90	810.18	794.23	780.56	758.60
75,000	888.10	868.05	850.96	836.31	812.79
80,000	947.31	925.92	907.69	892.06	866.97
85,000	1,006.52	983.79	964.42	947.82	921.16
90,000	1,065.72	1,041.66	1,021.15	1,003.57	975.34
95,000	1,124.93	1,099.53	1,077.88	1,059.32	1,029.53
100,000	1,184.14	1,157.40	1,134.61	1,115.08	1,083.71
110,000	1,302.55	1,273.14	1,248.07	1,226.58	1,192.08
120,000	1,420.96	1,388.88	1,361.53	1,338.09	1,300.45
125,000	1,480.17	1,446.75	1,418.26	1,393.85	1,354.64
130,000	1,539.38	1,504.62	1,474.99	1,449.60	1,408.82
140,000	1,657.79	1,620.36	1,588.45	1,561.11	1,517.19
150,000	1,776.20	1,736.10	1,701.91	1,672.61	1,625.57
160,000	1,894.62	1,851.84	1,815.37	1,784.12	1,733.94
170,000	2,013.03	1,967.58	1,928.84	1,895.63	1,842.31
175,000	2,072.23	2,025.45	1,985.57	1,951.38	1,896.49
180,000	2,131.44	2,083.32	2,042.30	2,007.14	1,950.68
190,000	2,249.85	2,199.06	2,155.76	2,118.64	2,059.05
200,000	2,368.27	2,314.80	2,269.22	2,230.15	2,167.42
220,000	2,605.09	2,546.28	2,496.14	2,453.16	2,384.16
225,000	2,664.30	2,604.15	2,552.87	2,508.92	2,438.35
230,000	2,723.51	2,662.02	2,609.60	2,564.67	2,492.53
240,000	2,841.92	2,777.76	2,723.06	2,676.18	2,600.90
$250,000	2,960.33	2,893.50	2,836.52	2,787.69	2,709.27

Table 1   113

11.75%   Monthly Payment Loans

Amortization Period in Years

	21	22	23	24	25
$ 100	1.08	1.07	1.06	1.05	1.04
200	2.15	2.13	2.11	2.09	2.07
300	3.22	3.19	3.16	3.13	3.11
400	4.29	4.25	4.21	4.17	4.14
500	5.36	5.31	5.26	5.22	5.18
600	6.43	6.37	6.31	6.26	6.21
700	7.50	7.43	7.36	7.30	7.25
800	8.57	8.49	8.41	8.34	8.28
900	9.64	9.55	9.46	9.38	9.32
1,000	10.72	10.61	10.51	10.43	10.35
2,000	21.43	21.21	21.02	20.85	20.70
3,000	32.14	31.81	31.52	31.27	31.05
4,000	42.85	42.41	42.03	41.69	41.40
5,000	53.56	53.01	52.53	52.11	51.74
6,000	64.27	63.61	63.04	62.53	62.09
7,000	74.98	74.21	73.54	72.95	72.44
8,000	85.69	84.81	84.05	83.38	82.79
9,000	96.40	95.41	94.55	93.80	93.14
10,000	107.11	106.02	105.06	104.22	103.48
15,000	160.67	159.02	157.58	156.33	155.22
20,000	214.22	212.03	210.11	208.43	206.96
25,000	267.78	265.03	262.64	260.54	258.70
30,000	321.33	318.04	315.16	312.65	310.44
35,000	374.89	371.04	367.69	364.75	362.18
40,000	428.44	424.05	420.21	416.86	413.92
45,000	481.99	477.05	472.74	468.97	465.66
50,000	535.55	530.06	525.27	521.08	517.40
55,000	589.10	583.06	577.79	573.18	569.14
60,000	642.66	636.07	630.32	625.29	620.88
65,000	696.21	689.07	682.85	677.40	672.62
70,000	749.77	742.08	735.37	729.50	724.36
75,000	803.32	795.08	787.90	781.61	776.10
80,000	856.88	848.09	840.42	833.72	827.84
85,000	910.43	901.09	892.95	885.83	879.58
90,000	963.98	954.10	945.48	937.93	931.32
95,000	1,017.54	1,007.11	998.00	990.04	983.06
100,000	1,071.09	1,060.11	1,050.53	1,042.15	1,034.80
110,000	1,178.20	1,166.12	1,155.58	1,146.36	1,138.28
120,000	1,285.31	1,272.13	1,260.63	1,250.58	1,241.76
125,000	1,338.86	1,325.14	1,313.16	1,302.68	1,293.50
130,000	1,392.42	1,378.14	1,365.69	1,354.79	1,345.24
140,000	1,499.53	1,484.15	1,470.74	1,459.00	1,448.72
150,000	1,606.64	1,590.16	1,575.79	1,563.22	1,552.20
160,000	1,713.75	1,696.17	1,680.84	1,667.43	1,655.68
170,000	1,820.85	1,802.18	1,785.89	1,771.65	1,759.16
175,000	1,874.41	1,855.19	1,838.42	1,823.75	1,810.90
180,000	1,927.96	1,908.20	1,890.95	1,875.86	1,862.64
190,000	2,035.07	2,014.21	1,996.00	1,980.08	1,966.12
200,000	2,142.18	2,120.22	2,101.05	2,084.29	2,069.60
220,000	2,356.40	2,332.24	2,311.16	2,292.72	2,276.56
225,000	2,409.95	2,385.24	2,363.68	2,344.83	2,328.30
230,000	2,463.51	2,438.25	2,416.21	2,396.93	2,380.04
240,000	2,570.62	2,544.26	2,521.26	2,501.15	2,483.52
$250,000	2,677.72	2,650.27	2,626.31	2,605.36	2,587.00

Monthly Payment Loans   **11.75%**

Amortization Period in Years

	26	27	28	29	30
$ 100	1.03	1.03	1.02	1.02	1.01
200	2.06	2.05	2.04	2.03	2.02
300	3.09	3.07	3.06	3.04	3.03
400	4.12	4.10	4.08	4.06	4.04
500	5.15	5.12	5.09	5.07	5.05
600	6.18	6.14	6.11	6.08	6.06
700	7.20	7.16	7.13	7.10	7.07
800	8.23	8.19	8.15	8.11	8.08
900	9.26	9.21	9.16	9.12	9.09
1,000	10.29	10.23	10.18	10.14	10.10
2,000	20.57	20.46	20.36	20.27	20.19
3,000	30.86	30.69	30.54	30.40	30.29
4,000	41.14	40.91	40.71	40.54	40.38
5,000	51.42	51.14	50.89	50.67	50.48
6,000	61.71	61.37	61.07	60.80	60.57
7,000	71.99	71.59	71.24	70.94	70.66
8,000	82.27	81.82	81.42	81.07	80.76
9,000	92.56	92.05	91.60	91.20	90.85
10,000	102.84	102.27	101.77	101.33	100.95
15,000	154.26	153.41	152.66	152.00	151.42
20,000	205.68	204.54	203.54	202.66	201.89
25,000	257.09	255.68	254.43	253.33	252.36
30,000	308.51	306.81	305.31	303.99	302.83
35,000	359.93	357.94	356.20	354.66	353.30
40,000	411.35	409.08	407.08	405.32	403.77
45,000	462.76	460.21	457.97	455.99	454.24
50,000	514.18	511.35	508.85	506.65	504.71
55,000	565.60	562.48	559.74	557.32	555.18
60,000	617.02	613.61	610.62	607.98	605.65
65,000	668.43	664.75	661.50	658.64	656.12
70,000	719.85	715.88	712.39	709.31	706.59
75,000	771.27	767.02	763.27	759.97	757.06
80,000	822.69	818.15	814.16	810.64	807.53
85,000	874.10	869.28	865.04	861.30	858.00
90,000	925.52	920.42	915.93	911.97	908.47
95,000	976.94	971.55	966.81	962.63	958.94
100,000	1,028.36	1,022.69	1,017.70	1,013.30	1,009.41
110,000	1,131.19	1,124.96	1,119.47	1,114.63	1,110.36
120,000	1,234.03	1,227.22	1,221.23	1,215.96	1,211.30
125,000	1,285.44	1,278.36	1,272.12	1,266.62	1,261.77
130,000	1,336.86	1,329.49	1,323.00	1,317.28	1,312.24
140,000	1,439.70	1,431.76	1,424.77	1,418.61	1,413.18
150,000	1,542.53	1,534.03	1,526.54	1,519.94	1,514.12
160,000	1,645.37	1,636.30	1,628.31	1,621.27	1,615.06
170,000	1,748.20	1,738.56	1,730.08	1,722.60	1,716.00
175,000	1,799.62	1,789.70	1,780.96	1,773.27	1,766.47
180,000	1,851.04	1,840.83	1,831.85	1,823.93	1,816.94
190,000	1,953.87	1,943.10	1,933.62	1,925.26	1,917.88
200,000	2,056.71	2,045.37	2,035.39	2,026.59	2,018.82
220,000	2,262.38	2,249.91	2,238.93	2,229.25	2,220.71
225,000	2,313.79	2,301.04	2,289.81	2,279.91	2,271.18
230,000	2,365.21	2,352.17	2,340.69	2,330.58	2,321.65
240,000	2,468.05	2,454.44	2,442.46	2,431.91	2,422.59
$250,000	2,570.88	2,556.71	2,544.23	2,533.23	2,523.53

Table 1   115

12.00%   Monthly Payment Loans

Amortization Period in Years

	5	7	8	10	12
$ 100	2.23	1.77	1.63	1.44	1.32
200	4.45	3.54	3.26	2.87	2.63
300	6.68	5.30	4.88	4.31	3.95
400	8.90	7.07	6.51	5.74	5.26
500	11.13	8.83	8.13	7.18	6.57
600	13.35	10.60	9.76	8.61	7.89
700	15.58	12.36	11.38	10.05	9.20
800	17.80	14.13	13.01	11.48	10.51
900	20.03	15.89	14.63	12.92	11.83
1,000	22.25	17.66	16.26	14.35	13.14
2,000	44.49	35.31	32.51	28.70	26.27
3,000	66.74	52.96	48.76	43.05	39.41
4,000	88.98	70.62	65.02	57.39	52.54
5,000	111.23	88.27	81.27	71.74	65.68
6,000	133.47	105.92	97.52	86.09	78.81
7,000	155.72	123.57	113.77	100.43	91.94
8,000	177.96	141.23	130.03	114.78	105.08
9,000	200.21	158.88	146.28	129.13	118.21
10,000	222.45	176.53	162.53	143.48	131.35
15,000	333.67	264.80	243.80	215.21	197.02
20,000	444.89	353.06	325.06	286.95	262.69
25,000	556.12	441.32	406.33	358.68	328.36
30,000	667.34	529.59	487.59	430.42	394.03
35,000	778.56	617.85	568.85	502.15	459.70
40,000	889.78	706.11	650.12	573.89	525.37
45,000	1,001.01	794.38	731.38	645.62	591.04
50,000	1,112.23	882.64	812.65	717.36	656.71
55,000	1,223.45	970.91	893.91	789.10	722.39
60,000	1,334.67	1,059.17	975.18	860.83	788.06
65,000	1,445.89	1,147.43	1,056.44	932.57	853.73
70,000	1,557.12	1,235.70	1,137.70	1,004.30	919.40
75,000	1,668.34	1,323.96	1,218.97	1,076.04	985.07
80,000	1,779.56	1,412.22	1,300.23	1,147.77	1,050.74
85,000	1,890.78	1,500.49	1,381.50	1,219.51	1,116.41
90,000	2,002.01	1,588.75	1,462.76	1,291.24	1,182.08
95,000	2,113.23	1,677.01	1,544.02	1,362.98	1,247.75
100,000	2,224.45	1,765.28	1,625.29	1,434.71	1,313.42
110,000	2,446.89	1,941.81	1,787.82	1,578.19	1,444.77
120,000	2,669.34	2,118.33	1,950.35	1,721.66	1,576.11
125,000	2,780.56	2,206.60	2,031.61	1,793.39	1,641.78
130,000	2,891.78	2,294.86	2,112.87	1,865.13	1,707.45
140,000	3,114.23	2,471.39	2,275.40	2,008.60	1,838.79
150,000	3,336.67	2,647.91	2,437.93	2,152.07	1,970.13
160,000	3,559.12	2,824.44	2,600.46	2,295.54	2,101.48
170,000	3,781.56	3,000.97	2,762.99	2,439.01	2,232.82
175,000	3,892.78	3,089.23	2,844.25	2,510.75	2,298.49
180,000	4,004.01	3,177.50	2,925.52	2,582.48	2,364.16
190,000	4,226.45	3,354.02	3,088.04	2,725.95	2,495.50
200,000	4,448.89	3,530.55	3,250.57	2,869.42	2,626.84
220,000	4,893.78	3,883.61	3,575.63	3,156.37	2,889.53
225,000	5,005.01	3,971.87	3,656.89	3,228.10	2,955.20
230,000	5,116.23	4,060.13	3,738.16	3,299.84	3,020.87
240,000	5,338.67	4,236.66	3,900.69	3,443.31	3,152.21
$250,000	5,561.12	4,413.19	4,063.22	3,586.78	3,283.55

Monthly Payment Loans   **12.00%**

Amortization Period in Years

	15	16	17	18	20
$ 100	1.21	1.18	1.16	1.14	1.11
200	2.41	2.35	2.31	2.27	2.21
300	3.61	3.53	3.46	3.40	3.31
400	4.81	4.70	4.61	4.53	4.41
500	6.01	5.87	5.76	5.66	5.51
600	7.21	7.05	6.91	6.80	6.61
700	8.41	8.22	8.06	7.93	7.71
800	9.61	9.39	9.21	9.06	8.81
900	10.81	10.57	10.37	10.19	9.91
1,000	12.01	11.74	11.52	11.32	11.02
2,000	24.01	23.48	23.03	22.64	22.03
3,000	36.01	35.22	34.54	33.96	33.04
4,000	48.01	46.95	46.05	45.28	44.05
5,000	60.01	58.69	57.57	56.60	55.06
6,000	72.02	70.43	69.08	67.92	66.07
7,000	84.02	82.17	80.59	79.24	77.08
8,000	96.02	93.90	92.10	90.56	88.09
9,000	108.02	105.64	103.61	101.88	99.10
10,000	120.02	117.38	115.13	113.20	110.11
15,000	180.03	176.06	172.69	169.80	165.17
20,000	240.04	234.75	230.25	226.40	220.22
25,000	300.05	293.44	287.81	282.99	275.28
30,000	360.06	352.12	345.37	339.59	330.33
35,000	420.06	410.81	402.93	396.19	385.39
40,000	480.07	469.50	460.49	452.79	440.44
45,000	540.08	528.18	518.05	509.38	495.49
50,000	600.09	586.87	575.61	565.98	550.55
55,000	660.10	645.55	633.17	622.58	605.60
60,000	720.11	704.24	690.73	679.18	660.66
65,000	780.11	762.93	748.30	735.77	715.71
70,000	840.12	821.61	805.86	792.37	770.77
75,000	900.13	880.30	863.42	848.97	825.82
80,000	960.14	938.99	920.98	905.57	880.87
85,000	1,020.15	997.67	978.54	962.16	935.93
90,000	1,080.16	1,056.36	1,036.10	1,018.76	990.98
95,000	1,140.16	1,115.04	1,093.66	1,075.36	1,046.04
100,000	1,200.17	1,173.73	1,151.22	1,131.96	1,101.09
110,000	1,320.19	1,291.10	1,266.34	1,245.15	1,211.20
120,000	1,440.21	1,408.48	1,381.46	1,358.35	1,321.31
125,000	1,500.22	1,467.16	1,439.02	1,414.94	1,376.36
130,000	1,560.22	1,525.85	1,496.59	1,471.54	1,431.42
140,000	1,680.24	1,643.22	1,611.71	1,584.74	1,541.53
150,000	1,800.26	1,760.59	1,726.83	1,697.93	1,651.63
160,000	1,920.27	1,877.97	1,841.95	1,811.13	1,761.74
170,000	2,040.29	1,995.34	1,957.07	1,924.32	1,871.85
175,000	2,100.30	2,054.02	2,014.63	1,980.92	1,926.91
180,000	2,160.31	2,112.71	2,072.19	2,037.52	1,981.96
190,000	2,280.32	2,230.08	2,187.31	2,150.71	2,092.07
200,000	2,400.34	2,347.46	2,302.44	2,263.91	2,202.18
220,000	2,640.37	2,582.20	2,532.68	2,490.30	2,422.39
225,000	2,700.38	2,640.89	2,590.24	2,546.89	2,477.45
230,000	2,760.39	2,699.57	2,647.80	2,603.49	2,532.50
240,000	2,880.41	2,816.95	2,762.92	2,716.69	2,642.61
$250,000	3,000.43	2,934.32	2,878.04	2,829.88	2,752.72

Table 1   117

12.00% Monthly Payment Loans

Amortization Period in Years

	21	22	23	24	25
$ 100	1.09	1.08	1.07	1.07	1.06
200	2.18	2.16	2.14	2.13	2.11
300	3.27	3.24	3.21	3.19	3.16
400	4.36	4.32	4.28	4.25	4.22
500	5.45	5.39	5.35	5.31	5.27
600	6.54	6.47	6.42	6.37	6.32
700	7.63	7.55	7.48	7.43	7.38
800	8.71	8.63	8.55	8.49	8.43
900	9.80	9.71	9.62	9.55	9.48
1,000	10.89	10.78	10.69	10.61	10.54
2,000	21.78	21.56	21.38	21.21	21.07
3,000	32.67	32.34	32.06	31.82	31.60
4,000	43.55	43.12	42.75	42.42	42.13
5,000	54.44	53.90	53.43	53.02	52.67
6,000	65.33	64.68	64.12	63.63	63.20
7,000	76.21	75.46	74.80	74.23	73.73
8,000	87.10	86.24	85.49	84.84	84.26
9,000	97.99	97.02	96.18	95.44	94.80
10,000	108.87	107.80	106.86	106.04	105.33
15,000	163.31	161.70	160.29	159.06	157.99
20,000	217.74	215.59	213.72	212.08	210.65
25,000	272.18	269.49	267.15	265.10	263.31
30,000	326.61	323.39	320.57	318.12	315.97
35,000	381.05	377.28	374.00	371.14	368.63
40,000	435.48	431.18	427.43	424.16	421.29
45,000	489.92	485.08	480.86	477.18	473.96
50,000	544.35	538.97	534.29	530.20	526.62
55,000	598.79	592.87	587.72	583.22	579.28
60,000	653.22	646.77	641.14	636.23	631.94
65,000	707.66	700.66	694.57	689.25	684.60
70,000	762.09	754.56	748.00	742.27	737.26
75,000	816.53	808.46	801.43	795.29	789.92
80,000	870.96	862.36	854.86	848.31	842.58
85,000	925.40	916.25	908.29	901.33	895.25
90,000	979.83	970.15	961.71	954.35	947.91
95,000	1,034.27	1,024.05	1,015.14	1,007.37	1,000.57
100,000	1,088.70	1,077.94	1,068.57	1,060.39	1,053.23
110,000	1,197.57	1,185.74	1,175.43	1,166.43	1,158.55
120,000	1,306.44	1,293.53	1,282.28	1,272.46	1,263.87
125,000	1,360.88	1,347.43	1,335.71	1,325.48	1,316.54
130,000	1,415.31	1,401.32	1,389.14	1,378.50	1,369.20
140,000	1,524.18	1,509.12	1,496.00	1,484.54	1,474.52
150,000	1,633.05	1,616.91	1,602.85	1,590.58	1,579.84
160,000	1,741.92	1,724.71	1,709.71	1,696.62	1,685.16
170,000	1,850.79	1,832.50	1,816.57	1,802.65	1,790.49
175,000	1,905.23	1,886.40	1,869.99	1,855.67	1,843.15
180,000	1,959.66	1,940.29	1,923.42	1,908.69	1,895.81
190,000	2,068.53	2,048.09	2,030.28	2,014.73	2,001.13
200,000	2,177.40	2,155.88	2,137.13	2,120.77	2,106.45
220,000	2,395.14	2,371.47	2,350.85	2,332.85	2,317.10
225,000	2,449.58	2,425.37	2,404.28	2,385.86	2,369.76
230,000	2,504.01	2,479.26	2,457.70	2,438.88	2,422.42
240,000	2,612.88	2,587.06	2,564.56	2,544.92	2,527.74
$250,000	2,721.75	2,694.85	2,671.42	2,650.96	2,633.07

Monthly Payment Loans   **12.00%**

Amortization Period in Years

$	26	27	28	29	30
100	1.05	1.05	1.04	1.04	1.03
200	2.10	2.09	2.08	2.07	2.06
300	3.15	3.13	3.11	3.10	3.09
400	4.19	4.17	4.15	4.13	4.12
500	5.24	5.21	5.19	5.17	5.15
600	6.29	6.25	6.22	6.20	6.18
700	7.33	7.30	7.26	7.23	7.21
800	8.38	8.34	8.30	8.26	8.23
900	9.43	9.38	9.33	9.30	9.26
1,000	10.47	10.42	10.37	10.33	10.29
2,000	20.94	20.83	20.74	20.65	20.58
3,000	31.41	31.25	31.10	30.98	30.86
4,000	41.88	41.66	41.47	41.30	41.15
5,000	52.35	52.08	51.84	51.62	51.44
6,000	62.82	62.49	62.20	61.95	61.72
7,000	73.29	72.91	72.57	72.27	72.01
8,000	83.76	83.32	82.93	82.59	82.29
9,000	94.23	93.74	93.30	92.92	92.58
10,000	104.70	104.15	103.67	103.24	102.87
15,000	157.05	156.22	155.50	154.86	154.30
20,000	209.40	208.29	207.33	206.48	205.73
25,000	261.74	260.37	259.16	258.09	257.16
30,000	314.09	312.44	310.99	309.71	308.59
35,000	366.44	364.51	362.82	361.33	360.02
40,000	418.79	416.58	414.65	412.95	411.45
45,000	471.13	468.66	466.48	464.57	462.88
50,000	523.48	520.73	518.31	516.18	514.31
55,000	575.83	572.80	570.14	567.80	565.74
60,000	628.18	624.87	621.97	619.42	617.17
65,000	680.52	676.95	673.80	671.04	668.60
70,000	732.87	729.02	725.63	722.66	720.03
75,000	785.22	781.09	777.46	774.27	771.46
80,000	837.57	833.16	829.30	825.89	822.90
85,000	889.91	885.24	881.13	877.51	874.33
90,000	942.26	937.31	932.96	929.13	925.76
95,000	994.61	989.38	984.79	980.75	977.19
100,000	1,046.96	1,041.45	1,036.62	1,032.36	1,028.62
110,000	1,151.65	1,145.60	1,140.28	1,135.60	1,131.48
120,000	1,256.35	1,249.74	1,243.94	1,238.84	1,234.34
125,000	1,308.70	1,301.82	1,295.77	1,290.45	1,285.77
130,000	1,361.04	1,353.89	1,347.60	1,342.07	1,337.20
140,000	1,465.74	1,458.03	1,451.26	1,445.31	1,440.06
150,000	1,570.43	1,562.18	1,554.92	1,548.54	1,542.92
160,000	1,675.13	1,666.32	1,658.59	1,651.78	1,645.79
170,000	1,779.82	1,770.47	1,762.25	1,755.01	1,748.65
175,000	1,832.17	1,822.54	1,814.08	1,806.63	1,800.08
180,000	1,884.52	1,874.61	1,865.91	1,858.25	1,851.51
190,000	1,989.21	1,978.76	1,969.57	1,961.49	1,954.37
200,000	2,093.91	2,082.90	2,073.23	2,064.72	2,057.23
220,000	2,303.30	2,291.19	2,280.55	2,271.19	2,262.95
225,000	2,355.65	2,343.26	2,332.38	2,322.81	2,314.38
230,000	2,408.00	2,395.34	2,384.21	2,374.43	2,365.81
240,000	2,512.69	2,499.48	2,487.88	2,477.67	2,468.68
$250,000	2,617.39	2,603.63	2,591.54	2,580.90	2,571.54

Table 1   119

12.25%   Monthly Payment Loans

Amortization Period in Years

	5	7	8	10	12
$ 100	2.24	1.78	1.64	1.45	1.33
200	4.48	3.56	3.28	2.90	2.66
300	6.72	5.34	4.92	4.35	3.99
400	8.95	7.12	6.56	5.80	5.32
500	11.19	8.90	8.20	7.25	6.65
600	13.43	10.68	9.84	8.70	7.98
700	15.66	12.46	11.48	10.15	9.31
800	17.90	14.23	13.12	11.60	10.63
900	20.14	16.01	14.76	13.05	11.96
1,000	22.38	17.79	16.40	14.50	13.29
2,000	44.75	35.58	32.79	28.99	26.58
3,000	67.12	53.37	49.18	43.48	39.86
4,000	89.49	71.15	65.57	57.97	53.15
5,000	111.86	88.94	81.96	72.46	66.43
6,000	134.23	106.73	98.35	86.96	79.72
7,000	156.60	124.51	114.74	101.45	93.01
8,000	178.97	142.30	131.13	115.94	106.29
9,000	201.34	160.09	147.52	130.43	119.58
10,000	223.71	177.87	163.91	144.92	132.86
15,000	335.57	266.81	245.86	217.38	199.29
20,000	447.42	355.74	327.82	289.84	265.72
25,000	559.28	444.67	409.77	362.30	332.15
30,000	671.13	533.61	491.72	434.76	398.58
35,000	782.99	622.54	573.67	507.22	465.01
40,000	894.84	711.47	655.63	579.68	531.44
45,000	1,006.70	800.41	737.58	652.14	597.87
50,000	1,118.55	889.34	819.53	724.60	664.30
55,000	1,230.41	978.27	901.48	797.06	730.73
60,000	1,342.26	1,067.21	983.44	869.52	797.16
65,000	1,454.12	1,156.14	1,065.39	941.98	863.59
70,000	1,565.97	1,245.07	1,147.34	1,014.44	930.02
75,000	1,677.83	1,334.01	1,229.29	1,086.90	996.45
80,000	1,789.68	1,422.94	1,311.25	1,159.36	1,062.88
85,000	1,901.54	1,511.88	1,393.20	1,231.82	1,129.31
90,000	2,013.39	1,600.81	1,475.15	1,304.28	1,195.74
95,000	2,125.25	1,689.74	1,557.10	1,376.74	1,262.17
100,000	2,237.10	1,778.68	1,639.06	1,449.20	1,328.60
110,000	2,460.81	1,956.54	1,802.96	1,594.12	1,461.46
120,000	2,684.52	2,134.41	1,966.87	1,739.04	1,594.32
125,000	2,796.38	2,223.34	2,048.82	1,811.50	1,660.75
130,000	2,908.23	2,312.28	2,130.77	1,883.96	1,727.18
140,000	3,131.94	2,490.14	2,294.68	2,028.88	1,860.04
150,000	3,355.65	2,668.01	2,458.58	2,173.80	1,992.90
160,000	3,579.36	2,845.88	2,622.49	2,318.72	2,125.76
170,000	3,803.07	3,023.75	2,786.39	2,463.64	2,258.62
175,000	3,914.93	3,112.68	2,868.34	2,536.10	2,325.05
180,000	4,026.78	3,201.61	2,950.30	2,608.56	2,391.48
190,000	4,250.49	3,379.48	3,114.20	2,753.48	2,524.34
200,000	4,474.20	3,557.35	3,278.11	2,898.40	2,657.20
220,000	4,921.62	3,913.08	3,605.92	3,188.24	2,922.92
225,000	5,033.48	4,002.01	3,687.87	3,260.70	2,989.35
230,000	5,145.33	4,090.95	3,769.82	3,333.16	3,055.78
240,000	5,369.04	4,268.81	3,933.73	3,478.08	3,188.64
$250,000	5,592.75	4,446.68	4,097.63	3,623.00	3,321.50

Monthly Payment Loans **12.25%**

Amortization Period in Years

	15	16	17	18	20
$ 100	1.22	1.20	1.17	1.15	1.12
200	2.44	2.39	2.34	2.30	2.24
300	3.65	3.58	3.51	3.45	3.36
400	4.87	4.77	4.68	4.60	4.48
500	6.09	5.96	5.84	5.75	5.60
600	7.30	7.15	7.01	6.90	6.72
700	8.52	8.34	8.18	8.05	7.83
800	9.74	9.53	9.35	9.20	8.95
900	10.95	10.72	10.52	10.35	10.07
1,000	12.17	11.91	11.68	11.49	11.19
2,000	24.33	23.81	23.36	22.98	22.38
3,000	36.49	35.71	35.04	34.47	33.56
4,000	48.66	47.61	46.72	45.96	44.75
5,000	60.82	59.51	58.40	57.45	55.93
6,000	72.98	71.41	70.08	68.94	67.12
7,000	85.15	83.32	81.76	80.43	78.30
8,000	97.31	95.22	93.44	91.92	89.49
9,000	109.47	107.12	105.12	103.41	100.68
10,000	121.63	119.02	116.80	114.90	111.86
15,000	182.45	178.53	175.19	172.34	167.79
20,000	243.26	238.04	233.59	229.79	223.72
25,000	304.08	297.54	291.99	287.24	279.65
30,000	364.89	357.05	350.38	344.68	335.57
35,000	425.71	416.56	408.78	402.13	391.50
40,000	486.52	476.07	467.17	459.58	447.43
45,000	547.34	535.57	525.57	517.02	503.36
50,000	608.15	595.08	583.97	574.47	559.29
55,000	668.97	654.59	642.36	631.91	615.22
60,000	729.78	714.10	700.76	689.36	671.14
65,000	790.60	773.60	759.15	746.81	727.07
70,000	851.41	833.11	817.55	804.25	783.00
75,000	912.23	892.62	875.95	861.70	838.93
80,000	973.04	952.13	934.34	919.15	894.86
85,000	1,033.86	1,011.63	992.74	976.59	950.78
90,000	1,094.67	1,071.14	1,051.14	1,034.04	1,006.71
95,000	1,155.49	1,130.65	1,109.53	1,091.49	1,062.64
100,000	1,216.30	1,190.16	1,167.93	1,148.93	1,118.57
110,000	1,337.93	1,309.17	1,284.72	1,263.82	1,230.43
120,000	1,459.56	1,428.19	1,401.51	1,378.72	1,342.28
125,000	1,520.38	1,487.69	1,459.91	1,436.16	1,398.21
130,000	1,581.19	1,547.20	1,518.30	1,493.61	1,454.14
140,000	1,702.82	1,666.22	1,635.10	1,608.50	1,566.00
150,000	1,824.45	1,785.23	1,751.89	1,723.40	1,677.85
160,000	1,946.08	1,904.25	1,868.68	1,838.29	1,789.71
170,000	2,067.71	2,023.26	1,985.47	1,953.18	1,901.56
175,000	2,128.53	2,082.77	2,043.87	2,010.63	1,957.49
180,000	2,189.34	2,142.28	2,102.27	2,068.07	2,013.42
190,000	2,310.97	2,261.29	2,219.06	2,182.97	2,125.28
200,000	2,432.60	2,380.31	2,335.85	2,297.86	2,237.13
220,000	2,675.86	2,618.34	2,569.43	2,527.64	2,460.85
225,000	2,736.68	2,677.84	2,627.83	2,585.09	2,516.78
230,000	2,797.49	2,737.35	2,686.23	2,642.54	2,572.70
240,000	2,919.12	2,856.37	2,803.02	2,757.43	2,684.56
$250,000	3,040.75	2,975.38	2,919.81	2,872.32	2,796.42

Table 1   121

12.25%   Monthly Payment Loans

Amortization Period in Years

	21	22	23	24	25
$ 100	1.11	1.10	1.09	1.08	1.08
200	2.22	2.20	2.18	2.16	2.15
300	3.32	3.29	3.27	3.24	3.22
400	4.43	4.39	4.35	4.32	4.29
500	5.54	5.48	5.44	5.40	5.36
600	6.64	6.58	6.53	6.48	6.44
700	7.75	7.68	7.61	7.56	7.51
800	8.86	8.77	8.70	8.63	8.58
900	9.96	9.87	9.79	9.71	9.65
1,000	11.07	10.96	10.87	10.79	10.72
2,000	22.13	21.92	21.74	21.58	21.44
3,000	33.20	32.88	32.61	32.37	32.16
4,000	44.26	43.84	43.47	43.15	42.87
5,000	55.33	54.80	54.34	53.94	53.59
6,000	66.39	65.76	65.21	64.73	64.31
7,000	77.45	76.72	76.07	75.52	75.03
8,000	88.52	87.67	86.94	86.30	85.74
9,000	99.58	98.63	97.81	97.09	96.46
10,000	110.65	109.59	108.68	107.88	107.18
15,000	165.97	164.39	163.01	161.81	160.77
20,000	221.29	219.18	217.35	215.75	214.35
25,000	276.61	273.97	271.68	269.68	267.94
30,000	331.93	328.77	326.02	323.62	321.53
35,000	387.25	383.56	380.35	377.56	375.12
40,000	442.57	438.35	434.69	431.49	428.70
45,000	497.89	493.15	489.02	485.43	482.29
50,000	553.21	547.94	543.36	539.36	535.88
55,000	608.53	602.73	597.69	593.30	589.46
60,000	663.85	657.53	652.03	647.24	643.05
65,000	719.17	712.32	706.36	701.17	696.64
70,000	774.49	767.11	760.70	755.11	750.23
75,000	829.81	821.91	815.03	809.04	803.81
80,000	885.13	876.70	869.37	862.98	857.40
85,000	940.45	931.49	923.70	916.91	910.99
90,000	995.77	986.29	978.04	970.85	964.57
95,000	1,051.09	1,041.08	1,032.37	1,024.79	1,018.16
100,000	1,106.42	1,095.87	1,086.71	1,078.72	1,071.75
110,000	1,217.06	1,205.46	1,195.38	1,186.59	1,178.92
120,000	1,327.70	1,315.05	1,304.05	1,294.47	1,286.10
125,000	1,383.02	1,369.84	1,358.38	1,348.40	1,339.68
130,000	1,438.34	1,424.63	1,412.72	1,402.34	1,393.27
140,000	1,548.98	1,534.22	1,521.39	1,510.21	1,500.45
150,000	1,659.62	1,643.81	1,630.06	1,618.08	1,607.62
160,000	1,770.26	1,753.40	1,738.73	1,725.95	1,714.80
170,000	1,880.90	1,862.98	1,847.40	1,833.82	1,821.97
175,000	1,936.22	1,917.78	1,901.74	1,887.76	1,875.56
180,000	1,991.54	1,972.57	1,956.07	1,941.70	1,929.14
190,000	2,102.18	2,082.16	2,064.74	2,049.57	2,036.32
200,000	2,212.83	2,191.74	2,173.41	2,157.44	2,143.49
220,000	2,434.11	2,410.92	2,390.75	2,373.18	2,357.84
225,000	2,489.43	2,465.71	2,445.09	2,427.12	2,411.43
230,000	2,544.75	2,520.50	2,499.42	2,481.05	2,465.02
240,000	2,655.39	2,630.09	2,608.09	2,588.93	2,572.19
$250,000	2,766.03	2,739.68	2,716.76	2,696.80	2,679.36

Monthly Payment Loans   **12.25%**

Amortization Period in Years

	26	27	28	29	30
$ 100	1.07	1.07	1.06	1.06	1.05
200	2.14	2.13	2.12	2.11	2.10
300	3.20	3.19	3.17	3.16	3.15
400	4.27	4.25	4.23	4.21	4.20
500	5.33	5.31	5.28	5.26	5.24
600	6.40	6.37	6.34	6.31	6.29
700	7.46	7.43	7.39	7.37	7.34
800	8.53	8.49	8.45	8.42	8.39
900	9.60	9.55	9.51	9.47	9.44
1,000	10.66	10.61	10.56	10.52	10.48
2,000	21.32	21.21	21.12	21.04	20.96
3,000	31.97	31.81	31.67	31.55	31.44
4,000	42.63	42.42	42.23	42.07	41.92
5,000	53.29	53.02	52.79	52.58	52.40
6,000	63.94	63.62	63.34	63.10	62.88
7,000	74.60	74.23	73.90	73.61	73.36
8,000	85.26	84.83	84.45	84.13	83.84
9,000	95.91	95.43	95.01	94.64	94.32
10,000	106.57	106.04	105.57	105.16	104.79
15,000	159.85	159.05	158.35	157.73	157.19
20,000	213.13	212.07	211.13	210.31	209.58
25,000	266.42	265.08	263.91	262.88	261.98
30,000	319.70	318.10	316.69	315.46	314.37
35,000	372.98	371.11	369.47	368.03	366.77
40,000	426.26	424.13	422.25	420.61	419.16
45,000	479.55	477.14	475.03	473.18	471.56
50,000	532.83	530.16	527.82	525.76	523.95
55,000	586.11	583.17	580.60	578.34	576.35
60,000	639.39	636.19	633.38	630.91	628.74
65,000	692.67	689.20	686.16	683.49	681.14
70,000	745.96	742.22	738.94	736.06	733.53
75,000	799.24	795.23	791.72	788.64	785.93
80,000	852.52	848.25	844.50	841.21	838.32
85,000	905.80	901.26	897.28	893.79	890.72
90,000	959.09	954.28	950.06	946.36	943.11
95,000	1,012.37	1,007.29	1,002.85	998.94	995.51
100,000	1,065.65	1,060.31	1,055.63	1,051.51	1,047.90
110,000	1,172.22	1,166.34	1,161.19	1,156.67	1,152.69
120,000	1,278.78	1,272.37	1,266.75	1,261.82	1,257.48
125,000	1,332.06	1,325.39	1,319.53	1,314.39	1,309.88
130,000	1,385.34	1,378.40	1,372.31	1,366.97	1,362.27
140,000	1,491.91	1,484.43	1,477.87	1,472.12	1,467.06
150,000	1,598.47	1,590.46	1,583.44	1,577.27	1,571.85
160,000	1,705.04	1,696.49	1,689.00	1,682.42	1,676.64
170,000	1,811.60	1,802.52	1,794.56	1,787.57	1,781.43
175,000	1,864.88	1,855.54	1,847.34	1,840.15	1,833.82
180,000	1,918.17	1,908.55	1,900.12	1,892.72	1,886.22
190,000	2,024.73	2,014.58	2,005.69	1,997.87	1,991.01
200,000	2,131.30	2,120.61	2,111.25	2,103.02	2,095.80
220,000	2,344.43	2,332.68	2,322.37	2,313.33	2,305.38
225,000	2,397.71	2,385.69	2,375.15	2,365.90	2,357.77
230,000	2,450.99	2,438.71	2,427.93	2,418.48	2,410.17
240,000	2,557.55	2,544.74	2,533.50	2,523.63	2,514.96
$250,000	2,664.12	2,650.77	2,639.06	2,628.78	2,619.75

Table 1   123

12.50%   Monthly Payment Loans

Amortization Period in Years

	5	7	8	10	12
$ 100	2.25	1.80	1.66	1.47	1.35
200	4.50	3.59	3.31	2.93	2.69
300	6.75	5.38	4.96	4.40	4.04
400	9.00	7.17	6.62	5.86	5.38
500	11.25	8.97	8.27	7.32	6.72
600	13.50	10.76	9.92	8.79	8.07
700	15.75	12.55	11.58	10.25	9.41
800	18.00	14.34	13.23	11.72	10.76
900	20.25	16.13	14.88	13.18	12.10
1,000	22.50	17.93	16.53	14.64	13.44
2,000	45.00	35.85	33.06	29.28	26.88
3,000	67.50	53.77	49.59	43.92	40.32
4,000	90.00	71.69	66.12	58.56	53.76
5,000	112.49	89.61	82.65	73.19	67.20
6,000	134.99	107.53	99.18	87.83	80.64
7,000	157.49	125.45	115.71	102.47	94.08
8,000	179.99	143.37	132.24	117.11	107.51
9,000	202.49	161.30	148.76	131.74	120.95
10,000	224.98	179.22	165.29	146.38	134.39
15,000	337.47	268.82	247.94	219.57	201.58
20,000	449.96	358.43	330.58	292.76	268.78
25,000	562.45	448.04	413.23	365.95	335.97
30,000	674.94	537.64	495.87	439.13	403.16
35,000	787.43	627.25	578.51	512.32	470.36
40,000	899.92	716.85	661.16	585.51	537.55
45,000	1,012.41	806.46	743.80	658.70	604.74
50,000	1,124.90	896.07	826.45	731.89	671.93
55,000	1,237.39	985.67	909.09	805.07	739.13
60,000	1,349.88	1,075.28	991.73	878.26	806.32
65,000	1,462.37	1,164.89	1,074.38	951.45	873.51
70,000	1,574.86	1,254.49	1,157.02	1,024.64	940.71
75,000	1,687.35	1,344.10	1,239.67	1,097.83	1,007.90
80,000	1,799.84	1,433.70	1,322.31	1,171.01	1,075.09
85,000	1,912.33	1,523.31	1,404.95	1,244.20	1,142.28
90,000	2,024.82	1,612.92	1,487.60	1,317.39	1,209.48
95,000	2,137.31	1,702.52	1,570.24	1,390.58	1,276.67
100,000	2,249.80	1,792.13	1,652.89	1,463.77	1,343.86
110,000	2,474.78	1,971.34	1,818.17	1,610.14	1,478.25
120,000	2,699.76	2,150.55	1,983.46	1,756.52	1,612.63
125,000	2,812.25	2,240.16	2,066.11	1,829.71	1,679.83
130,000	2,924.74	2,329.77	2,148.75	1,902.90	1,747.02
140,000	3,149.72	2,508.98	2,314.04	2,049.27	1,881.41
150,000	3,374.70	2,688.19	2,479.33	2,195.65	2,015.79
160,000	3,599.68	2,867.40	2,644.61	2,342.02	2,150.18
170,000	3,824.65	3,046.62	2,809.90	2,488.40	2,284.56
175,000	3,937.14	3,136.22	2,892.55	2,561.59	2,351.76
180,000	4,049.63	3,225.83	2,975.19	2,634.78	2,418.95
190,000	4,274.61	3,405.04	3,140.48	2,781.15	2,553.33
200,000	4,499.59	3,584.25	3,305.77	2,927.53	2,687.72
220,000	4,949.55	3,942.68	3,636.34	3,220.28	2,956.49
225,000	5,062.04	4,032.28	3,718.99	3,293.47	3,023.68
230,000	5,174.53	4,121.89	3,801.63	3,366.66	3,090.88
240,000	5,399.51	4,301.10	3,966.92	3,513.03	3,225.26
$250,000	5,624.49	4,480.31	4,132.21	3,659.41	3,359.65

Monthly Payment Loans   **12.50%**

Amortization Period in Years

	15	16	17	18	20
$ 100	1.24	1.21	1.19	1.17	1.14
200	2.47	2.42	2.37	2.34	2.28
300	3.70	3.63	3.56	3.50	3.41
400	4.94	4.83	4.74	4.67	4.55
500	6.17	6.04	5.93	5.84	5.69
600	7.40	7.25	7.11	7.00	6.82
700	8.63	8.45	8.30	8.17	7.96
800	9.87	9.66	9.48	9.33	9.09
900	11.10	10.87	10.67	10.50	10.23
1,000	12.33	12.07	11.85	11.67	11.37
2,000	24.66	24.14	23.70	23.33	22.73
3,000	36.98	36.21	35.55	34.99	34.09
4,000	49.31	48.27	47.39	46.65	45.45
5,000	61.63	60.34	59.24	58.31	56.81
6,000	73.96	72.41	71.09	69.97	68.17
7,000	86.28	84.47	82.94	81.63	79.53
8,000	98.61	96.54	94.78	93.29	90.90
9,000	110.93	108.61	106.63	104.95	102.26
10,000	123.26	120.67	118.48	116.61	113.62
15,000	184.88	181.01	177.71	174.91	170.43
20,000	246.51	241.34	236.95	233.21	227.23
25,000	308.14	301.67	296.19	291.51	284.04
30,000	369.76	362.01	355.42	349.81	340.85
35,000	431.39	422.34	414.66	408.11	397.65
40,000	493.01	482.67	473.90	466.41	454.46
45,000	554.64	543.01	533.13	524.71	511.27
50,000	616.27	603.34	592.37	583.01	568.08
55,000	677.89	663.67	651.60	641.31	624.88
60,000	739.52	724.01	710.84	699.61	681.69
65,000	801.14	784.34	770.08	757.91	738.50
70,000	862.77	844.67	829.31	816.21	795.30
75,000	924.40	905.01	888.55	874.51	852.11
80,000	986.02	965.34	947.79	932.81	908.92
85,000	1,047.65	1,025.67	1,007.02	991.11	965.72
90,000	1,109.27	1,086.01	1,066.26	1,049.41	1,022.53
95,000	1,170.90	1,146.34	1,125.49	1,107.71	1,079.34
100,000	1,232.53	1,206.67	1,184.73	1,166.01	1,136.15
110,000	1,355.78	1,327.34	1,303.20	1,282.61	1,249.76
120,000	1,479.03	1,448.01	1,421.68	1,399.21	1,363.37
125,000	1,540.66	1,508.34	1,480.91	1,457.51	1,420.18
130,000	1,602.28	1,568.68	1,540.15	1,515.81	1,476.99
140,000	1,725.54	1,689.34	1,658.62	1,632.41	1,590.60
150,000	1,848.79	1,810.01	1,777.09	1,749.01	1,704.22
160,000	1,972.04	1,930.68	1,895.57	1,865.61	1,817.83
170,000	2,095.29	2,051.34	2,014.04	1,982.21	1,931.44
175,000	2,156.92	2,111.68	2,073.28	2,040.51	1,988.25
180,000	2,218.54	2,172.01	2,132.51	2,098.81	2,045.06
190,000	2,341.80	2,292.68	2,250.98	2,215.41	2,158.67
200,000	2,465.05	2,413.34	2,369.46	2,332.01	2,272.29
220,000	2,711.55	2,654.68	2,606.40	2,565.21	2,499.51
225,000	2,773.18	2,715.01	2,665.64	2,623.51	2,556.32
230,000	2,834.81	2,775.35	2,724.87	2,681.81	2,613.13
240,000	2,958.06	2,896.01	2,843.35	2,798.41	2,726.74
$250,000	3,081.31	3,016.68	2,961.82	2,915.01	2,840.36

Table 1   125

12.50%   Monthly Payment Loans

Amortization Period in Years

	21	22	23	24	25
$ 100	1.13	1.12	1.11	1.10	1.10
200	2.25	2.23	2.21	2.20	2.19
300	3.38	3.35	3.32	3.30	3.28
400	4.50	4.46	4.42	4.39	4.37
500	5.63	5.57	5.53	5.49	5.46
600	6.75	6.69	6.63	6.59	6.55
700	7.87	7.80	7.74	7.69	7.64
800	9.00	8.92	8.84	8.78	8.73
900	10.12	10.03	9.95	9.88	9.82
1,000	11.25	11.14	11.05	10.98	10.91
2,000	22.49	22.28	22.10	21.95	21.81
3,000	33.73	33.42	33.15	32.92	32.72
4,000	44.97	44.56	44.20	43.89	43.62
5,000	56.22	55.70	55.25	54.86	54.52
6,000	67.46	66.84	66.30	65.83	65.43
7,000	78.70	77.98	77.35	76.81	76.33
8,000	89.94	89.12	88.40	87.78	87.23
9,000	101.18	100.26	99.45	98.75	98.14
10,000	112.43	111.39	110.50	109.72	109.04
15,000	168.64	167.09	165.75	164.58	163.56
20,000	224.85	222.78	220.99	219.43	218.08
25,000	281.06	278.48	276.24	274.29	272.59
30,000	337.27	334.17	331.49	329.15	327.11
35,000	393.48	389.87	386.73	384.01	381.63
40,000	449.69	445.56	441.98	438.86	436.15
45,000	505.90	501.26	497.23	493.72	490.66
50,000	562.11	556.95	552.47	548.58	545.18
55,000	618.32	612.65	607.72	603.43	599.70
60,000	674.54	668.34	662.97	658.29	654.22
65,000	730.75	724.04	718.21	713.15	708.74
70,000	786.96	779.73	773.46	768.01	763.25
75,000	843.17	835.43	828.71	822.86	817.77
80,000	899.38	891.12	883.95	877.72	872.29
85,000	955.59	946.82	939.20	932.58	926.81
90,000	1,011.80	1,002.51	994.45	987.44	981.32
95,000	1,068.01	1,058.21	1,049.70	1,042.29	1,035.84
100,000	1,124.22	1,113.90	1,104.94	1,097.15	1,090.36
110,000	1,236.64	1,225.29	1,215.44	1,206.86	1,199.39
120,000	1,349.07	1,336.68	1,325.93	1,316.58	1,308.43
125,000	1,405.28	1,392.37	1,381.18	1,371.44	1,362.95
130,000	1,461.49	1,448.07	1,436.42	1,426.29	1,417.47
140,000	1,573.91	1,559.46	1,546.92	1,536.01	1,526.50
150,000	1,686.33	1,670.85	1,657.41	1,645.72	1,635.54
160,000	1,798.75	1,782.24	1,767.90	1,755.44	1,744.57
170,000	1,911.18	1,893.63	1,878.40	1,865.15	1,853.61
175,000	1,967.39	1,949.32	1,933.64	1,920.01	1,908.12
180,000	2,023.60	2,005.02	1,988.89	1,974.87	1,962.64
190,000	2,136.02	2,116.41	2,099.39	2,084.58	2,071.68
200,000	2,248.44	2,227.80	2,209.88	2,194.29	2,180.71
220,000	2,473.28	2,450.58	2,430.87	2,413.72	2,398.78
225,000	2,529.50	2,506.27	2,486.11	2,468.58	2,453.30
230,000	2,585.71	2,561.97	2,541.36	2,523.44	2,507.82
240,000	2,698.13	2,673.35	2,651.85	2,633.15	2,616.85
$250,000	2,810.55	2,784.74	2,762.35	2,742.87	2,725.89

Monthly Payment Loans   __12.50%__

Amortization Period in Years

	26	27	28	29	30
$ 100	1.09	1.08	1.08	1.08	1.07
200	2.17	2.16	2.15	2.15	2.14
300	3.26	3.24	3.23	3.22	3.21
400	4.34	4.32	4.30	4.29	4.27
500	5.43	5.40	5.38	5.36	5.34
600	6.51	6.48	6.45	6.43	6.41
700	7.60	7.56	7.53	7.50	7.48
800	8.68	8.64	8.60	8.57	8.54
900	9.76	9.72	9.68	9.64	9.61
1,000	10.85	10.80	10.75	10.71	10.68
2,000	21.69	21.59	21.50	21.42	21.35
3,000	32.54	32.38	32.25	32.13	32.02
4,000	43.38	43.17	42.99	42.83	42.70
5,000	54.23	53.97	53.74	53.54	53.37
6,000	65.07	64.76	64.49	64.25	64.04
7,000	75.91	75.55	75.23	74.96	74.71
8,000	86.76	86.34	85.98	85.66	85.39
9,000	97.60	97.14	96.73	96.37	96.06
10,000	108.45	107.93	107.48	107.08	106.73
15,000	162.67	161.89	161.21	160.62	160.09
20,000	216.89	215.85	214.95	214.15	213.46
25,000	271.11	269.82	268.68	267.69	266.82
30,000	325.33	323.78	322.42	321.23	320.18
35,000	379.55	377.74	376.15	374.76	373.55
40,000	433.78	431.70	429.89	428.30	426.91
45,000	488.00	485.67	483.63	481.84	480.27
50,000	542.22	539.63	537.36	535.38	533.63
55,000	596.44	593.59	591.10	588.91	587.00
60,000	650.66	647.55	644.83	642.45	640.36
65,000	704.88	701.52	698.57	695.99	693.72
70,000	759.10	755.48	752.30	749.52	747.09
75,000	813.33	809.44	806.04	803.06	800.45
80,000	867.55	863.40	859.78	856.60	853.81
85,000	921.77	917.36	913.51	910.13	907.17
90,000	975.99	971.33	967.25	963.67	960.54
95,000	1,030.21	1,025.29	1,020.98	1,017.21	1,013.90
100,000	1,084.43	1,079.25	1,074.72	1,070.75	1,067.26
110,000	1,192.88	1,187.18	1,182.19	1,177.82	1,173.99
120,000	1,301.32	1,295.10	1,289.66	1,284.89	1,280.71
125,000	1,355.54	1,349.06	1,343.40	1,338.43	1,334.08
130,000	1,409.76	1,403.03	1,397.13	1,391.97	1,387.44
140,000	1,518.20	1,510.95	1,504.60	1,499.04	1,494.17
150,000	1,626.65	1,618.88	1,612.07	1,606.12	1,600.89
160,000	1,735.09	1,726.80	1,719.55	1,713.19	1,707.62
170,000	1,843.53	1,834.72	1,827.02	1,820.26	1,814.34
175,000	1,897.75	1,888.69	1,880.75	1,873.80	1,867.71
180,000	1,951.97	1,942.65	1,934.49	1,927.34	1,921.07
190,000	2,060.42	2,050.57	2,041.96	2,034.41	2,027.79
200,000	2,168.86	2,158.50	2,149.43	2,141.49	2,134.52
220,000	2,385.75	2,374.35	2,364.37	2,355.64	2,347.97
225,000	2,439.97	2,428.31	2,418.11	2,409.17	2,401.33
230,000	2,494.19	2,482.27	2,471.85	2,462.71	2,454.70
240,000	2,602.63	2,590.20	2,579.32	2,569.78	2,561.42
$250,000	2,711.07	2,698.12	2,686.79	2,676.86	2,668.15

Table 1   127

12.75%   Monthly Payment Loans

Amortization Period in Years

		5	7	8	10	12
$	100	2.27	1.81	1.67	1.48	1.36
	200	4.53	3.62	3.34	2.96	2.72
	300	6.79	5.42	5.01	4.44	4.08
	400	9.06	7.23	6.67	5.92	5.44
	500	11.32	9.03	8.34	7.40	6.80
	600	13.58	10.84	10.01	8.88	8.16
	700	15.84	12.64	11.67	10.35	9.52
	800	18.11	14.45	13.34	11.83	10.88
	900	20.37	16.26	15.01	13.31	12.24
	1,000	22.63	18.06	16.67	14.79	13.60
	2,000	45.26	36.12	33.34	29.57	27.19
	3,000	67.88	54.17	50.01	44.36	40.78
	4,000	90.51	72.23	66.68	59.14	54.37
	5,000	113.13	90.29	83.34	73.92	67.97
	6,000	135.76	108.34	100.01	88.71	81.56
	7,000	158.38	126.40	116.68	103.49	95.15
	8,000	181.01	144.46	133.35	118.28	108.74
	9,000	203.63	162.51	150.01	133.06	122.33
	10,000	226.26	180.57	166.68	147.84	135.93
	15,000	339.38	270.85	250.02	221.76	203.89
	20,000	452.51	361.13	333.36	295.68	271.85
	25,000	565.64	451.41	416.70	369.60	339.81
	30,000	678.76	541.69	500.04	443.52	407.77
	35,000	791.89	631.98	583.38	517.44	475.73
	40,000	905.02	722.26	666.71	591.36	543.69
	45,000	1,018.14	812.54	750.05	665.28	611.65
	50,000	1,131.27	902.82	833.39	739.20	679.61
	55,000	1,244.40	993.10	916.73	813.12	747.57
	60,000	1,357.52	1,083.38	1,000.07	887.04	815.53
	65,000	1,470.65	1,173.67	1,083.41	960.96	883.49
	70,000	1,583.78	1,263.95	1,166.75	1,034.88	951.45
	75,000	1,696.90	1,354.23	1,250.08	1,108.80	1,019.41
	80,000	1,810.03	1,444.51	1,333.42	1,182.72	1,087.37
	85,000	1,923.16	1,534.79	1,416.76	1,256.64	1,155.33
	90,000	2,036.28	1,625.07	1,500.10	1,330.56	1,223.29
	95,000	2,149.41	1,715.36	1,583.44	1,404.48	1,291.25
	100,000	2,262.54	1,805.64	1,666.78	1,478.40	1,359.21
	110,000	2,488.79	1,986.20	1,833.45	1,626.24	1,495.13
	120,000	2,715.04	2,166.76	2,000.13	1,774.08	1,631.05
	125,000	2,828.17	2,257.05	2,083.47	1,848.00	1,699.01
	130,000	2,941.29	2,347.33	2,166.81	1,921.92	1,766.97
	140,000	3,167.55	2,527.89	2,333.49	2,069.76	1,902.89
	150,000	3,393.80	2,708.45	2,500.16	2,217.60	2,038.81
	160,000	3,620.05	2,889.02	2,666.84	2,365.44	2,174.73
	170,000	3,846.31	3,069.58	2,833.52	2,513.28	2,310.65
	175,000	3,959.43	3,159.86	2,916.86	2,587.20	2,378.61
	180,000	4,072.56	3,250.14	3,000.20	2,661.12	2,446.57
	190,000	4,298.81	3,430.71	3,166.87	2,808.96	2,582.49
	200,000	4,525.07	3,611.27	3,333.55	2,956.80	2,718.41
	220,000	4,977.57	3,972.40	3,666.90	3,252.48	2,990.25
	225,000	5,090.70	4,062.68	3,750.24	3,326.40	3,058.21
	230,000	5,203.82	4,152.96	3,833.58	3,400.32	3,126.17
	240,000	5,430.08	4,333.52	4,000.26	3,548.16	3,262.09
$250,000		5,656.33	4,514.09	4,166.94	3,696.00	3,398.01

Monthly Payment Loans **12.75%**

Amortization Period in Years

	15	16	17	18	20
$ 100	1.25	1.23	1.21	1.19	1.16
200	2.50	2.45	2.41	2.37	2.31
300	3.75	3.67	3.61	3.55	3.47
400	5.00	4.90	4.81	4.74	4.62
500	6.25	6.12	6.01	5.92	5.77
600	7.50	7.34	7.21	7.10	6.93
700	8.75	8.57	8.42	8.29	8.08
800	10.00	9.79	9.62	9.47	9.24
900	11.24	11.01	10.82	10.65	10.39
1,000	12.49	12.24	12.02	11.84	11.54
2,000	24.98	24.47	24.04	23.67	23.08
3,000	37.47	36.70	36.05	35.50	34.62
4,000	49.96	48.94	48.07	47.33	46.16
5,000	62.45	61.17	60.09	59.16	57.70
6,000	74.94	73.40	72.10	71.00	69.23
7,000	87.42	85.63	84.12	82.83	80.77
8,000	99.91	97.87	96.13	94.66	92.31
9,000	112.40	110.10	108.15	106.49	103.85
10,000	124.89	122.33	120.17	118.32	115.39
15,000	187.33	183.50	180.25	177.48	173.08
20,000	249.77	244.66	240.33	236.64	230.77
25,000	312.21	305.83	300.41	295.80	288.46
30,000	374.66	366.99	360.49	354.96	346.15
35,000	437.10	428.15	420.57	414.11	403.84
40,000	499.54	489.32	480.65	473.27	461.53
45,000	561.98	550.48	540.74	532.43	519.22
50,000	624.42	611.65	600.82	591.59	576.91
55,000	686.87	672.81	660.90	650.75	634.60
60,000	749.31	733.97	720.98	709.91	692.29
65,000	811.75	795.14	781.06	769.07	749.98
70,000	874.19	856.30	841.14	828.22	807.67
75,000	936.63	917.47	901.22	887.38	865.36
80,000	999.07	978.63	961.30	946.54	923.05
85,000	1,061.52	1,039.80	1,021.39	1,005.70	980.74
90,000	1,123.96	1,100.96	1,081.47	1,064.86	1,038.44
95,000	1,186.40	1,162.12	1,141.55	1,124.02	1,096.13
100,000	1,248.84	1,223.29	1,201.63	1,183.17	1,153.82
110,000	1,373.73	1,345.62	1,321.79	1,301.49	1,269.20
120,000	1,498.61	1,467.94	1,441.95	1,419.81	1,384.58
125,000	1,561.05	1,529.11	1,502.03	1,478.97	1,442.27
130,000	1,623.49	1,590.27	1,562.12	1,538.13	1,499.96
140,000	1,748.38	1,712.60	1,682.28	1,656.44	1,615.34
150,000	1,873.26	1,834.93	1,802.44	1,774.76	1,730.72
160,000	1,998.14	1,957.26	1,922.60	1,893.08	1,846.10
170,000	2,123.03	2,079.59	2,042.77	2,011.39	1,961.48
175,000	2,185.47	2,140.75	2,102.85	2,070.55	2,019.18
180,000	2,247.91	2,201.91	2,162.93	2,129.71	2,076.87
190,000	2,372.80	2,324.24	2,283.09	2,248.03	2,192.25
200,000	2,497.68	2,446.57	2,403.25	2,366.34	2,307.63
220,000	2,747.45	2,691.23	2,643.58	2,602.98	2,538.39
225,000	2,809.89	2,752.39	2,703.66	2,662.14	2,596.08
230,000	2,872.33	2,813.56	2,763.74	2,721.30	2,653.77
240,000	2,997.21	2,935.88	2,883.90	2,839.61	2,769.15
$250,000	3,122.10	3,058.21	3,004.06	2,957.93	2,884.53

Table 1   129

12.75%   Monthly Payment Loans

Amortization Period in Years

	21	22	23	24	25
$ 100	1.15	1.14	1.13	1.12	1.11
200	2.29	2.27	2.25	2.24	2.22
300	3.43	3.40	3.37	3.35	3.33
400	4.57	4.53	4.50	4.47	4.44
500	5.72	5.67	5.62	5.58	5.55
600	6.86	6.80	6.74	6.70	6.66
700	8.00	7.93	7.87	7.81	7.77
800	9.14	9.06	8.99	8.93	8.88
900	10.28	10.19	10.11	10.05	9.99
1,000	11.43	11.33	11.24	11.16	11.10
2,000	22.85	22.65	22.47	22.32	22.19
3,000	34.27	33.97	33.70	33.47	33.28
4,000	45.69	45.29	44.94	44.63	44.37
5,000	57.11	56.61	56.17	55.79	55.46
6,000	68.53	67.93	67.40	66.94	66.55
7,000	79.95	79.25	78.63	78.10	77.64
8,000	91.37	90.57	89.87	89.26	88.73
9,000	102.80	101.89	101.10	100.41	99.82
10,000	114.22	113.21	112.33	111.57	110.91
15,000	171.32	169.81	168.49	167.35	166.36
20,000	228.43	226.41	224.66	223.14	221.82
25,000	285.54	283.01	280.82	278.92	277.27
30,000	342.64	339.61	336.98	334.70	332.72
35,000	399.75	396.21	393.15	390.49	388.17
40,000	456.85	452.81	449.31	446.27	443.63
45,000	513.96	509.41	505.47	502.05	499.08
50,000	571.07	566.01	561.64	557.84	554.53
55,000	628.17	622.61	617.80	613.62	609.98
60,000	685.28	679.21	673.96	669.40	665.44
65,000	742.38	735.82	730.13	725.19	720.89
70,000	799.49	792.42	786.29	780.97	776.34
75,000	856.60	849.02	842.45	836.75	831.79
80,000	913.70	905.62	898.61	892.53	887.25
85,000	970.81	962.22	954.78	948.32	942.70
90,000	1,027.91	1,018.82	1,010.94	1,004.10	998.15
95,000	1,085.02	1,075.42	1,067.10	1,059.88	1,053.60
100,000	1,142.13	1,132.02	1,123.27	1,115.67	1,109.06
110,000	1,256.34	1,245.22	1,235.59	1,227.23	1,219.96
120,000	1,370.55	1,358.42	1,347.92	1,338.80	1,330.87
125,000	1,427.66	1,415.02	1,404.08	1,394.58	1,386.32
130,000	1,484.76	1,471.63	1,460.25	1,450.37	1,441.77
140,000	1,598.97	1,584.83	1,572.57	1,561.93	1,552.68
150,000	1,713.19	1,698.03	1,684.90	1,673.50	1,663.58
160,000	1,827.40	1,811.23	1,797.22	1,785.06	1,774.49
170,000	1,941.61	1,924.43	1,909.55	1,896.63	1,885.39
175,000	1,998.72	1,981.03	1,965.71	1,952.41	1,940.85
180,000	2,055.82	2,037.63	2,021.88	2,008.20	1,996.30
190,000	2,170.03	2,150.83	2,134.20	2,119.76	2,107.20
200,000	2,284.25	2,264.04	2,246.53	2,231.33	2,218.11
220,000	2,512.67	2,490.44	2,471.18	2,454.46	2,439.92
225,000	2,569.78	2,547.04	2,527.34	2,510.24	2,495.37
230,000	2,626.88	2,603.64	2,583.51	2,566.03	2,550.83
240,000	2,741.09	2,716.84	2,695.83	2,677.59	2,661.73
$250,000	2,855.31	2,830.04	2,808.16	2,789.16	2,772.64

Monthly Payment Loans   **13.00%**

Amortization Period in Years

	15	16	17	18	20
$ 100	1.27	1.24	1.22	1.21	1.18
200	2.54	2.48	2.44	2.41	2.35
300	3.80	3.72	3.66	3.61	3.52
400	5.07	4.96	4.88	4.81	4.69
500	6.33	6.20	6.10	6.01	5.86
600	7.60	7.44	7.32	7.21	7.03
700	8.86	8.68	8.54	8.41	8.21
800	10.13	9.92	9.75	9.61	9.38
900	11.39	11.16	10.97	10.81	10.55
1,000	12.66	12.40	12.19	12.01	11.72
2,000	25.31	24.80	24.38	24.01	23.44
3,000	37.96	37.20	36.56	36.02	35.15
4,000	50.61	49.60	48.75	48.02	46.87
5,000	63.27	62.00	60.94	60.03	58.58
6,000	75.92	74.40	73.12	72.03	70.30
7,000	88.57	86.80	85.31	84.04	82.02
8,000	101.22	99.20	97.49	96.04	93.73
9,000	113.88	111.60	109.68	108.04	105.45
10,000	126.53	124.00	121.87	120.05	117.16
15,000	189.79	186.00	182.80	180.07	175.74
20,000	253.05	248.00	243.73	240.09	234.32
25,000	316.32	310.00	304.66	300.11	292.90
30,000	379.58	372.00	365.59	360.13	351.48
35,000	442.84	434.00	426.52	420.16	410.06
40,000	506.10	496.00	487.45	480.18	468.64
45,000	569.36	558.00	548.38	540.20	527.21
50,000	632.63	620.00	609.31	600.22	585.79
55,000	695.89	682.00	670.24	660.24	644.37
60,000	759.15	744.00	731.17	720.26	702.95
65,000	822.41	806.00	792.10	780.29	761.53
70,000	885.67	868.00	853.04	840.31	820.11
75,000	948.94	930.00	913.97	900.33	878.69
80,000	1,012.20	992.00	974.90	960.35	937.27
85,000	1,075.46	1,053.99	1,035.83	1,020.37	995.84
90,000	1,138.72	1,115.99	1,096.76	1,080.39	1,054.42
95,000	1,201.99	1,177.99	1,157.69	1,140.42	1,113.00
100,000	1,265.25	1,239.99	1,218.62	1,200.44	1,171.58
110,000	1,391.77	1,363.99	1,340.48	1,320.48	1,288.74
120,000	1,518.30	1,487.99	1,462.34	1,440.52	1,405.90
125,000	1,581.56	1,549.99	1,523.27	1,500.55	1,464.47
130,000	1,644.82	1,611.99	1,584.20	1,560.57	1,523.05
140,000	1,771.34	1,735.99	1,706.07	1,680.61	1,640.21
150,000	1,897.87	1,859.99	1,827.93	1,800.65	1,757.37
160,000	2,024.39	1,983.99	1,949.79	1,920.70	1,874.53
170,000	2,150.92	2,107.98	2,071.65	2,040.74	1,991.68
175,000	2,214.18	2,169.98	2,132.58	2,100.76	2,050.26
180,000	2,277.44	2,231.98	2,193.51	2,160.78	2,108.84
190,000	2,403.97	2,355.98	2,315.37	2,280.83	2,226.00
200,000	2,530.49	2,479.98	2,437.23	2,400.87	2,343.16
220,000	2,783.54	2,727.98	2,680.96	2,640.96	2,577.47
225,000	2,846.80	2,789.98	2,741.89	2,700.98	2,636.05
230,000	2,910.06	2,851.98	2,802.82	2,761.00	2,694.63
240,000	3,036.59	2,975.98	2,924.68	2,881.04	2,811.79
$250,000	3,163.11	3,099.97	3,046.54	3,001.09	2,928.94

Table 1   133

13.00%   Monthly Payment Loans

Amortization Period in Years

	21	22	23	24	25
$ 100	1.17	1.16	1.15	1.14	1.13
200	2.33	2.31	2.29	2.27	2.26
300	3.49	3.46	3.43	3.41	3.39
400	4.65	4.61	4.57	4.54	4.52
500	5.81	5.76	5.71	5.68	5.64
600	6.97	6.91	6.86	6.81	6.77
700	8.13	8.06	8.00	7.94	7.90
800	9.29	9.21	9.14	9.08	9.03
900	10.45	10.36	10.28	10.21	10.16
1,000	11.61	11.51	11.42	11.35	11.28
2,000	23.21	23.01	22.84	22.69	22.56
3,000	34.81	34.51	34.26	34.03	33.84
4,000	46.41	46.01	45.67	45.38	45.12
5,000	58.01	57.52	57.09	56.72	56.40
6,000	69.61	69.02	68.51	68.06	67.68
7,000	81.21	80.52	79.92	79.40	78.95
8,000	92.81	92.02	91.34	90.75	90.23
9,000	104.42	103.53	102.76	102.09	101.51
10,000	116.02	115.03	114.17	113.43	112.79
15,000	174.02	172.54	171.26	170.15	169.18
20,000	232.03	230.05	228.34	226.86	225.57
25,000	290.03	287.56	285.42	283.57	281.96
30,000	348.04	345.07	342.51	340.29	338.36
35,000	406.04	402.58	399.59	397.00	394.75
40,000	464.05	460.10	456.68	453.71	451.14
45,000	522.06	517.61	513.76	510.43	507.53
50,000	580.06	575.12	570.84	567.14	563.92
55,000	638.07	632.63	627.93	623.85	620.31
60,000	696.07	690.14	685.01	680.57	676.71
65,000	754.08	747.65	742.09	737.28	733.10
70,000	812.08	805.16	799.18	793.99	789.49
75,000	870.09	862.67	856.26	850.71	845.88
80,000	928.10	920.19	913.35	907.42	902.27
85,000	986.10	977.70	970.43	964.13	958.67
90,000	1,044.11	1,035.21	1,027.51	1,020.85	1,015.06
95,000	1,102.11	1,092.72	1,084.60	1,077.56	1,071.45
100,000	1,160.12	1,150.23	1,141.68	1,134.27	1,127.84
110,000	1,276.13	1,265.25	1,255.85	1,247.70	1,240.62
120,000	1,392.14	1,380.28	1,370.02	1,361.13	1,353.41
125,000	1,450.15	1,437.79	1,427.10	1,417.84	1,409.80
130,000	1,508.15	1,495.30	1,484.18	1,474.55	1,466.19
140,000	1,624.16	1,610.32	1,598.35	1,587.98	1,578.97
150,000	1,740.18	1,725.34	1,712.52	1,701.41	1,691.76
160,000	1,856.19	1,840.37	1,826.69	1,814.83	1,804.54
170,000	1,972.20	1,955.39	1,940.85	1,928.26	1,917.33
175,000	2,030.20	2,012.90	1,997.94	1,984.97	1,973.72
180,000	2,088.21	2,070.41	2,055.02	2,041.69	2,030.11
190,000	2,204.22	2,185.44	2,169.19	2,155.11	2,142.89
200,000	2,320.23	2,300.46	2,283.36	2,268.54	2,255.68
220,000	2,552.26	2,530.50	2,511.69	2,495.39	2,481.24
225,000	2,610.26	2,588.01	2,568.78	2,552.11	2,537.63
230,000	2,668.27	2,645.53	2,625.86	2,608.82	2,594.03
240,000	2,784.28	2,760.55	2,740.03	2,722.25	2,706.81
$250,000	2,900.29	2,875.57	2,854.19	2,835.67	2,819.59

Monthly Payment Loans   **13.00%**

Amortization Period in Years

	26	27	28	29	30
$ 100	1.13	1.12	1.12	1.11	1.11
200	2.25	2.24	2.23	2.22	2.22
300	3.37	3.36	3.34	3.33	3.32
400	4.49	4.47	4.46	4.44	4.43
500	5.62	5.59	5.57	5.55	5.54
600	6.74	6.71	6.68	6.66	6.64
700	7.86	7.83	7.80	7.77	7.75
800	8.98	8.94	8.91	8.88	8.85
900	10.11	10.06	10.02	9.99	9.96
1,000	11.23	11.18	11.14	11.10	11.07
2,000	22.45	22.35	22.27	22.19	22.13
3,000	33.67	33.53	33.40	33.29	33.19
4,000	44.89	44.70	44.53	44.38	44.25
5,000	56.12	55.87	55.66	55.48	55.31
6,000	67.34	67.05	66.79	66.57	66.38
7,000	78.56	78.22	77.92	77.67	77.44
8,000	89.78	89.40	89.06	88.76	88.50
9,000	101.01	100.57	100.19	99.85	99.56
10,000	112.23	111.74	111.32	110.95	110.62
15,000	168.34	167.61	166.98	166.42	165.93
20,000	224.45	223.48	222.63	221.89	221.24
25,000	280.57	279.35	278.29	277.36	276.55
30,000	336.68	335.22	333.95	332.83	331.86
35,000	392.79	391.09	389.60	388.31	387.17
40,000	448.90	446.96	445.26	443.78	442.48
45,000	505.01	502.82	500.92	499.25	497.79
50,000	561.13	558.69	556.57	554.72	553.10
55,000	617.24	614.56	612.23	610.19	608.41
60,000	673.35	670.43	667.89	665.66	663.72
65,000	729.46	726.30	723.54	721.14	719.03
70,000	785.58	782.17	779.20	776.61	774.34
75,000	841.69	838.04	834.86	832.08	829.65
80,000	897.80	893.91	890.51	887.55	884.96
85,000	953.91	949.77	946.17	943.02	940.27
90,000	1,010.02	1,005.64	1,001.83	998.49	995.58
95,000	1,066.14	1,061.51	1,057.48	1,053.97	1,050.89
100,000	1,122.25	1,117.38	1,113.14	1,109.44	1,106.20
110,000	1,234.47	1,229.12	1,224.45	1,220.38	1,216.82
120,000	1,346.70	1,340.86	1,335.77	1,331.32	1,327.44
125,000	1,402.81	1,396.73	1,391.42	1,386.79	1,382.75
130,000	1,458.92	1,452.59	1,447.08	1,442.27	1,438.06
140,000	1,571.15	1,564.33	1,558.39	1,553.21	1,548.68
150,000	1,683.37	1,676.07	1,669.71	1,664.15	1,659.30
160,000	1,795.60	1,787.81	1,781.02	1,775.10	1,769.92
170,000	1,907.82	1,899.54	1,892.33	1,886.04	1,880.54
175,000	1,963.93	1,955.41	1,947.99	1,941.51	1,935.85
180,000	2,020.04	2,011.28	2,003.65	1,996.98	1,991.16
190,000	2,132.27	2,123.02	2,114.96	2,107.93	2,101.78
200,000	2,244.49	2,234.76	2,226.27	2,218.87	2,212.40
220,000	2,468.94	2,458.23	2,448.90	2,440.76	2,433.64
225,000	2,525.05	2,514.10	2,504.56	2,496.23	2,488.95
230,000	2,581.17	2,569.97	2,560.21	2,551.70	2,544.26
240,000	2,693.39	2,681.71	2,671.53	2,662.64	2,654.88
$250,000	2,805.61	2,793.45	2,782.84	2,773.58	2,765.50

Table 1   135

13.25%   **Monthly Payment Loans**

Amortization Period in Years

	5	7	8	10	12
$ 100	2.29	1.84	1.70	1.51	1.40
200	4.58	3.67	3.39	3.02	2.79
300	6.87	5.50	5.09	4.53	4.18
400	9.16	7.34	6.78	6.04	5.57
500	11.45	9.17	8.48	7.54	6.96
600	13.73	11.00	10.17	9.05	8.35
700	16.02	12.83	11.87	10.56	9.74
800	18.31	14.67	13.56	12.07	11.13
900	20.60	16.50	15.26	13.58	12.52
1,000	22.89	18.33	16.95	15.08	13.91
2,000	45.77	36.66	33.90	30.16	27.81
3,000	68.65	54.99	50.85	45.24	41.71
4,000	91.53	73.32	67.79	60.32	55.61
5,000	114.41	91.65	84.74	75.40	69.51
6,000	137.29	109.97	101.69	90.48	83.41
7,000	160.17	128.30	118.64	105.56	97.31
8,000	183.06	146.63	135.58	120.64	111.22
9,000	205.94	164.96	152.53	135.72	125.12
10,000	228.82	183.29	169.48	150.79	139.02
15,000	343.22	274.93	254.22	226.19	208.52
20,000	457.63	366.57	338.95	301.58	278.03
25,000	572.04	458.21	423.69	376.98	347.54
30,000	686.44	549.85	508.43	452.37	417.04
35,000	800.85	641.49	593.16	527.77	486.55
40,000	915.26	733.13	677.90	603.16	556.06
45,000	1,029.66	824.77	762.64	678.56	625.56
50,000	1,144.07	916.41	847.38	753.95	695.07
55,000	1,258.47	1,008.05	932.11	829.34	764.58
60,000	1,372.88	1,099.69	1,016.85	904.74	834.08
65,000	1,487.29	1,191.33	1,101.59	980.13	903.59
70,000	1,601.69	1,282.98	1,186.32	1,055.53	973.10
75,000	1,716.10	1,374.62	1,271.06	1,130.92	1,042.60
80,000	1,830.51	1,466.26	1,355.80	1,206.32	1,112.11
85,000	1,944.91	1,557.90	1,440.53	1,281.71	1,181.62
90,000	2,059.32	1,649.54	1,525.27	1,357.11	1,251.12
95,000	2,173.72	1,741.18	1,610.01	1,432.50	1,320.63
100,000	2,288.13	1,832.82	1,694.75	1,507.89	1,390.14
110,000	2,516.94	2,016.10	1,864.22	1,658.68	1,529.15
120,000	2,745.76	2,199.38	2,033.69	1,809.47	1,668.16
125,000	2,860.16	2,291.02	2,118.43	1,884.87	1,737.67
130,000	2,974.57	2,382.66	2,203.17	1,960.26	1,807.18
140,000	3,203.38	2,565.95	2,372.64	2,111.05	1,946.19
150,000	3,432.19	2,749.23	2,542.12	2,261.84	2,085.20
160,000	3,661.01	2,932.51	2,711.59	2,412.63	2,224.21
170,000	3,889.82	3,115.79	2,881.06	2,563.42	2,363.23
175,000	4,004.22	3,207.43	2,965.80	2,638.81	2,432.73
180,000	4,118.63	3,299.07	3,050.54	2,714.21	2,502.24
190,000	4,347.44	3,482.35	3,220.01	2,864.99	2,641.25
200,000	4,576.26	3,665.64	3,389.49	3,015.78	2,780.27
220,000	5,033.88	4,032.20	3,728.43	3,317.36	3,058.29
225,000	5,148.29	4,123.84	3,813.17	3,392.76	3,127.80
230,000	5,262.69	4,215.48	3,897.91	3,468.15	3,197.31
240,000	5,491.51	4,398.76	4,067.38	3,618.94	3,336.32
$250,000	5,720.32	4,582.04	4,236.86	3,769.73	3,475.33

Monthly Payment Loans   **13.25%**

Amortization Period in Years

	15	16	17	18	20
$ 100	1.29	1.26	1.24	1.22	1.19
200	2.57	2.52	2.48	2.44	2.38
300	3.85	3.78	3.71	3.66	3.57
400	5.13	5.03	4.95	4.88	4.76
500	6.41	6.29	6.18	6.09	5.95
600	7.70	7.55	7.42	7.31	7.14
700	8.98	8.80	8.65	8.53	8.33
800	10.26	10.06	9.89	9.75	9.52
900	11.54	11.32	11.13	10.97	10.71
1,000	12.82	12.57	12.36	12.18	11.90
2,000	25.64	25.14	24.72	24.36	23.79
3,000	38.46	37.71	37.08	36.54	35.69
4,000	51.27	50.28	49.43	48.72	47.58
5,000	64.09	62.84	61.79	60.89	59.48
6,000	76.91	75.41	74.15	73.07	71.37
7,000	89.73	87.98	86.50	85.25	83.27
8,000	102.54	100.55	98.86	97.43	95.16
9,000	115.36	113.12	111.22	109.61	107.05
10,000	128.18	125.68	123.57	121.78	118.95
15,000	192.27	188.52	185.36	182.67	178.42
20,000	256.35	251.36	247.14	243.56	237.89
25,000	320.44	314.20	308.93	304.45	297.36
30,000	384.53	377.04	370.71	365.34	356.83
35,000	448.61	439.88	432.50	426.23	416.31
40,000	512.70	502.72	494.28	487.12	475.78
45,000	576.79	565.56	556.07	548.01	535.25
50,000	640.87	628.40	617.85	608.90	594.72
55,000	704.96	691.24	679.64	669.79	654.19
60,000	769.05	754.08	741.42	730.68	713.66
65,000	833.13	816.91	803.21	791.57	773.13
70,000	897.22	879.75	864.99	852.46	832.61
75,000	961.31	942.59	926.78	913.35	892.08
80,000	1,025.39	1,005.43	988.56	974.23	951.55
85,000	1,089.48	1,068.27	1,050.35	1,035.12	1,011.02
90,000	1,153.57	1,131.11	1,112.13	1,096.01	1,070.49
95,000	1,217.65	1,193.95	1,173.92	1,156.90	1,129.96
100,000	1,281.74	1,256.79	1,235.70	1,217.79	1,189.44
110,000	1,409.92	1,382.47	1,359.27	1,339.57	1,308.38
120,000	1,538.09	1,508.15	1,482.84	1,461.35	1,427.32
125,000	1,602.18	1,570.98	1,544.63	1,522.24	1,486.79
130,000	1,666.26	1,633.82	1,606.41	1,583.13	1,546.26
140,000	1,794.44	1,759.50	1,729.98	1,704.91	1,665.21
150,000	1,922.61	1,885.18	1,853.55	1,826.69	1,784.15
160,000	2,050.78	2,010.86	1,977.12	1,948.46	1,903.09
170,000	2,178.96	2,136.54	2,100.69	2,070.24	2,022.04
175,000	2,243.04	2,199.38	2,162.47	2,131.13	2,081.51
180,000	2,307.13	2,262.22	2,224.26	2,192.02	2,140.98
190,000	2,435.30	2,387.89	2,347.83	2,313.80	2,259.92
200,000	2,563.48	2,513.57	2,471.40	2,435.58	2,378.87
220,000	2,819.83	2,764.93	2,718.54	2,679.14	2,616.75
225,000	2,883.91	2,827.77	2,780.32	2,740.03	2,676.22
230,000	2,948.00	2,890.61	2,842.11	2,800.91	2,735.70
240,000	3,076.17	3,016.29	2,965.68	2,922.69	2,854.64
$250,000	3,204.35	3,141.96	3,089.25	3,044.47	2,973.58

Table 1   137

13.25%　　Monthly Payment Loans

Amortization Period in Years

	21	22	23	24	25
$ 100	1.18	1.17	1.17	1.16	1.15
200	2.36	2.34	2.33	2.31	2.30
300	3.54	3.51	3.49	3.46	3.45
400	4.72	4.68	4.65	4.62	4.59
500	5.90	5.85	5.81	5.77	5.74
600	7.07	7.02	6.97	6.92	6.89
700	8.25	8.18	8.13	8.08	8.03
800	9.43	9.35	9.29	9.23	9.18
900	10.61	10.52	10.45	10.38	10.33
1,000	11.79	11.69	11.61	11.53	11.47
2,000	23.57	23.38	23.21	23.06	22.94
3,000	35.35	35.06	34.81	34.59	34.41
4,000	47.13	46.75	46.41	46.12	45.87
5,000	58.91	58.43	58.01	57.65	57.34
6,000	70.70	70.12	69.62	69.18	68.81
7,000	82.48	81.80	81.22	80.71	80.27
8,000	94.26	93.49	92.82	92.24	91.74
9,000	106.04	105.17	104.42	103.77	103.21
10,000	117.82	116.86	116.02	115.30	114.68
15,000	176.73	175.28	174.03	172.95	172.01
20,000	235.64	233.71	232.04	230.60	229.35
25,000	294.55	292.14	290.05	288.24	286.68
30,000	353.46	350.56	348.06	345.89	344.02
35,000	412.37	408.99	406.07	403.54	401.35
40,000	471.28	467.42	464.08	461.19	458.69
45,000	530.19	525.84	522.08	518.84	516.02
50,000	589.10	584.27	580.09	576.48	573.36
55,000	648.01	642.69	638.10	634.13	630.69
60,000	706.92	701.12	696.11	691.78	688.03
65,000	765.83	759.55	754.12	749.43	745.36
70,000	824.74	817.97	812.13	807.07	802.70
75,000	883.65	876.40	870.14	864.72	860.03
80,000	942.56	934.83	928.15	922.37	917.37
85,000	1,001.47	993.25	986.16	980.02	974.70
90,000	1,060.38	1,051.68	1,044.16	1,037.67	1,032.04
95,000	1,119.29	1,110.10	1,102.17	1,095.31	1,089.37
100,000	1,178.20	1,168.53	1,160.18	1,152.96	1,146.71
110,000	1,296.02	1,285.38	1,276.20	1,268.26	1,261.38
120,000	1,413.84	1,402.24	1,392.22	1,383.55	1,376.05
125,000	1,472.75	1,460.66	1,450.23	1,441.20	1,433.38
130,000	1,531.66	1,519.09	1,508.23	1,498.85	1,490.72
140,000	1,649.48	1,635.94	1,624.25	1,614.14	1,605.39
150,000	1,767.30	1,752.79	1,740.27	1,729.44	1,720.06
160,000	1,885.12	1,869.65	1,856.29	1,844.73	1,834.73
170,000	2,002.94	1,986.50	1,972.31	1,960.03	1,949.40
175,000	2,061.85	2,044.92	2,030.31	2,017.68	2,006.73
180,000	2,120.76	2,103.35	2,088.32	2,075.33	2,064.07
190,000	2,238.58	2,220.20	2,204.34	2,190.62	2,178.74
200,000	2,356.40	2,337.06	2,320.36	2,305.92	2,293.41
220,000	2,592.04	2,570.76	2,552.39	2,536.51	2,522.75
225,000	2,650.95	2,629.19	2,610.40	2,594.16	2,580.08
230,000	2,709.86	2,687.61	2,668.41	2,651.80	2,637.42
240,000	2,827.68	2,804.47	2,784.43	2,767.10	2,752.09
$250,000	2,945.50	2,921.32	2,900.45	2,882.40	2,866.76

Monthly Payment Loans   **13.25%**

Amortization Period in Years

	26	27	28	29	30
$ 100	1.15	1.14	1.14	1.13	1.13
200	2.29	2.28	2.27	2.26	2.26
300	3.43	3.41	3.40	3.39	3.38
400	4.57	4.55	4.53	4.52	4.51
500	5.71	5.69	5.67	5.65	5.63
600	6.85	6.82	6.80	6.78	6.76
700	7.99	7.96	7.93	7.91	7.89
800	9.14	9.10	9.06	9.04	9.01
900	10.28	10.23	10.20	10.16	10.14
1,000	11.42	11.37	11.33	11.29	11.26
2,000	22.83	22.74	22.65	22.58	22.52
3,000	34.24	34.10	33.98	33.87	33.78
4,000	45.66	45.47	45.30	45.16	45.04
5,000	57.07	56.83	56.63	56.45	56.29
6,000	68.48	68.20	67.95	67.74	67.55
7,000	79.89	79.56	79.28	79.03	78.81
8,000	91.31	90.93	90.60	90.32	90.07
9,000	102.72	102.30	101.93	101.60	101.32
10,000	114.13	113.66	113.25	112.89	112.58
15,000	171.20	170.49	169.87	169.34	168.87
20,000	228.26	227.32	226.50	225.78	225.16
25,000	285.32	284.14	283.12	282.23	281.45
30,000	342.39	340.97	339.74	338.67	337.74
35,000	399.45	397.80	396.36	395.11	394.03
40,000	456.51	454.63	452.99	451.56	450.31
45,000	513.58	511.46	509.61	508.00	506.60
50,000	570.64	568.28	566.23	564.45	562.89
55,000	627.70	625.11	622.86	620.89	619.18
60,000	684.77	681.94	679.48	677.34	675.47
65,000	741.83	738.77	736.10	733.78	731.76
70,000	798.90	795.60	792.72	790.22	788.05
75,000	855.96	852.42	849.35	846.67	844.34
80,000	913.02	909.25	905.97	903.11	900.62
85,000	970.09	966.08	962.59	959.56	956.91
90,000	1,027.15	1,022.91	1,019.22	1,016.00	1,013.20
95,000	1,084.21	1,079.73	1,075.84	1,072.45	1,069.49
100,000	1,141.28	1,136.56	1,132.46	1,128.89	1,125.78
110,000	1,255.40	1,250.22	1,245.71	1,241.78	1,238.36
120,000	1,369.53	1,363.87	1,358.95	1,354.67	1,350.93
125,000	1,426.60	1,420.70	1,415.57	1,411.11	1,407.22
130,000	1,483.66	1,477.53	1,472.20	1,467.56	1,463.51
140,000	1,597.79	1,591.19	1,585.44	1,580.44	1,576.09
150,000	1,711.91	1,704.84	1,698.69	1,693.33	1,688.67
160,000	1,826.04	1,818.50	1,811.93	1,806.22	1,801.24
170,000	1,940.17	1,932.15	1,925.18	1,919.11	1,913.82
175,000	1,997.23	1,988.98	1,981.80	1,975.55	1,970.11
180,000	2,054.30	2,045.81	2,038.43	2,032.00	2,026.40
190,000	2,168.42	2,159.46	2,151.67	2,144.89	2,138.97
200,000	2,282.55	2,273.12	2,264.92	2,257.77	2,251.55
220,000	2,510.80	2,500.43	2,491.41	2,483.55	2,476.71
225,000	2,567.87	2,557.26	2,548.03	2,540.00	2,533.00
230,000	2,624.93	2,614.09	2,604.65	2,596.44	2,589.28
240,000	2,739.06	2,727.74	2,717.90	2,709.33	2,701.86
$250,000	2,853.19	2,841.40	2,831.14	2,822.22	2,814.44

Table 1   139

13.50%   Monthly Payment Loans

Amortization Period in Years

	5	7	8	10	12
$ 100	2.31	1.85	1.71	1.53	1.41
200	4.61	3.70	3.42	3.05	2.82
300	6.91	5.54	5.13	4.57	4.22
400	9.21	7.39	6.84	6.10	5.63
500	11.51	9.24	8.55	7.62	7.03
600	13.81	11.08	10.26	9.14	8.44
700	16.11	12.93	11.97	10.66	9.85
800	18.41	14.78	13.68	12.19	11.25
900	20.71	16.62	15.38	13.71	12.66
1,000	23.01	18.47	17.09	15.23	14.06
2,000	46.02	36.93	34.18	30.46	28.12
3,000	69.03	55.40	51.27	45.69	42.18
4,000	92.04	73.86	68.36	60.91	56.23
5,000	115.05	92.33	85.45	76.14	70.29
6,000	138.06	110.79	102.53	91.37	84.35
7,000	161.07	129.26	119.62	106.60	98.41
8,000	184.08	147.72	136.71	121.82	112.46
9,000	207.09	166.19	153.80	137.05	126.52
10,000	230.10	184.65	170.89	152.28	140.58
15,000	345.15	276.98	256.33	228.42	210.86
20,000	460.20	369.30	341.77	304.55	281.15
25,000	575.25	461.63	427.21	380.69	351.43
30,000	690.30	553.95	512.65	456.83	421.72
35,000	805.35	646.28	598.09	532.97	492.01
40,000	920.40	738.60	683.53	609.10	562.29
45,000	1,035.45	830.93	768.97	685.24	632.58
50,000	1,150.50	923.25	854.41	761.38	702.86
55,000	1,265.55	1,015.57	939.85	837.51	773.15
60,000	1,380.60	1,107.90	1,025.29	913.65	843.44
65,000	1,495.64	1,200.22	1,110.74	989.79	913.72
70,000	1,610.69	1,292.55	1,196.18	1,065.93	984.01
75,000	1,725.74	1,384.87	1,281.62	1,142.06	1,054.29
80,000	1,840.79	1,477.20	1,367.06	1,218.20	1,124.58
85,000	1,955.84	1,569.52	1,452.50	1,294.34	1,194.86
90,000	2,070.89	1,661.85	1,537.94	1,370.47	1,265.15
95,000	2,185.94	1,754.17	1,623.38	1,446.61	1,335.44
100,000	2,300.99	1,846.49	1,708.82	1,522.75	1,405.72
110,000	2,531.09	2,031.14	1,879.70	1,675.02	1,546.29
120,000	2,761.19	2,215.79	2,050.58	1,827.30	1,686.87
125,000	2,876.24	2,308.12	2,136.02	1,903.43	1,757.15
130,000	2,991.28	2,400.44	2,221.47	1,979.57	1,827.44
140,000	3,221.38	2,585.09	2,392.35	2,131.85	1,968.01
150,000	3,451.48	2,769.74	2,563.23	2,284.12	2,108.58
160,000	3,681.58	2,954.39	2,734.11	2,436.39	2,249.15
170,000	3,911.68	3,139.04	2,904.99	2,588.67	2,389.72
175,000	4,026.73	3,231.36	2,990.43	2,664.81	2,460.01
180,000	4,141.78	3,323.69	3,075.87	2,740.94	2,530.30
190,000	4,371.88	3,508.33	3,246.76	2,893.22	2,670.87
200,000	4,601.97	3,692.98	3,417.64	3,045.49	2,811.44
220,000	5,062.17	4,062.28	3,759.40	3,350.04	3,092.58
225,000	5,177.22	4,154.61	3,844.84	3,426.18	3,162.87
230,000	5,292.27	4,246.93	3,930.28	3,502.31	3,233.15
240,000	5,522.37	4,431.58	4,101.16	3,654.59	3,373.73
$250,000	5,752.47	4,616.23	4,272.04	3,806.86	3,514.30

Monthly Payment Loans · 13.50%

Amortization Period in Years

	15	16	17	18	20
$ 100	1.30	1.28	1.26	1.24	1.21
200	2.60	2.55	2.51	2.48	2.42
300	3.90	3.83	3.76	3.71	3.63
400	5.20	5.10	5.02	4.95	4.83
500	6.50	6.37	6.27	6.18	6.04
600	7.79	7.65	7.52	7.42	7.25
700	9.09	8.92	8.78	8.65	8.46
800	10.39	10.19	10.03	9.89	9.66
900	11.69	11.47	11.28	11.12	10.87
1,000	12.99	12.74	12.53	12.36	12.08
2,000	25.97	25.48	25.06	24.71	24.15
3,000	38.95	38.22	37.59	37.06	36.23
4,000	51.94	50.95	50.12	49.41	48.30
5,000	64.92	63.69	62.65	61.77	60.37
6,000	77.90	76.43	75.18	74.12	72.45
7,000	90.89	89.16	87.71	86.47	84.52
8,000	103.87	101.90	100.23	98.82	96.59
9,000	116.85	114.64	112.76	111.18	108.67
10,000	129.84	127.37	125.29	123.53	120.74
15,000	194.75	191.06	187.94	185.29	181.11
20,000	259.67	254.74	250.58	247.05	241.48
25,000	324.58	318.42	313.22	308.81	301.85
30,000	389.50	382.11	375.87	370.57	362.22
35,000	454.42	445.79	438.51	432.34	422.59
40,000	519.33	509.47	501.15	494.10	482.95
45,000	584.25	573.16	563.80	555.86	543.32
50,000	649.16	636.84	626.44	617.62	603.69
55,000	714.08	700.52	689.08	679.38	664.06
60,000	779.00	764.21	751.73	741.14	724.43
65,000	843.91	827.89	814.37	802.91	784.80
70,000	908.83	891.57	877.01	864.67	845.17
75,000	973.74	955.26	939.66	926.43	905.54
80,000	1,038.66	1,018.94	1,002.30	988.19	965.90
85,000	1,103.58	1,082.62	1,064.94	1,049.95	1,026.27
90,000	1,168.49	1,146.31	1,127.59	1,111.71	1,086.64
95,000	1,233.41	1,209.99	1,190.23	1,173.47	1,147.01
100,000	1,298.32	1,273.67	1,252.87	1,235.24	1,207.38
110,000	1,428.16	1,401.04	1,378.16	1,358.76	1,328.12
120,000	1,557.99	1,528.41	1,503.45	1,482.28	1,448.85
125,000	1,622.90	1,592.09	1,566.09	1,544.04	1,509.22
130,000	1,687.82	1,655.77	1,628.73	1,605.81	1,569.59
140,000	1,817.65	1,783.14	1,754.02	1,729.33	1,690.33
150,000	1,947.48	1,910.51	1,879.31	1,852.85	1,811.07
160,000	2,077.31	2,037.87	2,004.60	1,976.38	1,931.80
170,000	2,207.15	2,165.24	2,129.88	2,099.90	2,052.54
175,000	2,272.06	2,228.92	2,192.53	2,161.66	2,112.91
180,000	2,336.98	2,292.61	2,255.17	2,223.42	2,173.28
190,000	2,466.81	2,419.97	2,380.46	2,346.94	2,294.02
200,000	2,596.64	2,547.34	2,505.74	2,470.47	2,414.75
220,000	2,856.31	2,802.07	2,756.32	2,717.51	2,656.23
225,000	2,921.22	2,865.76	2,818.96	2,779.28	2,716.60
230,000	2,986.14	2,929.44	2,881.60	2,841.04	2,776.97
240,000	3,115.97	3,056.81	3,006.89	2,964.56	2,897.70
$250,000	3,245.80	3,184.18	3,132.18	3,088.08	3,018.44

Table 1   141

13.50%   Monthly Payment Loans

Amortization Period in Years

	21	22	23	24	25
$ 100	1.20	1.19	1.18	1.18	1.17
200	2.40	2.38	2.36	2.35	2.34
300	3.59	3.57	3.54	3.52	3.50
400	4.79	4.75	4.72	4.69	4.67
500	5.99	5.94	5.90	5.86	5.83
600	7.18	7.13	7.08	7.04	7.00
700	8.38	8.31	8.26	8.21	8.16
800	9.58	9.50	9.44	9.38	9.33
900	10.77	10.69	10.61	10.55	10.50
1,000	11.97	11.87	11.79	11.72	11.66
2,000	23.93	23.74	23.58	23.44	23.32
3,000	35.90	35.61	35.37	35.16	34.97
4,000	47.86	47.48	47.16	46.87	46.63
5,000	59.82	59.35	58.94	58.59	58.29
6,000	71.79	71.22	70.73	70.31	69.94
7,000	83.75	83.09	82.52	82.03	81.60
8,000	95.71	94.96	94.31	93.74	93.26
9,000	107.68	106.83	106.09	105.46	104.91
10,000	119.64	118.70	117.88	117.18	116.57
15,000	179.46	178.04	176.82	175.76	174.85
20,000	239.28	237.39	235.76	234.35	233.13
25,000	299.10	296.73	294.70	292.94	291.42
30,000	358.92	356.08	353.63	351.52	349.70
35,000	418.73	415.42	412.57	410.11	407.98
40,000	478.55	474.77	471.51	468.70	466.26
45,000	538.37	534.11	530.45	527.28	524.55
50,000	598.19	593.46	589.39	585.87	582.83
55,000	658.01	652.81	648.32	644.45	641.11
60,000	717.83	712.15	707.26	703.04	699.39
65,000	777.65	771.50	766.20	761.63	757.67
70,000	837.46	830.84	825.14	820.21	815.96
75,000	897.28	890.19	884.08	878.80	874.24
80,000	957.10	949.53	943.01	937.39	932.52
85,000	1,016.92	1,008.88	1,001.95	995.97	990.80
90,000	1,076.74	1,068.22	1,060.89	1,054.56	1,049.09
95,000	1,136.56	1,127.57	1,119.83	1,113.15	1,107.37
100,000	1,196.37	1,186.92	1,178.77	1,171.73	1,165.65
110,000	1,316.01	1,305.61	1,296.64	1,288.90	1,282.21
120,000	1,435.65	1,424.30	1,414.52	1,406.08	1,398.78
125,000	1,495.47	1,483.64	1,473.46	1,464.66	1,457.06
130,000	1,555.29	1,542.99	1,532.39	1,523.25	1,515.34
140,000	1,674.92	1,661.68	1,650.27	1,640.42	1,631.91
150,000	1,794.56	1,780.37	1,768.15	1,757.60	1,748.47
160,000	1,914.20	1,899.06	1,886.02	1,874.77	1,865.04
170,000	2,033.83	2,017.75	2,003.90	1,991.94	1,981.60
175,000	2,093.65	2,077.10	2,062.84	2,050.53	2,039.88
180,000	2,153.47	2,136.44	2,121.78	2,109.11	2,098.17
190,000	2,273.11	2,255.14	2,239.65	2,226.29	2,214.73
200,000	2,392.74	2,373.83	2,357.53	2,343.46	2,331.29
220,000	2,632.02	2,611.21	2,593.28	2,577.80	2,564.42
225,000	2,691.84	2,670.55	2,652.22	2,636.39	2,622.71
230,000	2,751.66	2,729.90	2,711.16	2,694.98	2,680.99
240,000	2,871.29	2,848.59	2,829.03	2,812.15	2,797.55
$250,000	2,990.93	2,967.28	2,946.91	2,929.32	2,914.12

Monthly Payment Loans   **13.50%**

Amortization Period in Years

	26	27	28	29	30
$ 100	1.17	1.16	1.16	1.15	1.15
200	2.33	2.32	2.31	2.30	2.30
300	3.49	3.47	3.46	3.45	3.44
400	4.65	4.63	4.61	4.60	4.59
500	5.81	5.78	5.76	5.75	5.73
600	6.97	6.94	6.92	6.90	6.88
700	8.13	8.10	8.07	8.04	8.02
800	9.29	9.25	9.22	9.19	9.17
900	10.45	10.41	10.37	10.34	10.31
1,000	11.61	11.56	11.52	11.49	11.46
2,000	23.21	23.12	23.04	22.97	22.91
3,000	34.82	34.68	34.56	34.46	34.37
4,000	46.42	46.24	46.08	45.94	45.82
5,000	58.02	57.80	57.60	57.43	57.28
6,000	69.63	69.35	69.12	68.91	68.73
7,000	81.23	80.91	80.63	80.39	80.18
8,000	92.84	92.47	92.15	91.88	91.64
9,000	104.44	104.03	103.67	103.36	103.09
10,000	116.04	115.59	115.19	114.85	114.55
15,000	174.06	173.38	172.78	172.27	171.82
20,000	232.08	231.17	230.37	229.69	229.09
25,000	290.10	288.96	287.97	287.11	286.36
30,000	348.12	346.75	345.56	344.53	343.63
35,000	406.14	404.54	403.15	401.95	400.90
40,000	464.16	462.33	460.74	459.37	458.17
45,000	522.18	520.12	518.34	516.79	515.44
50,000	580.19	577.91	575.93	574.21	572.71
55,000	638.21	635.70	633.52	631.63	629.98
60,000	696.23	693.49	691.11	689.05	687.25
65,000	754.25	751.28	748.71	746.47	744.52
70,000	812.27	809.07	806.30	803.89	801.79
75,000	870.29	866.86	863.89	861.31	859.06
80,000	928.31	924.65	921.48	918.73	916.33
85,000	986.33	982.45	979.08	976.15	973.61
90,000	1,044.35	1,040.24	1,036.67	1,033.57	1,030.88
95,000	1,102.36	1,098.03	1,094.26	1,090.99	1,088.15
100,000	1,160.38	1,155.82	1,151.85	1,148.41	1,145.42
110,000	1,276.42	1,271.40	1,267.04	1,263.25	1,259.96
120,000	1,392.46	1,386.98	1,382.22	1,378.09	1,374.50
125,000	1,450.48	1,444.77	1,439.82	1,435.51	1,431.77
130,000	1,508.50	1,502.56	1,497.41	1,492.93	1,489.04
140,000	1,624.54	1,618.14	1,612.59	1,607.77	1,603.58
150,000	1,740.57	1,733.72	1,727.78	1,722.61	1,718.12
160,000	1,856.61	1,849.30	1,842.96	1,837.45	1,832.66
170,000	1,972.65	1,964.89	1,958.15	1,952.30	1,947.21
175,000	2,030.67	2,022.68	2,015.74	2,009.72	2,004.48
180,000	2,088.69	2,080.47	2,073.33	2,067.14	2,061.75
190,000	2,204.72	2,196.05	2,188.52	2,181.98	2,176.29
200,000	2,320.76	2,311.63	2,303.70	2,296.82	2,290.83
220,000	2,552.84	2,542.79	2,534.07	2,526.50	2,519.91
225,000	2,610.86	2,600.58	2,591.67	2,583.92	2,577.18
230,000	2,668.88	2,658.37	2,649.26	2,641.34	2,634.45
240,000	2,784.91	2,773.95	2,764.44	2,756.18	2,748.99
$250,000	2,900.95	2,889.54	2,879.63	2,871.02	2,863.54

Table 1   143

13.75% Monthly Payment Loans

Amortization Period in Years

	5	7	8	10	12
$ 100	2.32	1.87	1.73	1.54	1.43
200	4.63	3.73	3.45	3.08	2.85
300	6.95	5.59	5.17	4.62	4.27
400	9.26	7.45	6.90	6.16	5.69
500	11.57	9.31	8.62	7.69	7.11
600	13.89	11.17	10.34	9.23	8.53
700	16.20	13.03	12.07	10.77	9.95
800	18.52	14.89	13.79	12.31	11.38
900	20.83	16.75	15.51	13.84	12.80
1,000	23.14	18.61	17.23	15.38	14.22
2,000	46.28	37.21	34.46	30.76	28.43
3,000	69.42	55.81	51.69	46.14	42.65
4,000	92.56	74.41	68.92	61.51	56.86
5,000	115.70	93.02	86.15	76.89	71.07
6,000	138.84	111.62	103.38	92.27	85.29
7,000	161.98	130.22	120.61	107.64	99.50
8,000	185.12	148.82	137.84	123.02	113.72
9,000	208.25	167.42	155.07	138.40	127.93
10,000	231.39	186.03	172.30	153.77	142.14
15,000	347.09	279.04	258.45	230.66	213.21
20,000	462.78	372.05	344.60	307.54	284.28
25,000	578.48	465.06	430.74	384.42	355.35
30,000	694.17	558.07	516.89	461.31	426.42
35,000	809.86	651.08	603.04	538.19	497.49
40,000	925.56	744.09	689.19	615.07	568.56
45,000	1,041.25	837.10	775.33	691.96	639.63
50,000	1,156.95	930.11	861.48	768.84	710.70
55,000	1,272.64	1,023.12	947.63	845.72	781.77
60,000	1,388.34	1,116.14	1,033.78	922.61	852.83
65,000	1,504.03	1,209.15	1,119.92	999.49	923.90
70,000	1,619.72	1,302.16	1,206.07	1,076.37	994.97
75,000	1,735.42	1,395.17	1,292.22	1,153.26	1,066.04
80,000	1,851.11	1,488.18	1,378.37	1,230.14	1,137.11
85,000	1,966.81	1,581.19	1,464.51	1,307.02	1,208.18
90,000	2,082.50	1,674.20	1,550.66	1,383.91	1,279.25
95,000	2,198.20	1,767.21	1,636.81	1,460.79	1,350.32
100,000	2,313.89	1,860.22	1,722.96	1,537.67	1,421.39
110,000	2,545.28	2,046.24	1,895.25	1,691.44	1,563.53
120,000	2,776.67	2,232.27	2,067.55	1,845.21	1,705.66
125,000	2,892.36	2,325.28	2,153.70	1,922.09	1,776.73
130,000	3,008.05	2,418.29	2,239.84	1,998.97	1,847.80
140,000	3,239.44	2,604.31	2,412.14	2,152.74	1,989.94
150,000	3,470.83	2,790.33	2,584.43	2,306.51	2,132.08
160,000	3,702.22	2,976.35	2,756.73	2,460.27	2,274.22
170,000	3,933.61	3,162.38	2,929.02	2,614.04	2,416.36
175,000	4,049.30	3,255.39	3,015.17	2,690.92	2,487.42
180,000	4,165.00	3,348.40	3,101.32	2,767.81	2,558.49
190,000	4,396.39	3,534.42	3,273.62	2,921.57	2,700.63
200,000	4,627.77	3,720.44	3,445.91	3,075.34	2,842.77
220,000	5,090.55	4,092.48	3,790.50	3,382.87	3,127.05
225,000	5,206.25	4,185.50	3,876.65	3,459.76	3,198.12
230,000	5,321.94	4,278.51	3,962.80	3,536.64	3,269.19
240,000	5,553.33	4,464.53	4,135.09	3,690.41	3,411.32
$250,000	5,784.72	4,650.55	4,307.39	3,844.18	3,553.46

Monthly Payment Loans **13.75%**

Amortization Period in Years

	15	16	17	18	20
$ 100	1.32	1.30	1.28	1.26	1.23
200	2.63	2.59	2.55	2.51	2.46
300	3.95	3.88	3.82	3.76	3.68
400	5.26	5.17	5.09	5.02	4.91
500	6.58	6.46	6.36	6.27	6.13
600	7.89	7.75	7.63	7.52	7.36
700	9.21	9.04	8.90	8.77	8.58
800	10.52	10.33	10.17	10.03	9.81
900	11.84	11.62	11.44	11.28	11.03
1,000	13.15	12.91	12.71	12.53	12.26
2,000	26.30	25.82	25.41	25.06	24.51
3,000	39.45	38.72	38.11	37.59	36.77
4,000	52.60	51.63	50.81	50.12	49.02
5,000	65.75	64.54	63.51	62.64	61.28
6,000	78.90	77.44	76.21	75.17	73.53
7,000	92.05	90.35	88.91	87.70	85.78
8,000	105.20	103.26	101.62	100.23	98.04
9,000	118.35	116.16	114.32	112.75	110.29
10,000	131.50	129.07	127.02	125.28	122.55
15,000	197.25	193.60	190.52	187.92	183.82
20,000	263.00	258.13	254.03	250.56	245.09
25,000	328.75	322.67	317.54	313.20	306.36
30,000	394.50	387.20	381.04	375.83	367.63
35,000	460.25	451.73	444.55	438.47	428.90
40,000	526.00	516.26	508.06	501.11	490.17
45,000	591.75	580.79	571.56	563.75	551.44
50,000	657.50	645.33	635.07	626.39	612.71
55,000	723.25	709.86	698.58	689.03	673.98
60,000	789.00	774.39	762.08	751.66	735.25
65,000	854.75	838.92	825.59	814.30	796.52
70,000	920.50	903.45	889.10	876.94	857.79
75,000	986.25	967.99	952.60	939.58	919.06
80,000	1,051.99	1,032.52	1,016.11	1,002.22	980.33
85,000	1,117.74	1,097.05	1,079.61	1,064.85	1,041.60
90,000	1,183.49	1,161.58	1,143.12	1,127.49	1,102.87
95,000	1,249.24	1,226.11	1,206.63	1,190.13	1,164.14
100,000	1,314.99	1,290.65	1,270.13	1,252.77	1,225.41
110,000	1,446.49	1,419.71	1,397.15	1,378.05	1,347.95
120,000	1,577.99	1,548.77	1,524.16	1,503.32	1,470.49
125,000	1,643.74	1,613.31	1,587.67	1,565.96	1,531.76
130,000	1,709.49	1,677.84	1,651.17	1,628.60	1,593.03
140,000	1,840.99	1,806.90	1,778.19	1,753.87	1,715.57
150,000	1,972.49	1,935.97	1,905.20	1,879.15	1,838.11
160,000	2,103.98	2,065.03	2,032.21	2,004.43	1,960.65
170,000	2,235.48	2,194.09	2,159.22	2,129.70	2,083.19
175,000	2,301.23	2,258.63	2,222.73	2,192.34	2,144.46
180,000	2,366.98	2,323.16	2,286.24	2,254.98	2,205.73
190,000	2,498.48	2,452.22	2,413.25	2,380.26	2,328.28
200,000	2,629.98	2,581.29	2,540.26	2,505.53	2,450.82
220,000	2,892.98	2,839.41	2,794.29	2,756.09	2,695.90
225,000	2,958.73	2,903.95	2,857.80	2,818.72	2,757.17
230,000	3,024.48	2,968.48	2,921.30	2,881.36	2,818.44
240,000	3,155.97	3,097.54	3,048.31	3,006.64	2,940.98
$250,000	3,287.47	3,226.61	3,175.33	3,131.91	3,063.52

Table 1   145

13.75%   Monthly Payment Loans

Amortization Period in Years

	21	22	23	24	25
$ 100	1.22	1.21	1.20	1.20	1.19
200	2.43	2.42	2.40	2.39	2.37
300	3.65	3.62	3.60	3.58	3.56
400	4.86	4.83	4.79	4.77	4.74
500	6.08	6.03	5.99	5.96	5.93
600	7.29	7.24	7.19	7.15	7.11
700	8.51	8.44	8.39	8.34	8.30
800	9.72	9.65	9.58	9.53	9.48
900	10.94	10.85	10.78	10.72	10.67
1,000	12.15	12.06	11.98	11.91	11.85
2,000	24.30	24.11	23.95	23.82	23.70
3,000	36.44	36.17	35.93	35.72	35.54
4,000	48.59	48.22	47.90	47.63	47.39
5,000	60.74	60.27	59.88	59.53	59.24
6,000	72.88	72.33	71.85	71.44	71.08
7,000	85.03	84.38	83.82	83.35	82.93
8,000	97.18	96.44	95.80	95.25	94.78
9,000	109.32	108.49	107.77	107.16	106.62
10,000	121.47	120.54	119.75	119.06	118.47
15,000	182.20	180.81	179.62	178.59	177.70
20,000	242.93	241.08	239.49	238.12	236.94
25,000	303.66	301.35	299.36	297.65	296.17
30,000	364.39	361.62	359.23	357.18	355.40
35,000	425.12	421.89	419.10	416.71	414.64
40,000	485.86	482.16	478.98	476.24	473.87
45,000	546.59	542.43	538.85	535.76	533.10
50,000	607.32	602.69	598.72	595.29	592.34
55,000	668.05	662.96	658.59	654.82	651.57
60,000	728.78	723.23	718.46	714.35	710.80
65,000	789.51	783.50	778.33	773.88	770.04
70,000	850.24	843.77	838.20	833.41	829.27
75,000	910.98	904.04	898.08	892.94	888.50
80,000	971.71	964.31	957.95	952.47	947.74
85,000	1,032.44	1,024.58	1,017.82	1,012.00	1,006.97
90,000	1,093.17	1,084.85	1,077.69	1,071.52	1,066.20
95,000	1,153.90	1,145.12	1,137.56	1,131.05	1,125.44
100,000	1,214.63	1,205.38	1,197.43	1,190.58	1,184.67
110,000	1,336.09	1,325.92	1,317.18	1,309.64	1,303.14
120,000	1,457.56	1,446.46	1,436.92	1,428.70	1,421.60
125,000	1,518.29	1,506.73	1,496.79	1,488.23	1,480.84
130,000	1,579.02	1,567.00	1,556.66	1,547.76	1,540.07
140,000	1,700.48	1,687.54	1,676.40	1,666.81	1,658.54
150,000	1,821.95	1,808.07	1,796.15	1,785.87	1,777.00
160,000	1,943.41	1,928.61	1,915.89	1,904.93	1,895.47
170,000	2,064.87	2,049.15	2,035.63	2,023.99	2,013.94
175,000	2,125.60	2,109.42	2,095.50	2,083.52	2,073.17
180,000	2,186.33	2,169.69	2,155.37	2,143.04	2,132.40
190,000	2,307.80	2,290.23	2,275.12	2,262.10	2,250.87
200,000	2,429.26	2,410.76	2,394.86	2,381.16	2,369.34
220,000	2,672.18	2,651.84	2,634.35	2,619.28	2,606.27
225,000	2,732.92	2,712.11	2,694.22	2,678.80	2,665.50
230,000	2,793.65	2,772.38	2,754.09	2,738.33	2,724.74
240,000	2,915.11	2,892.92	2,873.83	2,857.39	2,843.20
$250,000	3,036.57	3,013.45	2,993.57	2,976.45	2,961.67

Monthly Payment Loans   **13.75%**

Amortization Period in Years

	26	27	28	29	30
$ 100	1.18	1.18	1.18	1.17	1.17
200	2.36	2.36	2.35	2.34	2.34
300	3.54	3.53	3.52	3.51	3.50
400	4.72	4.71	4.69	4.68	4.67
500	5.90	5.88	5.86	5.84	5.83
600	7.08	7.06	7.03	7.01	7.00
700	8.26	8.23	8.20	8.18	8.16
800	9.44	9.41	9.38	9.35	9.33
900	10.62	10.58	10.55	10.52	10.49
1,000	11.80	11.76	11.72	11.68	11.66
2,000	23.60	23.51	23.43	23.36	23.31
3,000	35.39	35.26	35.14	35.04	34.96
4,000	47.19	47.01	46.86	46.72	46.61
5,000	58.98	58.76	58.57	58.40	58.26
6,000	70.78	70.51	70.28	70.08	69.91
7,000	82.57	82.26	82.00	81.76	81.56
8,000	94.37	94.02	93.71	93.44	93.21
9,000	106.17	105.77	105.42	105.12	104.87
10,000	117.96	117.52	117.14	116.80	116.52
15,000	176.94	176.28	175.70	175.20	174.77
20,000	235.92	235.03	234.27	233.60	233.03
25,000	294.89	293.79	292.83	292.00	291.28
30,000	353.87	352.55	351.40	350.40	349.54
35,000	412.85	411.30	409.96	408.80	407.79
40,000	471.83	470.06	468.53	467.20	466.05
45,000	530.81	528.82	527.09	525.60	524.31
50,000	589.78	587.57	585.66	584.00	582.56
55,000	648.76	646.33	644.23	642.40	640.82
60,000	707.74	705.09	702.79	700.80	699.07
65,000	766.72	763.84	761.36	759.20	757.33
70,000	825.70	822.60	819.92	817.60	815.58
75,000	884.67	881.36	878.49	876.00	873.84
80,000	943.65	940.12	937.05	934.40	932.10
85,000	1,002.63	998.87	995.62	992.80	990.35
90,000	1,061.61	1,057.63	1,054.18	1,051.20	1,048.61
95,000	1,120.58	1,116.39	1,112.75	1,109.60	1,106.86
100,000	1,179.56	1,175.14	1,171.32	1,168.00	1,165.12
110,000	1,297.52	1,292.66	1,288.45	1,284.80	1,281.63
120,000	1,415.47	1,410.17	1,405.58	1,401.59	1,398.14
125,000	1,474.45	1,468.93	1,464.14	1,459.99	1,456.40
130,000	1,533.43	1,527.68	1,522.71	1,518.39	1,514.65
140,000	1,651.39	1,645.20	1,639.84	1,635.19	1,631.16
150,000	1,769.34	1,762.71	1,756.97	1,751.99	1,747.67
160,000	1,887.30	1,880.23	1,874.10	1,868.79	1,864.19
170,000	2,005.25	1,997.74	1,991.23	1,985.59	1,980.70
175,000	2,064.23	2,056.50	2,049.80	2,043.99	2,038.95
180,000	2,123.21	2,115.25	2,108.36	2,102.39	2,097.21
190,000	2,241.16	2,232.77	2,225.49	2,219.19	2,213.72
200,000	2,359.12	2,350.28	2,342.63	2,335.99	2,330.23
220,000	2,595.03	2,585.31	2,576.89	2,569.59	2,563.25
225,000	2,654.01	2,644.07	2,635.45	2,627.99	2,621.51
230,000	2,712.99	2,702.82	2,694.02	2,686.39	2,679.76
240,000	2,830.94	2,820.34	2,811.15	2,803.18	2,796.28
$250,000	2,948.90	2,937.85	2,928.28	2,919.98	2,912.79

Table 1   147

14.00%   Monthly Payment Loans

Amortization Period in Years

	5	7	8	10	12
$ 100	2.33	1.88	1.74	1.56	1.44
200	4.66	3.75	3.48	3.11	2.88
300	6.99	5.63	5.22	4.66	4.32
400	9.31	7.50	6.95	6.22	5.75
500	11.64	9.38	8.69	7.77	7.19
600	13.97	11.25	10.43	9.32	8.63
700	16.29	13.12	12.17	10.87	10.06
800	18.62	15.00	13.90	12.43	11.50
900	20.95	16.87	15.64	13.98	12.94
1,000	23.27	18.75	17.38	15.53	14.38
2,000	46.54	37.49	34.75	31.06	28.75
3,000	69.81	56.23	52.12	46.58	43.12
4,000	93.08	74.97	69.49	62.11	57.49
5,000	116.35	93.71	86.86	77.64	71.86
6,000	139.61	112.45	104.23	93.16	86.23
7,000	162.88	131.19	121.61	108.69	100.60
8,000	186.15	149.93	138.98	124.22	114.98
9,000	209.42	168.67	156.35	139.74	129.35
10,000	232.69	187.41	173.72	155.27	143.72
15,000	349.03	281.11	260.58	232.90	215.57
20,000	465.37	374.81	347.44	310.54	287.43
25,000	581.71	468.51	434.29	388.17	359.29
30,000	698.05	562.21	521.15	465.80	431.14
35,000	814.39	655.91	608.01	543.44	503.00
40,000	930.74	749.61	694.87	621.07	574.86
45,000	1,047.08	843.31	781.72	698.70	646.71
50,000	1,163.42	937.01	868.58	776.34	718.57
55,000	1,279.76	1,030.71	955.44	853.97	790.42
60,000	1,396.10	1,124.41	1,042.30	931.60	862.28
65,000	1,512.44	1,218.11	1,129.15	1,009.24	934.14
70,000	1,628.78	1,311.81	1,216.01	1,086.87	1,005.99
75,000	1,745.12	1,405.51	1,302.87	1,164.50	1,077.85
80,000	1,861.47	1,499.21	1,389.73	1,242.14	1,149.71
85,000	1,977.81	1,592.91	1,476.58	1,319.77	1,221.56
90,000	2,094.15	1,686.61	1,563.44	1,397.40	1,293.42
95,000	2,210.49	1,780.31	1,650.30	1,475.04	1,365.28
100,000	2,326.83	1,874.01	1,737.16	1,552.67	1,437.13
110,000	2,559.51	2,061.41	1,910.87	1,707.94	1,580.84
120,000	2,792.20	2,248.81	2,084.59	1,863.20	1,724.56
125,000	2,908.54	2,342.51	2,171.44	1,940.84	1,796.41
130,000	3,024.88	2,436.21	2,258.30	2,018.47	1,868.27
140,000	3,257.56	2,623.61	2,432.02	2,173.74	2,011.98
150,000	3,490.24	2,811.01	2,605.73	2,329.00	2,155.70
160,000	3,722.93	2,998.41	2,779.45	2,484.27	2,299.41
170,000	3,955.61	3,185.81	2,953.16	2,639.53	2,443.12
175,000	4,071.95	3,279.51	3,040.02	2,717.17	2,514.98
180,000	4,188.29	3,373.21	3,126.88	2,794.80	2,586.83
190,000	4,420.97	3,560.61	3,300.59	2,950.07	2,730.55
200,000	4,653.66	3,748.01	3,474.31	3,105.33	2,874.26
220,000	5,119.02	4,122.81	3,821.74	3,415.87	3,161.68
225,000	5,235.36	4,216.51	3,908.59	3,493.50	3,233.54
230,000	5,351.70	4,310.21	3,995.45	3,571.13	3,305.40
240,000	5,584.39	4,497.61	4,169.17	3,726.40	3,449.11
$250,000	5,817.07	4,685.01	4,342.88	3,881.67	3,592.82

Monthly Payment Loans   14.00%

Amortization Period in Years

	15	16	17	18	20
$ 100	1.34	1.31	1.29	1.28	1.25
200	2.67	2.62	2.58	2.55	2.49
300	4.00	3.93	3.87	3.82	3.74
400	5.33	5.24	5.15	5.09	4.98
500	6.66	6.54	6.44	6.36	6.22
600	8.00	7.85	7.73	7.63	7.47
700	9.33	9.16	9.02	8.90	8.71
800	10.66	10.47	10.30	10.17	9.95
900	11.99	11.77	11.59	11.44	11.20
1,000	13.32	13.08	12.88	12.71	12.44
2,000	26.64	26.16	25.75	25.41	24.88
3,000	39.96	39.24	38.63	38.12	37.31
4,000	53.27	52.31	51.50	50.82	49.75
5,000	66.59	65.39	64.38	63.52	62.18
6,000	79.91	78.47	77.25	76.23	74.62
7,000	93.23	91.54	90.13	88.93	87.05
8,000	106.54	104.62	103.00	101.64	99.49
9,000	119.86	117.70	115.88	114.34	111.92
10,000	133.18	130.77	128.75	127.04	124.36
15,000	199.77	196.16	193.13	190.56	186.53
20,000	266.35	261.54	257.50	254.08	248.71
25,000	332.94	326.93	321.87	317.60	310.89
30,000	399.53	392.31	386.25	381.12	373.06
35,000	466.11	457.70	450.62	444.64	435.24
40,000	532.70	523.08	515.00	508.16	497.41
45,000	599.29	588.47	579.37	571.68	559.59
50,000	665.88	653.85	643.74	635.20	621.77
55,000	732.46	719.24	708.12	698.72	683.94
60,000	799.05	784.62	772.49	762.23	746.12
65,000	865.64	850.01	836.86	825.75	808.29
70,000	932.22	915.39	901.24	889.27	870.47
75,000	998.81	980.78	965.61	952.79	932.65
80,000	1,065.40	1,046.16	1,029.99	1,016.31	994.82
85,000	1,131.99	1,111.55	1,094.36	1,079.83	1,057.00
90,000	1,198.57	1,176.93	1,158.73	1,143.35	1,119.17
95,000	1,265.16	1,242.32	1,223.11	1,206.87	1,181.35
100,000	1,331.75	1,307.70	1,287.48	1,270.39	1,243.53
110,000	1,464.92	1,438.47	1,416.23	1,397.43	1,367.88
120,000	1,598.09	1,569.24	1,544.98	1,524.46	1,492.23
125,000	1,664.68	1,634.63	1,609.35	1,587.98	1,554.41
130,000	1,731.27	1,700.01	1,673.72	1,651.50	1,616.58
140,000	1,864.44	1,830.78	1,802.47	1,778.54	1,740.93
150,000	1,997.62	1,961.55	1,931.22	1,905.58	1,865.29
160,000	2,130.79	2,092.32	2,059.97	2,032.62	1,989.64
170,000	2,263.97	2,223.09	2,188.71	2,159.66	2,113.99
175,000	2,330.55	2,288.48	2,253.09	2,223.18	2,176.17
180,000	2,397.14	2,353.86	2,317.46	2,286.69	2,238.34
190,000	2,530.31	2,484.63	2,446.21	2,413.73	2,362.69
200,000	2,663.49	2,615.40	2,574.96	2,540.77	2,487.05
220,000	2,929.84	2,876.94	2,832.45	2,794.85	2,735.75
225,000	2,996.42	2,942.33	2,896.83	2,858.37	2,797.93
230,000	3,063.01	3,007.71	2,961.20	2,921.89	2,860.10
240,000	3,196.18	3,138.48	3,089.95	3,048.92	2,984.45
$250,000	3,329.36	3,269.25	3,218.70	3,175.96	3,108.81

Table 1   149

14.00% Monthly Payment Loans

Amortization Period in Years

	21	22	23	24	25
$ 100	1.24	1.23	1.22	1.21	1.21
200	2.47	2.45	2.44	2.42	2.41
300	3.70	3.68	3.65	3.63	3.62
400	4.94	4.90	4.87	4.84	4.82
500	6.17	6.12	6.09	6.05	6.02
600	7.40	7.35	7.30	7.26	7.23
700	8.64	8.57	8.52	8.47	8.43
800	9.87	9.80	9.73	9.68	9.64
900	11.10	11.02	10.95	10.89	10.84
1,000	12.33	12.24	12.17	12.10	12.04
2,000	24.66	24.48	24.33	24.20	24.08
3,000	36.99	36.72	36.49	36.29	36.12
4,000	49.32	48.96	48.65	48.39	48.16
5,000	61.65	61.20	60.81	60.48	60.19
6,000	73.98	73.44	72.98	72.58	72.23
7,000	86.31	85.68	85.14	84.67	84.27
8,000	98.64	97.92	97.30	96.77	96.31
9,000	110.97	110.16	109.46	108.86	108.34
10,000	123.30	122.40	121.62	120.96	120.38
15,000	184.95	183.59	182.43	181.43	180.57
20,000	246.60	244.79	243.24	241.91	240.76
25,000	308.25	305.99	304.05	302.38	300.95
30,000	369.90	367.18	364.86	362.86	361.13
35,000	431.54	428.38	425.67	423.33	421.32
40,000	493.19	489.58	486.47	483.81	481.51
45,000	554.84	550.77	547.28	544.28	541.70
50,000	616.49	611.97	608.09	604.76	601.89
55,000	678.14	673.17	668.90	665.23	662.07
60,000	739.79	734.36	729.71	725.71	722.26
65,000	801.43	795.56	790.52	786.18	782.45
70,000	863.08	856.76	851.33	846.66	842.64
75,000	924.73	917.95	912.13	907.13	902.83
80,000	986.38	979.15	972.94	967.61	963.01
85,000	1,048.03	1,040.34	1,033.75	1,028.08	1,023.20
90,000	1,109.68	1,101.54	1,094.56	1,088.56	1,083.39
95,000	1,171.32	1,162.74	1,155.37	1,149.03	1,143.58
100,000	1,232.97	1,223.93	1,216.18	1,209.51	1,203.77
110,000	1,356.27	1,346.33	1,337.80	1,330.46	1,324.14
120,000	1,479.57	1,468.72	1,459.41	1,451.41	1,444.52
125,000	1,541.21	1,529.92	1,520.22	1,511.89	1,504.71
130,000	1,602.86	1,591.11	1,581.03	1,572.36	1,564.89
140,000	1,726.16	1,713.51	1,702.65	1,693.31	1,685.27
150,000	1,849.46	1,835.90	1,824.26	1,814.26	1,805.65
160,000	1,972.75	1,958.29	1,945.88	1,935.21	1,926.02
170,000	2,096.05	2,080.68	2,067.50	2,056.16	2,046.40
175,000	2,157.70	2,141.88	2,128.31	2,116.64	2,106.59
180,000	2,219.35	2,203.08	2,189.12	2,177.11	2,166.77
190,000	2,342.64	2,325.47	2,310.73	2,298.06	2,287.15
200,000	2,465.94	2,447.86	2,432.35	2,419.01	2,407.53
220,000	2,712.53	2,692.65	2,675.59	2,660.91	2,648.28
225,000	2,774.18	2,753.85	2,736.39	2,721.39	2,708.47
230,000	2,835.83	2,815.04	2,797.20	2,781.86	2,768.66
240,000	2,959.13	2,937.44	2,918.82	2,902.82	2,889.03
$250,000	3,082.42	3,059.83	3,040.44	3,023.77	3,009.41

Monthly Payment Loans   14.00%

Amortization Period in Years

	26	27	28	29	30
$ 100	1.20	1.20	1.20	1.19	1.19
200	2.40	2.39	2.39	2.38	2.37
300	3.60	3.59	3.58	3.57	3.56
400	4.80	4.78	4.77	4.76	4.74
500	6.00	5.98	5.96	5.94	5.93
600	7.20	7.17	7.15	7.13	7.11
700	8.40	8.37	8.34	8.32	8.30
800	9.60	9.56	9.53	9.51	9.48
900	10.79	10.76	10.72	10.69	10.67
1,000	11.99	11.95	11.91	11.88	11.85
2,000	23.98	23.90	23.82	23.76	23.70
3,000	35.97	35.84	35.73	35.63	35.55
4,000	47.96	47.79	47.64	47.51	47.40
5,000	59.95	59.73	59.55	59.39	59.25
6,000	71.93	71.68	71.46	71.26	71.10
7,000	83.92	83.62	83.36	83.14	82.95
8,000	95.91	95.57	95.27	95.02	94.79
9,000	107.90	107.51	107.18	106.89	106.64
10,000	119.89	119.46	119.09	118.77	118.49
15,000	179.83	179.18	178.63	178.15	177.74
20,000	239.77	238.91	238.17	237.53	236.98
25,000	299.71	298.64	297.71	296.91	296.22
30,000	359.65	358.36	357.26	356.30	355.47
35,000	419.59	418.09	416.80	415.68	414.71
40,000	479.53	477.82	476.34	475.06	473.95
45,000	539.47	537.54	535.88	534.44	533.20
50,000	599.41	597.27	595.42	593.82	592.44
55,000	659.35	657.00	654.97	653.21	651.68
60,000	719.29	716.72	714.51	712.59	710.93
65,000	779.23	776.45	774.05	771.97	770.17
70,000	839.17	836.18	833.59	831.35	829.42
75,000	899.11	895.90	893.13	890.73	888.66
80,000	959.05	955.63	952.67	950.12	947.90
85,000	1,018.99	1,015.36	1,012.22	1,009.50	1,007.15
90,000	1,078.93	1,075.08	1,071.76	1,068.88	1,066.39
95,000	1,138.87	1,134.81	1,131.30	1,128.26	1,125.63
100,000	1,198.81	1,194.54	1,190.84	1,187.64	1,184.88
110,000	1,318.69	1,313.99	1,309.93	1,306.41	1,303.36
120,000	1,438.57	1,433.44	1,429.01	1,425.17	1,421.85
125,000	1,498.52	1,493.17	1,488.55	1,484.55	1,481.09
130,000	1,558.46	1,552.90	1,548.09	1,543.94	1,540.34
140,000	1,678.34	1,672.35	1,667.18	1,662.70	1,658.83
150,000	1,798.22	1,791.80	1,786.26	1,781.46	1,777.31
160,000	1,918.10	1,911.26	1,905.34	1,900.23	1,895.80
170,000	2,037.98	2,030.71	2,024.43	2,018.99	2,014.29
175,000	2,097.92	2,090.44	2,083.97	2,078.37	2,073.53
180,000	2,157.86	2,150.16	2,143.51	2,137.76	2,132.77
190,000	2,277.74	2,269.62	2,262.59	2,256.52	2,251.26
200,000	2,397.62	2,389.07	2,381.68	2,375.28	2,369.75
220,000	2,637.38	2,627.98	2,619.85	2,612.81	2,606.72
225,000	2,697.32	2,687.70	2,679.39	2,672.19	2,665.97
230,000	2,757.26	2,747.43	2,738.93	2,731.58	2,725.21
240,000	2,877.14	2,866.88	2,858.01	2,850.34	2,843.70
$250,000	2,997.03	2,986.34	2,977.10	2,969.10	2,962.18

Table 1   151

14.25%   Monthly Payment Loans

Amortization Period in Years

	5	7	8	10	12
$ 100	2.34	1.89	1.76	1.57	1.46
200	4.68	3.78	3.51	3.14	2.91
300	7.02	5.67	5.26	4.71	4.36
400	9.36	7.56	7.01	6.28	5.82
500	11.70	9.44	8.76	7.84	7.27
600	14.04	11.33	10.51	9.41	8.72
700	16.38	13.22	12.26	10.98	10.18
800	18.72	15.11	14.02	12.55	11.63
900	21.06	17.00	15.77	14.11	13.08
1,000	23.40	18.88	17.52	15.68	14.53
2,000	46.80	37.76	35.03	31.36	29.06
3,000	70.20	56.64	52.55	47.04	43.59
4,000	93.60	75.52	70.06	62.71	58.12
5,000	117.00	94.40	87.58	78.39	72.65
6,000	140.39	113.28	105.09	94.07	87.18
7,000	163.79	132.15	122.60	109.75	101.71
8,000	187.19	151.03	140.12	125.42	116.24
9,000	210.59	169.91	157.63	141.10	130.77
10,000	233.99	188.79	175.15	156.78	145.30
15,000	350.98	283.18	262.72	235.16	217.95
20,000	467.97	377.57	350.29	313.55	290.59
25,000	584.96	471.96	437.86	391.94	363.24
30,000	701.95	566.36	525.43	470.32	435.89
35,000	818.94	660.75	613.00	548.71	508.54
40,000	935.93	755.14	700.57	627.10	581.18
45,000	1,052.92	849.53	788.14	705.48	653.83
50,000	1,169.91	943.92	875.71	783.87	726.48
55,000	1,286.90	1,038.32	963.28	862.26	799.13
60,000	1,403.89	1,132.71	1,050.85	940.64	871.77
65,000	1,520.88	1,227.10	1,138.42	1,019.03	944.42
70,000	1,637.87	1,321.49	1,225.99	1,097.42	1,017.07
75,000	1,754.86	1,415.88	1,313.56	1,175.80	1,089.72
80,000	1,871.85	1,510.28	1,401.13	1,254.19	1,162.36
85,000	1,988.84	1,604.67	1,488.70	1,332.58	1,235.01
90,000	2,105.83	1,699.06	1,576.27	1,410.96	1,307.66
95,000	2,222.82	1,793.45	1,663.84	1,489.35	1,380.31
100,000	2,339.81	1,887.84	1,751.41	1,567.74	1,452.95
110,000	2,573.79	2,076.63	1,926.55	1,724.51	1,598.25
120,000	2,807.77	2,265.41	2,101.69	1,881.28	1,743.54
125,000	2,924.76	2,359.80	2,189.26	1,959.67	1,816.19
130,000	3,041.75	2,454.20	2,276.84	2,038.06	1,888.84
140,000	3,275.73	2,642.98	2,451.98	2,194.83	2,034.13
150,000	3,509.71	2,831.76	2,627.12	2,351.60	2,179.43
160,000	3,743.70	3,020.55	2,802.26	2,508.37	2,324.72
170,000	3,977.68	3,209.33	2,977.40	2,665.15	2,470.02
175,000	4,094.67	3,303.72	3,064.97	2,743.53	2,542.67
180,000	4,211.66	3,398.11	3,152.54	2,821.92	2,615.31
190,000	4,445.64	3,586.90	3,327.68	2,978.69	2,760.61
200,000	4,679.62	3,775.68	3,502.82	3,135.47	2,905.90
220,000	5,147.58	4,153.25	3,853.10	3,449.01	3,196.49
225,000	5,264.57	4,247.64	3,940.67	3,527.40	3,269.14
230,000	5,381.56	4,342.03	4,028.24	3,605.79	3,341.79
240,000	5,615.54	4,530.82	4,203.38	3,762.56	3,487.08
$250,000	5,849.52	4,719.60	4,378.52	3,919.33	3,632.38

Monthly Payment Loans   **14.25%**

Amortization Period in Years

	15	16	17	18	20
$ 100	1.35	1.33	1.31	1.29	1.27
200	2.70	2.65	2.61	2.58	2.53
300	4.05	3.98	3.92	3.87	3.79
400	5.40	5.30	5.22	5.16	5.05
500	6.75	6.63	6.53	6.45	6.31
600	8.10	7.95	7.83	7.73	7.58
700	9.45	9.28	9.14	9.02	8.84
800	10.79	10.60	10.44	10.31	10.10
900	12.14	11.93	11.75	11.60	11.36
1,000	13.49	13.25	13.05	12.89	12.62
2,000	26.98	26.50	26.10	25.77	25.24
3,000	40.46	39.75	39.15	38.65	37.86
4,000	53.95	53.00	52.20	51.53	50.47
5,000	67.43	66.25	65.25	64.41	63.09
6,000	80.92	79.50	78.30	77.29	75.71
7,000	94.41	92.74	91.35	90.17	88.33
8,000	107.89	105.99	104.40	103.05	100.94
9,000	121.38	119.24	117.45	115.93	113.56
10,000	134.86	132.49	130.50	128.81	126.18
15,000	202.29	198.73	195.74	193.22	189.26
20,000	269.72	264.97	260.99	257.62	252.35
25,000	337.15	331.22	326.23	322.03	315.43
30,000	404.58	397.46	391.48	386.43	378.52
35,000	472.01	463.70	456.72	450.84	441.61
40,000	539.44	529.94	521.97	515.24	504.69
45,000	606.87	596.18	587.21	579.64	567.78
50,000	674.29	662.43	652.46	644.05	630.86
55,000	741.72	728.67	717.70	708.45	693.95
60,000	809.15	794.91	782.95	772.86	757.04
65,000	876.58	861.15	848.20	837.26	820.12
70,000	944.01	927.40	913.44	901.67	883.21
75,000	1,011.44	993.64	978.69	966.07	946.29
80,000	1,078.87	1,059.88	1,043.93	1,030.47	1,009.38
85,000	1,146.30	1,126.12	1,109.18	1,094.88	1,072.47
90,000	1,213.73	1,192.36	1,174.42	1,159.28	1,135.55
95,000	1,281.16	1,258.61	1,239.67	1,223.69	1,198.64
100,000	1,348.58	1,324.85	1,304.91	1,288.09	1,261.72
110,000	1,483.44	1,457.33	1,435.40	1,416.90	1,387.90
120,000	1,618.30	1,589.82	1,565.90	1,545.71	1,514.07
125,000	1,685.73	1,656.06	1,631.14	1,610.11	1,577.15
130,000	1,753.16	1,722.30	1,696.39	1,674.52	1,640.24
140,000	1,888.02	1,854.79	1,826.88	1,803.33	1,766.41
150,000	2,022.87	1,987.27	1,957.37	1,932.14	1,892.58
160,000	2,157.73	2,119.75	2,087.86	2,060.94	2,018.76
170,000	2,292.59	2,252.24	2,218.35	2,189.75	2,144.93
175,000	2,360.02	2,318.48	2,283.59	2,254.16	2,208.01
180,000	2,427.45	2,384.72	2,348.84	2,318.56	2,271.10
190,000	2,562.31	2,517.21	2,479.33	2,447.37	2,397.27
200,000	2,697.16	2,649.69	2,609.82	2,576.18	2,523.44
220,000	2,966.88	2,914.66	2,870.80	2,833.80	2,775.79
225,000	3,034.31	2,980.90	2,936.05	2,898.20	2,838.87
230,000	3,101.74	3,047.14	3,001.29	2,962.61	2,901.96
240,000	3,236.60	3,179.63	3,131.79	3,091.41	3,028.13
$250,000	3,371.45	3,312.11	3,262.28	3,220.22	3,154.30

Table 1   153

14.25%   Monthly Payment Loans

Amortization Period in Years

	21	22	23	24	25
$ 100	1.26	1.25	1.24	1.23	1.23
200	2.51	2.49	2.47	2.46	2.45
300	3.76	3.73	3.71	3.69	3.67
400	5.01	4.98	4.94	4.92	4.90
500	6.26	6.22	6.18	6.15	6.12
600	7.51	7.46	7.41	7.38	7.34
700	8.76	8.70	8.65	8.60	8.57
800	10.02	9.95	9.88	9.83	9.79
900	11.27	11.19	11.12	11.06	11.01
1,000	12.52	12.43	12.35	12.29	12.23
2,000	25.03	24.86	24.70	24.58	24.46
3,000	37.55	37.28	37.05	36.86	36.69
4,000	50.06	49.71	49.40	49.15	48.92
5,000	62.57	62.13	61.75	61.43	61.15
6,000	75.09	74.56	74.10	73.72	73.38
7,000	87.60	86.98	86.45	86.00	85.61
8,000	100.12	99.41	98.80	98.29	97.84
9,000	112.63	111.84	111.15	110.57	110.07
10,000	125.14	124.26	123.50	122.86	122.30
15,000	187.71	186.39	185.25	184.28	183.44
20,000	250.28	248.52	247.00	245.71	244.59
25,000	312.85	310.64	308.75	307.13	305.74
30,000	375.42	372.77	370.50	368.56	366.88
35,000	437.99	434.90	432.25	429.98	428.03
40,000	500.56	497.03	494.00	491.41	489.18
45,000	563.13	559.16	555.75	552.83	550.32
50,000	625.70	621.28	617.50	614.26	611.47
55,000	688.27	683.41	679.25	675.68	672.62
60,000	750.84	745.54	741.00	737.11	733.76
65,000	813.41	807.67	802.75	798.53	794.91
70,000	875.98	869.80	864.50	859.96	856.05
75,000	938.55	931.92	926.25	921.38	917.20
80,000	1,001.12	994.05	988.00	982.81	978.35
85,000	1,063.69	1,056.18	1,049.75	1,044.23	1,039.49
90,000	1,126.25	1,118.31	1,111.50	1,105.66	1,100.64
95,000	1,188.82	1,180.44	1,173.25	1,167.08	1,161.79
100,000	1,251.39	1,242.56	1,235.00	1,228.51	1,222.93
110,000	1,376.53	1,366.82	1,358.50	1,351.36	1,345.23
120,000	1,501.67	1,491.08	1,482.00	1,474.21	1,467.52
125,000	1,564.24	1,553.20	1,543.75	1,535.64	1,528.66
130,000	1,626.81	1,615.33	1,605.50	1,597.06	1,589.81
140,000	1,751.95	1,739.59	1,729.00	1,719.91	1,712.10
150,000	1,877.09	1,863.84	1,852.50	1,842.76	1,834.40
160,000	2,002.23	1,988.10	1,976.00	1,965.61	1,956.69
170,000	2,127.37	2,112.35	2,099.50	2,088.46	2,078.98
175,000	2,189.93	2,174.48	2,161.25	2,149.89	2,140.13
180,000	2,252.50	2,236.61	2,223.00	2,211.31	2,201.27
190,000	2,377.64	2,360.87	2,346.50	2,334.16	2,323.57
200,000	2,502.78	2,485.12	2,470.00	2,457.02	2,445.86
220,000	2,753.06	2,733.63	2,716.99	2,702.72	2,690.45
225,000	2,815.63	2,795.76	2,778.74	2,764.14	2,751.59
230,000	2,878.20	2,857.89	2,840.49	2,825.57	2,812.74
240,000	3,003.34	2,982.15	2,963.99	2,948.42	2,935.03
$250,000	3,128.48	3,106.40	3,087.49	3,071.27	3,057.32

Monthly Payment Loans   **14.25%**

Amortization Period in Years

	26	27	28	29	30
$ 100	1.22	1.22	1.22	1.21	1.21
200	2.44	2.43	2.43	2.42	2.41
300	3.66	3.65	3.64	3.63	3.62
400	4.88	4.86	4.85	4.83	4.82
500	6.10	6.07	6.06	6.04	6.03
600	7.31	7.29	7.27	7.25	7.23
700	8.53	8.50	8.48	8.46	8.44
800	9.75	9.72	9.69	9.66	9.64
900	10.97	10.93	10.90	10.87	10.85
1,000	12.19	12.14	12.11	12.08	12.05
2,000	24.37	24.28	24.21	24.15	24.10
3,000	36.55	36.42	36.32	36.23	36.15
4,000	48.73	48.56	48.42	48.30	48.19
5,000	60.91	60.70	60.53	60.37	60.24
6,000	73.09	72.84	72.63	72.45	72.29
7,000	85.27	84.98	84.73	84.52	84.33
8,000	97.46	97.12	96.84	96.59	96.38
9,000	109.64	109.26	108.94	108.67	108.43
10,000	121.82	121.40	121.05	120.74	120.47
15,000	182.72	182.10	181.57	181.11	180.71
20,000	243.63	242.80	242.09	241.47	240.94
25,000	304.54	303.50	302.61	301.84	301.18
30,000	365.44	364.20	363.13	362.21	361.41
35,000	426.35	424.90	423.65	422.58	421.65
40,000	487.26	485.60	484.18	482.94	481.88
45,000	548.16	546.30	544.70	543.31	542.11
50,000	609.07	607.00	605.22	603.68	602.35
55,000	669.98	667.70	665.74	664.05	662.58
60,000	730.88	728.40	726.26	724.41	722.82
65,000	791.79	789.10	786.78	784.78	783.05
70,000	852.69	849.80	847.30	845.15	843.29
75,000	913.60	910.50	907.82	905.51	903.52
80,000	974.51	971.20	968.35	965.88	963.75
85,000	1,035.41	1,031.90	1,028.87	1,026.25	1,023.99
90,000	1,096.32	1,092.60	1,089.39	1,086.62	1,084.22
95,000	1,157.23	1,153.30	1,149.91	1,146.98	1,144.46
100,000	1,218.13	1,214.00	1,210.43	1,207.35	1,204.69
110,000	1,339.95	1,335.40	1,331.47	1,328.09	1,325.16
120,000	1,461.76	1,456.80	1,452.52	1,448.82	1,445.63
125,000	1,522.66	1,517.49	1,513.04	1,509.19	1,505.86
130,000	1,583.57	1,578.19	1,573.56	1,569.56	1,566.10
140,000	1,705.38	1,699.59	1,694.60	1,690.29	1,686.57
150,000	1,827.20	1,820.99	1,815.64	1,811.02	1,807.04
160,000	1,949.01	1,942.39	1,936.69	1,931.76	1,927.50
170,000	2,070.82	2,063.79	2,057.73	2,052.49	2,047.97
175,000	2,131.73	2,124.49	2,118.25	2,112.86	2,108.21
180,000	2,192.63	2,185.19	2,178.77	2,173.23	2,168.44
190,000	2,314.45	2,306.59	2,299.81	2,293.96	2,288.91
200,000	2,436.26	2,427.99	2,420.86	2,414.70	2,409.38
220,000	2,679.89	2,670.79	2,662.94	2,656.17	2,650.32
225,000	2,740.79	2,731.49	2,723.46	2,716.53	2,710.55
230,000	2,801.70	2,792.19	2,783.98	2,776.90	2,770.79
240,000	2,923.51	2,913.59	2,905.03	2,897.64	2,891.25
$250,000	3,045.32	3,034.98	3,026.07	3,018.37	3,011.72

Table 1   155

14.50%   Monthly Payment Loans
Amortization Period in Years

	5	7	8	10	12
$ 100	2.36	1.91	1.77	1.59	1.47
200	4.71	3.81	3.54	3.17	2.94
300	7.06	5.71	5.30	4.75	4.41
400	9.42	7.61	7.07	6.34	5.88
500	11.77	9.51	8.83	7.92	7.35
600	14.12	11.42	10.60	9.50	8.82
700	16.47	13.32	12.37	11.09	10.29
800	18.83	15.22	14.13	12.67	11.76
900	21.18	17.12	15.90	14.25	13.22
1,000	23.53	19.02	17.66	15.83	14.69
2,000	47.06	38.04	35.32	31.66	29.38
3,000	70.59	57.06	52.98	47.49	44.07
4,000	94.12	76.07	70.63	63.32	58.76
5,000	117.65	95.09	88.29	79.15	73.45
6,000	141.17	114.11	105.95	94.98	88.14
7,000	164.70	133.13	123.61	110.81	102.82
8,000	188.23	152.14	141.26	126.63	117.51
9,000	211.76	171.16	158.92	142.46	132.20
10,000	235.29	190.18	176.58	158.29	146.89
15,000	352.93	285.26	264.86	237.44	220.33
20,000	470.57	380.35	353.15	316.58	293.77
25,000	588.21	475.44	441.44	395.72	367.22
30,000	705.85	570.52	529.72	474.87	440.66
35,000	823.49	665.61	618.01	554.01	514.10
40,000	941.14	760.70	706.30	633.15	587.54
45,000	1,058.78	855.78	794.58	712.30	660.99
50,000	1,176.42	950.87	882.87	791.44	734.43
55,000	1,294.06	1,045.96	971.15	870.58	807.87
60,000	1,411.70	1,141.04	1,059.44	949.73	881.31
65,000	1,529.34	1,236.13	1,147.73	1,028.87	954.76
70,000	1,646.98	1,331.22	1,236.01	1,108.01	1,028.20
75,000	1,764.63	1,426.30	1,324.30	1,187.16	1,101.64
80,000	1,882.27	1,521.39	1,412.59	1,266.30	1,175.08
85,000	1,999.91	1,616.48	1,500.87	1,345.44	1,248.53
90,000	2,117.55	1,711.56	1,589.16	1,424.59	1,321.97
95,000	2,235.19	1,806.65	1,677.44	1,503.73	1,395.41
100,000	2,352.83	1,901.74	1,765.73	1,582.87	1,468.85
110,000	2,588.12	2,091.91	1,942.30	1,741.16	1,615.74
120,000	2,823.40	2,282.08	2,118.88	1,899.45	1,762.62
125,000	2,941.04	2,377.17	2,207.16	1,978.59	1,836.07
130,000	3,058.68	2,472.25	2,295.45	2,057.73	1,909.51
140,000	3,293.96	2,662.43	2,472.02	2,216.02	2,056.39
150,000	3,529.25	2,852.60	2,648.59	2,374.31	2,203.28
160,000	3,764.53	3,042.77	2,825.17	2,532.59	2,350.16
170,000	3,999.81	3,232.95	3,001.74	2,690.88	2,497.05
175,000	4,117.45	3,328.03	3,090.02	2,770.02	2,570.49
180,000	4,235.10	3,423.12	3,178.31	2,849.17	2,643.93
190,000	4,470.38	3,613.29	3,354.88	3,007.45	2,790.82
200,000	4,705.66	3,803.47	3,531.46	3,165.74	2,937.70
220,000	5,176.23	4,183.81	3,884.60	3,482.31	3,231.47
225,000	5,293.87	4,278.90	3,972.89	3,561.46	3,304.92
230,000	5,411.51	4,373.98	4,061.17	3,640.60	3,378.36
240,000	5,646.79	4,564.16	4,237.75	3,798.89	3,525.24
$250,000	5,882.08	4,754.33	4,414.32	3,957.17	3,672.13

Monthly Payment Loans   **14.50%**

Amortization Period in Years

	15	16	17	18	20
$ 100	1.37	1.35	1.33	1.31	1.28
200	2.74	2.69	2.65	2.62	2.56
300	4.10	4.03	3.97	3.92	3.84
400	5.47	5.37	5.29	5.23	5.12
500	6.83	6.72	6.62	6.53	6.40
600	8.20	8.06	7.94	7.84	7.68
700	9.56	9.40	9.26	9.15	8.96
800	10.93	10.74	10.58	10.45	10.24
900	12.29	12.08	11.91	11.76	11.52
1,000	13.66	13.43	13.23	13.06	12.80
2,000	27.32	26.85	26.45	26.12	25.60
3,000	40.97	40.27	39.68	39.18	38.40
4,000	54.63	53.69	52.90	52.24	51.20
5,000	68.28	67.11	66.13	65.30	64.00
6,000	81.94	80.53	79.35	78.36	76.80
7,000	95.59	93.95	92.57	91.42	89.60
8,000	109.25	107.37	105.80	104.47	102.40
9,000	122.90	120.79	119.02	117.53	115.20
10,000	136.56	134.21	132.25	130.59	128.00
15,000	204.83	201.32	198.37	195.89	192.00
20,000	273.11	268.42	264.49	261.18	256.00
25,000	341.38	335.52	330.61	326.47	320.00
30,000	409.66	402.63	396.73	391.77	384.00
35,000	477.93	469.73	462.85	457.06	448.00
40,000	546.21	536.83	528.97	522.35	512.00
45,000	614.48	603.94	595.10	587.65	576.00
50,000	682.76	671.04	661.22	652.94	640.00
55,000	751.03	738.14	727.34	718.24	704.00
60,000	819.31	805.25	793.46	783.53	768.00
65,000	887.58	872.35	859.58	848.82	832.00
70,000	955.86	939.45	925.70	914.12	896.00
75,000	1,024.13	1,006.56	991.82	979.41	960.00
80,000	1,092.41	1,073.66	1,057.94	1,044.70	1,024.00
85,000	1,160.68	1,140.76	1,124.07	1,110.00	1,088.00
90,000	1,228.96	1,207.87	1,190.19	1,175.29	1,152.00
95,000	1,297.23	1,274.97	1,256.31	1,240.59	1,216.00
100,000	1,365.51	1,342.08	1,322.43	1,305.88	1,280.00
110,000	1,502.06	1,476.28	1,454.67	1,436.47	1,408.00
120,000	1,638.61	1,610.49	1,586.91	1,567.05	1,536.00
125,000	1,706.88	1,677.59	1,653.04	1,632.35	1,600.00
130,000	1,775.16	1,744.70	1,719.16	1,697.64	1,664.00
140,000	1,911.71	1,878.90	1,851.40	1,828.23	1,792.00
150,000	2,048.26	2,013.11	1,983.64	1,958.82	1,920.00
160,000	2,184.81	2,147.32	2,115.88	2,089.40	2,048.00
170,000	2,321.36	2,281.52	2,248.13	2,219.99	2,176.00
175,000	2,389.63	2,348.63	2,314.25	2,285.28	2,240.00
180,000	2,457.91	2,415.73	2,380.37	2,350.58	2,304.00
190,000	2,594.46	2,549.94	2,512.61	2,481.17	2,432.00
200,000	2,731.01	2,684.15	2,644.85	2,611.75	2,560.00
220,000	3,004.11	2,952.56	2,909.34	2,872.93	2,816.00
225,000	3,072.38	3,019.66	2,975.46	2,938.22	2,880.00
230,000	3,140.66	3,086.77	3,041.58	3,003.52	2,944.00
240,000	3,277.21	3,220.97	3,173.82	3,134.10	3,072.00
$250,000	3,413.76	3,355.18	3,306.07	3,264.69	3,200.00

Table 1   157

14.50% Monthly Payment Loans

Amortization Period in Years

	21	22	23	24	25
$ 100	1.27	1.27	1.26	1.25	1.25
200	2.54	2.53	2.51	2.50	2.49
300	3.81	3.79	3.77	3.75	3.73
400	5.08	5.05	5.02	5.00	4.97
500	6.35	6.31	6.27	6.24	6.22
600	7.62	7.57	7.53	7.49	7.46
700	8.89	8.83	8.78	8.74	8.70
800	10.16	10.10	10.04	9.99	9.94
900	11.43	11.36	11.29	11.23	11.18
1,000	12.70	12.62	12.54	12.48	12.43
2,000	25.40	25.23	25.08	24.96	24.85
3,000	38.10	37.84	37.62	37.43	37.27
4,000	50.80	50.46	50.16	49.91	49.69
5,000	63.50	63.07	62.70	62.38	62.11
6,000	76.20	75.68	75.24	74.86	74.53
7,000	88.90	88.29	87.78	87.34	86.96
8,000	101.60	100.91	100.32	99.81	99.38
9,000	114.29	113.52	112.86	112.29	111.80
10,000	126.99	126.13	125.39	124.76	124.22
15,000	190.49	189.19	188.09	187.14	186.33
20,000	253.98	252.26	250.78	249.52	248.44
25,000	317.48	315.32	313.48	311.90	310.55
30,000	380.97	378.38	376.17	374.28	372.65
35,000	444.47	441.45	438.87	436.66	434.76
40,000	507.96	504.51	501.56	499.04	496.87
45,000	571.45	567.57	564.26	561.42	558.98
50,000	634.95	630.64	626.95	623.79	621.09
55,000	698.44	693.70	689.65	686.17	683.19
60,000	761.94	756.76	752.34	748.55	745.30
65,000	825.43	819.83	815.03	810.93	807.41
70,000	888.93	882.89	877.73	873.31	869.52
75,000	952.42	945.95	940.42	935.69	931.63
80,000	1,015.92	1,009.02	1,003.12	998.07	993.74
85,000	1,079.41	1,072.08	1,065.81	1,060.45	1,055.84
90,000	1,142.90	1,135.14	1,128.51	1,122.83	1,117.95
95,000	1,206.40	1,198.21	1,191.20	1,185.20	1,180.06
100,000	1,269.89	1,261.27	1,253.90	1,247.58	1,242.17
110,000	1,396.88	1,387.40	1,379.29	1,372.34	1,366.38
120,000	1,523.87	1,513.52	1,504.68	1,497.10	1,490.60
125,000	1,587.37	1,576.59	1,567.37	1,559.48	1,552.71
130,000	1,650.86	1,639.65	1,630.06	1,621.86	1,614.82
140,000	1,777.85	1,765.78	1,755.45	1,746.61	1,739.03
150,000	1,904.84	1,891.90	1,880.84	1,871.37	1,863.25
160,000	2,031.83	2,018.03	2,006.23	1,996.13	1,987.47
170,000	2,158.82	2,144.15	2,131.62	2,120.89	2,111.68
175,000	2,222.31	2,207.22	2,194.32	2,183.27	2,173.79
180,000	2,285.80	2,270.28	2,257.01	2,245.65	2,235.90
190,000	2,412.79	2,396.41	2,382.40	2,370.40	2,360.11
200,000	2,539.78	2,522.53	2,507.79	2,495.16	2,484.33
220,000	2,793.76	2,774.79	2,758.57	2,744.68	2,732.76
225,000	2,857.25	2,837.85	2,821.26	2,807.06	2,794.87
230,000	2,920.75	2,900.91	2,883.96	2,869.43	2,856.98
240,000	3,047.74	3,027.04	3,009.35	2,994.19	2,981.20
$250,000	3,174.73	3,153.17	3,134.73	3,118.95	3,105.41

Monthly Payment Loans   **14.50%**

Amortization Period in Years

	26	27	28	29	30
$ 100	1.24	1.24	1.24	1.23	1.23
200	2.48	2.47	2.47	2.46	2.45
300	3.72	3.71	3.70	3.69	3.68
400	4.96	4.94	4.93	4.91	4.90
500	6.19	6.17	6.16	6.14	6.13
600	7.43	7.41	7.39	7.37	7.35
700	8.67	8.64	8.62	8.59	8.58
800	9.91	9.87	9.85	9.82	9.80
900	11.14	11.11	11.08	11.05	11.03
1,000	12.38	12.34	12.31	12.28	12.25
2,000	24.76	24.68	24.61	24.55	24.50
3,000	37.13	37.01	36.91	36.82	36.74
4,000	49.51	49.35	49.21	49.09	48.99
5,000	61.88	61.68	61.51	61.36	61.23
6,000	74.26	74.02	73.81	73.63	73.48
7,000	86.63	86.35	86.11	85.90	85.72
8,000	99.01	98.69	98.41	98.17	97.97
9,000	111.38	111.02	110.71	110.44	110.22
10,000	123.76	123.36	123.01	122.72	122.46
15,000	185.63	185.03	184.52	184.07	183.69
20,000	247.51	246.71	246.02	245.43	244.92
25,000	309.38	308.38	307.52	306.78	306.14
30,000	371.26	370.06	369.03	368.14	367.37
35,000	433.13	431.73	430.53	429.49	428.60
40,000	495.01	493.41	492.03	490.85	489.83
45,000	556.89	555.09	553.54	552.20	551.06
50,000	618.76	616.76	615.04	613.56	612.28
55,000	680.64	678.44	676.55	674.92	673.51
60,000	742.51	740.11	738.05	736.27	734.74
65,000	804.39	801.79	799.55	797.63	795.97
70,000	866.26	863.46	861.06	858.98	857.19
75,000	928.14	925.14	922.56	920.34	918.42
80,000	990.01	986.82	984.06	981.69	979.65
85,000	1,051.89	1,048.49	1,045.57	1,043.05	1,040.88
90,000	1,113.77	1,110.17	1,107.07	1,104.40	1,102.11
95,000	1,175.64	1,171.84	1,168.57	1,165.76	1,163.33
100,000	1,237.52	1,233.52	1,230.08	1,227.12	1,224.56
110,000	1,361.27	1,356.87	1,353.09	1,349.83	1,347.02
120,000	1,485.02	1,480.22	1,476.09	1,472.54	1,469.47
125,000	1,546.90	1,541.90	1,537.60	1,533.89	1,530.70
130,000	1,608.77	1,603.57	1,599.10	1,595.25	1,591.93
140,000	1,732.52	1,726.92	1,722.11	1,717.96	1,714.38
150,000	1,856.27	1,850.28	1,845.12	1,840.67	1,836.84
160,000	1,980.02	1,973.63	1,968.12	1,963.38	1,959.29
170,000	2,103.78	2,096.98	2,091.13	2,086.09	2,081.75
175,000	2,165.65	2,158.65	2,152.63	2,147.45	2,142.98
180,000	2,227.53	2,220.33	2,214.14	2,208.80	2,204.21
190,000	2,351.28	2,343.68	2,337.14	2,331.51	2,326.66
200,000	2,475.03	2,467.03	2,460.15	2,454.23	2,449.12
220,000	2,722.53	2,713.74	2,706.17	2,699.65	2,694.03
225,000	2,784.41	2,775.41	2,767.67	2,761.00	2,755.26
230,000	2,846.28	2,837.09	2,829.17	2,822.36	2,816.48
240,000	2,970.03	2,960.44	2,952.18	2,945.07	2,938.94
$250,000	3,093.79	3,083.79	3,075.19	3,067.78	3,061.39

Table 1   159

14.75% Monthly Payment Loans

Amortization Period in Years

	5	7	8	10	12
$ 100	2.37	1.92	1.79	1.60	1.49
200	4.74	3.84	3.57	3.20	2.97
300	7.10	5.75	5.35	4.80	4.46
400	9.47	7.67	7.13	6.40	5.94
500	11.83	9.58	8.91	8.00	7.43
600	14.20	11.50	10.69	9.59	8.91
700	16.57	13.41	12.47	11.19	10.40
800	18.93	15.33	14.25	12.79	11.88
900	21.30	17.25	16.03	14.39	13.37
1,000	23.66	19.16	17.81	15.99	14.85
2,000	47.32	38.32	35.61	31.97	29.70
3,000	70.98	57.48	53.41	47.95	44.55
4,000	94.64	76.63	71.21	63.93	59.40
5,000	118.30	95.79	89.01	79.91	74.25
6,000	141.96	114.95	106.81	95.89	89.09
7,000	165.62	134.10	124.61	111.87	103.94
8,000	189.28	153.26	142.41	127.85	118.79
9,000	212.94	172.42	160.21	143.83	133.64
10,000	236.59	191.57	178.02	159.81	148.49
15,000	354.89	287.36	267.02	239.72	222.73
20,000	473.18	383.14	356.03	319.62	296.97
25,000	591.48	478.92	445.03	399.52	371.21
30,000	709.77	574.71	534.04	479.43	445.45
35,000	828.07	670.49	623.04	559.33	519.69
40,000	946.36	766.28	712.05	639.23	593.94
45,000	1,064.66	862.06	801.05	719.14	668.18
50,000	1,182.95	957.84	890.06	799.04	742.42
55,000	1,301.24	1,053.63	979.06	878.95	816.66
60,000	1,419.54	1,149.41	1,068.07	958.85	890.90
65,000	1,537.83	1,245.19	1,157.07	1,038.75	965.14
70,000	1,656.13	1,340.98	1,246.08	1,118.66	1,039.38
75,000	1,774.42	1,436.76	1,335.08	1,198.56	1,113.62
80,000	1,892.72	1,532.55	1,424.09	1,278.46	1,187.87
85,000	2,011.01	1,628.33	1,513.09	1,358.37	1,262.11
90,000	2,129.31	1,724.11	1,602.10	1,438.27	1,336.35
95,000	2,247.60	1,819.90	1,691.10	1,518.18	1,410.59
100,000	2,365.90	1,915.68	1,780.11	1,598.08	1,484.83
110,000	2,602.48	2,107.25	1,958.12	1,757.89	1,633.31
120,000	2,839.07	2,298.82	2,136.13	1,917.69	1,781.80
125,000	2,957.37	2,394.60	2,225.13	1,997.60	1,856.04
130,000	3,075.66	2,490.38	2,314.14	2,077.50	1,930.28
140,000	3,312.25	2,681.95	2,492.15	2,237.31	2,078.76
150,000	3,548.84	2,873.52	2,670.16	2,397.12	2,227.24
160,000	3,785.43	3,065.09	2,848.17	2,556.92	2,375.73
170,000	4,022.02	3,256.65	3,026.18	2,716.73	2,524.21
175,000	4,140.31	3,352.44	3,115.19	2,796.63	2,598.45
180,000	4,258.61	3,448.22	3,204.19	2,876.54	2,672.69
190,000	4,495.20	3,639.79	3,382.20	3,036.35	2,821.17
200,000	4,731.79	3,831.36	3,560.21	3,196.15	2,969.66
220,000	5,204.96	4,214.49	3,916.23	3,515.77	3,266.62
225,000	5,323.26	4,310.28	4,005.24	3,595.67	3,340.86
230,000	5,441.55	4,406.06	4,094.24	3,675.58	3,415.10
240,000	5,678.14	4,597.63	4,272.25	3,835.38	3,563.59
$250,000	5,914.73	4,789.20	4,450.26	3,995.19	3,712.07

Monthly Payment Loans   14.75%

Amortization Period in Years

	15	16	17	18	20
$ 100	1.39	1.36	1.35	1.33	1.30
200	2.77	2.72	2.69	2.65	2.60
300	4.15	4.08	4.03	3.98	3.90
400	5.54	5.44	5.37	5.30	5.20
500	6.92	6.80	6.71	6.62	6.50
600	8.30	8.16	8.05	7.95	7.80
700	9.68	9.52	9.39	9.27	9.09
800	11.07	10.88	10.73	10.59	10.39
900	12.45	12.24	12.07	11.92	11.69
1,000	13.83	13.60	13.41	13.24	12.99
2,000	27.66	27.19	26.81	26.48	25.97
3,000	41.48	40.79	40.21	39.72	38.96
4,000	55.31	54.38	53.61	52.95	51.94
5,000	69.13	67.97	67.01	66.19	64.92
6,000	82.96	81.57	80.41	79.43	77.91
7,000	96.78	95.16	93.81	92.67	90.89
8,000	110.61	108.76	107.21	105.90	103.87
9,000	124.43	122.35	120.61	119.14	116.86
10,000	138.26	135.94	134.01	132.38	129.84
15,000	207.38	203.91	201.01	198.57	194.76
20,000	276.51	271.88	268.01	264.75	259.68
25,000	345.63	339.85	335.01	330.94	324.59
30,000	414.76	407.82	402.01	397.13	389.51
35,000	483.88	475.79	469.01	463.31	454.43
40,000	553.01	543.76	536.01	529.50	519.35
45,000	622.13	611.73	603.01	595.69	584.26
50,000	691.26	679.69	670.02	661.88	649.18
55,000	760.38	747.66	737.02	728.06	714.10
60,000	829.51	815.63	804.02	794.25	779.02
65,000	898.63	883.60	871.02	860.44	843.94
70,000	967.76	951.57	938.02	926.62	908.85
75,000	1,036.88	1,019.54	1,005.02	992.81	973.77
80,000	1,106.01	1,087.51	1,072.02	1,059.00	1,038.69
85,000	1,175.13	1,155.48	1,139.02	1,125.19	1,103.61
90,000	1,244.26	1,223.45	1,206.02	1,191.37	1,168.52
95,000	1,313.38	1,291.42	1,273.03	1,257.56	1,233.44
100,000	1,382.51	1,359.38	1,340.03	1,323.75	1,298.36
110,000	1,520.76	1,495.32	1,474.03	1,456.12	1,428.20
120,000	1,659.01	1,631.26	1,608.03	1,588.50	1,558.03
125,000	1,728.13	1,699.23	1,675.03	1,654.68	1,622.95
130,000	1,797.26	1,767.20	1,742.03	1,720.87	1,687.87
140,000	1,935.51	1,903.14	1,876.04	1,853.24	1,817.70
150,000	2,073.76	2,039.07	2,010.04	1,985.62	1,947.54
160,000	2,212.01	2,175.01	2,144.04	2,117.99	2,077.37
170,000	2,350.26	2,310.95	2,278.04	2,250.37	2,207.21
175,000	2,419.39	2,378.92	2,345.04	2,316.55	2,272.13
180,000	2,488.51	2,446.89	2,412.04	2,382.74	2,337.04
190,000	2,626.76	2,582.83	2,546.05	2,515.12	2,466.88
200,000	2,765.01	2,718.76	2,680.05	2,647.49	2,596.72
220,000	3,041.51	2,990.64	2,948.05	2,912.24	2,856.39
225,000	3,110.64	3,058.61	3,015.05	2,978.43	2,921.30
230,000	3,179.76	3,126.58	3,082.06	3,044.61	2,986.22
240,000	3,318.01	3,262.52	3,216.06	3,176.99	3,116.06
$250,000	3,456.26	3,398.45	3,350.06	3,309.36	3,245.89

Table 1   161

14.75%   Monthly Payment Loans

Amortization Period in Years

	21	22	23	24	25
$ 100	1.29	1.29	1.28	1.27	1.27
200	2.58	2.57	2.55	2.54	2.53
300	3.87	3.85	3.82	3.81	3.79
400	5.16	5.13	5.10	5.07	5.05
500	6.45	6.41	6.37	6.34	6.31
600	7.74	7.69	7.64	7.61	7.57
700	9.02	8.97	8.92	8.87	8.84
800	10.31	10.25	10.19	10.14	10.10
900	11.60	11.53	11.46	11.41	11.36
1,000	12.89	12.81	12.73	12.67	12.62
2,000	25.77	25.61	25.46	25.34	25.23
3,000	38.66	38.41	38.19	38.01	37.85
4,000	51.54	51.21	50.92	50.67	50.46
5,000	64.43	64.01	63.65	63.34	63.08
6,000	77.31	76.81	76.38	76.01	75.69
7,000	90.20	89.61	89.11	88.68	88.31
8,000	103.08	102.41	101.83	101.34	100.92
9,000	115.97	115.21	114.56	114.01	113.54
10,000	128.85	128.01	127.29	126.68	126.15
15,000	193.27	192.01	190.93	190.01	189.22
20,000	257.70	256.01	254.58	253.35	252.30
25,000	322.12	320.02	318.22	316.69	315.37
30,000	386.54	384.02	381.86	380.02	378.44
35,000	450.97	448.02	445.51	443.36	441.52
40,000	515.39	512.02	509.15	506.69	504.59
45,000	579.81	576.03	572.79	570.03	567.66
50,000	644.24	640.03	636.44	633.37	630.74
55,000	708.66	704.03	700.08	696.70	693.81
60,000	773.08	768.03	763.72	760.04	756.88
65,000	837.51	832.03	827.36	823.37	819.96
70,000	901.93	896.04	891.01	886.71	883.03
75,000	966.35	960.04	954.65	950.05	946.10
80,000	1,030.78	1,024.04	1,018.29	1,013.38	1,009.18
85,000	1,095.20	1,088.04	1,081.94	1,076.72	1,072.25
90,000	1,159.62	1,152.05	1,145.58	1,140.05	1,135.32
95,000	1,224.05	1,216.05	1,209.22	1,203.39	1,198.40
100,000	1,288.47	1,280.05	1,272.87	1,266.73	1,261.47
110,000	1,417.32	1,408.05	1,400.15	1,393.40	1,387.62
120,000	1,546.16	1,536.06	1,527.44	1,520.07	1,513.76
125,000	1,610.59	1,600.06	1,591.08	1,583.41	1,576.84
130,000	1,675.01	1,664.06	1,654.72	1,646.74	1,639.91
140,000	1,803.86	1,792.07	1,782.01	1,773.41	1,766.06
150,000	1,932.70	1,920.07	1,909.30	1,900.09	1,892.20
160,000	2,061.55	2,048.08	2,036.58	2,026.76	2,018.35
170,000	2,190.40	2,176.08	2,163.87	2,153.43	2,144.50
175,000	2,254.82	2,240.08	2,227.51	2,216.77	2,207.57
180,000	2,319.24	2,304.09	2,291.15	2,280.10	2,270.64
190,000	2,448.09	2,432.09	2,418.44	2,406.77	2,396.79
200,000	2,576.94	2,560.09	2,545.73	2,533.45	2,522.93
220,000	2,834.63	2,816.10	2,800.30	2,786.79	2,775.23
225,000	2,899.05	2,880.11	2,863.94	2,850.13	2,838.30
230,000	2,963.48	2,944.11	2,927.58	2,913.46	2,901.37
240,000	3,092.32	3,072.11	3,054.87	3,040.13	3,027.52
$250,000	3,221.17	3,200.12	3,182.16	3,166.81	3,153.67

Monthly Payment Loans **14.75%**

Amortization Period in Years

	26	27	28	29	30
$ 100	1.26	1.26	1.25	1.25	1.25
200	2.52	2.51	2.50	2.50	2.49
300	3.78	3.76	3.75	3.75	3.74
400	5.03	5.02	5.00	4.99	4.98
500	6.29	6.27	6.25	6.24	6.23
600	7.55	7.52	7.50	7.49	7.47
700	8.80	8.78	8.75	8.73	8.72
800	10.06	10.03	10.00	9.98	9.96
900	11.32	11.28	11.25	11.23	11.21
1,000	12.57	12.54	12.50	12.47	12.45
2,000	25.14	25.07	25.00	24.94	24.89
3,000	37.71	37.60	37.50	37.41	37.34
4,000	50.28	50.13	50.00	49.88	49.78
5,000	62.85	62.66	62.49	62.35	62.23
6,000	75.42	75.19	74.99	74.82	74.67
7,000	87.99	87.72	87.49	87.29	87.12
8,000	100.56	100.25	99.99	99.76	99.56
9,000	113.13	112.78	112.49	112.23	112.01
10,000	125.70	125.31	124.98	124.70	124.45
15,000	188.55	187.97	187.47	187.04	186.68
20,000	251.40	250.62	249.96	249.39	248.90
25,000	314.25	313.28	312.45	311.74	311.12
30,000	377.09	375.93	374.94	374.08	373.35
35,000	439.94	438.59	437.43	436.43	435.57
40,000	502.79	501.24	499.92	498.78	497.80
45,000	565.64	563.90	562.41	561.12	560.02
50,000	628.49	626.55	624.89	623.47	622.24
55,000	691.33	689.21	687.38	685.82	684.47
60,000	754.18	751.86	749.87	748.16	746.69
65,000	817.03	814.52	812.36	810.51	808.91
70,000	879.88	877.17	874.85	872.85	871.14
75,000	942.73	939.83	937.34	935.20	933.36
80,000	1,005.57	1,002.48	999.83	997.55	995.59
85,000	1,068.42	1,065.14	1,062.32	1,059.89	1,057.81
90,000	1,131.27	1,127.79	1,124.81	1,122.24	1,120.03
95,000	1,194.12	1,190.45	1,187.30	1,184.59	1,182.26
100,000	1,256.97	1,253.10	1,249.78	1,246.93	1,244.48
110,000	1,382.66	1,378.41	1,374.76	1,371.63	1,368.93
120,000	1,508.36	1,503.72	1,499.74	1,496.32	1,493.38
125,000	1,571.21	1,566.38	1,562.23	1,558.66	1,555.60
130,000	1,634.05	1,629.03	1,624.72	1,621.01	1,617.82
140,000	1,759.75	1,754.34	1,749.70	1,745.70	1,742.27
150,000	1,885.45	1,879.65	1,874.67	1,870.40	1,866.72
160,000	2,011.14	2,004.96	1,999.65	1,995.09	1,991.17
170,000	2,136.84	2,130.27	2,124.63	2,119.78	2,115.61
175,000	2,199.69	2,192.92	2,187.12	2,182.13	2,177.84
180,000	2,262.53	2,255.58	2,249.61	2,244.48	2,240.06
190,000	2,388.23	2,380.89	2,374.59	2,369.17	2,364.51
200,000	2,513.93	2,506.20	2,499.56	2,493.86	2,488.96
220,000	2,765.32	2,756.82	2,749.52	2,743.25	2,737.85
225,000	2,828.17	2,819.47	2,812.01	2,805.59	2,800.08
230,000	2,891.02	2,882.13	2,874.50	2,867.94	2,862.30
240,000	3,016.71	3,007.44	2,999.48	2,992.63	2,986.75
$250,000	3,142.41	3,132.75	3,124.45	3,117.32	3,111.19

Table 1   163

15.00%   Monthly Payment Loans

Amortization Period in Years

	5	7	8	10	12
$ 100	2.38	1.93	1.80	1.62	1.51
200	4.76	3.86	3.59	3.23	3.01
300	7.14	5.79	5.39	4.85	4.51
400	9.52	7.72	7.18	6.46	6.01
500	11.90	9.65	8.98	8.07	7.51
600	14.28	11.58	10.77	9.69	9.01
700	16.66	13.51	12.57	11.30	10.51
800	19.04	15.44	14.36	12.91	12.01
900	21.42	17.37	16.16	14.53	13.51
1,000	23.79	19.30	17.95	16.14	15.01
2,000	47.58	38.60	35.90	32.27	30.02
3,000	71.37	57.90	53.84	48.41	45.03
4,000	95.16	77.19	71.79	64.54	60.04
5,000	118.95	96.49	89.73	80.67	75.05
6,000	142.74	115.79	107.68	96.81	90.06
7,000	166.53	135.08	125.62	112.94	105.07
8,000	190.32	154.38	143.57	129.07	120.08
9,000	214.11	173.68	161.51	145.21	135.08
10,000	237.90	192.97	179.46	161.34	150.09
15,000	356.85	289.46	269.19	242.01	225.14
20,000	475.80	385.94	358.91	322.67	300.18
25,000	594.75	482.42	448.64	403.34	375.22
30,000	713.70	578.91	538.37	484.01	450.27
35,000	832.65	675.39	628.09	564.68	525.31
40,000	951.60	771.88	717.82	645.34	600.36
45,000	1,070.55	868.36	807.55	726.01	675.40
50,000	1,189.50	964.84	897.28	806.68	750.44
55,000	1,308.45	1,061.33	987.00	887.35	825.49
60,000	1,427.40	1,157.81	1,076.73	968.01	900.53
65,000	1,546.35	1,254.29	1,166.46	1,048.68	975.57
70,000	1,665.30	1,350.78	1,256.18	1,129.35	1,050.62
75,000	1,784.25	1,447.26	1,345.91	1,210.02	1,125.66
80,000	1,903.20	1,543.75	1,435.64	1,290.68	1,200.71
85,000	2,022.15	1,640.23	1,525.36	1,371.35	1,275.75
90,000	2,141.10	1,736.71	1,615.09	1,452.02	1,350.79
95,000	2,260.05	1,833.20	1,704.82	1,532.69	1,425.84
100,000	2,379.00	1,929.68	1,794.55	1,613.35	1,500.88
110,000	2,616.90	2,122.65	1,974.00	1,774.69	1,650.97
120,000	2,854.80	2,315.62	2,153.45	1,936.02	1,801.06
125,000	2,973.75	2,412.10	2,243.18	2,016.69	1,876.10
130,000	3,092.70	2,508.58	2,332.91	2,097.36	1,951.14
140,000	3,330.60	2,701.55	2,512.36	2,258.69	2,101.23
150,000	3,568.49	2,894.52	2,691.82	2,420.03	2,251.32
160,000	3,806.39	3,087.49	2,871.27	2,581.36	2,401.41
170,000	4,044.29	3,280.45	3,050.72	2,742.70	2,551.50
175,000	4,163.24	3,376.94	3,140.45	2,823.37	2,626.54
180,000	4,282.19	3,473.42	3,230.18	2,904.03	2,701.58
190,000	4,520.09	3,666.39	3,409.63	3,065.37	2,851.67
200,000	4,757.99	3,859.36	3,589.09	3,226.70	3,001.76
220,000	5,233.79	4,245.29	3,947.99	3,549.37	3,301.93
225,000	5,352.74	4,341.77	4,037.72	3,630.04	3,376.98
230,000	5,471.69	4,438.26	4,127.45	3,710.71	3,452.02
240,000	5,709.59	4,631.23	4,306.90	3,872.04	3,602.11
$250,000	5,947.49	4,824.19	4,486.36	4,033.38	3,752.20

Monthly Payment Loans   **15.00%**

Amortization Period in Years

	15	16	17	18	20
$ 100	1.40	1.38	1.36	1.35	1.32
200	2.80	2.76	2.72	2.69	2.64
300	4.20	4.14	4.08	4.03	3.96
400	5.60	5.51	5.44	5.37	5.27
500	7.00	6.89	6.79	6.71	6.59
600	8.40	8.27	8.15	8.06	7.91
700	9.80	9.64	9.51	9.40	9.22
800	11.20	11.02	10.87	10.74	10.54
900	12.60	12.40	12.22	12.08	11.86
1,000	14.00	13.77	13.58	13.42	13.17
2,000	28.00	27.54	27.16	26.84	26.34
3,000	41.99	41.31	40.74	40.26	39.51
4,000	55.99	55.08	54.31	53.67	52.68
5,000	69.98	68.84	67.89	67.09	65.84
6,000	83.98	82.61	81.47	80.51	79.01
7,000	97.98	96.38	95.04	93.92	92.18
8,000	111.97	110.15	108.62	107.34	105.35
9,000	125.97	123.91	122.20	120.76	118.52
10,000	139.96	137.68	135.78	134.17	131.68
15,000	209.94	206.52	203.66	201.26	197.52
20,000	279.92	275.36	271.55	268.34	263.36
25,000	349.90	344.20	339.43	335.43	329.20
30,000	419.88	413.04	407.32	402.51	395.04
35,000	489.86	481.87	475.20	469.60	460.88
40,000	559.84	550.71	543.09	536.68	526.72
45,000	629.82	619.55	610.97	603.77	592.56
50,000	699.80	688.39	678.86	670.85	658.40
55,000	769.78	757.23	746.74	737.93	724.24
60,000	839.76	826.07	814.63	805.02	790.08
65,000	909.74	894.91	882.51	872.10	855.92
70,000	979.72	963.74	950.40	939.19	921.76
75,000	1,049.70	1,032.58	1,018.28	1,006.27	987.60
80,000	1,119.67	1,101.42	1,086.17	1,073.36	1,053.44
85,000	1,189.65	1,170.26	1,154.05	1,140.44	1,119.28
90,000	1,259.63	1,239.10	1,221.94	1,207.53	1,185.12
95,000	1,329.61	1,307.94	1,289.82	1,274.61	1,250.96
100,000	1,399.59	1,376.77	1,357.71	1,341.70	1,316.79
110,000	1,539.55	1,514.45	1,493.48	1,475.86	1,448.47
120,000	1,679.51	1,652.13	1,629.25	1,610.03	1,580.15
125,000	1,749.49	1,720.97	1,697.13	1,677.12	1,645.99
130,000	1,819.47	1,789.81	1,765.02	1,744.20	1,711.83
140,000	1,959.43	1,927.48	1,900.79	1,878.37	1,843.51
150,000	2,099.39	2,065.16	2,036.56	2,012.54	1,975.19
160,000	2,239.34	2,202.84	2,172.33	2,146.71	2,106.87
170,000	2,379.30	2,340.51	2,308.10	2,280.88	2,238.55
175,000	2,449.28	2,409.35	2,375.98	2,347.96	2,304.39
180,000	2,519.26	2,478.19	2,443.87	2,415.05	2,370.23
190,000	2,659.22	2,615.87	2,579.64	2,549.22	2,501.91
200,000	2,799.18	2,753.54	2,715.41	2,683.39	2,633.58
220,000	3,079.10	3,028.90	2,986.95	2,951.72	2,896.94
225,000	3,149.08	3,097.74	3,054.83	3,018.81	2,962.78
230,000	3,219.06	3,166.58	3,122.72	3,085.89	3,028.62
240,000	3,359.01	3,304.25	3,258.49	3,220.06	3,160.30
$250,000	3,498.97	3,441.93	3,394.26	3,354.23	3,291.98

Table 1   165

15.00%   Monthly Payment Loans

Amortization Period in Years

	21	22	23	24	25
$ 100	1.31	1.30	1.30	1.29	1.29
200	2.62	2.60	2.59	2.58	2.57
300	3.93	3.90	3.88	3.86	3.85
400	5.23	5.20	5.17	5.15	5.13
500	6.54	6.50	6.46	6.43	6.41
600	7.85	7.80	7.76	7.72	7.69
700	9.15	9.10	9.05	9.01	8.97
800	10.46	10.40	10.34	10.29	10.25
900	11.77	11.70	11.63	11.58	11.53
1,000	13.08	12.99	12.92	12.86	12.81
2,000	26.15	25.98	25.84	25.72	25.62
3,000	39.22	38.97	38.76	38.58	38.43
4,000	52.29	51.96	51.68	51.44	51.24
5,000	65.36	64.95	64.60	64.30	64.05
6,000	78.43	77.94	77.52	77.16	76.85
7,000	91.50	90.93	90.44	90.02	89.66
8,000	104.57	103.92	103.36	102.88	102.47
9,000	117.65	116.91	116.28	115.74	115.28
10,000	130.72	129.90	129.19	128.60	128.09
15,000	196.07	194.84	193.79	192.89	192.13
20,000	261.43	259.78	258.38	257.19	256.17
25,000	326.78	324.73	322.98	321.49	320.21
30,000	392.14	389.67	387.57	385.78	384.25
35,000	457.50	454.62	452.17	450.08	448.30
40,000	522.85	519.56	516.76	514.38	512.34
45,000	588.21	584.51	581.36	578.67	576.38
50,000	653.56	649.45	645.95	642.97	640.42
55,000	718.92	714.40	710.55	707.27	704.46
60,000	784.28	779.34	775.14	771.56	768.50
65,000	849.63	844.29	839.74	835.86	832.54
70,000	914.99	909.23	904.33	900.16	896.59
75,000	980.34	974.18	968.93	964.45	960.63
80,000	1,045.70	1,039.12	1,033.52	1,028.75	1,024.67
85,000	1,111.05	1,104.07	1,098.12	1,093.04	1,088.71
90,000	1,176.41	1,169.01	1,162.71	1,157.34	1,152.75
95,000	1,241.77	1,233.96	1,227.31	1,221.64	1,216.79
100,000	1,307.12	1,298.90	1,291.90	1,285.93	1,280.84
110,000	1,437.83	1,428.79	1,421.09	1,414.53	1,408.92
120,000	1,568.55	1,558.68	1,550.28	1,543.12	1,537.00
125,000	1,633.90	1,623.63	1,614.88	1,607.42	1,601.04
130,000	1,699.26	1,688.57	1,679.47	1,671.71	1,665.08
140,000	1,829.97	1,818.46	1,808.66	1,800.31	1,793.17
150,000	1,960.68	1,948.35	1,937.85	1,928.90	1,921.25
160,000	2,091.39	2,078.24	2,067.04	2,057.49	2,049.33
170,000	2,222.10	2,208.13	2,196.23	2,186.08	2,177.42
175,000	2,287.46	2,273.08	2,260.83	2,250.38	2,241.46
180,000	2,352.82	2,338.02	2,325.42	2,314.68	2,305.50
190,000	2,483.53	2,467.91	2,454.61	2,443.27	2,433.58
200,000	2,614.24	2,597.80	2,583.80	2,571.86	2,561.67
220,000	2,875.66	2,857.58	2,842.18	2,829.05	2,817.83
225,000	2,941.02	2,922.52	2,906.78	2,893.35	2,881.87
230,000	3,006.37	2,987.47	2,971.37	2,957.64	2,945.92
240,000	3,137.09	3,117.36	3,100.56	3,086.24	3,074.00
$250,000	3,267.80	3,247.25	3,229.75	3,214.83	3,202.08

Monthly Payment Loans   **15.00%**

Amortization Period in Years

	26	27	28	29	30
$ 100	1.28	1.28	1.27	1.27	1.27
200	2.56	2.55	2.54	2.54	2.53
300	3.83	3.82	3.81	3.81	3.80
400	5.11	5.10	5.08	5.07	5.06
500	6.39	6.37	6.35	6.34	6.33
600	7.66	7.64	7.62	7.61	7.59
700	8.94	8.91	8.89	8.87	8.86
800	10.22	10.19	10.16	10.14	10.12
900	11.49	11.46	11.43	11.41	11.38
1,000	12.77	12.73	12.70	12.67	12.65
2,000	25.53	25.46	25.40	25.34	25.29
3,000	38.30	38.19	38.09	38.01	37.94
4,000	51.06	50.91	50.79	50.68	50.58
5,000	63.83	63.64	63.48	63.34	63.23
6,000	76.59	76.37	76.18	76.01	75.87
7,000	89.36	89.10	88.87	88.68	88.52
8,000	102.12	101.82	101.57	101.35	101.16
9,000	114.89	114.55	114.26	114.02	113.80
10,000	127.65	127.28	126.96	126.68	126.45
15,000	191.48	190.92	190.44	190.02	189.67
20,000	255.30	254.55	253.91	253.36	252.89
25,000	319.12	318.19	317.39	316.70	316.12
30,000	382.95	381.83	380.87	380.04	379.34
35,000	446.77	445.46	444.34	443.38	442.56
40,000	510.59	509.10	507.82	506.72	505.78
45,000	574.42	572.74	571.30	570.06	569.00
50,000	638.24	636.37	634.77	633.40	632.23
55,000	702.06	700.01	698.25	696.74	695.45
60,000	765.89	763.65	761.73	760.08	758.67
65,000	829.71	827.28	825.21	823.42	821.89
70,000	893.53	890.92	888.68	886.76	885.12
75,000	957.36	954.56	952.16	950.10	948.34
80,000	1,021.18	1,018.20	1,015.64	1,013.44	1,011.56
85,000	1,085.00	1,081.83	1,079.11	1,076.78	1,074.78
90,000	1,148.83	1,145.47	1,142.59	1,140.12	1,138.00
95,000	1,212.65	1,209.11	1,206.07	1,203.46	1,201.23
100,000	1,276.48	1,272.74	1,269.54	1,266.80	1,264.45
110,000	1,404.12	1,400.02	1,396.50	1,393.48	1,390.89
120,000	1,531.77	1,527.29	1,523.45	1,520.16	1,517.34
125,000	1,595.59	1,590.93	1,586.93	1,583.50	1,580.56
130,000	1,659.42	1,654.56	1,650.41	1,646.84	1,643.78
140,000	1,787.06	1,781.84	1,777.36	1,773.52	1,770.23
150,000	1,914.71	1,909.11	1,904.31	1,900.20	1,896.67
160,000	2,042.36	2,036.39	2,031.27	2,026.88	2,023.12
170,000	2,170.00	2,163.66	2,158.22	2,153.56	2,149.56
175,000	2,233.83	2,227.30	2,221.70	2,216.90	2,212.78
180,000	2,297.65	2,290.93	2,285.18	2,280.24	2,276.00
190,000	2,425.30	2,418.21	2,412.13	2,406.92	2,402.45
200,000	2,552.95	2,545.48	2,539.08	2,533.60	2,528.89
220,000	2,808.24	2,800.03	2,792.99	2,786.96	2,781.78
225,000	2,872.06	2,863.67	2,856.47	2,850.30	2,845.00
230,000	2,935.89	2,927.30	2,919.95	2,913.64	2,908.23
240,000	3,063.53	3,054.58	3,046.90	3,040.32	3,034.67
$250,000	3,191.18	3,181.85	3,173.85	3,167.00	3,161.12

Table 1   167

15.25%   Monthly Payment Loans

Amortization Period in Years

	5	7	8	10	12
$ 100	2.40	1.95	1.81	1.63	1.52
200	4.79	3.89	3.62	3.26	3.04
300	7.18	5.84	5.43	4.89	4.56
400	9.57	7.78	7.24	6.52	6.07
500	11.97	9.72	9.05	8.15	7.59
600	14.36	11.67	10.86	9.78	9.11
700	16.75	13.61	12.67	11.41	10.62
800	19.14	15.55	14.48	13.03	12.14
900	21.53	17.50	16.29	14.66	13.66
1,000	23.93	19.44	18.10	16.29	15.18
2,000	47.85	38.88	36.19	32.58	30.35
3,000	71.77	58.32	54.28	48.87	45.52
4,000	95.69	77.75	72.37	65.15	60.69
5,000	119.61	97.19	90.46	81.44	75.86
6,000	143.53	116.63	108.55	97.73	91.03
7,000	167.45	136.07	126.64	114.01	106.20
8,000	191.38	155.50	144.73	130.30	121.37
9,000	215.30	174.94	162.82	146.59	136.54
10,000	239.22	194.38	180.91	162.87	151.71
15,000	358.83	291.56	271.36	244.31	227.56
20,000	478.43	388.75	361.81	325.74	303.41
25,000	598.04	485.94	452.26	407.18	379.26
30,000	717.65	583.12	542.72	488.61	455.11
35,000	837.25	680.31	633.17	570.05	530.96
40,000	956.86	777.50	723.62	651.48	606.81
45,000	1,076.47	874.68	814.07	732.92	682.66
50,000	1,196.07	971.87	904.52	814.35	758.51
55,000	1,315.68	1,069.06	994.98	895.79	834.36
60,000	1,435.29	1,166.24	1,085.43	977.22	910.21
65,000	1,554.89	1,263.43	1,175.88	1,058.66	986.06
70,000	1,674.50	1,360.61	1,266.33	1,140.09	1,061.91
75,000	1,794.11	1,457.80	1,356.78	1,221.53	1,137.76
80,000	1,913.71	1,554.99	1,447.23	1,302.96	1,213.61
85,000	2,033.32	1,652.17	1,537.69	1,384.39	1,289.46
90,000	2,152.93	1,749.36	1,628.14	1,465.83	1,365.31
95,000	2,272.53	1,846.55	1,718.59	1,547.26	1,441.16
100,000	2,392.14	1,943.73	1,809.04	1,628.70	1,517.01
110,000	2,631.35	2,138.11	1,989.95	1,791.57	1,668.71
120,000	2,870.57	2,332.48	2,170.85	1,954.44	1,820.41
125,000	2,990.17	2,429.67	2,261.30	2,035.87	1,896.26
130,000	3,109.78	2,526.85	2,351.75	2,117.31	1,972.11
140,000	3,349.00	2,721.22	2,532.66	2,280.18	2,123.81
150,000	3,588.21	2,915.60	2,713.56	2,443.05	2,275.51
160,000	3,827.42	3,109.97	2,894.46	2,605.91	2,427.21
170,000	4,066.64	3,304.34	3,075.37	2,768.78	2,578.91
175,000	4,186.24	3,401.53	3,165.82	2,850.22	2,654.76
180,000	4,305.85	3,498.72	3,256.27	2,931.65	2,730.61
190,000	4,545.06	3,693.09	3,437.18	3,094.52	2,882.31
200,000	4,784.28	3,887.46	3,618.08	3,257.39	3,034.01
220,000	5,262.70	4,276.21	3,979.89	3,583.13	3,337.41
225,000	5,382.31	4,373.39	4,070.34	3,664.57	3,413.26
230,000	5,501.92	4,470.58	4,160.79	3,746.00	3,489.11
240,000	5,741.13	4,664.95	4,341.69	3,908.87	3,640.81
$250,000	5,980.34	4,859.33	4,522.60	4,071.74	3,792.51

Monthly Payment Loans   **15.25%**

Amortization Period in Years

	15	16	17	18	20
$ 100	1.42	1.40	1.38	1.36	1.34
200	2.84	2.79	2.76	2.72	2.68
300	4.26	4.19	4.13	4.08	4.01
400	5.67	5.58	5.51	5.44	5.35
500	7.09	6.98	6.88	6.80	6.68
600	8.51	8.37	8.26	8.16	8.02
700	9.92	9.76	9.63	9.52	9.35
800	11.34	11.16	11.01	10.88	10.69
900	12.76	12.55	12.38	12.24	12.02
1,000	14.17	13.95	13.76	13.60	13.36
2,000	28.34	27.89	27.51	27.20	26.71
3,000	42.51	41.83	41.27	40.80	40.06
4,000	56.67	55.77	55.02	54.39	53.42
5,000	70.84	69.72	68.78	67.99	66.77
6,000	85.01	83.66	82.53	81.59	80.12
7,000	99.18	97.60	96.29	95.19	93.48
8,000	113.34	111.54	110.04	108.78	106.83
9,000	127.51	125.49	123.80	122.38	120.18
10,000	141.68	139.43	137.55	135.98	133.53
15,000	212.52	209.14	206.32	203.96	200.30
20,000	283.35	278.85	275.10	271.95	267.06
25,000	354.19	348.56	343.87	339.93	333.83
30,000	425.03	418.28	412.64	407.92	400.59
35,000	495.87	487.99	481.42	475.91	467.36
40,000	566.70	557.70	550.19	543.89	534.12
45,000	637.54	627.41	618.96	611.88	600.89
50,000	708.38	697.12	687.73	679.86	667.65
55,000	779.22	766.84	756.51	747.85	734.42
60,000	850.05	836.55	825.28	815.84	801.18
65,000	920.89	906.26	894.05	883.82	867.95
70,000	991.73	975.97	962.83	951.81	934.71
75,000	1,062.57	1,045.68	1,031.60	1,019.79	1,001.48
80,000	1,133.40	1,115.40	1,100.37	1,087.78	1,068.24
85,000	1,204.24	1,185.11	1,169.14	1,155.76	1,135.01
90,000	1,275.08	1,254.82	1,237.92	1,223.75	1,201.77
95,000	1,345.92	1,324.53	1,306.69	1,291.74	1,268.54
100,000	1,416.75	1,394.24	1,375.46	1,359.72	1,335.30
110,000	1,558.43	1,533.67	1,513.01	1,495.69	1,468.83
120,000	1,700.10	1,673.09	1,650.55	1,631.67	1,602.36
125,000	1,770.94	1,742.80	1,719.33	1,699.65	1,669.13
130,000	1,841.78	1,812.52	1,788.10	1,767.64	1,735.89
140,000	1,983.45	1,951.94	1,925.65	1,903.61	1,869.42
150,000	2,125.13	2,091.36	2,063.19	2,039.58	2,002.95
160,000	2,266.80	2,230.79	2,200.74	2,175.55	2,136.48
170,000	2,408.48	2,370.21	2,338.28	2,311.52	2,270.01
175,000	2,479.32	2,439.92	2,407.06	2,379.51	2,336.78
180,000	2,550.15	2,509.64	2,475.83	2,447.50	2,403.54
190,000	2,691.83	2,649.06	2,613.37	2,583.47	2,537.07
200,000	2,833.50	2,788.48	2,750.92	2,719.44	2,670.60
220,000	3,116.85	3,067.33	3,026.01	2,991.38	2,937.66
225,000	3,187.69	3,137.04	3,094.78	3,059.37	3,004.43
230,000	3,258.53	3,206.76	3,163.56	3,127.35	3,071.19
240,000	3,400.20	3,346.18	3,301.10	3,263.33	3,204.72
$250,000	3,541.88	3,485.60	3,438.65	3,399.30	3,338.25

Table 1   169

15.25% Monthly Payment Loans

Amortization Period in Years

$	21	22	23	24	25
100	1.33	1.32	1.32	1.31	1.31
200	2.66	2.64	2.63	2.62	2.61
300	3.98	3.96	3.94	3.92	3.91
400	5.31	5.28	5.25	5.23	5.21
500	6.63	6.59	6.56	6.53	6.51
600	7.96	7.91	7.87	7.84	7.81
700	9.29	9.23	9.18	9.14	9.11
800	10.61	10.55	10.49	10.45	10.41
900	11.94	11.87	11.80	11.75	11.71
1,000	13.26	13.18	13.12	13.06	13.01
2,000	26.52	26.36	26.23	26.11	26.01
3,000	39.78	39.54	39.34	39.16	39.01
4,000	53.04	52.72	52.45	52.21	52.02
5,000	66.30	65.90	65.56	65.27	65.02
6,000	79.56	79.07	78.67	78.32	78.02
7,000	92.81	92.25	91.78	91.37	91.02
8,000	106.07	105.43	104.89	104.42	104.03
9,000	119.33	118.61	118.00	117.47	117.03
10,000	132.59	131.79	131.11	130.53	130.03
15,000	198.88	197.68	196.66	195.79	195.04
20,000	265.17	263.57	262.21	261.05	260.06
25,000	331.47	329.46	327.76	326.31	325.07
30,000	397.76	395.35	393.31	391.57	390.08
35,000	464.05	461.24	458.86	456.83	455.10
40,000	530.34	527.13	524.41	522.09	520.11
45,000	596.63	593.02	589.96	587.35	585.12
50,000	662.93	658.92	655.51	652.61	650.13
55,000	729.22	724.81	721.06	717.87	715.15
60,000	795.51	790.70	786.61	783.13	780.16
65,000	861.80	856.59	852.16	848.39	845.17
70,000	928.09	922.48	917.71	913.65	910.19
75,000	994.39	988.37	983.26	978.91	975.20
80,000	1,060.68	1,054.26	1,048.81	1,044.17	1,040.21
85,000	1,126.97	1,120.15	1,114.36	1,109.43	1,105.22
90,000	1,193.26	1,186.04	1,179.91	1,174.69	1,170.24
95,000	1,259.55	1,251.93	1,245.46	1,239.95	1,235.25
100,000	1,325.85	1,317.83	1,311.01	1,305.21	1,300.26
110,000	1,458.43	1,449.61	1,442.11	1,435.73	1,430.29
120,000	1,591.01	1,581.39	1,573.21	1,566.25	1,560.31
125,000	1,657.31	1,647.28	1,638.76	1,631.51	1,625.33
130,000	1,723.60	1,713.17	1,704.31	1,696.77	1,690.34
140,000	1,856.18	1,844.95	1,835.41	1,827.29	1,820.37
150,000	1,988.77	1,976.74	1,966.51	1,957.81	1,950.39
160,000	2,121.35	2,108.52	2,097.61	2,088.33	2,080.42
170,000	2,253.94	2,240.30	2,228.71	2,218.85	2,210.44
175,000	2,320.23	2,306.19	2,294.26	2,284.11	2,275.46
180,000	2,386.52	2,372.08	2,359.81	2,349.37	2,340.47
190,000	2,519.10	2,503.86	2,490.91	2,479.89	2,470.50
200,000	2,651.69	2,635.65	2,622.01	2,610.41	2,600.52
220,000	2,916.86	2,899.21	2,884.21	2,871.45	2,860.57
225,000	2,983.15	2,965.10	2,949.77	2,936.71	2,925.59
230,000	3,049.44	3,030.99	3,015.32	3,001.97	2,990.60
240,000	3,182.02	3,162.77	3,146.42	3,132.49	3,120.62
$250,000	3,314.61	3,294.56	3,277.52	3,263.01	3,250.65

Monthly Payment Loans **15.25%**

Amortization Period in Years

	26	27	28	29	30
$ 100	1.30	1.30	1.29	1.29	1.29
200	2.60	2.59	2.58	2.58	2.57
300	3.89	3.88	3.87	3.87	3.86
400	5.19	5.17	5.16	5.15	5.14
500	6.49	6.47	6.45	6.44	6.43
600	7.78	7.76	7.74	7.73	7.71
700	9.08	9.05	9.03	9.01	9.00
800	10.37	10.34	10.32	10.30	10.28
900	11.67	11.64	11.61	11.59	11.57
1,000	12.97	12.93	12.90	12.87	12.85
2,000	25.93	25.85	25.79	25.74	25.69
3,000	38.89	38.78	38.69	38.61	38.54
4,000	51.85	51.70	51.58	51.47	51.38
5,000	64.81	64.63	64.47	64.34	64.23
6,000	77.77	77.55	77.37	77.21	77.07
7,000	90.73	90.48	90.26	90.08	89.92
8,000	103.69	103.40	103.15	102.94	102.76
9,000	116.65	116.32	116.05	115.81	115.61
10,000	129.61	129.25	128.94	128.68	128.45
15,000	194.41	193.87	193.41	193.01	192.67
20,000	259.21	258.49	257.88	257.35	256.90
25,000	324.01	323.11	322.34	321.68	321.12
30,000	388.82	387.74	386.81	386.02	385.34
35,000	453.62	452.36	451.28	450.36	449.57
40,000	518.42	516.98	515.75	514.69	513.79
45,000	583.22	581.60	580.21	579.03	578.01
50,000	648.02	646.22	644.68	643.36	642.23
55,000	712.83	710.84	709.15	707.70	706.46
60,000	777.63	775.47	773.62	772.03	770.68
65,000	842.43	840.09	838.08	836.37	834.90
70,000	907.23	904.71	902.55	900.71	899.13
75,000	972.03	969.33	967.02	965.04	963.35
80,000	1,036.84	1,033.95	1,031.49	1,029.38	1,027.57
85,000	1,101.64	1,098.57	1,095.95	1,093.71	1,091.79
90,000	1,166.44	1,163.20	1,160.42	1,158.05	1,156.02
95,000	1,231.24	1,227.82	1,224.89	1,222.38	1,220.24
100,000	1,296.04	1,292.44	1,289.36	1,286.72	1,284.46
110,000	1,425.65	1,421.68	1,418.29	1,415.39	1,412.91
120,000	1,555.25	1,550.93	1,547.23	1,544.06	1,541.36
125,000	1,620.05	1,615.55	1,611.70	1,608.40	1,605.58
130,000	1,684.86	1,680.17	1,676.16	1,672.74	1,669.80
140,000	1,814.46	1,809.41	1,805.10	1,801.41	1,798.25
150,000	1,944.06	1,938.66	1,934.03	1,930.08	1,926.69
160,000	2,073.67	2,067.90	2,062.97	2,058.75	2,055.14
170,000	2,203.27	2,197.14	2,191.90	2,187.42	2,183.58
175,000	2,268.07	2,261.76	2,256.37	2,251.76	2,247.81
180,000	2,332.87	2,326.39	2,320.84	2,316.09	2,312.03
190,000	2,462.48	2,455.63	2,449.77	2,444.76	2,440.48
200,000	2,592.08	2,584.87	2,578.71	2,573.44	2,568.92
220,000	2,851.29	2,843.36	2,836.58	2,830.78	2,825.81
225,000	2,916.09	2,907.98	2,901.05	2,895.12	2,890.04
230,000	2,980.89	2,972.60	2,965.52	2,959.45	2,954.26
240,000	3,110.50	3,101.85	3,094.45	3,088.12	3,082.71
$250,000	3,240.10	3,231.09	3,223.39	3,216.79	3,211.15

Table 1   171

15.50% Monthly Payment Loans

Amortization Period in Years

		5	7	8	10	12
$	100	2.41	1.96	1.83	1.65	1.54
	200	4.82	3.92	3.65	3.29	3.07
	300	7.22	5.88	5.48	4.94	4.60
	400	9.63	7.84	7.30	6.58	6.14
	500	12.03	9.79	9.12	8.23	7.67
	600	14.44	11.75	10.95	9.87	9.20
	700	16.84	13.71	12.77	11.51	10.74
	800	19.25	15.67	14.59	13.16	12.27
	900	21.65	17.63	16.42	14.80	13.80
	1,000	24.06	19.58	18.24	16.45	15.34
	2,000	48.11	39.16	36.48	32.89	30.67
	3,000	72.16	58.74	54.71	49.33	46.00
	4,000	96.22	78.32	72.95	65.77	61.33
	5,000	120.27	97.90	91.18	82.21	76.67
	6,000	144.32	117.48	109.42	98.65	92.00
	7,000	168.38	137.05	127.66	115.09	107.33
	8,000	192.43	156.63	145.89	131.53	122.66
	9,000	216.48	176.21	164.13	147.97	137.99
	10,000	240.54	195.79	182.36	164.42	153.33
	15,000	360.80	293.68	273.54	246.62	229.99
	20,000	481.07	391.57	364.72	328.83	306.65
	25,000	601.33	489.46	455.90	411.03	383.31
	30,000	721.60	587.36	547.08	493.24	459.97
	35,000	841.87	685.25	638.26	575.44	536.63
	40,000	962.13	783.14	729.44	657.65	613.29
	45,000	1,082.40	881.03	820.62	739.85	689.95
	50,000	1,202.66	978.92	911.80	822.06	766.61
	55,000	1,322.93	1,076.81	1,002.98	904.26	843.27
	60,000	1,443.20	1,174.71	1,094.16	986.47	919.93
	65,000	1,563.46	1,272.60	1,185.34	1,068.67	996.59
	70,000	1,683.73	1,370.49	1,276.52	1,150.88	1,073.25
	75,000	1,803.99	1,468.38	1,367.70	1,233.08	1,149.91
	80,000	1,924.26	1,566.27	1,458.88	1,315.29	1,226.57
	85,000	2,044.53	1,664.16	1,550.06	1,397.49	1,303.23
	90,000	2,164.79	1,762.06	1,641.24	1,479.70	1,379.89
	95,000	2,285.06	1,859.95	1,732.42	1,561.91	1,456.55
	100,000	2,405.32	1,957.84	1,823.60	1,644.11	1,533.21
	110,000	2,645.86	2,153.62	2,005.96	1,808.52	1,686.53
	120,000	2,886.39	2,349.41	2,188.32	1,972.93	1,839.85
	125,000	3,006.65	2,447.30	2,279.50	2,055.14	1,916.51
	130,000	3,126.92	2,545.19	2,370.67	2,137.34	1,993.17
	140,000	3,367.45	2,740.97	2,553.03	2,301.75	2,146.49
	150,000	3,607.98	2,936.76	2,735.39	2,466.16	2,299.81
	160,000	3,848.52	3,132.54	2,917.75	2,630.57	2,453.13
	170,000	4,089.05	3,328.32	3,100.11	2,794.98	2,606.45
	175,000	4,209.31	3,426.22	3,191.29	2,877.19	2,683.11
	180,000	4,329.58	3,524.11	3,282.47	2,959.39	2,759.77
	190,000	4,570.11	3,719.89	3,464.83	3,123.81	2,913.09
	200,000	4,810.64	3,915.67	3,647.19	3,288.22	3,066.41
	220,000	5,291.71	4,307.24	4,011.91	3,617.04	3,373.05
	225,000	5,411.97	4,405.13	4,103.09	3,699.24	3,449.71
	230,000	5,532.24	4,503.02	4,194.27	3,781.45	3,526.37
	240,000	5,772.77	4,698.81	4,376.63	3,945.86	3,679.70
$250,000		6,013.30	4,894.59	4,558.99	4,110.27	3,833.02

Monthly Payment Loans   **15.50%**

Amortization Period in Years

	15	16	17	18	20
$ 100	1.44	1.42	1.40	1.38	1.36
200	2.87	2.83	2.79	2.76	2.71
300	4.31	4.24	4.18	4.14	4.07
400	5.74	5.65	5.58	5.52	5.42
500	7.17	7.06	6.97	6.89	6.77
600	8.61	8.48	8.36	8.27	8.13
700	10.04	9.89	9.76	9.65	9.48
800	11.48	11.30	11.15	11.03	10.84
900	12.91	12.71	12.54	12.41	12.19
1,000	14.34	14.12	13.94	13.78	13.54
2,000	28.68	28.24	27.87	27.56	27.08
3,000	43.02	42.36	41.80	41.34	40.62
4,000	57.36	56.48	55.74	55.12	54.16
5,000	71.70	70.59	69.67	68.90	67.70
6,000	86.04	84.71	83.60	82.67	81.24
7,000	100.38	98.83	97.54	96.45	94.78
8,000	114.72	112.95	111.47	110.23	108.32
9,000	129.06	127.07	125.40	124.01	121.85
10,000	143.40	141.18	139.33	137.79	135.39
15,000	215.10	211.77	209.00	206.68	203.09
20,000	286.80	282.36	278.66	275.57	270.78
25,000	358.50	352.95	348.33	344.46	338.48
30,000	430.20	423.54	417.99	413.35	406.17
35,000	501.90	494.13	487.66	482.24	473.86
40,000	573.60	564.72	557.32	551.13	541.56
45,000	645.30	635.31	626.99	620.02	609.25
50,000	717.00	705.90	696.65	688.91	676.95
55,000	788.70	776.49	766.32	757.81	744.64
60,000	860.40	847.08	835.98	826.70	812.33
65,000	932.10	917.67	905.65	895.59	880.03
70,000	1,003.80	988.26	975.31	964.48	947.72
75,000	1,075.50	1,058.85	1,044.97	1,033.37	1,015.42
80,000	1,147.20	1,129.43	1,114.64	1,102.26	1,083.11
85,000	1,218.90	1,200.02	1,184.30	1,171.15	1,150.80
90,000	1,290.60	1,270.61	1,253.97	1,240.04	1,218.50
95,000	1,362.30	1,341.20	1,323.63	1,308.93	1,286.19
100,000	1,434.00	1,411.79	1,393.30	1,377.82	1,353.89
110,000	1,577.39	1,552.97	1,532.63	1,515.61	1,489.27
120,000	1,720.79	1,694.15	1,671.96	1,653.39	1,624.66
125,000	1,792.49	1,764.74	1,741.62	1,722.28	1,692.36
130,000	1,864.19	1,835.33	1,811.29	1,791.17	1,760.05
140,000	2,007.59	1,976.51	1,950.61	1,928.95	1,895.44
150,000	2,150.99	2,117.69	2,089.94	2,066.73	2,030.83
160,000	2,294.39	2,258.86	2,229.27	2,204.52	2,166.21
170,000	2,437.79	2,400.04	2,368.60	2,342.30	2,301.60
175,000	2,509.49	2,470.63	2,438.27	2,411.19	2,369.30
180,000	2,581.19	2,541.22	2,507.93	2,480.08	2,436.99
190,000	2,724.59	2,682.40	2,647.26	2,617.86	2,572.38
200,000	2,867.99	2,823.58	2,786.59	2,755.64	2,707.77
220,000	3,154.78	3,105.94	3,065.25	3,031.21	2,978.54
225,000	3,226.48	3,176.53	3,134.91	3,100.10	3,046.24
230,000	3,298.18	3,247.11	3,204.58	3,168.99	3,113.93
240,000	3,441.58	3,388.29	3,343.91	3,306.77	3,249.32
$250,000	3,584.98	3,529.47	3,483.24	3,444.55	3,384.71

Table 1   173

15.50%   Monthly Payment Loans

Amortization Period in Years

	21	22	23	24	25
$ 100	1.35	1.34	1.34	1.33	1.32
200	2.69	2.68	2.67	2.65	2.64
300	4.04	4.02	4.00	3.98	3.96
400	5.38	5.35	5.33	5.30	5.28
500	6.73	6.69	6.66	6.63	6.60
600	8.07	8.03	7.99	7.95	7.92
700	9.42	9.36	9.32	9.28	9.24
800	10.76	10.70	10.65	10.60	10.56
900	12.11	12.04	11.98	11.93	11.88
1,000	13.45	13.37	13.31	13.25	13.20
2,000	26.90	26.74	26.61	26.50	26.40
3,000	40.34	40.11	39.91	39.74	39.60
4,000	53.79	53.48	53.21	52.99	52.79
5,000	67.24	66.85	66.51	66.23	65.99
6,000	80.68	80.21	79.82	79.48	79.19
7,000	94.13	93.58	93.12	92.72	92.39
8,000	107.58	106.95	106.42	105.97	105.58
9,000	121.02	120.32	119.72	119.21	118.78
10,000	134.47	133.69	133.02	132.46	131.98
15,000	201.70	200.53	199.53	198.69	197.97
20,000	268.93	267.37	266.04	264.91	263.95
25,000	336.16	334.21	332.55	331.14	329.94
30,000	403.40	401.05	399.06	397.37	395.93
35,000	470.63	467.89	465.57	463.59	461.92
40,000	537.86	534.73	532.08	529.82	527.90
45,000	605.09	601.57	598.58	596.05	593.89
50,000	672.32	668.41	665.09	662.27	659.88
55,000	739.56	735.25	731.60	728.50	725.86
60,000	806.79	802.09	798.11	794.73	791.85
65,000	874.02	868.93	864.62	860.96	857.84
70,000	941.25	935.77	931.13	927.18	923.83
75,000	1,008.48	1,002.61	997.64	993.41	989.81
80,000	1,075.71	1,069.45	1,064.15	1,059.64	1,055.80
85,000	1,142.95	1,136.29	1,130.65	1,125.86	1,121.79
90,000	1,210.18	1,203.14	1,197.16	1,192.09	1,187.78
95,000	1,277.41	1,269.98	1,263.67	1,258.32	1,253.76
100,000	1,344.64	1,336.82	1,330.18	1,324.54	1,319.75
110,000	1,479.11	1,470.50	1,463.20	1,457.00	1,451.72
120,000	1,613.57	1,604.18	1,596.22	1,589.45	1,583.70
125,000	1,680.80	1,671.02	1,662.72	1,655.68	1,649.69
130,000	1,748.03	1,737.86	1,729.23	1,721.91	1,715.67
140,000	1,882.50	1,871.54	1,862.25	1,854.36	1,847.65
150,000	2,016.96	2,005.22	1,995.27	1,986.81	1,979.62
160,000	2,151.42	2,138.90	2,128.29	2,119.27	2,111.60
170,000	2,285.89	2,272.58	2,261.30	2,251.72	2,243.57
175,000	2,353.12	2,339.43	2,327.81	2,317.95	2,309.56
180,000	2,420.35	2,406.27	2,394.32	2,384.18	2,375.55
190,000	2,554.81	2,539.95	2,527.34	2,516.63	2,507.52
200,000	2,689.28	2,673.63	2,660.36	2,649.08	2,639.50
220,000	2,958.21	2,940.99	2,926.39	2,913.99	2,903.44
225,000	3,025.44	3,007.83	2,992.90	2,980.22	2,969.43
230,000	3,092.67	3,074.67	3,059.41	3,046.45	3,035.42
240,000	3,227.13	3,208.35	3,192.43	3,178.90	3,167.39
$250,000	3,361.60	3,342.03	3,325.44	3,311.35	3,299.37

Monthly Payment Loans   **15.50%**

Amortization Period in Years

	26	27	28	29	30
$ 100	1.32	1.32	1.31	1.31	1.31
200	2.64	2.63	2.62	2.62	2.61
300	3.95	3.94	3.93	3.93	3.92
400	5.27	5.25	5.24	5.23	5.22
500	6.58	6.57	6.55	6.54	6.53
600	7.90	7.88	7.86	7.85	7.83
700	9.21	9.19	9.17	9.15	9.14
800	10.53	10.50	10.48	10.46	10.44
900	11.85	11.81	11.79	11.77	11.75
1,000	13.16	13.13	13.10	13.07	13.05
2,000	26.32	26.25	26.19	26.14	26.10
3,000	39.47	39.37	39.28	39.21	39.14
4,000	52.63	52.49	52.37	52.27	52.19
5,000	65.79	65.61	65.47	65.34	65.23
6,000	78.94	78.74	78.56	78.41	78.28
7,000	92.10	91.86	91.65	91.47	91.32
8,000	105.26	104.98	104.74	104.54	104.37
9,000	118.41	118.10	117.83	117.61	117.41
10,000	131.57	131.22	130.93	130.67	130.46
15,000	197.35	196.83	196.39	196.01	195.68
20,000	263.14	262.44	261.85	261.34	260.91
25,000	328.92	328.05	327.31	326.68	326.13
30,000	394.70	393.66	392.77	392.01	391.36
35,000	460.49	459.27	458.23	457.34	456.59
40,000	526.27	524.88	523.69	522.68	521.81
45,000	592.05	590.49	589.15	588.01	587.04
50,000	657.84	656.10	654.61	653.35	652.26
55,000	723.62	721.71	720.07	718.68	717.49
60,000	789.40	787.32	785.53	784.01	782.72
65,000	855.19	852.92	850.99	849.35	847.94
70,000	920.97	918.53	916.46	914.68	913.17
75,000	986.75	984.14	981.92	980.02	978.39
80,000	1,052.54	1,049.75	1,047.38	1,045.35	1,043.62
85,000	1,118.32	1,115.36	1,112.84	1,110.68	1,108.84
90,000	1,184.10	1,180.97	1,178.30	1,176.02	1,174.07
95,000	1,249.88	1,246.58	1,243.76	1,241.35	1,239.30
100,000	1,315.67	1,312.19	1,309.22	1,306.69	1,304.52
110,000	1,447.23	1,443.41	1,440.14	1,437.35	1,434.97
120,000	1,578.80	1,574.63	1,571.06	1,568.02	1,565.43
125,000	1,644.58	1,640.23	1,636.52	1,633.36	1,630.65
130,000	1,710.37	1,705.84	1,701.98	1,698.69	1,695.88
140,000	1,841.93	1,837.06	1,832.91	1,829.36	1,826.33
150,000	1,973.50	1,968.28	1,963.83	1,960.03	1,956.78
160,000	2,105.07	2,099.50	2,094.75	2,090.70	2,087.23
170,000	2,236.63	2,230.72	2,225.67	2,221.36	2,217.68
175,000	2,302.42	2,296.33	2,291.13	2,286.70	2,282.91
180,000	2,368.20	2,361.94	2,356.59	2,352.03	2,348.14
190,000	2,499.76	2,493.15	2,487.51	2,482.70	2,478.59
200,000	2,631.33	2,624.37	2,618.44	2,613.37	2,609.04
220,000	2,894.46	2,886.81	2,880.28	2,874.70	2,869.94
225,000	2,960.25	2,952.42	2,945.74	2,940.04	2,935.17
230,000	3,026.03	3,018.03	3,011.20	3,005.37	3,000.39
240,000	3,157.60	3,149.25	3,142.12	3,136.04	3,130.85
$250,000	3,289.16	3,280.46	3,273.04	3,266.71	3,261.30

Table 1   175

15.75% Monthly Payment Loans

Amortization Period in Years

	5	7	8	10	12
$ 100	2.42	1.98	1.84	1.66	1.55
200	4.84	3.95	3.68	3.32	3.10
300	7.26	5.92	5.52	4.98	4.65
400	9.68	7.89	7.36	6.64	6.20
500	12.10	9.86	9.20	8.30	7.75
600	14.52	11.84	11.03	9.96	9.30
700	16.93	13.81	12.87	11.62	10.85
800	19.35	15.78	14.71	13.28	12.40
900	21.77	17.75	16.55	14.94	13.95
1,000	24.19	19.72	18.39	16.60	15.50
2,000	48.38	39.44	36.77	33.20	30.99
3,000	72.56	59.16	55.15	49.79	46.49
4,000	96.75	78.88	73.53	66.39	61.98
5,000	120.93	98.60	91.92	82.98	77.48
6,000	145.12	118.32	110.30	99.58	92.97
7,000	169.30	138.04	128.68	116.18	108.47
8,000	193.49	157.76	147.06	132.77	123.96
9,000	217.67	177.48	165.44	149.37	139.46
10,000	241.86	197.20	183.83	165.96	154.95
15,000	362.79	295.80	275.74	248.94	232.43
20,000	483.71	394.40	367.65	331.92	309.90
25,000	604.64	493.00	459.56	414.90	387.37
30,000	725.57	591.60	551.47	497.88	464.85
35,000	846.49	690.20	643.38	580.86	542.32
40,000	967.42	788.80	735.29	663.84	619.80
45,000	1,088.35	887.40	827.20	746.82	697.27
50,000	1,209.28	986.00	919.11	829.80	774.74
55,000	1,330.20	1,084.60	1,011.02	912.78	852.22
60,000	1,451.13	1,183.20	1,102.93	995.76	929.69
65,000	1,572.06	1,281.80	1,194.84	1,078.74	1,007.17
70,000	1,692.98	1,380.40	1,286.75	1,161.71	1,084.64
75,000	1,813.91	1,479.00	1,378.66	1,244.69	1,162.11
80,000	1,934.84	1,577.60	1,470.57	1,327.67	1,239.59
85,000	2,055.77	1,676.20	1,562.48	1,410.65	1,317.06
90,000	2,176.69	1,774.80	1,654.39	1,493.63	1,394.54
95,000	2,297.62	1,873.40	1,746.30	1,576.61	1,472.01
100,000	2,418.55	1,972.00	1,838.21	1,659.59	1,549.48
110,000	2,660.40	2,169.20	2,022.03	1,825.55	1,704.43
120,000	2,902.26	2,366.40	2,205.85	1,991.51	1,859.38
125,000	3,023.18	2,465.00	2,297.76	2,074.49	1,936.85
130,000	3,144.11	2,563.60	2,389.67	2,157.47	2,014.33
140,000	3,385.96	2,760.80	2,573.49	2,323.42	2,169.27
150,000	3,627.82	2,958.00	2,757.31	2,489.38	2,324.22
160,000	3,869.67	3,155.20	2,941.14	2,655.34	2,479.17
170,000	4,111.53	3,352.39	3,124.96	2,821.30	2,634.12
175,000	4,232.45	3,450.99	3,216.87	2,904.28	2,711.59
180,000	4,353.38	3,549.59	3,308.78	2,987.26	2,789.07
190,000	4,595.24	3,746.79	3,492.60	3,153.22	2,944.01
200,000	4,837.09	3,943.99	3,676.42	3,319.17	3,098.96
220,000	5,320.80	4,338.39	4,044.06	3,651.09	3,408.86
225,000	5,441.73	4,436.99	4,135.97	3,734.07	3,486.33
230,000	5,562.65	4,535.59	4,227.88	3,817.05	3,563.81
240,000	5,804.51	4,732.79	4,411.70	3,983.01	3,718.75
$250,000	6,046.36	4,929.99	4,595.52	4,148.97	3,873.70

Monthly Payment Loans   **15.75%**

Amortization Period in Years

	15	16	17	18	20
$ 100	1.46	1.43	1.42	1.40	1.38
200	2.91	2.86	2.83	2.80	2.75
300	4.36	4.29	4.24	4.19	4.12
400	5.81	5.72	5.65	5.59	5.50
500	7.26	7.15	7.06	6.98	6.87
600	8.71	8.58	8.47	8.38	8.24
700	10.16	10.01	9.88	9.78	9.61
800	11.62	11.44	11.29	11.17	10.99
900	13.07	12.87	12.71	12.57	12.36
1,000	14.52	14.30	14.12	13.96	13.73
2,000	29.03	28.59	28.23	27.92	27.46
3,000	43.54	42.89	42.34	41.88	41.18
4,000	58.06	57.18	56.45	55.84	54.91
5,000	72.57	71.48	70.57	69.80	68.63
6,000	87.08	85.77	84.68	83.76	82.36
7,000	101.60	100.06	98.79	97.72	96.08
8,000	116.11	114.36	112.90	111.68	109.81
9,000	130.62	128.65	127.01	125.64	123.53
10,000	145.14	142.95	141.13	139.60	137.26
15,000	217.70	214.42	211.69	209.40	205.89
20,000	290.27	285.89	282.25	279.20	274.51
25,000	362.83	357.36	352.81	349.00	343.14
30,000	435.40	428.83	423.37	418.80	411.77
35,000	507.96	500.30	493.93	488.60	480.39
40,000	580.53	571.77	564.49	558.40	549.02
45,000	653.09	643.24	635.05	628.20	617.65
50,000	725.66	714.71	705.61	698.00	686.27
55,000	798.22	786.18	776.17	767.80	754.90
60,000	870.79	857.65	846.73	837.60	823.53
65,000	943.36	929.12	917.29	907.40	892.15
70,000	1,015.92	1,000.59	987.85	977.20	960.78
75,000	1,088.49	1,072.06	1,058.41	1,047.00	1,029.41
80,000	1,161.05	1,143.53	1,128.97	1,116.80	1,098.03
85,000	1,233.62	1,215.00	1,199.53	1,186.60	1,166.66
90,000	1,306.18	1,286.47	1,270.09	1,256.40	1,235.29
95,000	1,378.75	1,357.95	1,340.65	1,326.20	1,303.91
100,000	1,451.31	1,429.42	1,411.21	1,396.00	1,372.54
110,000	1,596.44	1,572.36	1,552.33	1,535.60	1,509.79
120,000	1,741.57	1,715.30	1,693.45	1,675.20	1,647.05
125,000	1,814.14	1,786.77	1,764.01	1,745.00	1,715.67
130,000	1,886.71	1,858.24	1,834.57	1,814.80	1,784.30
140,000	2,031.84	2,001.18	1,975.69	1,954.40	1,921.55
150,000	2,176.97	2,144.12	2,116.81	2,094.00	2,058.81
160,000	2,322.10	2,287.06	2,257.93	2,233.60	2,196.06
170,000	2,467.23	2,430.00	2,399.05	2,373.20	2,333.31
175,000	2,539.79	2,501.47	2,469.61	2,443.00	2,401.94
180,000	2,612.36	2,572.94	2,540.17	2,512.80	2,470.57
190,000	2,757.49	2,715.89	2,681.29	2,652.40	2,607.82
200,000	2,902.62	2,858.83	2,822.41	2,792.00	2,745.07
220,000	3,192.88	3,144.71	3,104.65	3,071.20	3,019.58
225,000	3,265.45	3,216.18	3,175.21	3,141.00	3,088.21
230,000	3,338.01	3,287.65	3,245.77	3,210.80	3,156.83
240,000	3,483.14	3,430.59	3,386.89	3,350.40	3,294.09
$250,000	3,628.27	3,573.53	3,528.01	3,490.00	3,431.34

Table 1   177

15.75%   Monthly Payment Loans

Amortization Period in Years

	21	22	23	24	25
$ 100	1.37	1.36	1.35	1.35	1.34
200	2.73	2.72	2.70	2.69	2.68
300	4.10	4.07	4.05	4.04	4.02
400	5.46	5.43	5.40	5.38	5.36
500	6.82	6.78	6.75	6.72	6.70
600	8.19	8.14	8.10	8.07	8.04
700	9.55	9.50	9.45	9.41	9.38
800	10.91	10.85	10.80	10.76	10.72
900	12.28	12.21	12.15	12.10	12.06
1,000	13.64	13.56	13.50	13.44	13.40
2,000	27.28	27.12	26.99	26.88	26.79
3,000	40.91	40.68	40.49	40.32	40.18
4,000	54.55	54.24	53.98	53.76	53.58
5,000	68.18	67.80	67.48	67.20	66.97
6,000	81.82	81.36	80.97	80.64	80.36
7,000	95.45	94.92	94.46	94.08	93.76
8,000	109.09	108.47	107.96	107.52	107.15
9,000	122.72	122.03	121.45	120.96	120.54
10,000	136.36	135.59	134.95	134.40	133.93
15,000	204.53	203.39	202.42	201.60	200.90
20,000	272.71	271.18	269.89	268.79	267.86
25,000	340.88	338.97	337.36	335.99	334.83
30,000	409.06	406.77	404.83	403.19	401.79
35,000	477.23	474.56	472.30	470.38	468.76
40,000	545.41	542.35	539.77	537.58	535.72
45,000	613.58	610.15	607.24	604.78	602.69
50,000	681.76	677.94	674.71	671.97	669.65
55,000	749.93	745.73	742.18	739.17	736.61
60,000	818.11	813.53	809.65	806.37	803.58
65,000	886.28	881.32	877.12	873.56	870.54
70,000	954.46	949.11	944.59	940.76	937.51
75,000	1,022.63	1,016.91	1,012.06	1,007.96	1,004.47
80,000	1,090.81	1,084.70	1,079.53	1,075.15	1,071.44
85,000	1,158.98	1,152.49	1,147.00	1,142.35	1,138.40
90,000	1,227.16	1,220.29	1,214.47	1,209.55	1,205.37
95,000	1,295.33	1,288.08	1,281.94	1,276.74	1,272.33
100,000	1,363.51	1,355.87	1,349.42	1,343.94	1,339.29
110,000	1,499.86	1,491.46	1,484.36	1,478.33	1,473.22
120,000	1,636.21	1,627.05	1,619.30	1,612.73	1,607.15
125,000	1,704.38	1,694.84	1,686.77	1,679.92	1,674.12
130,000	1,772.56	1,762.63	1,754.24	1,747.12	1,741.08
140,000	1,908.91	1,898.22	1,889.18	1,881.52	1,875.01
150,000	2,045.26	2,033.81	2,024.12	2,015.91	2,008.94
160,000	2,181.61	2,169.40	2,159.06	2,150.30	2,142.87
170,000	2,317.96	2,304.98	2,294.00	2,284.70	2,276.80
175,000	2,386.13	2,372.78	2,361.47	2,351.89	2,343.76
180,000	2,454.31	2,440.57	2,428.94	2,419.09	2,410.73
190,000	2,590.66	2,576.16	2,563.88	2,553.48	2,544.66
200,000	2,727.01	2,711.74	2,698.83	2,687.88	2,678.58
220,000	2,999.71	2,982.92	2,968.71	2,956.66	2,946.44
225,000	3,067.88	3,050.71	3,036.18	3,023.86	3,013.41
230,000	3,136.06	3,118.50	3,103.65	3,091.06	3,080.37
240,000	3,272.41	3,254.09	3,238.59	3,225.45	3,214.30
$250,000	3,408.76	3,389.68	3,373.53	3,359.84	3,348.23

Monthly Payment Loans 15.75%

Amortization Period in Years

	26	27	28	29	30
$ 100	1.34	1.34	1.33	1.33	1.33
200	2.68	2.67	2.66	2.66	2.65
300	4.01	4.00	3.99	3.99	3.98
400	5.35	5.33	5.32	5.31	5.30
500	6.68	6.66	6.65	6.64	6.63
600	8.02	8.00	7.98	7.97	7.95
700	9.35	9.33	9.31	9.29	9.28
800	10.69	10.66	10.64	10.62	10.60
900	12.02	11.99	11.97	11.95	11.93
1,000	13.36	13.32	13.30	13.27	13.25
2,000	26.71	26.64	26.59	26.54	26.50
3,000	40.07	39.96	39.88	39.81	39.74
4,000	53.42	53.28	53.17	53.07	52.99
5,000	66.77	66.60	66.46	66.34	66.24
6,000	80.13	79.92	79.75	79.61	79.48
7,000	93.48	93.24	93.04	92.87	92.73
8,000	106.83	106.56	106.34	106.14	105.97
9,000	120.19	119.88	119.63	119.41	119.22
10,000	133.54	133.20	132.92	132.67	132.47
15,000	200.31	199.80	199.37	199.01	198.70
20,000	267.07	266.40	265.83	265.34	264.93
25,000	333.84	333.00	332.29	331.68	331.16
30,000	400.61	399.60	398.74	398.01	397.39
35,000	467.37	466.20	465.20	464.35	463.62
40,000	534.14	532.80	531.66	530.68	529.85
45,000	600.91	599.40	598.11	597.02	596.08
50,000	667.68	666.00	664.57	663.35	662.31
55,000	734.44	732.60	731.02	729.69	728.54
60,000	801.21	799.20	797.48	796.02	794.78
65,000	867.98	865.79	863.94	862.35	861.01
70,000	934.74	932.39	930.39	928.69	927.24
75,000	1,001.51	998.99	996.85	995.02	993.47
80,000	1,068.28	1,065.59	1,063.31	1,061.36	1,059.70
85,000	1,135.05	1,132.19	1,129.76	1,127.69	1,125.93
90,000	1,201.81	1,198.79	1,196.22	1,194.03	1,192.16
95,000	1,268.58	1,265.39	1,262.67	1,260.36	1,258.39
100,000	1,335.35	1,331.99	1,329.13	1,326.70	1,324.62
110,000	1,468.88	1,465.19	1,462.04	1,459.37	1,457.08
120,000	1,602.41	1,598.39	1,594.96	1,592.04	1,589.55
125,000	1,669.18	1,664.98	1,661.41	1,658.37	1,655.78
130,000	1,735.95	1,731.58	1,727.87	1,724.70	1,722.01
140,000	1,869.48	1,864.78	1,860.78	1,857.37	1,854.47
150,000	2,003.02	1,997.98	1,993.69	1,990.04	1,986.93
160,000	2,136.55	2,131.18	2,126.61	2,122.71	2,119.39
170,000	2,270.09	2,264.38	2,259.52	2,255.38	2,251.85
175,000	2,336.85	2,330.98	2,325.98	2,321.72	2,318.08
180,000	2,403.62	2,397.58	2,392.43	2,388.05	2,384.32
190,000	2,537.15	2,530.77	2,525.34	2,520.72	2,516.78
200,000	2,670.69	2,663.97	2,658.26	2,653.39	2,649.24
220,000	2,937.76	2,930.37	2,924.08	2,918.73	2,914.16
225,000	3,004.52	2,996.97	2,990.54	2,985.06	2,980.39
230,000	3,071.29	3,063.57	3,056.99	3,051.40	3,046.62
240,000	3,204.82	3,196.77	3,189.91	3,184.07	3,179.09
$250,000	3,338.36	3,329.96	3,322.82	3,316.73	3,311.55

Table 1   179

16.00% Monthly Payment Loans

Amortization Period in Years

	5	7	8	10	12
$ 100	2.44	1.99	1.86	1.68	1.57
200	4.87	3.98	3.71	3.36	3.14
300	7.30	5.96	5.56	5.03	4.70
400	9.73	7.95	7.42	6.71	6.27
500	12.16	9.94	9.27	8.38	7.83
600	14.60	11.92	11.12	10.06	9.40
700	17.03	13.91	12.98	11.73	10.97
800	19.46	15.89	14.83	13.41	12.53
900	21.89	17.88	16.68	15.08	14.10
1,000	24.32	19.87	18.53	16.76	15.66
2,000	48.64	39.73	37.06	33.51	31.32
3,000	72.96	59.59	55.59	50.26	46.98
4,000	97.28	79.45	74.12	67.01	62.64
5,000	121.60	99.32	92.65	83.76	78.30
6,000	145.91	119.18	111.18	100.51	93.95
7,000	170.23	139.04	129.71	117.26	109.61
8,000	194.55	158.90	148.24	134.02	125.27
9,000	218.87	178.76	166.76	150.77	140.93
10,000	243.19	198.63	185.29	167.52	156.59
15,000	364.78	297.94	277.94	251.27	234.88
20,000	486.37	397.25	370.58	335.03	313.17
25,000	607.96	496.56	463.22	418.79	391.46
30,000	729.55	595.87	555.87	502.54	469.75
35,000	851.14	695.18	648.51	586.30	548.04
40,000	972.73	794.49	741.16	670.06	626.34
45,000	1,094.32	893.80	833.80	753.81	704.63
50,000	1,215.91	993.11	926.44	837.57	782.92
55,000	1,337.50	1,092.42	1,019.09	921.33	861.21
60,000	1,459.09	1,191.73	1,111.73	1,005.08	939.50
65,000	1,580.68	1,291.04	1,204.38	1,088.84	1,017.79
70,000	1,702.27	1,390.35	1,297.02	1,172.60	1,096.08
75,000	1,823.86	1,489.66	1,389.66	1,256.35	1,174.37
80,000	1,945.45	1,588.97	1,482.31	1,340.11	1,252.67
85,000	2,067.04	1,688.28	1,574.95	1,423.87	1,330.96
90,000	2,188.63	1,787.59	1,667.60	1,507.62	1,409.25
95,000	2,310.22	1,886.90	1,760.24	1,591.38	1,487.54
100,000	2,431.81	1,986.21	1,852.88	1,675.14	1,565.83
110,000	2,674.99	2,184.83	2,038.17	1,842.65	1,722.41
120,000	2,918.17	2,383.45	2,223.46	2,010.16	1,879.00
125,000	3,039.76	2,482.76	2,316.10	2,093.92	1,957.29
130,000	3,161.35	2,582.07	2,408.75	2,177.68	2,035.58
140,000	3,404.53	2,780.69	2,594.04	2,345.19	2,192.16
150,000	3,647.71	2,979.31	2,779.32	2,512.70	2,348.74
160,000	3,890.89	3,177.94	2,964.61	2,680.21	2,505.33
170,000	4,134.07	3,376.56	3,149.90	2,847.73	2,661.91
175,000	4,255.66	3,475.87	3,242.54	2,931.48	2,740.20
180,000	4,377.26	3,575.18	3,335.19	3,015.24	2,818.49
190,000	4,620.44	3,773.80	3,520.47	3,182.75	2,975.07
200,000	4,863.62	3,972.42	3,705.76	3,350.27	3,131.66
220,000	5,349.98	4,369.66	4,076.34	3,685.29	3,444.82
225,000	5,471.57	4,468.97	4,168.98	3,769.05	3,523.11
230,000	5,593.16	4,568.28	4,261.63	3,852.81	3,601.40
240,000	5,836.34	4,766.90	4,446.91	4,020.32	3,757.99
$250,000	6,079.52	4,965.52	4,632.20	4,187.83	3,914.57

Monthly Payment Loans   **16.00%**

Amortization Period in Years

	15	16	17	18	20
$ 100	1.47	1.45	1.43	1.42	1.40
200	2.94	2.90	2.86	2.83	2.79
300	4.41	4.35	4.29	4.25	4.18
400	5.88	5.79	5.72	5.66	5.57
500	7.35	7.24	7.15	7.08	6.96
600	8.82	8.69	8.58	8.49	8.35
700	10.29	10.13	10.01	9.90	9.74
800	11.75	11.58	11.44	11.32	11.14
900	13.22	13.03	12.87	12.73	12.53
1,000	14.69	14.48	14.30	14.15	13.92
2,000	29.38	28.95	28.59	28.29	27.83
3,000	44.07	43.42	42.88	42.43	41.74
4,000	58.75	57.89	57.17	56.57	55.66
5,000	73.44	72.36	71.46	70.72	69.57
6,000	88.13	86.83	85.76	84.86	83.48
7,000	102.81	101.30	100.05	99.00	97.39
8,000	117.50	115.77	114.34	113.14	111.31
9,000	132.19	130.24	128.63	127.29	125.22
10,000	146.88	144.72	142.92	141.43	139.13
15,000	220.31	217.07	214.38	212.14	208.69
20,000	293.75	289.43	285.84	282.85	278.26
25,000	367.18	361.78	357.30	353.57	347.82
30,000	440.62	434.14	428.76	424.28	417.38
35,000	514.05	506.49	500.22	494.99	486.94
40,000	587.49	578.85	571.68	565.70	556.51
45,000	660.92	651.20	643.14	636.42	626.07
50,000	734.36	723.56	714.60	707.13	695.63
55,000	807.79	795.92	786.06	777.84	765.20
60,000	881.23	868.27	857.52	848.55	834.76
65,000	954.66	940.63	928.98	919.27	904.32
70,000	1,028.10	1,012.98	1,000.44	989.98	973.88
75,000	1,101.53	1,085.34	1,071.90	1,060.69	1,043.45
80,000	1,174.97	1,157.69	1,143.36	1,131.40	1,113.01
85,000	1,248.40	1,230.05	1,214.82	1,202.12	1,182.57
90,000	1,321.84	1,302.40	1,286.27	1,272.83	1,252.14
95,000	1,395.27	1,374.76	1,357.73	1,343.54	1,321.70
100,000	1,468.71	1,447.12	1,429.19	1,414.25	1,391.26
110,000	1,615.58	1,591.83	1,572.11	1,555.68	1,530.39
120,000	1,762.45	1,736.54	1,715.03	1,697.10	1,669.51
125,000	1,835.88	1,808.89	1,786.49	1,767.81	1,739.07
130,000	1,909.32	1,881.25	1,857.95	1,838.53	1,808.64
140,000	2,056.19	2,025.96	2,000.87	1,979.95	1,947.76
150,000	2,203.06	2,170.67	2,143.79	2,121.38	2,086.89
160,000	2,349.93	2,315.38	2,286.71	2,262.80	2,226.01
170,000	2,496.80	2,460.09	2,429.63	2,404.23	2,365.14
175,000	2,570.23	2,532.45	2,501.08	2,474.94	2,434.70
180,000	2,643.67	2,604.80	2,572.54	2,545.65	2,504.27
190,000	2,790.54	2,749.51	2,715.46	2,687.07	2,643.39
200,000	2,937.41	2,894.23	2,858.38	2,828.50	2,782.52
220,000	3,231.15	3,183.65	3,144.22	3,111.35	3,060.77
225,000	3,304.58	3,256.00	3,215.68	3,182.06	3,130.33
230,000	3,378.02	3,328.36	3,287.14	3,252.77	3,199.89
240,000	3,524.89	3,473.07	3,430.06	3,394.20	3,339.02
$250,000	3,671.76	3,617.78	3,572.98	3,535.62	3,478.14

Table 1   181

16.00%   Monthly Payment Loans

Amortization Period in Years

	21	22	23	24	25
$ 100	1.39	1.38	1.37	1.37	1.36
200	2.77	2.75	2.74	2.73	2.72
300	4.15	4.13	4.11	4.10	4.08
400	5.53	5.50	5.48	5.46	5.44
500	6.92	6.88	6.85	6.82	6.80
600	8.30	8.25	8.22	8.19	8.16
700	9.68	9.63	9.59	9.55	9.52
800	11.06	11.00	10.95	10.91	10.88
900	12.45	12.38	12.32	12.28	12.23
1,000	13.83	13.75	13.69	13.64	13.59
2,000	27.65	27.50	27.38	27.27	27.18
3,000	41.48	41.25	41.07	40.91	40.77
4,000	55.30	55.00	54.75	54.54	54.36
5,000	69.13	68.75	68.44	68.17	67.95
6,000	82.95	82.50	82.13	81.81	81.54
7,000	96.78	96.25	95.81	95.44	95.13
8,000	110.60	110.00	109.50	109.08	108.72
9,000	124.42	123.75	123.19	122.71	122.30
10,000	138.25	137.50	136.88	136.34	135.89
15,000	207.37	206.25	205.31	204.51	203.84
20,000	276.49	275.00	273.75	272.68	271.78
25,000	345.61	343.75	342.18	340.85	339.73
30,000	414.73	412.50	410.62	409.02	407.67
35,000	483.86	481.25	479.05	477.19	475.62
40,000	552.98	550.00	547.49	545.36	543.56
45,000	622.10	618.75	615.92	613.53	611.50
50,000	691.22	687.50	684.36	681.70	679.45
55,000	760.34	756.25	752.79	749.87	747.39
60,000	829.46	825.00	821.23	818.04	815.34
65,000	898.58	893.75	889.66	886.21	883.28
70,000	967.71	962.50	958.10	954.38	951.23
75,000	1,036.83	1,031.25	1,026.53	1,022.55	1,019.17
80,000	1,105.95	1,100.00	1,094.97	1,090.72	1,087.12
85,000	1,175.07	1,168.75	1,163.41	1,158.89	1,155.06
90,000	1,244.19	1,237.50	1,231.84	1,227.06	1,223.00
95,000	1,313.31	1,306.25	1,300.28	1,295.23	1,290.95
100,000	1,382.44	1,375.00	1,368.71	1,363.40	1,358.89
110,000	1,520.68	1,512.49	1,505.58	1,499.73	1,494.78
120,000	1,658.92	1,649.99	1,642.45	1,636.07	1,630.67
125,000	1,728.04	1,718.74	1,710.89	1,704.24	1,698.62
130,000	1,797.16	1,787.49	1,779.32	1,772.41	1,766.56
140,000	1,935.41	1,924.99	1,916.19	1,908.75	1,902.45
150,000	2,073.65	2,062.49	2,053.06	2,045.09	2,038.34
160,000	2,211.89	2,199.99	2,189.93	2,181.43	2,174.23
170,000	2,350.14	2,337.49	2,326.81	2,317.77	2,310.12
175,000	2,419.26	2,406.24	2,395.24	2,385.94	2,378.06
180,000	2,488.38	2,474.99	2,463.68	2,454.11	2,446.00
190,000	2,626.62	2,612.49	2,600.55	2,590.45	2,581.89
200,000	2,764.87	2,749.99	2,737.42	2,726.79	2,717.78
220,000	3,041.35	3,024.98	3,011.16	2,999.46	2,989.56
225,000	3,110.47	3,093.73	3,079.59	3,067.63	3,057.50
230,000	3,179.60	3,162.48	3,148.03	3,135.80	3,125.45
240,000	3,317.84	3,299.98	3,284.90	3,272.14	3,261.34
$250,000	3,456.08	3,437.48	3,421.77	3,408.48	3,397.23

Monthly Payment Loans   **16.00%**

Amortization Period in Years

	26	27	28	29	30
$ 100	1.36	1.36	1.35	1.35	1.35
200	2.72	2.71	2.70	2.70	2.69
300	4.07	4.06	4.05	4.05	4.04
400	5.43	5.41	5.40	5.39	5.38
500	6.78	6.76	6.75	6.74	6.73
600	8.14	8.12	8.10	8.09	8.07
700	9.49	9.47	9.45	9.43	9.42
800	10.85	10.82	10.80	10.78	10.76
900	12.20	12.17	12.15	12.13	12.11
1,000	13.56	13.52	13.50	13.47	13.45
2,000	27.11	27.04	26.99	26.94	26.90
3,000	40.66	40.56	40.48	40.41	40.35
4,000	54.21	54.08	53.97	53.87	53.80
5,000	67.76	67.60	67.46	67.34	67.24
6,000	81.31	81.11	80.95	80.81	80.69
7,000	94.86	94.63	94.44	94.28	94.14
8,000	108.41	108.15	107.93	107.74	107.59
9,000	121.96	121.67	121.42	121.21	121.03
10,000	135.51	135.19	134.91	134.68	134.48
15,000	203.27	202.78	202.37	202.02	201.72
20,000	271.02	270.37	269.82	269.35	268.96
25,000	338.77	337.96	337.28	336.69	336.19
30,000	406.53	405.55	404.73	404.03	403.43
35,000	474.28	473.15	472.18	471.37	470.67
40,000	542.03	540.74	539.64	538.70	537.91
45,000	609.79	608.33	607.09	606.04	605.15
50,000	677.54	675.92	674.55	673.38	672.38
55,000	745.29	743.51	742.00	740.71	739.62
60,000	813.05	811.10	809.45	808.05	806.86
65,000	880.80	878.70	876.91	875.39	874.10
70,000	948.56	946.29	944.36	942.73	941.33
75,000	1,016.31	1,013.88	1,011.82	1,010.06	1,008.57
80,000	1,084.06	1,081.47	1,079.27	1,077.40	1,075.81
85,000	1,151.82	1,149.06	1,146.73	1,144.74	1,143.05
90,000	1,219.57	1,216.65	1,214.18	1,212.08	1,210.29
95,000	1,287.32	1,284.25	1,281.63	1,279.41	1,277.52
100,000	1,355.08	1,351.84	1,349.09	1,346.75	1,344.76
110,000	1,490.58	1,487.02	1,484.00	1,481.42	1,479.24
120,000	1,626.09	1,622.20	1,618.90	1,616.10	1,613.71
125,000	1,693.85	1,689.80	1,686.36	1,683.44	1,680.95
130,000	1,761.60	1,757.39	1,753.81	1,750.77	1,748.19
140,000	1,897.11	1,892.57	1,888.72	1,885.45	1,882.66
150,000	2,032.61	2,027.75	2,023.63	2,020.12	2,017.14
160,000	2,168.12	2,162.94	2,158.54	2,154.80	2,151.62
170,000	2,303.63	2,298.12	2,293.45	2,289.47	2,286.09
175,000	2,371.38	2,365.71	2,360.90	2,356.81	2,353.33
180,000	2,439.13	2,433.30	2,428.35	2,424.15	2,420.57
190,000	2,574.64	2,568.49	2,563.26	2,558.82	2,555.04
200,000	2,710.15	2,703.67	2,698.17	2,693.49	2,689.52
220,000	2,981.16	2,974.04	2,967.99	2,962.84	2,958.47
225,000	3,048.92	3,041.63	3,035.44	3,030.18	3,025.71
230,000	3,116.67	3,109.22	3,102.89	3,097.52	3,092.95
240,000	3,252.18	3,244.40	3,237.80	3,232.19	3,227.42
$250,000	3,387.69	3,379.59	3,372.71	3,366.87	3,361.90

Table 1   183

16.25%   Monthly Payment Loans

Amortization Period in Years

	5	7	8	10	12
$ 100	2.45	2.01	1.87	1.70	1.59
200	4.90	4.01	3.74	3.39	3.17
300	7.34	6.01	5.61	5.08	4.75
400	9.79	8.01	7.48	6.77	6.33
500	12.23	10.01	9.34	8.46	7.92
600	14.68	12.01	11.21	10.15	9.50
700	17.12	14.01	13.08	11.84	11.08
800	19.57	16.01	14.95	13.53	12.66
900	22.01	18.01	16.81	15.22	14.25
1,000	24.46	20.01	18.68	16.91	15.83
2,000	48.91	40.01	37.36	33.82	31.65
3,000	73.36	60.02	56.03	50.73	47.47
4,000	97.81	80.02	74.71	67.63	63.29
5,000	122.26	100.03	93.39	84.54	79.12
6,000	146.71	120.03	112.06	101.45	94.94
7,000	171.16	140.04	130.74	118.36	110.76
8,000	195.61	160.04	149.41	135.26	126.58
9,000	220.06	180.05	168.09	152.17	142.41
10,000	244.52	200.05	186.77	169.08	158.23
15,000	366.77	300.08	280.15	253.62	237.34
20,000	489.03	400.10	373.53	338.15	316.45
25,000	611.28	500.12	466.91	422.69	395.57
30,000	733.54	600.15	560.29	507.23	474.68
35,000	855.79	700.17	653.67	591.77	553.79
40,000	978.05	800.19	747.05	676.30	632.90
45,000	1,100.30	900.22	840.43	760.84	712.01
50,000	1,222.56	1,000.24	933.81	845.38	791.13
55,000	1,344.81	1,100.26	1,027.19	929.91	870.24
60,000	1,467.07	1,200.29	1,120.57	1,014.45	949.35
65,000	1,589.33	1,300.31	1,213.95	1,098.99	1,028.46
70,000	1,711.58	1,400.33	1,307.33	1,183.53	1,107.58
75,000	1,833.84	1,500.36	1,400.71	1,268.06	1,186.69
80,000	1,956.09	1,600.38	1,494.09	1,352.60	1,265.80
85,000	2,078.35	1,700.41	1,587.47	1,437.14	1,344.91
90,000	2,200.60	1,800.43	1,680.85	1,521.67	1,424.02
95,000	2,322.86	1,900.45	1,774.23	1,606.21	1,503.14
100,000	2,445.11	2,000.48	1,867.61	1,690.75	1,582.25
110,000	2,689.62	2,200.52	2,054.37	1,859.82	1,740.47
120,000	2,934.14	2,400.57	2,241.14	2,028.90	1,898.70
125,000	3,056.39	2,500.59	2,334.52	2,113.44	1,977.81
130,000	3,178.65	2,600.62	2,427.90	2,197.97	2,056.92
140,000	3,423.16	2,800.66	2,614.66	2,367.05	2,215.15
150,000	3,667.67	3,000.71	2,801.42	2,536.12	2,373.37
160,000	3,912.18	3,200.76	2,988.18	2,705.20	2,531.60
170,000	4,156.69	3,400.81	3,174.94	2,874.27	2,689.82
175,000	4,278.95	3,500.83	3,268.32	2,958.81	2,768.93
180,000	4,401.20	3,600.85	3,361.70	3,043.34	2,848.04
190,000	4,645.71	3,800.90	3,548.46	3,212.42	3,006.27
200,000	4,890.22	4,000.95	3,735.22	3,381.49	3,164.49
220,000	5,379.24	4,401.04	4,108.74	3,719.64	3,480.94
225,000	5,501.50	4,501.07	4,202.13	3,804.18	3,560.05
230,000	5,623.76	4,601.09	4,295.51	3,888.72	3,639.17
240,000	5,868.27	4,801.14	4,482.27	4,057.79	3,797.39
$250,000	6,112.78	5,001.18	4,669.03	4,226.87	3,955.61

Monthly Payment Loans **16.25%**

Amortization Period in Years

	15	16	17	18	20
$ 100	1.49	1.47	1.45	1.44	1.42
200	2.98	2.93	2.90	2.87	2.83
300	4.46	4.40	4.35	4.30	4.24
400	5.95	5.86	5.79	5.74	5.65
500	7.44	7.33	7.24	7.17	7.06
600	8.92	8.79	8.69	8.60	8.47
700	10.41	10.26	10.14	10.03	9.88
800	11.89	11.72	11.58	11.47	11.29
900	13.38	13.19	13.03	12.90	12.70
1,000	14.87	14.65	14.48	14.33	14.11
2,000	29.73	29.30	28.95	28.66	28.21
3,000	44.59	43.95	43.42	42.98	42.31
4,000	59.45	58.60	57.89	57.31	56.41
5,000	74.31	73.25	72.37	71.63	70.51
6,000	89.18	87.90	86.84	85.96	84.61
7,000	104.04	102.55	101.31	100.28	98.71
8,000	118.90	117.20	115.78	114.61	112.81
9,000	133.76	131.84	130.26	128.94	126.91
10,000	148.62	146.49	144.73	143.26	141.01
15,000	222.93	219.74	217.09	214.89	211.51
20,000	297.24	292.98	289.45	286.52	282.01
25,000	371.55	366.23	361.82	358.15	352.52
30,000	445.86	439.47	434.18	429.78	423.02
35,000	520.16	512.71	506.54	501.40	493.52
40,000	594.47	585.96	578.90	573.03	564.02
45,000	668.78	659.20	651.27	644.66	634.53
50,000	743.09	732.45	723.63	716.29	705.03
55,000	817.40	805.69	795.99	787.92	775.53
60,000	891.71	878.94	868.35	859.55	846.03
65,000	966.01	952.18	940.72	931.17	916.53
70,000	1,040.32	1,025.42	1,013.08	1,002.80	987.04
75,000	1,114.63	1,098.67	1,085.44	1,074.43	1,057.54
80,000	1,188.94	1,171.91	1,157.80	1,146.06	1,128.04
85,000	1,263.25	1,245.16	1,230.16	1,217.69	1,198.54
90,000	1,337.56	1,318.40	1,302.53	1,289.32	1,269.05
95,000	1,411.86	1,391.64	1,374.89	1,360.95	1,339.55
100,000	1,486.17	1,464.89	1,447.25	1,432.57	1,410.05
110,000	1,634.79	1,611.38	1,591.98	1,575.83	1,551.06
120,000	1,783.41	1,757.87	1,736.70	1,719.09	1,692.06
125,000	1,857.72	1,831.11	1,809.06	1,790.72	1,762.56
130,000	1,932.02	1,904.35	1,881.43	1,862.34	1,833.06
140,000	2,080.64	2,050.84	2,026.15	2,005.60	1,974.07
150,000	2,229.26	2,197.33	2,170.87	2,148.86	2,115.07
160,000	2,377.87	2,343.82	2,315.60	2,292.12	2,256.08
170,000	2,526.49	2,490.31	2,460.32	2,435.37	2,397.08
175,000	2,600.80	2,563.55	2,532.69	2,507.00	2,467.58
180,000	2,675.11	2,636.80	2,605.05	2,578.63	2,538.09
190,000	2,823.72	2,783.28	2,749.77	2,721.89	2,679.09
200,000	2,972.34	2,929.77	2,894.50	2,865.14	2,820.10
220,000	3,269.57	3,222.75	3,183.95	3,151.66	3,102.11
225,000	3,343.88	3,295.99	3,256.31	3,223.28	3,172.61
230,000	3,418.19	3,369.24	3,328.67	3,294.91	3,243.11
240,000	3,566.81	3,515.73	3,473.40	3,438.17	3,384.11
$250,000	3,715.43	3,662.21	3,618.12	3,581.43	3,525.12

Table 1   185

16.25%   Monthly Payment Loans

Amortization Period in Years

	21	22	23	24	25
$ 100	1.41	1.40	1.39	1.39	1.38
200	2.81	2.79	2.78	2.77	2.76
300	4.21	4.19	4.17	4.15	4.14
400	5.61	5.58	5.56	5.54	5.52
500	7.01	6.98	6.95	6.92	6.90
600	8.41	8.37	8.33	8.30	8.28
700	9.81	9.76	9.72	9.69	9.65
800	11.22	11.16	11.11	11.07	11.03
900	12.62	12.55	12.50	12.45	12.41
1,000	14.02	13.95	13.89	13.83	13.79
2,000	28.03	27.89	27.77	27.66	27.58
3,000	42.05	41.83	41.65	41.49	41.36
4,000	56.06	55.77	55.53	55.32	55.15
5,000	70.08	69.71	69.41	69.15	68.93
6,000	84.09	83.66	83.29	82.98	82.72
7,000	98.10	97.60	97.17	96.81	96.50
8,000	112.12	111.54	111.05	110.64	110.29
9,000	126.13	125.48	124.93	124.47	124.07
10,000	140.15	139.42	138.81	138.30	137.86
15,000	210.22	209.13	208.21	207.44	206.79
20,000	280.29	278.84	277.62	276.59	275.71
25,000	350.36	348.55	347.02	345.73	344.64
30,000	420.43	418.26	416.42	414.88	413.57
35,000	490.50	487.97	485.83	484.02	482.49
40,000	560.58	557.67	555.23	553.17	551.42
45,000	630.65	627.38	624.63	622.31	620.35
50,000	700.72	697.09	694.04	691.46	689.28
55,000	770.79	766.80	763.44	760.60	758.20
60,000	840.86	836.51	832.84	829.75	827.13
65,000	910.93	906.22	902.24	898.89	896.06
70,000	981.00	975.93	971.65	968.04	964.98
75,000	1,051.07	1,045.64	1,041.05	1,037.18	1,033.91
80,000	1,121.15	1,115.34	1,110.45	1,106.33	1,102.84
85,000	1,191.22	1,185.05	1,179.86	1,175.47	1,171.77
90,000	1,261.29	1,254.76	1,249.26	1,244.62	1,240.69
95,000	1,331.36	1,324.47	1,318.66	1,313.76	1,309.62
100,000	1,401.43	1,394.18	1,388.07	1,382.91	1,378.55
110,000	1,541.57	1,533.60	1,526.87	1,521.20	1,516.40
120,000	1,681.72	1,673.01	1,665.68	1,659.49	1,654.25
125,000	1,751.79	1,742.72	1,735.08	1,728.63	1,723.18
130,000	1,821.86	1,812.43	1,804.48	1,797.78	1,792.11
140,000	1,962.00	1,951.85	1,943.29	1,936.07	1,929.96
150,000	2,102.14	2,091.27	2,082.10	2,074.36	2,067.82
160,000	2,242.29	2,230.68	2,220.90	2,212.65	2,205.67
170,000	2,382.43	2,370.10	2,359.71	2,350.94	2,343.53
175,000	2,452.50	2,439.81	2,429.11	2,420.08	2,412.45
180,000	2,522.57	2,509.52	2,498.51	2,489.23	2,481.38
190,000	2,662.71	2,648.93	2,637.32	2,627.52	2,619.23
200,000	2,802.86	2,788.35	2,776.13	2,765.81	2,757.09
220,000	3,083.14	3,067.19	3,053.74	3,042.39	3,032.80
225,000	3,153.21	3,136.90	3,123.14	3,111.53	3,101.72
230,000	3,223.28	3,206.60	3,192.54	3,180.68	3,170.65
240,000	3,363.43	3,346.02	3,331.35	3,318.97	3,308.50
$250,000	3,503.57	3,485.44	3,470.16	3,457.26	3,446.36

Monthly Payment Loans **16.25%**

Amortization Period in Years

	26	27	28	29	30
$ 100	1.38	1.38	1.37	1.37	1.37
200	2.75	2.75	2.74	2.74	2.73
300	4.13	4.12	4.11	4.11	4.10
400	5.50	5.49	5.48	5.47	5.46
500	6.88	6.86	6.85	6.84	6.83
600	8.25	8.24	8.22	8.21	8.19
700	9.63	9.61	9.59	9.57	9.56
800	11.00	10.98	10.96	10.94	10.92
900	12.38	12.35	12.33	12.31	12.29
1,000	13.75	13.72	13.70	13.67	13.65
2,000	27.50	27.44	27.39	27.34	27.30
3,000	41.25	41.16	41.08	41.01	40.95
4,000	55.00	54.87	54.77	54.68	54.60
5,000	68.75	68.59	68.46	68.35	68.25
6,000	82.50	82.31	82.15	82.02	81.90
7,000	96.24	96.03	95.84	95.68	95.55
8,000	109.99	109.74	109.53	109.35	109.20
9,000	123.74	123.46	123.22	123.02	122.85
10,000	137.49	137.18	136.91	136.69	136.50
15,000	206.23	205.76	205.37	205.03	204.75
20,000	274.98	274.35	273.82	273.37	272.99
25,000	343.72	342.94	342.28	341.71	341.24
30,000	412.46	411.52	410.73	410.06	409.49
35,000	481.20	480.11	479.18	478.40	477.73
40,000	549.95	548.70	547.64	546.74	545.98
45,000	618.69	617.28	616.09	615.08	614.23
50,000	687.43	685.87	684.55	683.42	682.47
55,000	756.17	754.46	753.00	751.77	750.72
60,000	824.92	823.04	821.45	820.11	818.97
65,000	893.66	891.63	889.91	888.45	887.21
70,000	962.40	960.22	958.36	956.79	955.46
75,000	1,031.14	1,028.80	1,026.82	1,025.13	1,023.71
80,000	1,099.89	1,097.39	1,095.27	1,093.48	1,091.95
85,000	1,168.63	1,165.97	1,163.73	1,161.82	1,160.20
90,000	1,237.37	1,234.56	1,232.18	1,230.16	1,228.45
95,000	1,306.11	1,303.15	1,300.63	1,298.50	1,296.69
100,000	1,374.86	1,371.73	1,369.09	1,366.84	1,364.94
110,000	1,512.34	1,508.91	1,506.00	1,503.53	1,501.43
120,000	1,649.83	1,646.08	1,642.90	1,640.21	1,637.93
125,000	1,718.57	1,714.67	1,711.36	1,708.55	1,706.17
130,000	1,787.31	1,783.25	1,779.81	1,776.89	1,774.42
140,000	1,924.80	1,920.43	1,916.72	1,913.58	1,910.91
150,000	2,062.28	2,057.60	2,053.63	2,050.26	2,047.41
160,000	2,199.77	2,194.77	2,190.54	2,186.95	2,183.90
170,000	2,337.25	2,331.94	2,327.45	2,323.63	2,320.39
175,000	2,406.00	2,400.53	2,395.90	2,391.97	2,388.64
180,000	2,474.74	2,469.12	2,464.35	2,460.31	2,456.89
190,000	2,612.22	2,606.29	2,601.26	2,597.00	2,593.38
200,000	2,749.71	2,743.46	2,738.17	2,733.68	2,729.87
220,000	3,024.68	3,017.81	3,011.99	3,007.05	3,002.86
225,000	3,093.42	3,086.40	3,080.44	3,075.39	3,071.11
230,000	3,162.17	3,154.98	3,148.89	3,143.73	3,139.35
240,000	3,299.65	3,292.16	3,285.80	3,280.42	3,275.85
$250,000	3,437.14	3,429.33	3,422.71	3,417.10	3,412.34

Table 1   187

16.50%   Monthly Payment Loans

Amortization Period in Years

	5	7	8	10	12
$ 100	2.46	2.02	1.89	1.71	1.60
200	4.92	4.03	3.77	3.42	3.20
300	7.38	6.05	5.65	5.12	4.80
400	9.84	8.06	7.53	6.83	6.40
500	12.30	10.08	9.42	8.54	8.00
600	14.76	12.09	11.30	10.24	9.60
700	17.21	14.11	13.18	11.95	11.20
800	19.67	16.12	15.06	13.66	12.79
900	22.13	18.14	16.95	15.36	14.39
1,000	24.59	20.15	18.83	17.07	15.99
2,000	49.17	40.30	37.65	34.13	31.98
3,000	73.76	60.45	56.48	51.20	47.97
4,000	98.34	80.60	75.30	68.26	63.95
5,000	122.93	100.74	94.12	85.33	79.94
6,000	147.51	120.89	112.95	102.39	95.93
7,000	172.10	141.04	131.77	119.45	111.92
8,000	196.68	161.19	150.60	136.52	127.90
9,000	221.27	181.34	169.42	153.58	143.89
10,000	245.85	201.48	188.24	170.65	159.88
15,000	368.77	302.22	282.36	255.97	239.82
20,000	491.70	402.96	376.48	341.29	319.75
25,000	614.62	503.70	470.60	426.61	399.69
30,000	737.54	604.44	564.72	511.93	479.63
35,000	860.46	705.18	658.84	597.25	559.56
40,000	983.39	805.92	752.96	682.57	639.50
45,000	1,106.31	906.66	847.08	767.90	719.44
50,000	1,229.23	1,007.40	941.20	853.22	799.37
55,000	1,352.15	1,108.14	1,035.32	938.54	879.31
60,000	1,475.08	1,208.88	1,129.44	1,023.86	959.25
65,000	1,598.00	1,309.62	1,223.56	1,109.18	1,039.18
70,000	1,720.92	1,410.36	1,317.68	1,194.50	1,119.12
75,000	1,843.84	1,511.10	1,411.80	1,279.82	1,199.06
80,000	1,966.77	1,611.84	1,505.92	1,365.14	1,278.99
85,000	2,089.69	1,712.58	1,600.04	1,450.46	1,358.93
90,000	2,212.61	1,813.32	1,694.16	1,535.79	1,438.87
95,000	2,335.53	1,914.05	1,788.28	1,621.11	1,518.80
100,000	2,458.46	2,014.79	1,882.40	1,706.43	1,598.74
110,000	2,704.30	2,216.27	2,070.64	1,877.07	1,758.61
120,000	2,950.15	2,417.75	2,258.88	2,047.71	1,918.49
125,000	3,073.07	2,518.49	2,353.00	2,133.03	1,998.42
130,000	3,195.99	2,619.23	2,447.12	2,218.35	2,078.36
140,000	3,441.84	2,820.71	2,635.36	2,389.00	2,238.23
150,000	3,687.68	3,022.19	2,823.60	2,559.64	2,398.11
160,000	3,933.53	3,223.67	3,011.84	2,730.28	2,557.98
170,000	4,179.37	3,425.15	3,200.08	2,900.92	2,717.85
175,000	4,302.30	3,525.89	3,294.20	2,986.25	2,797.79
180,000	4,425.22	3,626.63	3,388.32	3,071.57	2,877.73
190,000	4,671.06	3,828.10	3,576.56	3,242.21	3,037.60
200,000	4,916.91	4,029.58	3,764.80	3,412.85	3,197.47
220,000	5,408.60	4,432.54	4,141.28	3,754.14	3,517.22
225,000	5,531.52	4,533.28	4,235.40	3,839.46	3,597.16
230,000	5,654.44	4,634.02	4,329.52	3,924.78	3,677.09
240,000	5,900.29	4,835.50	4,517.76	4,095.42	3,836.97
$250,000	6,146.14	5,036.98	4,706.00	4,266.06	3,996.84

Monthly Payment Loans   **16.50%**

Amortization Period in Years

	15	16	17	18	20
$ 100	1.51	1.49	1.47	1.46	1.43
200	3.01	2.97	2.94	2.91	2.86
300	4.52	4.45	4.40	4.36	4.29
400	6.02	5.94	5.87	5.81	5.72
500	7.52	7.42	7.33	7.26	7.15
600	9.03	8.90	8.80	8.71	8.58
700	10.53	10.38	10.26	10.16	10.01
800	12.03	11.87	11.73	11.61	11.44
900	13.54	13.35	13.19	13.06	12.87
1,000	15.04	14.83	14.66	14.51	14.29
2,000	30.08	29.66	29.31	29.02	28.58
3,000	45.12	44.49	43.97	43.53	42.87
4,000	60.15	59.31	58.62	58.04	57.16
5,000	75.19	74.14	73.27	72.55	71.45
6,000	90.23	88.97	87.93	87.06	85.74
7,000	105.26	103.80	102.58	101.57	100.03
8,000	120.30	118.62	117.24	116.08	114.32
9,000	135.34	133.45	131.89	130.59	128.61
10,000	150.38	148.28	146.54	145.10	142.90
15,000	225.56	222.41	219.81	217.65	214.34
20,000	300.75	296.55	293.08	290.20	285.79
25,000	375.93	370.69	366.35	362.75	357.23
30,000	451.12	444.82	439.62	435.29	428.68
35,000	526.30	518.96	512.89	507.84	500.12
40,000	601.49	593.10	586.16	580.39	571.57
45,000	676.67	667.23	659.42	652.94	643.01
50,000	751.86	741.37	732.69	725.49	714.46
55,000	827.04	815.51	805.96	798.03	785.90
60,000	902.23	889.64	879.23	870.58	857.35
65,000	977.42	963.78	952.50	943.13	928.79
70,000	1,052.60	1,037.92	1,025.77	1,015.68	1,000.24
75,000	1,127.79	1,112.05	1,099.04	1,088.23	1,071.68
80,000	1,202.97	1,186.19	1,172.31	1,160.77	1,143.13
85,000	1,278.16	1,260.33	1,245.57	1,233.32	1,214.57
90,000	1,353.34	1,334.46	1,318.84	1,305.87	1,286.02
95,000	1,428.53	1,408.60	1,392.11	1,378.42	1,357.46
100,000	1,503.71	1,482.73	1,465.38	1,450.97	1,428.91
110,000	1,654.08	1,631.01	1,611.92	1,596.06	1,571.80
120,000	1,804.46	1,779.28	1,758.46	1,741.16	1,714.69
125,000	1,879.64	1,853.42	1,831.72	1,813.71	1,786.13
130,000	1,954.83	1,927.55	1,904.99	1,886.25	1,857.58
140,000	2,105.20	2,075.83	2,051.53	2,031.35	2,000.47
150,000	2,255.57	2,224.10	2,198.07	2,176.45	2,143.36
160,000	2,405.94	2,372.37	2,344.61	2,321.54	2,286.25
170,000	2,556.31	2,520.65	2,491.14	2,466.64	2,429.14
175,000	2,631.50	2,594.78	2,564.41	2,539.19	2,500.58
180,000	2,706.68	2,668.92	2,637.68	2,611.73	2,572.03
190,000	2,857.05	2,817.19	2,784.22	2,756.83	2,714.92
200,000	3,007.42	2,965.46	2,930.76	2,901.93	2,857.81
220,000	3,308.16	3,262.01	3,223.83	3,192.12	3,143.59
225,000	3,383.35	3,336.15	3,297.10	3,264.67	3,215.03
230,000	3,458.53	3,410.28	3,370.37	3,337.21	3,286.48
240,000	3,608.91	3,558.56	3,516.91	3,482.31	3,429.37
$250,000	3,759.28	3,706.83	3,663.44	3,627.41	3,572.26

Table 1   189

16.50%   Monthly Payment Loans

Amortization Period in Years

	21	22	23	24	25
$ 100	1.43	1.42	1.41	1.41	1.40
200	2.85	2.83	2.82	2.81	2.80
300	4.27	4.25	4.23	4.21	4.20
400	5.69	5.66	5.63	5.61	5.60
500	7.11	7.07	7.04	7.02	7.00
600	8.53	8.49	8.45	8.42	8.39
700	9.95	9.90	9.86	9.82	9.79
800	11.37	11.31	11.26	11.22	11.19
900	12.79	12.73	12.67	12.63	12.59
1,000	14.21	14.14	14.08	14.03	13.99
2,000	28.41	28.27	28.15	28.05	27.97
3,000	42.62	42.41	42.23	42.08	41.95
4,000	56.82	56.54	56.30	56.10	55.93
5,000	71.03	70.68	70.38	70.13	69.92
6,000	85.23	84.81	84.45	84.15	83.90
7,000	99.44	98.94	98.53	98.18	97.88
8,000	113.64	113.08	112.60	112.20	111.86
9,000	127.85	127.21	126.68	126.23	125.85
10,000	142.05	141.35	140.75	140.25	139.83
15,000	213.08	212.02	211.13	210.37	209.74
20,000	284.10	282.69	281.50	280.50	279.65
25,000	355.13	353.36	351.87	350.62	349.57
30,000	426.15	424.03	422.25	420.74	419.48
35,000	497.17	494.70	492.62	490.87	489.39
40,000	568.20	565.37	562.99	560.99	559.30
45,000	639.22	636.04	633.37	631.11	629.22
50,000	710.25	706.71	703.74	701.24	699.13
55,000	781.27	777.38	774.12	771.36	769.04
60,000	852.30	848.06	844.49	841.48	838.95
65,000	923.32	918.73	914.86	911.61	908.86
70,000	994.34	989.40	985.24	981.73	978.78
75,000	1,065.37	1,060.07	1,055.61	1,051.85	1,048.69
80,000	1,136.39	1,130.74	1,125.98	1,121.98	1,118.60
85,000	1,207.42	1,201.41	1,196.36	1,192.10	1,188.51
90,000	1,278.44	1,272.08	1,266.73	1,262.22	1,258.43
95,000	1,349.46	1,342.75	1,337.10	1,332.35	1,328.34
100,000	1,420.49	1,413.42	1,407.48	1,402.47	1,398.25
110,000	1,562.54	1,554.76	1,548.23	1,542.72	1,538.07
120,000	1,704.59	1,696.11	1,688.97	1,682.96	1,677.90
125,000	1,775.61	1,766.78	1,759.35	1,753.09	1,747.81
130,000	1,846.63	1,837.45	1,829.72	1,823.21	1,817.72
140,000	1,988.68	1,978.79	1,970.47	1,963.46	1,957.55
150,000	2,130.73	2,120.13	2,111.21	2,103.70	2,097.37
160,000	2,272.78	2,261.47	2,251.96	2,243.95	2,237.20
170,000	2,414.83	2,402.81	2,392.71	2,384.20	2,377.02
175,000	2,485.85	2,473.48	2,463.08	2,454.32	2,446.93
180,000	2,556.88	2,544.16	2,533.46	2,524.44	2,516.85
190,000	2,698.92	2,685.50	2,674.20	2,664.69	2,656.67
200,000	2,840.97	2,826.84	2,814.95	2,804.94	2,796.49
220,000	3,125.07	3,109.52	3,096.45	3,085.43	3,076.14
225,000	3,196.09	3,180.19	3,166.82	3,155.55	3,146.06
230,000	3,267.12	3,250.86	3,237.19	3,225.68	3,215.97
240,000	3,409.17	3,392.21	3,377.94	3,365.92	3,355.79
$250,000	3,551.21	3,533.55	3,518.69	3,506.17	3,495.62

Monthly Payment Loans   **16.50%**

Amortization Period in Years

	26	27	28	29	30
$ 100	1.40	1.40	1.39	1.39	1.39
200	2.79	2.79	2.78	2.78	2.78
300	4.19	4.18	4.17	4.17	4.16
400	5.58	5.57	5.56	5.55	5.55
500	6.98	6.96	6.95	6.94	6.93
600	8.37	8.36	8.34	8.33	8.32
700	9.77	9.75	9.73	9.71	9.70
800	11.16	11.14	11.12	11.10	11.09
900	12.56	12.53	12.51	12.49	12.47
1,000	13.95	13.92	13.90	13.87	13.86
2,000	27.90	27.84	27.79	27.74	27.71
3,000	41.85	41.76	41.68	41.61	41.56
4,000	55.79	55.67	55.57	55.48	55.41
5,000	69.74	69.59	69.46	69.35	69.26
6,000	83.69	83.51	83.35	83.22	83.11
7,000	97.63	97.42	97.24	97.09	96.97
8,000	111.58	111.34	111.13	110.96	110.82
9,000	125.53	125.26	125.03	124.83	124.67
10,000	139.47	139.17	138.92	138.70	138.52
15,000	209.21	208.76	208.37	208.05	207.78
20,000	278.94	278.34	277.83	277.40	277.03
25,000	348.68	347.92	347.29	346.75	346.29
30,000	418.41	417.51	416.74	416.10	415.55
35,000	488.14	487.09	486.20	485.44	484.81
40,000	557.88	556.67	555.65	554.79	554.06
45,000	627.61	626.26	625.11	624.14	623.32
50,000	697.35	695.84	694.57	693.49	692.58
55,000	767.08	765.42	764.02	762.84	761.84
60,000	836.81	835.01	833.48	832.19	831.09
65,000	906.55	904.59	902.94	901.54	900.35
70,000	976.28	974.17	972.39	970.88	969.61
75,000	1,046.02	1,043.76	1,041.85	1,040.23	1,038.87
80,000	1,115.75	1,113.34	1,111.30	1,109.58	1,108.12
85,000	1,185.48	1,182.92	1,180.76	1,178.93	1,177.38
90,000	1,255.22	1,252.51	1,250.22	1,248.28	1,246.64
95,000	1,324.95	1,322.09	1,319.67	1,317.63	1,315.90
100,000	1,394.69	1,391.67	1,389.13	1,386.98	1,385.15
110,000	1,534.15	1,530.84	1,528.04	1,525.67	1,523.67
120,000	1,673.62	1,670.01	1,666.95	1,664.37	1,662.18
125,000	1,743.36	1,739.59	1,736.41	1,733.72	1,731.44
130,000	1,813.09	1,809.18	1,805.87	1,803.07	1,800.70
140,000	1,952.56	1,948.34	1,944.78	1,941.76	1,939.21
150,000	2,092.03	2,087.51	2,083.69	2,080.46	2,077.73
160,000	2,231.49	2,226.68	2,222.60	2,219.16	2,216.24
170,000	2,370.96	2,365.84	2,361.52	2,357.86	2,354.76
175,000	2,440.70	2,435.43	2,430.97	2,427.20	2,424.01
180,000	2,510.43	2,505.01	2,500.43	2,496.55	2,493.27
190,000	2,649.90	2,644.18	2,639.34	2,635.25	2,631.79
200,000	2,789.37	2,783.34	2,778.25	2,773.95	2,770.30
220,000	3,068.30	3,061.68	3,056.08	3,051.34	3,047.33
225,000	3,138.04	3,131.26	3,125.53	3,120.69	3,116.59
230,000	3,207.77	3,200.85	3,194.99	3,190.04	3,185.85
240,000	3,347.24	3,340.01	3,333.90	3,328.74	3,324.36
$250,000	3,486.71	3,479.18	3,472.82	3,467.43	3,462.88

Table 1   191

16.75% Monthly Payment Loans
Amortization Period in Years

	5	7	8	10	12
$ 100	2.48	2.03	1.90	1.73	1.62
200	4.95	4.06	3.80	3.45	3.24
300	7.42	6.09	5.70	5.17	4.85
400	9.89	8.12	7.59	6.89	6.47
500	12.36	10.15	9.49	8.62	8.08
600	14.84	12.18	11.39	10.34	9.70
700	17.31	14.21	13.29	12.06	11.31
800	19.78	16.24	15.18	13.78	12.93
900	22.25	18.27	17.08	15.50	14.54
1,000	24.72	20.30	18.98	17.23	16.16
2,000	49.44	40.59	37.95	34.45	32.31
3,000	74.16	60.88	56.92	51.67	48.46
4,000	98.88	81.17	75.89	68.89	64.62
5,000	123.60	101.46	94.87	86.11	80.77
6,000	148.32	121.75	113.84	103.34	96.92
7,000	173.03	142.05	132.81	120.56	113.08
8,000	197.75	162.34	151.78	137.78	129.23
9,000	222.47	182.63	170.76	155.00	145.38
10,000	247.19	202.92	189.73	172.22	161.53
15,000	370.78	304.38	284.59	258.33	242.30
20,000	494.37	405.84	379.45	344.44	323.06
25,000	617.96	507.29	474.32	430.55	403.83
30,000	741.56	608.75	569.18	516.66	484.59
35,000	865.15	710.21	664.04	602.76	565.36
40,000	988.74	811.67	758.90	688.87	646.12
45,000	1,112.33	913.13	853.76	774.98	726.89
50,000	1,235.92	1,014.58	948.63	861.09	807.65
55,000	1,359.51	1,116.04	1,043.49	947.20	888.42
60,000	1,483.11	1,217.50	1,138.35	1,033.31	969.18
65,000	1,606.70	1,318.96	1,233.21	1,119.41	1,049.95
70,000	1,730.29	1,420.42	1,328.07	1,205.52	1,130.71
75,000	1,853.88	1,521.87	1,422.94	1,291.63	1,211.48
80,000	1,977.47	1,623.33	1,517.80	1,377.74	1,292.24
85,000	2,101.06	1,724.79	1,612.66	1,463.85	1,373.00
90,000	2,224.66	1,826.25	1,707.52	1,549.96	1,453.77
95,000	2,348.25	1,927.71	1,802.39	1,636.06	1,534.53
100,000	2,471.84	2,029.16	1,897.25	1,722.17	1,615.30
110,000	2,719.02	2,232.08	2,086.97	1,894.39	1,776.83
120,000	2,966.21	2,435.00	2,276.70	2,066.61	1,938.36
125,000	3,089.80	2,536.45	2,371.56	2,152.71	2,019.12
130,000	3,213.39	2,637.91	2,466.42	2,238.82	2,099.89
140,000	3,460.57	2,840.83	2,656.14	2,411.04	2,261.42
150,000	3,707.76	3,043.74	2,845.87	2,583.26	2,422.95
160,000	3,954.94	3,246.66	3,035.59	2,755.47	2,584.47
170,000	4,202.12	3,449.57	3,225.32	2,927.69	2,746.00
175,000	4,325.72	3,551.03	3,320.18	3,013.80	2,826.77
180,000	4,449.31	3,652.49	3,415.04	3,099.91	2,907.53
190,000	4,696.49	3,855.41	3,604.77	3,272.12	3,069.06
200,000	4,943.68	4,058.32	3,794.49	3,444.34	3,230.59
220,000	5,438.04	4,464.15	4,173.94	3,788.77	3,553.65
225,000	5,561.63	4,565.61	4,268.80	3,874.88	3,634.42
230,000	5,685.23	4,667.07	4,363.66	3,960.99	3,715.18
240,000	5,932.41	4,869.99	4,553.39	4,133.21	3,876.71
$250,000	6,179.59	5,072.90	4,743.11	4,305.42	4,038.24

Monthly Payment Loans   **16.75%**

Amortization Period in Years

	15	16	17	18	20
$ 100	1.53	1.51	1.49	1.47	1.45
200	3.05	3.01	2.97	2.94	2.90
300	4.57	4.51	4.46	4.41	4.35
400	6.09	6.01	5.94	5.88	5.80
500	7.61	7.51	7.42	7.35	7.24
600	9.13	9.01	8.91	8.82	8.69
700	10.65	10.51	10.39	10.29	10.14
800	12.18	12.01	11.87	11.76	11.59
900	13.70	13.51	13.36	13.23	13.04
1,000	15.22	15.01	14.84	14.70	14.48
2,000	30.43	30.02	29.68	29.39	28.96
3,000	45.64	45.02	44.51	44.09	43.44
4,000	60.86	60.03	59.35	58.78	57.92
5,000	76.07	75.04	74.18	73.48	72.40
6,000	91.28	90.04	89.02	88.17	86.87
7,000	106.50	105.05	103.86	102.86	101.35
8,000	121.71	120.06	118.69	117.56	115.83
9,000	136.92	135.06	133.53	132.25	130.31
10,000	152.14	150.07	148.36	146.95	144.79
15,000	228.20	225.10	222.54	220.42	217.18
20,000	304.27	300.13	296.72	293.89	289.57
25,000	380.34	375.17	370.90	367.36	361.96
30,000	456.40	450.20	445.08	440.83	434.35
35,000	532.47	525.23	519.26	514.30	506.74
40,000	608.53	600.26	593.44	587.77	579.13
45,000	684.60	675.30	667.61	661.24	651.52
50,000	760.67	750.33	741.79	734.72	723.91
55,000	836.73	825.36	815.97	808.19	796.31
60,000	912.80	900.39	890.15	881.66	868.70
65,000	988.86	975.43	964.33	955.13	941.09
70,000	1,064.93	1,050.46	1,038.51	1,028.60	1,013.48
75,000	1,141.00	1,125.49	1,112.69	1,102.07	1,085.87
80,000	1,217.06	1,200.52	1,186.87	1,175.54	1,158.26
85,000	1,293.13	1,275.55	1,261.04	1,249.01	1,230.65
90,000	1,369.19	1,350.59	1,335.22	1,322.48	1,303.04
95,000	1,445.26	1,425.62	1,409.40	1,395.95	1,375.43
100,000	1,521.33	1,500.65	1,483.58	1,469.43	1,447.82
110,000	1,673.46	1,650.72	1,631.94	1,616.37	1,592.61
120,000	1,825.59	1,800.78	1,780.30	1,763.31	1,737.39
125,000	1,901.66	1,875.81	1,854.47	1,836.78	1,809.78
130,000	1,977.72	1,950.85	1,928.65	1,910.25	1,882.17
140,000	2,129.85	2,100.91	2,077.01	2,057.19	2,026.95
150,000	2,281.99	2,250.98	2,225.37	2,204.14	2,171.73
160,000	2,434.12	2,401.04	2,373.73	2,351.08	2,316.52
170,000	2,586.25	2,551.10	2,522.08	2,498.02	2,461.30
175,000	2,662.32	2,626.14	2,596.26	2,571.49	2,533.69
180,000	2,738.38	2,701.17	2,670.44	2,644.96	2,606.08
190,000	2,890.52	2,851.23	2,818.80	2,791.90	2,750.86
200,000	3,042.65	3,001.30	2,967.16	2,938.85	2,895.64
220,000	3,346.91	3,301.43	3,263.87	3,232.73	3,185.21
225,000	3,422.98	3,376.46	3,338.05	3,306.20	3,257.60
230,000	3,499.04	3,451.49	3,412.23	3,379.67	3,329.99
240,000	3,651.18	3,601.56	3,560.59	3,526.61	3,474.77
$250,000	3,803.31	3,751.62	3,708.94	3,673.56	3,619.55

Table 1   193

16.75% Monthly Payment Loans

Amortization Period in Years

	21	22	23	24	25
$ 100	1.44	1.44	1.43	1.43	1.42
200	2.88	2.87	2.86	2.85	2.84
300	4.32	4.30	4.29	4.27	4.26
400	5.76	5.74	5.71	5.69	5.68
500	7.20	7.17	7.14	7.12	7.09
600	8.64	8.60	8.57	8.54	8.51
700	10.08	10.03	9.99	9.96	9.93
800	11.52	11.47	11.42	11.38	11.35
900	12.96	12.90	12.85	12.80	12.77
1,000	14.40	14.33	14.27	14.23	14.18
2,000	28.80	28.66	28.54	28.45	28.36
3,000	43.19	42.99	42.81	42.67	42.54
4,000	57.59	57.31	57.08	56.89	56.72
5,000	71.99	71.64	71.35	71.11	70.90
6,000	86.38	85.97	85.62	85.33	85.08
7,000	100.78	100.30	99.89	99.55	99.26
8,000	115.17	114.62	114.16	113.77	113.44
9,000	129.57	128.95	128.43	127.99	127.62
10,000	143.97	143.28	142.70	142.21	141.80
15,000	215.95	214.91	214.05	213.32	212.70
20,000	287.93	286.55	285.39	284.42	283.60
25,000	359.91	358.18	356.74	355.53	354.50
30,000	431.89	429.82	428.09	426.63	425.40
35,000	503.87	501.46	499.43	497.73	496.30
40,000	575.85	573.09	570.78	568.84	567.20
45,000	647.83	644.73	642.13	639.94	638.10
50,000	719.81	716.36	713.48	711.05	709.00
55,000	791.79	788.00	784.82	782.15	779.90
60,000	863.77	859.64	856.17	853.26	850.80
65,000	935.75	931.27	927.52	924.36	921.70
70,000	1,007.73	1,002.91	998.86	995.46	992.60
75,000	1,079.71	1,074.54	1,070.21	1,066.57	1,063.50
80,000	1,151.69	1,146.18	1,141.56	1,137.67	1,134.40
85,000	1,223.67	1,217.82	1,212.90	1,208.78	1,205.30
90,000	1,295.65	1,289.45	1,284.25	1,279.88	1,276.20
95,000	1,367.63	1,361.09	1,355.60	1,350.98	1,347.10
100,000	1,439.61	1,432.72	1,426.95	1,422.09	1,418.00
110,000	1,583.57	1,576.00	1,569.64	1,564.30	1,559.80
120,000	1,727.53	1,719.27	1,712.33	1,706.51	1,701.60
125,000	1,799.51	1,790.90	1,783.68	1,777.61	1,772.50
130,000	1,871.49	1,862.54	1,855.03	1,848.71	1,843.40
140,000	2,015.45	2,005.81	1,997.72	1,990.92	1,985.20
150,000	2,159.41	2,149.08	2,140.42	2,133.13	2,127.00
160,000	2,303.37	2,292.35	2,283.11	2,275.34	2,268.80
170,000	2,447.33	2,435.63	2,425.80	2,417.55	2,410.60
175,000	2,519.31	2,507.26	2,497.15	2,488.65	2,481.50
180,000	2,591.29	2,578.90	2,568.50	2,559.76	2,552.40
190,000	2,735.25	2,722.17	2,711.19	2,701.96	2,694.20
200,000	2,879.21	2,865.44	2,853.89	2,844.17	2,836.00
220,000	3,167.13	3,151.99	3,139.27	3,128.59	3,119.60
225,000	3,239.11	3,223.62	3,210.62	3,199.69	3,190.50
230,000	3,311.09	3,295.26	3,281.97	3,270.80	3,261.40
240,000	3,455.05	3,438.53	3,424.66	3,413.01	3,403.20
$250,000	3,599.01	3,581.80	3,567.36	3,555.21	3,545.00

Monthly Payment Loans   **16.75%**

Amortization Period in Years

	26	27	28	29	30
$ 100	1.42	1.42	1.41	1.41	1.41
200	2.83	2.83	2.82	2.82	2.82
300	4.25	4.24	4.23	4.23	4.22
400	5.66	5.65	5.64	5.63	5.63
500	7.08	7.06	7.05	7.04	7.03
600	8.49	8.47	8.46	8.45	8.44
700	9.91	9.89	9.87	9.85	9.84
800	11.32	11.30	11.28	11.26	11.25
900	12.74	12.71	12.69	12.67	12.65
1,000	14.15	14.12	14.10	14.08	14.06
2,000	28.30	28.24	28.19	28.15	28.11
3,000	42.44	42.35	42.28	42.22	42.17
4,000	56.59	56.47	56.37	56.29	56.22
5,000	70.73	70.59	70.47	70.36	70.27
6,000	84.88	84.70	84.56	84.43	84.33
7,000	99.02	98.82	98.65	98.50	98.38
8,000	113.17	112.94	112.74	112.58	112.44
9,000	127.31	127.05	126.83	126.65	126.49
10,000	141.46	141.17	140.93	140.72	140.54
15,000	212.19	211.75	211.39	211.08	210.81
20,000	282.92	282.34	281.85	281.43	281.08
25,000	353.64	352.92	352.31	351.79	351.35
30,000	424.37	423.50	422.77	422.15	421.62
35,000	495.10	494.08	493.23	492.50	491.89
40,000	565.83	564.67	563.69	562.86	562.16
45,000	636.55	635.25	634.15	633.22	632.43
50,000	707.28	705.83	704.61	703.58	702.70
55,000	778.01	776.41	775.07	773.93	772.97
60,000	848.74	847.00	845.53	844.29	843.24
65,000	919.47	917.58	915.99	914.65	913.51
70,000	990.19	988.16	986.45	985.00	983.78
75,000	1,060.92	1,058.75	1,056.91	1,055.36	1,054.05
80,000	1,131.65	1,129.33	1,127.37	1,125.72	1,124.32
85,000	1,202.38	1,199.91	1,197.83	1,196.07	1,194.59
90,000	1,273.10	1,270.49	1,268.29	1,266.43	1,264.86
95,000	1,343.83	1,341.08	1,338.75	1,336.79	1,335.13
100,000	1,414.56	1,411.66	1,409.21	1,407.15	1,405.40
110,000	1,556.02	1,552.82	1,550.13	1,547.86	1,545.94
120,000	1,697.47	1,693.99	1,691.05	1,688.57	1,686.48
125,000	1,768.20	1,764.57	1,761.51	1,758.93	1,756.75
130,000	1,838.93	1,835.15	1,831.97	1,829.29	1,827.02
140,000	1,980.38	1,976.32	1,972.89	1,970.00	1,967.56
150,000	2,121.84	2,117.49	2,113.81	2,110.72	2,108.10
160,000	2,263.29	2,258.65	2,254.73	2,251.43	2,248.64
170,000	2,404.75	2,399.82	2,395.66	2,392.14	2,389.18
175,000	2,475.48	2,470.40	2,466.12	2,462.50	2,459.45
180,000	2,546.20	2,540.98	2,536.58	2,532.86	2,529.72
190,000	2,687.66	2,682.15	2,677.50	2,673.57	2,670.26
200,000	2,829.12	2,823.31	2,818.42	2,814.29	2,810.80
220,000	3,112.03	3,105.64	3,100.26	3,095.71	3,091.88
225,000	3,182.75	3,176.23	3,170.72	3,166.07	3,162.15
230,000	3,253.48	3,246.81	3,241.18	3,236.43	3,232.41
240,000	3,394.94	3,387.97	3,382.10	3,377.14	3,372.95
$250,000	3,536.39	3,529.14	3,523.02	3,517.86	3,513.49

Table 1   195

17.00%   Monthly Payment Loans

Amortization Period in Years

	5	7	8	10	12
$ 100	2.49	2.05	1.92	1.74	1.64
200	4.98	4.09	3.83	3.48	3.27
300	7.46	6.14	5.74	5.22	4.90
400	9.95	8.18	7.65	6.96	6.53
500	12.43	10.22	9.57	8.69	8.16
600	14.92	12.27	11.48	10.43	9.80
700	17.40	14.31	13.39	12.17	11.43
800	19.89	16.35	15.30	13.91	13.06
900	22.37	18.40	17.21	15.65	14.69
1,000	24.86	20.44	19.13	17.38	16.32
2,000	49.71	40.88	38.25	34.76	32.64
3,000	74.56	61.31	57.37	52.14	48.96
4,000	99.42	81.75	76.49	69.52	65.28
5,000	124.27	102.18	95.61	86.90	81.60
6,000	149.12	122.62	114.73	104.28	97.92
7,000	173.97	143.06	133.86	121.66	114.24
8,000	198.83	163.49	152.98	139.04	130.56
9,000	223.68	183.93	172.10	156.42	146.88
10,000	248.53	204.36	191.22	173.80	163.20
15,000	372.79	306.54	286.83	260.70	244.79
20,000	497.06	408.72	382.43	347.60	326.39
25,000	621.32	510.90	478.04	434.50	407.99
30,000	745.58	613.08	573.65	521.40	489.58
35,000	869.85	715.26	669.26	608.30	571.18
40,000	994.11	817.44	764.86	695.20	652.77
45,000	1,118.37	919.62	860.47	782.09	734.37
50,000	1,242.63	1,021.80	956.08	868.99	815.97
55,000	1,366.90	1,123.97	1,051.68	955.89	897.56
60,000	1,491.16	1,226.15	1,147.29	1,042.79	979.16
65,000	1,615.42	1,328.33	1,242.90	1,129.69	1,060.75
70,000	1,739.69	1,430.51	1,338.51	1,216.59	1,142.35
75,000	1,863.95	1,532.69	1,434.11	1,303.49	1,223.95
80,000	1,988.21	1,634.87	1,529.72	1,390.39	1,305.54
85,000	2,112.47	1,737.05	1,625.33	1,477.29	1,387.14
90,000	2,236.74	1,839.23	1,720.94	1,564.18	1,468.74
95,000	2,361.00	1,941.41	1,816.54	1,651.08	1,550.33
100,000	2,485.26	2,043.59	1,912.15	1,737.98	1,631.93
110,000	2,733.79	2,247.94	2,103.36	1,911.78	1,795.12
120,000	2,982.31	2,452.30	2,294.58	2,085.58	1,958.31
125,000	3,106.58	2,554.48	2,390.19	2,172.48	2,039.91
130,000	3,230.84	2,656.66	2,485.79	2,259.37	2,121.50
140,000	3,479.37	2,861.02	2,677.01	2,433.17	2,284.70
150,000	3,727.89	3,065.38	2,868.22	2,606.97	2,447.89
160,000	3,976.42	3,269.73	3,059.44	2,780.77	2,611.08
170,000	4,224.94	3,474.09	3,250.65	2,954.57	2,774.27
175,000	4,349.21	3,576.27	3,346.26	3,041.46	2,855.87
180,000	4,473.47	3,678.45	3,441.87	3,128.36	2,937.47
190,000	4,721.99	3,882.81	3,633.08	3,302.16	3,100.66
200,000	4,970.52	4,087.17	3,824.30	3,475.96	3,263.85
220,000	5,467.57	4,495.88	4,206.72	3,823.55	3,590.24
225,000	5,591.83	4,598.06	4,302.33	3,910.45	3,671.83
230,000	5,716.10	4,700.24	4,397.94	3,997.35	3,753.43
240,000	5,964.62	4,904.60	4,589.15	4,171.15	3,916.62
$250,000	6,213.15	5,108.96	4,780.37	4,344.95	4,079.81

Monthly Payment Loans   **17.00%**

Amortization Period in Years

	15	16	17	18	20
$ 100	1.54	1.52	1.51	1.49	1.47
200	3.08	3.04	3.01	2.98	2.94
300	4.62	4.56	4.51	4.47	4.41
400	6.16	6.08	6.01	5.96	5.87
500	7.70	7.60	7.51	7.44	7.34
600	9.24	9.12	9.02	8.93	8.81
700	10.78	10.64	10.52	10.42	10.27
800	12.32	12.15	12.02	11.91	11.74
900	13.86	13.67	13.52	13.40	13.21
1,000	15.40	15.19	15.02	14.88	14.67
2,000	30.79	30.38	30.04	29.76	29.34
3,000	46.18	45.56	45.06	44.64	44.01
4,000	61.57	60.75	60.08	59.52	58.68
5,000	76.96	75.94	75.10	74.40	73.35
6,000	92.35	91.12	90.12	89.28	88.01
7,000	107.74	106.31	105.13	104.16	102.68
8,000	123.13	121.50	120.15	119.04	117.35
9,000	138.52	136.68	135.17	133.92	132.02
10,000	153.91	151.87	150.19	148.80	146.69
15,000	230.86	227.80	225.28	223.20	220.03
20,000	307.81	303.73	300.37	297.59	293.37
25,000	384.76	379.66	375.47	371.99	366.71
30,000	461.71	455.60	450.56	446.39	440.05
35,000	538.66	531.53	525.65	520.79	513.39
40,000	615.61	607.46	600.74	595.18	586.73
45,000	692.56	683.39	675.83	669.58	660.07
50,000	769.51	759.32	750.93	743.98	733.41
55,000	846.46	835.25	826.02	818.38	806.75
60,000	923.41	911.19	901.11	892.77	880.09
65,000	1,000.36	987.12	976.20	967.17	953.43
70,000	1,077.31	1,063.05	1,051.30	1,041.57	1,026.77
75,000	1,154.26	1,138.98	1,126.39	1,115.97	1,100.11
80,000	1,231.21	1,214.91	1,201.48	1,190.36	1,173.45
85,000	1,308.16	1,290.84	1,276.57	1,264.76	1,246.79
90,000	1,385.11	1,366.78	1,351.66	1,339.16	1,320.13
95,000	1,462.06	1,442.71	1,426.76	1,413.55	1,393.47
100,000	1,539.01	1,518.64	1,501.85	1,487.95	1,466.81
110,000	1,692.91	1,670.50	1,652.03	1,636.75	1,613.49
120,000	1,846.81	1,822.37	1,802.22	1,785.54	1,760.17
125,000	1,923.76	1,898.30	1,877.31	1,859.94	1,833.51
130,000	2,000.71	1,974.23	1,952.40	1,934.34	1,906.85
140,000	2,154.61	2,126.09	2,102.59	2,083.13	2,053.53
150,000	2,308.51	2,277.96	2,252.77	2,231.93	2,200.21
160,000	2,462.41	2,429.82	2,402.95	2,380.72	2,346.89
170,000	2,616.31	2,581.68	2,553.14	2,529.52	2,493.57
175,000	2,693.26	2,657.61	2,628.23	2,603.91	2,566.91
180,000	2,770.21	2,733.55	2,703.32	2,678.31	2,640.25
190,000	2,924.11	2,885.41	2,853.51	2,827.10	2,786.93
200,000	3,078.01	3,037.27	3,003.69	2,975.90	2,933.61
220,000	3,385.81	3,341.00	3,304.06	3,273.49	3,226.97
225,000	3,462.76	3,416.93	3,379.15	3,347.89	3,300.31
230,000	3,539.71	3,492.86	3,454.24	3,422.28	3,373.65
240,000	3,693.62	3,644.73	3,604.43	3,571.08	3,520.33
$250,000	3,847.52	3,796.59	3,754.61	3,719.87	3,667.01

Table 1   197

17.00% Monthly Payment Loans

Amortization Period in Years

	21	22	23	24	25
$ 100	1.46	1.46	1.45	1.45	1.44
200	2.92	2.91	2.90	2.89	2.88
300	4.38	4.36	4.34	4.33	4.32
400	5.84	5.81	5.79	5.77	5.76
500	7.30	7.27	7.24	7.21	7.19
600	8.76	8.72	8.68	8.66	8.63
700	10.22	10.17	10.13	10.10	10.07
800	11.68	11.62	11.58	11.54	11.51
900	13.13	13.07	13.02	12.98	12.95
1,000	14.59	14.53	14.47	14.42	14.38
2,000	29.18	29.05	28.93	28.84	28.76
3,000	43.77	43.57	43.40	43.26	43.14
4,000	58.36	58.09	57.86	57.68	57.52
5,000	72.94	72.61	72.33	72.09	71.89
6,000	87.53	87.13	86.79	86.51	86.27
7,000	102.12	101.65	101.26	100.93	100.65
8,000	116.71	116.17	115.72	115.35	115.03
9,000	131.30	130.69	130.19	129.76	129.41
10,000	145.88	145.21	144.65	144.18	143.78
15,000	218.82	217.82	216.97	216.27	215.67
20,000	291.76	290.42	289.30	288.36	287.56
25,000	364.70	363.02	361.62	360.44	359.45
30,000	437.64	435.63	433.94	432.53	431.34
35,000	510.58	508.23	506.27	504.62	503.23
40,000	583.52	580.84	578.59	576.71	575.12
45,000	656.46	653.44	650.91	648.79	647.01
50,000	729.40	726.04	723.24	720.88	718.90
55,000	802.34	798.65	795.56	792.97	790.79
60,000	875.27	871.25	867.88	865.06	862.68
65,000	948.21	943.85	940.20	937.14	934.57
70,000	1,021.15	1,016.46	1,012.53	1,009.23	1,006.46
75,000	1,094.09	1,089.06	1,084.85	1,081.32	1,078.35
80,000	1,167.03	1,161.67	1,157.17	1,153.41	1,150.24
85,000	1,239.97	1,234.27	1,229.50	1,225.49	1,222.13
90,000	1,312.91	1,306.87	1,301.82	1,297.58	1,294.02
95,000	1,385.85	1,379.48	1,374.14	1,369.67	1,365.91
100,000	1,458.79	1,452.08	1,446.47	1,441.76	1,437.80
110,000	1,604.67	1,597.29	1,591.11	1,585.93	1,581.58
120,000	1,750.54	1,742.50	1,735.76	1,730.11	1,725.36
125,000	1,823.48	1,815.10	1,808.08	1,802.19	1,797.25
130,000	1,896.42	1,887.70	1,880.40	1,874.28	1,869.14
140,000	2,042.30	2,032.91	2,025.05	2,018.46	2,012.92
150,000	2,188.18	2,178.12	2,169.70	2,162.63	2,156.70
160,000	2,334.06	2,323.33	2,314.34	2,306.81	2,300.48
170,000	2,479.93	2,468.54	2,458.99	2,450.98	2,444.26
175,000	2,552.87	2,541.14	2,531.31	2,523.07	2,516.15
180,000	2,625.81	2,613.74	2,603.63	2,595.16	2,588.04
190,000	2,771.69	2,758.95	2,748.28	2,739.33	2,731.82
200,000	2,917.57	2,904.16	2,892.93	2,883.51	2,875.60
220,000	3,209.33	3,194.57	3,182.22	3,171.86	3,163.16
225,000	3,282.26	3,267.18	3,254.54	3,243.94	3,235.05
230,000	3,355.20	3,339.78	3,326.86	3,316.03	3,306.94
240,000	3,501.08	3,484.99	3,471.51	3,460.21	3,450.72
$250,000	3,646.96	3,630.20	3,616.16	3,604.38	3,594.50

Monthly Payment Loans   **17.00%**

Amortization Period in Years

	26	27	28	29	30
$ 100	1.44	1.44	1.43	1.43	1.43
200	2.87	2.87	2.86	2.86	2.86
300	4.31	4.30	4.29	4.29	4.28
400	5.74	5.73	5.72	5.71	5.71
500	7.18	7.16	7.15	7.14	7.13
600	8.61	8.60	8.58	8.57	8.56
700	10.05	10.03	10.01	10.00	9.98
800	11.48	11.46	11.44	11.42	11.41
900	12.92	12.89	12.87	12.85	12.84
1,000	14.35	14.32	14.30	14.28	14.26
2,000	28.69	28.64	28.59	28.55	28.52
3,000	43.04	42.96	42.88	42.83	42.78
4,000	57.38	57.27	57.18	57.10	57.03
5,000	71.73	71.59	71.47	71.37	71.29
6,000	86.07	85.91	85.76	85.65	85.55
7,000	100.42	100.22	100.06	99.92	99.80
8,000	114.76	114.54	114.35	114.19	114.06
9,000	129.11	128.86	128.64	128.47	128.32
10,000	143.45	143.17	142.94	142.74	142.57
15,000	215.18	214.76	214.40	214.11	213.86
20,000	286.90	286.34	285.87	285.47	285.14
25,000	358.62	357.92	357.34	356.84	356.42
30,000	430.35	429.51	428.80	428.21	427.71
35,000	502.07	501.09	500.27	499.58	498.99
40,000	573.79	572.68	571.74	570.94	570.28
45,000	645.52	644.26	643.20	642.31	641.56
50,000	717.24	715.84	714.67	713.68	712.84
55,000	788.97	787.43	786.13	785.04	784.13
60,000	860.69	859.01	857.60	856.41	855.41
65,000	932.41	930.60	929.07	927.78	926.69
70,000	1,004.14	1,002.18	1,000.53	999.15	997.98
75,000	1,075.86	1,073.76	1,072.00	1,070.51	1,069.26
80,000	1,147.58	1,145.35	1,143.47	1,141.88	1,140.55
85,000	1,219.31	1,216.93	1,214.93	1,213.25	1,211.83
90,000	1,291.03	1,288.52	1,286.40	1,284.62	1,283.11
95,000	1,362.75	1,360.10	1,357.86	1,355.98	1,354.40
100,000	1,434.48	1,431.68	1,429.33	1,427.35	1,425.68
110,000	1,577.93	1,574.85	1,572.26	1,570.08	1,568.25
120,000	1,721.37	1,718.02	1,715.20	1,712.82	1,710.82
125,000	1,793.10	1,789.60	1,786.66	1,784.19	1,782.10
130,000	1,864.82	1,861.19	1,858.13	1,855.55	1,853.38
140,000	2,008.27	2,004.35	2,001.06	1,998.29	1,995.95
150,000	2,151.71	2,147.52	2,143.99	2,141.02	2,138.52
160,000	2,295.16	2,290.69	2,286.93	2,283.76	2,281.09
170,000	2,438.61	2,433.86	2,429.86	2,426.49	2,423.65
175,000	2,510.33	2,505.44	2,501.32	2,497.86	2,494.94
180,000	2,582.06	2,577.03	2,572.79	2,569.23	2,566.22
190,000	2,725.50	2,720.19	2,715.72	2,711.96	2,708.79
200,000	2,868.95	2,863.36	2,858.66	2,854.69	2,851.36
220,000	3,155.85	3,149.70	3,144.52	3,140.16	3,136.49
225,000	3,227.57	3,221.28	3,215.99	3,211.53	3,207.57
230,000	3,299.29	3,292.86	3,287.45	3,282.90	3,279.06
240,000	3,442.74	3,436.03	3,430.39	3,425.63	3,421.63
$250,000	3,586.19	3,579.20	3,573.32	3,568.37	3,564.19

Table 1   199

17.25%   Monthly Payment Loans

Amortization Period in Years

		5	7	8	10	12
$	100	2.50	2.06	1.93	1.76	1.65
	200	5.00	4.12	3.86	3.51	3.30
	300	7.50	6.18	5.79	5.27	4.95
	400	10.00	8.24	7.71	7.02	6.60
	500	12.50	10.30	9.64	8.77	8.25
	600	15.00	12.35	11.57	10.53	9.90
	700	17.50	14.41	13.49	12.28	11.55
	800	19.99	16.47	15.42	14.04	13.19
	900	22.49	18.53	17.35	15.79	14.84
	1,000	24.99	20.59	19.28	17.54	16.49
	2,000	49.98	41.17	38.55	35.08	32.98
	3,000	74.97	61.75	57.82	52.62	49.46
	4,000	99.95	82.33	77.09	70.16	65.95
	5,000	124.94	102.91	96.36	87.70	82.44
	6,000	149.93	123.49	115.63	105.24	98.92
	7,000	174.92	144.07	134.90	122.77	115.41
	8,000	199.90	164.65	154.17	140.31	131.89
	9,000	224.89	185.23	173.44	157.85	148.38
	10,000	249.88	205.81	192.72	175.39	164.87
	15,000	374.81	308.71	289.07	263.08	247.30
	20,000	499.75	411.62	385.43	350.78	329.73
	25,000	624.68	514.52	481.78	438.47	412.16
	30,000	749.62	617.42	578.14	526.16	494.59
	35,000	874.56	720.32	674.49	613.85	577.02
	40,000	999.49	823.23	770.85	701.55	659.45
	45,000	1,124.43	926.13	867.20	789.24	741.88
	50,000	1,249.36	1,029.03	963.56	876.93	824.32
	55,000	1,374.30	1,131.93	1,059.91	964.62	906.75
	60,000	1,499.24	1,234.84	1,156.27	1,052.32	989.18
	65,000	1,624.17	1,337.74	1,252.62	1,140.01	1,071.61
	70,000	1,749.11	1,440.64	1,348.98	1,227.70	1,154.04
	75,000	1,874.04	1,543.55	1,445.33	1,315.39	1,236.47
	80,000	1,998.98	1,646.45	1,541.69	1,403.09	1,318.90
	85,000	2,123.92	1,749.35	1,638.04	1,490.78	1,401.33
	90,000	2,248.85	1,852.25	1,734.40	1,578.47	1,483.76
	95,000	2,373.79	1,955.16	1,830.75	1,666.16	1,566.19
	100,000	2,498.72	2,058.06	1,927.11	1,753.86	1,648.63
	110,000	2,748.60	2,263.86	2,119.82	1,929.24	1,813.49
	120,000	2,998.47	2,469.67	2,312.53	2,104.63	1,978.35
	125,000	3,123.40	2,572.57	2,408.89	2,192.32	2,060.78
	130,000	3,248.34	2,675.48	2,505.24	2,280.01	2,143.21
	140,000	3,498.21	2,881.28	2,697.95	2,455.40	2,308.07
	150,000	3,748.08	3,087.09	2,890.66	2,630.78	2,472.94
	160,000	3,997.96	3,292.89	3,083.37	2,806.17	2,637.80
	170,000	4,247.83	3,498.70	3,276.08	2,981.55	2,802.66
	175,000	4,372.76	3,601.60	3,372.44	3,069.24	2,885.09
	180,000	4,497.70	3,704.50	3,468.79	3,156.94	2,967.52
	190,000	4,747.57	3,910.31	3,661.50	3,332.32	3,132.38
	200,000	4,997.44	4,116.11	3,854.21	3,507.71	3,297.25
	220,000	5,497.19	4,527.72	4,239.64	3,858.48	3,626.97
	225,000	5,622.12	4,630.63	4,335.99	3,946.17	3,709.40
	230,000	5,747.06	4,733.53	4,432.35	4,033.86	3,791.83
	240,000	5,996.93	4,939.33	4,625.06	4,209.25	3,956.70
$250,000		6,246.80	5,145.14	4,817.77	4,384.63	4,121.56

Monthly Payment Loans   **17.25%**

Amortization Period in Years

	15	16	17	18	20
$ 100	1.56	1.54	1.53	1.51	1.49
200	3.12	3.08	3.05	3.02	2.98
300	4.68	4.62	4.57	4.52	4.46
400	6.23	6.15	6.09	6.03	5.95
500	7.79	7.69	7.61	7.54	7.43
600	9.35	9.23	9.13	9.04	8.92
700	10.90	10.76	10.65	10.55	10.41
800	12.46	12.30	12.17	12.06	11.89
900	14.02	13.84	13.69	13.56	13.38
1,000	15.57	15.37	15.21	15.07	14.86
2,000	31.14	30.74	30.41	30.14	29.72
3,000	46.71	46.11	45.61	45.20	44.58
4,000	62.28	61.47	60.81	60.27	59.44
5,000	77.84	76.84	76.01	75.33	74.30
6,000	93.41	92.21	91.22	90.40	89.16
7,000	108.98	107.57	106.42	105.46	104.01
8,000	124.55	122.94	121.62	120.53	118.87
9,000	140.11	138.31	136.82	135.59	133.73
10,000	155.68	153.67	152.02	150.66	148.59
15,000	233.52	230.51	228.03	225.99	222.88
20,000	311.36	307.34	304.04	301.31	297.17
25,000	389.19	384.18	380.05	376.64	371.47
30,000	467.03	461.01	456.06	451.97	445.76
35,000	544.87	537.85	532.07	527.29	520.05
40,000	622.71	614.68	608.08	602.62	594.34
45,000	700.55	691.52	684.09	677.95	668.63
50,000	778.38	768.35	760.09	753.27	742.93
55,000	856.22	845.18	836.10	828.60	817.22
60,000	934.06	922.02	912.11	903.93	891.51
65,000	1,011.90	998.85	988.12	979.26	965.80
70,000	1,089.73	1,075.69	1,064.13	1,054.58	1,040.09
75,000	1,167.57	1,152.52	1,140.14	1,129.91	1,114.39
80,000	1,245.41	1,229.36	1,216.15	1,205.24	1,188.68
85,000	1,323.25	1,306.19	1,292.16	1,280.56	1,262.97
90,000	1,401.09	1,383.03	1,368.17	1,355.89	1,337.26
95,000	1,478.92	1,459.86	1,444.17	1,431.22	1,411.55
100,000	1,556.76	1,536.69	1,520.18	1,506.54	1,485.85
110,000	1,712.44	1,690.36	1,672.20	1,657.20	1,634.43
120,000	1,868.11	1,844.03	1,824.22	1,807.85	1,783.02
125,000	1,945.95	1,920.87	1,900.23	1,883.18	1,857.31
130,000	2,023.79	1,997.70	1,976.24	1,958.51	1,931.60
140,000	2,179.46	2,151.37	2,128.26	2,109.16	2,080.18
150,000	2,335.14	2,305.04	2,280.27	2,259.81	2,228.77
160,000	2,490.82	2,458.71	2,432.29	2,410.47	2,377.35
170,000	2,646.49	2,612.38	2,584.31	2,561.12	2,525.94
175,000	2,724.33	2,689.21	2,660.32	2,636.45	2,600.23
180,000	2,802.17	2,766.05	2,736.33	2,711.78	2,674.52
190,000	2,957.84	2,919.72	2,888.34	2,862.43	2,823.10
200,000	3,113.52	3,073.38	3,040.36	3,013.08	2,971.69
220,000	3,424.87	3,380.72	3,344.40	3,314.39	3,268.86
225,000	3,502.71	3,457.56	3,420.41	3,389.72	3,343.15
230,000	3,580.55	3,534.39	3,496.42	3,465.05	3,417.44
240,000	3,736.22	3,688.06	3,648.43	3,615.70	3,566.03
$250,000	3,891.90	3,841.73	3,800.45	3,766.35	3,714.61

Table 1   201

17.25%   Monthly Payment Loans

Amortization Period in Years

	21	22	23	24	25
$ 100	1.48	1.48	1.47	1.47	1.46
200	2.96	2.95	2.94	2.93	2.92
300	4.44	4.42	4.40	4.39	4.38
400	5.92	5.89	5.87	5.85	5.84
500	7.40	7.36	7.34	7.31	7.29
600	8.87	8.83	8.80	8.77	8.75
700	10.35	10.31	10.27	10.24	10.21
800	11.83	11.78	11.73	11.70	11.67
900	13.31	13.25	13.20	13.16	13.12
1,000	14.79	14.72	14.67	14.62	14.58
2,000	29.57	29.43	29.33	29.23	29.16
3,000	44.35	44.15	43.99	43.85	43.73
4,000	59.13	58.86	58.65	58.46	58.31
5,000	73.91	73.58	73.31	73.08	72.89
6,000	88.69	88.29	87.97	87.69	87.46
7,000	103.47	103.01	102.63	102.31	102.04
8,000	118.25	117.72	117.29	116.92	116.62
9,000	133.03	132.44	131.95	131.54	131.19
10,000	147.81	147.15	146.61	146.15	145.77
15,000	221.71	220.73	219.91	219.23	218.65
20,000	295.61	294.30	293.21	292.30	291.53
25,000	369.51	367.88	366.51	365.37	364.42
30,000	443.41	441.45	439.81	438.45	437.30
35,000	517.31	515.03	513.12	511.52	510.18
40,000	591.21	588.60	586.42	584.59	583.06
45,000	665.11	662.18	659.72	657.67	655.94
50,000	739.01	735.75	733.02	730.74	728.83
55,000	812.91	809.32	806.32	803.81	801.71
60,000	886.82	882.90	879.62	876.89	874.59
65,000	960.72	956.47	952.93	949.96	947.47
70,000	1,034.62	1,030.05	1,026.23	1,023.03	1,020.35
75,000	1,108.52	1,103.62	1,099.53	1,096.11	1,093.24
80,000	1,182.42	1,177.20	1,172.83	1,169.18	1,166.12
85,000	1,256.32	1,250.77	1,246.13	1,242.25	1,239.00
90,000	1,330.22	1,324.35	1,319.43	1,315.33	1,311.88
95,000	1,404.12	1,397.92	1,392.74	1,388.40	1,384.76
100,000	1,478.02	1,471.49	1,466.04	1,461.47	1,457.65
110,000	1,625.82	1,618.64	1,612.64	1,607.62	1,603.41
120,000	1,773.63	1,765.79	1,759.24	1,753.77	1,749.17
125,000	1,847.53	1,839.37	1,832.55	1,826.84	1,822.06
130,000	1,921.43	1,912.94	1,905.85	1,899.91	1,894.94
140,000	2,069.23	2,060.09	2,052.45	2,046.06	2,040.70
150,000	2,217.03	2,207.24	2,199.05	2,192.21	2,186.47
160,000	2,364.83	2,354.39	2,345.66	2,338.35	2,332.23
170,000	2,512.64	2,501.54	2,492.26	2,484.50	2,478.00
175,000	2,586.54	2,575.11	2,565.56	2,557.57	2,550.88
180,000	2,660.44	2,648.69	2,638.86	2,630.65	2,623.76
190,000	2,808.24	2,795.83	2,785.47	2,776.79	2,769.52
200,000	2,956.04	2,942.98	2,932.07	2,922.94	2,915.29
220,000	3,251.64	3,237.28	3,225.28	3,215.23	3,206.82
225,000	3,325.55	3,310.86	3,298.58	3,288.31	3,279.70
230,000	3,399.45	3,384.43	3,371.88	3,361.38	3,352.58
240,000	3,547.25	3,531.58	3,518.48	3,507.53	3,498.34
$250,000	3,695.05	3,678.73	3,665.09	3,653.67	3,644.11

Monthly Payment Loans   **17.25%**

Amortization Period in Years

	26	27	28	29	30
$ 100	1.46	1.46	1.45	1.45	1.45
200	2.91	2.91	2.90	2.90	2.90
300	4.37	4.36	4.35	4.35	4.34
400	5.82	5.81	5.80	5.80	5.79
500	7.28	7.26	7.25	7.24	7.23
600	8.73	8.72	8.70	8.69	8.68
700	10.19	10.17	10.15	10.14	10.13
800	11.64	11.62	11.60	11.59	11.57
900	13.09	13.07	13.05	13.03	13.02
1,000	14.55	14.52	14.50	14.48	14.46
2,000	29.09	29.04	28.99	28.96	28.92
3,000	43.64	43.56	43.49	43.43	43.38
4,000	58.18	58.07	57.98	57.91	57.84
5,000	72.73	72.59	72.48	72.38	72.30
6,000	87.27	87.11	86.97	86.86	86.76
7,000	101.82	101.63	101.47	101.34	101.22
8,000	116.36	116.14	115.96	115.81	115.68
9,000	130.90	130.66	130.46	130.29	130.14
10,000	145.45	145.18	144.95	144.76	144.60
15,000	218.17	217.77	217.43	217.14	216.90
20,000	290.89	290.35	289.90	289.52	289.20
25,000	363.61	362.94	362.38	361.90	361.50
30,000	436.34	435.53	434.85	434.28	433.80
35,000	509.06	508.11	507.32	506.66	506.10
40,000	581.78	580.70	579.80	579.04	578.40
45,000	654.50	653.29	652.27	651.42	650.70
50,000	727.22	725.88	724.75	723.80	723.00
55,000	799.94	798.46	797.22	796.18	795.30
60,000	872.67	871.05	869.69	868.55	867.60
65,000	945.39	943.64	942.17	940.93	939.90
70,000	1,018.11	1,016.22	1,014.64	1,013.31	1,012.20
75,000	1,090.83	1,088.81	1,087.12	1,085.69	1,084.49
80,000	1,163.55	1,161.40	1,159.59	1,158.07	1,156.79
85,000	1,236.27	1,233.99	1,232.06	1,230.45	1,229.09
90,000	1,309.00	1,306.57	1,304.54	1,302.83	1,301.39
95,000	1,381.72	1,379.16	1,377.01	1,375.21	1,373.69
100,000	1,454.44	1,451.75	1,449.49	1,447.59	1,445.99
110,000	1,599.88	1,596.92	1,594.43	1,592.35	1,590.59
120,000	1,745.33	1,742.10	1,739.38	1,737.10	1,735.19
125,000	1,818.05	1,814.68	1,811.86	1,809.48	1,807.49
130,000	1,890.77	1,887.27	1,884.33	1,881.86	1,879.79
140,000	2,036.21	2,032.44	2,029.28	2,026.62	2,024.39
150,000	2,181.66	2,177.62	2,174.23	2,171.38	2,168.98
160,000	2,327.10	2,322.79	2,319.18	2,316.14	2,313.58
170,000	2,472.54	2,467.97	2,464.12	2,460.89	2,458.18
175,000	2,545.26	2,540.55	2,536.60	2,533.27	2,530.48
180,000	2,617.99	2,613.14	2,609.07	2,605.65	2,602.78
190,000	2,763.43	2,758.31	2,754.02	2,750.41	2,747.38
200,000	2,908.87	2,903.49	2,898.97	2,895.17	2,891.98
220,000	3,199.76	3,193.84	3,188.86	3,184.69	3,181.17
225,000	3,272.48	3,266.42	3,261.34	3,257.06	3,253.47
230,000	3,345.20	3,339.01	3,333.81	3,329.44	3,325.77
240,000	3,490.65	3,484.19	3,478.76	3,474.20	3,470.37
$250,000	3,636.09	3,629.36	3,623.71	3,618.96	3,614.97

Table 1   203

17.50% Monthly Payment Loans

Amortization Period in Years

	5	7	8	10	12
$ 100	2.52	2.08	1.95	1.77	1.67
200	5.03	4.15	3.89	3.54	3.34
300	7.54	6.22	5.83	5.31	5.00
400	10.05	8.30	7.77	7.08	6.67
500	12.57	10.37	9.72	8.85	8.33
600	15.08	12.44	11.66	10.62	10.00
700	17.59	14.51	13.60	12.39	11.66
800	20.10	16.59	15.54	14.16	13.33
900	22.61	18.66	17.48	15.93	14.99
1,000	25.13	20.73	19.43	17.70	16.66
2,000	50.25	41.46	38.85	35.40	33.31
3,000	75.37	62.18	58.27	53.10	49.97
4,000	100.49	82.91	77.69	70.80	66.62
5,000	125.62	103.63	97.11	88.49	83.27
6,000	150.74	124.36	116.53	106.19	99.93
7,000	175.86	145.09	135.95	123.89	116.58
8,000	200.98	165.81	155.37	141.59	133.24
9,000	226.10	186.54	174.80	159.29	149.89
10,000	251.23	207.26	194.22	176.98	166.54
15,000	376.84	310.89	291.32	265.47	249.81
20,000	502.45	414.52	388.43	353.96	333.08
25,000	628.06	518.15	485.54	442.45	416.35
30,000	753.67	621.78	582.64	530.94	499.62
35,000	879.28	725.41	679.75	619.43	582.89
40,000	1,004.89	829.04	776.85	707.92	666.16
45,000	1,130.50	932.67	873.96	796.41	749.43
50,000	1,256.12	1,036.29	971.07	884.90	832.70
55,000	1,381.73	1,139.92	1,068.17	973.39	915.97
60,000	1,507.34	1,243.55	1,165.28	1,061.88	999.24
65,000	1,632.95	1,347.18	1,262.38	1,150.37	1,082.51
70,000	1,758.56	1,450.81	1,359.49	1,238.86	1,165.78
75,000	1,884.17	1,554.44	1,456.60	1,327.35	1,249.05
80,000	2,009.78	1,658.07	1,553.70	1,415.84	1,332.31
85,000	2,135.39	1,761.70	1,650.81	1,504.32	1,415.58
90,000	2,261.00	1,865.33	1,747.91	1,592.81	1,498.85
95,000	2,386.62	1,968.96	1,845.02	1,681.30	1,582.12
100,000	2,512.23	2,072.58	1,942.13	1,769.79	1,665.39
110,000	2,763.45	2,279.84	2,136.34	1,946.77	1,831.93
120,000	3,014.67	2,487.10	2,330.55	2,123.75	1,998.47
125,000	3,140.28	2,590.73	2,427.66	2,212.24	2,081.74
130,000	3,265.89	2,694.36	2,524.76	2,300.73	2,165.01
140,000	3,517.11	2,901.62	2,718.97	2,477.71	2,331.55
150,000	3,768.34	3,108.87	2,913.19	2,654.69	2,498.09
160,000	4,019.56	3,316.13	3,107.40	2,831.67	2,664.62
170,000	4,270.78	3,523.39	3,301.61	3,008.64	2,831.16
175,000	4,396.39	3,627.02	3,398.72	3,097.13	2,914.43
180,000	4,522.00	3,730.65	3,495.82	3,185.62	2,997.70
190,000	4,773.23	3,937.91	3,690.03	3,362.60	3,164.24
200,000	5,024.45	4,145.16	3,884.25	3,539.58	3,330.78
220,000	5,526.89	4,559.68	4,272.67	3,893.54	3,663.86
225,000	5,652.50	4,663.31	4,369.78	3,982.03	3,747.13
230,000	5,778.11	4,766.94	4,466.88	4,070.52	3,830.40
240,000	6,029.34	4,974.20	4,661.10	4,247.50	3,996.93
$250,000	6,280.56	5,181.45	4,855.31	4,424.47	4,163.47

Monthly Payment Loans   **17.50%**

Amortization Period in Years

	15	16	17	18	20
$ 100	1.58	1.56	1.54	1.53	1.51
200	3.15	3.11	3.08	3.06	3.01
300	4.73	4.67	4.62	4.58	4.52
400	6.30	6.22	6.16	6.11	6.02
500	7.88	7.78	7.70	7.63	7.53
600	9.45	9.33	9.24	9.16	9.03
700	11.03	10.89	10.78	10.68	10.54
800	12.60	12.44	12.31	12.21	12.04
900	14.18	14.00	13.85	13.73	13.55
1,000	15.75	15.55	15.39	15.26	15.05
2,000	31.50	31.10	30.78	30.51	30.10
3,000	47.24	46.65	46.16	45.76	45.15
4,000	62.99	62.20	61.55	61.01	60.20
5,000	78.73	77.75	76.93	76.26	75.25
6,000	94.48	93.29	92.32	91.52	90.30
7,000	110.23	108.84	107.71	106.77	105.35
8,000	125.97	124.39	123.09	122.02	120.40
9,000	141.72	139.94	138.48	137.27	135.45
10,000	157.46	155.49	153.86	152.52	150.50
15,000	236.19	233.23	230.79	228.78	225.75
20,000	314.92	310.97	307.72	305.04	300.99
25,000	393.65	388.71	384.65	381.30	376.24
30,000	472.38	466.45	461.58	457.56	451.49
35,000	551.11	544.19	538.51	533.82	526.73
40,000	629.84	621.93	615.44	610.08	601.98
45,000	708.57	699.67	692.37	686.34	677.23
50,000	787.29	777.41	769.29	762.60	752.48
55,000	866.02	855.15	846.22	838.86	827.72
60,000	944.75	932.89	923.15	915.12	902.97
65,000	1,023.48	1,010.63	1,000.08	991.38	978.22
70,000	1,102.21	1,088.37	1,077.01	1,067.64	1,053.46
75,000	1,180.94	1,166.11	1,153.94	1,143.90	1,128.71
80,000	1,259.67	1,243.86	1,230.87	1,220.16	1,203.96
85,000	1,338.40	1,321.60	1,307.80	1,296.42	1,279.21
90,000	1,417.13	1,399.34	1,384.73	1,372.68	1,354.45
95,000	1,495.85	1,477.08	1,461.66	1,448.94	1,429.70
100,000	1,574.58	1,554.82	1,538.58	1,525.20	1,504.95
110,000	1,732.04	1,710.30	1,692.44	1,677.72	1,655.44
120,000	1,889.50	1,865.78	1,846.30	1,830.24	1,805.94
125,000	1,968.23	1,943.52	1,923.23	1,906.50	1,881.18
130,000	2,046.96	2,021.26	2,000.16	1,982.76	1,956.43
140,000	2,204.41	2,176.74	2,154.02	2,135.28	2,106.92
150,000	2,361.87	2,332.22	2,307.87	2,287.80	2,257.42
160,000	2,519.33	2,487.71	2,461.73	2,440.32	2,407.91
170,000	2,676.79	2,643.19	2,615.59	2,592.84	2,558.41
175,000	2,755.52	2,720.93	2,692.52	2,669.10	2,633.65
180,000	2,834.25	2,798.67	2,769.45	2,745.36	2,708.90
190,000	2,991.70	2,954.15	2,923.31	2,897.88	2,859.39
200,000	3,149.16	3,109.63	3,077.16	3,050.39	3,009.89
220,000	3,464.08	3,420.59	3,384.88	3,355.43	3,310.88
225,000	3,542.81	3,498.33	3,461.81	3,431.69	3,386.12
230,000	3,621.53	3,576.07	3,538.74	3,507.95	3,461.37
240,000	3,778.99	3,731.56	3,692.60	3,660.47	3,611.87
$250,000	3,936.45	3,887.04	3,846.45	3,812.99	3,762.36

Table 1   205

17.50% Monthly Payment Loans

Amortization Period in Years

	21	22	23	24	25
$ 100	1.50	1.50	1.49	1.49	1.48
200	3.00	2.99	2.98	2.97	2.96
300	4.50	4.48	4.46	4.45	4.44
400	5.99	5.97	5.95	5.93	5.92
500	7.49	7.46	7.43	7.41	7.39
600	8.99	8.95	8.92	8.89	8.87
700	10.49	10.44	10.40	10.37	10.35
800	11.98	11.93	11.89	11.85	11.83
900	13.48	13.42	13.38	13.34	13.30
1,000	14.98	14.91	14.86	14.82	14.78
2,000	29.95	29.82	29.72	29.63	29.56
3,000	44.92	44.73	44.57	44.44	44.33
4,000	59.90	59.64	59.43	59.25	59.11
5,000	74.87	74.55	74.29	74.07	73.88
6,000	89.84	89.46	89.14	88.88	88.66
7,000	104.82	104.37	104.00	103.69	103.43
8,000	119.79	119.28	118.86	118.50	118.21
9,000	134.76	134.19	133.71	133.32	132.98
10,000	149.74	149.10	148.57	148.13	147.76
15,000	224.60	223.65	222.85	222.19	221.63
20,000	299.47	298.20	297.14	296.25	295.51
25,000	374.33	372.74	371.42	370.31	369.39
30,000	449.20	447.29	445.70	444.37	443.26
35,000	524.06	521.84	519.98	518.44	517.14
40,000	598.93	596.39	594.27	592.50	591.02
45,000	673.79	670.93	668.55	666.56	664.89
50,000	748.66	745.48	742.83	740.62	738.77
55,000	823.53	820.03	817.12	814.68	812.65
60,000	898.39	894.58	891.40	888.74	886.52
65,000	973.26	969.13	965.68	962.80	960.40
70,000	1,048.12	1,043.67	1,039.96	1,036.87	1,034.28
75,000	1,122.99	1,118.22	1,114.25	1,110.93	1,108.15
80,000	1,197.85	1,192.77	1,188.53	1,184.99	1,182.03
85,000	1,272.72	1,267.32	1,262.81	1,259.05	1,255.91
90,000	1,347.58	1,341.86	1,337.09	1,333.11	1,329.78
95,000	1,422.45	1,416.41	1,411.38	1,407.17	1,403.66
100,000	1,497.32	1,490.96	1,485.66	1,481.23	1,477.53
110,000	1,647.05	1,640.06	1,634.23	1,629.36	1,625.29
120,000	1,796.78	1,789.15	1,782.79	1,777.48	1,773.04
125,000	1,871.64	1,863.70	1,857.07	1,851.54	1,846.92
130,000	1,946.51	1,938.25	1,931.36	1,925.60	1,920.79
140,000	2,096.24	2,087.34	2,079.92	2,073.73	2,068.55
150,000	2,245.97	2,236.44	2,228.49	2,221.85	2,216.30
160,000	2,395.70	2,385.53	2,377.05	2,369.97	2,364.05
170,000	2,545.43	2,534.63	2,525.62	2,518.09	2,511.81
175,000	2,620.30	2,609.18	2,599.90	2,592.16	2,585.68
180,000	2,695.16	2,683.72	2,674.18	2,666.22	2,659.56
190,000	2,844.89	2,832.82	2,822.75	2,814.34	2,807.31
200,000	2,994.63	2,981.91	2,971.31	2,962.46	2,955.06
220,000	3,294.09	3,280.11	3,268.45	3,258.71	3,250.57
225,000	3,368.95	3,354.65	3,342.73	3,332.77	3,324.45
230,000	3,443.82	3,429.20	3,417.01	3,406.83	3,398.32
240,000	3,593.55	3,578.30	3,565.58	3,554.96	3,546.08
$250,000	3,743.28	3,727.39	3,714.14	3,703.08	3,693.83

Monthly Payment Loans 17.50%

Amortization Period in Years

	26	27	28	29	30
$ 100	1.48	1.48	1.47	1.47	1.47
200	2.95	2.95	2.94	2.94	2.94
300	4.43	4.42	4.41	4.41	4.40
400	5.90	5.89	5.88	5.88	5.87
500	7.38	7.36	7.35	7.34	7.34
600	8.85	8.84	8.82	8.81	8.80
700	10.33	10.31	10.29	10.28	10.27
800	11.80	11.78	11.76	11.75	11.74
900	13.27	13.25	13.23	13.22	13.20
1,000	14.75	14.72	14.70	14.68	14.67
2,000	29.49	29.44	29.40	29.36	29.33
3,000	44.24	44.16	44.10	44.04	43.99
4,000	58.98	58.88	58.79	58.72	58.66
5,000	73.73	73.60	73.49	73.40	73.32
6,000	88.47	88.32	88.19	88.08	87.98
7,000	103.22	103.03	102.88	102.75	102.65
8,000	117.96	117.75	117.58	117.43	117.31
9,000	132.70	132.47	132.28	132.11	131.97
10,000	147.45	147.19	146.97	146.79	146.64
15,000	221.17	220.78	220.46	220.18	219.95
20,000	294.89	294.37	293.94	293.58	293.27
25,000	368.61	367.97	367.42	366.97	366.59
30,000	442.34	441.56	440.91	440.36	439.90
35,000	516.06	515.15	514.39	513.75	513.22
40,000	589.78	588.74	587.87	587.15	586.54
45,000	663.50	662.33	661.36	660.54	659.85
50,000	737.22	735.93	734.84	733.93	733.17
55,000	810.94	809.52	808.32	807.32	806.48
60,000	884.67	883.11	881.81	880.72	879.80
65,000	958.39	956.70	955.29	954.11	953.12
70,000	1,032.11	1,030.29	1,028.78	1,027.50	1,026.43
75,000	1,105.83	1,103.89	1,102.26	1,100.89	1,099.75
80,000	1,179.55	1,177.48	1,175.74	1,174.29	1,173.07
85,000	1,253.27	1,251.07	1,249.23	1,247.68	1,246.38
90,000	1,327.00	1,324.66	1,322.71	1,321.07	1,319.70
95,000	1,400.72	1,398.26	1,396.19	1,394.46	1,393.01
100,000	1,474.44	1,471.85	1,469.68	1,467.86	1,466.33
110,000	1,621.88	1,619.03	1,616.64	1,614.64	1,612.96
120,000	1,769.33	1,766.22	1,763.61	1,761.43	1,759.60
125,000	1,843.05	1,839.81	1,837.09	1,834.82	1,832.91
130,000	1,916.77	1,913.40	1,910.58	1,908.21	1,906.23
140,000	2,064.21	2,060.58	2,057.55	2,055.00	2,052.86
150,000	2,211.66	2,207.77	2,204.51	2,201.78	2,199.49
160,000	2,359.10	2,354.95	2,351.48	2,348.57	2,346.13
170,000	2,506.54	2,502.14	2,498.45	2,495.35	2,492.76
175,000	2,580.27	2,575.73	2,571.93	2,568.75	2,566.07
180,000	2,653.99	2,649.32	2,645.41	2,642.14	2,639.39
190,000	2,801.43	2,796.51	2,792.38	2,788.92	2,786.02
200,000	2,948.87	2,943.69	2,939.35	2,935.71	2,932.66
220,000	3,243.76	3,238.06	3,233.28	3,229.28	3,225.92
225,000	3,317.48	3,311.65	3,306.77	3,302.67	3,299.24
230,000	3,391.20	3,385.24	3,380.25	3,376.06	3,372.55
240,000	3,538.65	3,532.43	3,527.22	3,522.85	3,519.19
$250,000	3,686.09	3,679.61	3,674.18	3,669.63	3,665.82

Table 1   207

17.75%   **Monthly Payment Loans**

Amortization Period in Years

	5	7	8	10	12
$ 100	2.53	2.09	1.96	1.79	1.69
200	5.06	4.18	3.92	3.58	3.37
300	7.58	6.27	5.88	5.36	5.05
400	10.11	8.35	7.83	7.15	6.73
500	12.63	10.44	9.79	8.93	8.42
600	15.16	12.53	11.75	10.72	10.10
700	17.69	14.62	13.71	12.51	11.78
800	20.21	16.70	15.66	14.29	13.46
900	22.74	18.79	17.62	16.08	15.14
1,000	25.26	20.88	19.58	17.86	16.83
2,000	50.52	41.75	39.15	35.72	33.65
3,000	75.78	62.62	58.72	53.58	50.47
4,000	101.04	83.49	78.29	71.44	67.29
5,000	126.29	104.36	97.86	89.29	84.12
6,000	151.55	125.23	117.44	107.15	100.94
7,000	176.81	146.11	137.01	125.01	117.76
8,000	202.07	166.98	156.58	142.87	134.58
9,000	227.32	187.85	176.15	160.73	151.40
10,000	252.58	208.72	195.72	178.58	168.23
15,000	378.87	313.08	293.58	267.87	252.34
20,000	505.16	417.44	391.44	357.16	336.45
25,000	631.45	521.79	489.30	446.45	420.56
30,000	757.73	626.15	587.16	535.74	504.67
35,000	884.02	730.51	685.02	625.03	588.78
40,000	1,010.31	834.87	782.88	714.32	672.89
45,000	1,136.60	939.23	880.74	803.61	757.00
50,000	1,262.89	1,043.58	978.60	892.90	841.12
55,000	1,389.17	1,147.94	1,076.46	982.19	925.23
60,000	1,515.46	1,252.30	1,174.32	1,071.48	1,009.34
65,000	1,641.75	1,356.66	1,272.18	1,160.77	1,093.45
70,000	1,768.04	1,461.01	1,370.04	1,250.06	1,177.56
75,000	1,894.33	1,565.37	1,467.90	1,339.35	1,261.67
80,000	2,020.61	1,669.73	1,565.76	1,428.64	1,345.78
85,000	2,146.90	1,774.09	1,663.62	1,517.93	1,429.89
90,000	2,273.19	1,878.45	1,761.48	1,607.21	1,514.00
95,000	2,399.48	1,982.80	1,859.34	1,696.50	1,598.11
100,000	2,525.77	2,087.16	1,957.20	1,785.79	1,682.23
110,000	2,778.34	2,295.88	2,152.92	1,964.37	1,850.45
120,000	3,030.92	2,504.59	2,348.64	2,142.95	2,018.67
125,000	3,157.21	2,608.95	2,446.50	2,232.24	2,102.78
130,000	3,283.50	2,713.31	2,544.36	2,321.53	2,186.89
140,000	3,536.07	2,922.02	2,740.08	2,500.11	2,355.11
150,000	3,788.65	3,130.74	2,935.79	2,678.69	2,523.34
160,000	4,041.22	3,339.45	3,131.51	2,857.27	2,691.56
170,000	4,293.80	3,548.17	3,327.23	3,035.85	2,859.78
175,000	4,420.09	3,652.53	3,425.09	3,125.13	2,943.89
180,000	4,546.38	3,756.89	3,522.95	3,214.42	3,028.00
190,000	4,798.95	3,965.60	3,718.67	3,393.00	3,196.22
200,000	5,051.53	4,174.32	3,914.39	3,571.58	3,364.45
220,000	5,556.68	4,591.75	4,305.83	3,928.74	3,700.89
225,000	5,682.97	4,696.11	4,403.69	4,018.03	3,785.00
230,000	5,809.26	4,800.46	4,501.55	4,107.32	3,869.11
240,000	6,061.83	5,009.18	4,697.27	4,285.90	4,037.33
$250,000	6,314.41	5,217.90	4,892.99	4,464.48	4,205.56

Monthly Payment Loans   17.75%

Amortization Period in Years

	15	16	17	18	20
$ 100	1.60	1.58	1.56	1.55	1.53
200	3.19	3.15	3.12	3.09	3.05
300	4.78	4.72	4.68	4.64	4.58
400	6.37	6.30	6.23	6.18	6.10
500	7.97	7.87	7.79	7.72	7.63
600	9.56	9.44	9.35	9.27	9.15
700	11.15	11.02	10.90	10.81	10.67
800	12.74	12.59	12.46	12.36	12.20
900	14.34	14.16	14.02	13.90	13.72
1,000	15.93	15.74	15.58	15.44	15.25
2,000	31.85	31.47	31.15	30.88	30.49
3,000	47.78	47.20	46.72	46.32	45.73
4,000	63.70	62.93	62.29	61.76	60.97
5,000	79.63	78.66	77.86	77.20	76.21
6,000	95.55	94.39	93.43	92.64	91.45
7,000	111.48	110.12	109.00	108.08	106.69
8,000	127.40	125.85	124.57	123.52	121.93
9,000	143.33	141.58	140.14	138.96	137.17
10,000	159.25	157.31	155.71	154.40	152.41
15,000	238.87	235.96	233.56	231.59	228.62
20,000	318.50	314.61	311.41	308.79	304.82
25,000	398.12	393.26	389.27	385.98	381.03
30,000	477.74	471.91	467.12	463.18	457.23
35,000	557.37	550.56	544.97	540.37	533.44
40,000	636.99	629.21	622.82	617.57	609.64
45,000	716.61	707.86	700.68	694.77	685.85
50,000	796.24	786.51	778.53	771.96	762.05
55,000	875.86	865.16	856.38	849.16	838.26
60,000	955.48	943.81	934.23	926.35	914.46
65,000	1,035.11	1,022.46	1,012.08	1,003.55	990.67
70,000	1,114.73	1,101.11	1,089.94	1,080.74	1,066.87
75,000	1,194.35	1,179.76	1,167.79	1,157.94	1,143.08
80,000	1,273.98	1,258.41	1,245.64	1,235.14	1,219.28
85,000	1,353.60	1,337.06	1,323.49	1,312.33	1,295.49
90,000	1,433.22	1,415.71	1,401.35	1,389.53	1,371.69
95,000	1,512.85	1,494.36	1,479.20	1,466.72	1,447.90
100,000	1,592.47	1,573.01	1,557.05	1,543.92	1,524.10
110,000	1,751.72	1,730.31	1,712.75	1,698.31	1,676.51
120,000	1,910.96	1,887.61	1,868.46	1,852.70	1,828.92
125,000	1,990.59	1,966.26	1,946.31	1,929.90	1,905.13
130,000	2,070.21	2,044.91	2,024.16	2,007.09	1,981.33
140,000	2,229.46	2,202.21	2,179.87	2,161.48	2,133.74
150,000	2,388.70	2,359.51	2,335.57	2,315.87	2,286.15
160,000	2,547.95	2,516.81	2,491.28	2,470.27	2,438.56
170,000	2,707.20	2,674.11	2,646.98	2,624.66	2,590.97
175,000	2,786.82	2,752.76	2,724.83	2,701.85	2,667.18
180,000	2,866.44	2,831.41	2,802.69	2,779.05	2,743.38
190,000	3,025.69	2,988.71	2,958.39	2,933.44	2,895.79
200,000	3,184.94	3,146.01	3,114.09	3,087.83	3,048.20
220,000	3,503.43	3,460.61	3,425.50	3,396.61	3,353.02
225,000	3,583.05	3,539.26	3,503.36	3,473.81	3,429.23
230,000	3,662.68	3,617.91	3,581.21	3,551.00	3,505.43
240,000	3,821.92	3,775.21	3,736.91	3,705.40	3,657.84
$250,000	3,981.17	3,932.51	3,892.62	3,859.79	3,810.25

Table 1   209

17.75%   Monthly Payment Loans

Amortization Period in Years

	21	22	23	24	25
$ 100	1.52	1.52	1.51	1.51	1.50
200	3.04	3.03	3.02	3.01	3.00
300	4.55	4.54	4.52	4.51	4.50
400	6.07	6.05	6.03	6.01	5.99
500	7.59	7.56	7.53	7.51	7.49
600	9.10	9.07	9.04	9.01	8.99
700	10.62	10.58	10.54	10.51	10.49
800	12.14	12.09	12.05	12.01	11.98
900	13.65	13.60	13.55	13.51	13.48
1,000	15.17	15.11	15.06	15.02	14.98
2,000	30.34	30.21	30.11	30.03	29.95
3,000	45.50	45.32	45.16	45.04	44.93
4,000	60.67	60.42	60.22	60.05	59.90
5,000	75.84	75.53	75.27	75.06	74.88
6,000	91.00	90.63	90.32	90.07	89.85
7,000	106.17	105.74	105.38	105.08	104.83
8,000	121.34	120.84	120.43	120.09	119.80
9,000	136.50	135.95	135.48	135.10	134.78
10,000	151.67	151.05	150.54	150.11	149.75
15,000	227.50	226.58	225.80	225.16	224.62
20,000	303.34	302.10	301.07	300.21	299.50
25,000	379.17	377.62	376.34	375.26	374.37
30,000	455.00	453.15	451.60	450.32	449.24
35,000	530.83	528.67	526.87	525.37	524.12
40,000	606.67	604.19	602.13	600.42	598.99
45,000	682.50	679.72	677.40	675.47	673.86
50,000	758.33	755.24	752.67	750.52	748.73
55,000	834.17	830.76	827.93	825.58	823.61
60,000	910.00	906.29	903.20	900.63	898.48
65,000	985.83	981.81	978.47	975.68	973.35
70,000	1,061.66	1,057.34	1,053.73	1,050.73	1,048.23
75,000	1,137.50	1,132.86	1,129.00	1,125.78	1,123.10
80,000	1,213.33	1,208.38	1,204.26	1,200.83	1,197.97
85,000	1,289.16	1,283.91	1,279.53	1,275.89	1,272.85
90,000	1,365.00	1,359.43	1,354.80	1,350.94	1,347.72
95,000	1,440.83	1,434.95	1,430.06	1,425.99	1,422.59
100,000	1,516.66	1,510.48	1,505.33	1,501.04	1,497.46
110,000	1,668.33	1,661.52	1,655.86	1,651.15	1,647.21
120,000	1,819.99	1,812.57	1,806.39	1,801.25	1,796.96
125,000	1,895.83	1,888.09	1,881.66	1,876.30	1,871.83
130,000	1,971.66	1,963.62	1,956.93	1,951.35	1,946.70
140,000	2,123.32	2,114.67	2,107.46	2,101.46	2,096.45
150,000	2,274.99	2,265.71	2,257.99	2,251.56	2,246.19
160,000	2,426.65	2,416.76	2,408.52	2,401.66	2,395.94
170,000	2,578.32	2,567.81	2,559.06	2,551.77	2,545.69
175,000	2,654.15	2,643.33	2,634.32	2,626.82	2,620.56
180,000	2,729.99	2,718.85	2,709.59	2,701.87	2,695.43
190,000	2,881.65	2,869.90	2,860.12	2,851.97	2,845.18
200,000	3,033.32	3,020.95	3,010.65	3,002.08	2,994.92
220,000	3,336.65	3,323.04	3,311.72	3,302.29	3,294.42
225,000	3,412.48	3,398.57	3,386.99	3,377.34	3,369.29
230,000	3,488.31	3,474.09	3,462.25	3,452.39	3,444.16
240,000	3,639.98	3,625.14	3,612.78	3,602.49	3,593.91
$250,000	3,791.65	3,776.18	3,763.32	3,752.60	3,743.65

Monthly Payment Loans   17.75%

Amortization Period in Years

	26	27	28	29	30
$ 100	1.50	1.50	1.49	1.49	1.49
200	2.99	2.99	2.98	2.98	2.98
300	4.49	4.48	4.47	4.47	4.47
400	5.98	5.97	5.96	5.96	5.95
500	7.48	7.46	7.45	7.45	7.44
600	8.97	8.96	8.94	8.93	8.93
700	10.47	10.45	10.43	10.42	10.41
800	11.96	11.94	11.92	11.91	11.90
900	13.46	13.43	13.41	13.40	13.39
1,000	14.95	14.92	14.90	14.89	14.87
2,000	29.89	29.84	29.80	29.77	29.74
3,000	44.84	44.76	44.70	44.65	44.61
4,000	59.78	59.68	59.60	59.53	59.47
5,000	74.73	74.60	74.50	74.41	74.34
6,000	89.67	89.52	89.40	89.29	89.21
7,000	104.62	104.44	104.30	104.18	104.07
8,000	119.56	119.36	119.20	119.06	118.94
9,000	134.51	134.28	134.10	133.94	133.81
10,000	149.45	149.20	148.99	148.82	148.67
15,000	224.18	223.80	223.49	223.23	223.01
20,000	298.90	298.40	297.98	297.64	297.34
25,000	373.62	373.00	372.48	372.04	371.68
30,000	448.35	447.60	446.97	446.45	446.01
35,000	523.07	522.20	521.47	520.86	520.35
40,000	597.79	596.80	595.96	595.27	594.68
45,000	672.52	671.40	670.46	669.67	669.02
50,000	747.24	745.99	744.95	744.08	743.35
55,000	821.97	820.59	819.45	818.49	817.69
60,000	896.69	895.19	893.94	892.90	892.02
65,000	971.41	969.79	968.44	967.30	966.35
70,000	1,046.14	1,044.39	1,042.93	1,041.71	1,040.69
75,000	1,120.86	1,118.99	1,117.43	1,116.12	1,115.02
80,000	1,195.58	1,193.59	1,191.92	1,190.53	1,189.36
85,000	1,270.31	1,268.19	1,266.42	1,264.93	1,263.69
90,000	1,345.03	1,342.79	1,340.91	1,339.34	1,338.03
95,000	1,419.76	1,417.39	1,415.40	1,413.75	1,412.36
100,000	1,494.48	1,491.98	1,489.90	1,488.16	1,486.70
110,000	1,643.93	1,641.18	1,638.89	1,636.97	1,635.37
120,000	1,793.37	1,790.38	1,787.88	1,785.79	1,784.04
125,000	1,868.10	1,864.98	1,862.37	1,860.19	1,858.37
130,000	1,942.82	1,939.58	1,936.87	1,934.60	1,932.70
140,000	2,092.27	2,088.78	2,085.86	2,083.42	2,081.37
150,000	2,241.72	2,237.97	2,234.85	2,232.23	2,230.04
160,000	2,391.16	2,387.17	2,383.84	2,381.05	2,378.71
170,000	2,540.61	2,536.37	2,532.83	2,529.86	2,527.38
175,000	2,615.33	2,610.97	2,607.32	2,604.27	2,601.72
180,000	2,690.06	2,685.57	2,681.82	2,678.68	2,676.05
190,000	2,839.51	2,834.77	2,830.80	2,827.49	2,824.72
200,000	2,988.95	2,983.96	2,979.79	2,976.31	2,973.39
220,000	3,287.85	3,282.36	3,277.77	3,273.94	3,270.73
225,000	3,362.57	3,356.96	3,352.27	3,348.34	3,345.06
230,000	3,437.30	3,431.56	3,426.76	3,422.75	3,419.40
240,000	3,586.74	3,580.76	3,575.75	3,571.57	3,568.07
$250,000	3,736.19	3,729.95	3,724.74	3,720.38	3,716.74

Table 1   211

18.00%   Monthly Payment Loans

Amortization Period in Years

	5	7	8	10	12
$ 100	2.54	2.11	1.98	1.81	1.70
200	5.08	4.21	3.95	3.61	3.40
300	7.62	6.31	5.92	5.41	5.10
400	10.16	8.41	7.89	7.21	6.80
500	12.70	10.51	9.87	9.01	8.50
600	15.24	12.62	11.84	10.82	10.20
700	17.78	14.72	13.81	12.62	11.90
800	20.32	16.82	15.78	14.42	13.60
900	22.86	18.92	17.76	16.22	15.30
1,000	25.40	21.02	19.73	18.02	17.00
2,000	50.79	42.04	39.45	36.04	33.99
3,000	76.19	63.06	59.17	54.06	50.98
4,000	101.58	84.08	78.90	72.08	67.97
5,000	126.97	105.09	98.62	90.10	84.96
6,000	152.37	126.11	118.34	108.12	101.95
7,000	177.76	147.13	138.07	126.13	118.94
8,000	203.15	168.15	157.79	144.15	135.93
9,000	228.55	189.17	177.51	162.17	152.93
10,000	253.94	210.18	197.24	180.19	169.92
15,000	380.91	315.27	295.85	270.28	254.87
20,000	507.87	420.36	394.47	360.38	339.83
25,000	634.84	525.45	493.09	450.47	424.78
30,000	761.81	630.54	591.70	540.56	509.74
35,000	888.77	735.63	690.32	630.65	594.70
40,000	1,015.74	840.72	788.93	720.75	679.65
45,000	1,142.71	945.81	887.55	810.84	764.61
50,000	1,269.68	1,050.90	986.17	900.93	849.56
55,000	1,396.64	1,155.99	1,084.78	991.02	934.52
60,000	1,523.61	1,261.08	1,183.40	1,081.12	1,019.48
65,000	1,650.58	1,366.16	1,282.01	1,171.21	1,104.43
70,000	1,777.54	1,471.25	1,380.63	1,261.30	1,189.39
75,000	1,904.51	1,576.34	1,479.25	1,351.39	1,274.34
80,000	2,031.48	1,681.43	1,577.86	1,441.49	1,359.30
85,000	2,158.45	1,786.52	1,676.48	1,531.58	1,444.26
90,000	2,285.41	1,891.61	1,775.09	1,621.67	1,529.21
95,000	2,412.38	1,996.70	1,873.71	1,711.76	1,614.17
100,000	2,539.35	2,101.79	1,972.33	1,801.86	1,699.12
110,000	2,793.28	2,311.97	2,169.56	1,982.04	1,869.04
120,000	3,047.22	2,522.15	2,366.79	2,162.23	2,038.95
125,000	3,174.18	2,627.23	2,465.41	2,252.32	2,123.90
130,000	3,301.15	2,732.32	2,564.02	2,342.41	2,208.86
140,000	3,555.08	2,942.50	2,761.25	2,522.60	2,378.77
150,000	3,809.02	3,152.68	2,958.49	2,702.78	2,548.68
160,000	4,062.95	3,362.86	3,155.72	2,882.97	2,718.60
170,000	4,316.89	3,573.04	3,352.95	3,063.15	2,888.51
175,000	4,443.85	3,678.13	3,451.57	3,153.25	2,973.46
180,000	4,570.82	3,783.22	3,550.18	3,243.34	3,058.42
190,000	4,824.76	3,993.39	3,747.42	3,423.52	3,228.33
200,000	5,078.69	4,203.57	3,944.65	3,603.71	3,398.24
220,000	5,586.56	4,623.93	4,339.11	3,964.08	3,738.07
225,000	5,713.53	4,729.02	4,437.73	4,054.17	3,823.02
230,000	5,840.49	4,834.11	4,536.34	4,144.26	3,907.98
240,000	6,094.43	5,044.29	4,733.58	4,324.45	4,077.89
$250,000	6,348.36	5,254.46	4,930.81	4,504.63	4,247.80

Monthly Payment Loans   **18.00%**

Amortization Period in Years

	15	16	17	18	20
$ 100	1.62	1.60	1.58	1.57	1.55
200	3.23	3.19	3.16	3.13	3.09
300	4.84	4.78	4.73	4.69	4.63
400	6.45	6.37	6.31	6.26	6.18
500	8.06	7.96	7.88	7.82	7.72
600	9.67	9.55	9.46	9.38	9.26
700	11.28	11.14	11.03	10.94	10.81
800	12.89	12.74	12.61	12.51	12.35
900	14.50	14.33	14.19	14.07	13.89
1,000	16.11	15.92	15.76	15.63	15.44
2,000	32.21	31.83	31.52	31.26	30.87
3,000	48.32	47.74	47.27	46.89	46.30
4,000	64.42	63.66	63.03	62.51	61.74
5,000	80.53	79.57	78.78	78.14	77.17
6,000	96.63	95.48	94.54	93.77	92.60
7,000	112.73	111.39	110.30	109.39	108.04
8,000	128.84	127.31	126.05	125.02	123.47
9,000	144.94	143.22	141.81	140.65	138.90
10,000	161.05	159.13	157.56	156.27	154.34
15,000	241.57	238.69	236.34	234.41	231.50
20,000	322.09	318.26	315.12	312.54	308.67
25,000	402.61	397.82	393.90	390.68	385.83
30,000	483.13	477.38	472.68	468.81	463.00
35,000	563.65	556.94	551.46	546.95	540.16
40,000	644.17	636.51	630.23	625.08	617.33
45,000	724.69	716.07	709.01	703.22	694.50
50,000	805.22	795.63	787.79	781.35	771.66
55,000	885.74	875.20	866.57	859.49	848.83
60,000	966.26	954.76	945.35	937.62	925.99
65,000	1,046.78	1,034.32	1,024.13	1,015.75	1,003.16
70,000	1,127.30	1,113.88	1,102.91	1,093.89	1,080.32
75,000	1,207.82	1,193.45	1,181.68	1,172.02	1,157.49
80,000	1,288.34	1,273.01	1,260.46	1,250.16	1,234.65
85,000	1,368.86	1,352.57	1,339.24	1,328.29	1,311.82
90,000	1,449.38	1,432.14	1,418.02	1,406.43	1,388.99
95,000	1,529.90	1,511.70	1,496.80	1,484.56	1,466.15
100,000	1,610.43	1,591.26	1,575.58	1,562.70	1,543.32
110,000	1,771.47	1,750.39	1,733.14	1,718.97	1,697.65
120,000	1,932.51	1,909.51	1,890.69	1,875.23	1,851.98
125,000	2,013.03	1,989.07	1,969.47	1,953.37	1,929.14
130,000	2,093.55	2,068.64	2,048.25	2,031.50	2,006.31
140,000	2,254.59	2,227.76	2,205.81	2,187.77	2,160.64
150,000	2,415.64	2,386.89	2,363.36	2,344.04	2,314.97
160,000	2,576.68	2,546.01	2,520.92	2,500.31	2,469.30
170,000	2,737.72	2,705.14	2,678.48	2,656.58	2,623.63
175,000	2,818.24	2,784.70	2,757.26	2,734.71	2,700.80
180,000	2,898.76	2,864.27	2,836.04	2,812.85	2,777.97
190,000	3,059.80	3,023.39	2,993.59	2,969.12	2,932.30
200,000	3,220.85	3,182.52	3,151.15	3,125.39	3,086.63
220,000	3,542.93	3,500.77	3,466.27	3,437.93	3,395.29
225,000	3,623.45	3,580.33	3,545.04	3,516.06	3,472.46
230,000	3,703.97	3,659.89	3,623.82	3,594.20	3,549.62
240,000	3,865.02	3,819.02	3,781.38	3,750.46	3,703.95
$250,000	4,026.06	3,978.14	3,938.94	3,906.73	3,858.28

Table 1   213

18.00%   Monthly Payment Loans

Amortization Period in Years

	21	22	23	24	25
$ 100	1.54	1.54	1.53	1.53	1.52
200	3.08	3.07	3.06	3.05	3.04
300	4.61	4.60	4.58	4.57	4.56
400	6.15	6.13	6.11	6.09	6.07
500	7.69	7.66	7.63	7.61	7.59
600	9.22	9.19	9.16	9.13	9.11
700	10.76	10.72	10.68	10.65	10.63
800	12.29	12.25	12.21	12.17	12.14
900	13.83	13.78	13.73	13.69	13.66
1,000	15.37	15.31	15.26	15.21	15.18
2,000	30.73	30.61	30.51	30.42	30.35
3,000	46.09	45.91	45.76	45.63	45.53
4,000	61.45	61.21	61.01	60.84	60.70
5,000	76.81	76.51	76.26	76.05	75.88
6,000	92.17	91.81	91.51	91.26	91.05
7,000	107.53	107.11	106.76	106.47	106.23
8,000	122.89	122.41	122.01	121.68	121.40
9,000	138.25	137.71	137.26	136.88	136.57
10,000	153.61	153.01	152.51	152.09	151.75
15,000	230.41	229.51	228.76	228.14	227.62
20,000	307.22	306.01	305.01	304.18	303.49
25,000	384.02	382.51	381.27	380.23	379.36
30,000	460.82	459.02	457.52	456.27	455.23
35,000	537.62	535.52	533.77	532.32	531.11
40,000	614.43	612.02	610.02	608.36	606.98
45,000	691.23	688.52	686.27	684.40	682.85
50,000	768.03	765.02	762.53	760.45	758.72
55,000	844.84	841.53	838.78	836.49	834.59
60,000	921.64	918.03	915.03	912.54	910.46
65,000	998.44	994.53	991.28	988.58	986.33
70,000	1,075.24	1,071.03	1,067.53	1,064.63	1,062.21
75,000	1,152.05	1,147.53	1,143.79	1,140.67	1,138.08
80,000	1,228.85	1,224.04	1,220.04	1,216.71	1,213.95
85,000	1,305.65	1,300.54	1,296.29	1,292.76	1,289.82
90,000	1,382.45	1,377.04	1,372.54	1,368.80	1,365.69
95,000	1,459.26	1,453.54	1,448.79	1,444.85	1,441.56
100,000	1,536.06	1,530.04	1,525.05	1,520.89	1,517.43
110,000	1,689.67	1,683.05	1,677.55	1,672.98	1,669.18
120,000	1,843.27	1,836.05	1,830.05	1,825.07	1,820.92
125,000	1,920.07	1,912.55	1,906.31	1,901.11	1,896.79
130,000	1,996.88	1,989.05	1,982.56	1,977.16	1,972.66
140,000	2,150.48	2,142.06	2,135.06	2,129.25	2,124.41
150,000	2,304.09	2,295.06	2,287.57	2,281.34	2,276.15
160,000	2,457.69	2,448.07	2,440.07	2,433.42	2,427.89
170,000	2,611.30	2,601.07	2,592.57	2,585.51	2,579.64
175,000	2,688.10	2,677.57	2,668.83	2,661.56	2,655.51
180,000	2,764.90	2,754.07	2,745.08	2,737.60	2,731.38
190,000	2,918.51	2,907.08	2,897.58	2,889.69	2,883.12
200,000	3,072.11	3,060.08	3,050.09	3,041.78	3,034.86
220,000	3,379.33	3,366.09	3,355.10	3,345.96	3,338.35
225,000	3,456.13	3,442.59	3,431.35	3,422.00	3,414.22
230,000	3,532.93	3,519.09	3,507.60	3,498.05	3,490.09
240,000	3,686.54	3,672.10	3,660.10	3,650.13	3,641.84
$250,000	3,840.14	3,825.10	3,812.61	3,802.22	3,793.58

Monthly Payment Loans   18.00%

Amortization Period in Years

	26	27	28	29	30
$ 100	1.52	1.52	1.52	1.51	1.51
200	3.03	3.03	3.03	3.02	3.02
300	4.55	4.54	4.54	4.53	4.53
400	6.06	6.05	6.05	6.04	6.03
500	7.58	7.57	7.56	7.55	7.54
600	9.09	9.08	9.07	9.06	9.05
700	10.61	10.59	10.58	10.56	10.55
800	12.12	12.10	12.09	12.07	12.06
900	13.64	13.61	13.60	13.58	13.57
1,000	15.15	15.13	15.11	15.09	15.08
2,000	30.30	30.25	30.21	30.17	30.15
3,000	45.44	45.37	45.31	45.26	45.22
4,000	60.59	60.49	60.41	60.34	60.29
5,000	75.73	75.61	75.51	75.43	75.36
6,000	90.88	90.73	90.61	90.51	90.43
7,000	106.02	105.86	105.72	105.60	105.50
8,000	121.17	120.98	120.82	120.68	120.57
9,000	136.31	136.10	135.92	135.77	135.64
10,000	151.46	151.22	151.02	150.85	150.71
15,000	227.19	226.83	226.53	226.28	226.07
20,000	302.92	302.44	302.03	301.70	301.42
25,000	378.64	378.04	377.54	377.12	376.78
30,000	454.37	453.65	453.05	452.55	452.13
35,000	530.10	529.26	528.56	527.97	527.48
40,000	605.83	604.87	604.06	603.40	602.84
45,000	681.55	680.47	679.57	678.82	678.19
50,000	757.28	756.08	755.08	754.24	753.55
55,000	833.01	831.69	830.59	829.67	828.90
60,000	908.74	907.30	906.09	905.09	904.26
65,000	984.46	982.90	981.60	980.52	979.61
70,000	1,060.19	1,058.51	1,057.11	1,055.94	1,054.96
75,000	1,135.92	1,134.12	1,132.62	1,131.36	1,130.32
80,000	1,211.65	1,209.73	1,208.12	1,206.79	1,205.67
85,000	1,287.37	1,285.34	1,283.63	1,282.21	1,281.03
90,000	1,363.10	1,360.94	1,359.14	1,357.64	1,356.38
95,000	1,438.83	1,436.55	1,434.65	1,433.06	1,431.74
100,000	1,514.56	1,512.16	1,510.15	1,508.48	1,507.09
110,000	1,666.01	1,663.37	1,661.17	1,659.33	1,657.80
120,000	1,817.47	1,814.59	1,812.18	1,810.18	1,808.51
125,000	1,893.19	1,890.19	1,887.69	1,885.60	1,883.86
130,000	1,968.92	1,965.80	1,963.20	1,961.03	1,959.22
140,000	2,120.38	2,117.02	2,114.21	2,111.88	2,109.92
150,000	2,271.83	2,268.23	2,265.23	2,262.72	2,260.63
160,000	2,423.29	2,419.45	2,416.24	2,413.57	2,411.34
170,000	2,574.74	2,570.66	2,567.26	2,564.42	2,562.05
175,000	2,650.47	2,646.27	2,642.77	2,639.84	2,637.40
180,000	2,726.20	2,721.88	2,718.27	2,715.27	2,712.76
190,000	2,877.65	2,873.09	2,869.29	2,866.12	2,863.47
200,000	3,029.11	3,024.31	3,020.30	3,016.96	3,014.18
220,000	3,332.02	3,326.74	3,322.33	3,318.66	3,315.59
225,000	3,407.74	3,402.34	3,397.84	3,394.08	3,390.95
230,000	3,483.47	3,477.95	3,473.35	3,469.51	3,466.30
240,000	3,634.93	3,629.17	3,624.36	3,620.36	3,617.01
$250,000	3,786.38	3,780.38	3,775.38	3,771.20	3,767.72

Table 1   215

18.25%   Monthly Payment Loans

Amortization Period in Years

	5	7	8	10	12
$ 100	2.56	2.12	1.99	1.82	1.72
200	5.11	4.24	3.98	3.64	3.44
300	7.66	6.35	5.97	5.46	5.15
400	10.22	8.47	7.96	7.28	6.87
500	12.77	10.59	9.94	9.09	8.59
600	15.32	12.70	11.93	10.91	10.30
700	17.88	14.82	13.92	12.73	12.02
800	20.43	16.94	15.91	14.55	13.73
900	22.98	19.05	17.89	16.37	15.45
1,000	25.53	21.17	19.88	18.18	17.17
2,000	51.06	42.33	39.76	36.36	34.33
3,000	76.59	63.50	59.63	54.54	51.49
4,000	102.12	84.66	79.51	72.72	68.65
5,000	127.65	105.83	99.38	90.90	85.81
6,000	153.18	126.99	119.26	109.08	102.97
7,000	178.71	148.16	139.13	127.26	120.13
8,000	204.24	169.32	159.01	145.44	137.29
9,000	229.77	190.49	178.88	163.62	154.45
10,000	255.30	211.65	198.76	181.80	171.61
15,000	382.95	317.47	298.13	272.70	257.42
20,000	510.60	423.30	397.51	363.60	343.22
25,000	638.25	529.12	496.88	454.50	429.03
30,000	765.89	634.94	596.26	545.40	514.83
35,000	893.54	740.77	695.63	636.30	600.63
40,000	1,021.19	846.59	795.01	727.20	686.44
45,000	1,148.84	952.41	894.38	818.10	772.24
50,000	1,276.49	1,058.24	993.76	908.99	858.05
55,000	1,404.13	1,164.06	1,093.13	999.89	943.85
60,000	1,531.78	1,269.88	1,192.51	1,090.79	1,029.66
65,000	1,659.43	1,375.71	1,291.88	1,181.69	1,115.46
70,000	1,787.08	1,481.53	1,391.26	1,272.59	1,201.26
75,000	1,914.73	1,587.35	1,490.63	1,363.49	1,287.07
80,000	2,042.37	1,693.18	1,590.01	1,454.39	1,372.87
85,000	2,170.02	1,799.00	1,689.38	1,545.29	1,458.68
90,000	2,297.67	1,904.82	1,788.76	1,636.19	1,544.48
95,000	2,425.32	2,010.64	1,888.13	1,727.08	1,630.29
100,000	2,552.97	2,116.47	1,987.51	1,817.98	1,716.09
110,000	2,808.26	2,328.11	2,186.26	1,999.78	1,887.70
120,000	3,063.56	2,539.76	2,385.01	2,181.58	2,059.31
125,000	3,191.21	2,645.58	2,484.39	2,272.48	2,145.11
130,000	3,318.86	2,751.41	2,583.76	2,363.38	2,230.91
140,000	3,574.15	2,963.05	2,782.51	2,545.17	2,402.52
150,000	3,829.45	3,174.70	2,981.26	2,726.97	2,574.13
160,000	4,084.74	3,386.35	3,180.01	2,908.77	2,745.74
170,000	4,340.04	3,597.99	3,378.76	3,090.57	2,917.35
175,000	4,467.69	3,703.81	3,478.14	3,181.47	3,003.15
180,000	4,595.34	3,809.64	3,577.51	3,272.37	3,088.96
190,000	4,850.63	4,021.28	3,776.26	3,454.16	3,260.57
200,000	5,105.93	4,232.93	3,975.02	3,635.96	3,432.17
220,000	5,616.52	4,656.22	4,372.52	3,999.56	3,775.39
225,000	5,744.17	4,762.05	4,471.89	4,090.46	3,861.20
230,000	5,871.82	4,867.87	4,571.27	4,181.35	3,947.00
240,000	6,127.11	5,079.52	4,770.02	4,363.15	4,118.61
$250,000	6,382.41	5,291.16	4,968.77	4,544.95	4,290.22

Monthly Payment Loans   **18.25%**

Amortization Period in Years

	15	16	17	18	20
$ 100	1.63	1.61	1.60	1.59	1.57
200	3.26	3.22	3.19	3.17	3.13
300	4.89	4.83	4.79	4.75	4.69
400	6.52	6.44	6.38	6.33	6.26
500	8.15	8.05	7.98	7.91	7.82
600	9.78	9.66	9.57	9.49	9.38
700	11.40	11.27	11.16	11.08	10.94
800	13.03	12.88	12.76	12.66	12.51
900	14.66	14.49	14.35	14.24	14.07
1,000	16.29	16.10	15.95	15.82	15.63
2,000	32.57	32.20	31.89	31.64	31.26
3,000	48.86	48.29	47.83	47.45	46.88
4,000	65.14	64.39	63.77	63.27	62.51
5,000	81.43	80.48	79.71	79.08	78.13
6,000	97.71	96.58	95.65	94.90	93.76
7,000	114.00	112.68	111.60	110.71	109.39
8,000	130.28	128.77	127.54	126.53	125.01
9,000	146.56	144.87	143.48	142.34	140.64
10,000	162.85	160.96	159.42	158.16	156.26
15,000	244.27	241.44	239.13	237.23	234.39
20,000	325.69	321.92	318.84	316.31	312.52
25,000	407.12	402.40	398.55	395.39	390.65
30,000	488.54	482.88	478.25	474.46	468.78
35,000	569.96	563.36	557.96	553.54	546.91
40,000	651.38	643.83	637.67	632.62	625.04
45,000	732.80	724.31	717.38	711.69	703.17
50,000	814.23	804.79	797.09	790.77	781.29
55,000	895.65	885.27	876.79	869.85	859.42
60,000	977.07	965.75	956.50	948.92	937.55
65,000	1,058.49	1,046.23	1,036.21	1,028.00	1,015.68
70,000	1,139.91	1,126.71	1,115.92	1,107.08	1,093.81
75,000	1,221.34	1,207.18	1,195.63	1,186.15	1,171.94
80,000	1,302.76	1,287.66	1,275.34	1,265.23	1,250.07
85,000	1,384.18	1,368.14	1,355.04	1,344.30	1,328.20
90,000	1,465.60	1,448.62	1,434.75	1,423.38	1,406.33
95,000	1,547.02	1,529.10	1,514.46	1,502.46	1,484.45
100,000	1,628.45	1,609.58	1,594.17	1,581.53	1,562.58
110,000	1,791.29	1,770.54	1,753.58	1,739.69	1,718.84
120,000	1,954.13	1,931.49	1,913.00	1,897.84	1,875.10
125,000	2,035.56	2,011.97	1,992.71	1,976.92	1,953.23
130,000	2,116.98	2,092.45	2,072.42	2,055.99	2,031.36
140,000	2,279.82	2,253.41	2,231.83	2,214.15	2,187.61
150,000	2,442.67	2,414.36	2,391.25	2,372.30	2,343.87
160,000	2,605.51	2,575.32	2,550.67	2,530.45	2,500.13
170,000	2,768.35	2,736.28	2,710.08	2,688.60	2,656.39
175,000	2,849.78	2,816.76	2,789.79	2,767.68	2,734.52
180,000	2,931.20	2,897.24	2,869.50	2,846.76	2,812.65
190,000	3,094.04	3,058.19	3,028.91	3,004.91	2,968.90
200,000	3,256.89	3,219.15	3,188.33	3,163.06	3,125.16
220,000	3,582.57	3,541.07	3,507.16	3,479.37	3,437.68
225,000	3,664.00	3,621.54	3,586.87	3,558.45	3,515.81
230,000	3,745.42	3,702.02	3,666.58	3,637.52	3,593.93
240,000	3,908.26	3,862.98	3,826.00	3,795.68	3,750.19
$250,000	4,071.11	4,023.94	3,985.41	3,953.83	3,906.45

Table 1   217

18.25% Monthly Payment Loans

Amortization Period in Years

		21	22	23	24	25
$	100	1.56	1.55	1.55	1.55	1.54
	200	3.12	3.10	3.09	3.09	3.08
	300	4.67	4.65	4.64	4.63	4.62
	400	6.23	6.20	6.18	6.17	6.15
	500	7.78	7.75	7.73	7.71	7.69
	600	9.34	9.30	9.27	9.25	9.23
	700	10.89	10.85	10.82	10.79	10.77
	800	12.45	12.40	12.36	12.33	12.30
	900	14.00	13.95	13.91	13.87	13.84
	1,000	15.56	15.50	15.45	15.41	15.38
	2,000	31.12	31.00	30.90	30.82	30.75
	3,000	46.67	46.49	46.35	46.23	46.13
	4,000	62.23	61.99	61.80	61.64	61.50
	5,000	77.78	77.49	77.25	77.04	76.88
	6,000	93.34	92.98	92.69	92.45	92.25
	7,000	108.89	108.48	108.14	107.86	107.63
	8,000	124.45	123.98	123.59	123.27	123.00
	9,000	140.00	139.47	139.04	138.68	138.37
	10,000	155.56	154.97	154.49	154.08	153.75
	15,000	233.33	232.45	231.73	231.12	230.62
	20,000	311.11	309.94	308.97	308.16	307.49
	25,000	388.88	387.42	386.21	385.20	384.36
	30,000	466.66	464.90	463.45	462.24	461.24
	35,000	544.43	542.38	540.69	539.28	538.11
	40,000	622.21	619.87	617.93	616.32	614.98
	45,000	699.98	697.35	695.17	693.36	691.85
	50,000	777.76	774.83	772.41	770.39	768.72
	55,000	855.53	852.31	849.65	847.43	845.60
	60,000	933.31	929.80	926.89	924.47	922.47
	65,000	1,011.08	1,007.28	1,004.13	1,001.51	999.34
	70,000	1,088.86	1,084.76	1,081.37	1,078.55	1,076.21
	75,000	1,166.63	1,162.24	1,158.61	1,155.59	1,153.08
	80,000	1,244.41	1,239.73	1,235.85	1,232.63	1,229.96
	85,000	1,322.18	1,317.21	1,313.09	1,309.67	1,306.83
	90,000	1,399.96	1,394.69	1,390.33	1,386.71	1,383.70
	95,000	1,477.73	1,472.17	1,467.57	1,463.75	1,460.57
	100,000	1,555.51	1,549.66	1,544.81	1,540.78	1,537.44
	110,000	1,711.06	1,704.62	1,699.29	1,694.86	1,691.19
	120,000	1,866.61	1,859.59	1,853.77	1,848.94	1,844.93
	125,000	1,944.39	1,937.07	1,931.01	1,925.98	1,921.80
	130,000	2,022.16	2,014.55	2,008.25	2,003.02	1,998.68
	140,000	2,177.71	2,169.52	2,162.73	2,157.10	2,152.42
	150,000	2,333.26	2,324.48	2,317.21	2,311.17	2,306.16
	160,000	2,488.81	2,479.45	2,471.69	2,465.25	2,459.91
	170,000	2,644.36	2,634.41	2,626.17	2,619.33	2,613.65
	175,000	2,722.14	2,711.90	2,703.41	2,696.37	2,690.52
	180,000	2,799.91	2,789.38	2,780.65	2,773.41	2,767.39
	190,000	2,955.46	2,944.34	2,935.13	2,927.49	2,921.14
	200,000	3,111.01	3,099.31	3,089.61	3,081.56	3,074.88
	220,000	3,422.11	3,409.24	3,398.57	3,389.72	3,382.37
	225,000	3,499.89	3,486.72	3,475.81	3,466.76	3,459.24
	230,000	3,577.67	3,564.20	3,553.05	3,543.80	3,536.11
	240,000	3,733.22	3,719.17	3,707.53	3,697.87	3,689.86
$250,000		3,888.77	3,874.13	3,862.01	3,851.95	3,843.60

Monthly Payment Loans   **18.25%**

Amortization Period in Years

	26	27	28	29	30
$ 100	1.54	1.54	1.54	1.53	1.53
200	3.07	3.07	3.07	3.06	3.06
300	4.61	4.60	4.60	4.59	4.59
400	6.14	6.13	6.13	6.12	6.12
500	7.68	7.67	7.66	7.65	7.64
600	9.21	9.20	9.19	9.18	9.17
700	10.75	10.73	10.72	10.71	10.70
800	12.28	12.26	12.25	12.24	12.23
900	13.82	13.80	13.78	13.76	13.75
1,000	15.35	15.33	15.31	15.29	15.28
2,000	30.70	30.65	30.61	30.58	30.56
3,000	46.04	45.98	45.92	45.87	45.83
4,000	61.39	61.30	61.22	61.16	61.11
5,000	76.74	76.62	76.53	76.45	76.38
6,000	92.08	91.95	91.83	91.74	91.66
7,000	107.43	107.27	107.14	107.02	106.93
8,000	122.78	122.59	122.44	122.31	122.21
9,000	138.12	137.92	137.74	137.60	137.48
10,000	153.47	153.24	153.05	152.89	152.76
15,000	230.20	229.86	229.57	229.33	229.13
20,000	306.94	306.48	306.09	305.77	305.51
25,000	383.67	383.09	382.61	382.21	381.88
30,000	460.40	459.71	459.14	458.66	458.26
35,000	537.14	536.33	535.66	535.10	534.63
40,000	613.87	612.95	612.18	611.54	611.01
45,000	690.60	689.56	688.70	687.98	687.38
50,000	767.34	766.18	765.22	764.42	763.76
55,000	844.07	842.80	841.74	840.86	840.13
60,000	920.80	919.42	918.27	917.31	916.51
65,000	997.54	996.04	994.79	993.75	992.88
70,000	1,074.27	1,072.65	1,071.31	1,070.19	1,069.26
75,000	1,151.00	1,149.27	1,147.83	1,146.63	1,145.63
80,000	1,227.74	1,225.89	1,224.35	1,223.07	1,222.01
85,000	1,304.47	1,302.51	1,300.87	1,299.51	1,298.38
90,000	1,381.20	1,379.12	1,377.40	1,375.96	1,374.76
95,000	1,457.93	1,455.74	1,453.92	1,452.40	1,451.13
100,000	1,534.67	1,532.36	1,530.44	1,528.84	1,527.51
110,000	1,688.13	1,685.59	1,683.48	1,681.72	1,680.26
120,000	1,841.60	1,838.83	1,836.53	1,834.61	1,833.01
125,000	1,918.33	1,915.45	1,913.05	1,911.05	1,909.38
130,000	1,995.07	1,992.07	1,989.57	1,987.49	1,985.76
140,000	2,148.53	2,145.30	2,142.61	2,140.37	2,138.51
150,000	2,302.00	2,298.54	2,295.66	2,293.26	2,291.26
160,000	2,455.47	2,451.77	2,448.70	2,446.14	2,444.01
170,000	2,608.93	2,605.01	2,601.74	2,599.02	2,596.76
175,000	2,685.66	2,681.62	2,678.26	2,675.47	2,673.14
180,000	2,762.40	2,758.24	2,754.79	2,751.91	2,749.51
190,000	2,915.86	2,911.48	2,907.83	2,904.79	2,902.26
200,000	3,069.33	3,064.71	3,060.87	3,057.67	3,055.01
220,000	3,376.26	3,371.18	3,366.96	3,363.44	3,360.51
225,000	3,453.00	3,447.80	3,443.48	3,439.88	3,436.89
230,000	3,529.73	3,524.42	3,520.00	3,516.32	3,513.26
240,000	3,683.20	3,677.65	3,673.05	3,669.21	3,666.01
$250,000	3,836.66	3,830.89	3,826.09	3,822.09	3,818.76

Table 1   219

18.50%   Monthly Payment Loans

Amortization Period in Years

	5	7	8	10	12
$ 100	2.57	2.14	2.01	1.84	1.74
200	5.14	4.27	4.01	3.67	3.47
300	7.70	6.40	6.01	5.51	5.20
400	10.27	8.53	8.02	7.34	6.94
500	12.84	10.66	10.02	9.18	8.67
600	15.40	12.79	12.02	11.01	10.40
700	17.97	14.92	14.02	12.84	12.14
800	20.54	17.05	16.03	14.68	13.87
900	23.10	19.19	18.03	16.51	15.60
1,000	25.67	21.32	20.03	18.35	17.34
2,000	51.34	42.63	40.06	36.69	34.67
3,000	77.00	63.94	60.09	55.03	52.00
4,000	102.67	85.25	80.11	73.37	69.33
5,000	128.34	106.56	100.14	91.71	86.66
6,000	154.00	127.88	120.17	110.05	103.99
7,000	179.67	149.19	140.20	128.40	121.32
8,000	205.33	170.50	160.22	146.74	138.65
9,000	231.00	191.81	180.25	165.08	155.99
10,000	256.67	213.12	200.28	183.42	173.32
15,000	385.00	319.68	300.42	275.13	259.97
20,000	513.33	426.24	400.55	366.84	346.63
25,000	641.66	532.80	500.69	458.55	433.28
30,000	769.99	639.36	600.83	550.25	519.94
35,000	898.32	745.92	700.97	641.96	606.59
40,000	1,026.65	852.48	801.10	733.67	693.25
45,000	1,154.98	959.04	901.24	825.38	779.91
50,000	1,283.32	1,065.60	1,001.38	917.09	866.56
55,000	1,411.65	1,172.16	1,101.51	1,008.80	953.22
60,000	1,539.98	1,278.72	1,201.65	1,100.50	1,039.87
65,000	1,668.31	1,385.28	1,301.79	1,192.21	1,126.53
70,000	1,796.64	1,491.84	1,401.93	1,283.92	1,213.18
75,000	1,924.97	1,598.40	1,502.06	1,375.63	1,299.84
80,000	2,053.30	1,704.96	1,602.20	1,467.34	1,386.50
85,000	2,181.63	1,811.52	1,702.34	1,559.05	1,473.15
90,000	2,309.96	1,918.08	1,802.47	1,650.75	1,559.81
95,000	2,438.29	2,024.64	1,902.61	1,742.46	1,646.46
100,000	2,566.63	2,131.20	2,002.75	1,834.17	1,733.12
110,000	2,823.29	2,344.32	2,203.02	2,017.59	1,906.43
120,000	3,079.95	2,557.44	2,403.30	2,201.00	2,079.74
125,000	3,208.28	2,663.99	2,503.44	2,292.71	2,166.40
130,000	3,336.61	2,770.55	2,603.57	2,384.42	2,253.05
140,000	3,593.27	2,983.67	2,803.85	2,567.84	2,426.36
150,000	3,849.94	3,196.79	3,004.12	2,751.25	2,599.68
160,000	4,106.60	3,409.91	3,204.40	2,934.67	2,772.99
170,000	4,363.26	3,623.03	3,404.67	3,118.09	2,946.30
175,000	4,491.59	3,729.59	3,504.81	3,209.79	3,032.95
180,000	4,619.92	3,836.15	3,604.94	3,301.50	3,119.61
190,000	4,876.58	4,049.27	3,805.22	3,484.92	3,292.92
200,000	5,133.25	4,262.39	4,005.49	3,668.34	3,466.23
220,000	5,646.57	4,688.63	4,406.04	4,035.17	3,812.86
225,000	5,774.90	4,795.19	4,506.18	4,126.88	3,899.51
230,000	5,903.23	4,901.75	4,606.32	4,218.59	3,986.17
240,000	6,159.90	5,114.87	4,806.59	4,402.00	4,159.48
$250,000	6,416.56	5,327.98	5,006.87	4,585.42	4,332.79

Monthly Payment Loans   18.50%

Amortization Period in Years

	15	16	17	18	20
$ 100	1.65	1.63	1.62	1.61	1.59
200	3.30	3.26	3.23	3.21	3.17
300	4.94	4.89	4.84	4.81	4.75
400	6.59	6.52	6.46	6.41	6.33
500	8.24	8.14	8.07	8.01	7.91
600	9.88	9.77	9.68	9.61	9.50
700	11.53	11.40	11.29	11.21	11.08
800	13.18	13.03	12.91	12.81	12.66
900	14.82	14.66	14.52	14.41	14.24
1,000	16.47	16.28	16.13	16.01	15.82
2,000	32.94	32.56	32.26	32.01	31.64
3,000	49.40	48.84	48.39	48.02	47.46
4,000	65.87	65.12	64.52	64.02	63.28
5,000	82.33	81.40	80.65	80.03	79.10
6,000	98.80	97.68	96.77	96.03	94.92
7,000	115.26	113.96	112.90	112.03	110.74
8,000	131.73	130.24	129.03	128.04	126.56
9,000	148.19	146.52	145.16	144.04	142.38
10,000	164.66	162.80	161.29	160.05	158.19
15,000	246.98	244.20	241.93	240.07	237.29
20,000	329.31	325.60	322.57	320.09	316.38
25,000	411.64	406.99	403.21	400.11	395.48
30,000	493.96	488.39	483.85	480.13	474.57
35,000	576.29	569.79	564.49	560.15	553.67
40,000	658.61	651.19	645.13	640.17	632.76
45,000	740.94	732.58	725.77	720.20	711.86
50,000	823.27	813.98	806.41	800.22	790.95
55,000	905.59	895.38	887.05	880.24	870.05
60,000	987.92	976.78	967.69	960.26	949.14
65,000	1,070.25	1,058.17	1,048.33	1,040.28	1,028.24
70,000	1,152.57	1,139.57	1,128.97	1,120.30	1,107.33
75,000	1,234.90	1,220.97	1,209.61	1,200.32	1,186.43
80,000	1,317.22	1,302.37	1,290.25	1,280.34	1,265.52
85,000	1,399.55	1,383.76	1,370.90	1,360.37	1,344.62
90,000	1,481.88	1,465.16	1,451.54	1,440.39	1,423.71
95,000	1,564.20	1,546.56	1,532.18	1,520.41	1,502.81
100,000	1,646.53	1,627.96	1,612.82	1,600.43	1,581.90
110,000	1,811.18	1,790.75	1,774.10	1,760.47	1,740.09
120,000	1,975.83	1,953.55	1,935.38	1,920.51	1,898.28
125,000	2,058.16	2,034.95	2,016.02	2,000.54	1,977.38
130,000	2,140.49	2,116.34	2,096.66	2,080.56	2,056.47
140,000	2,305.14	2,279.14	2,257.94	2,240.60	2,214.66
150,000	2,469.79	2,441.93	2,419.22	2,400.64	2,372.85
160,000	2,634.44	2,604.73	2,580.50	2,560.68	2,531.04
170,000	2,799.09	2,767.52	2,741.79	2,720.73	2,689.23
175,000	2,881.42	2,848.92	2,822.43	2,800.75	2,768.32
180,000	2,963.75	2,930.32	2,903.07	2,880.77	2,847.42
190,000	3,128.40	3,093.11	3,064.35	3,040.81	3,005.61
200,000	3,293.05	3,255.91	3,225.63	3,200.85	3,163.80
220,000	3,622.36	3,581.50	3,548.19	3,520.94	3,480.18
225,000	3,704.68	3,662.90	3,628.83	3,600.96	3,559.27
230,000	3,787.01	3,744.30	3,709.47	3,680.98	3,638.37
240,000	3,951.66	3,907.09	3,870.75	3,841.02	3,796.56
$250,000	4,116.31	4,069.89	4,032.04	4,001.07	3,954.75

Table 1   221

18.50%   Monthly Payment Loans

Amortization Period in Years

	21	22	23	24	25
$ 100	1.58	1.57	1.57	1.57	1.56
200	3.16	3.14	3.13	3.13	3.12
300	4.73	4.71	4.70	4.69	4.68
400	6.31	6.28	6.26	6.25	6.23
500	7.88	7.85	7.83	7.81	7.79
600	9.46	9.42	9.39	9.37	9.35
700	11.03	10.99	10.96	10.93	10.91
800	12.61	12.56	12.52	12.49	12.46
900	14.18	14.13	14.09	14.05	14.02
1,000	15.76	15.70	15.65	15.61	15.58
2,000	31.51	31.39	31.30	31.22	31.15
3,000	47.26	47.08	46.94	46.83	46.73
4,000	63.01	62.78	62.59	62.43	62.30
5,000	78.76	78.47	78.24	78.04	77.88
6,000	94.51	94.16	93.88	93.65	93.45
7,000	110.26	109.86	109.53	109.25	109.03
8,000	126.01	125.55	125.17	124.86	124.60
9,000	141.76	141.24	140.82	140.47	140.18
10,000	157.51	156.94	156.47	156.08	155.75
15,000	236.26	235.40	234.70	234.11	233.63
20,000	315.01	313.87	312.93	312.15	311.50
25,000	393.76	392.33	391.16	390.18	389.38
30,000	472.51	470.80	469.39	468.22	467.25
35,000	551.26	549.26	547.62	546.25	545.12
40,000	630.01	627.73	625.85	624.29	623.00
45,000	708.76	706.20	704.08	702.32	700.87
50,000	787.51	784.66	782.31	780.36	778.75
55,000	866.26	863.13	860.54	858.40	856.62
60,000	945.01	941.59	938.77	936.43	934.50
65,000	1,023.76	1,020.06	1,017.00	1,014.47	1,012.37
70,000	1,102.51	1,098.52	1,095.23	1,092.50	1,090.24
75,000	1,181.26	1,176.99	1,173.46	1,170.54	1,168.12
80,000	1,260.01	1,255.45	1,251.69	1,248.57	1,245.99
85,000	1,338.76	1,333.92	1,329.92	1,326.61	1,323.87
90,000	1,417.51	1,412.39	1,408.15	1,404.64	1,401.74
95,000	1,496.26	1,490.85	1,486.38	1,482.68	1,479.61
100,000	1,575.01	1,569.32	1,564.61	1,560.72	1,557.49
110,000	1,732.51	1,726.25	1,721.07	1,716.79	1,713.24
120,000	1,890.01	1,883.18	1,877.53	1,872.86	1,868.99
125,000	1,968.76	1,961.64	1,955.76	1,950.89	1,946.86
130,000	2,047.51	2,040.11	2,033.99	2,028.93	2,024.73
140,000	2,205.01	2,197.04	2,190.45	2,185.00	2,180.48
150,000	2,362.51	2,353.97	2,346.91	2,341.07	2,336.23
160,000	2,520.01	2,510.90	2,503.37	2,497.14	2,491.98
170,000	2,677.51	2,667.83	2,659.84	2,653.21	2,647.73
175,000	2,756.26	2,746.30	2,738.07	2,731.25	2,725.60
180,000	2,835.01	2,824.77	2,816.30	2,809.28	2,803.48
190,000	2,992.51	2,981.70	2,972.76	2,965.36	2,959.22
200,000	3,150.01	3,138.63	3,129.22	3,121.43	3,114.97
220,000	3,465.01	3,452.49	3,442.14	3,433.57	3,426.47
225,000	3,543.76	3,530.96	3,520.37	3,511.60	3,504.34
230,000	3,622.51	3,609.42	3,598.60	3,589.64	3,582.22
240,000	3,780.01	3,766.35	3,755.06	3,745.71	3,737.97
$250,000	3,937.51	3,923.28	3,911.52	3,901.78	3,893.72

Monthly Payment Loans   18.50%

Amortization Period in Years

	26	27	28	29	30
$ 100	1.56	1.56	1.56	1.55	1.55
200	3.11	3.11	3.11	3.10	3.10
300	4.67	4.66	4.66	4.65	4.65
400	6.22	6.22	6.21	6.20	6.20
500	7.78	7.77	7.76	7.75	7.74
600	9.33	9.32	9.31	9.30	9.29
700	10.89	10.87	10.86	10.85	10.84
800	12.44	12.43	12.41	12.40	12.39
900	14.00	13.98	13.96	13.95	13.94
1,000	15.55	15.53	15.51	15.50	15.48
2,000	31.10	31.06	31.02	30.99	30.96
3,000	46.65	46.58	46.53	46.48	46.44
4,000	62.20	62.11	62.03	61.97	61.92
5,000	77.75	77.63	77.54	77.47	77.40
6,000	93.29	93.16	93.05	92.96	92.88
7,000	108.84	108.69	108.56	108.45	108.36
8,000	124.39	124.21	124.06	123.94	123.84
9,000	139.94	139.74	139.57	139.43	139.32
10,000	155.49	155.26	155.08	154.93	154.80
15,000	233.23	232.89	232.62	232.39	232.20
20,000	310.97	310.52	310.15	309.85	309.59
25,000	388.71	388.15	387.69	387.31	386.99
30,000	466.45	465.78	465.23	464.77	464.39
35,000	544.19	543.41	542.77	542.23	541.79
40,000	621.93	621.04	620.30	619.69	619.18
45,000	699.67	698.67	697.84	697.15	696.58
50,000	777.41	776.30	775.38	774.61	773.98
55,000	855.15	853.93	852.92	852.07	851.37
60,000	932.89	931.56	930.45	929.53	928.77
65,000	1,010.63	1,009.19	1,007.99	1,007.00	1,006.17
70,000	1,088.37	1,086.82	1,085.53	1,084.46	1,083.57
75,000	1,166.11	1,164.45	1,163.06	1,161.92	1,160.96
80,000	1,243.85	1,242.08	1,240.60	1,239.38	1,238.36
85,000	1,321.59	1,319.71	1,318.14	1,316.84	1,315.76
90,000	1,399.33	1,397.33	1,395.68	1,394.30	1,393.16
95,000	1,477.07	1,474.96	1,473.21	1,471.76	1,470.55
100,000	1,554.81	1,552.59	1,550.75	1,549.22	1,547.95
110,000	1,710.29	1,707.85	1,705.83	1,704.14	1,702.74
120,000	1,865.78	1,863.11	1,860.90	1,859.06	1,857.54
125,000	1,943.52	1,940.74	1,938.44	1,936.52	1,934.94
130,000	2,021.26	2,018.37	2,015.97	2,013.99	2,012.33
140,000	2,176.74	2,173.63	2,171.05	2,168.91	2,167.13
150,000	2,332.22	2,328.89	2,326.12	2,323.83	2,321.92
160,000	2,487.70	2,484.15	2,481.20	2,478.75	2,476.72
170,000	2,643.18	2,639.41	2,636.27	2,633.67	2,631.51
175,000	2,720.92	2,717.04	2,713.81	2,711.13	2,708.91
180,000	2,798.66	2,794.66	2,791.35	2,788.59	2,786.31
190,000	2,954.14	2,949.92	2,946.42	2,943.52	2,941.10
200,000	3,109.62	3,105.18	3,101.50	3,098.44	3,095.89
220,000	3,420.58	3,415.70	3,411.65	3,408.28	3,405.48
225,000	3,498.32	3,493.33	3,489.18	3,485.74	3,482.88
230,000	3,576.06	3,570.96	3,566.72	3,563.20	3,560.28
240,000	3,731.55	3,726.22	3,721.80	3,718.12	3,715.07
$250,000	3,887.03	3,881.48	3,876.87	3,873.04	3,869.87

Table 1   223

18.75%   Monthly Payment Loans

Amortization Period in Years

	5	7	8	10	12
$ 100	2.59	2.15	2.02	1.86	1.76
200	5.17	4.30	4.04	3.71	3.51
300	7.75	6.44	6.06	5.56	5.26
400	10.33	8.59	8.08	7.41	7.01
500	12.91	10.73	10.10	9.26	8.76
600	15.49	12.88	12.11	11.11	10.51
700	18.07	15.03	14.13	12.96	12.26
800	20.65	17.17	16.15	14.81	14.01
900	23.23	19.32	18.17	16.66	15.76
1,000	25.81	21.46	20.19	18.51	17.51
2,000	51.61	42.92	40.37	37.01	35.01
3,000	77.41	64.38	60.55	55.52	52.51
4,000	103.22	85.84	80.73	74.02	70.01
5,000	129.02	107.30	100.91	92.53	87.52
6,000	154.82	128.76	121.09	111.03	105.02
7,000	180.63	150.22	141.27	129.53	122.52
8,000	206.43	171.68	161.45	148.04	140.02
9,000	232.23	193.14	181.63	166.54	157.52
10,000	258.04	214.60	201.81	185.05	175.03
15,000	387.05	321.90	302.71	277.57	262.54
20,000	516.07	429.20	403.61	370.09	350.05
25,000	645.08	536.50	504.51	462.61	437.56
30,000	774.10	643.80	605.42	555.13	525.07
35,000	903.12	751.10	706.32	647.65	612.58
40,000	1,032.13	858.39	807.22	740.17	700.09
45,000	1,161.15	965.69	908.12	832.69	787.60
50,000	1,290.16	1,072.99	1,009.02	925.21	875.11
55,000	1,419.18	1,180.29	1,109.93	1,017.73	962.62
60,000	1,548.20	1,287.59	1,210.83	1,110.25	1,050.13
65,000	1,677.21	1,394.89	1,311.73	1,202.77	1,137.64
70,000	1,806.23	1,502.19	1,412.63	1,295.29	1,225.15
75,000	1,935.24	1,609.48	1,513.53	1,387.82	1,312.66
80,000	2,064.26	1,716.78	1,614.44	1,480.34	1,400.17
85,000	2,193.28	1,824.08	1,715.34	1,572.86	1,487.68
90,000	2,322.29	1,931.38	1,816.24	1,665.38	1,575.19
95,000	2,451.31	2,038.68	1,917.14	1,757.90	1,662.70
100,000	2,580.32	2,145.98	2,018.04	1,850.42	1,750.21
110,000	2,838.36	2,360.57	2,219.85	2,035.46	1,925.23
120,000	3,096.39	2,575.17	2,421.65	2,220.50	2,100.25
125,000	3,225.40	2,682.47	2,522.55	2,313.02	2,187.76
130,000	3,354.42	2,789.77	2,623.45	2,405.54	2,275.28
140,000	3,612.45	3,004.37	2,825.26	2,590.58	2,450.30
150,000	3,870.48	3,218.96	3,027.06	2,775.63	2,625.32
160,000	4,128.51	3,433.56	3,228.87	2,960.67	2,800.34
170,000	4,386.55	3,648.16	3,430.67	3,145.71	2,975.36
175,000	4,515.56	3,755.46	3,531.57	3,238.23	3,062.87
180,000	4,644.58	3,862.75	3,632.47	3,330.75	3,150.38
190,000	4,902.61	4,077.35	3,834.28	3,515.79	3,325.40
200,000	5,160.64	4,291.95	4,036.08	3,700.83	3,500.42
220,000	5,676.71	4,721.14	4,439.69	4,070.92	3,850.46
225,000	5,805.72	4,828.44	4,540.59	4,163.44	3,937.97
230,000	5,934.74	4,935.74	4,641.49	4,255.96	4,025.48
240,000	6,192.77	5,150.34	4,843.30	4,441.00	4,200.50
$250,000	6,450.80	5,364.93	5,045.10	4,626.04	4,375.52

Monthly Payment Loans   **18.75%**

Amortization Period in Years

	15	16	17	18	20
$ 100	1.67	1.65	1.64	1.62	1.61
200	3.33	3.30	3.27	3.24	3.21
300	5.00	4.94	4.90	4.86	4.81
400	6.66	6.59	6.53	6.48	6.41
500	8.33	8.24	8.16	8.10	8.01
600	9.99	9.88	9.79	9.72	9.61
700	11.66	11.53	11.43	11.34	11.21
800	13.32	13.18	13.06	12.96	12.82
900	14.99	14.82	14.69	14.58	14.42
1,000	16.65	16.47	16.32	16.20	16.02
2,000	33.30	32.93	32.64	32.39	32.03
3,000	49.95	49.40	48.95	48.59	48.04
4,000	66.59	65.86	65.27	64.78	64.06
5,000	83.24	82.32	81.58	80.97	80.07
6,000	99.89	98.79	97.90	97.17	96.08
7,000	116.53	115.25	114.21	113.36	112.09
8,000	133.18	131.72	130.53	129.56	128.11
9,000	149.83	148.18	146.84	145.75	144.12
10,000	166.47	164.64	163.16	161.94	160.13
15,000	249.71	246.96	244.73	242.91	240.19
20,000	332.94	329.28	326.31	323.88	320.26
25,000	416.17	411.60	407.89	404.85	400.32
30,000	499.41	493.92	489.46	485.82	480.38
35,000	582.64	576.24	571.04	566.79	560.45
40,000	665.87	658.56	652.61	647.76	640.51
45,000	749.11	740.88	734.19	728.72	720.57
50,000	832.34	823.20	815.77	809.69	800.64
55,000	915.57	905.52	897.34	890.66	880.70
60,000	998.81	987.84	978.92	971.63	960.76
65,000	1,082.04	1,070.16	1,060.49	1,052.60	1,040.83
70,000	1,165.27	1,152.48	1,142.07	1,133.57	1,120.89
75,000	1,248.51	1,234.80	1,223.65	1,214.54	1,200.95
80,000	1,331.74	1,317.12	1,305.22	1,295.51	1,281.02
85,000	1,414.97	1,399.44	1,386.80	1,376.48	1,361.08
90,000	1,498.21	1,481.76	1,468.37	1,457.44	1,441.14
95,000	1,581.44	1,564.08	1,549.95	1,538.41	1,521.21
100,000	1,664.67	1,646.40	1,631.53	1,619.38	1,601.27
110,000	1,831.14	1,811.04	1,794.68	1,781.32	1,761.40
120,000	1,997.61	1,975.68	1,957.83	1,943.26	1,921.52
125,000	2,080.84	2,058.00	2,039.41	2,024.23	2,001.59
130,000	2,164.07	2,140.32	2,120.98	2,105.20	2,081.65
140,000	2,330.54	2,304.95	2,284.13	2,267.13	2,241.78
150,000	2,497.01	2,469.59	2,447.29	2,429.07	2,401.90
160,000	2,663.48	2,634.23	2,610.44	2,591.01	2,562.03
170,000	2,829.94	2,798.87	2,773.59	2,752.95	2,722.16
175,000	2,913.18	2,881.19	2,855.17	2,833.91	2,802.22
180,000	2,996.41	2,963.51	2,936.74	2,914.88	2,882.28
190,000	3,162.88	3,128.15	3,099.90	3,076.82	3,042.41
200,000	3,329.34	3,292.79	3,263.05	3,238.76	3,202.54
220,000	3,662.28	3,622.07	3,589.35	3,562.63	3,522.79
225,000	3,745.51	3,704.39	3,670.93	3,643.60	3,602.85
230,000	3,828.74	3,786.71	3,752.50	3,724.57	3,682.92
240,000	3,995.21	3,951.35	3,915.66	3,886.51	3,843.04
$250,000	4,161.68	4,115.99	4,078.81	4,048.45	4,003.17

Table 1   225

18.75% Monthly Payment Loans

Amortization Period in Years

	21	22	23	24	25
$ 100	1.60	1.59	1.59	1.59	1.58
200	3.19	3.18	3.17	3.17	3.16
300	4.79	4.77	4.76	4.75	4.74
400	6.38	6.36	6.34	6.33	6.32
500	7.98	7.95	7.93	7.91	7.89
600	9.57	9.54	9.51	9.49	9.47
700	11.17	11.13	11.10	11.07	11.05
800	12.76	12.72	12.68	12.65	12.63
900	14.36	14.31	14.27	14.23	14.20
1,000	15.95	15.90	15.85	15.81	15.78
2,000	31.90	31.79	31.69	31.62	31.56
3,000	47.84	47.68	47.54	47.43	47.33
4,000	63.79	63.57	63.38	63.23	63.11
5,000	79.73	79.46	79.23	79.04	78.88
6,000	95.68	95.35	95.07	94.85	94.66
7,000	111.62	111.24	110.92	110.65	110.43
8,000	127.57	127.13	126.76	126.46	126.21
9,000	143.51	143.02	142.61	142.27	141.99
10,000	159.46	158.91	158.45	158.07	157.76
15,000	239.19	238.36	237.67	237.11	236.64
20,000	318.91	317.81	316.90	316.14	315.52
25,000	398.64	397.26	396.12	395.18	394.40
30,000	478.37	476.71	475.34	474.21	473.27
35,000	558.10	556.16	554.56	553.24	552.15
40,000	637.82	635.61	633.79	632.28	631.03
45,000	717.55	715.06	713.01	711.31	709.91
50,000	797.28	794.51	792.23	790.35	788.79
55,000	877.01	873.96	871.45	869.38	867.67
60,000	956.73	953.41	950.68	948.41	946.54
65,000	1,036.46	1,032.87	1,029.90	1,027.45	1,025.42
70,000	1,116.19	1,112.32	1,109.12	1,106.48	1,104.30
75,000	1,195.92	1,191.77	1,188.34	1,185.52	1,183.18
80,000	1,275.64	1,271.22	1,267.57	1,264.55	1,262.06
85,000	1,355.37	1,350.67	1,346.79	1,343.58	1,340.94
90,000	1,435.10	1,430.12	1,426.01	1,422.62	1,419.81
95,000	1,514.83	1,509.57	1,505.23	1,501.65	1,498.69
100,000	1,594.55	1,589.02	1,584.46	1,580.69	1,577.57
110,000	1,754.01	1,747.92	1,742.90	1,738.75	1,735.33
120,000	1,913.46	1,906.82	1,901.35	1,896.82	1,893.08
125,000	1,993.19	1,986.28	1,980.57	1,975.86	1,971.96
130,000	2,072.92	2,065.73	2,059.79	2,054.89	2,050.84
140,000	2,232.37	2,224.63	2,218.24	2,212.96	2,208.60
150,000	2,391.83	2,383.53	2,376.68	2,371.03	2,366.35
160,000	2,551.28	2,542.43	2,535.13	2,529.10	2,524.11
170,000	2,710.74	2,701.33	2,693.57	2,687.16	2,681.87
175,000	2,790.47	2,780.78	2,772.80	2,766.20	2,760.74
180,000	2,870.19	2,860.23	2,852.02	2,845.23	2,839.62
190,000	3,029.65	3,019.14	3,010.46	3,003.30	2,997.38
200,000	3,189.10	3,178.04	3,168.91	3,161.37	3,155.14
220,000	3,508.01	3,495.84	3,485.80	3,477.50	3,470.65
225,000	3,587.74	3,575.29	3,565.02	3,556.54	3,549.53
230,000	3,667.47	3,654.74	3,644.24	3,635.57	3,628.40
240,000	3,826.92	3,813.64	3,802.69	3,793.64	3,786.16
$250,000	3,986.38	3,972.55	3,961.13	3,951.71	3,943.92

226   Table 1

Monthly Payment Loans   **18.75%**

Amortization Period in Years

	26	27	28	29	30
$ 100	1.58	1.58	1.58	1.57	1.57
200	3.15	3.15	3.15	3.14	3.14
300	4.73	4.72	4.72	4.71	4.71
400	6.30	6.30	6.29	6.28	6.28
500	7.88	7.87	7.86	7.85	7.85
600	9.45	9.44	9.43	9.42	9.42
700	11.03	11.01	11.00	10.99	10.98
800	12.60	12.59	12.57	12.56	12.55
900	14.18	14.16	14.14	14.13	14.12
1,000	15.75	15.73	15.72	15.70	15.69
2,000	31.50	31.46	31.43	31.40	31.37
3,000	47.25	47.19	47.14	47.09	47.06
4,000	63.00	62.92	62.85	62.79	62.74
5,000	78.75	78.65	78.56	78.49	78.43
6,000	94.50	94.38	94.27	94.18	94.11
7,000	110.25	110.10	109.98	109.88	109.79
8,000	126.00	125.83	125.69	125.57	125.48
9,000	141.75	141.56	141.40	141.27	141.16
10,000	157.50	157.29	157.11	156.97	156.85
15,000	236.25	235.93	235.67	235.45	235.27
20,000	315.00	314.58	314.22	313.93	313.69
25,000	393.75	393.22	392.78	392.41	392.11
30,000	472.50	471.86	471.33	470.89	470.53
35,000	551.25	550.50	549.89	549.37	548.95
40,000	630.00	629.15	628.44	627.85	627.37
45,000	708.75	707.79	706.99	706.33	705.79
50,000	787.50	786.43	785.55	784.82	784.21
55,000	866.25	865.07	864.10	863.30	862.63
60,000	945.00	943.72	942.66	941.78	941.05
65,000	1,023.75	1,022.36	1,021.21	1,020.26	1,019.47
70,000	1,102.50	1,101.00	1,099.77	1,098.74	1,097.89
75,000	1,181.25	1,179.64	1,178.32	1,177.22	1,176.31
80,000	1,259.99	1,258.29	1,256.87	1,255.70	1,254.73
85,000	1,338.74	1,336.93	1,335.43	1,334.18	1,333.15
90,000	1,417.49	1,415.57	1,413.98	1,412.66	1,411.57
95,000	1,496.24	1,494.22	1,492.54	1,491.15	1,489.99
100,000	1,574.99	1,572.86	1,571.09	1,569.63	1,568.41
110,000	1,732.49	1,730.14	1,728.20	1,726.59	1,725.25
120,000	1,889.99	1,887.43	1,885.31	1,883.55	1,882.09
125,000	1,968.74	1,966.07	1,963.86	1,962.03	1,960.52
130,000	2,047.49	2,044.71	2,042.42	2,040.51	2,038.94
140,000	2,204.99	2,202.00	2,199.53	2,197.48	2,195.78
150,000	2,362.49	2,359.28	2,356.63	2,354.44	2,352.62
160,000	2,519.98	2,516.57	2,513.74	2,511.40	2,509.46
170,000	2,677.48	2,673.86	2,670.85	2,668.36	2,666.30
175,000	2,756.23	2,752.50	2,749.41	2,746.84	2,744.72
180,000	2,834.98	2,831.14	2,827.96	2,825.32	2,823.14
190,000	2,992.48	2,988.43	2,985.07	2,982.29	2,979.98
200,000	3,149.98	3,145.71	3,142.18	3,139.25	3,136.82
220,000	3,464.98	3,460.28	3,456.39	3,453.17	3,450.50
225,000	3,543.73	3,538.92	3,534.95	3,531.65	3,528.92
230,000	3,622.48	3,617.57	3,613.50	3,610.13	3,607.34
240,000	3,779.97	3,774.85	3,770.61	3,767.10	3,764.18
$250,000	3,937.47	3,932.14	3,927.72	3,924.06	3,921.03

Table 1   227

19.00% Monthly Payment Loans

Amortization Period in Years

	5	7	8	10	12
$ 100	2.60	2.17	2.04	1.87	1.77
200	5.19	4.33	4.07	3.74	3.54
300	7.79	6.49	6.11	5.61	5.31
400	10.38	8.65	8.14	7.47	7.07
500	12.98	10.81	10.17	9.34	8.84
600	15.57	12.97	12.21	11.21	10.61
700	18.16	15.13	14.24	13.07	12.38
800	20.76	17.29	16.27	14.94	14.14
900	23.35	19.45	18.31	16.81	15.91
1,000	25.95	21.61	20.34	18.67	17.68
2,000	51.89	43.22	40.67	37.34	35.35
3,000	77.83	64.83	61.01	56.01	53.03
4,000	103.77	86.44	81.34	74.67	70.70
5,000	129.71	108.05	101.67	93.34	88.37
6,000	155.65	129.65	122.01	112.01	106.05
7,000	181.59	151.26	142.34	130.68	123.72
8,000	207.53	172.87	162.68	149.34	141.39
9,000	233.47	194.48	183.01	168.01	159.07
10,000	259.41	216.09	203.34	186.68	176.74
15,000	389.11	324.13	305.01	280.01	265.11
20,000	518.82	432.17	406.68	373.35	353.48
25,000	648.52	540.21	508.35	466.69	441.85
30,000	778.22	648.25	610.02	560.02	530.21
35,000	907.92	756.29	711.69	653.36	618.58
40,000	1,037.63	864.33	813.36	746.69	706.95
45,000	1,167.33	972.37	915.03	840.03	795.32
50,000	1,297.03	1,080.41	1,016.70	933.37	883.69
55,000	1,426.74	1,188.45	1,118.37	1,026.70	972.06
60,000	1,556.44	1,296.49	1,220.04	1,120.04	1,060.42
65,000	1,686.14	1,404.53	1,321.71	1,213.38	1,148.79
70,000	1,815.84	1,512.57	1,423.38	1,306.71	1,237.16
75,000	1,945.55	1,620.61	1,525.04	1,400.05	1,325.53
80,000	2,075.25	1,728.65	1,626.71	1,493.38	1,413.90
85,000	2,204.95	1,836.69	1,728.38	1,586.72	1,502.27
90,000	2,334.65	1,944.73	1,830.05	1,680.06	1,590.63
95,000	2,464.36	2,052.77	1,931.72	1,773.39	1,679.00
100,000	2,594.06	2,160.81	2,033.39	1,866.73	1,767.37
110,000	2,853.47	2,376.89	2,236.73	2,053.40	1,944.11
120,000	3,112.87	2,592.97	2,440.07	2,240.07	2,120.84
125,000	3,242.57	2,701.01	2,541.74	2,333.41	2,209.21
130,000	3,372.28	2,809.05	2,643.41	2,426.75	2,297.58
140,000	3,631.68	3,025.13	2,846.75	2,613.42	2,474.32
150,000	3,891.09	3,241.21	3,050.08	2,800.09	2,651.05
160,000	4,150.49	3,457.29	3,253.42	2,986.76	2,827.79
170,000	4,409.90	3,673.37	3,456.76	3,173.44	3,004.53
175,000	4,539.60	3,781.41	3,558.43	3,266.77	3,092.89
180,000	4,669.30	3,889.45	3,660.10	3,360.11	3,181.26
190,000	4,928.71	4,105.53	3,863.44	3,546.78	3,358.00
200,000	5,188.12	4,321.61	4,066.78	3,733.45	3,534.73
220,000	5,706.93	4,753.77	4,473.46	4,106.80	3,888.21
225,000	5,836.63	4,861.81	4,575.12	4,200.13	3,976.58
230,000	5,966.33	4,969.85	4,676.79	4,293.47	4,064.94
240,000	6,225.74	5,185.93	4,880.13	4,480.14	4,241.68
$250,000	6,485.14	5,402.01	5,083.47	4,666.81	4,418.42

228   Table 1

Monthly Payment Loans **19.00%**

Amortization Period in Years

	15	16	17	18	20
$ 100	1.69	1.67	1.66	1.64	1.63
200	3.37	3.33	3.31	3.28	3.25
300	5.05	5.00	4.96	4.92	4.87
400	6.74	6.66	6.61	6.56	6.49
500	8.42	8.33	8.26	8.20	8.11
600	10.10	9.99	9.91	9.84	9.73
700	11.79	11.66	11.56	11.47	11.35
800	13.47	13.32	13.21	13.11	12.97
900	15.15	14.99	14.86	14.75	14.59
1,000	16.83	16.65	16.51	16.39	16.21
2,000	33.66	33.30	33.01	32.77	32.42
3,000	50.49	49.95	49.51	49.16	48.63
4,000	67.32	66.60	66.02	65.54	64.83
5,000	84.15	83.25	82.52	81.92	81.04
6,000	100.98	99.90	99.02	98.31	97.25
7,000	117.81	116.55	115.53	114.69	113.45
8,000	134.64	133.20	132.03	131.08	129.66
9,000	151.46	149.85	148.53	147.46	145.87
10,000	168.29	166.49	165.03	163.84	162.07
15,000	252.44	249.74	247.55	245.76	243.11
20,000	336.58	332.98	330.06	327.68	324.14
25,000	420.72	416.23	412.58	409.60	405.18
30,000	504.87	499.47	495.09	491.52	486.21
35,000	589.01	582.72	577.61	573.44	567.24
40,000	673.16	665.96	660.12	655.36	648.28
45,000	757.30	749.21	742.63	737.28	729.31
50,000	841.44	832.45	825.15	819.20	810.35
55,000	925.59	915.70	907.66	901.12	891.38
60,000	1,009.73	998.94	990.18	983.04	972.42
65,000	1,093.87	1,082.19	1,072.69	1,064.95	1,053.45
70,000	1,178.02	1,165.43	1,155.21	1,146.87	1,134.48
75,000	1,262.16	1,248.67	1,237.72	1,228.79	1,215.52
80,000	1,346.31	1,331.92	1,320.24	1,310.71	1,296.55
85,000	1,430.45	1,415.16	1,402.75	1,392.63	1,377.59
90,000	1,514.59	1,498.41	1,485.26	1,474.55	1,458.62
95,000	1,598.74	1,581.65	1,567.78	1,556.47	1,539.66
100,000	1,682.88	1,664.90	1,650.29	1,638.39	1,620.69
110,000	1,851.17	1,831.39	1,815.32	1,802.23	1,782.76
120,000	2,019.46	1,997.88	1,980.35	1,966.07	1,944.83
125,000	2,103.60	2,081.12	2,062.86	2,047.99	2,025.86
130,000	2,187.74	2,164.37	2,145.38	2,129.90	2,106.90
140,000	2,356.03	2,330.85	2,310.41	2,293.74	2,268.96
150,000	2,524.32	2,497.34	2,475.44	2,457.58	2,431.03
160,000	2,692.61	2,663.83	2,640.47	2,621.42	2,593.10
170,000	2,860.89	2,830.32	2,805.49	2,785.26	2,755.17
175,000	2,945.04	2,913.57	2,888.01	2,867.18	2,836.20
180,000	3,029.18	2,996.81	2,970.52	2,949.10	2,917.24
190,000	3,197.47	3,163.30	3,135.55	3,112.94	3,079.31
200,000	3,365.76	3,329.79	3,300.58	3,276.77	3,241.37
220,000	3,702.33	3,662.77	3,630.64	3,604.45	3,565.51
225,000	3,786.48	3,746.01	3,713.15	3,686.37	3,646.55
230,000	3,870.62	3,829.26	3,795.67	3,768.29	3,727.58
240,000	4,038.91	3,995.75	3,960.70	3,932.13	3,889.65
$250,000	4,207.20	4,162.24	4,125.72	4,095.97	4,051.72

Table 1   229

19.00% Monthly Payment Loans

Amortization Period in Years

	21	22	23	24	25
$ 100	1.62	1.61	1.61	1.61	1.60
200	3.23	3.22	3.21	3.21	3.20
300	4.85	4.83	4.82	4.81	4.80
400	6.46	6.44	6.42	6.41	6.40
500	8.08	8.05	8.03	8.01	7.99
600	9.69	9.66	9.63	9.61	9.59
700	11.30	11.27	11.24	11.21	11.19
800	12.92	12.88	12.84	12.81	12.79
900	14.53	14.48	14.44	14.41	14.38
1,000	16.15	16.09	16.05	16.01	15.98
2,000	32.29	32.18	32.09	32.02	31.96
3,000	48.43	48.27	48.14	48.03	47.94
4,000	64.57	64.36	64.18	64.03	63.91
5,000	80.71	80.44	80.22	80.04	79.89
6,000	96.85	96.53	96.27	96.05	95.87
7,000	112.99	112.62	112.31	112.05	111.84
8,000	129.14	128.71	128.35	128.06	127.82
9,000	145.28	144.79	144.40	144.07	143.80
10,000	161.42	160.88	160.44	160.07	159.77
15,000	242.13	241.32	240.66	240.11	239.66
20,000	322.83	321.76	320.87	320.14	319.54
25,000	403.54	402.20	401.09	400.18	399.43
30,000	484.25	482.63	481.31	480.21	479.31
35,000	564.95	563.07	561.52	560.25	559.19
40,000	645.66	643.51	641.74	640.28	639.08
45,000	726.37	723.95	721.96	720.32	718.96
50,000	807.08	804.39	802.17	800.35	798.85
55,000	887.78	884.83	882.39	880.38	878.73
60,000	968.49	965.26	962.61	960.42	958.61
65,000	1,049.20	1,045.70	1,042.82	1,040.45	1,038.50
70,000	1,129.90	1,126.14	1,123.04	1,120.49	1,118.38
75,000	1,210.61	1,206.58	1,203.26	1,200.52	1,198.27
80,000	1,291.32	1,287.02	1,283.47	1,280.56	1,278.15
85,000	1,372.03	1,367.45	1,363.69	1,360.59	1,358.03
90,000	1,452.73	1,447.89	1,443.91	1,440.63	1,437.92
95,000	1,533.44	1,528.33	1,524.13	1,520.66	1,517.80
100,000	1,614.15	1,608.77	1,604.34	1,600.69	1,597.69
110,000	1,775.56	1,769.65	1,764.78	1,760.76	1,757.45
120,000	1,936.98	1,930.52	1,925.21	1,920.83	1,917.22
125,000	2,017.68	2,010.96	2,005.43	2,000.87	1,997.11
130,000	2,098.39	2,091.40	2,085.64	2,080.90	2,076.99
140,000	2,259.80	2,252.28	2,246.08	2,240.97	2,236.76
150,000	2,421.22	2,413.15	2,406.51	2,401.04	2,396.53
160,000	2,582.63	2,574.03	2,566.94	2,561.11	2,556.29
170,000	2,744.05	2,734.90	2,727.38	2,721.18	2,716.06
175,000	2,824.75	2,815.34	2,807.59	2,801.21	2,795.95
180,000	2,905.46	2,895.78	2,887.81	2,881.25	2,875.83
190,000	3,066.88	3,056.66	3,048.25	3,041.31	3,035.60
200,000	3,228.29	3,217.53	3,208.68	3,201.38	3,195.37
220,000	3,551.12	3,539.29	3,529.55	3,521.52	3,514.90
225,000	3,631.83	3,619.72	3,609.76	3,601.56	3,594.79
230,000	3,712.53	3,700.16	3,689.98	3,681.59	3,674.67
240,000	3,873.95	3,861.04	3,850.41	3,841.66	3,834.44
$250,000	4,035.36	4,021.92	4,010.85	4,001.73	3,994.21

Monthly Payment Loans   **19.00%**

Amortization Period in Years

	26	27	28	29	30
$ 100	1.60	1.60	1.60	1.60	1.59
200	3.20	3.19	3.19	3.19	3.18
300	4.79	4.78	4.78	4.78	4.77
400	6.39	6.38	6.37	6.37	6.36
500	7.98	7.97	7.96	7.96	7.95
600	9.58	9.56	9.55	9.55	9.54
700	11.17	11.16	11.15	11.14	11.13
800	12.77	12.75	12.74	12.73	12.72
900	14.36	14.34	14.33	14.32	14.31
1,000	15.96	15.94	15.92	15.91	15.89
2,000	31.91	31.87	31.83	31.81	31.78
3,000	47.86	47.80	47.75	47.71	47.67
4,000	63.81	63.73	63.66	63.61	63.56
5,000	79.76	79.66	79.58	79.51	79.45
6,000	95.72	95.59	95.49	95.41	95.34
7,000	111.67	111.53	111.41	111.31	111.23
8,000	127.62	127.46	127.32	127.21	127.12
9,000	143.57	143.39	143.24	143.11	143.01
10,000	159.52	159.32	159.15	159.01	158.89
15,000	239.28	238.98	238.72	238.51	238.34
20,000	319.04	318.63	318.30	318.02	317.78
25,000	398.80	398.29	397.87	397.52	397.23
30,000	478.56	477.95	477.44	477.02	476.67
35,000	558.32	557.61	557.01	556.52	556.12
40,000	638.08	637.26	636.59	636.03	635.56
45,000	717.84	716.92	716.16	715.53	715.01
50,000	797.60	796.58	795.73	795.03	794.45
55,000	877.36	876.24	875.30	874.53	873.90
60,000	957.12	955.89	954.88	954.04	953.34
65,000	1,036.88	1,035.55	1,034.45	1,033.54	1,032.79
70,000	1,116.64	1,115.21	1,114.02	1,113.04	1,112.23
75,000	1,196.40	1,194.86	1,193.59	1,192.54	1,191.67
80,000	1,276.16	1,274.52	1,273.17	1,272.05	1,271.12
85,000	1,355.92	1,354.18	1,352.74	1,351.55	1,350.56
90,000	1,435.68	1,433.84	1,432.31	1,431.05	1,430.01
95,000	1,515.44	1,513.49	1,511.88	1,510.55	1,509.45
100,000	1,595.20	1,593.15	1,591.46	1,590.06	1,588.90
110,000	1,754.72	1,752.47	1,750.60	1,749.06	1,747.79
120,000	1,914.24	1,911.78	1,909.75	1,908.07	1,906.68
125,000	1,994.00	1,991.44	1,989.32	1,987.57	1,986.12
130,000	2,073.76	2,071.09	2,068.89	2,067.07	2,065.57
140,000	2,233.28	2,230.41	2,228.04	2,226.08	2,224.45
150,000	2,392.80	2,389.72	2,387.18	2,385.08	2,383.34
160,000	2,552.32	2,549.04	2,546.33	2,544.09	2,542.23
170,000	2,711.84	2,708.35	2,705.47	2,703.09	2,701.12
175,000	2,791.60	2,788.01	2,785.04	2,782.59	2,780.57
180,000	2,871.36	2,867.67	2,864.62	2,862.10	2,860.01
190,000	3,030.88	3,026.98	3,023.76	3,021.10	3,018.90
200,000	3,190.40	3,186.30	3,182.91	3,180.11	3,177.79
220,000	3,509.44	3,504.93	3,501.20	3,498.12	3,495.57
225,000	3,589.20	3,584.58	3,580.77	3,577.62	3,575.01
230,000	3,668.96	3,664.24	3,660.34	3,657.12	3,654.46
240,000	3,828.48	3,823.55	3,819.49	3,816.13	3,813.35
$250,000	3,988.00	3,982.87	3,978.63	3,975.13	3,972.24

Table 1   231

19.25% Monthly Payment Loans

Amortization Period in Years

		5	7	8	10	12
$	100	2.61	2.18	2.05	1.89	1.79
	200	5.22	4.36	4.10	3.77	3.57
	300	7.83	6.53	6.15	5.65	5.36
	400	10.44	8.71	8.20	7.54	7.14
	500	13.04	10.88	10.25	9.42	8.93
	600	15.65	13.06	12.30	11.30	10.71
	700	18.26	15.23	14.35	13.19	12.50
	800	20.87	17.41	16.40	15.07	14.28
	900	23.48	19.59	18.44	16.95	16.07
	1,000	26.08	21.76	20.49	18.84	17.85
	2,000	52.16	43.52	40.98	37.67	35.70
	3,000	78.24	65.28	61.47	56.50	53.54
	4,000	104.32	87.03	81.96	75.33	71.39
	5,000	130.40	108.79	102.44	94.16	89.23
	6,000	156.47	130.55	122.93	112.99	107.08
	7,000	182.55	152.30	143.42	131.82	124.93
	8,000	208.63	174.06	163.91	150.65	142.77
	9,000	234.71	195.82	184.40	169.48	160.62
	10,000	260.79	217.57	204.88	188.31	178.46
	15,000	391.18	326.36	307.32	282.47	267.69
	20,000	521.57	435.14	409.76	376.62	356.92
	25,000	651.96	543.93	512.20	470.78	446.15
	30,000	782.35	652.71	614.64	564.93	535.38
	35,000	912.75	761.49	717.08	659.09	624.61
	40,000	1,043.14	870.28	819.52	753.24	713.84
	45,000	1,173.53	979.06	921.96	847.40	803.07
	50,000	1,303.92	1,087.85	1,024.40	941.55	892.30
	55,000	1,434.31	1,196.63	1,126.84	1,035.71	981.53
	60,000	1,564.70	1,305.41	1,229.28	1,129.86	1,070.76
	65,000	1,695.09	1,414.20	1,331.72	1,224.02	1,159.98
	70,000	1,825.49	1,522.98	1,434.16	1,318.17	1,249.21
	75,000	1,955.88	1,631.77	1,536.60	1,412.32	1,338.44
	80,000	2,086.27	1,740.55	1,639.04	1,506.48	1,427.67
	85,000	2,216.66	1,849.33	1,741.48	1,600.63	1,516.90
	90,000	2,347.05	1,958.12	1,843.92	1,694.79	1,606.13
	95,000	2,477.44	2,066.90	1,946.35	1,788.94	1,695.36
	100,000	2,607.84	2,175.69	2,048.79	1,883.10	1,784.59
	110,000	2,868.62	2,393.26	2,253.67	2,071.41	1,963.05
	120,000	3,129.40	2,610.82	2,458.55	2,259.72	2,141.51
	125,000	3,259.79	2,719.61	2,560.99	2,353.87	2,230.74
	130,000	3,390.18	2,828.39	2,663.43	2,448.03	2,319.96
	140,000	3,650.97	3,045.96	2,868.31	2,636.34	2,498.42
	150,000	3,911.75	3,263.53	3,073.19	2,824.64	2,676.88
	160,000	4,172.53	3,481.10	3,278.07	3,012.95	2,855.34
	170,000	4,433.32	3,698.66	3,482.95	3,201.26	3,033.80
	175,000	4,563.71	3,807.45	3,585.39	3,295.42	3,123.03
	180,000	4,694.10	3,916.23	3,687.83	3,389.57	3,212.26
	190,000	4,954.88	4,133.80	3,892.70	3,577.88	3,390.71
	200,000	5,215.67	4,351.37	4,097.58	3,766.19	3,569.17
	220,000	5,737.23	4,786.51	4,507.34	4,142.81	3,926.09
	225,000	5,867.62	4,895.29	4,609.78	4,236.96	4,015.32
	230,000	5,998.02	5,004.07	4,712.22	4,331.12	4,104.55
	240,000	6,258.80	5,221.64	4,917.10	4,519.43	4,283.01
$250,000		6,519.58	5,439.21	5,121.98	4,707.74	4,461.47

Monthly Payment Loans   **19.25%**

Amortization Period in Years

	15	16	17	18	20
$ 100	1.71	1.69	1.67	1.66	1.65
200	3.41	3.37	3.34	3.32	3.29
300	5.11	5.06	5.01	4.98	4.93
400	6.81	6.74	6.68	6.63	6.57
500	8.51	8.42	8.35	8.29	8.21
600	10.21	10.11	10.02	9.95	9.85
700	11.91	11.79	11.69	11.61	11.49
800	13.61	13.47	13.36	13.26	13.13
900	15.32	i5.16	15.03	14.92	14.77
1,000	17.02	16.84	16.70	16.58	16.41
2,000	34.03	33.67	33.39	33.15	32.81
3,000	51.04	50.51	50.08	49.73	49.21
4,000	68.05	67.34	66.77	66.30	65.61
5,000	85.06	84.18	83.46	82.88	82.01
6,000	102.07	101.01	100.15	99.45	98.41
7,000	119.09	117.85	116.84	116.03	114.82
8,000	136.10	134.68	133.53	132.60	131.22
9,000	153.11	151.52	150.22	149.18	147.62
10,000	170.12	168.35	166.92	165.75	164.02
15,000	255.18	252.52	250.37	248.62	246.03
20,000	340.23	336.70	333.83	331.49	328.04
25,000	425.29	420.87	417.28	414.37	410.04
30,000	510.35	505.04	500.74	497.24	492.05
35,000	595.41	589.21	584.19	580.11	574.06
40,000	680.46	673.39	667.65	662.98	656.07
45,000	765.52	757.56	751.10	745.86	738.07
50,000	850.58	841.73	834.56	828.73	820.08
55,000	935.63	925.90	918.02	911.60	902.09
60,000	1,020.69	1,010.08	1,001.47	994.47	984.10
65,000	1,105.75	1,094.25	1,084.93	1,077.34	1,066.10
70,000	1,190.81	1,178.42	1,168.38	1,160.22	1,148.11
75,000	1,275.86	1,262.59	1,251.84	1,243.09	1,230.12
80,000	1,360.92	1,346.77	1,335.29	1,325.96	1,312.13
85,000	1,445.98	1,430.94	1,418.75	1,408.83	1,394.13
90,000	1,531.03	1,515.11	1,502.20	1,491.71	1,476.14
95,000	1,616.09	1,599.28	1,585.66	1,574.58	1,558.15
100,000	1,701.15	1,683.46	1,669.12	1,657.45	1,640.16
110,000	1,871.26	1,851.80	1,836.03	1,823.19	1,804.17
120,000	2,041.38	2,020.15	2,002.94	1,988.94	1,968.19
125,000	2,126.43	2,104.32	2,086.39	2,071.81	2,050.19
130,000	2,211.49	2,188.49	2,169.85	2,154.68	2,132.20
140,000	2,381.61	2,356.84	2,336.76	2,320.43	2,296.22
150,000	2,551.72	2,525.18	2,503.67	2,486.17	2,460.23
160,000	2,721.83	2,693.53	2,670.58	2,651.92	2,624.25
170,000	2,891.95	2,861.87	2,837.49	2,817.66	2,788.26
175,000	2,977.01	2,946.04	2,920.95	2,900.53	2,870.27
180,000	3,062.06	3,030.22	3,004.40	2,983.41	2,952.28
190,000	3,232.18	3,198.56	3,171.31	3,149.15	3,116.29
200,000	3,402.29	3,366.91	3,338.23	3,314.90	3,280.31
220,000	3,742.52	3,703.60	3,672.05	3,646.38	3,608.34
225,000	3,827.58	3,787.77	3,755.50	3,729.26	3,690.35
230,000	3,912.63	3,871.94	3,838.96	3,812.13	3,772.35
240,000	4,082.75	4,040.29	4,005.87	3,977.87	3,936.37
$250,000	4,252.86	4,208.63	4,172.78	4,143.62	4,100.38

Table 1   233

19.25%   Monthly Payment Loans

Amortization Period in Years

	21	22	23	24	25
$ 100	1.64	1.63	1.63	1.63	1.62
200	3.27	3.26	3.25	3.25	3.24
300	4.91	4.89	4.88	4.87	4.86
400	6.54	6.52	6.50	6.49	6.48
500	8.17	8.15	8.13	8.11	8.09
600	9.81	9.78	9.75	9.73	9.71
700	11.44	11.40	11.37	11.35	11.33
800	13.08	13.03	13.00	12.97	12.95
900	14.71	14.66	14.62	14.59	14.57
1,000	16.34	16.29	16.25	16.21	16.18
2,000	32.68	32.58	32.49	32.42	32.36
3,000	49.02	48.86	48.73	48.63	48.54
4,000	65.36	65.15	64.98	64.83	64.72
5,000	81.69	81.43	81.22	81.04	80.90
6,000	98.03	97.72	97.46	97.25	97.07
7,000	114.37	114.00	113.70	113.46	113.25
8,000	130.71	130.29	129.95	129.66	129.43
9,000	147.05	146.57	146.19	145.87	145.61
10,000	163.38	162.86	162.43	162.08	161.79
15,000	245.07	244.29	243.64	243.11	242.68
20,000	326.76	325.72	324.86	324.15	323.57
25,000	408.45	407.14	406.07	405.19	404.46
30,000	490.14	488.57	487.28	486.22	485.35
35,000	571.83	570.00	568.50	567.26	566.24
40,000	653.52	651.43	649.71	648.30	647.14
45,000	735.21	732.85	730.92	729.33	728.03
50,000	816.90	814.28	812.14	810.37	808.92
55,000	898.58	895.71	893.35	891.41	889.81
60,000	980.27	977.14	974.56	972.44	970.70
65,000	1,061.96	1,058.56	1,055.77	1,053.48	1,051.59
70,000	1,143.65	1,139.99	1,136.99	1,134.52	1,132.48
75,000	1,225.34	1,221.42	1,218.20	1,215.55	1,213.38
80,000	1,307.03	1,302.85	1,299.41	1,296.59	1,294.27
85,000	1,388.72	1,384.28	1,380.63	1,377.63	1,375.16
90,000	1,470.41	1,465.70	1,461.84	1,458.66	1,456.05
95,000	1,552.10	1,547.13	1,543.05	1,539.70	1,536.94
100,000	1,633.79	1,628.56	1,624.27	1,620.74	1,617.83
110,000	1,797.16	1,791.41	1,786.69	1,782.81	1,779.62
120,000	1,960.54	1,954.27	1,949.12	1,944.88	1,941.40
125,000	2,042.23	2,035.70	2,030.33	2,025.92	2,022.29
130,000	2,123.92	2,117.12	2,111.54	2,106.96	2,103.18
140,000	2,287.30	2,279.98	2,273.97	2,269.03	2,264.96
150,000	2,450.68	2,442.84	2,436.40	2,431.10	2,426.75
160,000	2,614.05	2,605.69	2,598.82	2,593.18	2,588.53
170,000	2,777.43	2,768.55	2,761.25	2,755.25	2,750.31
175,000	2,859.12	2,849.97	2,842.46	2,836.29	2,831.20
180,000	2,940.81	2,931.40	2,923.68	2,917.32	2,912.09
190,000	3,104.19	3,094.26	3,086.10	3,079.40	3,073.88
200,000	3,267.57	3,257.11	3,248.53	3,241.47	3,235.66
220,000	3,594.32	3,582.82	3,573.38	3,565.61	3,559.23
225,000	3,676.01	3,664.25	3,654.59	3,646.65	3,640.12
230,000	3,757.70	3,745.68	3,735.81	3,727.69	3,721.01
240,000	3,921.08	3,908.53	3,898.23	3,889.76	3,882.79
$250,000	4,084.46	4,071.39	4,060.66	4,051.83	4,044.57

Monthly Payment Loans **19.25%**

Amortization Period in Years

	26	27	28	29	30
$ 100	1.62	1.62	1.62	1.62	1.61
200	3.24	3.23	3.23	3.23	3.22
300	4.85	4.85	4.84	4.84	4.83
400	6.47	6.46	6.45	6.45	6.44
500	8.08	8.07	8.06	8.06	8.05
600	9.70	9.69	9.68	9.67	9.66
700	11.31	11.30	11.29	11.28	11.27
800	12.93	12.91	12.90	12.89	12.88
900	14.54	14.53	14.51	14.50	14.49
1,000	16.16	16.14	16.12	16.11	16.10
2,000	32.31	32.27	32.24	32.22	32.19
3,000	48.47	48.41	48.36	48.32	48.29
4,000	64.62	64.54	64.48	64.43	64.38
5,000	80.78	80.68	80.60	80.53	80.47
6,000	96.93	96.81	96.72	96.64	96.57
7,000	113.09	112.95	112.83	112.74	112.66
8,000	129.24	129.08	128.95	128.85	128.76
9,000	145.39	145.22	145.07	144.95	144.85
10,000	161.55	161.35	161.19	161.06	160.94
15,000	242.32	242.02	241.78	241.58	241.41
20,000	323.09	322.70	322.37	322.11	321.88
25,000	403.86	403.37	402.97	402.63	402.35
30,000	484.64	484.04	483.56	483.16	482.82
35,000	565.41	564.72	564.15	563.68	563.29
40,000	646.18	645.39	644.74	644.21	643.76
45,000	726.95	726.06	725.33	724.73	724.23
50,000	807.72	806.74	805.93	805.26	804.70
55,000	888.49	887.41	886.52	885.78	885.17
60,000	969.27	968.08	967.11	966.31	965.64
65,000	1,050.04	1,048.76	1,047.70	1,046.83	1,046.11
70,000	1,130.81	1,129.43	1,128.29	1,127.36	1,126.58
75,000	1,211.58	1,210.10	1,208.89	1,207.88	1,207.05
80,000	1,292.35	1,290.78	1,289.48	1,288.41	1,287.52
85,000	1,373.13	1,371.45	1,370.07	1,368.93	1,367.99
90,000	1,453.90	1,452.12	1,450.66	1,449.46	1,448.46
95,000	1,534.67	1,532.80	1,531.25	1,529.98	1,528.93
100,000	1,615.44	1,613.47	1,611.85	1,610.51	1,609.40
110,000	1,776.98	1,774.82	1,773.03	1,771.56	1,770.34
120,000	1,938.53	1,936.16	1,934.21	1,932.61	1,931.28
125,000	2,019.30	2,016.84	2,014.81	2,013.13	2,011.75
130,000	2,100.07	2,097.51	2,095.40	2,093.66	2,092.22
140,000	2,261.62	2,258.86	2,256.58	2,254.71	2,253.16
150,000	2,423.16	2,420.20	2,417.77	2,415.76	2,414.10
160,000	2,584.70	2,581.55	2,578.95	2,576.81	2,575.04
170,000	2,746.25	2,742.90	2,740.14	2,737.86	2,735.98
175,000	2,827.02	2,823.57	2,820.73	2,818.38	2,816.45
180,000	2,907.79	2,904.24	2,901.32	2,898.91	2,896.92
190,000	3,069.33	3,065.59	3,062.50	3,059.96	3,057.86
200,000	3,230.88	3,226.94	3,223.69	3,221.01	3,218.80
220,000	3,553.96	3,549.63	3,546.06	3,543.11	3,540.68
225,000	3,634.74	3,630.30	3,626.65	3,623.63	3,621.15
230,000	3,715.51	3,710.98	3,707.24	3,704.16	3,701.62
240,000	3,877.05	3,872.32	3,868.42	3,865.21	3,862.56
$250,000	4,038.59	4,033.67	4,029.61	4,026.26	4,023.50

Table 1   235

19.50%   Monthly Payment Loans

Amortization Period in Years

	5	7	8	10	12
$ 100	2.63	2.20	2.07	1.90	1.81
200	5.25	4.39	4.13	3.80	3.61
300	7.87	6.58	6.20	5.70	5.41
400	10.49	8.77	8.26	7.60	7.21
500	13.11	10.96	10.33	9.50	9.01
600	15.73	13.15	12.39	11.40	10.82
700	18.36	15.34	14.45	13.30	12.62
800	20.98	17.53	16.52	15.20	14.42
900	23.60	19.72	18.58	17.10	16.22
1,000	26.22	21.91	20.65	19.00	18.02
2,000	52.44	43.82	41.29	38.00	36.04
3,000	78.65	65.72	61.93	56.99	54.06
4,000	104.87	87.63	82.57	75.99	72.08
5,000	131.09	109.54	103.22	94.98	90.10
6,000	157.30	131.44	123.86	113.98	108.12
7,000	183.52	153.35	144.50	132.97	126.14
8,000	209.74	175.25	165.14	151.97	144.15
9,000	235.95	197.16	185.79	170.96	162.17
10,000	262.17	219.07	206.43	189.96	180.19
15,000	393.25	328.60	309.64	284.93	270.28
20,000	524.33	438.13	412.85	379.91	360.38
25,000	655.42	547.66	516.07	474.89	450.47
30,000	786.50	657.19	619.28	569.86	540.56
35,000	917.58	766.72	722.49	664.84	630.66
40,000	1,048.66	876.25	825.70	759.81	720.75
45,000	1,179.75	985.78	928.92	854.79	810.84
50,000	1,310.83	1,095.31	1,032.13	949.77	900.94
55,000	1,441.91	1,204.84	1,135.34	1,044.74	991.03
60,000	1,572.99	1,314.37	1,238.55	1,139.72	1,081.12
65,000	1,704.07	1,423.90	1,341.76	1,234.69	1,171.22
70,000	1,835.16	1,533.43	1,444.98	1,329.67	1,261.31
75,000	1,966.24	1,642.96	1,548.19	1,424.65	1,351.40
80,000	2,097.32	1,752.49	1,651.40	1,519.62	1,441.50
85,000	2,228.40	1,862.03	1,754.61	1,614.60	1,531.59
90,000	2,359.49	1,971.56	1,857.83	1,709.57	1,621.68
95,000	2,490.57	2,081.09	1,961.04	1,804.55	1,711.78
100,000	2,621.65	2,190.62	2,064.25	1,899.53	1,801.87
110,000	2,883.81	2,409.68	2,270.68	2,089.48	1,982.06
120,000	3,145.98	2,628.74	2,477.10	2,279.43	2,162.24
125,000	3,277.06	2,738.27	2,580.31	2,374.41	2,252.34
130,000	3,408.14	2,847.80	2,683.52	2,469.38	2,342.43
140,000	3,670.31	3,066.86	2,889.95	2,659.34	2,522.62
150,000	3,932.47	3,285.92	3,096.37	2,849.29	2,702.80
160,000	4,194.64	3,504.98	3,302.80	3,039.24	2,882.99
170,000	4,456.80	3,724.05	3,509.22	3,229.19	3,063.18
175,000	4,587.88	3,833.58	3,612.44	3,324.17	3,153.27
180,000	4,718.97	3,943.11	3,715.65	3,419.14	3,243.36
190,000	4,981.13	4,162.17	3,922.07	3,609.10	3,423.55
200,000	5,243.29	4,381.23	4,128.50	3,799.05	3,603.73
220,000	5,767.62	4,819.35	4,541.35	4,178.95	3,964.11
225,000	5,898.71	4,928.88	4,644.56	4,273.93	4,054.20
230,000	6,029.79	5,038.41	4,747.77	4,368.91	4,144.29
240,000	6,291.95	5,257.47	4,954.20	4,558.86	4,324.48
$250,000	6,554.12	5,476.53	5,160.62	4,748.81	4,504.67

Monthly Payment Loans   **19.50%**

Amortization Period in Years

	15	16	17	18	20
$ 100	1.72	1.71	1.69	1.68	1.66
200	3.44	3.41	3.38	3.36	3.32
300	5.16	5.11	5.07	5.03	4.98
400	6.88	6.81	6.76	6.71	6.64
500	8.60	8.52	8.44	8.39	8.30
600	10.32	10.22	10.13	10.06	9.96
700	12.04	11.92	11.82	11.74	11.62
800	13.76	13.62	13.51	13.42	13.28
900	15.48	15.32	15.20	15.09	14.94
1,000	17.20	17.03	16.88	16.77	16.60
2,000	34.39	34.05	33.76	33.54	33.20
3,000	51.59	51.07	50.64	50.30	49.79
4,000	68.78	68.09	67.52	67.07	66.39
5,000	85.98	85.11	84.40	83.83	82.99
6,000	103.17	102.13	101.28	100.60	99.58
7,000	120.37	119.15	118.16	117.36	116.18
8,000	137.56	136.17	135.04	134.13	132.78
9,000	154.76	153.19	151.92	150.90	149.37
10,000	171.95	170.21	168.80	167.66	165.97
15,000	257.93	255.32	253.20	251.49	248.95
20,000	343.90	340.42	337.60	335.32	331.94
25,000	429.87	425.52	422.00	419.14	414.92
30,000	515.85	510.63	506.40	502.97	497.90
35,000	601.82	595.73	590.80	586.80	580.89
40,000	687.79	680.83	675.20	670.63	663.87
45,000	773.77	765.94	759.60	754.46	746.85
50,000	859.74	851.04	844.00	838.28	829.84
55,000	945.71	936.14	928.40	922.11	912.82
60,000	1,031.69	1,021.25	1,012.80	1,005.94	995.80
65,000	1,117.66	1,106.35	1,097.20	1,089.77	1,078.79
70,000	1,203.63	1,191.45	1,181.60	1,173.60	1,161.77
75,000	1,289.61	1,276.56	1,266.00	1,257.42	1,244.75
80,000	1,375.58	1,361.66	1,350.40	1,341.25	1,327.74
85,000	1,461.55	1,446.76	1,434.79	1,425.08	1,410.72
90,000	1,547.53	1,531.87	1,519.19	1,508.91	1,493.70
95,000	1,633.50	1,616.97	1,603.59	1,592.74	1,576.69
100,000	1,719.48	1,702.07	1,687.99	1,676.56	1,659.67
110,000	1,891.42	1,872.28	1,856.79	1,844.22	1,825.64
120,000	2,063.37	2,042.49	2,025.59	2,011.87	1,991.60
125,000	2,149.34	2,127.59	2,109.99	2,095.70	2,074.59
130,000	2,235.32	2,212.69	2,194.39	2,179.53	2,157.57
140,000	2,407.26	2,382.90	2,363.19	2,347.19	2,323.54
150,000	2,579.21	2,553.11	2,531.99	2,514.84	2,489.50
160,000	2,751.16	2,723.31	2,700.79	2,682.50	2,655.47
170,000	2,923.10	2,893.52	2,869.58	2,850.15	2,821.43
175,000	3,009.08	2,978.62	2,953.98	2,933.98	2,904.42
180,000	3,095.05	3,063.73	3,038.38	3,017.81	2,987.40
190,000	3,267.00	3,233.93	3,207.18	3,185.47	3,153.37
200,000	3,438.95	3,404.14	3,375.98	3,353.12	3,319.33
220,000	3,782.84	3,744.55	3,713.58	3,688.43	3,651.27
225,000	3,868.81	3,829.66	3,797.98	3,772.26	3,734.25
230,000	3,954.79	3,914.76	3,882.38	3,856.09	3,817.23
240,000	4,126.73	4,084.97	4,051.18	4,023.74	3,983.20
$250,000	4,298.68	4,255.17	4,219.97	4,191.40	4,149.17

Table 1   237

19.50%   Monthly Payment Loans

Amortization Period in Years

	21	22	23	24	25
$ 100	1.66	1.65	1.65	1.65	1.64
200	3.31	3.30	3.29	3.29	3.28
300	4.97	4.95	4.94	4.93	4.92
400	6.62	6.60	6.58	6.57	6.56
500	8.27	8.25	8.23	8.21	8.20
600	9.93	9.90	9.87	9.85	9.83
700	11.58	11.54	11.51	11.49	11.47
800	13.23	13.19	13.16	13.13	13.11
900	14.89	14.84	14.80	14.77	14.75
1,000	16.54	16.49	16.45	16.41	16.39
2,000	33.07	32.97	32.89	32.82	32.77
3,000	49.61	49.46	49.33	49.23	49.15
4,000	66.14	65.94	65.77	65.64	65.53
5,000	82.68	82.42	82.22	82.05	81.91
6,000	99.21	98.91	98.66	98.45	98.29
7,000	115.75	115.39	115.10	114.86	114.67
8,000	132.28	131.88	131.54	131.27	131.05
9,000	148.82	148.36	147.99	147.68	147.43
10,000	165.35	164.84	164.43	164.09	163.81
15,000	248.02	247.26	246.64	246.13	245.71
20,000	330.70	329.68	328.85	328.17	327.61
25,000	413.37	412.10	411.06	410.21	409.51
30,000	496.04	494.52	493.27	492.25	491.41
35,000	578.72	576.94	575.48	574.29	573.31
40,000	661.39	659.36	657.69	656.33	655.21
45,000	744.06	741.78	739.91	738.37	737.11
50,000	826.74	824.20	822.12	820.41	819.01
55,000	909.41	906.62	904.33	902.45	900.91
60,000	992.08	989.04	986.54	984.49	982.81
65,000	1,074.75	1,071.45	1,068.75	1,066.53	1,064.71
70,000	1,157.43	1,153.87	1,150.96	1,148.57	1,146.61
75,000	1,240.10	1,236.29	1,233.17	1,230.61	1,228.51
80,000	1,322.77	1,318.71	1,315.38	1,312.65	1,310.41
85,000	1,405.45	1,401.13	1,397.59	1,394.69	1,392.31
90,000	1,488.12	1,483.55	1,479.81	1,476.73	1,474.21
95,000	1,570.79	1,565.97	1,562.02	1,558.77	1,556.11
100,000	1,653.47	1,648.39	1,644.23	1,640.81	1,638.01
110,000	1,818.81	1,813.23	1,808.65	1,804.89	1,801.81
120,000	1,984.16	1,978.07	1,973.07	1,968.98	1,965.61
125,000	2,066.83	2,060.48	2,055.28	2,051.02	2,047.51
130,000	2,149.50	2,142.90	2,137.49	2,133.06	2,129.41
140,000	2,314.85	2,307.74	2,301.92	2,297.14	2,293.21
150,000	2,480.20	2,472.58	2,466.34	2,461.22	2,457.01
160,000	2,645.54	2,637.42	2,630.76	2,625.30	2,620.81
170,000	2,810.89	2,802.26	2,795.18	2,789.38	2,784.62
175,000	2,893.56	2,884.68	2,877.39	2,871.42	2,866.52
180,000	2,976.24	2,967.10	2,959.61	2,953.46	2,948.42
190,000	3,141.58	3,131.93	3,124.03	3,117.54	3,112.22
200,000	3,306.93	3,296.77	3,288.45	3,281.62	3,276.02
220,000	3,637.62	3,626.45	3,617.29	3,609.78	3,603.62
225,000	3,720.29	3,708.87	3,699.51	3,691.82	3,685.52
230,000	3,802.97	3,791.29	3,781.72	3,773.87	3,767.42
240,000	3,968.31	3,956.13	3,946.14	3,937.95	3,931.22
$250,000	4,133.66	4,120.96	4,110.56	4,102.03	4,095.02

Monthly Payment Loans   **19.50%**

Amortization Period in Years

	26	27	28	29	30
$ 100	1.64	1.64	1.64	1.64	1.63
200	3.28	3.27	3.27	3.27	3.26
300	4.91	4.91	4.90	4.90	4.89
400	6.55	6.54	6.53	6.53	6.52
500	8.18	8.17	8.17	8.16	8.15
600	9.82	9.81	9.80	9.79	9.78
700	11.45	11.44	11.43	11.42	11.41
800	13.09	13.08	13.06	13.05	13.04
900	14.73	14.71	14.70	14.68	14.67
1,000	16.36	16.34	16.33	16.31	16.30
2,000	32.72	32.68	32.65	32.62	32.60
3,000	49.08	49.02	48.97	48.93	48.90
4,000	65.43	65.36	65.30	65.24	65.20
5,000	81.79	81.70	81.62	81.55	81.50
6,000	98.15	98.03	97.94	97.86	97.80
7,000	114.50	114.37	114.26	114.17	114.10
8,000	130.86	130.71	130.59	130.48	130.40
9,000	147.22	147.05	146.91	146.79	146.70
10,000	163.58	163.39	163.23	163.10	163.00
15,000	245.36	245.08	244.84	244.65	244.49
20,000	327.15	326.77	326.46	326.20	325.99
25,000	408.93	408.46	408.07	407.75	407.49
30,000	490.72	490.15	489.68	489.30	488.98
35,000	572.50	571.84	571.29	570.85	570.48
40,000	654.29	653.53	652.91	652.39	651.97
45,000	736.07	735.22	734.52	733.94	733.47
50,000	817.86	816.91	816.13	815.49	814.97
55,000	899.64	898.60	897.74	897.04	896.46
60,000	981.43	980.29	979.36	978.59	977.96
65,000	1,063.21	1,061.98	1,060.97	1,060.14	1,059.45
70,000	1,145.00	1,143.67	1,142.58	1,141.69	1,140.95
75,000	1,226.78	1,225.36	1,224.20	1,223.24	1,222.45
80,000	1,308.57	1,307.05	1,305.81	1,304.78	1,303.94
85,000	1,390.35	1,388.74	1,387.42	1,386.33	1,385.44
90,000	1,472.14	1,470.43	1,469.03	1,467.88	1,466.93
95,000	1,553.92	1,552.13	1,550.65	1,549.43	1,548.43
100,000	1,635.71	1,633.82	1,632.26	1,630.98	1,629.93
110,000	1,799.28	1,797.20	1,795.48	1,794.08	1,792.92
120,000	1,962.85	1,960.58	1,958.71	1,957.17	1,955.91
125,000	2,044.63	2,042.27	2,040.32	2,038.72	2,037.41
130,000	2,126.42	2,123.96	2,121.94	2,120.27	2,118.90
140,000	2,289.99	2,287.34	2,285.16	2,283.37	2,281.89
150,000	2,453.56	2,450.72	2,448.39	2,446.47	2,444.89
160,000	2,617.13	2,614.10	2,611.61	2,609.56	2,607.88
170,000	2,780.70	2,777.48	2,774.84	2,772.66	2,770.87
175,000	2,862.49	2,859.17	2,856.45	2,854.21	2,852.37
180,000	2,944.27	2,940.86	2,938.06	2,935.76	2,933.86
190,000	3,107.84	3,104.25	3,101.29	3,098.86	3,096.85
200,000	3,271.41	3,267.63	3,264.51	3,261.95	3,259.85
220,000	3,598.55	3,594.39	3,590.96	3,588.15	3,585.83
225,000	3,680.34	3,676.08	3,672.58	3,669.70	3,667.33
230,000	3,762.12	3,757.77	3,754.19	3,751.24	3,748.82
240,000	3,925.69	3,921.15	3,917.42	3,914.34	3,911.81
$250,000	4,089.26	4,084.53	4,080.64	4,077.44	4,074.81

Table 1   239

19.75%   Monthly Payment Loans

Amortization Period in Years

	5	7	8	10	12
$ 100	2.64	2.21	2.08	1.92	1.82
200	5.28	4.42	4.16	3.84	3.64
300	7.91	6.62	6.24	5.75	5.46
400	10.55	8.83	8.32	7.67	7.28
500	13.18	11.03	10.40	9.59	9.10
600	15.82	13.24	12.48	11.50	10.92
700	18.45	15.44	14.56	13.42	12.74
800	21.09	17.65	16.64	15.33	14.56
900	23.72	19.86	18.72	17.25	16.38
1,000	26.36	22.06	20.80	19.17	18.20
2,000	52.71	44.12	41.60	38.33	36.39
3,000	79.07	66.17	62.40	57.49	54.58
4,000	105.42	88.23	83.20	76.65	72.77
5,000	131.78	110.28	103.99	95.81	90.97
6,000	158.13	132.34	124.79	114.97	109.16
7,000	184.49	154.40	145.59	134.13	127.35
8,000	210.84	176.45	166.39	153.29	145.54
9,000	237.20	198.51	187.18	172.45	163.73
10,000	263.55	220.56	207.98	191.61	181.93
15,000	395.33	330.84	311.97	287.41	272.89
20,000	527.10	441.12	415.96	383.21	363.85
25,000	658.88	551.40	519.94	479.01	454.81
30,000	790.65	661.68	623.93	574.81	545.77
35,000	922.43	771.96	727.92	670.61	636.73
40,000	1,054.20	882.24	831.91	766.41	727.69
45,000	1,185.98	992.52	935.90	862.21	818.65
50,000	1,317.75	1,102.80	1,039.88	958.01	909.61
55,000	1,449.53	1,213.08	1,143.87	1,053.81	1,000.57
60,000	1,581.30	1,323.36	1,247.86	1,149.61	1,091.53
65,000	1,713.08	1,433.64	1,351.85	1,245.41	1,182.49
70,000	1,844.85	1,543.92	1,455.83	1,341.21	1,273.45
75,000	1,976.63	1,654.20	1,559.82	1,437.01	1,364.41
80,000	2,108.40	1,764.48	1,663.81	1,532.81	1,455.37
85,000	2,240.18	1,874.76	1,767.80	1,628.61	1,546.33
90,000	2,371.95	1,985.04	1,871.79	1,724.41	1,637.29
95,000	2,503.73	2,095.32	1,975.77	1,820.21	1,728.25
100,000	2,635.50	2,205.60	2,079.76	1,916.02	1,819.21
110,000	2,899.05	2,426.16	2,287.74	2,107.62	2,001.13
120,000	3,162.60	2,646.71	2,495.71	2,299.22	2,183.05
125,000	3,294.38	2,756.99	2,599.70	2,395.02	2,274.01
130,000	3,426.15	2,867.27	2,703.69	2,490.82	2,364.97
140,000	3,689.70	3,087.83	2,911.66	2,682.42	2,546.89
150,000	3,953.25	3,308.39	3,119.64	2,874.02	2,728.82
160,000	4,216.80	3,528.95	3,327.62	3,065.62	2,910.74
170,000	4,480.35	3,749.51	3,535.59	3,257.22	3,092.66
175,000	4,612.13	3,859.79	3,639.58	3,353.02	3,183.62
180,000	4,743.90	3,970.07	3,743.57	3,448.82	3,274.58
190,000	5,007.45	4,190.63	3,951.54	3,640.42	3,456.50
200,000	5,271.00	4,411.19	4,159.52	3,832.03	3,638.42
220,000	5,798.10	4,852.31	4,575.47	4,215.23	4,002.26
225,000	5,929.87	4,962.59	4,679.46	4,311.03	4,093.22
230,000	6,061.65	5,072.86	4,783.44	4,406.83	4,184.18
240,000	6,325.20	5,293.42	4,991.42	4,598.43	4,366.10
$250,000	6,588.75	5,513.98	5,199.40	4,790.03	4,548.02

Monthly Payment Loans   **19.75%**

Amortization Period in Years

	15	16	17	18	20
$ 100	1.74	1.73	1.71	1.70	1.68
200	3.48	3.45	3.42	3.40	3.36
300	5.22	5.17	5.13	5.09	5.04
400	6.96	6.89	6.83	6.79	6.72
500	8.69	8.61	8.54	8.48	8.40
600	10.43	10.33	10.25	10.18	10.08
700	12.17	12.05	11.95	11.88	11.76
800	13.91	13.77	13.66	13.57	13.44
900	15.65	15.49	15.37	15.27	15.12
1,000	17.38	17.21	17.07	16.96	16.80
2,000	34.76	34.42	34.14	33.92	33.59
3,000	52.14	51.63	51.21	50.88	50.38
4,000	69.52	68.83	68.28	67.83	67.17
5,000	86.90	86.04	85.35	84.79	83.97
6,000	104.28	103.25	102.42	101.75	100.76
7,000	121.65	120.46	119.49	118.71	117.55
8,000	139.03	137.66	136.56	135.66	134.34
9,000	156.41	154.87	153.63	152.62	151.14
10,000	173.79	172.08	170.70	169.58	167.93
15,000	260.68	258.12	256.04	254.36	251.89
20,000	347.58	344.15	341.39	339.15	335.85
25,000	434.47	430.19	426.73	423.94	419.81
30,000	521.36	516.23	512.08	508.72	503.77
35,000	608.25	602.26	597.43	593.51	587.73
40,000	695.15	688.30	682.77	678.29	671.69
45,000	782.04	774.34	768.12	763.08	755.66
50,000	868.93	860.37	853.46	847.87	839.62
55,000	955.83	946.41	938.81	932.65	923.58
60,000	1,042.72	1,032.45	1,024.16	1,017.44	1,007.54
65,000	1,129.61	1,118.49	1,109.50	1,102.22	1,091.50
70,000	1,216.50	1,204.52	1,194.85	1,187.01	1,175.46
75,000	1,303.40	1,290.56	1,280.19	1,271.80	1,259.42
80,000	1,390.29	1,376.60	1,365.54	1,356.58	1,343.38
85,000	1,477.18	1,462.63	1,450.89	1,441.37	1,427.34
90,000	1,564.07	1,548.67	1,536.23	1,526.16	1,511.31
95,000	1,650.97	1,634.71	1,621.58	1,610.94	1,595.27
100,000	1,737.86	1,720.74	1,706.92	1,695.73	1,679.23
110,000	1,911.65	1,892.82	1,877.62	1,865.30	1,847.15
120,000	2,085.43	2,064.89	2,048.31	2,034.87	2,015.07
125,000	2,172.32	2,150.93	2,133.65	2,119.66	2,099.03
130,000	2,259.22	2,236.97	2,219.00	2,204.44	2,182.99
140,000	2,433.00	2,409.04	2,389.69	2,374.02	2,350.92
150,000	2,606.79	2,581.11	2,560.38	2,543.59	2,518.84
160,000	2,780.57	2,753.19	2,731.08	2,713.16	2,686.76
170,000	2,954.36	2,925.26	2,901.77	2,882.73	2,854.68
175,000	3,041.25	3,011.30	2,987.11	2,967.52	2,938.64
180,000	3,128.14	3,097.34	3,072.46	3,052.31	3,022.61
190,000	3,301.93	3,269.41	3,243.15	3,221.88	3,190.53
200,000	3,475.71	3,441.48	3,413.84	3,391.45	3,358.45
220,000	3,823.29	3,785.63	3,755.23	3,730.59	3,694.30
225,000	3,910.18	3,871.67	3,840.57	3,815.38	3,778.26
230,000	3,997.07	3,957.71	3,925.92	3,900.17	3,862.22
240,000	4,170.86	4,129.78	4,096.61	4,069.74	4,030.14
$250,000	4,344.64	4,301.85	4,267.30	4,239.31	4,198.06

Table 1   241

19.75%   Monthly Payment Loans

Amortization Period in Years

	21	22	23	24	25
$ 100	1.68	1.67	1.67	1.67	1.66
200	3.35	3.34	3.33	3.33	3.32
300	5.02	5.01	5.00	4.99	4.98
400	6.70	6.68	6.66	6.65	6.64
500	8.37	8.35	8.33	8.31	8.30
600	10.04	10.01	9.99	9.97	9.95
700	11.72	11.68	11.65	11.63	11.61
800	13.39	13.35	13.32	13.29	13.27
900	15.06	15.02	14.98	14.95	14.93
1,000	16.74	16.69	16.65	16.61	16.59
2,000	33.47	33.37	33.29	33.22	33.17
3,000	50.20	50.05	49.93	49.83	49.75
4,000	66.93	66.74	66.57	66.44	66.33
5,000	83.66	83.42	83.22	83.05	82.92
6,000	100.40	100.10	99.86	99.66	99.50
7,000	117.13	116.78	116.50	116.27	116.08
8,000	133.86	133.47	133.14	132.88	132.66
9,000	150.59	150.15	149.78	149.49	149.24
10,000	167.32	166.83	166.43	166.10	165.83
15,000	250.98	250.24	249.64	249.14	248.74
20,000	334.64	333.66	332.85	332.19	331.65
25,000	418.30	417.07	416.06	415.23	414.56
30,000	501.96	500.48	499.27	498.28	497.47
35,000	585.62	583.89	582.48	581.33	580.38
40,000	669.28	667.31	665.69	664.37	663.29
45,000	752.94	750.72	748.90	747.42	746.20
50,000	836.60	834.13	832.11	830.46	829.11
55,000	920.26	917.54	915.33	913.51	912.02
60,000	1,003.92	1,000.96	998.54	996.56	994.93
65,000	1,087.57	1,084.37	1,081.75	1,079.60	1,077.84
70,000	1,171.23	1,167.78	1,164.96	1,162.65	1,160.76
75,000	1,254.89	1,251.19	1,248.17	1,245.69	1,243.67
80,000	1,338.55	1,334.61	1,331.38	1,328.74	1,326.58
85,000	1,422.21	1,418.02	1,414.59	1,411.79	1,409.49
90,000	1,505.87	1,501.43	1,497.80	1,494.83	1,492.40
95,000	1,589.53	1,584.84	1,581.01	1,577.88	1,575.31
100,000	1,673.19	1,668.26	1,664.22	1,660.92	1,658.22
110,000	1,840.51	1,835.08	1,830.65	1,827.02	1,824.04
120,000	2,007.83	2,001.91	1,997.07	1,993.11	1,989.86
125,000	2,091.49	2,085.32	2,080.28	2,076.15	2,072.77
130,000	2,175.14	2,168.73	2,163.49	2,159.20	2,155.68
140,000	2,342.46	2,335.56	2,329.91	2,325.29	2,321.51
150,000	2,509.78	2,502.38	2,496.33	2,491.38	2,487.33
160,000	2,677.10	2,669.21	2,662.76	2,657.47	2,653.15
170,000	2,844.42	2,836.03	2,829.18	2,823.57	2,818.97
175,000	2,928.08	2,919.45	2,912.39	2,906.61	2,901.88
180,000	3,011.74	3,002.86	2,995.60	2,989.66	2,984.79
190,000	3,179.05	3,169.68	3,162.02	3,155.75	3,150.61
200,000	3,346.37	3,336.51	3,328.44	3,321.84	3,316.43
220,000	3,681.01	3,670.16	3,661.29	3,654.03	3,648.08
225,000	3,764.67	3,753.57	3,744.50	3,737.07	3,730.99
230,000	3,848.33	3,836.98	3,827.71	3,820.12	3,813.90
240,000	4,015.65	4,003.81	3,994.13	3,986.21	3,979.72
$250,000	4,182.97	4,170.64	4,160.55	4,152.30	4,145.54

Monthly Payment Loans   **19.75%**

Amortization Period in Years

	26	27	28	29	30
$ 100	1.66	1.66	1.66	1.66	1.66
200	3.32	3.31	3.31	3.31	3.31
300	4.97	4.97	4.96	4.96	4.96
400	6.63	6.62	6.62	6.61	6.61
500	8.28	8.28	8.27	8.26	8.26
600	9.94	9.93	9.92	9.91	9.91
700	11.60	11.58	11.57	11.57	11.56
800	13.25	13.24	13.23	13.22	13.21
900	14.91	14.89	14.88	14.87	14.86
1,000	16.56	16.55	16.53	16.52	16.51
2,000	33.12	33.09	33.06	33.03	33.01
3,000	49.68	49.63	49.59	49.55	49.52
4,000	66.24	66.17	66.11	66.06	66.02
5,000	82.80	82.71	82.64	82.58	82.53
6,000	99.36	99.26	99.17	99.09	99.03
7,000	115.92	115.80	115.69	115.61	115.54
8,000	132.48	132.34	132.22	132.12	132.04
9,000	149.04	148.88	148.75	148.64	148.55
10,000	165.60	165.42	165.27	165.15	165.05
15,000	248.40	248.13	247.91	247.72	247.57
20,000	331.20	330.84	330.54	330.30	330.10
25,000	414.00	413.55	413.18	412.87	412.62
30,000	496.80	496.26	495.81	495.44	495.14
35,000	579.60	578.97	578.45	578.02	577.67
40,000	662.40	661.68	661.08	660.59	660.19
45,000	745.20	744.39	743.72	743.16	742.71
50,000	828.00	827.10	826.35	825.74	825.24
55,000	910.80	909.80	908.98	908.31	907.76
60,000	993.60	992.51	991.62	990.88	990.28
65,000	1,076.40	1,075.22	1,074.25	1,073.46	1,072.80
70,000	1,159.20	1,157.93	1,156.89	1,156.03	1,155.33
75,000	1,242.00	1,240.64	1,239.52	1,238.60	1,237.85
80,000	1,324.80	1,323.35	1,322.16	1,321.18	1,320.37
85,000	1,407.60	1,406.06	1,404.79	1,403.75	1,402.90
90,000	1,490.40	1,488.77	1,487.43	1,486.32	1,485.42
95,000	1,573.20	1,571.48	1,570.06	1,568.90	1,567.94
100,000	1,656.00	1,654.19	1,652.69	1,651.47	1,650.47
110,000	1,821.60	1,819.60	1,817.96	1,816.62	1,815.51
120,000	1,987.20	1,985.02	1,983.23	1,981.76	1,980.56
125,000	2,070.00	2,067.73	2,065.87	2,064.34	2,063.08
130,000	2,152.80	2,150.44	2,148.50	2,146.91	2,145.60
140,000	2,318.40	2,315.86	2,313.77	2,312.06	2,310.65
150,000	2,484.00	2,481.28	2,479.04	2,477.20	2,475.70
160,000	2,649.60	2,646.69	2,644.31	2,642.35	2,640.74
170,000	2,815.20	2,812.11	2,809.58	2,807.50	2,805.79
175,000	2,898.00	2,894.82	2,892.21	2,890.07	2,888.31
180,000	2,980.80	2,977.53	2,974.85	2,972.64	2,970.83
190,000	3,146.40	3,142.95	3,140.12	3,137.79	3,135.88
200,000	3,312.00	3,308.37	3,305.38	3,302.94	3,300.93
220,000	3,643.20	3,639.20	3,635.92	3,633.23	3,631.02
225,000	3,726.00	3,721.91	3,718.56	3,715.80	3,713.54
230,000	3,808.80	3,804.62	3,801.19	3,798.38	3,796.07
240,000	3,974.40	3,970.04	3,966.46	3,963.52	3,961.11
$250,000	4,140.00	4,135.46	4,131.73	4,128.67	4,126.16

Table 1   243

20.00%   **Monthly Payment Loans**

Amortization Period in Years

	5	7	8	10	12
$ 100	2.65	2.23	2.10	1.94	1.84
200	5.30	4.45	4.20	3.87	3.68
300	7.95	6.67	6.29	5.80	5.51
400	10.60	8.89	8.39	7.74	7.35
500	13.25	11.11	10.48	9.67	9.19
600	15.90	13.33	12.58	11.60	11.02
700	18.55	15.55	14.67	13.53	12.86
800	21.20	17.77	16.77	15.47	14.70
900	23.85	19.99	18.86	17.40	16.53
1,000	26.50	22.21	20.96	19.33	18.37
2,000	52.99	44.42	41.91	38.66	36.74
3,000	79.49	66.62	62.86	57.98	55.10
4,000	105.98	88.83	83.82	77.31	73.47
5,000	132.47	111.04	104.77	96.63	91.84
6,000	158.97	133.24	125.72	115.96	110.20
7,000	185.46	155.45	146.68	135.28	128.57
8,000	211.96	177.65	167.63	154.61	146.93
9,000	238.45	199.86	188.58	173.94	165.30
10,000	264.94	222.07	209.54	193.26	183.67
15,000	397.41	333.10	314.30	289.89	275.50
20,000	529.88	444.13	419.07	386.52	367.33
25,000	662.35	555.16	523.84	483.14	459.16
30,000	794.82	666.19	628.60	579.77	550.99
35,000	927.29	777.22	733.37	676.40	642.82
40,000	1,059.76	888.25	838.13	773.03	734.65
45,000	1,192.23	999.28	942.90	869.66	826.48
50,000	1,324.70	1,110.31	1,047.67	966.28	918.31
55,000	1,457.17	1,221.35	1,152.43	1,062.91	1,010.14
60,000	1,589.64	1,332.38	1,257.20	1,159.54	1,101.97
65,000	1,722.11	1,443.41	1,361.96	1,256.17	1,193.80
70,000	1,854.58	1,554.44	1,466.73	1,352.79	1,285.63
75,000	1,987.05	1,665.47	1,571.50	1,449.42	1,377.46
80,000	2,119.52	1,776.50	1,676.26	1,546.05	1,469.29
85,000	2,251.99	1,887.53	1,781.03	1,642.68	1,561.12
90,000	2,384.45	1,998.56	1,885.79	1,739.31	1,652.95
95,000	2,516.92	2,109.59	1,990.56	1,835.93	1,744.78
100,000	2,649.39	2,220.62	2,095.33	1,932.56	1,836.61
110,000	2,914.33	2,442.69	2,304.86	2,125.82	2,020.27
120,000	3,179.27	2,664.75	2,514.39	2,319.07	2,203.94
125,000	3,311.74	2,775.78	2,619.16	2,415.70	2,295.77
130,000	3,444.21	2,886.81	2,723.92	2,512.33	2,387.60
140,000	3,709.15	3,108.87	2,933.45	2,705.58	2,571.26
150,000	3,974.09	3,330.93	3,142.99	2,898.84	2,754.92
160,000	4,239.03	3,553.00	3,352.52	3,092.10	2,938.58
170,000	4,503.97	3,775.06	3,562.05	3,285.35	3,122.24
175,000	4,636.43	3,886.09	3,666.82	3,381.98	3,214.07
180,000	4,768.90	3,997.12	3,771.58	3,478.61	3,305.90
190,000	5,033.84	4,219.18	3,981.11	3,671.86	3,489.56
200,000	5,298.78	4,441.24	4,190.65	3,865.12	3,673.22
220,000	5,828.66	4,885.37	4,609.71	4,251.63	4,040.54
225,000	5,961.13	4,996.40	4,714.48	4,348.26	4,132.37
230,000	6,093.60	5,107.43	4,819.24	4,444.89	4,224.20
240,000	6,358.54	5,329.49	5,028.77	4,638.14	4,407.87
$250,000	6,623.48	5,551.55	5,238.31	4,831.40	4,591.53

Monthly Payment Loans   <u>**20.00%**</u>

Amortization Period in Years

	15	16	17	18	20
$ 100	1.76	1.74	1.73	1.72	1.70
200	3.52	3.48	3.46	3.43	3.40
300	5.27	5.22	5.18	5.15	5.10
400	7.03	6.96	6.91	6.86	6.80
500	8.79	8.70	8.63	8.58	8.50
600	10.54	10.44	10.36	10.29	10.20
700	12.30	12.18	12.09	12.01	11.90
800	14.06	13.92	13.81	13.72	13.60
900	15.81	15.66	15.54	15.44	15.29
1,000	17.57	17.40	17.26	17.15	16.99
2,000	35.13	34.79	34.52	34.30	33.98
3,000	52.69	52.19	51.78	51.45	50.97
4,000	70.26	69.58	69.04	68.60	67.96
5,000	87.82	86.98	86.30	85.75	84.95
6,000	105.38	104.37	103.56	102.90	101.93
7,000	122.95	121.77	120.82	120.05	118.92
8,000	140.51	139.16	138.08	137.20	135.91
9,000	158.07	156.56	155.34	154.35	152.90
10,000	175.63	173.95	172.60	171.50	169.89
15,000	263.45	260.92	258.89	257.25	254.83
20,000	351.26	347.90	345.19	342.99	339.77
25,000	439.08	434.87	431.48	428.74	424.71
30,000	526.89	521.84	517.78	514.49	509.65
35,000	614.71	608.82	604.07	600.23	594.59
40,000	702.52	695.79	690.37	685.98	679.53
45,000	790.34	782.76	776.66	771.73	764.48
50,000	878.15	869.74	862.96	857.47	849.42
55,000	965.97	956.71	949.25	943.22	934.36
60,000	1,053.78	1,043.68	1,035.55	1,028.97	1,019.30
65,000	1,141.60	1,130.66	1,121.84	1,114.71	1,104.24
70,000	1,229.41	1,217.63	1,208.14	1,200.46	1,189.18
75,000	1,317.23	1,304.60	1,294.43	1,286.21	1,274.12
80,000	1,405.04	1,391.58	1,380.73	1,371.95	1,359.06
85,000	1,492.86	1,478.55	1,467.02	1,457.70	1,444.01
90,000	1,580.67	1,565.52	1,553.32	1,543.45	1,528.95
95,000	1,668.49	1,652.50	1,639.61	1,629.19	1,613.89
100,000	1,756.30	1,739.47	1,725.91	1,714.94	1,698.83
110,000	1,931.93	1,913.42	1,898.50	1,886.43	1,868.71
120,000	2,107.56	2,087.36	2,071.09	2,057.93	2,038.59
125,000	2,195.38	2,174.34	2,157.38	2,143.68	2,123.54
130,000	2,283.19	2,261.31	2,243.68	2,229.42	2,208.48
140,000	2,458.82	2,435.26	2,416.27	2,400.92	2,378.36
150,000	2,634.45	2,609.20	2,588.86	2,572.41	2,548.24
160,000	2,810.08	2,783.15	2,761.45	2,743.90	2,718.12
170,000	2,985.71	2,957.10	2,934.04	2,915.40	2,888.01
175,000	3,073.52	3,044.07	3,020.33	3,001.14	2,972.95
180,000	3,161.34	3,131.04	3,106.63	3,086.89	3,057.89
190,000	3,336.97	3,304.99	3,279.22	3,258.38	3,227.77
200,000	3,512.60	3,478.94	3,451.81	3,429.88	3,397.65
220,000	3,863.86	3,826.83	3,796.99	3,772.86	3,737.42
225,000	3,951.67	3,913.80	3,883.29	3,858.61	3,822.36
230,000	4,039.49	4,000.78	3,969.58	3,944.36	3,907.30
240,000	4,215.12	4,174.72	4,142.17	4,115.85	4,077.18
$250,000	4,390.75	4,348.67	4,314.76	4,287.35	4,247.07

Table 1   245

20.00%   Monthly Payment Loans

Amortization Period in Years

	21	22	23	24	25
$ 100	1.70	1.69	1.69	1.69	1.68
200	3.39	3.38	3.37	3.37	3.36
300	5.08	5.07	5.06	5.05	5.04
400	6.78	6.76	6.74	6.73	6.72
500	8.47	8.45	8.43	8.41	8.40
600	10.16	10.13	10.11	10.09	10.08
700	11.86	11.82	11.79	11.77	11.75
800	13.55	13.51	13.48	13.45	13.43
900	15.24	15.20	15.16	15.13	15.11
1,000	16.93	16.89	16.85	16.82	16.79
2,000	33.86	33.77	33.69	33.63	33.57
3,000	50.79	50.65	50.53	50.44	50.36
4,000	67.72	67.53	67.38	67.25	67.14
5,000	84.65	84.41	84.22	84.06	83.93
6,000	101.58	101.29	101.06	100.87	100.71
7,000	118.51	118.18	117.90	117.68	117.50
8,000	135.44	135.06	134.75	134.49	134.28
9,000	152.37	151.94	151.59	151.30	151.07
10,000	169.30	168.82	168.43	168.11	167.85
15,000	253.95	253.23	252.64	252.16	251.77
20,000	338.59	337.64	336.86	336.22	335.70
25,000	423.24	422.04	421.07	420.27	419.62
30,000	507.89	506.45	505.28	504.32	503.54
35,000	592.54	590.86	589.49	588.38	587.46
40,000	677.18	675.27	673.71	672.43	671.39
45,000	761.83	759.68	757.92	756.48	755.31
50,000	846.48	844.08	842.13	840.53	839.23
55,000	931.13	928.49	926.34	924.59	923.15
60,000	1,015.77	1,012.90	1,010.56	1,008.64	1,007.08
65,000	1,100.42	1,097.31	1,094.77	1,092.69	1,091.00
70,000	1,185.07	1,181.72	1,178.98	1,176.75	1,174.92
75,000	1,269.72	1,266.12	1,263.19	1,260.80	1,258.84
80,000	1,354.36	1,350.53	1,347.41	1,344.85	1,342.77
85,000	1,439.01	1,434.94	1,431.62	1,428.91	1,426.69
90,000	1,523.66	1,519.35	1,515.83	1,512.96	1,510.61
95,000	1,608.31	1,603.76	1,600.04	1,597.01	1,594.53
100,000	1,692.95	1,688.16	1,684.26	1,681.06	1,678.46
110,000	1,862.25	1,856.98	1,852.68	1,849.17	1,846.30
120,000	2,031.54	2,025.79	2,021.11	2,017.28	2,014.15
125,000	2,116.19	2,110.20	2,105.32	2,101.33	2,098.07
130,000	2,200.84	2,194.61	2,189.53	2,185.38	2,181.99
140,000	2,370.13	2,363.43	2,357.96	2,353.49	2,349.84
150,000	2,539.43	2,532.24	2,526.38	2,521.59	2,517.68
160,000	2,708.72	2,701.06	2,694.81	2,689.70	2,685.53
170,000	2,878.02	2,869.87	2,863.23	2,857.81	2,853.37
175,000	2,962.66	2,954.28	2,947.44	2,941.86	2,937.30
180,000	3,047.31	3,038.69	3,031.66	3,025.91	3,021.22
190,000	3,216.61	3,207.51	3,200.08	3,194.02	3,189.06
200,000	3,385.90	3,376.32	3,368.51	3,362.12	3,356.91
220,000	3,724.49	3,713.95	3,705.36	3,698.34	3,692.60
225,000	3,809.14	3,798.36	3,789.57	3,782.39	3,776.52
230,000	3,893.78	3,882.77	3,873.78	3,866.44	3,860.44
240,000	4,063.08	4,051.58	4,042.21	4,034.55	4,028.29
$250,000	4,232.37	4,220.40	4,210.63	4,202.65	4,196.13

Monthly Payment Loans   **20.00%**

Amortization Period in Years

	26	27	28	29	30
$ 100	1.68	1.68	1.68	1.68	1.68
200	3.36	3.35	3.35	3.35	3.35
300	5.03	5.03	5.02	5.02	5.02
400	6.71	6.70	6.70	6.69	6.69
500	8.39	8.38	8.37	8.36	8.36
600	10.06	10.05	10.04	10.04	10.03
700	11.74	11.73	11.72	11.71	11.70
800	13.42	13.40	13.39	13.38	13.37
900	15.09	15.08	15.06	15.05	15.04
1,000	16.77	16.75	16.74	16.72	16.72
2,000	33.53	33.50	33.47	33.44	33.43
3,000	50.29	50.24	50.20	50.16	50.14
4,000	67.06	66.99	66.93	66.88	66.85
5,000	83.82	83.73	83.66	83.60	83.56
6,000	100.58	100.48	100.39	100.32	100.27
7,000	117.35	117.23	117.13	117.04	116.98
8,000	134.11	133.97	133.86	133.76	133.69
9,000	150.87	150.72	150.59	150.48	150.40
10,000	167.64	167.46	167.32	167.20	167.11
15,000	251.45	251.19	250.98	250.80	250.66
20,000	335.27	334.92	334.63	334.40	334.21
25,000	419.08	418.65	418.29	418.00	417.76
30,000	502.90	502.38	501.95	501.60	501.31
35,000	586.72	586.11	585.61	585.20	584.86
40,000	670.53	669.83	669.26	668.80	668.41
45,000	754.35	753.56	752.92	752.39	751.96
50,000	838.16	837.29	836.58	835.99	835.51
55,000	921.98	921.02	920.24	919.59	919.07
60,000	1,005.80	1,004.75	1,003.89	1,003.19	1,002.62
65,000	1,089.61	1,088.48	1,087.55	1,086.79	1,086.17
70,000	1,173.43	1,172.21	1,171.21	1,170.39	1,169.72
75,000	1,257.24	1,255.94	1,254.86	1,253.99	1,253.27
80,000	1,341.06	1,339.66	1,338.52	1,337.59	1,336.82
85,000	1,424.88	1,423.39	1,422.18	1,421.19	1,420.37
90,000	1,508.69	1,507.12	1,505.84	1,504.78	1,503.92
95,000	1,592.51	1,590.85	1,589.49	1,588.38	1,587.47
100,000	1,676.32	1,674.58	1,673.15	1,671.98	1,671.02
110,000	1,843.96	1,842.04	1,840.47	1,839.18	1,838.13
120,000	2,011.59	2,009.49	2,007.78	2,006.38	2,005.23
125,000	2,095.40	2,093.22	2,091.44	2,089.98	2,088.78
130,000	2,179.22	2,176.95	2,175.09	2,173.57	2,172.33
140,000	2,346.85	2,344.41	2,342.41	2,340.77	2,339.43
150,000	2,514.48	2,511.87	2,509.72	2,507.97	2,506.53
160,000	2,682.12	2,679.32	2,677.04	2,675.17	2,673.63
170,000	2,849.75	2,846.78	2,844.35	2,842.37	2,840.74
175,000	2,933.56	2,930.51	2,928.01	2,925.96	2,924.29
180,000	3,017.38	3,014.24	3,011.67	3,009.56	3,007.84
190,000	3,185.01	3,181.70	3,178.98	3,176.76	3,174.94
200,000	3,352.64	3,349.15	3,346.30	3,343.96	3,342.04
220,000	3,687.91	3,684.07	3,680.93	3,678.35	3,676.25
225,000	3,771.72	3,767.80	3,764.58	3,761.95	3,759.80
230,000	3,855.54	3,851.53	3,848.24	3,845.55	3,843.35
240,000	4,023.17	4,018.98	4,015.56	4,012.75	4,010.45
$250,000	4,190.80	4,186.44	4,182.87	4,179.95	4,177.55

Table 1   247

Table 2
Monthly Loan Factors on $1000

For less common loan cases than those in Table 1, Table 2 provides the payment information. It gives amortization periods from 1 to 40 years, at interest rates from 5 percent to 20 percent. Table 2 also supplements Table 3, the remaining loan balance table, allowing loan balances to be figured for cases not covered there.

Example 4.   Monthly Payment on a Loan

Glenda Dallious will take back a purchase money mortgage of $350,000 for a term of 21 years at 11.25 percent.

To find the payment, enter Table 2 at the page for 21 years. On the 11.25 percent line under 21 years, read $10.3617. Divide the loan amount by $1000 and multiply by this payment to get

$$\frac{\$350,000}{\$1000} \times \$10.3617 = \$3,626.60$$

the monthly payment for a loan with this data.

Example 5.   Loan Balance Not Given in Table 3

Table 2 may also be used to find the mortgage loan balance on a loan for less common cases. For the balance at the end of any year, divide the factor in Table 2 for the *original* term of the loan by the factor for the number of years remaining.

For a 9.00 percent loan that has 22 of 30 years remaining, this will be the original 30-year payment divided by the payment for a 22-year loan. Using $100,000 principal amount will give

$$\frac{\$8.0462}{8.7117} = 92.361 \text{ percent}$$

the remaining balance on the loan.

This case could have been solved more quickly using Table 3. The terms were selected, though, to let you confirm that the method gives the same answer as Table 3.

Example 6.   The Annual Mortgage Constant

Real estate persons prefer the annual mortgage constant to the actual monthly payment. Annual mortgage constants express the *rate* of mortgage payment as a percentage of the loan represented by one year's payments. Comparison of loan plans is simplified using the "constant."

Kursten has offers for a mortgage loan, one at 10.00 percent interest for 21 years, another at 10.25 percent amortized over 25 years.

Enter Table 2 on the page containing loan factors for 21 and 25 years. On the 10.00 percent line, take the factor under 21 years; it is 9.5078 per $1000. Multiply this by 1.2 to get 11.409 percent, the annual mortgage constant on a 10.00 percent, 21-year loan.

On 10.25 percent line, take the factor under 25 years; it is 9.2638 per $1000. Multiply this also by 1.2, to get 11.117 percent, the annual mortgage constant for a 10.25 percent, 25-year loan.

Even though the interest rate is higher, many persons would prefer the loan with the lower annual constant, since it will lower cash needs.

Monthly Payment Factors
Payment per $1000

Interest Rate	Amortization Period in Years				
	1	2	3	4	5
5.00%	85.6075	43.8714	29.9709	23.0293	18.8712
.25	85.7221	43.9834	30.0833	23.1427	18.9860
.50	85.8368	44.0957	30.1959	23.2565	19.1012
.75	85.9516	44.2080	30.3088	23.3706	19.2168
6.00	86.0664	44.3206	30.4219	23.4850	19.3328
.25	86.1814	44.4333	30.5353	23.5998	19.4493
.50	86.2964	44.5463	30.6490	23.7150	19.5661
.75	86.4115	44.6593	30.7629	23.8304	19.6835
7.00	86.5267	44.7726	30.8771	23.9462	19.8012
.25	86.6420	44.8860	30.9915	24.0624	19.9194
.50	86.7574	44.9996	31.1062	24.1789	20.0379
.75	86.8729	45.1134	31.2212	24.2957	20.1570
8.00	86.9884	45.2273	31.3364	24.4129	20.2764
.25	87.1041	45.3414	31.4518	24.5304	20.3963
.50	87.2198	45.4557	31.5675	24.6483	20.5165
.75	87.3356	45.5701	31.6835	24.7665	20.6372
9.00	87.4515	45.6847	31.7997	24.8850	20.7584
.25	87.5675	45.7995	31.9162	25.0039	20.8799
.50	87.6835	45.9145	32.0329	25.1231	21.0019
.75	87.7997	46.0296	32.1499	25.2427	21.1242
10.00	87.9159	46.1449	32.2672	25.3626	21.2470
.25	88.0322	46.2604	32.3847	25.4828	21.3703
.50	88.1486	46.3760	32.5024	25.6034	21.4939
.75	88.2651	46.4919	32.6205	25.7243	21.6180
11.00	88.3817	46.6078	32.7387	25.8455	21.7424
.25	88.4983	46.7240	32.8572	25.9671	21.8673
.50	88.6151	46.8403	32.9760	26.0890	21.9926
.75	88.7319	46.9568	33.0950	26.2113	22.1183
12.00	88.8488	47.0735	33.2143	26.3338	22.2444
.25	88.9658	47.1903	33.3338	26.4568	22.3710
.50	89.0829	47.3073	33.4536	26.5800	22.4979
.75	89.2000	47.4245	33.5737	26.7036	22.6253
13.00	89.3173	47.5418	33.6940	26.8275	22.7531
.25	89.4346	47.6593	33.8145	26.9517	22.8813
.50	89.5520	47.7770	33.9353	27.0763	23.0098
.75	89.6695	47.8949	34.0563	27.2012	23.1388
14.00	89.7871	48.0129	34.1776	27.3265	23.2683
.25	89.9048	48.1311	34.2992	27.4520	23.3981
.50	90.0225	48.2494	34.4210	27.5780	23.5283
.75	90.1404	48.3680	34.5430	27.7042	23.6589
15.00	90.2583	48.4866	34.6653	27.8307	23.7899
.25	90.3763	48.6055	34.7879	27.9576	23.9214
.50	90.4944	48.7245	34.9107	28.0849	24.0532
.75	90.6126	48.8437	35.0337	28.2124	24.1854
16.00	90.7309	48.9631	35.1570	28.3403	24.3181
.25	90.8492	49.0826	35.2806	28.4685	24.4511
.50	90.9676	49.2024	35.4044	28.5970	24.5845
.75	91.0862	49.3222	35.5284	28.7259	24.7184
17.00	91.2048	49.4423	35.6527	28.8550	24.8526
.25	91.3234	49.5625	35.7773	28.9845	24.9872
.50	91.4422	49.6828	35.9021	29.1144	25.1222
.75	91.5611	49.8034	36.0271	29.2445	25.2576
18.00	91.6800	49.9241	36.1524	29.3750	25.3934
.25	91.7990	50.0450	36.2779	29.5058	25.5296
.50	91.9181	50.1660	36.4037	29.6369	25.6662
.75	92.0373	50.2872	36.5297	29.7684	25.8032
19.00	92.1566	50.4086	36.6560	29.9001	25.9406
.25	92.2759	50.5302	36.7825	30.0322	26.0783
.50	92.3954	50.6519	36.9093	30.1646	26.2164
.75	92.5149	50.7738	37.0363	30.2973	26.3550
20.00%	92.6345	50.8958	37.1636	30.4304	26.4939

Table 2   251

Monthly Payment Factors
Payment per $1000

Interest Rate	Amortization Period in Years 6	7	8	9	10
5.00%	16.1049	14.1339	12.6599	11.5173	10.6066
.25	16.2212	14.2517	12.7793	11.6383	10.7292
.50	16.3379	14.3700	12.8993	11.7600	10.8526
.75	16.4551	14.4890	13.0200	11.8825	10.9769
6.00	16.5729	14.6086	13.1414	12.0057	11.1021
.25	16.6912	14.7287	13.2635	12.1298	11.2280
.50	16.8099	14.8494	13.3862	12.2545	11.3548
.75	16.9292	14.9708	13.5096	12.3800	11.4824
7.00	17.0490	15.0927	13.6337	12.5063	11.6108
.25	17.1693	15.2152	13.7585	12.6333	11.7401
.50	17.2901	15.3383	13.8839	12.7610	11.8702
.75	17.4114	15.4620	14.0099	12.8895	12.0011
8.00	17.5332	15.5862	14.1367	13.0187	12.1328
.25	17.6556	15.7111	14.2641	13.1487	12.2653
.50	17.7784	15.8365	14.3921	13.2794	12.3986
.75	17.9017	15.9625	14.5208	13.4108	12.5327
9.00	18.0255	16.0891	14.6502	13.5429	12.6676
.25	18.1499	16.2162	14.7802	13.6758	12.8033
.50	18.2747	16.3440	14.9109	13.8094	12.9398
.75	18.4000	16.4723	15.0422	13.9437	13.0770
10.00	18.5258	16.6012	15.1742	14.0787	13.2151
.25	18.6522	16.7306	15.3068	14.2144	13.3539
.50	18.7790	16.8607	15.4400	14.3509	13.4935
.75	18.9063	16.9913	15.5739	14.4880	13.6339
11.00	19.0341	17.1224	15.7084	14.6259	13.7750
.25	19.1624	17.2542	15.8436	14.7644	13.9169
.50	19.2912	17.3865	15.9794	14.9037	14.0595
.75	19.4204	17.5193	16.1158	15.0436	14.2029
12.00	19.5502	17.6527	16.2528	15.1842	14.3471
.25	19.6804	17.7867	16.3905	15.3256	14.4920
.50	19.8112	17.9212	16.5288	15.4676	14.6376
.75	19.9424	18.0563	16.6677	15.6102	14.7840
13.00	20.0741	18.1920	16.8073	15.7536	14.9311
.25	20.2063	18.3282	16.9474	15.8976	15.0789
.50	20.3390	18.4649	17.0882	16.0423	15.2274
.75	20.4721	18.6022	17.2295	16.1877	15.3767
14.00	20.6057	18.7400	17.3715	16.3337	15.5266
.25	20.7398	18.8784	17.5141	16.4804	15.6773
.50	20.8744	19.0173	17.6573	16.6277	15.8287
.75	21.0095	19.1568	17.8010	16.7757	15.9807
15.00	21.1450	19.2968	17.9454	16.9243	16.1335
.25	21.2810	19.4373	18.0904	17.0736	16.2869
.50	21.4175	19.5783	18.2359	17.2235	16.4411
.75	21.5544	19.7199	18.3821	17.3741	16.5958
16.00	21.6918	19.8621	18.5288	17.5253	16.7513
.25	21.8297	20.0047	18.6761	17.6771	16.9074
.50	21.9681	20.1479	18.8240	17.8295	17.0642
.75	22.1069	20.2916	18.9724	17.9825	17.2217
17.00	22.2461	20.4358	19.1215	18.1362	17.3798
.25	22.3859	20.5805	19.2710	18.2905	17.5385
.50	22.5260	20.7258	19.4212	18.4453	17.6979
.75	22.6667	20.8716	19.5719	18.6008	17.8579
18.00	22.8078	21.0178	19.7232	18.7569	18.0185
.25	22.9493	21.1646	19.8751	18.9136	18.1798
.50	23.0914	21.3119	20.0274	19.0708	18.3417
.75	23.2338	21.4597	20.1804	19.2287	18.5041
19.00	23.3767	21.6080	20.3339	19.3871	18.6672
.25	23.5201	21.7568	20.4879	19.5461	18.8309
.50	23.6639	21.9061	20.6425	19.7057	18.9952
.75	23.8081	22.0559	20.7976	19.8658	19.1601
20.00%	23.9528	22.2062	20.9532	20.0265	19.3256

Monthly Payment Factors
Payment per $1000

Interest Rate	Amortization Period in Years				
	11	12	13	14	15
5.00%	9.8645	9.2489	8.7306	8.2887	7.9079
.25	9.9888	9.3748	8.8582	8.4179	8.0388
.50	10.1139	9.5017	8.9868	8.5483	8.1708
.75	10.2400	9.6296	9.1165	8.6797	8.3041
6.00	10.3670	9.7585	9.2472	8.8124	8.4386
.25	10.4949	9.8884	9.3790	8.9461	8.5742
.50	10.6238	10.0192	9.5119	9.0810	8.7111
.75	10.7535	10.1510	9.6458	9.2169	8.8491
7.00	10.8841	10.2838	9.7807	9.3540	8.9883
.25	11.0156	10.4176	9.9167	9.4922	9.1286
.50	11.1480	10.5523	10.0537	9.6314	9.2701
.75	11.2813	10.6879	10.1917	9.7718	9.4128
8.00	11.4154	10.8245	10.3307	9.9132	9.5565
.25	11.5505	10.9621	10.4708	10.0557	9.7014
.50	11.6864	11.1006	10.6118	10.1992	9.8474
.75	11.8232	11.2400	10.7538	10.3438	9.9945
9.00	11.9608	11.3803	10.8968	10.4894	10.1427
.25	12.0993	11.5216	11.0408	10.6360	10.2919
.50	12.2386	11.6637	11.1857	10.7837	10.4422
.75	12.3788	11.8068	11.3316	10.9324	10.5936
10.00	12.5199	11.9508	11.4785	11.0820	10.7461
.25	12.6618	12.0957	11.6263	11.2327	10.8995
.50	12.8045	12.2414	11.7750	11.3843	11.0540
.75	12.9480	12.3880	11.9247	11.5370	11.2095
11.00	13.0923	12.5356	12.0753	11.6905	11.3660
.25	13.2375	12.6839	12.2268	11.8451	11.5234
.50	13.3835	12.8332	12.3792	12.0006	11.6819
.75	13.5303	12.9833	12.5325	12.1570	11.8413
12.00	13.6779	13.1342	12.6867	12.3143	12.0017
.25	13.8263	13.2860	12.8417	12.4725	12.1630
.50	13.9754	13.4386	12.9977	12.6317	12.3252
.75	14.1254	13.5920	13.1545	12.7917	12.4884
13.00	14.2761	13.7463	13.3121	12.9526	12.6524
.25	14.4276	13.9013	13.4706	13.1144	12.8174
.50	14.5799	14.0572	13.6299	13.2771	12.9832
.75	14.7329	14.2138	13.7901	13.4406	13.1499
14.00	14.8867	14.3713	13.9510	13.6049	13.3174
.25	15.0412	14.5295	14.1128	13.7701	13.4858
.50	15.1964	14.6885	14.2754	13.9360	13.6550
.75	15.3524	14.8483	14.4387	14.1028	13.8250
15.00	15.5091	15.0088	14.6029	14.2704	13.9959
.25	15.6666	15.1700	14.7678	14.4388	14.1675
.50	15.8247	15.3320	14.9335	14.6079	14.3399
.75	15.9836	15.4948	15.0999	14.7778	14.5131
16.00	16.1432	15.6583	15.2670	14.9485	14.6870
.25	16.3034	15.8224	15.4349	15.1199	14.8617
.50	16.4644	15.9873	15.6036	15.2920	15.0371
.75	16.6260	16.1529	15.7729	15.4648	15.2132
17.00	16.7883	16.3192	15.9430	15.6384	15.3900
.25	16.9513	16.4862	16.1137	15.8126	15.5676
.50	17.1149	16.6539	16.2851	15.9876	15.7458
.75	17.2792	16.8222	16.4572	16.1632	15.9247
18.00	17.4442	16.9912	16.6300	16.3395	16.1042
.25	17.6098	17.1608	16.8034	16.5165	16.2844
.50	17.7760	17.3311	16.9775	16.6941	16.4652
.75	17.9428	17.5021	17.1523	16.8723	16.6467
19.00	18.1103	17.6736	17.3276	17.0511	16.8288
.25	18.2784	17.8458	17.5036	17.2306	17.0114
.50	18.4471	18.0186	17.6802	17.4107	17.1947
.75	18.6164	18.1921	17.8574	17.5914	17.3785
20.00%	18.7863	18.3661	18.0352	17.7727	17.5630

Table 2   253

Monthly Payment Factors
Payment per $1000

Interest Rate	Amortization Period in Years				
	16	17	18	19	20
5.00%	7.5768	7.2866	7.0303	6.8028	6.5996
.25	7.7093	7.4206	7.1660	6.9401	6.7384
.50	7.8430	7.5561	7.3032	7.0789	6.8789
.75	7.9781	7.6929	7.4417	7.2191	7.0208
6.00	8.1144	7.8310	7.5816	7.3608	7.1643
.25	8.2519	7.9705	7.7229	7.5040	7.3093
.50	8.3908	8.1112	7.8656	7.6486	7.4557
.75	8.5308	8.2533	8.0096	7.7945	7.6036
7.00	8.6721	8.3966	8.1550	7.9419	7.7530
.25	8.8146	8.5412	8.3017	8.0907	7.9038
.50	8.9583	8.6871	8.4497	8.2408	8.0559
.75	9.1032	8.8342	8.5990	8.3922	8.2095
8.00	9.2493	8.9826	8.7496	8.5450	8.3644
.25	9.3965	9.1321	8.9015	8.6991	8.5207
.50	9.5449	9.2829	9.0546	8.8545	8.6782
.75	9.6945	9.4349	9.2089	9.0111	8.8371
9.00	9.8452	9.5880	9.3644	9.1690	8.9973
.25	9.9970	9.7423	9.5212	9.3281	9.1587
.50	10.1499	9.8978	9.6791	9.4884	9.3213
.75	10.3039	10.0544	9.8382	9.6499	9.4852
10.00	10.4590	10.2121	9.9984	9.8126	9.6502
.25	10.6152	10.3709	10.1598	9.9764	9.8164
.50	10.7724	10.5308	10.3223	10.1414	9.9838
.75	10.9307	10.6918	10.4858	10.3075	10.1523
11.00	11.0900	10.8538	10.6505	10.4746	10.3219
.25	11.2503	11.0169	10.8162	10.6429	10.4926
.50	11.4116	11.1810	10.9830	10.8122	10.6643
.75	11.5740	11.3461	11.1507	10.9825	10.8371
12.00	11.7373	11.5122	11.3195	11.1539	11.0109
.25	11.9015	11.6792	11.4893	11.3262	11.1856
.50	12.0667	11.8473	11.6600	11.4995	11.3614
.75	12.2328	12.0162	11.8317	11.6738	11.5381
13.00	12.3999	12.1861	12.0043	11.8490	11.7158
.25	12.5678	12.3570	12.1779	12.0251	11.8943
.50	12.7367	12.5287	12.3523	12.2021	12.0737
.75	12.9064	12.7013	12.5276	12.3800	12.2541
14.00	13.0770	12.8748	12.7038	12.5588	12.4352
.25	13.2484	13.0491	12.8809	12.7384	12.6172
.50	13.4207	13.2242	13.0587	12.9188	12.8000
.75	13.5938	13.4002	13.2374	13.1000	12.9836
15.00	13.7677	13.5770	13.4169	13.2820	13.1679
.25	13.9424	13.7546	13.5972	13.4647	13.3530
.50	14.1179	13.9329	13.7782	13.6483	13.5388
.75	14.2941	14.1120	13.9600	13.8325	13.7253
16.00	14.4711	14.2919	14.1425	14.0175	13.9126
.25	14.6488	14.4725	14.3257	14.2031	14.1005
.50	14.8273	14.6538	14.5096	14.3894	14.2890
.75	15.0065	14.8358	14.6942	14.5764	14.4782
17.00	15.1863	15.0184	14.8795	14.7641	14.6680
.25	15.3669	15.2018	15.0654	14.9524	14.8584
.50	15.5481	15.3858	15.2519	15.1412	15.0494
.75	15.7300	15.5704	15.4391	15.3307	15.2410
18.00	15.9126	15.7557	15.6269	15.5208	15.4331
.25	16.0957	15.9416	15.8153	15.7114	15.6258
.50	16.2795	16.1281	16.0042	15.9026	15.8190
.75	16.4639	16.3152	16.1938	16.0943	16.0127
19.00	16.6489	16.5029	16.3838	16.2866	16.2068
.25	16.8345	16.6911	16.5745	16.4793	16.4015
.50	17.0207	16.8799	16.7656	16.6725	16.5966
.75	17.2074	17.0692	16.9572	16.8663	16.7922
20.00%	17.3947	17.2590	17.1494	17.0605	16.9882

Monthly Payment Factors
Payment per $1000

Interest Rate	Amortization Period in Years				
	21	22	23	24	25
5.00%	6.4172	6.2528	6.1041	5.9690	5.8459
.25	6.5576	6.3948	6.2476	6.1140	5.9925
.50	6.6997	6.5385	6.3929	6.2609	6.1409
.75	6.8434	6.6838	6.5398	6.4095	6.2911
6.00	6.9886	6.8307	6.6885	6.5598	6.4430
.25	7.1353	6.9793	6.8387	6.7118	6.5967
.50	7.2836	7.1294	6.9906	6.8654	6.7521
.75	7.4334	7.2811	7.1441	7.0207	6.9091
7.00	7.5847	7.4342	7.2992	7.1776	7.0678
.25	7.7375	7.5889	7.4558	7.3361	7.2281
.50	7.8917	7.7451	7.6139	7.4960	7.3899
.75	8.0473	7.9027	7.7735	7.6576	7.5533
8.00	8.2043	8.0618	7.9345	7.8205	7.7182
.25	8.3627	8.2222	8.0970	7.9850	7.8845
.50	8.5224	8.3841	8.2609	8.1508	8.0523
.75	8.6834	8.5472	8.4261	8.3181	8.2214
9.00	8.8458	8.7117	8.5927	8.4866	8.3920
.25	9.0094	8.8775	8.7606	8.6566	8.5638
.50	9.1743	9.0446	8.9297	8.8277	8.7370
.75	9.3405	9.2129	9.1002	9.0002	8.9114
10.00	9.5078	9.3825	9.2718	9.1739	9.0870
.25	9.6763	9.5532	9.4447	9.3488	9.2638
.50	9.8460	9.7251	9.6187	9.5248	9.4418
.75	10.0168	9.8981	9.7938	9.7020	9.6209
11.00	10.1887	10.0722	9.9701	9.8803	9.8011
.25	10.3617	10.2475	10.1474	10.0596	9.9824
.50	10.5358	10.4237	10.3258	10.2400	10.1647
.75	10.7109	10.6011	10.5052	10.4214	10.3480
12.00	10.8870	10.7794	10.6856	10.6038	10.5322
.25	11.0641	10.9587	10.8670	10.7872	10.7174
.50	11.2422	11.1390	11.0494	10.9714	10.9035
.75	11.4212	11.3202	11.2326	11.1566	11.0905
13.00	11.6011	11.5023	11.4168	11.3427	11.2784
.25	11.7820	11.6853	11.6018	11.5296	11.4670
.50	11.9637	11.8691	11.7876	11.7173	11.6564
.75	12.1463	12.0538	11.9743	11.9058	11.8467
14.00	12.3297	12.2393	12.1617	12.0950	12.0376
.25	12.5139	12.4256	12.3500	12.2851	12.2293
.50	12.6989	12.6126	12.5389	12.4758	12.4216
.75	12.8847	12.8004	12.7286	12.6672	12.6146
15.00	13.0712	12.9890	12.9190	12.8593	12.8083
.25	13.2584	13.1782	13.1100	13.0520	13.0026
.50	13.4464	13.3681	13.3018	13.2454	13.1975
.75	13.6350	13.5587	13.4941	13.4394	13.3929
16.00	13.8243	13.7499	13.6871	13.6339	13.5889
.25	14.0143	13.9417	13.8806	13.8290	13.7854
.50	14.2048	14.1342	14.0747	14.0247	13.9824
.75	14.3960	14.3272	14.2694	14.2208	14.1800
17.00	14.5878	14.5208	14.4646	14.4175	14.3780
.25	14.7802	14.7149	14.6603	14.6147	14.5764
.50	14.9731	14.9095	14.8565	14.8123	14.7753
.75	15.1666	15.1047	15.0532	15.0104	14.9746
18.00	15.3605	15.3004	15.2504	15.2089	15.1743
.25	15.5550	15.4965	15.4480	15.4078	15.3744
.50	15.7500	15.6931	15.6461	15.6071	15.5748
.75	15.9455	15.8902	15.8445	15.8068	15.7757
19.00	16.1414	16.0876	16.0434	16.0069	15.9768
.25	16.3378	16.2855	16.2426	16.2073	16.1783
.50	16.5346	16.4838	16.4422	16.4081	16.3801
.75	16.7318	16.6825	16.6422	16.6092	16.5821
20.00%	16.9295	16.8816	16.8425	16.8106	16.7845

Table 2   255

Monthly Payment Factors
Payment per $1000

Interest Rate	Amortization Period in Years				
	26	27	28	29	30
5.00%	5.7334	5.6304	5.5357	5.4486	5.3682
.25	5.8815	5.7799	5.6867	5.6010	5.5220
.50	6.0314	5.9314	5.8397	5.7554	5.6779
.75	6.1832	6.0847	5.9945	5.9118	5.8357
6.00	6.3368	6.2399	6.1512	6.0700	5.9955
.25	6.4921	6.3968	6.3098	6.2302	6.1572
.50	6.6492	6.5555	6.4702	6.3921	6.3207
.75	6.8079	6.7160	6.6323	6.5558	6.4860
7.00	6.9684	6.8781	6.7961	6.7213	6.6530
.25	7.1304	7.0419	6.9616	6.8884	6.8218
.50	7.2941	7.2073	7.1287	7.0572	6.9921
.75	7.4593	7.3743	7.2974	7.2276	7.1641
8.00	7.6260	7.5428	7.4676	7.3995	7.3376
.25	7.7942	7.7128	7.6393	7.5729	7.5127
.50	7.9638	7.8842	7.8125	7.7477	7.6891
.75	8.1348	8.0570	7.9871	7.9240	7.8670
9.00	8.3072	8.2313	8.1630	8.1016	8.0462
.25	8.4810	8.4068	8.3403	8.2805	8.2268
.50	8.6560	8.5836	8.5188	8.4607	8.4085
.75	8.8323	8.7617	8.6986	8.6421	8.5915
10.00	9.0098	8.9410	8.8796	8.8248	8.7757
.25	9.1885	9.1214	9.0618	9.0085	8.9610
.50	9.3683	9.3030	9.2450	9.1934	9.1474
.75	9.5492	9.4857	9.4294	9.3793	9.3348
11.00	9.7313	9.6695	9.6148	9.5663	9.5232
.25	9.9143	9.8543	9.8012	9.7542	9.7126
.50	10.0984	10.0401	9.9886	9.9431	9.9029
.75	10.2835	10.2268	10.1769	10.1329	10.0941
12.00	10.4695	10.4145	10.3661	10.3236	10.2861
.25	10.6565	10.6030	10.5562	10.5151	10.4790
.50	10.8443	10.7925	10.7471	10.7074	10.6726
.75	11.0329	10.9827	10.9388	10.9005	10.8669
13.00	11.2224	11.1738	11.1313	11.0943	11.0620
.25	11.4127	11.3656	11.3246	11.2888	11.2577
.50	11.6038	11.5581	11.5185	11.4841	11.4541
.75	11.7956	11.7514	11.7131	11.6799	11.6511
14.00	11.9881	11.9453	11.9084	11.8764	11.8487
.25	12.1813	12.1399	12.1043	12.0735	12.0469
.50	12.3751	12.3351	12.3007	12.2711	12.2456
.75	12.5696	12.5310	12.4978	12.4693	12.4448
15.00	12.7647	12.7274	12.6954	12.6680	12.6444
.25	12.9604	12.9243	12.8935	12.8672	12.8446
.50	13.1566	13.1218	13.0922	13.0668	13.0452
.75	13.3534	13.3198	13.2913	13.2669	13.2462
16.00	13.5507	13.5183	13.4908	13.4674	13.4476
.25	13.7485	13.7173	13.6908	13.6684	13.6493
.50	13.9468	13.9167	13.8912	13.8697	13.8515
.75	14.1456	14.1165	14.0921	14.0714	14.0540
17.00	14.3447	14.3168	14.2933	14.2734	14.2568
.25	14.5443	14.5174	14.4948	14.4758	14.4599
.50	14.7443	14.7184	14.6967	14.6785	14.6633
.75	14.9447	14.9198	14.8989	14.8815	14.8669
18.00	15.1455	15.1215	15.1015	15.0848	15.0709
.25	15.3466	15.3235	15.3043	15.2883	15.2750
.50	15.5481	15.5259	15.5075	15.4922	15.4794
.75	15.7499	15.7285	15.7109	15.6962	15.6841
19.00	15.9520	15.9315	15.9145	15.9005	15.8889
.25	16.1544	16.1349	16.1184	16.1050	16.0940
.50	16.3570	16.3381	16.3225	16.3097	16.2992
.75	16.5600	16.5418	16.5269	16.5147	16.5046
20.00%	16.7632	16.7457	16.7315	16.7198	16.7102

Monthly Payment Factors
Payment per $1000

Interest	Amortization Period in Years				
Rate	31	32	33	34	35
5.00%	5.2939	5.2251	5.1613	5.1020	5.0469
.25	5.4491	5.3817	5.3192	5.2613	5.2074
.50	5.6064	5.5404	5.4793	5.4227	5.3702
.75	5.7657	5.7011	5.6414	5.5862	5.5350
6.00	5.9269	5.8638	5.8055	5.7517	5.7019
.25	6.0901	6.0284	5.9716	5.9192	5.8708
.50	6.2552	6.1950	6.1396	6.0886	6.0415
.75	6.4220	6.3633	6.3094	6.2598	6.2142
7.00	6.5906	6.5334	6.4810	6.4328	6.3886
.25	6.7609	6.7052	6.6543	6.6075	6.5647
.50	6.9328	6.8787	6.8292	6.7839	6.7424
.75	7.1064	7.0538	7.0057	6.9619	6.9218
8.00	7.2815	7.2304	7.1838	7.1414	7.1026
.25	7.4581	7.4085	7.3634	7.3223	7.2849
.50	7.6361	7.5880	7.5444	7.5047	7.4686
.75	7.8155	7.7689	7.7267	7.6884	7.6536
9.00	7.9963	7.9512	7.9103	7.8734	7.8399
.25	8.1783	8.1347	8.0953	8.0596	8.0274
.50	8.3616	8.3194	8.2814	8.2471	8.2161
.75	8.5461	8.5053	8.4687	8.4356	8.4059
10.00	8.7318	8.6924	8.6570	8.6253	8.5967
.25	8.9185	8.8805	8.8465	8.8159	8.7886
.50	9.1063	9.0697	9.0369	9.0076	8.9813
.75	9.2952	9.2598	9.2283	9.2002	9.1750
11.00	9.4850	9.4509	9.4206	9.3936	9.3696
.25	9.6757	9.6429	9.6138	9.5880	9.5649
.50	9.8673	9.8358	9.8079	9.7831	9.7611
.75	10.0598	10.0295	10.0027	9.9790	9.9579
12.00	10.2531	10.2240	10.1983	10.1756	10.1555
.25	10.4472	10.4192	10.3946	10.3729	10.3537
.50	10.6420	10.6152	10.5916	10.5708	10.5525
.75	10.8375	10.8118	10.7892	10.7694	10.7520
13.00	11.0337	11.0090	10.9874	10.9685	10.9519
.25	11.2306	11.2069	11.1863	11.1682	11.1524
.50	11.4281	11.4054	11.3856	11.3684	11.3534
.75	11.6261	11.6044	11.5855	11.5691	11.5549
14.00	11.8247	11.8040	11.7859	11.7703	11.7567
.25	12.0239	12.0040	11.9868	11.9719	11.9590
.50	12.2235	12.2045	12.1881	12.1739	12.1617
.75	12.4237	12.4055	12.3898	12.3764	12.3647
15.00	12.6242	12.6069	12.5920	12.5792	12.5681
.25	12.8252	12.8087	12.7945	12.7823	12.7718
.50	13.0267	13.0109	12.9973	12.9858	12.9758
.75	13.2285	13.2134	13.2005	13.1895	13.1801
16.00	13.4307	13.4163	13.4040	13.3936	13.3847
.25	13.6332	13.6195	13.6078	13.5979	13.5895
.50	13.8360	13.8230	13.8119	13.8025	13.7945
.75	14.0392	14.0268	14.0162	14.0073	13.9998
17.00	14.2427	14.2308	14.2208	14.2124	14.2053
.25	14.4464	14.4351	14.4256	14.4176	14.4109
.50	14.6504	14.6397	14.6307	14.6231	14.6168
.75	14.8547	14.8445	14.8359	14.8288	14.8228
18.00	15.0592	15.0495	15.0414	15.0346	15.0289
.25	15.2639	15.2547	15.2470	15.2406	15.2352
.50	15.4689	15.4601	15.4528	15.4467	15.4417
.75	15.6740	15.6657	15.6588	15.6530	15.6483
19.00	15.8793	15.8714	15.8649	15.8594	15.8549
.25	16.0849	16.0773	16.0711	16.0660	16.0618
.50	16.2905	16.2834	16.2775	16.2727	16.2687
.75	16.4964	16.4896	16.4840	16.4794	16.4757
20.00%	16.7023	16.6959	16.6906	16.6863	16.6828

Table 2   257

Monthly Payment Factors
Payment per $1000

Interest Rate	Amortization Period in Years				
	36	37	38	39	40
5.00%	4.9955	4.9476	4.9029	4.8611	4.8220
.25	5.1573	5.1107	5.0672	5.0266	4.9887
.50	5.3214	5.2760	5.2338	5.1944	5.1577
.75	5.4875	5.4435	5.4025	5.3644	5.3289
6.00	5.6558	5.6130	5.5733	5.5364	5.5021
.25	5.8260	5.7845	5.7461	5.7105	5.6774
.50	5.9981	5.9580	5.9208	5.8864	5.8546
.75	6.1721	6.1333	6.0974	6.0642	6.0336
7.00	6.3478	6.3103	6.2757	6.2438	6.2143
.25	6.5253	6.4891	6.4557	6.4250	6.3967
.50	6.7044	6.6694	6.6374	6.6079	6.5807
.75	6.8850	6.8514	6.8205	6.7922	6.7662
8.00	7.0672	7.0348	7.0052	6.9780	6.9531
.25	7.2508	7.2196	7.1912	7.1652	7.1414
.50	7.4358	7.4058	7.3786	7.3537	7.3309
.75	7.6220	7.5933	7.5672	7.5434	7.5217
9.00	7.8096	7.7820	7.7570	7.7343	7.7136
.25	7.9983	7.9719	7.9480	7.9263	7.9066
.50	8.1882	8.1629	8.1400	8.1193	8.1006
.75	8.3791	8.3549	8.3331	8.3134	8.2956
10.00	8.5710	8.5479	8.5271	8.5084	8.4915
.25	8.7640	8.7419	8.7221	8.7042	8.6882
.50	8.9578	8.9368	8.9179	8.9009	8.8857
.75	9.1526	9.1325	9.1145	9.0984	9.0840
11.00	9.3481	9.3290	9.3119	9.2966	9.2829
.25	9.5445	9.5262	9.5100	9.4955	9.4826
.50	9.7415	9.7242	9.7087	9.6950	9.6828
.75	9.9393	9.9228	9.9082	9.8952	9.8836
12.00	10.1378	10.1221	10.1082	10.0959	10.0850
.25	10.3368	10.3219	10.3088	10.2971	10.2869
.50	10.5365	10.5223	10.5099	10.4989	10.4892
.75	10.7367	10.7233	10.7115	10.7011	10.6920
13.00	10.9374	10.9247	10.9135	10.9037	10.8951
.25	11.1386	11.1266	11.1160	11.1068	11.0987
.50	11.3403	11.3289	11.3189	11.3102	11.3026
.75	11.5424	11.5316	11.5222	11.5140	11.5069
14.00	11.7450	11.7347	11.7258	11.7181	11.7114
.25	11.9479	11.9382	11.9298	11.9225	11.9162
.50	12.1511	12.1420	12.1341	12.1272	12.1213
.75	12.3547	12.3461	12.3386	12.3322	12.3267
15.00	12.5587	12.5505	12.5435	12.5374	12.5322
.25	12.7629	12.7552	12.7486	12.7429	12.7380
.50	12.9674	12.9601	12.9539	12.9486	12.9440
.75	13.1721	13.1653	13.1594	13.1544	13.1502
16.00	13.3771	13.3707	13.3652	13.3605	13.3565
.25	13.5823	13.5763	13.5711	13.5667	13.5630
.50	13.7878	13.7821	13.7772	13.7731	13.7696
.75	13.9934	13.9880	13.9835	13.9796	13.9764
17.00	14.1993	14.1942	14.1899	14.1863	14.1832
.25	14.4053	14.4005	14.3965	14.3931	14.3902
.50	14.6114	14.6069	14.6032	14.6000	14.5973
.75	14.8177	14.8135	14.8100	14.8070	14.8045
18.00	15.0242	15.0202	15.0169	15.0141	15.0118
.25	15.2308	15.2270	15.2239	15.2214	15.2192
.50	15.4375	15.4340	15.4311	15.4287	15.4266
.75	15.6443	15.6410	15.6383	15.6360	15.6342
19.00	15.8512	15.8482	15.8456	15.8435	15.8417
.25	16.0583	16.0554	16.0530	16.0510	16.0494
.50	16.2654	16.2627	16.2604	16.2586	16.2571
.75	16.4726	16.4701	16.4680	16.4663	16.4648
20.00%	16.6799	16.6775	16.6756	16.6740	16.6726

Table 3
Remaining Loan Balance

Table 3 shows the remaining balance on a loan at the end of each year, and allows you to figure the interest or principal paid during each year. Balloon payments of the entire balance remaining are given as well.

Example 7.   Remaining Balance on a Loan

Sarah Janing's loan, taken out four years ago, had an original amount of $85,000 and a loan term of 30 years and bears interest at 11.50 percent. She is considering refinancing at a lower interest rate and wishes to know the current balance.

Enter Table 3 in the section marked 30 years. On the line for 11.50 percent under 4 years, read the percent remaining; it is 98.064, the percentage balance on the loan. Multiply the original loan amount by the percentage balance to get

$$\$85{,}000 \quad \times \quad 0.98064 \quad = \quad \$83{,}354$$

the balance on the loan after four years.

Example 8.   Amount of a Balloon Payment

Steve Morrissey has a proposal for a loan at 9.00 percent interest. The amortization period of the loan will be 20 years, but there will be a balloon payment at the end of 7 years.

A balloon payment is the same as the balance due. The balance is controlled entirely by the interest rate and the amortization period. Enter Table 3 in the section marked 20 years. On the line for 9.00 percent, read the figure under percent remaining for 7 years. The answer, 82.568, is the percentage of the original loan that will be due as a balloon payment after 7 years.

Example 9.   Interest or Principal Paid in a Year

The Calvets are considering the effect of income tax deductions for interest on their home mortgage loan. The loan they plan is for $160,000, calls for 30-year amortization and a rate of 10.00 percent. From Table 1, they find that the payments will be $1404.12 per month, or $16,849.44 per year. They want to calculate the principal and interest for the first year.

Principal: Enter Table 3 at the section for 30 years. On the line for 10 percent, read under year 1 the percentage, 99.444. Multiply the original loan amount by the percentage to get

$$\$160,000 \quad \times \quad 0.99444 \quad = \quad \$159,110.40$$

remaining balance. Subtracting from $160,000 gives $889.60 principal paid in the first year.

Interest: Subtract the principal paid from the payments in one year, to get

$$\$16,849.44 \quad - \quad 889.60 \quad = \quad \$15,959.84$$

interest paid in the first year. The procedure for the second and succeeding years is similar: Subtract the percent remaining at the end of the year in question from the percent remaining the previous year. Multiply that percentage by the original loan amount to get the principal paid for that year. Subtract the principal paid from the total payments for the year to get the interest paid.

Example 10.   Principal, Interest since Loan Began

Clarence Stedley took out a 12.00 percent loan on a 15-year amortization schedule nine years ago in the original amount of $100,000. He is making payments of $1,200.17 per month.

Principal: To find the principal paydown, enter Table 3 at the section for 15-year amortization. On the line for 12 percent, find the percent remaining under 9 years; it is 61.389 percent. Subtract this from 100 percent, and multiply it by the original loan amount, to get

$$\$100,000 \quad \times \quad 0.38611 \quad = \quad \$38,611$$

the principal paid off over 9 years.

Interest: Take the total loan payments made and subtract the total principal paid. Since Stedley has made 108 payments of $1200.17, his total payments have been

$$\$1,200.17 \quad \times \quad 108 \quad = \quad \$129,618$$

Subtracting the $38,611 of principal payments gives $91,007 total interest paid from the start of the loan through the end of the ninth year.

30 Years — Remaining Loan Balance

Interest Rate	Percent remaining in year					
	1	2	3	4	5	6
5.00%	98.525	96.974	95.344	93.630	91.829	89.935
.25	98.590	97.104	95.538	93.888	92.149	90.317
.50	98.653	97.230	95.726	94.138	92.461	90.688
.75	98.714	97.351	95.908	94.380	92.762	91.048
6.00	98.772	97.468	96.084	94.615	93.054	91.398
.25	98.828	97.581	96.254	94.841	93.337	91.737
.50	98.882	97.690	96.417	95.060	93.611	92.065
.75	98.934	97.794	96.575	95.271	93.876	92.384
7.00	98.984	97.895	96.727	95.475	94.132	92.692
.25	99.032	97.992	96.873	95.671	94.379	92.990
.50	99.078	98.085	97.014	95.861	94.617	93.278
.75	99.122	98.174	97.150	96.043	94.848	93.556
8.00	99.165	98.260	97.280	96.219	95.070	93.825
.25	99.205	98.342	97.405	96.388	95.284	94.085
.50	99.244	98.421	97.526	96.551	95.490	94.336
.75	99.281	98.497	97.641	96.708	95.689	94.577
9.00	99.317	98.570	97.752	96.858	95.880	94.810
.25	99.351	98.639	97.858	97.003	96.064	95.035
.50	99.383	98.706	97.960	97.141	96.241	95.251
.75	99.414	98.769	98.058	97.274	96.411	95.459
10.00	99.444	98.830	98.152	97.402	96.574	95.660
.25	99.472	98.888	98.241	97.525	96.731	95.852
.50	99.499	98.944	98.327	97.642	96.882	96.038
.75	99.525	98.997	98.409	97.754	97.026	96.215
11.00	99.550	99.048	98.487	97.862	97.165	96.386
.25	99.573	99.096	98.562	97.965	97.297	96.551
.50	99.596	99.142	98.634	98.064	97.425	96.708
.75	99.617	99.186	98.702	98.158	97.547	96.859
12.00	99.637	99.228	98.767	98.248	97.663	97.004
.25	99.656	99.268	98.830	98.334	97.775	97.143
.50	99.675	99.306	98.889	98.417	97.882	97.276
.75	99.692	99.343	98.946	98.495	97.984	97.403
13.00	99.709	99.377	99.000	98.570	98.082	97.526
.25	99.724	99.410	99.051	98.642	98.175	97.642
.50	99.739	99.441	99.100	98.710	98.264	97.754
.75	99.753	99.471	99.147	98.775	98.349	97.861
14.00	99.767	99.499	99.191	98.837	98.431	97.963
.25	99.780	99.526	99.234	98.897	98.508	98.061
.50	99.792	99.551	99.274	98.953	98.583	98.155
.75	99.803	99.576	99.312	99.007	98.653	98.244
15.00	99.814	99.599	99.348	99.058	98.721	98.329
.25	99.825	99.620	99.383	99.107	98.785	98.411
.50	99.834	99.641	99.416	99.153	98.846	98.488
.75	99.844	99.661	99.447	99.197	98.904	98.563
16.00	99.852	99.679	99.477	99.239	98.960	98.633
.25	99.861	99.697	99.505	99.279	99.013	98.701
.50	99.869	99.714	99.531	99.316	99.063	98.765
.75	99.876	99.730	99.557	99.352	99.111	98.827
17.00	99.883	99.745	99.581	99.387	99.157	98.885
.25	99.890	99.759	99.604	99.419	99.200	98.941
.50	99.896	99.772	99.625	99.450	99.242	98.994
.75	99.902	99.785	99.646	99.479	99.281	99.044
18.00	99.908	99.797	99.665	99.507	99.318	99.093
.25	99.913	99.809	99.683	99.533	99.354	99.138
.50	99.918	99.819	99.701	99.559	99.388	99.182
.75	99.923	99.830	99.717	99.582	99.420	99.224
19.00	99.927	99.839	99.733	99.605	99.450	99.263
.25	99.931	99.848	99.748	99.626	99.479	99.301
.50	99.935	99.857	99.762	99.646	99.506	99.336
.75	99.939	99.865	99.775	99.666	99.532	99.370
20.00%	99.943	99.873	99.788	99.684	99.557	99.403

Remaining Loan Balance   **30 Years**

Interest Rate	Percent remaining in year					
	7	8	9	10	11	12
5.00%	87.945	85.853	83.654	81.342	78.912	76.358
.25	88.386	86.352	84.208	81.948	79.567	77.058
.50	88.816	86.838	84.748	82.541	80.209	77.746
.75	89.234	87.311	85.276	83.120	80.837	78.419
6.00	89.639	87.772	85.790	83.686	81.451	79.079
.25	90.034	88.221	86.291	84.238	82.052	79.726
.50	90.416	88.657	86.779	84.776	82.639	80.358
.75	90.787	89.080	87.254	85.301	83.212	80.977
7.00	91.147	89.492	87.716	85.812	83.771	81.582
.25	91.496	89.891	88.165	86.310	84.316	82.173
.50	91.834	90.278	88.602	86.795	84.848	82.750
.75	92.161	90.654	89.025	87.266	85.366	83.313
8.00	92.477	91.018	89.437	87.725	85.870	83.862
.25	92.783	91.370	89.836	88.170	86.361	84.398
.50	93.079	91.711	90.223	88.603	86.839	84.920
.75	93.365	92.041	90.598	89.022	87.304	85.428
9.00	93.640	92.361	90.961	89.430	87.755	85.923
.25	93.907	92.669	91.313	89.825	88.193	86.405
.50	94.163	92.967	91.653	90.208	88.619	86.873
.75	94.411	93.255	91.982	90.579	89.032	87.328
10.00	94.649	93.533	92.300	90.938	89.433	87.771
.25	94.879	93.801	92.608	91.286	89.822	88.201
.50	95.100	94.060	92.905	91.622	90.199	88.618
.75	95.313	94.309	93.192	91.948	90.564	89.023
11.00	95.518	94.549	93.468	92.263	90.917	89.416
.25	95.715	94.781	93.736	92.567	91.259	89.797
.50	95.904	95.003	93.993	92.860	91.590	90.166
.75	96.086	95.218	94.242	93.144	91.911	90.524
12.00	96.261	95.424	94.481	93.418	92.220	90.871
.25	96.429	95.622	94.711	93.682	92.520	91.207
.50	96.590	95.813	94.933	93.937	92.809	91.531
.75	96.744	95.996	95.147	94.183	93.088	91.846
13.00	96.893	96.172	95.353	94.420	93.358	92.150
.25	97.035	96.341	95.550	94.648	93.619	92.444
.50	97.171	96.504	95.741	94.868	93.870	92.729
.75	97.301	96.659	95.923	95.080	94.112	93.003
14.00	97.426	96.809	96.099	95.284	94.346	93.269
.25	97.546	96.952	96.268	95.480	94.572	93.525
.50	97.660	97.090	96.430	95.669	94.789	93.773
.75	97.770	97.221	96.586	95.850	94.998	94.012
15.00	97.875	97.347	96.735	96.025	95.200	94.243
.25	97.975	97.468	96.879	96.193	95.394	94.465
.50	98.071	97.584	97.016	96.354	95.581	94.680
.75	98.163	97.695	97.148	96.509	95.761	94.887
16.00	98.250	97.801	97.275	96.658	95.934	95.086
.25	98.334	97.903	97.396	96.801	96.101	95.279
.50	98.414	98.000	97.512	96.938	96.261	95.464
.75	98.490	98.093	97.624	97.070	96.416	95.643
17.00	98.563	98.182	97.731	97.196	96.564	95.815
.25	98.633	98.267	97.833	97.318	96.706	95.981
.50	98.699	98.348	97.931	97.434	96.843	96.140
.75	98.762	98.426	98.024	97.546	96.975	96.294
18.00	98.823	98.500	98.114	97.653	97.101	96.442
.25	98.880	98.571	98.200	97.755	97.223	96.584
.50	98.935	98.638	98.282	97.854	97.339	96.721
.75	98.987	98.703	98.361	97.948	97.451	96.853
19.00	99.037	98.765	98.436	98.038	97.559	96.979
.25	99.085	98.824	98.508	98.125	97.662	97.101
.50	99.130	98.880	98.576	98.208	97.761	97.218
.75	99.173	98.934	98.642	98.287	97.856	97.331
20.00%	99.214	98.985	98.705	98.363	97.947	97.439

Table 3   263

__30 Years__   __Remaining Loan Balance__

Interest Rate	Percent remaining in year					
	13	14	15	16	17	18
5.00%	73.673	70.851	67.884	64.765	61.487	58.042
.25	74.415	71.628	68.693	65.599	62.338	58.903
.50	75.143	72.394	69.490	66.422	63.180	59.756
.75	75.859	73.147	70.275	67.234	64.013	60.602
6.00	76.561	73.887	71.049	68.035	64.836	61.439
.25	77.250	74.615	71.810	68.825	65.648	62.267
.50	77.925	75.329	72.559	69.604	66.450	63.086
.75	78.587	76.030	73.295	70.370	67.241	63.895
7.00	79.235	76.718	74.019	71.125	68.022	64.694
.25	79.869	77.392	74.729	71.867	68.791	65.483
.50	80.489	78.052	75.427	72.597	69.548	66.262
.75	81.095	78.699	76.111	73.314	70.294	67.030
8.00	81.688	79.332	76.782	74.019	71.027	67.787
.25	82.266	79.952	77.439	74.711	71.749	68.533
.50	82.831	80.557	78.083	75.390	72.458	69.268
.75	83.382	81.149	78.713	76.056	73.156	69.991
9.00	83.919	81.728	79.330	76.708	73.840	70.703
.25	84.443	82.292	79.934	77.348	74.512	71.403
.50	84.954	82.844	80.524	77.975	75.172	72.091
.75	85.451	83.381	81.101	78.588	75.819	72.768
10.00	85.934	83.906	81.665	79.189	76.454	73.432
.25	86.405	84.417	82.215	79.776	77.075	74.085
.50	86.863	84.915	82.752	80.351	77.685	74.725
.75	87.308	85.400	83.276	80.912	78.281	75.353
11.00	87.741	85.872	83.787	81.461	78.866	75.970
.25	88.161	86.332	84.286	81.997	79.437	76.574
.50	88.569	86.779	84.771	82.520	79.997	77.167
.75	88.966	87.214	85.245	83.031	80.544	77.747
12.00	89.350	87.637	85.706	83.530	81.078	78.316
.25	89.723	88.047	86.155	84.016	81.601	78.872
.50	90.085	88.447	86.591	84.491	82.111	79.417
.75	90.435	88.834	87.016	84.953	82.610	79.951
13.00	90.775	89.211	87.430	85.403	83.097	80.473
.25	91.104	89.576	87.832	85.842	83.573	80.983
.50	91.423	89.930	88.223	86.270	84.037	81.482
.75	91.732	90.274	88.603	86.686	84.489	81.970
14.00	92.031	90.607	88.972	87.092	84.931	82.447
.25	92.320	90.931	89.330	87.486	85.361	82.913
.50	92.599	91.244	89.678	87.870	85.781	83.368
.75	92.870	91.547	90.016	88.243	86.190	83.813
15.00	93.131	91.841	90.344	88.606	86.589	84.247
.25	93.384	92.126	90.662	88.959	86.977	84.671
.50	93.628	92.402	90.971	89.302	87.355	85.084
.75	93.864	92.669	91.271	89.636	87.724	85.488
16.00	94.092	92.927	91.561	89.960	88.082	85.882
.25	94.313	93.177	91.843	90.274	88.432	86.266
.50	94.525	93.419	92.115	90.580	88.771	86.640
.75	94.730	93.653	92.380	90.877	89.102	87.006
17.00	94.928	93.879	92.636	91.165	89.424	87.362
.25	95.119	94.097	92.885	91.445	89.736	87.709
.50	95.304	94.309	93.125	91.717	90.041	88.047
.75	95.482	94.513	93.358	91.980	90.337	88.377
18.00	95.653	94.710	93.583	92.236	90.625	88.698
.25	95.818	94.901	93.802	92.484	90.904	89.011
.50	95.978	95.085	94.013	92.724	91.176	89.316
.75	96.132	95.263	94.217	92.958	91.440	89.613
19.00	96.280	95.435	94.415	93.184	91.697	89.902
.25	96.422	95.601	94.607	93.403	91.947	90.183
.50	96.560	95.761	94.792	93.616	92.189	90.457
.75	96.692	95.916	94.971	93.822	92.424	90.724
20.00%	96.820	96.065	95.144	94.022	92.653	90.984

Remaining Loan Balance   **30 Years**

Interest Rate	Percent remaining in year					
	19	20	21	22	23	24
5.00%	54.420	50.612	46.610	42.403	37.981	33.333
.25	55.283	51.468	47.447	43.211	38.747	34.042
.50	56.139	52.318	48.281	44.017	39.512	34.753
.75	56.989	53.164	49.112	44.821	40.277	35.464
6.00	57.832	54.004	49.939	45.623	41.041	36.177
.25	58.668	54.838	50.761	46.422	41.804	36.889
.50	59.496	55.665	51.578	47.218	42.565	37.601
.75	60.315	56.486	52.391	48.010	43.324	38.312
7.00	61.126	57.300	53.197	48.798	44.081	39.023
.25	61.928	58.107	53.998	49.582	44.835	39.732
.50	62.721	58.905	54.793	50.362	45.586	40.440
.75	63.504	59.696	55.581	51.136	46.334	41.146
8.00	64.278	60.478	56.362	51.905	47.078	41.850
.25	65.042	61.252	57.136	52.668	47.818	42.551
.50	65.796	62.016	57.903	53.426	48.553	43.250
.75	66.539	62.772	58.662	54.177	49.284	43.946
9.00	67.272	63.518	59.413	54.922	50.010	44.638
.25	67.994	64.255	60.156	55.661	50.732	45.327
.50	68.705	64.982	60.890	56.392	51.447	46.012
.75	69.405	65.700	61.616	57.116	52.158	46.693
10.00	70.094	66.407	62.333	57.833	52.862	47.370
.25	70.772	67.104	63.042	58.543	53.560	48.043
.50	71.439	67.791	63.741	59.245	54.253	48.711
.75	72.095	68.468	64.431	59.939	54.939	49.374
11.00	72.739	69.134	65.112	60.625	55.618	50.033
.25	73.372	69.790	65.784	61.303	56.291	50.686
.50	73.993	70.436	66.446	61.973	56.958	51.334
.75	74.604	71.070	67.099	62.635	57.617	51.977
12.00	75.203	71.695	67.742	63.288	58.269	52.614
.25	75.790	72.309	68.376	63.933	58.915	53.245
.50	76.367	72.912	69.000	64.569	59.553	53.871
.75	76.932	73.505	69.614	65.197	60.183	54.492
13.00	77.486	74.087	70.219	65.817	60.807	55.106
.25	78.029	74.659	70.814	66.427	61.423	55.714
.50	78.561	75.220	71.399	67.029	62.032	56.316
.75	79.082	75.771	71.975	67.623	62.633	56.912
14.00	79.593	76.312	72.542	68.208	63.227	57.502
.25	80.093	76.843	73.098	68.784	63.813	58.086
.50	80.582	77.363	73.645	69.351	64.392	58.663
.75	81.061	77.873	74.183	69.910	64.963	59.234
15.00	81.529	78.374	74.712	70.461	65.526	59.799
.25	81.987	78.864	75.231	71.002	66.082	60.357
.50	82.435	79.345	75.740	71.535	66.630	60.909
.75	82.874	79.816	76.241	72.060	67.172	61.455
16.00	83.302	80.278	76.733	72.577	67.705	61.994
.25	83.721	80.730	77.215	73.085	68.231	62.527
.50	84.130	81.173	77.689	73.584	68.749	63.053
.75	84.530	81.606	78.154	74.076	69.260	63.573
17.00	84.921	82.031	78.610	74.559	69.764	64.087
.25	85.302	82.446	79.057	75.034	70.260	64.594
.50	85.675	82.853	79.496	75.501	70.749	65.095
.75	86.039	83.251	79.926	75.960	71.230	65.589
18.00	86.395	83.641	80.348	76.412	71.705	66.078
.25	86.742	84.022	80.762	76.855	72.172	66.559
.50	87.081	84.395	81.168	77.291	72.633	67.035
.75	87.411	84.760	81.566	77.720	73.086	67.506
19.00	87.734	85.117	81.956	78.140	73.533	67.969
.25	88.049	85.466	82.339	78.554	73.972	68.426
.50	88.356	85.807	82.713	78.959	74.405	68.878
.75	88.656	86.141	83.081	79.358	74.831	69.323
20.00%	88.949	86.467	83.440	79.750	75.250	69.763

Table 3   265

30 Years   Remaining Loan Balance

Interest Rate	Percent remaining in year				
	25	26	27	28	29
5.00%	28.447	23.310	17.911	12.236	6.271
.25	29.085	23.861	18.356	12.555	6.442
.50	29.725	24.414	18.804	12.876	6.615
.75	30.368	24.970	19.254	13.201	6.790
6.00	31.012	25.529	19.708	13.528	6.966
.25	31.658	26.090	20.164	13.857	7.144
.50	32.304	26.653	20.623	14.189	7.324
.75	32.951	27.217	21.084	14.523	7.506
7.00	33.599	27.783	21.547	14.860	7.689
.25	34.247	28.350	22.012	15.198	7.874
.50	34.894	28.918	22.478	15.538	8.059
.75	35.542	29.487	22.946	15.880	8.247
8.00	36.188	30.056	23.416	16.224	8.435
.25	36.834	30.626	23.886	16.569	8.625
.50	37.478	31.195	24.358	16.916	8.816
.75	38.120	31.765	24.830	17.264	9.008
9.00	38.761	32.334	25.303	17.612	9.201
.25	39.400	32.902	25.776	17.963	9.395
.50	40.037	33.469	26.250	18.314	9.590
.75	40.671	34.036	26.723	18.665	9.785
10.00	41.303	34.601	27.197	19.018	9.982
.25	41.932	35.165	27.670	19.371	10.179
.50	42.558	35.727	28.144	19.724	10.377
.75	43.181	36.288	28.616	20.078	10.576
11.00	43.800	36.847	29.089	20.433	10.775
.25	44.416	37.403	29.560	20.787	10.975
.50	45.028	37.958	30.031	21.142	11.175
.75	45.637	38.511	30.500	21.497	11.376
12.00	46.241	39.061	30.969	21.851	11.577
.25	46.842	39.608	31.436	22.206	11.778
.50	47.438	40.153	31.902	22.560	11.980
.75	48.030	40.695	32.367	22.914	12.183
13.00	48.618	41.234	32.831	23.268	12.385
.25	49.201	41.770	33.293	23.621	12.588
.50	49.779	42.303	33.753	23.974	12.790
.75	50.353	42.833	34.211	24.326	12.993
14.00	50.922	43.360	34.668	24.678	13.197
.25	51.487	43.883	35.123	25.029	13.399
.50	52.046	44.404	35.576	25.380	13.603
.75	52.601	44.920	36.027	25.729	13.806
15.00	53.151	45.434	36.476	26.078	14.009
.25	53.695	45.943	36.923	26.426	14.212
.50	54.234	46.449	37.367	26.773	14.415
.75	54.769	46.952	37.810	27.120	14.619
16.00	55.299	47.451	38.250	27.465	14.822
.25	55.823	47.946	38.688	27.809	15.025
.50	56.342	48.437	39.124	28.152	15.227
.75	56.857	48.925	39.557	28.495	15.430
17.00	57.366	49.408	39.988	28.836	15.632
.25	57.869	49.888	40.417	29.175	15.834
.50	58.368	50.365	40.843	29.514	16.036
.75	58.861	50.837	41.266	29.851	16.237
18.00	59.350	51.305	41.687	30.188	16.439
.25	59.832	51.769	42.105	30.522	16.639
.50	60.310	52.230	42.521	30.856	16.840
.75	60.784	52.688	42.936	31.190	17.042
19.00	61.252	53.140	43.346	31.521	17.242
.25	61.714	53.589	43.754	31.850	17.441
.50	62.171	54.034	44.160	32.178	17.640
.75	62.624	54.475	44.563	32.506	17.840
20.00%	63.072	54.913	44.964	32.832	18.039

Remaining Loan Balance   **25 Years**

Interest Rate	Percent remaining in year				
	1	2	3	4	5
5.00%	97.938	95.771	93.492	91.098	88.580
.25	98.012	95.916	93.708	91.382	88.930
.50	98.083	96.058	93.919	91.659	89.272
.75	98.153	96.196	94.124	91.930	89.606
6.00	98.220	96.330	94.324	92.194	89.932
.25	98.285	96.461	94.518	92.451	90.251
.50	98.349	96.587	94.708	92.702	90.562
.75	98.410	96.710	94.892	92.947	90.866
7.00	98.470	96.830	95.071	93.185	91.162
.25	98.528	96.946	95.245	93.416	91.451
.50	98.584	97.058	95.414	93.642	91.733
.75	98.638	97.167	95.578	93.861	92.007
8.00	98.691	97.273	95.738	94.075	92.274
.25	98.742	97.376	95.892	94.282	92.534
.50	98.791	97.475	96.043	94.484	92.787
.75	98.838	97.571	96.188	94.679	93.033
9.00	98.884	97.664	96.329	94.869	93.272
.25	98.929	97.754	96.466	95.054	93.505
.50	98.972	97.841	96.599	95.233	93.731
.75	99.013	97.925	96.727	95.406	93.951
10.00	99.053	98.007	96.851	95.574	94.164
.25	99.092	98.085	96.971	95.737	94.371
.50	99.129	98.161	97.087	95.895	94.571
.75	99.165	98.235	97.200	96.048	94.766
11.00	99.199	98.305	97.308	96.196	94.955
.25	99.232	98.374	97.413	96.339	95.138
.50	99.264	98.440	97.515	96.478	95.315
.75	99.295	98.503	97.613	96.612	95.487
12.00	99.325	98.564	97.707	96.741	95.653
.25	99.354	98.623	97.799	96.867	95.814
.50	99.381	98.680	97.887	96.988	95.970
.75	99.408	98.735	97.971	97.105	96.121
13.00	99.433	98.788	98.053	97.218	96.267
.25	99.457	98.838	98.132	97.327	96.407
.50	99.481	98.887	98.208	97.432	96.544
.75	99.503	98.934	98.282	97.533	96.675
14.00	99.525	98.979	98.352	97.631	96.803
.25	99.546	99.023	98.420	97.726	96.926
.50	99.566	99.065	98.486	97.817	97.044
.75	99.585	99.105	98.548	97.904	97.159
15.00	99.604	99.143	98.609	97.989	97.269
.25	99.621	99.180	98.667	98.070	97.376
.50	99.638	99.216	98.723	98.149	97.479
.75	99.654	99.250	98.777	98.224	97.578
16.00	99.670	99.283	98.829	98.297	97.674
.25	99.685	99.314	98.879	98.367	97.766
.50	99.699	99.344	98.927	98.434	97.855
.75	99.713	99.373	98.972	98.499	97.940
17.00	99.726	99.401	99.017	98.561	98.023
.25	99.738	99.428	99.059	98.621	98.102
.50	99.750	99.453	99.100	98.679	98.179
.75	99.762	99.478	99.139	98.734	98.252
18.00	99.773	99.501	99.176	98.787	98.323
.25	99.783	99.523	99.212	98.839	98.391
.50	99.793	99.545	99.246	98.888	98.457
.75	99.803	99.565	99.279	98.935	98.520
19.00	99.812	99.585	99.311	98.980	98.581
.25	99.821	99.604	99.341	99.024	98.639
.50	99.829	99.622	99.370	99.065	98.695
.75	99.837	99.639	99.398	99.105	98.749
20.00%	99.845	99.656	99.425	99.144	98.801

Table 3   267

25 Years — Remaining Loan Balance

Interest Rate	Percent remaining in year				
	6	7	8	9	10
5.00%	85.934	83.152	80.229	77.155	73.924
.25	86.346	83.623	80.754	77.731	74.545
.50	86.749	84.085	81.271	78.297	75.156
.75	87.144	84.538	81.778	78.854	75.759
6.00	87.531	84.982	82.276	79.402	76.352
.25	87.909	85.417	82.764	79.941	76.936
.50	88.279	85.843	83.244	80.470	77.511
.75	88.640	86.260	83.714	80.990	78.077
7.00	88.993	86.668	84.174	81.501	78.633
.25	89.338	87.067	84.626	82.001	79.180
.50	89.675	87.457	85.068	82.493	79.718
.75	90.003	87.839	85.500	82.974	80.245
8.00	90.324	88.211	85.924	83.446	80.763
.25	90.636	88.575	86.338	83.909	81.272
.50	90.940	88.930	86.743	84.362	81.771
.75	91.237	89.277	87.139	84.805	82.260
9.00	91.526	89.615	87.525	85.240	82.739
.25	91.807	89.945	87.903	85.664	83.209
.50	92.081	90.266	88.272	86.079	83.669
.75	92.347	90.579	88.632	86.485	84.120
10.00	92.606	90.884	88.983	86.882	84.561
.25	92.857	91.181	89.325	87.270	84.993
.50	93.102	91.470	89.659	87.648	85.415
.75	93.339	91.752	89.984	88.017	85.828
11.00	93.570	92.025	90.301	88.378	86.232
.25	93.794	92.291	90.610	88.730	86.627
.50	94.011	92.550	90.911	89.073	87.012
.75	94.222	92.801	91.203	89.407	87.389
12.00	94.427	93.045	91.488	89.733	87.756
.25	94.625	93.282	91.765	90.051	88.115
.50	94.817	93.512	92.034	90.361	88.465
.75	95.004	93.736	92.296	90.662	88.807
13.00	95.184	93.952	92.551	90.955	89.140
.25	95.359	94.163	92.798	91.241	89.465
.50	95.528	94.367	93.038	91.519	89.781
.75	95.692	94.564	93.271	91.789	90.090
14.00	95.850	94.756	93.498	92.052	90.390
.25	96.004	94.941	93.718	92.307	90.683
.50	96.152	95.121	93.931	92.556	90.968
.75	96.295	95.295	94.138	92.797	91.245
15.00	96.434	95.464	94.338	93.032	91.515
.25	96.568	95.627	94.533	93.259	91.778
.50	96.697	95.785	94.721	93.481	92.033
.75	96.822	95.938	94.904	93.695	92.282
16.00	96.943	96.086	95.081	93.904	92.523
.25	97.059	96.229	95.253	94.106	92.758
.50	97.172	96.367	95.419	94.302	92.986
.75	97.280	96.500	95.580	94.492	93.208
17.00	97.385	96.630	95.735	94.677	93.424
.25	97.486	96.754	95.886	94.856	93.633
.50	97.583	96.875	96.032	95.029	93.837
.75	97.677	96.991	96.173	95.198	94.034
18.00	97.768	97.104	96.310	95.361	94.226
.25	97.855	97.212	96.442	95.518	94.412
.50	97.939	97.317	96.569	95.671	94.592
.75	98.020	97.418	96.693	95.820	94.768
19.00	98.098	97.516	96.812	95.963	94.937
.25	98.173	97.610	96.928	96.102	95.102
.50	98.246	97.701	97.039	96.236	95.262
.75	98.315	97.788	97.147	96.366	95.417
20.00%	98.383	97.873	97.251	96.492	95.568

Remaining Loan Balance   **25 Years**

Interest Rate	Percent remaining in year				
	11	12	13	14	15
5.00%	70.528	66.959	63.206	59.262	55.116
.25	71.187	67.649	63.921	59.992	55.852
.50	71.838	68.332	64.629	60.717	56.584
.75	72.480	69.008	65.330	61.436	57.312
6.00	73.113	69.675	66.025	62.149	58.034
.25	73.738	70.334	66.712	62.856	58.752
.50	74.354	70.986	67.391	63.556	59.464
.75	74.961	71.628	68.063	64.250	60.171
7.00	75.559	72.262	68.727	64.937	60.872
.25	76.148	72.888	69.384	65.617	61.567
.50	76.727	73.504	70.032	66.289	62.256
.75	77.297	74.112	70.671	66.954	62.938
8.00	77.858	74.711	71.303	67.612	63.614
.25	78.409	75.300	71.925	68.261	64.283
.50	78.950	75.880	72.539	68.903	64.945
.75	79.482	76.451	73.145	69.537	65.600
9.00	80.004	77.013	73.741	70.162	66.248
.25	80.517	77.565	74.329	70.779	66.888
.50	81.020	78.108	74.907	71.388	67.520
.75	81.514	78.642	75.477	71.989	68.145
10.00	81.998	79.166	76.037	72.581	68.762
.25	82.472	79.680	76.588	73.164	69.372
.50	82.937	80.185	77.130	73.739	69.973
.75	83.392	80.681	77.663	74.304	70.566
11.00	83.838	81.167	78.187	74.862	71.152
.25	84.275	81.644	78.701	75.410	71.729
.50	84.702	82.111	79.206	75.949	72.297
.75	85.120	82.569	79.703	76.480	72.858
12.00	85.529	83.018	80.190	77.002	73.410
.25	85.928	83.458	80.667	77.515	73.954
.50	86.319	83.888	81.136	78.019	74.490
.75	86.701	84.310	81.596	78.515	75.017
13.00	87.074	84.723	82.047	79.002	75.536
.25	87.438	85.126	82.489	79.480	76.047
.50	87.794	85.521	82.922	79.949	76.549
.75	88.141	85.907	83.346	80.410	77.043
14.00	88.480	86.285	83.762	80.862	77.529
.25	88.811	86.654	84.169	81.305	78.006
.50	89.133	87.014	84.567	81.740	78.475
.75	89.448	87.367	84.957	82.167	78.937
15.00	89.754	87.711	85.339	82.586	79.390
.25	90.053	88.047	85.712	82.996	79.834
.50	90.345	88.375	86.078	83.398	80.271
.75	90.628	88.695	86.435	83.791	80.700
16.00	90.905	89.008	86.784	84.177	81.121
.25	91.174	89.313	87.126	84.555	81.535
.50	91.436	89.611	87.460	84.925	81.940
.75	91.692	89.901	87.786	85.288	82.338
17.00	91.940	90.184	88.104	85.643	82.728
.25	92.182	90.460	88.416	85.990	83.111
.50	92.417	90.729	88.720	86.330	83.486
.75	92.646	90.991	89.017	86.662	83.854
18.00	92.869	91.247	89.307	86.988	84.215
.25	93.085	91.495	89.590	87.306	84.569
.50	93.296	91.738	89.866	87.617	84.915
.75	93.500	91.974	90.136	87.922	85.255
19.00	93.699	92.204	90.399	88.219	85.587
.25	93.893	92.428	90.656	88.510	85.913
.50	94.080	92.646	90.906	88.795	86.233
.75	94.263	92.859	91.150	89.073	86.545
20.00%	94.440	93.065	91.389	89.344	86.851

Table 3   269

25 Years   Remaining Loan Balance

Interest Rate	16	17	18	19	20
5.00%	50.758	46.176	41.361	36.299	30.978
.25	51.489	46.892	42.048	36.942	31.563
.50	52.218	47.606	42.734	37.587	32.149
.75	52.944	48.318	43.420	38.232	32.737
6.00	53.666	49.028	44.104	38.877	33.327
.25	54.384	49.736	44.788	39.522	33.917
.50	55.099	50.440	45.470	40.167	34.509
.75	55.809	51.142	46.151	40.812	35.101
7.00	56.514	51.841	46.829	41.456	35.694
.25	57.215	52.535	47.506	42.099	36.287
.50	57.910	53.227	48.180	42.741	36.880
.75	58.600	53.914	48.851	43.381	37.472
8.00	59.285	54.597	49.519	44.020	38.065
.25	59.964	55.275	50.184	44.657	38.657
.50	60.638	55.949	50.846	45.292	39.248
.75	61.305	56.618	51.505	45.925	39.838
9.00	61.966	57.282	52.159	46.556	40.427
.25	62.620	57.941	52.810	47.184	41.015
.50	63.268	58.595	53.457	47.809	41.601
.75	63.910	59.242	54.099	48.431	42.186
10.00	64.544	59.885	54.737	49.050	42.768
.25	65.172	60.521	55.370	49.666	43.349
.50	65.793	61.152	55.999	50.279	43.928
.75	66.406	61.776	56.623	50.887	44.504
11.00	67.012	62.394	57.241	51.493	45.078
.25	67.611	63.006	57.855	52.094	45.650
.50	68.203	63.611	58.463	52.691	46.219
.75	68.787	64.210	59.066	53.284	46.785
12.00	69.363	64.802	59.664	53.873	47.348
.25	69.932	65.388	60.255	54.457	47.908
.50	70.493	65.967	60.841	55.037	48.465
.75	71.047	66.539	61.422	55.613	49.018
13.00	71.592	67.104	61.996	56.184	49.568
.25	72.130	67.662	62.565	56.750	50.115
.50	72.661	68.214	63.128	57.311	50.659
.75	73.183	68.758	63.684	57.867	51.198
14.00	73.698	69.295	64.235	58.419	51.734
.25	74.205	69.825	64.779	58.965	52.266
.50	74.704	70.349	65.317	59.506	52.794
.75	75.196	70.865	65.850	60.043	53.319
15.00	75.680	71.374	66.375	60.574	53.839
.25	76.156	71.876	66.895	61.099	54.356
.50	76.625	72.371	67.408	61.620	54.868
.75	77.085	72.858	67.915	62.135	55.376
16.00	77.539	73.339	68.416	62.645	55.880
.25	77.985	73.813	68.911	63.150	56.380
.50	78.423	74.280	69.399	63.649	56.875
.75	78.854	74.740	69.881	64.143	57.366
17.00	79.278	75.193	70.357	64.631	57.853
.25	79.694	75.639	70.826	65.114	58.336
.50	80.103	76.078	71.289	65.592	58.814
.75	80.505	76.511	71.747	66.064	59.288
18.00	80.900	76.936	72.197	66.531	59.757
.25	81.288	77.355	72.642	66.993	60.222
.50	81.668	77.768	73.080	67.449	60.682
.75	82.042	78.173	73.513	67.900	61.139
19.00	82.409	78.572	73.939	68.345	61.590
.25	82.770	78.965	74.360	68.785	62.037
.50	83.124	79.351	74.774	69.220	62.480
.75	83.471	79.731	75.182	69.649	62.919
20.00%	83.812	80.105	75.585	70.073	63.352

Remaining Loan Balance   **25 Years**

Interest Rate	Percent remaining in year			
	21	22	23	24
5.00%	25.385	19.505	13.325	6.829
.25	25.894	19.920	13.624	6.991
.50	26.405	20.337	13.926	7.154
.75	26.919	20.757	14.231	7.319
6.00	27.435	21.179	14.537	7.486
.25	27.952	21.603	14.846	7.654
.50	28.472	22.030	15.157	7.824
.75	28.993	22.459	15.471	7.996
7.00	29.515	22.890	15.786	8.168
.25	30.039	23.323	16.103	8.342
.50	30.563	23.757	16.422	8.518
.75	31.089	24.193	16.743	8.695
8.00	31.615	24.630	17.065	8.873
.25	32.142	25.069	17.389	9.052
.50	32.669	25.508	17.715	9.232
.75	33.196	25.949	18.041	9.414
9.00	33.723	26.390	18.369	9.596
.25	34.250	26.832	18.698	9.780
.50	34.777	27.275	19.029	9.964
.75	35.303	27.718	19.360	10.150
10.00	35.828	28.162	19.692	10.336
.25	36.353	28.606	20.025	10.523
.50	36.877	29.050	20.359	10.711
.75	37.400	29.494	20.694	10.900
11.00	37.922	29.937	21.029	11.090
.25	38.442	30.381	21.365	11.280
.50	38.962	30.824	21.701	11.471
.75	39.479	31.267	22.037	11.662
12.00	39.995	31.710	22.374	11.854
.25	40.509	32.152	22.711	12.047
.50	41.022	32.593	23.048	12.240
.75	41.532	33.033	23.386	12.433
13.00	42.040	33.473	23.723	12.627
.25	42.546	33.911	24.060	12.822
.50	43.050	34.349	24.398	13.016
.75	43.552	34.785	24.735	13.211
14.00	44.051	35.221	25.072	13.407
.25	44.548	35.655	25.408	13.603
.50	45.042	36.087	25.745	13.798
.75	45.533	36.519	26.081	13.994
15.00	46.022	36.949	26.416	14.191
.25	46.508	37.377	26.751	14.387
.50	46.991	37.803	27.086	14.584
.75	47.472	38.228	27.420	14.780
16.00	47.949	38.652	27.753	14.977
.25	48.423	39.074	28.086	15.174
.50	48.895	39.494	28.418	15.371
.75	49.363	39.912	28.750	15.568
17.00	49.828	40.328	29.080	15.764
.25	50.290	40.742	29.410	15.961
.50	50.749	41.155	29.739	16.158
.75	51.205	41.565	30.068	16.355
18.00	51.657	41.973	30.395	16.551
.25	52.106	42.379	30.721	16.748
.50	52.552	42.784	31.047	16.944
.75	52.995	43.186	31.371	17.141
19.00	53.434	43.586	31.694	17.336
.25	53.870	43.983	32.017	17.532
.50	54.302	44.379	32.339	17.728
.75	54.732	44.773	32.659	17.924
20.00%	55.157	45.164	32.978	18.119

Table 3   271

__20 Years__   **Remaining Loan Balance**

Interest Rate	1	2	3	4	5
		Percent remaining in year			
5.00%	97.013	93.873	90.572	87.102	83.455
.25	97.095	94.033	90.807	87.407	83.824
.50	97.175	94.190	91.037	87.707	84.188
.75	97.253	94.345	91.264	88.002	84.547
6.00	97.330	94.496	91.486	88.292	84.900
.25	97.405	94.644	91.705	88.577	85.247
.50	97.479	94.789	91.919	88.857	85.589
.75	97.551	94.931	92.129	89.132	85.926
7.00	97.621	95.070	92.335	89.402	86.257
.25	97.690	95.206	92.537	89.667	86.582
.50	97.757	95.339	92.734	89.927	86.902
.75	97.822	95.470	92.928	90.183	87.217
8.00	97.886	95.597	93.118	90.433	87.526
.25	97.949	95.722	93.304	90.679	87.829
.50	98.010	95.844	93.486	90.920	88.127
.75	98.069	95.963	93.664	91.156	88.420
9.00	98.127	96.079	93.838	91.388	88.707
.25	98.184	96.192	94.009	91.614	88.989
.50	98.239	96.303	94.176	91.837	89.265
.75	98.293	96.412	94.339	92.054	89.537
10.00	98.345	96.517	94.498	92.267	89.802
.25	98.396	96.620	94.654	92.475	90.063
.50	98.446	96.721	94.806	92.679	90.319
.75	98.495	96.819	94.954	92.879	90.569
11.00	98.542	96.915	95.099	93.074	90.814
.25	98.588	97.008	95.241	93.265	91.054
.50	98.632	97.099	95.379	93.451	91.289
.75	98.676	97.187	95.514	93.633	91.519
12.00	98.718	97.273	95.646	93.811	91.744
.25	98.759	97.357	95.774	93.985	91.965
.50	98.799	97.439	95.899	94.155	92.180
.75	98.838	97.519	96.021	94.321	92.391
13.00	98.876	97.596	96.140	94.483	92.597
.25	98.912	97.672	96.256	94.641	92.798
.50	98.948	97.745	96.369	94.795	92.995
.75	98.983	97.816	96.479	94.946	93.188
14.00	99.016	97.886	96.586	95.092	93.376
.25	99.049	97.953	96.690	95.235	93.559
.50	99.081	98.018	96.792	95.375	93.738
.75	99.111	98.082	96.891	95.511	93.913
15.00	99.141	98.144	96.987	95.643	94.084
.25	99.170	98.204	97.080	95.773	94.251
.50	99.198	98.263	97.171	95.898	94.414
.75	99.225	98.319	97.260	96.021	94.572
16.00	99.252	98.374	97.346	96.140	94.727
.25	99.277	98.428	97.430	96.256	94.878
.50	99.302	98.480	97.511	96.370	95.025
.75	99.326	98.530	97.590	96.480	95.169
17.00	99.349	98.579	97.667	96.587	95.308
.25	99.372	98.626	97.741	96.691	95.445
.50	99.394	98.672	97.814	96.792	95.577
.75	99.415	98.717	97.884	96.891	95.707
18.00	99.435	98.760	97.952	96.987	95.833
.25	99.455	98.802	98.019	97.080	95.955
.50	99.474	98.842	98.083	97.171	96.075
.75	99.493	98.882	98.146	97.259	96.191
19.00	99.511	98.920	98.206	97.345	96.304
.25	99.528	98.957	98.265	97.428	96.415
.50	99.545	98.992	98.322	97.509	96.522
.75	99.561	99.027	98.377	97.587	96.626
20.00%	99.577	99.061	98.431	97.664	96.728

Remaining Loan Balance   **20 Years**

Interest	Percent remaining in year				
Rate	6	7	8	9	10
5.00%	79.621	75.591	71.355	66.902	62.222
.25	80.049	76.070	71.878	67.460	62.805
.50	80.471	76.544	72.396	68.014	63.384
.75	80.888	77.013	72.909	68.563	63.960
6.00	81.298	77.475	73.416	69.107	64.531
.25	81.704	77.932	73.918	69.646	65.099
.50	82.103	78.383	74.414	70.180	65.662
.75	82.496	78.828	74.905	70.709	66.220
7.00	82.884	79.268	75.390	71.232	66.774
.25	83.266	79.701	75.870	71.751	67.323
.50	83.642	80.129	76.343	72.263	67.867
.75	84.012	80.551	76.811	72.771	68.406
8.00	84.377	80.966	77.273	73.273	68.941
.25	84.735	81.376	77.729	73.769	69.470
.50	85.088	81.779	78.178	74.259	69.994
.75	85.434	82.177	78.622	74.744	70.513
9.00	85.775	82.568	79.060	75.223	71.026
.25	86.110	82.953	79.492	75.696	71.534
.50	86.439	83.332	79.917	76.163	72.036
.75	86.762	83.705	80.336	76.624	72.533
10.00	87.080	84.072	80.750	77.079	73.024
.25	87.392	84.433	81.157	77.528	73.510
.50	87.698	84.788	81.558	77.971	73.990
.75	87.998	85.137	81.952	78.408	74.464
11.00	88.293	85.480	82.341	78.839	74.932
.25	88.582	85.816	82.723	79.264	75.394
.50	88.865	86.147	83.099	79.682	75.851
.75	89.143	86.472	83.470	80.095	76.302
12.00	89.415	86.791	83.834	80.501	76.746
.25	89.682	87.104	84.191	80.901	77.185
.50	89.944	87.411	84.543	81.296	77.618
.75	90.200	87.713	84.889	81.684	78.045
13.00	90.451	88.008	85.229	82.065	78.466
.25	90.696	88.298	85.562	82.441	78.881
.50	90.937	88.583	85.890	82.811	79.289
.75	91.172	88.861	86.212	83.175	79.692
14.00	91.402	89.135	86.528	83.533	80.089
.25	91.628	89.402	86.838	83.884	80.481
.50	91.848	89.665	87.143	84.230	80.866
.75	92.064	89.922	87.442	84.570	81.245
15.00	92.274	90.173	87.735	84.904	81.618
.25	92.480	90.420	88.022	85.232	81.986
.50	92.681	90.661	88.304	85.555	82.348
.75	92.878	90.897	88.580	85.871	82.703
16.00	93.070	91.128	88.851	86.182	83.054
.25	93.258	91.354	89.117	86.488	83.398
.50	93.441	91.575	89.377	86.787	83.737
.75	93.620	91.792	89.632	87.082	84.070
17.00	93.795	92.003	89.882	87.370	84.397
.25	93.965	92.210	90.126	87.654	84.719
.50	94.132	92.412	90.366	87.931	85.035
.75	94.294	92.610	90.600	88.204	85.346
18.00	94.453	92.803	90.830	88.471	85.651
.25	94.607	92.992	91.055	88.734	85.951
.50	94.758	93.176	91.275	88.991	86.246
.75	94.905	93.356	91.490	89.243	86.536
19.00	95.048	93.532	91.701	89.490	86.820
.25	95.188	93.704	91.907	89.732	87.099
.50	95.324	93.871	92.108	89.969	87.373
.75	95.457	94.035	92.305	90.201	87.642
20.00%	95.586	94.195	92.498	90.429	87.906

Table 3   273

20 Years **Remaining Loan Balance**

Interest Rate	11	12	13	14	15
		Percent remaining in year			
5.00%	57.301	52.130	46.693	40.978	34.972
.25	57.899	52.729	47.282	41.541	35.492
.50	58.494	53.327	47.870	42.104	36.013
.75	59.086	53.923	48.456	42.667	36.535
6.00	59.674	54.517	49.042	43.229	37.058
.25	60.259	55.108	49.626	43.791	37.581
.50	60.841	55.697	50.209	44.353	38.105
.75	61.419	56.283	50.790	44.914	38.630
7.00	61.993	56.866	51.369	45.475	39.154
.25	62.563	57.447	51.947	46.034	39.679
.50	63.129	58.024	52.522	46.593	40.203
.75	63.691	58.598	53.095	47.150	40.728
8.00	64.249	59.168	53.665	47.706	41.252
.25	64.802	59.735	54.233	48.260	41.776
.50	65.351	60.298	54.799	48.813	42.299
.75	65.896	60.858	55.362	49.365	42.821
9.00	66.435	61.414	55.922	49.914	43.343
.25	66.970	61.966	56.478	50.461	43.864
.50	67.500	62.513	57.032	51.007	44.383
.75	68.025	63.057	57.583	51.550	44.902
10.00	68.545	63.596	58.130	52.091	45.419
.25	69.060	64.131	58.673	52.629	45.935
.50	69.569	64.662	59.214	53.165	46.449
.75	70.074	65.188	59.750	53.698	46.962
11.00	70.573	65.709	60.283	54.228	47.473
.25	71.067	66.226	60.812	54.756	47.983
.50	71.555	66.738	61.337	55.281	48.490
.75	72.038	67.245	61.858	55.802	48.996
12.00	72.515	67.747	62.375	56.321	49.499
.25	72.987	68.245	62.888	56.836	50.001
.50	73.453	68.737	63.396	57.348	50.500
.75	73.914	69.224	63.901	57.857	50.997
13.00	74.369	69.707	64.401	58.363	51.491
.25	74.818	70.184	64.896	58.864	51.983
.50	75.262	70.656	65.388	59.363	52.472
.75	75.700	71.122	65.874	59.857	52.959
14.00	76.132	71.584	66.356	60.348	53.443
.25	76.559	72.040	66.834	60.835	53.924
.50	76.980	72.491	67.307	61.319	54.402
.75	77.395	72.937	67.775	61.799	54.878
15.00	77.805	73.378	68.239	62.274	55.351
.25	78.208	73.813	68.698	62.746	55.820
.50	78.606	74.242	69.152	63.214	56.287
.75	78.999	74.667	69.601	63.678	56.750
16.00	79.386	75.086	70.046	64.137	57.211
.25	79.767	75.500	70.486	64.593	57.668
.50	80.143	75.909	70.921	65.044	58.122
.75	80.513	76.312	71.351	65.492	58.573
17.00	80.877	76.710	71.776	65.935	59.020
.25	81.236	77.102	72.196	66.374	59.464
.50	81.589	77.490	72.612	66.809	59.905
.75	81.937	77.872	73.023	67.240	60.342
18.00	82.280	78.248	73.429	67.666	60.776
.25	82.617	78.620	73.830	68.088	61.206
.50	82.949	78.986	74.226	68.506	61.633
.75	83.275	79.348	74.617	68.920	62.057
19.00	83.596	79.704	75.004	69.329	62.477
.25	83.912	80.055	75.386	69.734	62.893
.50	84.223	80.401	75.763	70.135	63.306
.75	84.528	80.741	76.135	70.531	63.716
20.00%	84.829	81.077	76.502	70.924	64.121

Remaining Loan Balance **20 Years**

Interest Rate	Percent remaining in year			
	16	17	18	19
5.00%	28.657	22.020	15.043	7.709
.25	29.117	22.399	15.320	7.861
.50	29.578	22.781	15.600	8.014
.75	30.041	23.164	15.881	8.168
6.00	30.506	23.550	16.165	8.324
.25	30.972	23.937	16.450	8.481
.50	31.439	24.326	16.737	8.640
.75	31.907	24.717	17.026	8.799
7.00	32.377	25.109	17.316	8.960
.25	32.847	25.503	17.609	9.122
.50	33.318	25.898	17.902	9.286
.75	33.790	26.295	18.197	9.450
8.00	34.262	26.692	18.494	9.616
.25	34.735	27.091	18.792	9.782
.50	35.208	27.491	19.092	9.950
.75	35.682	27.892	19.392	10.119
9.00	36.155	28.294	19.694	10.288
.25	36.629	28.696	19.997	10.459
.50	37.103	29.099	20.301	10.631
.75	37.576	29.503	20.607	10.803
10.00	38.049	29.907	20.913	10.977
.25	38.522	30.312	21.220	11.151
.50	38.994	30.717	21.528	11.326
.75	39.466	31.122	21.837	11.502
11.00	39.937	31.528	22.146	11.679
.25	40.407	31.934	22.456	11.856
.50	40.877	32.340	22.767	12.034
.75	41.345	32.745	23.079	12.213
12.00	41.813	33.151	23.391	12.393
.25	42.279	33.556	23.703	12.573
.50	42.744	33.962	24.016	12.754
.75	43.208	34.367	24.329	12.935
13.00	43.671	34.771	24.643	13.117
.25	44.132	35.175	24.957	13.299
.50	44.592	35.579	25.271	13.482
.75	45.050	35.982	25.585	13.666
14.00	45.506	36.384	25.900	13.850
.25	45.961	36.786	26.214	14.034
.50	46.414	37.187	26.529	14.219
.75	46.865	37.587	26.843	14.404
15.00	47.314	37.986	27.158	14.589
.25	47.761	38.384	27.472	14.775
.50	48.207	38.781	27.786	14.961
.75	48.650	39.178	28.101	15.147
16.00	49.091	39.573	28.414	15.334
.25	49.530	39.967	28.728	15.521
.50	49.967	40.359	29.041	15.708
.75	50.401	40.751	29.354	15.895
17.00	50.833	41.141	29.667	16.083
.25	51.263	41.530	29.979	16.270
.50	51.691	41.918	30.291	16.458
.75	52.116	42.304	30.602	16.646
18.00	52.538	42.689	30.913	16.834
.25	52.958	43.072	31.223	17.022
.50	53.376	43.454	31.533	17.210
.75	53.791	43.835	31.842	17.398
19.00	54.203	44.213	32.151	17.586
.25	54.613	44.591	32.459	17.774
.50	55.020	44.966	32.766	17.963
.75	55.425	45.340	33.073	18.151
20.00%	55.827	45.712	33.379	18.339

Table 3   275

18 Years   Remaining Loan Balance

Rate	1	2	3	4	5	6
5.00%	96.484	92.788	88.902	84.818	80.525	76.013
.25	96.569	92.953	89.143	85.129	80.898	76.439
.50	96.653	93.117	89.381	85.435	81.266	76.861
.75	96.735	93.277	89.615	85.736	81.629	77.279
6.00	96.815	93.434	89.845	86.034	81.988	77.692
.25	96.895	93.589	90.071	86.327	82.342	78.101
.50	96.972	93.741	90.294	86.617	82.692	78.505
.75	97.048	93.891	90.514	86.901	83.038	78.905
7.00	97.123	94.038	90.729	87.182	83.378	79.300
.25	97.196	94.182	90.942	87.459	83.714	79.690
.50	97.268	94.323	91.150	87.731	84.046	80.075
.75	97.338	94.462	91.355	87.999	84.373	80.456
8.00	97.407	94.598	91.557	88.263	84.695	80.832
.25	97.474	94.732	91.755	88.522	85.013	81.203
.50	97.540	94.863	91.949	88.777	85.326	81.569
.75	97.605	94.991	92.140	89.029	85.634	81.930
9.00	97.668	95.117	92.327	89.276	85.938	82.286
.25	97.730	95.241	92.511	89.518	86.237	82.638
.50	97.791	95.362	92.692	89.757	86.531	82.985
.75	97.850	95.480	92.869	89.992	86.821	83.327
10.00	97.908	95.596	93.043	90.222	87.106	83.663
.25	97.964	95.710	93.213	90.448	87.387	83.995
.50	98.020	95.821	93.381	90.671	87.663	84.323
.75	98.074	95.930	93.544	90.889	87.934	84.645
11.00	98.127	96.037	93.705	91.104	88.201	84.962
.25	98.179	96.141	93.863	91.314	88.463	85.275
.50	98.229	96.243	94.017	91.520	88.721	85.583
.75	98.278	96.343	94.168	91.723	88.975	85.885
12.00	98.327	96.441	94.316	91.922	89.224	86.183
.25	98.374	96.536	94.461	92.117	89.468	86.477
.50	98.419	96.630	94.603	92.308	89.709	86.765
.75	98.464	96.721	94.742	92.495	89.944	87.049
13.00	98.508	96.810	94.878	92.679	90.176	87.328
.25	98.551	96.897	95.011	92.859	90.403	87.602
.50	98.592	96.982	95.141	93.035	90.626	87.872
.75	98.633	97.065	95.268	93.208	90.845	88.137
14.00	98.672	97.146	95.393	93.377	91.060	88.397
.25	98.711	97.226	95.514	93.543	91.271	88.653
.50	98.749	97.303	95.633	93.705	91.477	88.905
.75	98.785	97.378	95.750	93.864	91.680	89.151
15.00	98.821	97.452	95.863	94.019	91.879	89.394
.25	98.856	97.524	95.974	94.171	92.073	89.632
.50	98.889	97.594	96.083	94.320	92.264	89.865
.75	98.922	97.662	96.189	94.466	92.451	90.095
16.00	98.955	97.729	96.292	94.608	92.634	90.320
.25	98.986	97.794	96.393	94.748	92.813	90.540
.50	99.016	97.857	96.492	94.884	92.989	90.757
.75	99.046	97.919	96.588	95.017	93.161	90.969
17.00	99.075	97.979	96.682	95.147	93.329	91.178
.25	99.103	98.038	96.774	95.274	93.494	91.382
.50	99.130	98.095	96.864	95.399	93.656	91.582
.75	99.157	98.151	96.951	95.520	93.814	91.778
18.00	99.182	98.205	97.036	95.639	93.968	91.971
.25	99.208	98.258	97.119	95.755	94.119	92.159
.50	99.232	98.309	97.200	95.868	94.267	92.344
.75	99.256	98.359	97.279	95.979	94.412	92.525
19.00	99.279	98.408	97.356	96.086	94.553	92.702
.25	99.301	98.455	97.431	96.192	94.692	92.876
.50	99.323	98.501	97.504	96.295	94.827	93.046
.75	99.344	98.546	97.576	96.395	94.959	93.212
20.00%	99.365	98.590	97.645	96.493	95.088	93.375

Percent remaining in year

Remaining Loan Balance ## 18 Years

Interest Rate	Percent remaining in year					
	7	8	9	10	11	12
5.00%	71.269	66.283	61.042	55.532	49.741	43.653
.25	71.741	66.790	61.573	56.075	50.282	44.177
.50	72.209	67.294	62.102	56.617	50.822	44.701
.75	72.673	67.794	62.627	57.156	51.361	45.224
6.00	73.132	68.290	63.150	57.693	51.899	45.747
.25	73.587	68.783	63.669	58.227	52.435	46.270
.50	74.038	69.271	64.185	58.759	52.969	46.791
.75	74.484	69.756	64.698	59.288	53.502	47.313
7.00	74.926	70.236	65.207	59.815	54.033	47.833
.25	75.363	70.713	65.713	60.339	54.562	48.352
.50	75.796	71.185	66.215	60.860	55.089	48.870
.75	76.224	71.652	66.714	61.378	55.614	49.387
8.00	76.647	72.116	67.208	61.893	56.137	49.903
.25	77.066	72.575	67.699	62.405	56.657	50.417
.50	77.480	73.029	68.185	62.913	57.175	50.930
.75	77.889	73.479	68.668	63.419	57.691	51.441
9.00	78.293	73.925	69.147	63.920	58.204	51.951
.25	78.692	74.365	69.621	64.418	58.714	52.459
.50	79.086	74.801	70.091	64.913	59.221	52.965
.75	79.476	75.233	70.557	65.404	59.726	53.468
10.00	79.861	75.659	71.018	65.891	60.227	53.970
.25	80.240	76.081	71.475	66.375	60.726	54.470
.50	80.615	76.498	71.928	66.854	61.221	54.967
.75	80.984	76.910	72.376	67.330	61.713	55.462
11.00	81.349	77.318	72.820	67.801	62.202	55.955
.25	81.709	77.720	73.259	68.269	62.687	56.445
.50	82.063	78.117	73.693	68.732	63.170	56.933
.75	82.413	78.510	74.123	69.191	63.648	57.417
12.00	82.758	78.898	74.548	69.646	64.123	57.900
.25	83.097	79.280	74.968	70.097	64.595	58.379
.50	83.432	79.658	75.384	70.544	65.063	58.856
.75	83.762	80.031	75.795	70.986	65.527	59.329
13.00	84.087	80.398	76.201	71.423	65.987	59.800
.25	84.407	80.761	76.602	71.857	66.444	60.268
.50	84.722	81.119	76.998	72.286	66.896	60.732
.75	85.032	81.472	77.390	72.710	67.345	61.194
14.00	85.337	81.820	77.777	73.130	67.790	61.652
.25	85.637	82.163	78.159	73.546	68.231	62.107
.50	85.933	82.501	78.536	73.957	68.668	62.559
.75	86.224	82.834	78.908	74.363	69.101	63.007
15.00	86.510	83.162	79.276	74.765	69.529	63.452
.25	86.791	83.485	79.639	75.162	69.954	63.893
.50	87.067	83.804	79.996	75.555	70.375	64.332
.75	87.339	84.117	80.349	75.943	70.791	64.766
16.00	87.607	84.426	80.698	76.327	71.203	65.197
.25	87.869	84.730	81.041	76.706	71.612	65.625
.50	88.127	85.029	81.380	77.080	72.016	66.049
.75	88.381	85.324	81.714	77.450	72.415	66.469
17.00	88.630	85.614	82.043	77.816	72.811	66.886
.25	88.875	85.899	82.368	78.176	73.202	67.299
.50	89.115	86.180	82.687	78.532	73.589	67.708
.75	89.351	86.456	83.002	78.884	73.972	68.114
18.00	89.582	86.727	83.313	79.231	74.351	68.516
.25	89.810	86.994	83.619	79.574	74.725	68.914
.50	90.033	87.256	83.920	79.912	75.095	69.308
.75	90.252	87.514	84.217	80.245	75.461	69.699
19.00	90.467	87.768	84.509	80.574	75.823	70.086
.25	90.678	88.017	84.797	80.899	76.180	70.469
.50	90.885	88.262	85.080	81.219	76.534	70.849
.75	91.087	88.503	85.359	81.535	76.883	71.224
20.00%	91.286	88.739	85.633	81.846	77.228	71.596

Table 3   277

18 Years   Remaining Loan Balance

Interest Rate	Percent remaining in year				
	13	14	15	16	17
5.00%	37.254	30.528	23.457	16.025	8.212
.25	37.744	30.965	23.821	16.293	8.360
.50	38.234	31.403	24.186	16.562	8.508
.75	38.725	31.842	24.553	16.833	8.658
6.00	39.216	32.283	24.922	17.106	8.809
.25	39.708	32.725	25.292	17.381	8.961
.50	40.200	33.167	25.664	17.657	9.115
.75	40.692	33.611	26.037	17.935	9.269
7.00	41.184	34.056	26.411	18.214	9.425
.25	41.677	34.501	26.787	18.495	9.582
.50	42.169	34.947	27.164	18.777	9.739
.75	42.660	35.393	27.542	19.061	9.898
8.00	43.152	35.840	27.922	19.346	10.058
.25	43.643	36.287	28.302	19.632	10.219
.50	44.133	36.735	28.683	19.920	10.381
.75	44.623	37.183	29.065	20.208	10.544
9.00	45.112	37.631	29.448	20.498	10.708
.25	45.600	38.079	29.832	20.789	10.873
.50	46.087	38.527	30.216	21.081	11.039
.75	46.573	38.974	30.601	21.374	11.205
10.00	47.058	39.422	30.986	21.667	11.373
.25	47.542	39.869	31.372	21.962	11.541
.50	48.024	40.316	31.758	22.258	11.710
.75	48.505	40.762	32.145	22.554	11.880
11.00	48.985	41.208	32.532	22.851	12.051
.25	49.463	41.653	32.919	23.149	12.222
.50	49.939	42.098	33.306	23.448	12.394
.75	50.414	42.542	33.693	23.747	12.567
12.00	50.887	42.985	34.080	24.046	12.740
.25	51.358	43.427	34.467	24.347	12.914
.50	51.827	43.868	34.854	24.647	13.089
.75	52.294	44.308	35.241	24.949	13.264
13.00	52.759	44.746	35.628	25.250	13.440
.25	53.222	45.184	36.014	25.552	13.617
.50	53.683	45.620	36.400	25.854	13.793
.75	54.141	46.055	36.785	26.157	13.971
14.00	54.597	46.489	37.170	26.459	14.149
.25	55.051	46.921	37.554	26.762	14.327
.50	55.502	47.352	37.938	27.065	14.506
.75	55.951	47.781	38.322	27.368	14.685
15.00	56.397	48.209	38.704	27.671	14.865
.25	56.841	48.635	39.086	27.975	15.045
.50	57.282	49.059	39.467	28.278	15.225
.75	57.721	49.482	39.847	28.581	15.406
16.00	58.156	49.902	40.227	28.884	15.587
.25	58.589	50.321	40.605	29.187	15.769
.50	59.019	50.738	40.983	29.490	15.950
.75	59.447	51.153	41.359	29.792	16.132
17.00	59.871	51.566	41.734	30.095	16.314
.25	60.292	51.977	42.109	30.397	16.497
.50	60.711	52.386	42.482	30.699	16.679
.75	61.127	52.793	42.854	31.000	16.862
18.00	61.539	53.198	43.225	31.301	17.045
.25	61.949	53.601	43.595	31.602	17.228
.50	62.355	54.001	43.963	31.903	17.411
.75	62.759	54.399	44.330	32.203	17.595
19.00	63.159	54.795	44.696	32.502	17.778
.25	63.556	55.189	45.061	32.801	17.962
.50	63.951	55.580	45.424	33.100	18.145
.75	64.342	55.969	45.785	33.398	18.329
20.00%	64.730	56.356	46.146	33.695	18.513

Remaining Loan Balance **15 Years**

Interest Rate	Percent remaining in year				
	1	2	3	4	5
5.00%	95.406	90.577	85.501	80.166	74.557
.25	95.496	90.750	85.749	80.478	74.925
.50	95.585	90.921	85.993	80.788	75.289
.75	95.672	91.089	86.235	81.095	75.651
6.00	95.758	91.255	86.474	81.398	76.009
.25	95.843	91.419	86.710	81.699	76.365
.50	95.927	91.581	86.944	81.996	76.717
.75	96.009	91.740	87.174	82.290	77.067
7.00	96.090	91.898	87.402	82.582	77.413
.25	96.170	92.053	87.627	82.870	77.756
.50	96.249	92.206	87.850	83.155	78.096
.75	96.326	92.357	88.069	83.437	78.433
8.00	96.402	92.506	88.286	83.716	78.766
.25	96.477	92.652	88.500	83.991	79.097
.50	96.551	92.797	88.711	84.264	79.424
.75	96.623	92.939	88.919	84.533	79.747
9.00	96.695	93.079	89.125	84.799	80.068
.25	96.765	93.217	89.327	85.062	80.385
.50	96.834	93.353	89.527	85.322	80.699
.75	96.902	93.487	89.725	85.579	81.009
10.00	96.968	93.619	89.919	85.832	81.317
.25	97.034	93.749	90.111	86.082	81.620
.50	97.098	93.877	90.300	86.329	81.921
.75	97.161	94.002	90.486	86.573	82.218
11.00	97.224	94.126	90.670	86.814	82.512
.25	97.285	94.248	90.851	87.051	82.802
.50	97.345	94.367	91.029	87.286	83.089
.75	97.404	94.485	91.205	87.517	83.372
12.00	97.461	94.601	91.377	87.745	83.652
.25	97.518	94.715	91.548	87.970	83.929
.50	97.574	94.826	91.715	88.192	84.202
.75	97.629	94.936	91.880	88.411	84.472
13.00	97.682	95.045	92.043	88.627	84.739
.25	97.735	95.151	92.203	88.839	85.002
.50	97.787	95.255	92.360	89.049	85.262
.75	97.837	95.358	92.515	89.255	85.518
14.00	97.887	95.458	92.667	89.459	85.771
.25	97.936	95.557	92.817	89.659	86.021
.50	97.983	95.654	92.964	89.857	86.268
.75	98.030	95.750	93.109	90.051	86.511
15.00	98.076	95.843	93.251	90.243	86.750
.25	98.121	95.935	93.391	90.431	86.987
.50	98.165	96.025	93.529	90.617	87.220
.75	98.209	96.114	93.664	90.800	87.450
16.00	98.251	96.201	93.797	90.980	87.677
.25	98.293	96.286	93.928	91.157	87.900
.50	98.333	96.370	94.056	91.331	88.121
.75	98.373	96.452	94.182	91.502	88.338
17.00	98.412	96.532	94.306	91.671	88.552
.25	98.450	96.611	94.428	91.837	88.762
.50	98.488	96.688	94.547	92.000	88.970
.75	98.524	96.764	94.665	92.161	89.174
18.00	98.560	96.838	94.780	92.319	89.376
.25	98.595	96.911	94.893	92.474	89.574
.50	98.629	96.982	95.004	92.626	89.770
.75	98.663	97.052	95.113	92.776	89.962
19.00	98.696	97.121	95.220	92.924	90.151
.25	98.728	97.188	95.324	93.068	90.338
.50	98.759	97.254	95.427	93.211	90.521
.75	98.790	97.318	95.528	93.351	90.702
20.00%	98.820	97.381	95.627	93.488	90.879

Table 3   279

15 Years   Remaining Loan Balance

Interest Rate	Percent remaining in year				
	6	7	8	9	10
5.00%	68.662	62.464	55.950	49.103	41.905
.25	69.072	62.905	56.406	49.557	42.341
.50	69.480	63.343	56.860	50.012	42.777
.75	69.885	63.779	57.313	50.465	43.213
6.00	70.288	64.213	57.765	50.918	43.649
.25	70.688	64.645	58.214	51.370	44.085
.50	71.085	65.075	58.663	51.821	44.521
.75	71.479	65.502	59.109	52.271	44.957
7.00	71.870	65.927	59.554	52.720	45.393
.25	72.259	66.349	59.997	53.168	45.828
.50	72.644	66.769	60.438	53.615	46.263
.75	73.027	67.186	60.877	54.061	46.697
8.00	73.406	67.601	61.314	54.505	47.131
.25	73.782	68.013	61.749	54.948	47.565
.50	74.156	68.422	62.182	55.390	47.997
.75	74.526	68.829	62.612	55.830	48.429
9.00	74.893	69.232	63.041	56.268	48.861
.25	75.257	69.633	63.467	56.705	49.291
.50	75.617	70.031	63.890	57.140	49.721
.75	75.974	70.426	64.312	57.574	50.149
10.00	76.329	70.818	64.731	58.006	50.577
.25	76.679	71.207	65.147	58.436	51.003
.50	77.027	71.593	65.561	58.864	51.428
.75	77.371	71.976	65.972	59.290	51.853
11.00	77.711	72.356	66.381	59.714	52.276
.25	78.049	72.733	66.786	60.136	52.697
.50	78.383	73.106	67.190	60.556	53.117
.75	78.713	73.476	67.590	60.973	53.536
12.00	79.040	73.844	67.988	61.389	53.954
.25	79.364	74.207	68.382	61.802	54.369
.50	79.684	74.568	68.774	62.213	54.784
.75	80.001	74.925	69.163	62.622	55.196
13.00	80.315	75.280	69.550	63.029	55.608
.25	80.624	75.630	69.933	63.433	56.017
.50	80.931	75.978	70.313	63.834	56.424
.75	81.234	76.322	70.690	64.233	56.830
14.00	81.533	76.662	71.064	64.630	57.234
.25	81.829	77.000	71.435	65.024	57.636
.50	82.122	77.334	71.803	65.415	58.037
.75	82.411	77.664	72.168	65.804	58.435
15.00	82.697	77.991	72.530	66.190	58.831
.25	82.979	78.315	72.888	66.573	59.225
.50	83.258	78.635	73.244	66.954	59.617
.75	83.533	78.952	73.596	67.332	60.008
16.00	83.805	79.266	73.945	67.708	60.395
.25	84.073	79.576	74.291	68.080	60.781
.50	84.338	79.883	74.634	68.450	61.165
.75	84.600	80.186	74.973	68.817	61.546
17.00	84.858	80.486	75.309	69.181	61.925
.25	85.113	80.782	75.642	69.542	62.302
.50	85.365	81.075	75.972	69.900	62.677
.75	85.613	81.365	76.298	70.256	63.049
18.00	85.858	81.651	76.622	70.608	63.419
.25	86.099	81.934	76.942	70.958	63.786
.50	86.337	82.213	77.258	71.305	64.151
.75	86.572	82.489	77.572	71.649	64.514
19.00	86.804	82.762	77.882	71.989	64.874
.25	87.032	83.032	78.189	72.327	65.232
.50	87.258	83.298	78.493	72.662	65.587
.75	87.480	83.561	78.793	72.994	65.940
20.00%	87.699	83.820	79.090	73.323	66.291

Remaining Loan Balance   **15 Years**

Interest Rate	Percent remaining in year			
	11	12	13	14
5.00%	34.339	26.385	18.025	9.237
.25	34.736	26.722	18.277	9.378
.50	35.134	27.059	18.530	9.519
.75	35.532	27.398	18.784	9.661
6.00	35.932	27.738	19.040	9.805
.25	36.332	28.080	19.297	9.949
.50	36.732	28.422	19.555	10.094
.75	37.134	28.765	19.815	10.241
7.00	37.535	29.110	20.075	10.388
.25	37.937	29.455	20.337	10.536
.50	38.340	29.802	20.600	10.685
.75	38.742	30.149	20.865	10.835
8.00	39.145	30.497	21.130	10.986
.25	39.548	30.845	21.396	11.138
.50	39.952	31.195	21.664	11.290
.75	40.355	31.545	21.932	11.444
9.00	40.758	31.895	22.201	11.598
.25	41.161	32.247	22.472	11.753
.50	41.564	32.598	22.743	11.909
.75	41.967	32.951	23.015	12.066
10.00	42.370	33.303	23.288	12.223
.25	42.772	33.656	23.561	12.381
.50	43.174	34.010	23.836	12.540
.75	43.575	34.363	24.111	12.700
11.00	43.977	34.717	24.386	12.860
.25	44.377	35.071	24.663	13.021
.50	44.777	35.425	24.940	13.183
.75	45.176	35.780	25.217	13.345
12.00	45.575	36.134	25.496	13.508
.25	45.973	36.488	25.774	13.672
.50	46.370	36.843	26.054	13.836
.75	46.767	37.197	26.333	14.000
13.00	47.162	37.551	26.613	14.166
.25	47.557	37.905	26.894	14.332
.50	47.950	38.259	27.175	14.498
.75	48.343	38.612	27.456	14.665
14.00	48.734	38.965	27.737	14.832
.25	49.125	39.318	28.019	15.000
.50	49.514	39.671	28.301	15.168
.75	49.902	40.023	28.583	15.337
15.00	50.289	40.374	28.865	15.506
.25	50.675	40.725	29.148	15.676
.50	51.059	41.076	29.431	15.846
.75	51.442	41.426	29.713	16.017
16.00	51.824	41.775	29.996	16.187
.25	52.204	42.124	30.279	16.359
.50	52.583	42.472	30.562	16.530
.75	52.960	42.820	30.845	16.702
17.00	53.336	43.167	31.127	16.874
.25	53.710	43.512	31.410	17.047
.50	54.083	43.858	31.693	17.219
.75	54.453	44.202	31.975	17.392
18.00	54.823	44.545	32.257	17.566
.25	55.191	44.888	32.540	17.739
.50	55.557	45.230	32.822	17.913
.75	55.921	45.570	33.103	18.087
19.00	56.283	45.910	33.385	18.261
.25	56.644	46.249	33.666	18.435
.50	57.003	46.586	33.947	18.610
.75	57.360	46.923	34.227	18.785
20.00%	57.715	47.259	34.508	18.959

Table 3   281

12 Years   Remaining Loan Balance

Interest Rate	Percent remaining in year					
	1	2	3	4	5	6
5.00%	93.760	87.200	80.305	73.057	65.438	57.429
.25	93.854	87.377	80.552	73.359	65.780	57.794
.50	93.947	87.552	80.797	73.661	66.122	58.158
.75	94.039	87.726	81.040	73.960	66.462	58.520
6.00	94.130	87.898	81.282	74.258	66.800	58.882
.25	94.220	88.069	81.522	74.553	67.137	59.243
.50	94.309	88.238	81.759	74.847	67.472	59.603
.75	94.398	88.405	81.995	75.139	67.806	59.962
7.00	94.485	88.571	82.229	75.429	68.138	60.319
.25	94.571	88.735	82.461	75.717	68.468	60.675
.50	94.656	88.897	82.691	76.004	68.797	61.031
.75	94.740	89.058	82.920	76.288	69.124	61.385
8.00	94.823	89.217	83.146	76.570	69.449	61.737
.25	94.906	89.375	83.370	76.851	69.773	62.088
.50	94.987	89.531	83.593	77.129	70.095	62.438
.75	95.067	89.685	83.813	77.406	70.415	62.787
9.00	95.147	89.838	84.031	77.680	70.733	63.134
.25	95.225	89.989	84.248	77.953	71.050	63.480
.50	95.302	90.139	84.463	78.223	71.364	63.825
.75	95.379	90.287	84.675	78.491	71.677	64.167
10.00	95.454	90.433	84.886	78.757	71.988	64.509
.25	95.529	90.578	85.094	79.022	72.296	64.849
.50	95.603	90.721	85.301	79.284	72.603	65.187
.75	95.675	90.862	85.505	79.544	72.908	65.523
11.00	95.747	91.002	85.708	79.801	73.211	65.858
.25	95.818	91.141	85.909	80.057	73.512	66.192
.50	95.888	91.277	86.107	80.311	73.811	66.524
.75	95.957	91.412	86.304	80.562	74.108	66.854
12.00	96.025	91.546	86.499	80.812	74.403	67.182
.25	96.092	91.678	86.692	81.059	74.696	67.508
.50	96.159	91.808	86.882	81.304	74.987	67.833
.75	96.224	91.937	87.071	81.547	75.276	68.156
13.00	96.289	92.065	87.258	81.788	75.562	68.478
.25	96.352	92.191	87.443	82.026	75.847	68.797
.50	96.415	92.315	87.626	82.263	76.129	69.114
.75	96.477	92.438	87.806	82.497	76.409	69.430
14.00	96.538	92.559	87.985	82.729	76.688	69.744
.25	96.598	92.678	88.162	82.959	76.964	70.056
.50	96.657	92.797	88.337	83.187	77.237	70.366
.75	96.716	92.913	88.510	83.412	77.509	70.674
15.00	96.774	93.029	88.682	83.636	77.779	70.980
.25	96.830	93.142	88.851	83.857	78.046	71.284
.50	96.887	93.255	89.018	84.076	78.311	71.587
.75	96.942	93.365	89.183	84.293	78.574	71.887
16.00	96.996	93.475	89.347	84.508	78.835	72.185
.25	97.050	93.583	89.508	84.720	79.094	72.481
.50	97.103	93.689	89.668	84.931	79.350	72.775
.75	97.155	93.794	89.826	85.139	79.604	73.068
17.00	97.206	93.898	89.982	85.345	79.856	73.358
.25	97.256	94.000	90.136	85.549	80.106	73.646
.50	97.306	94.101	90.288	85.751	80.353	73.932
.75	97.355	94.200	90.438	85.951	80.599	74.216
18.00	97.403	94.299	90.586	86.148	80.842	74.497
.25	97.451	94.395	90.733	86.344	81.083	74.777
.50	97.497	94.491	90.878	86.537	81.321	75.055
.75	97.543	94.585	91.021	86.728	81.558	75.330
19.00	97.589	94.677	91.162	86.917	81.792	75.604
.25	97.633	94.769	91.301	87.104	82.024	75.875
.50	97.677	94.859	91.439	87.289	82.254	76.144
.75	97.720	94.948	91.575	87.472	82.482	76.411
20.00%	97.763	95.035	91.709	87.653	82.707	76.676

Remaining Loan Balance   **12 Years**

Interest Rate	Percent remaining in year				
	7	8	9	10	11
5.00%	49.011	40.161	30.860	21.082	10.804
.25	49.378	40.509	31.163	21.314	10.936
.50	49.744	40.856	31.467	21.548	11.070
.75	50.111	41.204	31.772	21.783	11.204
6.00	50.476	41.552	32.077	22.018	11.338
.25	50.842	41.900	32.383	22.254	11.474
.50	51.207	42.248	32.690	22.492	11.610
.75	51.571	42.597	32.998	22.730	11.747
7.00	51.935	42.945	33.306	22.969	11.885
.25	52.299	43.294	33.614	23.209	12.024
.50	52.661	43.642	33.923	23.450	12.163
.75	53.023	43.991	34.233	23.691	12.303
8.00	53.385	44.339	34.543	23.934	12.444
.25	53.746	44.688	34.854	24.177	12.585
.50	54.105	45.036	35.164	24.421	12.727
.75	54.465	45.384	35.476	24.665	12.870
9.00	54.823	45.732	35.787	24.911	13.013
.25	55.180	46.079	36.099	25.157	13.157
.50	55.537	46.426	36.412	25.403	13.302
.75	55.892	46.773	36.724	25.650	13.447
10.00	56.247	47.120	37.037	25.898	13.593
.25	56.600	47.466	37.350	26.147	13.740
.50	56.953	47.812	37.663	26.396	13.887
.75	57.304	48.157	37.976	26.646	14.035
11.00	57.655	48.502	38.290	26.896	14.183
.25	58.004	48.846	38.603	27.146	14.332
.50	58.352	49.190	38.917	27.398	14.482
.75	58.699	49.533	39.230	27.649	14.632
12.00	59.045	49.876	39.544	27.901	14.783
.25	59.389	50.218	39.857	28.154	14.934
.50	59.732	50.559	40.171	28.407	15.085
.75	60.074	50.900	40.484	28.660	15.238
13.00	60.415	51.239	40.797	28.914	15.390
.25	60.754	51.579	41.111	29.168	15.544
.50	61.092	51.917	41.423	29.422	15.697
.75	61.428	52.254	41.736	29.677	15.851
14.00	61.763	52.591	42.049	29.932	16.006
.25	62.097	52.927	42.361	30.187	16.161
.50	62.429	53.262	42.673	30.443	16.316
.75	62.760	53.596	42.985	30.699	16.472
15.00	63.089	53.929	43.296	30.954	16.629
.25	63.416	54.261	43.607	31.211	16.785
.50	63.742	54.592	43.918	31.467	16.943
.75	64.067	54.922	44.228	31.723	17.100
16.00	64.389	55.251	44.538	31.980	17.258
.25	64.711	55.579	44.847	32.236	17.416
.50	65.030	55.906	45.156	32.493	17.575
.75	65.348	56.231	45.465	32.750	17.734
17.00	65.664	56.556	45.773	33.007	17.893
.25	65.979	56.879	46.080	33.264	18.053
.50	66.291	57.202	46.387	33.520	18.212
.75	66.602	57.523	46.693	33.777	18.373
18.00	66.912	57.842	46.999	34.034	18.533
.25	67.219	58.161	47.304	34.291	18.694
.50	67.525	58.478	47.608	34.548	18.855
.75	67.829	58.794	47.912	34.804	19.016
19.00	68.131	59.109	48.215	35.061	19.178
.25	68.432	59.422	48.517	35.317	19.340
.50	68.730	59.734	48.819	35.573	19.502
.75	69.027	60.045	49.120	35.830	19.664
20.00%	69.322	60.354	49.420	36.086	19.826

Table 3   283

<u>10 Years</u>   Remaining Loan Balance

Interest Rate	1	2	3	4	5
5.00%	92.093	83.781	75.043	65.859	56.205
.25	92.189	83.958	75.284	66.143	56.511
.50	92.284	84.133	75.523	66.426	56.817
.75	92.379	84.308	75.760	66.708	57.122
6.00	92.473	84.481	75.997	66.989	57.426
.25	92.566	84.653	76.232	67.269	57.730
.50	92.658	84.824	76.466	67.548	58.033
.75	92.750	84.994	76.699	67.826	58.335
7.00	92.840	85.163	76.930	68.103	58.637
.25	92.930	85.330	77.160	68.378	58.938
.50	93.019	85.496	77.389	68.653	59.238
.75	93.107	85.661	77.617	68.926	59.538
8.00	93.195	85.825	77.843	69.199	59.837
.25	93.281	85.987	78.068	69.470	60.135
.50	93.367	86.148	78.291	69.740	60.432
.75	93.452	86.308	78.513	70.008	60.728
9.00	93.537	86.467	78.734	70.276	61.024
.25	93.620	86.624	78.953	70.542	61.319
.50	93.703	86.781	79.171	70.807	61.612
.75	93.785	86.936	79.388	71.071	61.905
10.00	93.866	87.089	79.603	71.333	62.197
.25	93.946	87.242	79.817	71.594	62.488
.50	94.026	87.393	80.029	71.854	62.778
.75	94.104	87.543	80.240	72.113	63.067
11.00	94.182	87.692	80.450	72.370	63.355
.25	94.260	87.839	80.658	72.626	63.642
.50	94.336	87.986	80.865	72.881	63.929
.75	94.412	88.131	81.070	73.134	64.213
12.00	94.487	88.274	81.274	73.386	64.497
.25	94.561	88.417	81.477	73.636	64.780
.50	94.634	88.558	81.677	73.886	65.062
.75	94.707	88.698	81.877	74.133	65.343
13.00	94.779	88.837	82.075	74.380	65.622
.25	94.850	88.975	82.272	74.625	65.901
.50	94.920	89.111	82.467	74.868	66.178
.75	94.990	89.246	82.661	75.110	66.454
14.00	95.059	89.380	82.853	75.351	66.729
.25	95.127	89.513	83.044	75.590	67.003
.50	95.195	89.644	83.233	75.828	67.275
.75	95.261	89.774	83.421	76.064	67.546
15.00	95.327	89.903	83.607	76.299	67.816
.25	95.392	90.031	83.792	76.533	68.085
.50	95.457	90.158	83.976	76.765	68.353
.75	95.521	90.283	84.158	76.995	68.619
16.00	95.584	90.407	84.338	77.224	68.884
.25	95.646	90.530	84.517	77.451	69.148
.50	95.708	90.652	84.695	77.677	69.410
.75	95.769	90.772	84.871	77.902	69.672
17.00	95.829	90.891	85.046	78.125	69.931
.25	95.889	91.010	85.219	78.346	70.190
.50	95.948	91.127	85.391	78.566	70.447
.75	96.006	91.242	85.561	78.785	70.703
18.00	96.063	91.357	85.730	79.002	70.957
.25	96.120	91.470	85.897	79.217	71.211
.50	96.177	91.583	86.063	79.431	71.462
.75	96.232	91.694	86.227	79.643	71.713
19.00	96.287	91.804	86.390	79.854	71.962
.25	96.341	91.912	86.552	80.063	72.209
.50	96.395	92.020	86.712	80.271	72.455
.75	96.448	92.127	86.871	80.477	72.700
20.00%	96.500	92.232	87.028	80.682	72.943

Remaining Loan Balance   **10 Years**

Interest Rate	Percent remaining in year			
	6	7	8	9
5.00%	46.057	35.390	24.176	12.390
.25	46.361	35.665	24.394	12.516
.50	46.665	35.941	24.612	12.643
.75	46.969	36.217	24.830	12.771
6.00	47.273	36.494	25.049	12.899
.25	47.577	36.771	25.269	13.028
.50	47.880	37.048	25.490	13.158
.75	48.184	37.325	25.711	13.288
7.00	48.487	37.603	25.933	13.419
.25	48.790	37.882	26.155	13.550
.50	49.093	38.160	26.378	13.682
.75	49.396	38.439	26.602	13.815
8.00	49.698	38.718	26.826	13.948
.25	50.000	38.997	27.051	14.081
.50	50.302	39.276	27.276	14.215
.75	50.603	39.556	27.502	14.350
9.00	50.904	39.835	27.728	14.485
.25	51.205	40.115	27.955	14.621
.50	51.505	40.395	28.182	14.757
.75	51.805	40.675	28.410	14.894
10.00	52.105	40.955	28.638	15.032
.25	52.404	41.235	28.867	15.169
.50	52.702	41.515	29.096	15.308
.75	53.000	41.795	29.325	15.446
11.00	53.297	42.076	29.555	15.586
.25	53.594	42.356	29.785	15.726
.50	53.891	42.636	30.016	15.866
.75	54.186	42.916	30.247	16.007
12.00	54.482	43.196	30.478	16.148
.25	54.776	43.475	30.710	16.289
.50	55.070	43.755	30.942	16.431
.75	55.363	44.034	31.174	16.574
13.00	55.656	44.314	31.406	16.717
.25	55.948	44.593	31.639	16.860
.50	56.239	44.872	31.872	17.004
.75	56.529	45.151	32.105	17.148
14.00	56.819	45.429	32.339	17.293
.25	57.108	45.708	32.572	17.438
.50	57.396	45.986	32.806	17.583
.75	57.683	46.263	33.040	17.729
15.00	57.970	46.541	33.274	17.875
.25	58.256	46.818	33.508	18.021
.50	58.541	47.095	33.743	18.168
.75	58.825	47.371	33.977	18.315
16.00	59.108	47.647	34.212	18.463
.25	59.390	47.923	34.447	18.610
.50	59.671	48.198	34.682	18.759
.75	59.952	48.473	34.917	18.907
17.00	60.231	48.747	35.152	19.056
.25	60.510	49.021	35.387	19.205
.50	60.787	49.295	35.622	19.354
.75	61.064	49.568	35.857	19.504
18.00	61.340	49.840	36.092	19.654
.25	61.614	50.113	36.327	19.804
.50	61.888	50.384	36.562	19.954
.75	62.160	50.655	36.797	20.105
19.00	62.432	50.925	37.032	20.256
.25	62.702	51.195	37.267	20.407
.50	62.972	51.465	37.502	20.559
.75	63.240	51.733	37.736	20.710
20.00%	63.508	52.001	37.971	20.862

Table 3   285

5 Years   Remaining Loan Balance

Interest Rate	Percent remaining in year			
	1	2	3	4
5.00%	81.944	62.965	43.015	22.044
.25	82.039	63.111	43.166	22.148
.50	82.133	63.257	43.318	22.253
.75	82.226	63.403	43.469	22.358
6.00	82.320	63.549	43.620	22.463
.25	82.413	63.694	43.772	22.568
.50	82.506	63.839	43.923	22.673
.75	82.598	63.984	44.075	22.779
7.00	82.690	64.129	44.226	22.884
.25	82.782	64.274	44.378	22.990
.50	82.874	64.418	44.529	23.097
.75	82.965	64.562	44.681	23.203
8.00	83.056	64.706	44.832	23.309
.25	83.147	64.849	44.984	23.416
.50	83.237	64.993	45.135	23.523
.75	83.327	65.136	45.287	23.630
9.00	83.417	65.278	45.438	23.737
.25	83.507	65.421	45.590	23.844
.50	83.596	65.563	45.741	23.952
.75	83.685	65.705	45.893	24.060
10.00	83.773	65.847	46.044	24.167
.25	83.861	65.989	46.196	24.276
.50	83.949	66.130	46.347	24.384
.75	84.037	66.271	46.498	24.492
11.00	84.125	66.412	46.650	24.601
.25	84.212	66.552	46.801	24.709
.50	84.298	66.693	46.952	24.818
.75	84.385	66.833	47.104	24.927
12.00	84.471	66.972	47.255	25.036
.25	84.557	67.112	47.406	25.146
.50	84.642	67.251	47.557	25.255
.75	84.728	67.390	47.708	25.365
13.00	84.813	67.529	47.859	25.474
.25	84.897	67.667	48.010	25.584
.50	84.981	67.805	48.161	25.694
.75	85.065	67.943	48.312	25.805
14.00	85.149	68.080	48.463	25.915
.25	85.232	68.218	48.613	26.025
.50	85.316	68.354	48.764	26.136
.75	85.398	68.491	48.914	26.247
15.00	85.481	68.627	49.065	26.358
.25	85.563	68.763	49.215	26.469
.50	85.645	68.899	49.366	26.580
.75	85.726	69.035	49.516	26.691
16.00	85.807	69.170	49.666	26.802
.25	85.888	69.305	49.816	26.914
.50	85.969	69.439	49.966	27.026
.75	86.049	69.573	50.116	27.137
17.00	86.129	69.707	50.266	27.249
.25	86.209	69.841	50.416	27.361
.50	86.288	69.974	50.565	27.473
.75	86.367	70.107	50.715	27.586
18.00	86.446	70.240	50.864	27.698
.25	86.524	70.372	51.013	27.810
.50	86.602	70.504	51.163	27.923
.75	86.680	70.636	51.312	28.036
19.00	86.757	70.768	51.461	28.148
.25	86.834	70.899	51.609	28.261
.50	86.911	71.029	51.758	28.374
.75	86.988	71.160	51.907	28.487
20.00%	87.064	71.290	52.055	28.600

Table 4
Daily Interest on $1000

Interest for a day, a week, a month, or fractions of a month is calculated on $1000 in Table 4. Two bases for interest are shown, a 360-day year, called ordinary interest, and a 365-day year, called exact interest. A 360-day year is used in mortgage loans, The 365-day year is used for prorations at closing and for other loans, unless specified differently.

Example 11. Interest on Loan for Given Period

Coronado Manor will be sold subject to a loan of $299,600 at 10 percent. At the closing, the buyer will receive credit for 10 days of interest.

Enter Table 4 on the page for 360-day years. On the line for 10 percent, read the factor under 10 days, $2.77778 per $1000 of loan. Multiply this by the number of thousands in the loan to get

$$\$2.77778 \times 299.6 = \$832.22$$

the proration credit for 10 days' interest.

Example 12. Short-term Rental of a House

The seller agrees the Fords may move into their new, $150,000 home 5 days before closing, if they will pay rent at 9 percent, the fair market rate.

Enter Table 4 at the page for 365-day years. On the 9 percent line under 5 days, find $1.23288 per $1000. Multiply it by the thousands of value to get

$$\$1.23288 \times 150 = \$184.93$$

the fair rental by reference to interest rates.

360 Day Daily Interest on $1000

Interest Rate	Number of days in a 360-day year					
	1	5	7	10	15	30
5.00%	0.13889	0.69444	0.97222	1.38889	2.08333	4.16667
.25	0.14583	0.72917	1.02083	1.45833	2.18750	4.37500
.50	0.15278	0.76389	1.06944	1.52778	2.29167	4.58333
.75	0.15972	0.79861	1.11806	1.59722	2.39583	4.79167
6.00	0.16667	0.83333	1.16667	1.66667	2.50000	5.00000
.25	0.17361	0.86806	1.21528	1.73611	2.60417	5.20833
.50	0.18056	0.90278	1.26389	1.80556	2.70833	5.41667
.75	0.18750	0.93750	1.31250	1.87500	2.81250	5.62500
7.00	0.19444	0.97222	1.36111	1.94444	2.91667	5.83333
.25	0.20139	1.00694	1.40972	2.01389	3.02083	6.04167
.50	0.20833	1.04167	1.45833	2.08333	3.12500	6.25000
.75	0.21528	1.07639	1.50694	2.15278	3.22917	6.45833
8.00	0.22222	1.11111	1.55556	2.22222	3.33333	6.66667
.25	0.22917	1.14583	1.60417	2.29167	3.43750	6.87500
.50	0.23611	1.18056	1.65278	2.36111	3.54167	7.08333
.75	0.24306	1.21528	1.70139	2.43056	3.64583	7.29167
9.00	0.25000	1.25000	1.75000	2.50000	3.75000	7.50000
.25	0.25694	1.28472	1.79861	2.56944	3.85417	7.70833
.50	0.26389	1.31944	1.84722	2.63889	3.95833	7.91667
.75	0.27083	1.35417	1.89583	2.70833	4.06250	8.12500
10.00	0.27778	1.38889	1.94444	2.77778	4.16667	8.33333
.25	0.28472	1.42361	1.99306	2.84722	4.27083	8.54167
.50	0.29167	1.45833	2.04167	2.91667	4.37500	8.75000
.75	0.29861	1.49306	2.09028	2.98611	4.47917	8.95833
11.00	0.30556	1.52778	2.13889	3.05556	4.58333	9.16667
.25	0.31250	1.56250	2.18750	3.12500	4.68750	9.37500
.50	0.31944	1.59722	2.23611	3.19444	4.79167	9.58333
.75	0.32639	1.63194	2.28472	3.26389	4.89583	9.79167
12.00	0.33333	1.66667	2.33333	3.33333	5.00000	10.00000
.25	0.34028	1.70139	2.38194	3.40278	5.10417	10.20833
.50	0.34722	1.73611	2.43056	3.47222	5.20833	10.41667
.75	0.35417	1.77083	2.47917	3.54167	5.31250	10.62500
13.00	0.36111	1.80556	2.52778	3.61111	5.41667	10.83333
.25	0.36806	1.84028	2.57639	3.68056	5.52083	11.04167
.50	0.37500	1.87500	2.62500	3.75000	5.62500	11.25000
.75	0.38194	1.90972	2.67361	3.81944	5.72917	11.45833
14.00	0.38889	1.94444	2.72222	3.88889	5.83333	11.66667
.25	0.39583	1.97917	2.77083	3.95833	5.93750	11.87500
.50	0.40278	2.01389	2.81944	4.02778	6.04167	12.08333
.75	0.40972	2.04861	2.86806	4.09722	6.14583	12.29167
15.00	0.41667	2.08333	2.91667	4.16667	6.25000	12.50000
.25	0.42361	2.11806	2.96528	4.23611	6.35417	12.70833
.50	0.43056	2.15278	3.01389	4.30556	6.45833	12.91667
.75	0.43750	2.18750	3.06250	4.37500	6.56250	13.12500
16.00	0.44444	2.22222	3.11111	4.44444	6.66667	13.33333
.25	0.45139	2.25694	3.15972	4.51389	6.77083	13.54167
.50	0.45833	2.29167	3.20833	4.58333	6.87500	13.75000
.75	0.46528	2.32639	3.25694	4.65278	6.97917	13.95833
17.00	0.47222	2.36111	3.30556	4.72222	7.08333	14.16667
.25	0.47917	2.39583	3.35417	4.79167	7.18750	14.37500
.50	0.48611	2.43056	3.40278	4.86111	7.29167	14.58333
.75	0.49306	2.46528	3.45139	4.93056	7.39583	14.79167
18.00	0.50000	2.50000	3.50000	5.00000	7.50000	15.00000
.25	0.50694	2.53472	3.54861	5.06944	7.60417	15.20833
.50	0.51389	2.56944	3.59722	5.13889	7.70833	15.41667
.75	0.52083	2.60417	3.64583	5.20833	7.81250	15.62500
19.00	0.52778	2.63889	3.69444	5.27778	7.91667	15.83333
.25	0.53472	2.67361	3.74306	5.34722	8.02083	16.04167
.50	0.54167	2.70833	3.79167	5.41667	8.12500	16.25000
.75	0.54861	2.74306	3.84028	5.48611	8.22917	16.45833
20.00%	0.55556	2.77778	3.88889	5.55556	8.33333	16.66667

Daily Interest on $1000   <u>365 Day</u>

Interest Rate						

Number of days in a 360-day year

Interest Rate	1	5	7	10	15	30
5.00%	0.13699	0.68493	0.95890	1.36986	2.05479	4.10959
.25	0.14384	0.71918	1.00685	1.43836	2.15753	4.31507
.50	0.15068	0.75342	1.05479	1.50685	2.26027	4.52055
.75	0.15753	0.78767	1.10274	1.57534	2.36301	4.72603
6.00	0.16438	0.82192	1.15069	1.64384	2.46575	4.93151
.25	0.17123	0.85616	1.19863	1.71233	2.56849	5.13699
.50	0.17808	0.89041	1.24658	1.78082	2.67123	5.34247
.75	0.18493	0.92466	1.29452	1.84932	2.77397	5.54795
7.00	0.19178	0.95890	1.34247	1.91781	2.87671	5.75342
.25	0.19863	0.99315	1.39041	1.98630	2.97945	5.95890
.50	0.20548	1.02740	1.43836	2.05479	3.08219	6.16438
.75	0.21233	1.06164	1.48630	2.12329	3.18493	6.36986
8.00	0.21918	1.09589	1.53425	2.19178	3.28767	6.57534
.25	0.22603	1.13014	1.58219	2.26027	3.39041	6.78082
.50	0.23288	1.16438	1.63014	2.32877	3.49315	6.98630
.75	0.23973	1.19863	1.67808	2.39726	3.59589	7.19178
9.00	0.24658	1.23288	1.72603	2.46575	3.69863	7.39726
.25	0.25342	1.26712	1.77397	2.53425	3.80137	7.60274
.50	0.26027	1.30137	1.82192	2.60274	3.90411	7.80822
.75	0.26712	1.33562	1.86986	2.67123	4.00685	8.01370
10.00	0.27397	1.36986	1.91781	2.73973	4.10959	8.21918
.25	0.28082	1.40411	1.96575	2.80822	4.21233	8.42466
.50	0.28767	1.43836	2.01370	2.87671	4.31507	8.63014
.75	0.29452	1.47260	2.06164	2.94521	4.41781	8.83562
11.00	0.30137	1.50685	2.10959	3.01370	4.52055	9.04110
.25	0.30822	1.54110	2.15753	3.08219	4.62329	9.24658
.50	0.31507	1.57534	2.20548	3.15068	4.72603	9.45206
.75	0.32192	1.60959	2.25342	3.21918	4.82877	9.65753
12.00	0.32877	1.64384	2.30137	3.28767	4.93151	9.86301
.25	0.33562	1.67808	2.34932	3.35616	5.03425	10.06849
.50	0.34247	1.71233	2.39726	3.42466	5.13699	10.27397
.75	0.34932	1.74658	2.44521	3.49315	5.23973	10.47945
13.00	0.35616	1.78082	2.49315	3.56164	5.34247	10.68493
.25	0.36301	1.81507	2.54110	3.63014	5.44521	10.89041
.50	0.36986	1.84932	2.58904	3.69863	5.54795	11.09589
.75	0.37671	1.88356	2.63699	3.76712	5.65069	11.30137
14.00	0.38356	1.91781	2.68493	3.83562	5.75342	11.50685
.25	0.39041	1.95205	2.73288	3.90411	5.85616	11.71233
.50	0.39726	1.98630	2.78082	3.97260	5.95890	11.91781
.75	0.40411	2.02055	2.82877	4.04110	6.06164	12.12329
15.00	0.41096	2.05479	2.87671	4.10959	6.16438	12.32877
.25	0.41781	2.08904	2.92466	4.17808	6.26712	12.53425
.50	0.42466	2.12329	2.97260	4.24658	6.36986	12.73973
.75	0.43151	2.15753	3.02055	4.31507	6.47260	12.94521
16.00	0.43836	2.19178	3.06849	4.38356	6.57534	13.15069
.25	0.44521	2.22603	3.11644	4.45206	6.67808	13.35616
.50	0.45205	2.26027	3.16438	4.52055	6.78082	13.56164
.75	0.45890	2.29452	3.21233	4.58904	6.88356	13.76712
17.00	0.46575	2.32877	3.26027	4.65753	6.98630	13.97260
.25	0.47260	2.36301	3.30822	4.72603	7.08904	14.17808
.50	0.47945	2.39726	3.35616	4.79452	7.19178	14.38356
.75	0.48630	2.43151	3.40411	4.86301	7.29452	14.58904
18.00	0.49315	2.46575	3.45205	4.93151	7.39726	14.79452
.25	0.50000	2.50000	3.50000	5.00000	7.50000	15.00000
.50	0.50685	2.53425	3.54795	5.06849	7.60274	15.20548
.75	0.51370	2.56849	3.59589	5.13699	7.70548	15.41096
19.00	0.52055	2.60274	3.64384	5.20548	7.80822	15.61644
.25	0.52740	2.63699	3.69178	5.27397	7.91096	15.82192
.50	0.53425	2.67123	3.73973	5.34247	8.01370	16.02740
.75	0.54110	2.70548	3.78767	5.41096	8.11644	16.23288
20.00%	0.54795	2.73973	3.83562	5.47945	8.21918	16.43836

Table 4   289

Table 5
Benefits of Regular Prepayment

Prepaying a mortgage loan regularly cuts interest expense and builds equity that can cushion future emergencies. Even $50 per month added to $1,000 of loan payment can cut five years or more from the loan term. Table 5 gives the particulars of the shortened loan life and the interest savings that steady prepayments bring.

The secret to substantial savings that come from small prepayments lies in interest compounding. Principal payments reduce future interest expense at the compounded mortgage rate.

Example 13.   Benefits of Regular Prepayment

Paul Tinnuba has taken out a 30-year loan at 9.50 percent interest. He can put an additional $100 per month, or 6 percent of the total, toward the mortgage.

To find the benefits of such a program, enter Table 5 at 9.50 percent interest; in the section for added pay of 6 percent, read across on the line for an original term of 30 years. Under 9.50 percent, the new term is shown to be 23Y 2m, or 23 years and 2 months. Adding 6 percent to the monthly payment cuts the loan payoff from 30 years to just over 23 years, 2 months.

Next to new term, read under interest savings, 55.0 percent. The prepayments will save interest equal to 55 percent of the loan, compared to what the interest would be without prepayments.

Benefits of Regular Prepayment

Reduced Term and Interest Savings

Added Pay	Orig'l Term	5.00% Interest		5.50% Interest		6.00% Interest	
		New Term	Interest Savings	New Term	Interest Savings	New Term	Interest Savings
	15	14Y 6m	1.7%	14Y 5m	1.9%	14Y 5m	2.2%
2.5%	20	19Y 2m	2.7%	19Y 2m	3.2%	19Y 1m	3.8%
	25	23Y 10m	4.1%	23Y 9m	4.9%	23Y 8m	5.9%
	30	28Y 4m	5.9%	28Y 3m	7.3%	28Y 1m	8.8%
	15	14Y 2m	2.6%	14Y 2m	3.0%	14Y 1m	3.5%
4%	20	18Y 9m	4.2%	18Y 8m	5.0%	18Y 7m	5.8%
	25	23Y 2m	6.3%	23Y 1m	7.6%	22Y 11m	9.1%
	30	27Y 6m	9.1%	27Y 3m	11.1%	27Y 1m	13.4%
	15	13Y 12m	3.2%	13Y 11m	3.7%	13Y 11m	4.3%
5%	20	18Y 5m	5.1%	18Y 4m	6.1%	18Y 3m	7.1%
	25	22Y 9m	7.7%	22Y 7m	9.3%	22Y 5m	11.1%
	30	26Y 11m	11.1%	26Y 8m	13.5%	26Y 5m	16.3%
	15	13Y 9m	3.8%	13Y 9m	4.4%	13Y 8m	5.1%
6%	20	18Y 2m	6.1%	18Y 1m	7.2%	17Y 11m	8.4%
	25	22Y 4m	9.1%	22Y 2m	10.9%	22Y 0m	12.9%
	30	26Y 5m	12.9%	26Y 1m	15.7%	25Y 10m	18.9%
	15	13Y 6m	4.6%	13Y 5m	5.4%	13Y 5m	6.2%
7.5%	20	17Y 9m	7.4%	17Y 7m	8.7%	17Y 6m	10.2%
	25	21Y 10m	11.0%	21Y 7m	13.1%	21Y 5m	15.6%
	30	25Y 8m	15.6%	25Y 4m	18.9%	24Y 12m	22.6%
	15	13Y 1m	5.9%	12Y 12m	6.9%	12Y 11m	7.9%
10%	20	17Y 1m	9.4%	16Y 12m	11.1%	16Y 10m	12.9%
	25	20Y 11m	13.9%	20Y 8m	16.6%	20Y 5m	19.6%
	30	24Y 6m	19.6%	24Y 1m	23.6%	23Y 9m	28.1%
	15	12Y 8m	7.2%	12Y 7m	8.3%	12Y 6m	9.5%
12.5%	20	16Y 6m	11.3%	16Y 4m	13.3%	16Y 2m	15.4%
	25	20Y 1m	16.6%	19Y 10m	19.7%	19Y 7m	23.2%
	30	23Y 6m	23.2%	23Y 0m	27.8%	22Y 7m	33.0%
	15	12Y 3m	8.3%	12Y 2m	9.6%	12Y 1m	11.0%
15%	20	15Y 12m	13.0%	15Y 9m	15.3%	15Y 7m	17.7%
	25	19Y 5m	19.0%	19Y 1m	22.5%	18Y 9m	26.4%
	30	22Y 6m	26.4%	22Y 1m	31.6%	21Y 7m	37.3%
	15	11Y 7m	10.4%	11Y 6m	12.0%	11Y 4m	13.7%
20%	20	14Y 12m	16.1%	14Y 9m	18.8%	14Y 7m	21.8%
	25	18Y 1m	23.3%	17Y 9m	27.5%	17Y 5m	32.0%
	30	20Y 10m	32.0%	20Y 4m	38.0%	19Y 10m	44.6%
	15	10Y 12m	12.2%	10Y 10m	14.1%	10Y 9m	16.0%
25%	20	14Y 1m	18.8%	13Y 11m	21.9%	13Y 8m	25.2%
	25	16Y 11m	27.0%	16Y 7m	31.6%	16Y 2m	36.7%
	30	19Y 5m	36.7%	18Y 11m	43.3%	18Y 5m	50.5%
	15	10Y 1m	14.8%	9Y 11m	17.0%	9Y 10m	19.3%
33.3%	20	12Y 10m	22.6%	12Y 7m	26.2%	12Y 5m	30.0%
	25	15Y 4m	32.0%	14Y 11m	37.3%	14Y 7m	43.0%
	30	17Y 6m	43.0%	16Y 11m	50.5%	16Y 5m	58.4%

Benefits of Regular Prepayment

Reduced Term and Interest Savings

Added Pay	Orig'l Term	6.50% Interest		7.00% Interest		7.50% Interest	
		New Term	Interest Savings	New Term	Interest Savings	New Term	Interest Savings
	15	14Y 5m	2.6%	14Y 4m	2.9%	14Y 4m	3.3%
2.5%	20	19Y 0m	4.4%	18Y 12m	5.1%	18Y 11m	5.9%
	25	23Y 7m	7.0%	23Y 5m	8.3%	23Y 4m	9.7%
	30	27Y 11m	10.7%	27Y 8m	12.8%	27Y 6m	15.2%
	15	14Y 1m	4.0%	14Y 0m	4.6%	13Y 12m	5.2%
4%	20	18Y 6m	6.8%	18Y 5m	7.9%	18Y 4m	9.1%
	25	22Y 9m	10.7%	22Y 7m	12.6%	22Y 5m	14.7%
	30	26Y 10m	16.1%	26Y 6m	19.2%	26Y 3m	22.7%
	15	13Y 10m	4.9%	13Y 9m	5.6%	13Y 9m	6.3%
5%	20	18Y 2m	8.3%	18Y 1m	9.6%	17Y 12m	11.0%
	25	22Y 3m	13.0%	22Y 1m	15.3%	21Y 11m	17.8%
	30	26Y 2m	19.5%	25Y 10m	23.1%	25Y 6m	27.1%
	15	13Y 8m	5.8%	13Y 7m	6.6%	13Y 6m	7.5%
6%	20	17Y 10m	9.8%	17Y 9m	11.3%	17Y 7m	12.9%
	25	21Y 10m	15.2%	21Y 7m	17.8%	21Y 5m	20.7%
	30	25Y 6m	22.6%	25Y 2m	26.7%	24Y 9m	31.3%
	15	13Y 4m	7.1%	13Y 3m	8.0%	13Y 2m	9.1%
7.5%	20	17Y 5m	11.8%	17Y 3m	13.6%	17Y 1m	15.6%
	25	21Y 2m	18.3%	20Y 11m	21.3%	20Y 8m	24.7%
	30	24Y 7m	26.9%	24Y 3m	31.6%	23Y 10m	36.9%
	15	12Y 10m	9.0%	12Y 9m	10.2%	12Y 8m	11.5%
10%	20	16Y 8m	14.9%	16Y 6m	17.2%	16Y 4m	19.6%
	25	20Y 2m	22.9%	19Y 11m	26.6%	19Y 7m	30.6%
	30	23Y 4m	33.2%	22Y 10m	38.8%	22Y 5m	45.0%
	15	12Y 5m	10.8%	12Y 4m	12.3%	12Y 3m	13.8%
12.5%	20	16Y 0m	17.8%	15Y 10m	20.4%	15Y 8m	23.2%
	25	19Y 3m	27.0%	18Y 11m	31.2%	18Y 8m	35.8%
	30	22Y 2m	38.7%	21Y 8m	45.0%	21Y 2m	51.9%
	15	12Y 0m	12.5%	11Y 11m	14.1%	11Y 10m	15.9%
15%	20	15Y 5m	20.4%	15Y 3m	23.3%	15Y 0m	26.4%
	25	18Y 5m	30.7%	18Y 1m	35.3%	17Y 9m	40.3%
	30	21Y 1m	43.6%	20Y 7m	50.4%	20Y 1m	57.9%
	15	11Y 3m	15.5%	11Y 2m	17.5%	11Y 0m	19.5%
20%	20	14Y 4m	24.9%	14Y 2m	28.3%	13Y 11m	32.0%
	25	17Y 0m	36.9%	16Y 8m	42.3%	16Y 4m	48.0%
	30	19Y 4m	51.7%	18Y 10m	59.5%	18Y 3m	67.8%
	15	10Y 7m	18.1%	10Y 6m	20.3%	10Y 4m	22.7%
25%	20	13Y 5m	28.8%	13Y 2m	32.6%	12Y 12m	36.7%
	25	15Y 10m	42.2%	15Y 6m	48.0%	15Y 1m	54.3%
	30	17Y 10m	58.3%	17Y 4m	66.7%	16Y 10m	75.6%
	15	9Y 8m	21.8%	9Y 7m	24.4%	9Y 5m	27.1%
33.3%	20	12Y 2m	34.1%	11Y 11m	38.4%	11Y 8m	43.0%
	25	14Y 2m	49.2%	13Y 10m	55.7%	13Y 5m	62.6%
	30	15Y 11m	67.0%	15Y 4m	76.1%	14Y 10m	85.6%

Table 5   293

Benefits of Regular Prepayment

Reduced Term and Interest Savings

Added Pay	Orig'l Term	8.00% Interest		8.50% Interest		9.00% Interest	
		New Term	Interest Savings	New Term	Interest Savings	New Term	Interest Savings
2.5%	15	14Y 4m	3.8%	14Y 3m	4.2%	14Y 3m	4.7%
	20	18Y 10m	6.8%	18Y 9m	7.8%	18Y 9m	8.8%
	25	23Y 2m	11.3%	23Y 1m	13.1%	22Y 11m	15.2%
	30	27Y 3m	18.0%	27Y 0m	21.1%	26Y 9m	24.6%
4%	15	13Y 11m	5.8%	13Y 11m	6.5%	13Y 10m	7.3%
	20	18Y 3m	10.4%	18Y 2m	11.8%	18Y 0m	13.4%
	25	22Y 3m	17.1%	22Y 1m	19.7%	21Y 10m	22.7%
	30	25Y 11m	26.6%	25Y 7m	31.0%	25Y 3m	35.9%
5%	15	13Y 8m	7.1%	13Y 8m	8.0%	13Y 7m	8.9%
	20	17Y 10m	12.6%	17Y 9m	14.4%	17Y 7m	16.3%
	25	21Y 8m	20.6%	21Y 6m	23.7%	21Y 3m	27.1%
	30	25Y 2m	31.7%	24Y 9m	36.8%	24Y 5m	42.4%
6%	15	13Y 6m	8.4%	13Y 5m	9.4%	13Y 4m	10.5%
	20	17Y 6m	14.7%	17Y 4m	16.7%	17Y 3m	18.9%
	25	21Y 2m	23.9%	20Y 11m	27.4%	20Y 8m	31.2%
	30	24Y 5m	36.4%	24Y 0m	42.0%	23Y 7m	48.3%
7.5%	15	13Y 2m	10.2%	13Y 1m	11.4%	12Y 12m	12.7%
	20	16Y 12m	17.7%	16Y 10m	20.1%	16Y 8m	22.6%
	25	20Y 5m	28.4%	20Y 2m	32.4%	19Y 10m	36.9%
	30	23Y 5m	42.7%	22Y 11m	49.1%	22Y 6m	56.1%
10%	15	12Y 7m	12.9%	12Y 6m	14.4%	12Y 5m	16.0%
	20	16Y 2m	22.2%	15Y 12m	25.0%	15Y 10m	28.1%
	25	19Y 4m	35.0%	18Y 12m	39.8%	18Y 8m	45.0%
	30	21Y 11m	51.8%	21Y 5m	59.1%	20Y 12m	67.0%
12.5%	15	12Y 2m	15.4%	12Y 1m	17.2%	11Y 11m	19.0%
	20	15Y 6m	26.2%	15Y 3m	29.4%	15Y 1m	32.9%
	25	18Y 4m	40.7%	17Y 12m	46.1%	17Y 8m	51.9%
	30	20Y 8m	59.4%	20Y 2m	67.4%	19Y 8m	76.0%
15%	15	11Y 8m	17.7%	11Y 7m	19.7%	11Y 6m	21.8%
	20	14Y 10m	29.8%	14Y 7m	33.4%	14Y 5m	37.2%
	25	17Y 5m	45.8%	17Y 1m	51.6%	16Y 9m	57.9%
	30	19Y 7m	65.9%	19Y 1m	74.5%	18Y 7m	83.7%
20%	15	10Y 11m	21.7%	10Y 10m	24.1%	10Y 8m	26.6%
	20	13Y 8m	35.9%	13Y 6m	40.1%	13Y 3m	44.5%
	25	15Y 11m	54.2%	15Y 7m	60.8%	15Y 3m	67.7%
	30	17Y 9m	76.6%	17Y 3m	86.0%	16Y 9m	95.9%
25%	15	10Y 3m	25.2%	10Y 1m	27.8%	9Y 12m	30.6%
	20	12Y 9m	41.0%	12Y 6m	45.6%	12Y 3m	50.5%
	25	14Y 9m	61.0%	14Y 4m	68.1%	13Y 12m	75.5%
	30	16Y 3m	85.0%	15Y 9m	95.0%	15Y 3m	105.4%
33.3%	15	9Y 3m	30.0%	9Y 2m	33.0%	9Y 0m	36.2%
	20	11Y 5m	47.9%	11Y 2m	53.0%	10Y 11m	58.4%
	25	13Y 1m	69.9%	12Y 9m	77.6%	12Y 4m	85.6%
	30	14Y 4m	95.7%	13Y 10m	106.3%	13Y 5m	117.2%

Benefits of Regular Prepayment

Reduced Term and Interest Savings

Added Pay	Orig'l Term	9.50% Interest		10.00% Interest		10.50% Interest	
		New Term	Interest Savings	New Term	Interest Savings	New Term	Interest Savings
2.5%	15	14Y 3m	5.3%	14Y 2m	5.9%	14Y 2m	6.5%
	20	18Y 8m	10.0%	18Y 7m	11.3%	18Y 6m	12.8%
	25	22Y 9m	17.5%	22Y 7m	20.0%	22Y 5m	22.8%
	30	26Y 6m	28.6%	26Y 2m	33.1%	25Y 11m	38.0%
4%	15	13Y 10m	8.2%	13Y 9m	9.1%	13Y 8m	10.0%
	20	17Y 11m	15.2%	17Y 10m	17.1%	17Y 8m	19.2%
	25	21Y 8m	25.9%	21Y 5m	29.4%	21Y 2m	33.3%
	30	24Y 11m	41.3%	24Y 6m	47.3%	24Y 2m	53.8%
5%	15	13Y 6m	9.9%	13Y 6m	11.0%	13Y 5m	12.2%
	20	17Y 6m	18.3%	17Y 4m	20.6%	17Y 3m	23.0%
	25	21Y 0m	30.9%	20Y 9m	35.0%	20Y 6m	39.5%
	30	23Y 12m	48.6%	23Y 7m	55.3%	23Y 2m	62.6%
6%	15	13Y 3m	11.6%	13Y 2m	12.9%	13Y 2m	14.3%
	20	17Y 1m	21.3%	16Y 11m	23.8%	16Y 9m	26.6%
	25	20Y 5m	35.5%	20Y 1m	40.1%	19Y 10m	45.0%
	30	23Y 2m	55.0%	22Y 9m	62.4%	22Y 3m	70.3%
7.5%	15	12Y 11m	14.1%	12Y 10m	15.5%	12Y 9m	17.1%
	20	16Y 6m	25.4%	16Y 4m	28.3%	16Y 2m	31.6%
	25	19Y 7m	41.7%	19Y 3m	46.9%	18Y 11m	52.5%
	30	22Y 1m	63.6%	21Y 7m	71.7%	21Y 1m	80.3%
10%	15	12Y 4m	17.7%	12Y 3m	19.6%	12Y 2m	21.5%
	20	15Y 8m	31.4%	15Y 5m	35.0%	15Y 3m	38.8%
	25	18Y 4m	50.6%	18Y 0m	56.5%	17Y 8m	62.9%
	30	20Y 6m	75.5%	19Y 12m	84.5%	19Y 6m	94.0%
12.5%	15	11Y 10m	21.0%	11Y 9m	23.1%	11Y 8m	25.4%
	20	14Y 10m	36.7%	14Y 8m	40.7%	14Y 5m	45.0%
	25	17Y 4m	58.1%	16Y 11m	64.6%	16Y 7m	71.6%
	30	19Y 2m	85.2%	18Y 8m	94.8%	18Y 2m	105.0%
15%	15	11Y 5m	24.0%	11Y 3m	26.4%	11Y 2m	28.9%
	20	14Y 2m	41.4%	13Y 11m	45.7%	13Y 9m	50.4%
	25	16Y 5m	64.5%	16Y 0m	71.5%	15Y 8m	79.0%
	30	18Y 1m	93.3%	17Y 7m	103.5%	17Y 1m	114.1%
20%	15	10Y 7m	29.2%	10Y 5m	32.0%	10Y 4m	34.9%
	20	13Y 0m	49.2%	12Y 9m	54.2%	12Y 6m	59.4%
	25	14Y 10m	75.1%	14Y 6m	82.8%	14Y 2m	90.8%
	30	16Y 3m	106.3%	15Y 9m	117.1%	15Y 3m	128.3%
25%	15	9Y 10m	33.6%	9Y 9m	36.7%	9Y 7m	39.9%
	20	12Y 0m	55.6%	11Y 9m	61.0%	11Y 7m	66.6%
	25	13Y 8m	83.4%	13Y 3m	91.5%	12Y 11m	100.0%
	30	14Y 9m	116.2%	14Y 4m	127.5%	13Y 10m	139.1%
33.3%	15	8Y 11m	39.5%	8Y 9m	43.0%	8Y 7m	46.6%
	20	10Y 9m	64.0%	10Y 6m	69.9%	10Y 3m	76.0%
	25	12Y 0m	94.0%	11Y 8m	102.7%	11Y 4m	111.6%
	30	12Y 11m	128.6%	12Y 6m	140.3%	12Y 1m	152.4%

Table 5   295

Benefits of Regular Prepayment

Reduced Term and Interest Savings

Added Pay	Orig'l Term	11.00% Interest		11.50% Interest		12.00% Interest	
		New Term	Interest Savings	New Term	Interest Savings	New Term	Interest Savings
	15	14Y 1m	7.2%	14Y 1m	8.0%	14Y 0m	8.8%
2.5%	20	18Y 5m	14.3%	18Y 3m	16.0%	18Y 2m	17.9%
	25	22Y 3m	25.9%	22Y 1m	29.3%	21Y 10m	33.0%
	30	25Y 7m	43.5%	25Y 2m	49.5%	24Y 10m	56.1%
	15	13Y 8m	11.1%	13Y 7m	12.2%	13Y 6m	13.4%
4%	20	17Y 7m	21.4%	17Y 5m	23.9%	17Y 4m	26.5%
	25	20Y 12m	37.6%	20Y 9m	42.2%	20Y 5m	47.2%
	30	23Y 9m	60.9%	23Y 4m	68.6%	22Y 10m	76.8%
	15	13Y 4m	13.4%	13Y 3m	14.8%	13Y 3m	16.2%
5%	20	17Y 1m	25.7%	16Y 11m	28.6%	16Y 9m	31.6%
	25	20Y 3m	44.3%	19Y 11m	49.6%	19Y 8m	55.2%
	30	22Y 8m	70.5%	22Y 3m	78.9%	21Y 10m	87.8%
	15	13Y 1m	15.7%	12Y 12m	17.2%	12Y 11m	18.9%
6%	20	16Y 7m	29.6%	16Y 5m	32.8%	16Y 3m	36.3%
	25	19Y 7m	50.4%	19Y 3m	56.2%	18Y 11m	62.3%
	30	21Y 10m	78.8%	21Y 4m	87.8%	20Y 10m	97.4%
	15	12Y 8m	18.8%	12Y 7m	20.6%	12Y 6m	22.6%
7.5%	20	15Y 12m	35.0%	15Y 10m	38.7%	15Y 7m	42.6%
	25	18Y 8m	58.4%	18Y 4m	64.8%	17Y 12m	71.6%
	30	20Y 7m	89.5%	20Y 2m	99.3%	19Y 8m	109.5%
	15	12Y 1m	23.6%	11Y 12m	25.8%	11Y 10m	28.1%
10%	20	15Y 0m	42.8%	14Y 10m	47.1%	14Y 8m	51.7%
	25	17Y 4m	69.7%	16Y 12m	76.9%	16Y 8m	84.4%
	30	18Y 12m	104.1%	18Y 6m	114.6%	18Y 0m	125.5%
	15	11Y 6m	27.8%	11Y 5m	30.3%	11Y 4m	32.9%
12.5%	20	14Y 3m	49.5%	14Y 0m	54.3%	13Y 9m	59.3%
	25	16Y 3m	79.0%	15Y 11m	86.7%	15Y 7m	94.8%
	30	17Y 8m	115.6%	17Y 2m	126.7%	16Y 9m	138.1%
	15	11Y 0m	31.5%	10Y 11m	34.3%	10Y 10m	37.2%
15%	20	13Y 6m	55.3%	13Y 3m	60.4%	13Y 1m	65.8%
	25	15Y 4m	86.7%	14Y 12m	94.9%	14Y 8m	103.4%
	30	16Y 7m	125.1%	16Y 1m	136.6%	15Y 8m	148.4%
	15	10Y 2m	37.9%	10Y 1m	41.1%	9Y 11m	44.5%
20%	20	12Y 4m	64.8%	12Y 1m	70.5%	11Y 10m	76.5%
	25	13Y 10m	99.2%	13Y 5m	108.0%	13Y 1m	117.0%
	30	14Y 10m	139.9%	14Y 4m	151.9%	13Y 11m	164.2%
	15	9Y 6m	43.3%	9Y 4m	46.8%	9Y 2m	50.4%
25%	20	11Y 4m	72.5%	11Y 1m	78.6%	10Y 10m	84.9%
	25	12Y 7m	108.9%	12Y 3m	118.0%	11Y 11m	127.4%
	30	13Y 5m	151.1%	13Y 0m	163.4%	12Y 7m	176.0%
	15	8Y 6m	50.4%	8Y 4m	54.3%	8Y 3m	58.3%
33.3%	20	10Y 0m	82.3%	9Y 10m	88.9%	9Y 7m	95.6%
	25	11Y 0m	120.9%	10Y 9m	130.5%	10Y 5m	140.2%
	30	11Y 8m	164.7%	11Y 4m	177.4%	10Y 11m	190.3%

Benefits of Regular Prepayment

Reduced Term and Interest Savings

Added Pay	Orig'l Term	12.50% Interest		13.00% Interest		13.50% Interest	
		New Term	Interest Savings	New Term	Interest Savings	New Term	Interest Savings
2.5%	15	13Y 12m	9.7%	13Y 11m	10.6%	13Y 11m	11.6%
	20	18Y 1m	19.9%	17Y 12m	22.2%	17Y 10m	24.6%
	25	21Y 7m	37.1%	21Y 5m	41.5%	21Y 2m	46.4%
	30	24Y 5m	63.2%	24Y 1m	70.9%	23Y 8m	79.1%
4%	15	13Y 6m	14.7%	13Y 5m	16.1%	13Y 4m	17.6%
	20	17Y 2m	29.4%	17Y 0m	32.5%	16Y 10m	35.8%
	25	20Y 2m	52.6%	19Y 11m	58.4%	19Y 7m	64.6%
	30	22Y 5m	85.5%	21Y 12m	94.8%	21Y 6m	104.7%
5%	15	13Y 2m	17.8%	13Y 1m	19.4%	12Y 12m	21.1%
	20	16Y 7m	34.9%	16Y 5m	38.5%	16Y 3m	42.3%
	25	19Y 4m	61.3%	19Y 1m	67.7%	18Y 9m	74.5%
	30	21Y 4m	97.3%	20Y 10m	107.3%	20Y 5m	117.8%
6%	15	12Y 10m	20.6%	12Y 9m	22.5%	12Y 8m	24.5%
	20	16Y 1m	40.0%	15Y 11m	43.9%	15Y 9m	48.1%
	25	18Y 7m	68.9%	18Y 4m	75.8%	17Y 12m	83.1%
	30	20Y 5m	107.4%	19Y 11m	117.9%	19Y 5m	128.9%
7.5%	15	12Y 5m	24.6%	12Y 4m	26.8%	12Y 3m	29.1%
	20	15Y 5m	46.8%	15Y 3m	51.2%	15Y 0m	55.9%
	25	17Y 8m	78.8%	17Y 4m	86.3%	16Y 12m	94.2%
	30	19Y 2m	120.1%	18Y 9m	131.2%	18Y 3m	142.8%
10%	15	11Y 9m	30.5%	11Y 8m	33.1%	11Y 7m	35.8%
	20	14Y 5m	56.5%	14Y 2m	61.5%	13Y 12m	66.8%
	25	16Y 4m	92.3%	15Y 12m	100.6%	15Y 8m	109.1%
	30	17Y 7m	136.9%	17Y 1m	148.7%	16Y 8m	160.8%
12.5%	15	11Y 2m	35.7%	11Y 1m	38.6%	10Y 11m	41.7%
	20	13Y 7m	64.6%	13Y 4m	70.1%	13Y 1m	75.9%
	25	15Y 3m	103.2%	14Y 10m	111.9%	14Y 6m	121.0%
	30	16Y 3m	150.0%	15Y 10m	162.1%	15Y 4m	174.6%
15%	15	10Y 8m	40.3%	10Y 7m	43.5%	10Y 5m	46.8%
	20	12Y 10m	71.5%	12Y 7m	77.4%	12Y 5m	83.5%
	25	14Y 3m	112.2%	13Y 11m	121.3%	13Y 7m	130.7%
	30	15Y 2m	160.5%	14Y 9m	173.0%	14Y 4m	185.7%
20%	15	9Y 10m	48.0%	9Y 8m	51.6%	9Y 6m	55.4%
	20	11Y 7m	82.7%	11Y 5m	89.1%	11Y 2m	95.7%
	25	12Y 9m	126.3%	12Y 6m	135.9%	12Y 2m	145.8%
	30	13Y 6m	176.8%	13Y 1m	189.6%	12Y 9m	202.7%
25%	15	9Y 1m	54.2%	8Y 11m	58.2%	8Y 10m	62.3%
	20	10Y 8m	91.5%	10Y 5m	98.2%	10Y 2m	105.2%
	25	11Y 7m	137.0%	11Y 4m	146.9%	11Y 0m	157.1%
	30	12Y 2m	188.8%	11Y 10m	201.9%	11Y 6m	215.2%
33.3%	15	8Y 1m	62.5%	7Y 11m	66.8%	7Y 10m	71.3%
	20	9Y 4m	102.6%	9Y 2m	109.7%	8Y 11m	117.1%
	25	10Y 2m	150.3%	9Y 10m	160.5%	9Y 7m	170.9%
	30	10Y 7m	203.4%	10Y 3m	216.7%	9Y 11m	230.2%

Table 5   297

Table 6
Adjustable Rate Mortgages

Adjustable Rate Mortgages (ARMs) have benefits for borrowers and lenders. Borrowers get a lower rate of interest at the start and qualify for a larger loan than with a fixed-rate plan. Lenders avoid the interest rate risk they face with fixed-rate loans.

The payment in the first year of an ARM is the same as in the customary 30-year case. Each year after that, the rate is adjusted according to one of several indexes. Rate increases are limited in any one year and in total over the life of the loan.

If the interest rate goes up and the lender permits the loan payment to remain constant, the result is negative amortization: The loan balance goes up. To avoid negative amortization, the payment can be increased. Table 6 shows the payments that will keep the loan amortizing on its original 30-year schedule, if the interest rate rises at any of four rates of increase, 1/4, 1/2, 3/4, or 1 percent per year.

Example 11. Finding the Payments on an ARM

Pat Brannell is looking at a $90,000 ARM with an initial interest rate of 11.00 percent per year. The rate may rise by 1 percent in any year and by a maximum of 4 percent over the loan term.

Brannell wants to see the payments that would keep the loan on the original schedule and avoid negative amortization.

Enter Table 6 on the page for rate increases of 1 percent per year. Under column 1 on the 11.00 percent line, read $9.5233 per $1000, the payment on a usual 30-year loan. Multiply this by the number of thousands to get

$$\$9.5233 \times 90 = \$857.10$$

the payment in the first year. Repeat the process, using the figure from column 2, $10.2771, for the second year, that from column 3, $11.0358, for the third year and so on, always staying on the line for 11.00 percent interest. The interest rates built into these columns is 1 percent higher in each column.

Example 12. Maximum Payment on an ARM

The Schaeffers are offered a $110,000 loan that could rise 1/2 percent per year or a maximum of 2 percent over the life of the loan, starting from a 7.50 percent rate.

To find the maximum payment, enter Table 6 on the page for rate increases of 1/2 percent per year. On the line for 7.50 percent interest, read the payment under column 4, $8.0074, which contains a rate 2 percent higher than at the start. This will be the maximum payment on a $1000 loan with this data.

Next, multiply the payment by the number of thousands to get

$$\$8.0074 \times 110 = \$880.81$$

the maximum payment on $110,000 that begins at 7.50 percent and rises 1/2 percent per year, with a maximum 2 percent increase.

Adjustable Rate Mortgages
Rate increases 1/4% per year

Interest Rate	Payment per $1000				
	1	2	3	4	5
5.00%	5.3682	5.5184	5.6668	5.8133	5.9577
.25	5.5220	5.6743	5.8247	5.9733	6.1197
.50	5.6779	5.8321	5.9846	6.1352	6.2836
.75	5.8357	5.9920	6.1464	6.2989	6.4493
6.00	5.9955	6.1537	6.3101	6.4645	6.6168
.25	6.1572	6.3172	6.4755	6.6318	6.7861
.50	6.3207	6.4826	6.6427	6.8009	6.9570
.75	6.4860	6.6497	6.8116	6.9716	7.1295
7.00	6.6530	6.8185	6.9821	7.1439	7.3035
.25	6.8218	6.9889	7.1543	7.3177	7.4791
.50	6.9921	7.1609	7.3280	7.4931	7.6562
.75	7.1641	7.3345	7.5032	7.6699	7.8347
8.00	7.3376	7.5096	7.6798	7.8482	8.0145
.25	7.5127	7.6861	7.8579	8.0278	8.1957
.50	7.6891	7.8641	8.0373	8.2087	8.3781
.75	7.8670	8.0433	8.2180	8.3909	8.5617
9.00	8.0462	8.2239	8.4000	8.5743	8.7466
.25	8.2268	8.4058	8.5832	8.7588	8.9325
.50	8.4085	8.5889	8.7676	8.9445	9.1196
.75	8.5915	8.7731	8.9531	9.1313	9.3077
10.00	8.7757	8.9585	9.1396	9.3191	9.4968
.25	8.9610	9.1449	9.3273	9.5080	9.6868
.50	9.1474	9.3324	9.5159	9.6977	9.8778
.75	9.3348	9.5209	9.7055	9.8885	10.0697
11.00	9.5232	9.7103	9.8960	10.0800	10.2624
.25	9.7126	9.9007	10.0874	10.2725	10.4559
.50	9.9029	10.0919	10.2796	10.4657	10.6502
.75	10.0941	10.2840	10.4726	10.6597	10.8452
12.00	10.2861	10.4769	10.6664	10.8544	11.0409
.25	10.4790	10.6706	10.8610	11.0499	11.2373
.50	10.6726	10.8650	11.0562	11.2460	11.4343
.75	10.8669	11.0602	11.2521	11.4428	11.6319
13.00	11.0620	11.2560	11.4487	11.6401	11.8301
.25	11.2577	11.4524	11.6459	11.8381	12.0289
.50	11.4541	11.6495	11.8437	12.0366	12.2282
.75	11.6511	11.8471	12.0420	12.2356	12.4279
14.00	11.8487	12.0453	12.2409	12.4352	12.6282
.25	12.0469	12.2441	12.4402	12.6352	12.8289
.50	12.2456	12.4433	12.6401	12.8357	13.0300
.75	12.4448	12.6431	12.8404	13.0366	13.2316
15.00	12.6444	12.8433	13.0411	13.2379	13.4335
.25	12.8446	13.0439	13.2423	13.4396	13.6358
.50	13.0452	13.2449	13.4438	13.6417	13.8384
.75	13.2462	13.4464	13.6457	13.8441	14.0414
16.00%	13.4476	13.6482	13.8480	14.0469	14.2446

Table 6   301

Adjustable Rate Mortgages
Rate increases 1/2% per year

Interest Rate	Payment per $1000				
	1	2	3	4	5
5.00%	5.3682	5.6705	5.9731	6.2753	6.5765
.25	5.5220	5.8284	6.1350	6.4411	6.7462
.50	5.6779	5.9883	6.2987	6.6087	6.9176
.75	5.8357	6.1500	6.4643	6.7781	7.0906
6.00	5.9955	6.3136	6.6317	6.9491	7.2653
.25	6.1572	6.4790	6.8007	7.1217	7.4414
.50	6.3207	6.6462	6.9714	7.2959	7.6191
.75	6.4860	6.8150	7.1437	7.4716	7.7982
7.00	6.6530	6.9855	7.3176	7.6488	7.9787
.25	6.8218	7.1576	7.4930	7.8275	8.1605
.50	6.9921	7.3312	7.6698	8.0074	8.3436
.75	7.1641	7.5064	7.8481	8.1888	8.5280
8.00	7.3376	7.6830	8.0277	8.3713	8.7135
.25	7.5127	7.8610	8.2086	8.5552	8.9002
.50	7.6891	8.0403	8.3908	8.7401	9.0879
.75	7.8670	8.2210	8.5742	8.9263	9.2768
9.00	8.0462	8.4029	8.7588	9.1135	9.4666
.25	8.2268	8.5860	8.9445	9.3017	9.6574
.50	8.4085	8.7704	9.1313	9.4910	9.8491
.75	8.5915	8.9558	9.3191	9.6812	10.0417
10.00	8.7757	9.1423	9.5080	9.8723	10.2351
.25	8.9610	9.3299	9.6977	10.0644	10.4294
.50	9.1474	9.5184	9.8885	10.2572	10.6244
.75	9.3348	9.7079	10.0801	10.4509	10.8201
11.00	9.5232	9.8984	10.2725	10.6453	11.0165
.25	9.7126	10.0897	10.4657	10.8405	11.2136
.50	9.9029	10.2818	10.6597	11.0363	11.4114
.75	10.0941	10.4748	10.8545	11.2329	11.6097
12.00	10.2861	10.6686	11.0499	11.4301	11.8086
.25	10.4790	10.8630	11.2461	11.6278	12.0080
.50	10.6726	11.0582	11.4428	11.8262	12.2080
.75	10.8669	11.2541	11.6402	12.0251	12.4084
13.00	11.0620	11.4506	11.8382	12.2245	12.6093
.25	11.2577	11.6477	12.0367	12.4244	12.8107
.50	11.4541	11.8454	12.2357	12.6248	13.0124
.75	11.6511	12.0437	12.4353	12.8256	13.2146
14.00	11.8487	12.2425	12.6353	13.0269	13.4171
.25	12.0469	12.4418	12.8358	13.2286	13.6200
.50	12.2456	12.6416	13.0367	13.4306	13.8232
.75	12.4448	12.8419	13.2380	13.6330	14.0267
15.00	12.6444	13.0425	13.4397	13.8358	14.2305
.25	12.8446	13.2436	13.6418	14.0388	14.4346
.50	13.0452	13.4451	13.8442	14.2422	14.6390
.75	13.2462	13.6470	14.0470	14.4459	14.8436
16.00%	13.4476	13.8492	14.2500	14.6498	15.0484

Adjustable Rate Mortgages
Rate increases 3/4% per year

Interest Rate	Payment per $1000				
	1	2	3	4	5
5.00%	5.3682	5.8246	6.2867	6.7532	7.2225
.25	5.5220	5.9845	6.4524	6.9245	7.3992
.50	5.6779	6.1463	6.6199	7.0975	7.5775
.75	5.8357	6.3099	6.7891	7.2720	7.7572
6.00	5.9955	6.4753	6.9600	7.4481	7.9384
.25	6.1572	6.6425	7.1325	7.6257	8.1209
.50	6.3207	6.8114	7.3065	7.8047	8.3047
.75	6.4860	6.9820	7.4821	7.9851	8.4898
7.00	6.6530	7.1541	7.6591	8.1668	8.6760
.25	6.8218	7.3278	7.8376	8.3498	8.8634
.50	6.9921	7.5030	8.0174	8.5341	9.0520
.75	7.1641	7.6797	8.1985	8.7195	9.2416
8.00	7.3376	7.8578	8.3809	8.9060	9.4322
.25	7.5127	8.0372	8.5645	9.0937	9.6238
.50	7.6891	8.2179	8.7493	9.2824	9.8163
.75	7.8670	8.3999	8.9353	9.4721	10.0097
9.00	8.0462	8.5831	9.1223	9.6628	10.2039
.25	8.2268	8.7675	9.3103	9.8544	10.3990
.50	8.4085	8.9530	9.4994	10.0469	10.5948
.75	8.5915	9.1396	9.6894	10.2402	10.7913
10.00	8.7757	9.3272	9.8803	10.4344	10.9885
.25	8.9610	9.5158	10.0722	10.6292	11.1864
.50	9.1474	9.7054	10.2648	10.8249	11.3849
.75	9.3348	9.8959	10.4583	11.0212	11.5841
11.00	9.5232	10.0873	10.6525	11.2182	11.7837
.25	9.7126	10.2795	10.8475	11.4158	11.9839
.50	9.9029	10.4726	11.0431	11.6140	12.1846
.75	10.0941	10.6664	11.2395	11.8128	12.3858
12.00	10.2861	10.8609	11.4365	12.0121	12.5875
.25	10.4790	11.0562	11.6340	12.2120	12.7895
.50	10.6726	11.2521	11.8322	12.4123	12.9920
.75	10.8669	11.4487	12.0309	12.6131	13.1948
13.00	11.0620	11.6459	12.2301	12.8143	13.3980
.25	11.2577	11.8437	12.4299	13.0160	13.6016
.50	11.4541	12.0420	12.6301	13.2180	13.8054
.75	11.6511	12.2409	12.8308	13.4204	14.0096
14.00	11.8487	12.4402	13.0318	13.6232	14.2140
.25	12.0469	12.6401	13.2333	13.8263	14.4187
.50	12.2456	12.8404	13.4352	14.0297	14.6236
.75	12.4448	13.0411	13.6375	14.2335	14.8288
15.00	12.6444	13.2423	13.8400	14.4375	15.0342
.25	12.8446	13.4438	14.0430	14.6417	15.2398
.50	13.0452	13.6457	14.2462	14.8462	15.4456
.75	13.2462	13.8480	14.4497	15.0510	15.6516
16.00%	13.4476	14.0506	14.6535	15.2560	15.8577

Table 6   303

Adjustable Rate Mortgages
Rate increases 1% per year

Interest Rate	Payment per $1000				
	1	2	3	4	5
5.00%	5.3682	5.9805	6.6074	7.2459	7.8932
.25	5.5220	6.1423	6.7768	7.4224	8.0764
.50	5.6779	6.3060	6.9478	7.6003	8.2609
.75	5.8357	6.4715	7.1205	7.7797	8.4467
6.00	5.9955	6.6388	7.2947	7.9605	8.6337
.25	6.1572	6.8077	7.4705	8.1427	8.8219
.50	6.3207	6.9783	7.6477	8.3261	9.0113
.75	6.4860	7.1505	7.8263	8.5108	9.2017
7.00	6.6530	7.3243	8.0064	8.6967	9.3931
.25	6.8218	7.4996	8.1877	8.8837	9.5855
.50	6.9921	7.6763	8.3703	9.0719	9.7789
.75	7.1641	7.8544	8.5542	9.2611	9.9732
8.00	7.3376	8.0339	8.7392	9.4513	10.1683
.25	7.5127	8.2147	8.9253	9.6424	10.3642
.50	7.6891	8.3968	9.1126	9.8345	10.5609
.75	7.8670	8.5800	9.3009	10.0275	10.7583
9.00	8.0462	8.7645	9.4901	10.2213	10.9564
.25	8.2268	8.9501	9.6804	10.4159	11.1551
.50	8.4085	9.1367	9.8716	10.6113	11.3545
.75	8.5915	9.3244	10.0636	10.8074	11.5545
10.00	8.7757	9.5131	10.2565	11.0043	11.7550
.25	8.9610	9.7028	10.4502	11.2017	11.9561
.50	9.1474	9.8934	10.6447	11.3998	12.1576
.75	9.3348	10.0848	10.8399	11.5985	12.3596
11.00	9.5232	10.2771	11.0358	11.7978	12.5621
.25	9.7126	10.4702	11.2323	11.9976	12.7649
.50	9.9029	10.6641	11.4295	12.1979	12.9682
.75	10.0941	10.8587	11.6273	12.3987	13.1718
12.00	10.2861	11.0541	11.8257	12.5999	13.3758
.25	10.4790	11.2501	12.0246	12.8016	13.5801
.50	10.6726	11.4467	12.2241	13.0037	13.7847
.75	10.8669	11.6440	12.4240	13.2061	13.9895
13.00	11.0620	11.8418	12.6244	13.4090	14.1947
.25	11.2577	12.0402	12.8253	13.6122	14.4001
.50	11.4541	12.2391	13.0266	13.8157	14.6057
.75	11.6511	12.4385	13.2282	14.0195	14.8115
14.00	11.8487	12.6385	13.4303	14.2236	15.0176
.25	12.0469	12.8388	13.6327	14.4279	15.2238
.50	12.2456	13.0396	13.8355	14.6326	15.4302
.75	12.4448	13.2408	14.0386	14.8374	15.6368
15.00	12.6444	13.4424	14.2420	15.0425	15.8435
.25	12.8446	13.6444	14.4457	15.2478	16.0503
.50	13.0452	13.8467	14.6496	15.4533	16.2573
.75	13.2462	14.0494	14.8538	15.6590	16.4644
16.00%	13.4476	14.2524	15.0583	15.8649	16.6717

Table 7
Biweekly Payment Loans

Biweekly loans combine convenience with thrift. Every two weeks, biweekly borrowers pay one-half the payment on a normal 30-year loan. This works out to 13 months' of payments yearly, prepaying the loan a full month every year and bringing important interest savings as well.

Studies show that biweekly loans are particularly convenient for households with weekly or biweekly paychecks. But smoothing out household bills also suits the convenience of many families with monthly pay, or that receive commission income.

Example 16.   Biweekly Payments and Savings

The Radecks need a $130,000 loan at the current loan rate of 9.75 percent interest. They want to check the features of a biweekly payment loan.

To find the payment, enter Table 7 on the page for 30-year base. On the line for 9.75 percent, the biweekly payment is $4.2958 per $1000. For a loan of $130,000, this will be $558.45 every two weeks.

On the same line, the biweekly full term is shown to be 21 years 10 weeks. The prepayment feature of the biweekly has cut the loan term from 30 years to just over 21 years, 2 months.

Still on the 9.75 percent line under total interest are the figures $1368 per $1000 interest paid. This seems to be a large amount, until it is considered that this is a savings, shown in the next column, of 72.51 percent of the loan amount compared to what would be paid on an ordinary 30-year loan.

Example 17. Biweekly versus Other Loans

The Adelsons have the possibility to take a loan with a 20-year amortization plan, or a biweekly. Either way, the loan would be for $100,000 at an interest rate of 10.50 percent.

In Table 7, on the line for 10.50 percent interest, find the full amortization of the biweekly, 20 years and 25 weeks. The biweekly plan requires about 6 months longer to full payoff than the 20-year loan.

The payment on the 20-year loan is found in Table 1, using Example 1. For $100,000 at 10.50 percent for 20 years, it is $998.38 per month, or $11,980.56 per year. The biweekly payment, on the 10.50 percent line is $4.5737 per $1000 every two weeks, a total in 1 year of $11,891.88, or $90 per year less.

For total interest, Table 7 shows the total interest on this biweekly to be $143,500 over its life. For the 20-year loan, multiply $11,981 times 20 and subtract $100,000, to get $139,620. The plans are very similar in total interest cost. The advantage of the biweekly plan is its lower payment. Both save a great deal of interest compared to a 30-year loan, the 20-year plan having a small edge over a biweekly.

Biweekly Payment Loans
Payment per $1000 on 30-year base

Interest Rate	Biweekly Payment	Ordinary Payment	Biweekly Full Term		Total Interest Paid	Saved
5.00%	$2.6841	$5.3682	25 yrs	12 wks	$ 761	17.16%
.25	2.7610	5.5220	25 yrs	3 wks	799	18.90
.50	2.8389	5.6779	24 yrs	46 wks	837	20.75
.75	2.9179	5.8357	24 yrs	36 wks	874	22.72
6.00	2.9978	5.9955	24 yrs	26 wks	910	24.81
.25	3.0786	6.1572	24 yrs	16 wks	946	27.03
.50	3.1603	6.3207	24 yrs	6 wks	982	29.37
.75	3.2430	6.4860	23 yrs	48 wks	1,016	31.85
7.00	3.3265	6.6530	23 yrs	37 wks	1,050	34.46
.25	3.4109	6.8218	23 yrs	26 wks	1,084	37.21
.50	3.4961	6.9921	23 yrs	15 wks	1,116	40.10
.75	3.5821	7.1641	23 yrs	3 wks	1,148	43.13
8.00	3.6688	7.3376	22 yrs	44 wks	1,179	46.30
.25	3.7563	7.5127	22 yrs	32 wks	1,208	49.61
.50	3.8446	7.6891	22 yrs	20 wks	1,237	53.07
.75	3.9335	7.8670	22 yrs	8 wks	1,265	56.67
9.00	4.0231	8.0462	21 yrs	48 wks	1,292	60.42
.25	4.1134	8.2268	21 yrs	35 wks	1,319	64.31
.50	4.2043	8.4085	21 yrs	23 wks	1,344	68.34
.75	4.2958	8.5915	21 yrs	10 wks	1,368	72.51
10.00	4.3879	8.7757	20 yrs	50 wks	1,391	76.82
.25	4.4805	8.9610	20 yrs	37 wks	1,413	81.26
.50	4.5737	9.1474	20 yrs	25 wks	1,435	85.85
.75	4.6674	9.3348	20 yrs	12 wks	1,455	90.56
11.00	4.7616	9.5232	19 yrs	51 wks	1,474	95.40
.25	4.8563	9.7126	19 yrs	39 wks	1,493	100.37
.50	4.9515	9.9029	19 yrs	26 wks	1,510	105.46
.75	5.0470	10.0941	19 yrs	13 wks	1,527	110.67
12.00	5.1431	10.2861	19 yrs	1 wks	1,543	115.99
.25	5.2395	10.4790	18 yrs	40 wks	1,558	121.43
.50	5.3363	10.6726	18 yrs	28 wks	1,572	126.97
.75	5.4335	10.8669	18 yrs	16 wks	1,586	132.62
13.00	5.5310	11.0620	18 yrs	4 wks	1,599	138.36
.25	5.6289	11.2577	17 yrs	44 wks	1,611	144.20
.50	5.7271	11.4541	17 yrs	32 wks	1,622	150.13
.75	5.8256	11.6511	17 yrs	20 wks	1,633	156.15
14.00	5.9244	11.8487	17 yrs	8 wks	1,643	162.26
.25	6.0234	12.0469	16 yrs	49 wks	1,652	168.44
.50	6.1228	12.2456	16 yrs	37 wks	1,661	174.70
.75	6.2224	12.4448	16 yrs	26 wks	1,670	181.03
15.00	6.3222	12.6444	16 yrs	15 wks	1,678	187.43
.25	6.4223	12.8446	16 yrs	4 wks	1,685	193.89
.50	6.5226	13.0452	15 yrs	45 wks	1,692	200.42
.75	6.6231	13.2462	15 yrs	35 wks	1,699	207.00
16.00	6.7238	13.4476	15 yrs	25 wks	1,705	213.64
.25	6.8247	13.6493	15 yrs	14 wks	1,710	220.33
.50	6.9257	13.8515	15 yrs	4 wks	1,716	227.07
.75	7.0270	14.0540	14 yrs	46 wks	1,721	233.86
17.00	7.1284	14.2568	14 yrs	37 wks	1,726	240.69
.25	7.2299	14.4599	14 yrs	27 wks	1,730	247.56
.50	7.3316	14.6633	14 yrs	18 wks	1,734	254.47
.75	7.4335	14.8669	14 yrs	9 wks	1,738	261.42
18.00	7.5354	15.0709	13 yrs	52 wks	1,742	268.40
.25	7.6375	15.2750	13 yrs	43 wks	1,745	275.41
.50	7.7397	15.4794	13 yrs	34 wks	1,748	282.45
.75	7.8420	15.6841	13 yrs	26 wks	1,751	289.53
19.00	7.9445	15.8889	13 yrs	17 wks	1,754	296.63
.25	8.0470	16.0940	13 yrs	9 wks	1,756	303.75
.50	8.1496	16.2992	13 yrs	1 wks	1,759	310.90
.75	8.2523	16.5046	12 yrs	45 wks	1,761	318.07
20.00%	8.3551	16.7102	12 yrs	37 wks	$1,763	325.26%

Table 7   307

Biweekly Payment Loans
Payment per $1000 on 25-year base

Interest Rate	Biweekly Payment	Ordinary Payment	Biweekly Full Term		Total Interest Paid	Saved
5.00%	$2.9230	$5.8459	21 yrs	25 wks	$ 632	12.17%
.25	2.9962	5.9925	21 yrs	19 wks	665	13.32
.50	3.0704	6.1409	21 yrs	13 wks	697	14.54
.75	3.1455	6.2911	21 yrs	7 wks	729	15.83
6.00	3.2215	6.4430	21 yrs	1 wks	761	17.20
.25	3.2983	6.5967	20 yrs	47 wks	793	18.64
.50	3.3760	6.7521	20 yrs	41 wks	824	20.16
.75	3.4546	6.9091	20 yrs	34 wks	855	21.76
7.00	3.5339	7.0678	20 yrs	27 wks	886	23.44
.25	3.6140	7.2281	20 yrs	20 wks	916	25.21
.50	3.6950	7.3899	20 yrs	13 wks	946	27.07
.75	3.7766	7.5533	20 yrs	6 wks	976	29.01
8.00	3.8591	7.7182	19 yrs	51 wks	1,005	31.05
.25	3.9423	7.8845	19 yrs	44 wks	1,034	33.18
.50	4.0261	8.0523	19 yrs	36 wks	1,062	35.40
.75	4.1107	8.2214	19 yrs	28 wks	1,089	37.72
9.00	4.1960	8.3920	19 yrs	21 wks	1,116	40.14
.25	4.2819	8.5638	19 yrs	13 wks	1,143	42.65
.50	4.3685	8.7370	19 yrs	5 wks	1,168	45.27
.75	4.4557	8.9114	18 yrs	49 wks	1,194	47.98
10.00	4.5435	9.0870	18 yrs	40 wks	1,218	50.79
.25	4.6319	9.2638	18 yrs	32 wks	1,242	53.70
.50	4.7209	9.4418	18 yrs	24 wks	1,265	56.71
.75	4.8105	9.6209	18 yrs	15 wks	1,288	59.82
11.00	4.9006	9.8011	18 yrs	7 wks	1,310	63.03
.25	4.9912	9.9824	17 yrs	50 wks	1,331	66.33
.50	5.0823	10.1647	17 yrs	42 wks	1,352	69.74
.75	5.1740	10.3480	17 yrs	33 wks	1,372	73.24
12.00	5.2661	10.5322	17 yrs	24 wks	1,391	76.84
.25	5.3587	10.7174	17 yrs	15 wks	1,410	80.54
.50	5.4518	10.9035	17 yrs	7 wks	1,428	84.32
.75	5.5453	11.0905	16 yrs	50 wks	1,445	88.20
13.00	5.6392	11.2784	16 yrs	41 wks	1,462	92.17
.25	5.7335	11.4670	16 yrs	32 wks	1,478	96.23
.50	5.8282	11.6564	16 yrs	24 wks	1,493	100.38
.75	5.9233	11.8467	16 yrs	15 wks	1,508	104.61
14.00	6.0188	12.0376	16 yrs	6 wks	1,522	108.92
.25	6.1146	12.2293	15 yrs	49 wks	1,536	113.31
.50	6.2108	12.4216	15 yrs	41 wks	1,549	117.78
.75	6.3073	12.6146	15 yrs	32 wks	1,561	122.33
15.00	6.4042	12.8083	15 yrs	24 wks	1,573	126.95
.25	6.5013	13.0026	15 yrs	15 wks	1,584	131.65
.50	6.5987	13.1975	15 yrs	7 wks	1,595	136.41
.75	6.6964	13.3929	14 yrs	50 wks	1,605	141.24
16.00	6.7944	13.5889	14 yrs	42 wks	1,615	146.14
.25	6.8927	13.7854	14 yrs	34 wks	1,625	151.10
.50	6.9912	13.9824	14 yrs	25 wks	1,634	156.11
.75	7.0900	14.1800	14 yrs	17 wks	1,642	161.19
17.00	7.1890	14.3780	14 yrs	9 wks	1,650	166.32
.25	7.2882	14.5764	14 yrs	1 wks	1,658	171.51
.50	7.3876	14.7753	13 yrs	46 wks	1,665	176.74
.75	7.4873	14.9746	13 yrs	38 wks	1,672	182.03
18.00	7.5871	15.1743	13 yrs	30 wks	1,679	187.36
.25	7.6872	15.3744	13 yrs	23 wks	1,685	192.74
.50	7.7874	15.5748	13 yrs	15 wks	1,691	198.16
.75	7.8878	15.7757	13 yrs	8 wks	1,696	203.62
19.00	7.9884	15.9768	13 yrs	0 wks	1,702	209.12
.25	8.0891	16.1783	12 yrs	45 wks	1,707	214.66
.50	8.1900	16.3801	12 yrs	38 wks	1,712	220.24
.75	8.2911	16.5821	12 yrs	31 wks	1,716	225.84
20.00%	8.3923	16.7845	12 yrs	24 wks	$1,720	231.49%

Biweekly Payment Loans
Payment per $1000 on 20-year base

Interest Rate	Biweekly Payment	Ordinary Payment	Biweekly Full Term		Total Interest Paid	Saved
5.00%	$3.2998	$6.5996	17 yrs	26 wks	$ 501	8.25%
.25	3.3692	6.7384	17 yrs	23 wks	528	8.96
.50	3.4394	6.8789	17 yrs	19 wks	554	9.72
.75	3.5104	7.0208	17 yrs	16 wks	580	10.51
6.00	3.5822	7.1643	17 yrs	13 wks	606	11.34
.25	3.6546	7.3093	17 yrs	9 wks	632	12.21
.50	3.7279	7.4557	17 yrs	6 wks	658	13.13
.75	3.8018	7.6036	17 yrs	2 wks	684	14.09
7.00	3.8765	7.7530	16 yrs	50 wks	710	15.09
.25	3.9519	7.9038	16 yrs	46 wks	735	16.15
.50	4.0280	8.0559	16 yrs	42 wks	761	17.25
.75	4.1047	8.2095	16 yrs	38 wks	786	18.39
8.00	4.1822	8.3644	16 yrs	34 wks	812	19.59
.25	4.2603	8.5207	16 yrs	30 wks	837	20.84
.50	4.3391	8.6782	16 yrs	26 wks	861	22.14
.75	4.4186	8.8371	16 yrs	22 wks	886	23.50
9.00	4.4986	8.9973	16 yrs	17 wks	910	24.91
.25	4.5793	9.1587	16 yrs	13 wks	934	26.37
.50	4.6607	9.3213	16 yrs	8 wks	958	27.89
.75	4.7426	9.4852	16 yrs	4 wks	982	29.47
10.00	4.8251	9.6502	15 yrs	51 wks	1,005	31.11
.25	4.9082	9.8164	15 yrs	46 wks	1,028	32.81
.50	4.9919	9.9838	15 yrs	42 wks	1,050	34.56
.75	5.0761	10.1523	15 yrs	37 wks	1,073	36.38
11.00	5.1609	10.3219	15 yrs	32 wks	1,095	38.26
.25	5.2463	10.4926	15 yrs	27 wks	1,116	40.20
.50	5.3321	10.6643	15 yrs	22 wks	1,137	42.20
.75	5.4185	10.8371	15 yrs	17 wks	1,158	44.27
12.00	5.5054	11.0109	15 yrs	11 wks	1,179	46.40
.25	5.5928	11.1856	15 yrs	6 wks	1,199	48.59
.50	5.6807	11.3614	15 yrs	1 wks	1,218	50.84
.75	5.7691	11.5381	14 yrs	48 wks	1,238	53.16
13.00	5.8579	11.7158	14 yrs	42 wks	1,256	55.55
.25	5.9472	11.8943	14 yrs	37 wks	1,275	57.99
.50	6.0369	12.0737	14 yrs	32 wks	1,293	60.50
.75	6.1270	12.2541	14 yrs	26 wks	1,310	63.08
14.00	6.2176	12.4352	14 yrs	21 wks	1,327	65.71
.25	6.3086	12.6172	14 yrs	15 wks	1,344	68.41
.50	6.4000	12.8000	14 yrs	10 wks	1,360	71.17
.75	6.4918	12.9836	14 yrs	4 wks	1,376	74.00
15.00	6.5839	13.1679	13 yrs	50 wks	1,392	76.88
.25	6.6765	13.3530	13 yrs	45 wks	1,406	79.82
.50	6.7694	13.5388	13 yrs	39 wks	1,421	82.83
.75	6.8627	13.7253	13 yrs	34 wks	1,435	85.89
16.00	6.9563	13.9126	13 yrs	28 wks	1,449	89.01
.25	7.0502	14.1005	13 yrs	22 wks	1,462	92.19
.50	7.1445	14.2890	13 yrs	17 wks	1,475	95.43
.75	7.2391	14.4782	13 yrs	11 wks	1,488	98.72
17.00	7.3340	14.6680	13 yrs	6 wks	1,500	102.07
.25	7.4292	14.8584	13 yrs	0 wks	1,511	105.47
.50	7.5247	15.0494	12 yrs	47 wks	1,523	108.92
.75	7.6205	15.2410	12 yrs	41 wks	1,534	112.42
18.00	7.7166	15.4331	12 yrs	35 wks	1,544	115.98
.25	7.8129	15.6258	12 yrs	30 wks	1,554	119.58
.50	7.9095	15.8190	12 yrs	24 wks	1,564	123.23
.75	8.0063	16.0127	12 yrs	19 wks	1,574	126.93
19.00	8.1034	16.2068	12 yrs	13 wks	1,583	130.68
.25	8.2008	16.4015	12 yrs	8 wks	1,592	134.47
.50	8.2983	16.5966	12 yrs	3 wks	1,600	138.30
.75	8.3961	16.7922	11 yrs	49 wks	1,608	142.17
20.00%	8.4941	16.9882	11 yrs	44 wks	$1,616	146.09%

Table 7   309

Glossary

adjustable rate mortgage (ARM)   loan with an interest rate that varies according to an index

amortization   reduction of a loan amount by principal payments at regular intervals

amortization period   time required to pay a loan entirely through periodic payments

Annual Percentage Rate (APR)   yield to maturity to a lender from interest, points, and certain fees

appraisal   estimate of the present value of real estate prepared according to formal regulations

balloon   loan clause making the entire balance due before the end of the amortization period

balloon payment   entire remaining balance of a loan required as a single payment

closing costs   charges related to a sale or loan, such as legal fees, transfer taxes, title insurance

commitment   agreement binding a lender to lend on given terms, if closing is within a stated time

debt service   payments required on a loan for both principal and interest

discount   reduction in the proceeds loaned to a borrower to increase the yield of a lender

equity   share of sale price or property value held by the owner, opposed to debt held by the lender